SRI LANKA MALDIVES

Note to readers

Because of the political situation and the conflict which has raged between the Liberation Tigers of Tamil Eelam (LTTE) and the Sri Lankan government since 1983, visitors are strongly advised not to visit the north of the island and the jungle around Batticaloa (east of Polonnaruwa) which are not described in this guide. The government declines all responsibility for travellers visiting these areas. The army controls the rest of the island which is more vulnerable to terrorism: terrorist attacks are mainly aimed at Sri Lankan institutions (especially in Colombo) and its sacred symbols (in 1998, it was the Temple of the Tooth at Kandy that was targeted), and sometimes public transport. Before undertaking a trip, it is advisable to consult the advice sheets for travellers issued by the Foreign Office or the Sri Lanka Consular Information Sheet (www.travel.state.gov/sri_lanka.html).

In this guide Sri Lanka is presented by region and the Maldives by atoll. The tour itineraries described and shown on the maps give ideas for excursions off the beaten track; ■ indicates possible overnight stops en route. When organising a trip according to the number of days at your disposal, consult the map of itineraries on p 111.

Just one point here about the **practical information**. The chapters entitled "Practical information" give general information to help you plan your trip. In the "Exploring Sri Lanka" and "Exploring the Maldives" sections, after each description of a town, site or itinerary, there is a practical section giving information about the place in question: access, useful addresses, accommodation, eating out, other things to do, shopping guide, etc.

Prices are generally given in the local currency but to help you plan your budget hotels and restaurants are classed by price in US dollars. Given the difficulty of quoting specific prices for hotels in the Maldives, we have opted for four classification categories *(see "Practical information" on p 367)*.

We are obliged to point out that living costs vary constantly and opening hours may change, so that prices and practical information may have changed since publication.

Sights and other features on the **maps** are marked in their local name. However, on town plans some of the sights and landmarks have been given their English name for ease of reference. On the inside cover a lexicon lists all the names commonly used in the text and in the maps.

Michelin Travel Publications
Published in 2001

New - In the NEOS guides emphasis is placed on the discovery and enjoyment of a new destination through meeting the people, tasting the food and absorbing the exotic atmosphere. In addition to recommendations on which sights to see, we give details on the most suitable places to stay and eat, on what to look out for in traditional markets and where to go in search of the hidden character of the region, its crafts and its dancing rhythms. For those keen to explore places on foot, we provide guidelines and useful addresses in order to help organise walks to suit all tastes.

Expert - The NEOS guides are written by people who have travelled in the country and researched the sites before recommending them by the allocation of stars. Accommodation and restaurants are similarly recommended by a on the grounds of quality and value for money. Cartographers have drawn easy-to-use maps with clearly marked itineraries, as well as detailed plans of towns, archeological sites and large museums.

Open to all cultures, the NEOS guides provide an insight into the daily lives of the local people. In a world that is becoming ever more accessible, it is vital that religious practices, regional etiquette, traditional customs and languages be understood and respected by all travellers. Equipped with this knowledge, visitors can seek to share and enjoy with confidence the best of the local cuisine, musical harmonies and the skills involved in the production of arts and crafts.

Sensitive to the atmosphere and heritage of a foreign land, the NEOS guides encourage travellers to see, hear, smell and feel a country, through words and images. Take inspiration from the enthusiasm of our experienced travel writers and make this a journey full of discovery and enchantment.

S. Held

Sri Lanka

The Maldives

SRI LANKA

Official name: Democratic Socialist Republic
of Sri Lanka
Surface area: 65 610sqkm
Population: 18 721 000
Capital: Colombo
Currency: Sri Lankan rupee (LKR)

Setting the scene

B Morandi / DIAF

Cliff sculptures at Buduruvegala

The garden island

On a map of the world, Sri Lanka looks like a pearl hanging from the end of the Indian sub-continent from which it is separated only by the Palk Strait less than 100km wide. Covering 65 610sqkm (about the size of the Benelux countries) Sri Lanka reproduces in microcosm many of the features of the southern tip of India. Sri Lanka means the "Venerable Place". While it harks back to the original name of the island, Sri Lanka does not conjure up the same exotic image as the name Ceylon, although it still hints at the country's tropical aura.
In contrast to coastlines of watery mazes bordered by mangrove trees, beaches fringed with palms and jungles infested with tangles of ancient trees, there are also stretches of land that are almost desert, scattered with huge boulders and dotted with scrub. All this has been turned into an immense garden through the efforts of the island's population. In turn mysterious and wild or disciplined and cultivated, the natural environment of Sri Lanka is the most enchanting aspect of the island.

A stepped landscape

Sri Lanka comprises several levels of eroded hills. In the centre and in the south is a mountainous massif consisting of metamorphic rocks with rich deposits of garnets and graphite, as well as crystalline limestone, granite and quartzite which are resistant to erosion. The **massif** culminates at 2 524m in the Piduru Talagala peak which breaks up the relief of the surrounding undulating **plateaux** composed of ancient rock formations of shale and gneiss, varying in altitude between 300m and 900m. This area is in turn surrounded by the **coastal plains** long since reclaimed from lagoons or tracts of alluvium. Unlike the other stretches of coastline, the Jaffna peninsula has inherited a thick layer of marine limestone which forms a low karst. *See map inside front cover.*

Monsoon landscape on the west coast

P Le Floc'h / EXPLORER

A temperate tropical climate

It is always warm in Sri Lanka and the temperature varies little during the course of the year *(see table p 80)*. However, variations in rainfall levels and altitude result in climatic conditions which differ considerably from region to region. The **summer monsoon**, which is the most important, arrives in Sri Lanka in the southwest, an area with high rainfall levels all year round although May to September are the wettest months. This part of the island has an annual rainfall of more than 2.5m. Combined with high temperatures (between 22°C and 30°C), this produces an almost equatorial type of vegetation in the area, although the Sinharaja rainforest is now all that remains. The rains then reach the hills, the western slopes attracting the heaviest rain in the island (Adam's Peak holds the record with 7m of rain in one year). It is also cooler up here. In contrast, less rain falls in the northeast and southeast (the Ruhunu), the highlands acting as a barrier. These two regions have two highly contrasting seasons; the wet season runs from December to February, when the **winter monsoon** blows, with the dry season lasting for several months in the middle of the year. Irregular rainfall has also created semi-arid areas.

A landscape of contrasts

Whereas erosion has carved out the contours on the map and the monsoons are responsible for the type of vegetation, in the end it is human intervention that has changed the landscape of the island in a profound and enduring way, initially transforming the semi-arid areas in the northwest and southeast, then the western coastal strip and the central more mountainous area.

The dry region

In the southeast and northwest of the island, the semi-arid landscape is scattered with vegetation in the form of shrubs, savannah and tall acacia trees. Yet water is present everywhere, in the form of reservoirs, often forming huge lakes attracting herds of wild elephant that come to drink. These reservoirs, which look completely natural, demonstrate the hard work of generations who have shaped this landscape and established village communities at the water's edge.

The miracle of water on barren land – In the southeast, in the area around the Yala National Park, the low-lying land, flooded by **salty lagoons** or buried beneath **untamed jungle**, looks as though it has always been wild. Yet, in ancient times, it was criss-crossed by an ingenious **irrigation system**. The problem was not clearing the vegetation to create paddy fields; this was relatively straightforward, but the lack of water in the summer required a solution that would make rice production possible. Today, only the oasis at Tissamaharama, together with certain maps dating back to the colonial era and aerial photographs testify to this massive modification of the landscape, which village communities carried out by constructing barrages of hard-packed earth across rivers flowing down from the mountains, or by storing the rains brought by the winter monsoon. The southeast served as a laboratory for the plains in the central northern part of the island, where one of the best examples of **hydraulic engineering** in the ancient world was implemented around the 1C AD, remaining operational into the 12C. Over time, techniques were refined and brought to a high pitch of perfection, with devices for lifting water from wells, conduits for reducing pressure, and chains of reservoirs or "tanks". Water from rivers originating in the wetter

P Le Floc'h / EXPLORER

Dry landscape in the Sigiriya region

parts of the country was drawn off into canals, stored in "tanks" sometimes several square miles in extent, then distributed over ever more extensive areas of the eastern arid zone. In total, the sovereigns who ruled from Anuradhapura and Polonnaruwa built around 80 000 artificial lakes, reservoirs and pools, linked by a network of almost 1 000km of water **channels**.

Following the example of the Ancients – During the 13C, the hydraulic system gradually deteriorated and the areas that had been successfully irrigated by the Sinhalese sovereigns became one large **swamp**. Having grown to more than 10 million in the 13C, the population fell to around 3.5 million by 1900, the year in which the colonial administration set about improving the region, by now strongly malarial. The results were largely disappointing until the long drought of the 1970s when the government launched the **Mahaweli Development Plan**: based on the same principle that had been used by engineers in ancient times, the aim was to divert water from the wet region towards the drier areas. This made it possible to irrigate 265 000 hectares of new land and to support 100 000 hectares of flooded paddy fields. Unfortunately, the tensions prevailing among the communities of the north have not made it possible to extend irrigation to this part of the island.

The wet region

The low-lying land of the southwest – In this region of lush vegetation, not a patch of land lies uncultivated. Being as well watered as it is, this area can support both crops for food production and commercial plantations. The smallest hollows are carpeted with **paddy-fields**, the sandy areas are planted with **coconut palms** and the hilly land with **heveas** (from which rubber is taken), **pepper plants** and **cacao trees**. In addition to supporting intensive farming, this southwestern quarter is densely populated, the entire region scattered with village communities. Along the coast is a string of fishing hamlets, seaside resorts and beaches which provide an idyllic setting for a well-earned rest after travelling around the island.

The transformation of the highlands – Forming a bastion of moderately-high, rounded peaks, the mountains in the centre of the island benefit from high rainfall levels and cool temperatures. Further to the south the lower-lying land forms a rocky escarpment.
Until the 16C, the mountainous region was home to aboriginal hunter-gatherers, the Veddas. They were able to obtain everything they needed from the thick forests where the vegetation thrived on the damp conditions. With the establishment of Sinhalese kingdoms along the northern edge of the area, at Gampol and then Kandy, the first clearance campaigns were implemented and the mountain slopes were given over to **paddy fields** and **crops for food production**.
When the kingdom of Kandy fell in 1815 the landscape was changed forever; the British introduced **coffee** and then **tea plantations**, transforming whole sections of the wild heart of the island into fields as straight as a die. Further change came with the building of the railway which was to link this mountain stronghold and its traditions with Colombo and the modern world.
As the state took control after Independence, the development of the plantations accelerated the rate of **deforestation**. This both eroded the slopes and upset the micro-climate. In the first decade after Independence, the forest covered around 44 % of the land but by the beginning of the 1990s this figure had fallen to 24 %.

Exotic flora and fauna

Jungle and gardens

On the back of their experience gained in the tropical colonies of Malaysia and Singapore, the British created several **botanical gardens** in Ceylon. These provided an answer to the dual need to take an inventory of the species native to the island and to acclimatise plants from other continents (such as tea, coffee and hevea) with a view to their commercial cultivation. But where man has let nature take its own course, the vegetation has spread according to the climate and the type of soil; the salty water of the lagoons fringed with **mangroves** with their gnarled aerial roots, while the jungles of the dry region are studded by giant trees such as **kapok**, **ebony** and **acacia**. The word jungle has a special meaning in Sri Lanka: rather than an impenetrable forest, it refers to a space that has not been affected by human activity, a home to wildlife.
In the tropical rainforest of Sinharaja, you can see what the heart of Ceylon was like before human intervention: a continuous canopy, with a fantastic variety of plants, dominated by trees several hundreds of years old.

Sanctuaries for wildlife

In the numerous parks where wildlife is protected, and sometimes just outside them, the presence of wild animals is one of the wonders of the island. It is impossible to visit Sri Lanka without glimpsing at least one herd of **wild elephant** plucking delicately at the leaves of bushes, a solitary **monitor lizard** dragging itself heavily across the ground or swimming skilfully through the waters of a canal, the metallic flash of a **kingfisher**, the sinewy silhouette of a **cormorant**, or ancient **turtles** depositing their eggs on the beach.
One tenth of the island is set aside for wildlife and is protected by the Wildlife Department. This department ensures both control of and respect for the environment. Most of the **national parks** were created in the colonial period when they were used as hunting reserves. Today, the peaceful co-existence of animals and people brings hope of peace to an island where human conflict has only brought suffering.

FLORA

Coconut palm
Tree palm
Pepper plant
Rotang palm
Tallipot palm
Croton
H. Choimet

Frangipani
Anthurium
Hibiscus
Caladium
Cardamom
Bougainvillea
H. Choimet

FAUNA

Langur
Porcupine
Varan
(Water-monitor)
Indian star tortoise
Sambur
Panther
H. Choimet

BIRDS

Kingfisher
Sea Eagle
Bird of paradise
Great cormorant
Parakeet
Painted stork
H. Choimet

Chronology

The Anuradhapura period (3C BC-993 AD)

247-207 BC	Reign of Devanampiya Tissa and introduction of Buddhism.
204-161 BC	Indian occupation overthrown by Dutugemunu (161-137).
1C BC	Buddhist doctrine recorded in writing for the first time.
312	The sacred tooth of Buddha taken to Anuradhapura.
535-620	Important irrigation work.
993	The sacking and burning of Anuradhapura by the Chola rulers who occupied the island until 1070.

The Polonnaruwa period (1070-1235)

1070	Vijayabahu I (1055-1110) recaptures Anuradhapura and declares himself king at Polonnaruwa. War of succession upon his death.
1153-1186	Period of material, political and religious reformation during the reign of Parakramabahu.
1196-1235	Raids by Malay pirates.
1235	Fall of the kingdom of Polonnaruwa.

The period of ephemeral capitals (1236-1597)

1236	Parakramabahu II makes Dambadeniya the capital.
1272	Yapahuwa becomes the seat of power.
1344	The Jaffna region emerges as an independent Tamil kingdom.
1415	The Sinhalese capital is established at Kotte, on the outskirts of modern Colombo.
1505	The Portuguese settle near the coast and convert part of the population to Catholicism.
1597	The Portuguese seize Kotte, then Jaffna. Sinhalese power shifts to Kandy.

The Kandyan period (1597-1815)

1656	The trading-post at Colombo falls into the hands of the Dutch.
1747-1780	Reign of Kirti Sri Rajasinha and campaigns to restore Buddhist monuments.
1796	Great Britain annexes Ceylon.
1815	Submission of the Kandyan Kingdom to the British.
1817-1818	Insurrection against the colonial administration.

Colonial and contemporary period

1830-1870	Increase in the number of coffee, then tea plantations in the highlands.
1931	The island becomes constitutionally autonomous on the basis of a representative system.
1948	Independence. The UNP seizes power.
1956	The UNP loses the elections to Solomon Bandaranaike (SLFP).
1959	Assassination of Solomon Bandaranaike. His widow, Sirimavo, becomes the world's first elected female leader, and puts the economy under state control.
1965	Return to power of the UNP.
1970	Tamils start armed separatist movement.
1972	Ceylon officially returns to its pre-colonial name of Sri Lanka.
1972-1975	Nationalisation of the plantations.
1977	Collapse of the left. J R Jayawardene (UNP) begins liberalisation of trade.
1978	Institution of a presidential regime based on the French model.
1983	Anti-Tamil pogroms – "Black July".
1988-1989	Ruthless suppression of fledgling youth movement.
1990	Withdrawal of Indian troops and resumption of fighting between the Sri Lankan army and the Tamil Tigers.
1991	Assassination of Rajiv Gandhi by the LTTE.
1994	The UNP loses the legislative, then the presidential elections, won by the daughter of Mrs Bandaranaike, Chandrika Kumaratunga.
1995	The Sri Lankan army controls the Jaffna peninsula.
1999	Chandrika Kumaratunga is re-elected.
2000	Death of Sirimavo Bandaranaike. Chandrika Kumaratunga is re-elected President and forms a coalition government.

THE FATE OF AN ISLAND
FROM TAPROBANE TO SRI LANKA

The island's situation at the crossroads of the monsoons of the Indian Ocean, together with the reputation of its famous spices made it a highly suitable stopping-place on the trade route between the Arabian peninsula and the Malaysian straits, and then between Europe and the China Sea. Intertwined over the centuries and fundamental to our understanding of Sri Lanka's history are its ancient kingdoms and the island's links with the outside world.

The era of the ancient kingdoms

Taprobane, the promised land of Buddhism

Several prehistoric and proto-historic sites in the central highlands testify to human occupation since very early times. Only a tiny aboriginal population remains although nowadays the **Veddahs** of the Mahiyangana region are closely integrated into society in general.

The island was largely dependent on India during its early history. Still somewhat of a mystery to Ancient Greek geographers, it was known as **Taprobane**. In the 5C BC, the main components of its modern population crossed over from the continent: **Dravidians** from the southern tip of India, and the **Sinhala**, or Sons of the Lion, who spoke an Indo-European language.

In the 3C BC, Ceylon entered the orbit of the immense Indian **Maurya** empire, the springboard for the spread of Buddhism in Asia. The Sons of the Lion, whose sovereign Mahasena embraced the new doctrine, played a major role in the spread of Buddhism overseas. On a domestic level, Buddhism constituted both a social model and the basis for the monarchy: the secular power of the monarch was exercised within the framework of the Buddhist doctrine and priesthood, over which the monarch presided.

The capital, **Anuradhapura**, became the economic and cultural centre of one of the most brilliant ancient civilisations in Asia although it was occupied at different periods by regional Dravidian powers, the most important being the reign of Elara (204-161 BC). This king, described in chronicles of the time as a wise monarch, was eventually put to flight by Dutugemunu, a Sinhalese prince from the southeast, a conquest that has been portrayed as a crusade of Buddhism against Hinduism. The Buddhist capital was then adorned with magnificent monuments and relations with the Indianised states that were emerging to the west of the Indonesian archipelago were established.

During the early Middle Ages, a network of Buddhist universities spread from the Bay of Bengal to Sumatra. We know about their development, daily life and teaching thanks to the journals kept by pilgrims who travelled from China to study the **teachings of Buddha**. Ceylon became one of the very first guardians of Buddhist doctrine and also of a number of its most outstanding relics, including the sacred tooth of Buddha, and from the 5C onwards took up a position as champion of the orthodoxy in a context of gradual disaffection on the part of the Indian monarchs for Buddhist teaching.

Serendib, at the heart of the routes of Capricorn

The Chola dominion – The **Chola** dynasty emerged in the 5C and 6C in the south of India. Using its immense and highly disciplined navy, it came to control trade up the Coromandel coast and across the Bay of Bengal, pushing into southeast Asia and Indonesia and eventually taking control of Ceylon itself. The Shiva-worshipping, Tamil-speaking Chola made the island a province of their kingdom, with **Polonnaruwa** as its administrative capital. The decline of Chola power in the early 12C resulted in the emergence of a new Sinhalese kingdom. A Buddhist state was reconstructed on the model of Anuradhapura, its overseas influence a testament to the nautical prowess of the Chola fleet. The religious foundations of the ancient royal capital were rebuilt and a model city with great palaces and monasteries was constructed at Polonnaruwa.

Muslim trading-posts – The 12C also saw a new trading network spreading across the Indian Ocean: **Arab seafarers and merchants** established a chain of trading-posts within the triangle of Djibouti, Zanzibar and Ceylon, which they named **Serendib**. However, unlike the Indian sub-continent the island did not welcome the influence of Islam which had spread rapidly from the coast of Oman during this period.

The brief Polonnaruwa period was a golden age for Ceylon with **Parakramabahu**, son of its greatest sovereign, leading military expeditions to the subcontinent. It also marked the beginnings of a decline. Torn by quarrels about the succession, and weakened by an extravagant rebuilding programme as well as raids by Malay pirates, the kingdom sank into oblivion in the 13C, unleashing two centuries of political instability. Against this backdrop the Tamils and the Sinhalese increasingly withdrew into their separate communities. The Tamils established a kingdom on the Jaffna peninsula, while the Sinhalese eventually settled at Kotte, now a suburb to the east of Colombo.

In the 13C, the state was no longer a powerful force to be reckoned with in this part of Asia. When **Marco Polo** stopped here, he was fascinated not so much by the customs and the people as by the prodigious wealth of the region. Now it was the growing demand for spices and silks on the markets of Europe and the Middle East that accelerated the development of Arab trading-posts all over the Indian Ocean, as far as the Strait of Malacca in Malaysia and even Canton in southern China.

The significance of the monsoon

The term "monsoon" comes from the Arabic word "mausim", meaning "season". Nowadays used to refer to the alternating periods of rain and drought which govern the lives of agricultural populations living around the Indian ocean, the word monsoon originally meant the pattern of winds and currents familiar to those sailing the seas of the region. During the age of sail, the only way of getting to India was in summer, while the return journey had to be made in winter, using the monsoon and the currents it generated to sail along the African coast. Before caravels arrived on the scene, the dhow was the boat of the Indian coast for which the Arabs invented the triangular sail, called a "lateen" sail. And so the spice route and its trading-posts were born.

Ceylon, the island trading-post

No longer a political force, Ceylon was merely a stopping-place on the maritime trading route, with Colombo as its main port. The choice of Kotte as capital (1415-1597), only a few kilometres from this trading emporium, was also significant, since it heralded the increasing importance of the island's maritime trading activities to its economy. But while the island set out to become a trading nation, it lost its prestige as the chosen land of Buddhism as Islam tightened its grasp on the coastal states of Malaysia, Sumatra and Java.

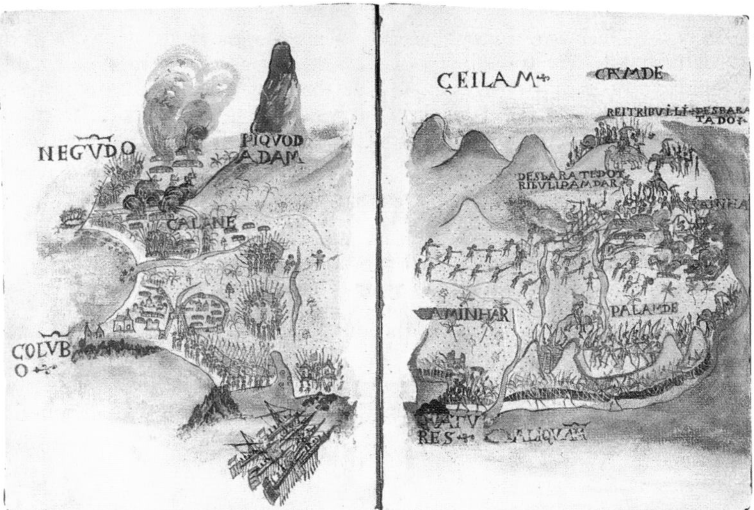

AKG Paris

Map from the "Livro de Lisuarte de Abreu" (1565)

The Portuguese missions – Pepper from Malabar, cloves from the Moluccas, cinnamon from Ceylon. As **Portuguese sailors** explored the Atlantic in their search for these spices, navigating their way with the help of the stars, they discovered a way through to the Indian Ocean via the tip of Southern Africa, which they rounded at the end of the 15C, and named the Cape of Good Hope. Onwards they went following the old Arab trail almost to the island of Malacca (Malaysia); but it was in India, on the Malabar coast, that they established their bridgehead in Asia: **Goa** became an administrative, religious and cultural metropolis with a strong racial mix. And it was here that the Portuguese set about their mission: to acquire spices and convert the people to Christianity. Along the coastline at Colombo, Galle and Puttalam the Portuguese-Goan missions converted the fishing communities and built churches.

Their doctrines won over the kingdom of Jaffna and the Sinhalese at Kotte withdrew to **Kandy** in the foothills. From then on, Ceylon was pulled in two directions. Whereas the Kandy stronghold upheld the traditions of the ancient Buddhist kingdons, the communities on the coastline nurtured an increasingly wide mix of cultures and peoples.

The Dutch period – By the end of the 16C, the spice trade had become a bone of contention between the Catholic Habsburgs and the Protestant nations, which, hitherto, had been excluded from maritime trade in these seas. In 1595, various expeditions funded by Dutch companies set out to challenge Portuguese power. In Ceylon, they secretly plotted with the Kandyan court against the Portuguese, whom they first drove out of Java (1619), then evicted permanently from the coasts of the cinnamon isle. They imposed reforms and rationalised the way in which trade was organised with the **island trading-post**, unwittingly laying the foundations for the systematic exploitation of its riches during the era of the planters. However, like the Portuguese, they never succeeded in taking possession of Kandy, the kingdom of the island's interior.

A British colony

In 1639, the Dutch were under attack from their European rivals who had settled in southern Asia. The **British**, who had obtained concessions from the Grand Moghul to open trading-posts in India, made their way around the Bay of Bengal, hotly pursued by the vessels of the French East India Company founded by Colbert, French finance minister under Louis XIV. In 1763, the Treaty of Paris ousted France, which renounced its expansionist policy in the region. The European wars and the vicissitudes of the late 18C saw Ceylon fall under the control of the British **East India Company**, which by 1815 reigned as absolute master over the Indian Ocean. This time the entire island came under British rule: the Kandyan kingdom, sapped by quarrels over the succession between factions of the aristocracy, fell into its hands like a ripe fruit.

It was at this point in the island's history that Ceylon became geared to the **plantation economy**, developed in the New and Old Worlds to satisfy the demand for products which Europe craved: **coffee** and **sugar**. Like the other islands in the Indian Ocean, it suffered the consequences of the abolition of slavery and the development of seasonal migration of workers under contract. The **coolie trade** found its labour among the Tamil peasants of southern India, who came to pick coffee and then, after 1840, **tea**. The shock waves of British "railwaymania" had repercussions in Ceylon, where the first railway line linking Colombo and Kandy was built in 1867. The opening of the Suez Canal (1869) and the appearance of tea-clippers (1870) shortened the route and journey time still further.

Colombo, Main Street

Towards the Republic of Sri Lanka

A peaceful road to independence

In imposing its economic and social system, colonisation brought about the disintegration of society with its long-standing traditions. It also encouraged the emergence of a new social contract and a middle-class of entrepreneurs that was highly Westernised: known as the "sunburnt English", they assimilated the principles of liberalism in teaching establishments both here and in Britain. When, in 1931, the British prepared to relinquish the colony, giving the island a status of **internal autonomy** and a representative system based on universal suffrage, it was this Westernised middle-class that created the first political party, the **United National Party (UNP)**, assuming responsibility for the destiny of the island.

Neither Communist leanings prevalent in South-East Asia, nor religious or ethnic strife rife in India or Pakistan marked the years of transition towards independence, which was achieved peacefully in **February 1948**, just after the end of the Second World War. But trouble was brewing as the population expanded rapidly, boosted by an improvement in living conditions and the presence of the expatriate labour from the coolie trade. By this stage, the population no longer identified themselves with their conservative rulers, who were more inclined to speak English than Sinhalese or Tamil and the economy, which had inherited the 19C plantations, was totally dependent on the vicissitudes of world markets.

1948-1977: Growing pains

The end of the 1950s was dominated by the figure of **Solomon Bandaranaike**, father of the current president, Chandrika Kumaratunga. Following in the footsteps of the first two prime ministers of the independent island, DS Senanayake and his son Dudley, he had come to power by distancing himself from the UNP and creating his own political party, the **Sri Lanka Freedom Party (SLFP)**.

The seeds of revolt – The profound social changes taking place also encouraged the formation of new political groups. Sinhalese nationalism, fuelled by Buddhist activists, succeeded in imposing Sinhalese as the official language of the country while unrest among the educated young, who were finding it hard to get jobs (the unemployment rate had reached 32 % of the working population) resulted in a swing towards the far left with Maoist tendencies. The latter was represented by the **Janatha Vimuthi Peramuna (JVP)**, who advocated revolution based on the Chinese model. The murder of Solomon Bandaranaike by a Buddhist extremist in 1959 marked the beginning of a series of political assassinations which undermined Ceylon's commitment to democracy. The widespread discontent with the conservatives who had returned to power led to victory for a united left front, headed by Mrs **Sirimavo Bandaranaike**, the Prime Minister's widow, in the 1970 elections. The new government adopted an **interventionist strategy** for the country, which became Sri Lanka in 1972.

1977-1990: separatist demands

The new liberal policy – Mrs Sirimavo Bandaranaike's nationalisation policy only partially achieved its aims. Although the irrigation programme made it possible to achieve virtual self-sufficiency in food production for the first time, the cost of the social policy was too high. The left front then suffered a crushing and unexpected defeat in the elections of 1977, leading to the return to power of the UNP, under the leadership of **JR Jayawardene**. The new head of state initiated a radical change in economic policy, replacing the socialist model applied in India by Indira Ghandi and advocated by the Bandaranaikes, with **liberalism** based on the Singaporean model, exercised within a framework of political authoritarianism. When the profits from the plantation system proved to be insufficient, the government made a massive appeal for foreign aid to develop the country's infrastructure. But, in doing so, Sri Lanka entered into a new era of dependence, with international aid and development bodies (the IMF, the World Bank) rather than private investors responding to the appeal.

Birth of the Tigers – On a general level the economy improved (unemployment levels fell, inflation dropped, the island returned to growth), but social inequalities were accentuated and tensions between the communities increased. The most serious was the increase in separatist activity by the **Tamils** in the north and east of the country. In 1981, the Liberation Tigers of Tamil Eelam (LTTE) established themselves as the spearhead of separatism and became a focus for all kinds of discontent. In essence they regarded themselves as being the victims of discrimination: in terms of culture (the official language of the country was Sinhalese, with the Tamil language being regarded as a minority language), religion (Buddhism was protected by the state within the framework of the new constitution of 1978) and political representation (there was a Sinhalese monopoly of power). Following in the footsteps of revolutionary Sinhalese youth, whose hopes had been dashed in the 1970s, young Tamils militated in favour of independence.

The start of a war – The conflict flared up when, in July 1983, the Tigers killed 13 soldiers of the Sri Lankan army in an ambush. The killings were fiercely condemned by the government which organised a state funeral thereby triggering off violent riots against the Tamil communities. Now the tragedy of the Partition of India and Pakistan was revisited upon Sri Lanka. During the conflict that has ensued it has become apparent what lies at the heart of the problem: both communities fear seeing their identity absorbed, even obliterated to the advantage of their rivals.

In 1985, peace negotiations initiated by the kingdom of Bhutan were suspended, each side refusing to budge: the Tamils demanded a federalist solution while the state insisted on maintaining the unitarian Constitution.

Mediation fails – Pressure from the Tamils of Tamil Nadu, who were worried about their cousins in Sri Lanka, combined with India's wish to establish herself as a regional superpower, led Prime Minister **Rajiv Gandhi** to intervene. By virtue of a **peace accord** signed by president Jayawardene, but not ratified by the government, Rajiv Gandhi sent an expeditionary force to Sri Lanka in 1987. While the conflict raged causing heavy losses among civilians caught in the cross-fire, the initial deployment of 1 700 soldiers rapidly increased to 45 000. Not only did the Tigers not lay down their arms but they turned against the Indian troops. Rajiv Gandhi ended up by giving into the government in Colombo, which was demanding the withdrawal of his troops. Without even an outline for a peace settlement being drawn up the retreat began in July 1989. But the Tigers did not forget the man who was responsible for the death of 2 200 of their fighters. In 1991, they orchestrated the suicide attack that caused the death of Indira Ghandhi's son.

Red revolt – The political authoritarianism of the Jayawardene government ended up prohibiting the formation of extremist leftist movements such as the JVP. The result was a **clandestine insurrection** by the JVP on the model of the Khmer Rouge which led to a reign of terror between 1987 and 1990. When **Ranasinghe Premadasa** succeeded Jayawardene as the head of the country in

1988, he clamped down hard, sending in armed militia against JVP sympathisers. The operation destroyed the framework of the JVP, and human rights organisations pointed an accusing finger at Sri Lanka.

The 1990s: a period of uncertainty

1990 saw a brief respite. But the retreat of Indian troops from the north of the island led to a resumption of fighting between the Tigers and the army. As for the UNP in power, their credibility had been undermined by tensions within the party and years of chaos ended in the assassination of R Premadasa in 1993. In 1994, a short, televised speech by the new president **Ranil Wikremesinghe** precipitated the fall of the UNP. By declaring that the minorities in the country should be kept in their place and recognise their status as subordinate members of the great Sinhalese family, he lost the support of the two largest political groups: the Ceylon Workers Congress (CWC), representing the Tamil workers in the plantations, and the Muslim Congress (SLMC). They rejoined the ranks of the SLPF the leader of which, **Chandrika Kumaratunga**, won the elections hands down (with more than 60 % of the vote).

Democracy and war – It looked as though peace had been restored but, in April 1995, the LTTE resumed hostilities after a 100-day truce. With the occupation of the Jaffna peninsula by the Sri Lankan army in December of the same year the actions of the Tigers escalated into guerrilla warfare on the northern and eastern fronts, and acts of terrorism in the rest of the country. Unable to negotiate with the Tigers the new president was forced to abandon her peace policy and restart a ruthless war against the Tigers.

At the end of 1999, when the army was still engaged in the bloodiest campaign since the end of the conflict and two top-rank Tamil politicians were murdered in the centre of Colombo during the course of the year, Chandrika Kumaratunga set the cat among the pigeons by calling presidential elections a year early. She was re-elected in December, after an attempt on her life during which she lost an eye. Democracy is still in place, even though the war continues.

Electoral campaign at Chilaw

C Bourzat

Sri Lanka today

The period following the 50th anniversary of Independence celebrations in 1988 has hardly been glorious in the political sphere. The federal organisation plan is still waiting to be implemented due to an insufficient parliamentary majority, and the reputation for corruption that has beleaguered every government since Independence persists.

However, Sri Lanka can congratulate itself on having achieved some important economic goals. The economic growth which occurred between 1991 and 1995 is all the more remarkable, given that the conflict has deprived the country of a third of its land and has weighed heavily on the state coffers. The island has also achieved almost complete economic independence from its colonial legacy and has even emerged relatively unscathed from the economic turmoil in South-East Asia

The political chessboard

In 1978, the Jayawardene government abandoned the British parliamentary regime in favour of a presidential model based on the French system, and renamed the island the Democratic Socialist Republic of Sri Lanka. The **President**, elected for a six-year term, is not only the head of the state and Commander-in-chief of the armed forces, but also head of the government. The last presidential elections, held a year early, took place in December 1999. The President appoints his cabinet of ministers, headed by a Prime Minister who has the role of arbitrator in the legislature.

The **Parliament**, the only body able to pass legislation, takes the form of a chamber of 225 deputies, elected for six years by universal suffrage according to the rules of proportional representation (a minimum of 12.5 % of the vote in a constituency is required to obtain a seat).

The government grants a considerable amount of **autonomy** to the eight provinces of the country. These are administered by a council, elected for five years, at the head of which is the Provincial Prime Minister, assisted by a governor appointed by the President.

The party currently in power is the People's Alliance, a coalition of the left formed around the **Sri Lanka Freedom Party (SLFP)**, led by Chandrika Kumaratunga Bandaranaike. The Prime Minister is none other than Mrs Sirimavo Bandaranaike, mother of the President. The main opposition party is the **United National Party**, a traditionally conservative party. Differences in the economic policy of government and opposition have become increasingly blurred over the years, the SLFP though maintains a marked leftward orientation in social policy. The ethnic and religious minorities in the country are mainly represented by the Tamil United Liberation Front (TULF), the Eelam People's Democratic Party (EPDP) and the Sri Lanka Muslim Congress (SLMC), all three of which are represented in Parliament.

Revitalising the economy

A shift in emphasis

During the second half of the 20C, the Sri Lankan economy retained much of the framework of the colonial period, relying on exports of tea, rubber and coconut derivatives. Today, the economy has really taken off, based on an increasingly wide range of resources and turning more and more towards **industry**.

In terms of volume, industry now represents 60 % of Sri Lanka's exports, compared to 2 % in 1970, while production from plantations has fallen from 90 % of exports to 3 % in twenty years.

In 1992, an overly bureaucratic management structure and generous salary system undermined revenues and the government was forced to cede the management of industries that had previously been nationalised back to private enterprise. But the coconut palm plantations were only of interest to the domestic market, while tea and rubber remained too sensitive to the fluctuations in world markets.

The "re-colonisation" of the dry area

The land improvement programme is part of a vast "re-colonisation" project, which aims to ease congestion on the over-populated southwest coast whilst compensating for the lack of land available in the higher areas of the country around Kandy. Today, the land supports two types of cultivation. The peasants continue to practise traditional farming methods, or "chena", based on crop rotation (millet, maize and cotton) over three years. Large areas are then more or less abandoned to the jungle which forms pockets of varying density, providing a refuge for wild elephants. Elsewhere, areas that have recently been re-colonised are irrigated and planted with rice.

Furthermore, latex was partly imported from Indonesia and Malaysia at lower cost. Having generated a deficit in the 1990s, tea has made a recovery since 1995, thanks to the increase in the area under cultivation.

Rice-growing has benefited enormously from large-scale irrigation projects which have enabled Sri Lanka to become virtually self-sufficient in terms of rice production. However, the Mahaweli Project has not generated enough jobs in agriculture, while the civil war has had the effect of cutting rice-production by nearly a quarter. The ambitious rice policy of the 1970s is gradually being abandoned in favour of products that are more profitable for domestic and export markets: vegetables, fruit and spices. The whole agricultural sector is still sensitive to the vagaries of the weather: hit by the drought in 1996, it still dreads the repercussions of El Niño.

Finally, **fishing** has been directly affected by the conflict, the northern and eastern coasts having provided more than half the national catch until 1983. Since then, the volume of imported fish, particularly from the Maldives, has considerably increased, together with the price of fish.

The commercial triangle

Sri Lanka's present choice of commercial partners is evidence of a complete break with the island's colonial past. Trade is now conducted with three main partners: the Western industrial powers, the "Dragons" of Asia and Japan, and the oil-producing countries.

Sri Lanka's principal trading partners in the West are the United States (65 %) and Germany, the main destinations for products from the island's **clothing industry**, which, with a value of around US$1.6 billion, constitutes Sri Lanka's main export. The **textile industry** developed after 1977 within the framework of joint-ventures funded with European and Asian capital and established in the newly created tax-free areas. However, this dynamic industry is now under threat. On the one hand Sri Lanka is not a producer and has to buy in its raw materials; on the other hand, the collapse of the stock exchange and the devaluation of the currencies of South-East Asia make these countries fierce competitors with their low prices.

Tourism constitutes the fourth source of income for the island. Having begun to develop in the late 1960s, this sector was very successful, attracting as many as 400 000 visitors in 1982. Having been badly affected by the civil war and undermined by the social instability of the late 1990s, tourism showed signs of recovery in 1997, attracting 366 200 visitors that year. Here too, Sri Lanka must compete with destinations such as Thailand which, like Sri Lanka, favours mass tourism, but has the advantage of being a more stable environment and benefiting from highly competitive prices.

Sri Lanka's Asian partners – Japan, Korea, Hong Kong and Singapore – have become its main suppliers of both **consumer goods** and the **raw materials** required by its textile industry, as well as of motor vehicles.
As for the Gulf States, they are Sri Lanka's main purchasers of **tea** and supply Sri Lanka with petroleum, which is refined near Colombo, and which still supplies two-thirds of the country's energy. But Sri Lanka has a very special link with the Gulf States since it supplies most of the emigrant work force to those countries. In fact, 1.2 million Sri Lankans, 80 % of whom are (often unqualified) women, work abroad, and through their earnings carefully saved and sent back, they constitute the country's third-highest source of revenue (US$880 million in 1998). The Middle East is the largest labour market, with 250 000 Sri Lankans in Saudi Arabia, 125 000 in Kuwait, and 105 000 in the United Arab Emirates *(see insert p 64)*.

The social sphere

Sri Lanka can pride itself on its leaders' genuine concern for the social welfare of its people, and this has been so since the earliest years of independence. The country has several remarkable achievements including its extremely high **literacy rate** (89 %), the highest in Asia, made possible by free education. The **social security** system is the most successful in Asia. Finally, a national awareness programme has achieved **population control**, all the more remarkable for a population that increased at an alarming rate during the 20C (2.4 million in 1870, 6.6 million in 1946, 18.7 million in 1997).
Successive governments have financed the cost of these programmes by various means. Under the SLFP leadership in the 1970s, profits from the plantations were diverted to this end. Then, from the 1980s onwards, appeals were made for international financial aid. Initially they led to a worrying level of foreign debt, which has now been brought under control and represents 69.7 % of the GDP.

The price of war

Today the problem is that more than a quarter of government revenue is absorbed by the **cost of the war**. In the absence of conscription, the government has had to mount an intensive recruitment campaign for an army which, when the conflict started in 1983, numbered only 9 000 men. Now there are 165 000 men and women, although still not enough to cope with the onslaught by the Tamil rebel guerrillas, estimated to number only 10 000. In a country where the unemployment rate stands at 12 % and the average monthly salary of a civil servant is about 3 000Rs, a soldier's pay of 7 000Rs (including a risk premium), added to which is an undertaking to reimburse the cost of food, travel and medical care, is regarded as attractive. However, the Sri Lankan army has the highest desertion rate in the world and it is struggling to maintain a large enough force.
Since the conflict began, this problem has continued to dog the government: the population has been taught to depend on a providential State but the price of the war for peace is high.

Tea in Sri Lanka

We owe the invention of Ceylon tea to a Scotsman, James Taylor. Between 1860 and 1870, he conducted experiments on various young plants imported from Assam and China, at a time when the coffee grown by the first planters, which was ravaged by disease, was threatened with ruin. Tea proved to be a much more attractive crop, being hardy enough to be planted on high ground where coffee would not grow. Suddenly, new land was turned over to tea plantations. Today, tea bushes, carefully trimmed like Bonsai plants, hug every curve and slope of the mountainous region.

An army of pickers

Native to China, the tea plant has white flowers and evergreen leaves and belongs to the camellia family. In the wild, it takes the form of a small tree, but when cultivated, it is a **bush**, no more than a metre and a half in height.

Picking, which takes place up to fifteen times a year, is done by hand, the pickers selecting the **bud** and the two young leaves which are used to make tea. Six hundred thousand pickers draped in the boldly coloured saris traditionally worn by Tamil women work the 220 000ha of Sri Lanka's plantations. In the space of a couple of hours, they fill the basket

The tea coolies

When coffee was the main crop, planters recruited hundreds of thousands of Tamils from southern India who would come over for the harvest from mid August to November, while their paddy fields were inactive. Labour was cheap. However, this new industry required harvesting throughout the year and instead of being seasonal, the Tamil migration became permanent, leading to a considerable change in the composition of the population. Today, the plantation region is dotted with their churches, mosques and Hindu temples, often modest in size, but always brilliantly coloured.

Blenders of the Lipton company in Colombo

R Holzbachova-Ph Bénet

carried on their backs, slung from a headband. A stick is used to flatten the bush, enabling the pickers to see which shoots to pick. Working eight hours a day, up to their waists in a sea of green tea bushes, on average they collect 18kg per day, which translates into a monthly wage of about US$50.

The different stages of tea production

The tea plant may have a docile temperament, but processing the leaves is a different story altogether: the vine does not produce the wine!

Once harvested, the alchemy of tea takes place in three stages at the factory. First, the **withering process** involves spreading the pickings on grids to extract some of the 70 % of water contained in the leaves. Then comes the **rolling process**: machines grind the tea for an hour and a half so that the essential oils are released. The leaves are then placed on a conveyor belt so that the leaves ready for the **fermentation** process, a key stage in the production of black tea because it releases the tannins, can be selected. At this stage, the leaves, which have been roughly treated in the previous operations, are left to rest for three hours. They still retain 30 % of their water but after the **drying** process, the tea contains no more than 2 % of water. At the end of this cycle, 100kg of leaves produces 20kg of tea. The last stage, **sifting**, when the leaves are graded according to size, determines the quality of the tea. In Sri Lanka, they like **strong tea**, made with microscopically small particles of tea. Coarser fibres are used to make a lighter drink, while blending yields teas of widely different strengths. The tea from the tea plantations is not what you put in your teapot at the breakfast table. It is sent to Colombo where it is blended and packaged for distribution.

The tea auction

On June 29, 1998, the Chamber of Commerce in London witnessed the last sitting of a ritual introduced in 1679 by the East India Company: the tea auction. Orchestrated by distinguished connoisseurs, the tea "noses", who taste and compare hundreds of varieties, the teas are classified according to grade, season and plantation of origin, then auctioned off to the highest bidder. Fast losing momentum in the UK where tea is a national institution, and now at the mercy of the Internet, the tea auction is currently held in cities in the large tea-producing regions: Mombassa in Kenya, Calcutta in India and Colombo.

Small businesses win the day

While Sri Lanka remains the second-largest producer of tea in the world after India, which dominates the industry with its low production costs, its reputation for quality makes it the largest exporter. At the end of the 1990s, the drought which had a severe impact on production in India and Kenya enabled Sri Lanka to expand sales significantly. The island also gained two new, important customers: Russia and the Gulf States.

The bureaucratic nature of the large plantations (half of which still belong to the state) prevented them from being able to cope with this additional demand and it was the small, private producers in the heart of the island who responded to the opportunity. Whereas their fields comprise 40 % of the land devoted to tea cultivation, they now provide 60 % of national production. Industry analysts anticipate that they could soon be supplying as much as two-thirds of the national quota. The low costs associated with family farming make them much more competitive and the cultivation of spices, fruit and vegetables in addition to tea shelters them from the dangers of monoculture.

THE ISLAND'S ARTISTIC HERITAGE

What better place for an artistic melting-pot, than an island at the crossroads of the Asian trading routes? The fusion of the many different Sri Lankan identities has resulted in works of powerful originality, even more remarkable for having developed independently from the island's mighty neighbour, India. Spread out over three important periods in history, the island's artistic prowess is almost entirely dedicated to Buddhism. At **Anuradhapura**, the first great capital, religious architecture assumed magnificent proportions under royal patronage. Royal patronage was also in evidence at **Polonnaruwa**, but the results were stylistically different and new to Asia. Finally, during the **Kandyan** era, we see the triumph of regional artistic schools, financed by local dignitaries, monks and other worthies.

Whether they are profane or sacred works, paintings or engravings, on rock or on buildings, the island's creative expression always exudes a sense of harmony with the environment and the landscape, with a subtle evocation of the natural world that no modern landscape painter could fail to admire.

Buddhist art

Monasteries and community life

At several places on the island, natural **caves**, with their inscriptions, provide some idea of what the very first monasteries were like: shelters carved into the rock, their sparseness conducive to a life of meditation. The monastery of Vesagiriya, to the south of Anuradhapura *(see p 184)*, and the caves of Mulgirigala, to the north of Tangalle *(see p 300)*, are good examples of these austere, rocky retreats.

Generously endowed by the sovereigns, the monasteries built in the capital gradually helped to shape the architectural structure of these places devoted to community life. The religious buildings stood inside a protective inner wall: the sacred **Bo tree** (*bodhighara*), **reliquary monument** (*stupa or dagoba*) and its chapel, and the **image hall** (*patimaghara, pilimage* or *gedige*). In this same complex, a room, usually a hypostyle was used by the Venerables when preaching; another was used by the monks during the fasting ceremony and for confession (*uposathaghara* or *poyage*). The monastery of Jetavanarama at Anuradhapura *(see p 176)*, which has been painstakingly restored by UNESCO, and the Pirivena monastery at Polonnaruwa *(see p 196)* are amongst some of the finest examples of these old monastic complexes.

Environmentally-friendly monks

Visitors to Sri Lanka today are often struck by the high standards of hygiene in the country's ancient monasteries. The baths, which still stand beside the latrines, were fed by underground water channels, and effluent was removed with real concern for the environment. In the museum at Jetavanarama at Anuradhapura, a device found at the entrance to the conduit indicated how water was removed from the latrines: it consisted of three superimposed earthenware jars, the first filled with coal, the second with lime and the third with sand, which acted as a septic tank.

The community buildings were laid out within an external wall where the monastic cells, the refectory, the dispensaries, the wells and the pools were situated. Only the architectural form and the scale of the buildings have changed over the years. Today's monasteries retain the same basic layout, though the architecture is more subdued, with pink tiled roofs and whitewashed walls dating from the Kandyan period.

From a cult of symbols...

In its early days, Buddhism relied solely on symbols, since it abstained from any human representation of Buddha. The appearance of the latter is still a bone of contention among scholars of Buddhist art in Asia who seem unclear whether it originated in India or Ceylon. No firm conclusion has yet been reached. However, there is no doubt that, for five hundred years, the objects of Buddhist devotion consisted of either **symbolic images** or **holy relics**.

The former often refer to events from the life of Buddha: the tree represents his Enlightenment; the *stupa* his Extinction. These symbols are still indisputably part of any modern representation. Two footprints *(sri pada)*, carved in the hollow of a paving stone, evoke his immortal presence. Other images, such as the jar of abundance, the parasol or the fly-swat are popular symbols associated with royalty and prosperity. We find the same tendency towards symbolism in the architecture: the main buildings erected for worship are the **bodhighara**, an enclosure built around a cutting from the tree of Enlightenment, or the **dagoba**, a monumental shrine in its own right. This architectural form, which pervades the history of the art of Ceylon, is more than a mere shrine. Built to house relics and accompanied by other treasures, the *stupa* assumed the form of a tumulus, or burial mound, thus perpetuating the memory of the *Parinirvana*, "the great Extinction", the final aim of Buddhists, which occurred at the death of Buddha. From the Anuradhapura period onwards, they assumed a cosmogonic connotation – they became an ideal representation of the world – with buttresses engraved with symbols built around the central dome, representing the four cardinal points. At Anuradhapura, and at all the other sacred sites on the island, the *stupa* is a priceless object of pilgrimage and veneration.

The legend of the "dagoba"

According to popular belief, the form of this building was dictated by Buddha himself. When his disciples asked him about the possibility of erecting a memorial to him after his death, the Master replied that his teachings alone must be the object of veneration. On saying this, he spread out the robe that he wore on his shoulders, folded it carefully into a square and covered it with his begging bowl, thus sketching out the form of the "dagoba": a dome placed above a square terrace.

...to a cult of images

In the 2C and 3C AD, Buddha ceased to be worshipped exclusively in symbolic form and the first effigies appeared.

The Buddha in samadhi – The Master is depicted sitting, in the position which led him to Enlightenment: the *samadhi* or position of mental calm. His legs are crossed, as in the statues of Southern India. The smooth robe that swathes his

B Simmons / DIAF

The giant Buddha of Gal Vihara at Polonnaruwa

body is gathered at the front, on the left side of his body. His hands are placed on his lap, palms upwards, in an expression of meditation *(dhyana mudra)*. The Buddha in *samadhi* at Anuradhapura is a serene expression of these early images *(see p 178)*.

Giant statuary – In the 8C and 9C, changes in devotional practice led to the replacement of the *dagoba* by giant statues of Buddha, draped in a folded robe. Most often he is depicted **standing**, with one hand raised in a sign of peace *(abhaya mudra)*. This is how he is portrayed at several places on the island, at Avukana, Sasseruwa and Maligawila, sculpted in the living rock, the statues assuming gigantic proportions.

He is sometimes portrayed **supine**, as at Gal Vihara at Polonnaruwa, his head resting on the open palm of his hand. When the soles of his feet are parallel it means that he is resting. If his right foot is slightly withdrawn, it means that he is dead and about to enter *Parinirvana*.

This vogue of creating giant statues was accompanied by the depiction of deities associated with the "large vehicle" trend of Buddhism: the **bodhisattvas**. These "beings of the Enlightenment", who are the saints of Buddhism, invested with the virtues of wisdom and compassion, were not depicted as monks, but as princes sporting an array of jewels.

There are still some splendid examples in the south of the island: the statue of Avalokiteshvara, standing in the forest of Maligawila *(see p 272)*, the silent dialogue of the figures carved in the rock at Buduruvegala *(see p 270)*, or the solitary statue of the king of Weligama, who was mysteriously cured of leprosy *(see p 288)*.

The hall of the image – Other signs of a new era in the Buddhist religion include the appearance and development at Polonnaruwa from the 11C onwards, of the **patimaghara** or **gedige**, the "hall of the image", which often housed huge statues of Buddha, created from a core of bricks *(see p 197)*. These constitute one of the most original creations in medieval architecture in Ceylon. Their form has varied considerably over the centuries, ending, during the Kandyan period, with more austere, modest buildings, housing a contrasting profusion of brightly-coloured statues and paintings.

The anonymous world of the natural spirits

A whole series of worshippers gathers around the religious images. The "yakkhini", the tree spirits, are depicted as three female deities, whose bodies are coiled around the fetish tree like a creeper. The trees of the forest spring up from the depths of the earth where treasure, precious stones and precious metals are hidden, guarded by "yakkha", the partners of the "yakkhini". Snakes or "naga" are the masters of this underground world. Powerful beings, protectors of the fertility of the sun and water, they are generally depicted as hybrid man-serpents, their coiled or twisted tails representing their body, with a cobra's hood for a tiara.

The miniature world of the kandyan temples

During the Kandyan period, religious architecture ceased to be ostentatious in size and appearance. On the contrary, builders played the card of modesty, sometimes even drawing their inspiration from such humble buildings as rice stores built on piles. They also erected numerous **rock temples**, sometimes over earlier ancient religious foundations, hidden in caves or under rocky escarpments, to which they would add a simple whitewashed façade, pierced with baluster windows and heavy wooden doors. On entering the Silver Temple *(see p 168)* or the one at Degaldoruwa *(see p 230)*, you have the feeling of opening a door into another world.

The **hall of the image** is the most important building: the richness of its interior decoration provides a marked contrast to the austerity of the building as a whole. But this prolific ornamentation has a meaning, the temple being a representation of the **supernatural world**. At the far end, the main image is a Buddha bathed in colour, seated under a *makara torana* or lying down. On the ceiling, painted panels depict the battle against "and defeat of Mara", or portray deities in their palaces or their vehicle. On the walls at the side are depicted the last existence of Buddha or his former lives *(jataka)*, the Seven Weeks after the Enlightenment *(Sat Sati)*, the Sixteen Pilgrimage Sites *(Solosmasthana)* on the island, or the 24 previous Buddhas (the *suvisi vivarana* or 24 Annunciations). Often, on either side of the door, there are portraits of the people who commissioned the paintings: monks, sovereigns or dignitaries, in the costume appropriate to their standing. You will see these shimmering universes, which always have a didactic message, at the Vijaya Sundarama Vihara at Kandy *(see p 225)*, at the Temple of Delgadoruwa *(see p 230)* and at the monastery of Purvarama, in the south of the island *(see p 287)*.

The image hall stands beside a sanctuary, preceded by an antechamber or surrounded by an ambulatory. Secondary oratories *(devala)* are dedicated to other deities. A **dagoba** houses the holy relics that have been there since the foundation of the temple and a **bodhighara** protects the Bo tree, surrounded by a terrace dotted with altars for receiving offerings of flowers. Monastic life unfolds around the residences *(avasa)*, the preaching halls *(bana maduwa)*, the chapter-house *(poyage)* and the library.

The teaching of the "jatakas"

The former lives of Buddha are the subject of an anthology of 547 fables and parables, which provide the subjects for the decoration of temples and the edification of the faithful. Prince Siddharta becomes Buddha at the end of a long journey of re-births which see him as a lion or a rabbit, a naga or a spirit, a Brahman or a king. The panorama of these successive lives is a model of progression. His ten former existences thus exalt the ten greatest virtues of Buddhist philosophy. The 547th fable portrays him with the traits of Prince Vessantara who does not hesitate to give away what is most precious to him: the lucky elephant of his father's kingdom, his wife and his two children. The Vessantara jataka emphasises the importance that Buddhists place on giving: the intention to give has its value and extreme generosity frees the giver from all attachment.

The landscape

All the art of ancient Ceylon is pervaded by a love of nature, which finds its most eloquent expression in **gardens**, majestic compositions created with the aim of pleasing royalty or providing solitary environments suited to monastic meditation. When a *Sangha* received a piece of land on which to establish his community, it was usually in the form of a park or garden. The latter have not survived to the present day, but from the ruins of certain monasteries and the spatial layout of this "open" architecture, it is easy to imagine the harmony that existed between the monks and their surroundings. Sri Lanka also boasts examples of gardens conceived for the pleasure of the king and his gynaeceum (women's living quarters), some of them among the most ancient in the world: the Park of the Goldfish at Anuradhapura *(see p 182)* and the terraced gardens at Sigiriya *(see p 205)*. These artificial landscapes combine the fantasy of outcrops of natural rock with man-made pavilions and pools, all linked by **water**. Transported in channels or stored in reservoirs, water is used to create subtle plays of waterfalls or streams, bringing life and freshness to this recreation of nature.

Other forms of art

The Dravidian legacy

The presence of Hindu communities throughout Ceylon's history together with the patronage of Southern Indian powers have endowed the island with some fine, albeit rare, examples of Dravidian art.

During the period when the island was dominated by the Cholas of Tanjore, the medieval city of Polonnaruwa accommodated several Hindu buildings, mainly dedicated to Shiva, the form and construction of which were quite distinct from their Buddhist counterparts. The first were built in stone, whereas later buildings were mostly built in brick. The nearer you get to the holy of holies inside, the smaller the building becomes, whereas the halls of the image of Buddha are built around a giant statue.

Gopuram of a Hindu temple

C Bowman / SCOPE

The Hindu temples of Polonnaruwa have also produced some magnificent examples of medieval **statuary** from Southern India, with dancing Shivas, sensuously feminine Parvatis and hieratic Vishnus. Today, you will find these stone or bronze statues in the museums in Colombo *(see p 127)* and Polonnaruwa *(see p 200)*.

The prevailing model in the architecture of temples built in our time is that of the last phase of the Tamil Nadu style, where the sanctuary is preceded by a monumental porch, the **gopuram**, decorated with coloured statues of the heroes and gods of the Indian pantheon.

Western influences

As the Portuguese, Dutch and British settled in Ceylon, completely new architectural forms, suitable for their religions and ways of life, sprang up across the island. To begin with, they conducted their affairs from the shelter of the ramparts of a fort. Built by the Portuguese, but considerably altered by their successors, the Dutch, these constructions punctuate the coasts of Sri Lanka. Often, all that remains are a few fragments of wall, or an imposing gateway that guarded access to the fort. The stronghold that once protected the important harbour of Galle is the largest surviving Dutch citadel in the world. None of the **churches** built by the Portuguese has survived on the island and the Roman Catholic churches that can still be seen, especially along the west coast, were built during the period of British colonisation, according to the neo-Gothic or neo-Renaissance models which were in vogue at the time in Victorian England. There are two rare examples of 17C Protestant churches surviving in Galle and Colombo.

Finally, Sri Lanka is a veritable anthology of **colonial houses**, skilfully combining Western comforts (the fireplaces of the homes of the tea planters in the mountainous regions) with features necessitated by the tropical climate (the cool verandas of the houses in Galle).

Lexicon of architecture and imagery

Abhaya	Canonical gesture of Buddha: his hand is raised level with his shoulder, his palm held towards the body.
Anda	Dome of a dagoba.
Arama or -rama	Park, garden, monastic residence.
Bodhighara	Enclosure or building erected around the Tree of Enlightenment.
Chaitya	Monumental reliquary.
Chattravali	Pile of masonry disks on the top of a monumental reliquary, featuring a parasol, a symbol of royalty.
Dagoba	Monumental reliquary.
Devale	Temple dedicated to a god of the Sinhalese pantheon.
Dig-ge	"Long house", the hypostyle of the tambourine players in front of a Sinhalese temple.
Gana	Pot-bellied dwarfs and dancers depicted in friezes.
Ge	Hall, house.
Gedige	Temple of the image (or patimaghara).
Gopuram	The sculpted porch of a Hindu temple.
Hamsa	Goose or swan, mythical bird of the Indian bestiary.
Harmika	Small pavilion or palace forming the base of the finial of a monumental reliquary.
Jataka	A story of one of Buddha's 547 previous lives.
Kovil	Temple of a Hindu god.
Kuti	Monk's cell.
Linga	The phallic stone symbol of the god Shiva.
Makara	Mythical, composite animal borrowed from Indian bestiary.
Makara torana	Porch with a canopy terminating with the mouths of makaras, surmounted by two rows of deities.
Mudra	Particular gestures used in Buddhist and Hindu statues.
Nagaraja	King-serpent, guardian spirit.
Nataraja	"King of the dance", aspect of the god Shiva often depicted in medieval Hindu statuary.
Ola	Manuscript written on tallipot leaves.
Padapittika	Flagstones engraved with a footprint.
Padma	Lotus, sacred flower sometimes personified by a dwarf.
Pasada	Palace.
Pokuna	Pool.
Potgul	Library and room set apart for scribes in a monastery.
Poyage	"Hall of the full moon", where the monastery chapter would meet to recite Buddhist doctrine on nights with a full moon (or Uposathaghara).
Punkalasa	Jar of abundance, symbolic motif.
Samadhi	The seated lotus position, the bodily attitude suited to meditation.
Sandakada pahana	Stone threshold in the shape of a half-moon.
Sri pada	Holy footprint.
Tampita vihara	Buddhist temple built on piles.
Thûpa	Monumental reliquary.
Tribangha	Characteristic sensual pose of much statuary of the Indian tradition.
Vahalkada	Buttresses built at the four cardinal points of a dagoba.
Vajra	Symbol of purification and wisdom of esoteric Buddhism, in the form of a sceptre bulging at either end.
Vatadage	Circular temple sheltering a dagoba under a roof over a structure supported by several concentric rows of pillars, sometimes with external walls and balustrades (pali thûpaghara).
Vihara	A Buddhist temple complex, a temple on its own or a complex of buildings (viharaya in the case of a large complex).
Yoni	Sculpted flagstone symbolising the womb, into which a linga is inserted.

MONUMENTAL RELIQUARY

DAGOBA

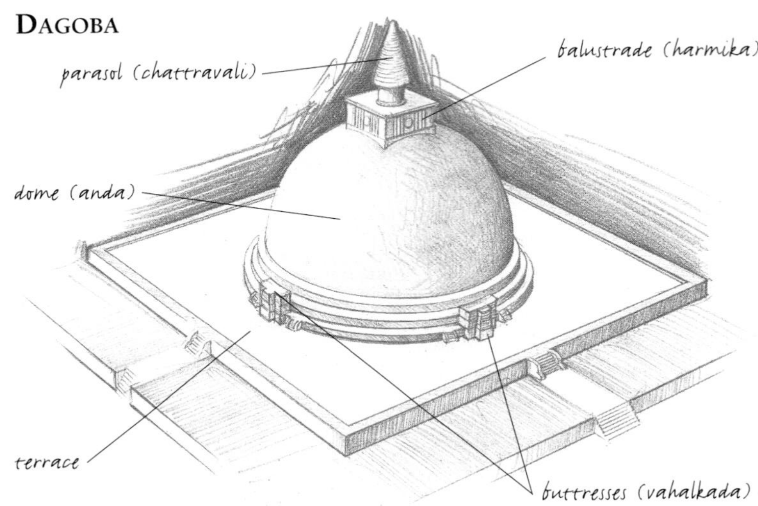

RECONSTRUCTION OF A VATADAGE

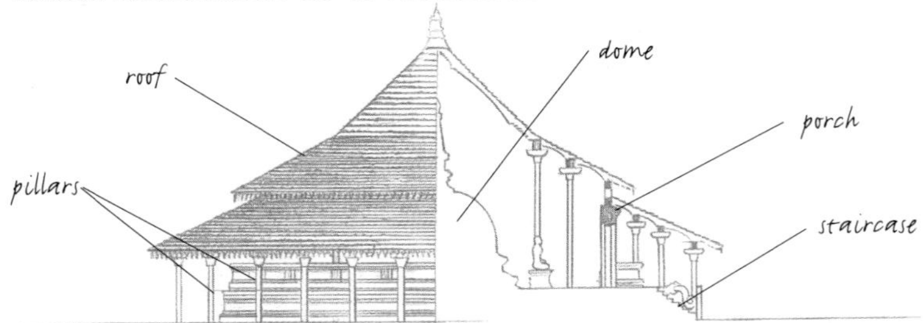

RUINED VATADAGE

ARCHITECTURAL ELEMENTS

HALL OF THE IMAGE IN THE KANDYAN PERIOD

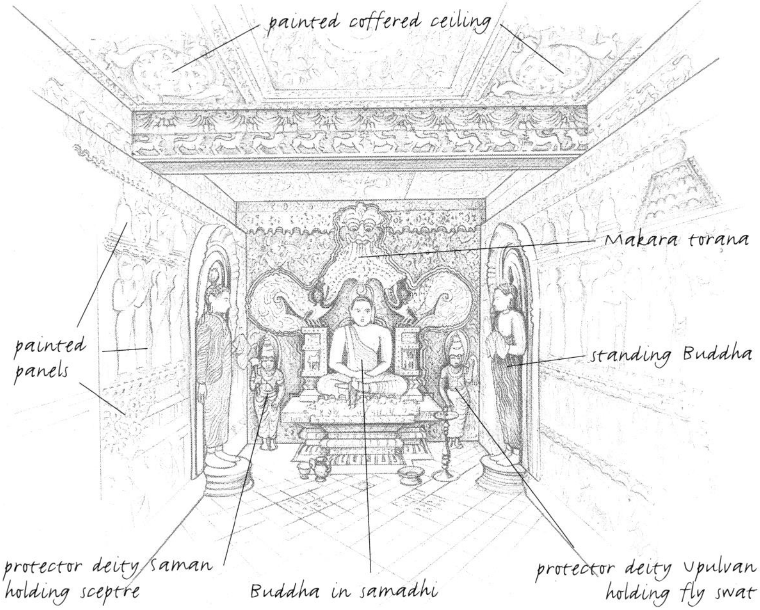

painted coffered ceiling
Makara torana
painted panels
standing Buddha
protector deity Saman holding sceptre
Buddha in samadhi
protector deity Upulvan holding fly swat

STAIRCASE

ramp (makara)
decorated stelae
stone threshold in the shape of a half moon (sandakada pahana)
king-serpent (nagaraja)
dwarfs (gana)

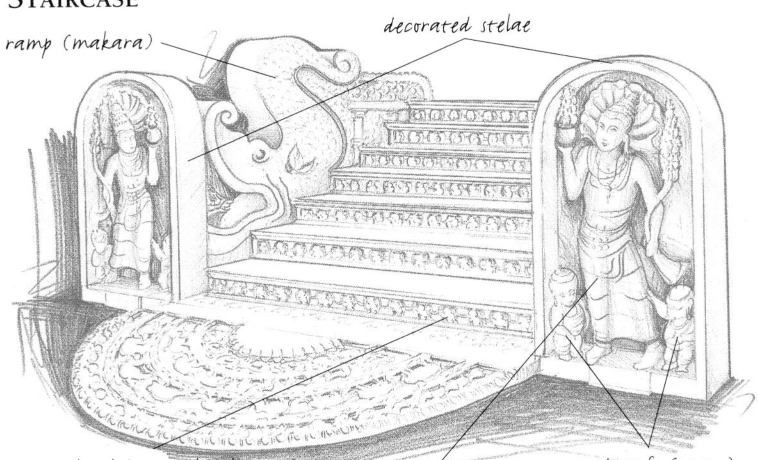

H. Choimet

BUDDHIST TEMPLE

BUDDHIST TEMPLE DURING MEDIEVAL TIMES

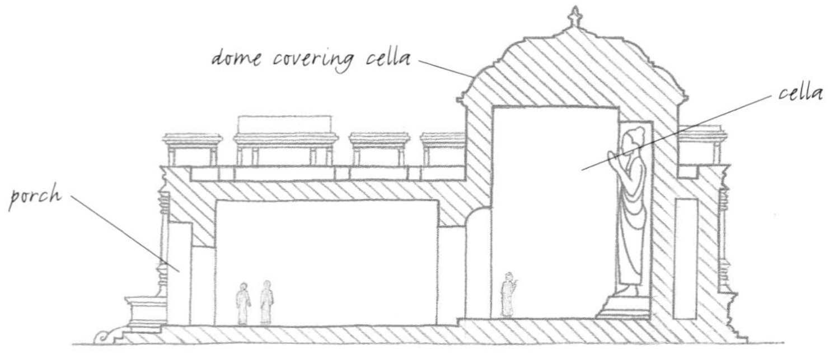

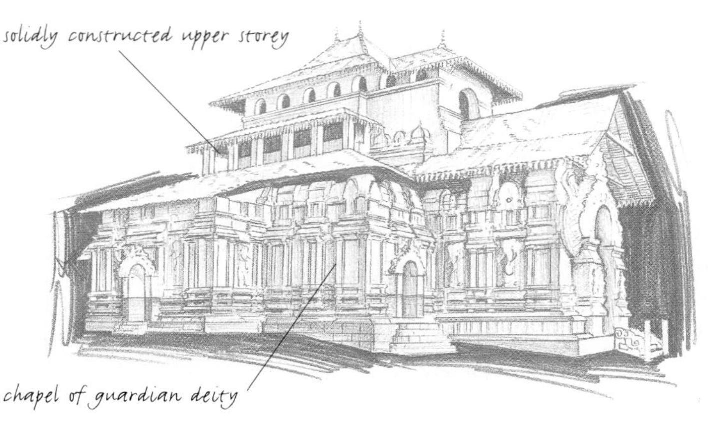

H. Choinet

CLASSIC KANDYAN TEMPLE

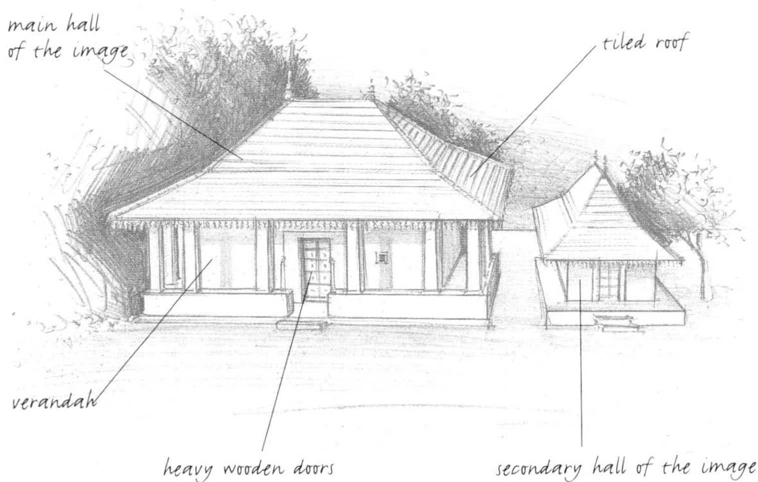

KANDYAN SEMI-ROCK TEMPLE

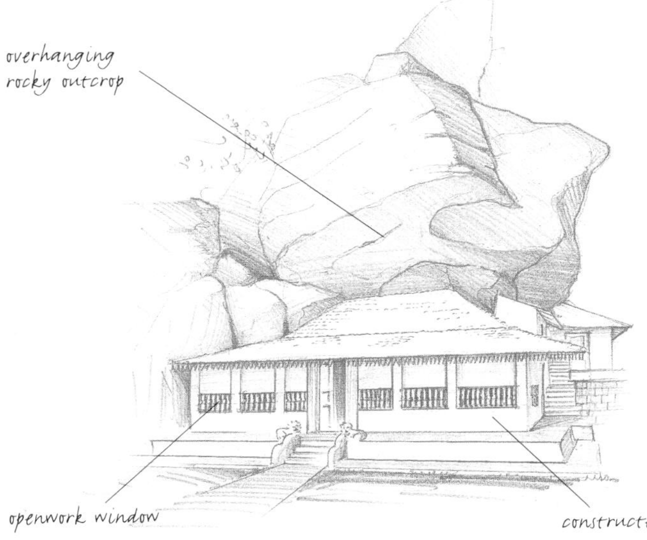

H. Choinet

Meeting the people

B Brillion

Sri Lankan faces

AN ETHNIC MELTING-POT

The population of Sri Lanka is 18 721 000, of whom 74% are Sinhalese and 18% Tamils. One of the legends in the chronicle known as the *Mahavamsa* describes the people of the island before the era of great maritime trade. Since then, history has made this country a melting-pot of cultures and ethnic groups, and mixed marriages have erased the differences to such an extent that, nowadays, it is impossible to distinguish a Tamil from a Sinhalese on the basis of physical appearance alone. As for the aboriginal inhabitants of the island, they have long since been absorbed and constitute less than 1% of the population.

Origins – the myth

When the prophets announced that a princess from Magadha, a province of north-eastern India, would lie with a lion her father locked her up to protect her from her fate. But the young girl managed to escape and as she ran through the forest, was carried off by a lion. The prophecy having come true, the girl gave birth to twins, a boy, Sinha Bahu and a girl, Sinha Valli. Ashamed of his paternal origins, Sinha Bahu, now a young man, killed his father and then married his sister. From their numerous descendants **Vijaya**, the Victorious, was born, who set off for Ceylon with 800 companions. When they arrived, the magic spells of the *yakkhini* **Kuveni** brought about their capture. But then smitten by Vijaya, Kuveni helped him to conquer her people, the *Yakkhas*, the earliest inhabitants of the island. However, Vijaya soon forgot her treacherous assistance. Once the *Yakkhas* had been conquered, he abandoned Kuveni to marry a princess from southern India.

The peoples of legend...

Three peoples appear in this legend: the **Sinhalas**, the descendants of the lion *(sinha)*; the **Dravidians**, represented by the Indian princess who married Vijaya; the **Yakkhas**, the native inhabitants of Ceylon from whom the Veddas are possibly descended.

The Sinhalese – They consider themselves to be the Sinhalas, and it is the lion from which they are descended that appears on the Sri Lankan flag brandishing a sword. Legend suggests that they originated in northern India, and this seems to be confirmed by their language, **Sinhalese** or **Sinhala**, which became Sri Lanka's official language *(see p 76)*.

The other common denominator of this ethnic majority is its widespread allegiance to **Buddhism**, although one factor distinguishes theirs from other societies professing this religion: **a caste system**, similar to the one in India.
Based on socio-economic principles, it has evolved over the centuries, and been strongly influenced by the Tamil tradition which places those who work on the land, the **Vallalas**, very high in the hierarchy: during the Kandyan period, members of the nobility took Vallala as a name for the caste. From the 16C onwards, European occupation was responsible for the partial disintegration of this system, although it was soon to be replaced by another. The **Udaratas**, the "people of the highlands", who had withdrawn to the interior of the island under the aegis of the kingdom of Kandy, passed themselves off as a conservative aristocracy upholding traditions in contrast to the **Pataratas**, the "people of the lowlands" who lived in the coastal provinces and who were subject to foreign influences. Even today, surnames still reveal aristocratic or common origins.

The Tamils – Originally from the south of India, they are divided into the **Sri Lankan Tamils**, who have lived on the island for more than 2 000 years, and the **immigrant Tamils**, who arrived in the 19C to work on the tea plantations. In the early 20C, Tamils constituted more than 28 % of the population. Having been pressed into service as *coolies* or having migrated in search of other work, the Tamils have created a diaspora throughout the countries bordering the Indian Ocean: there are some 62 million of them, of whom the majority live in Sri Lanka, Malaysia, South Africa and Singapore. These figures also highlight one of the issues at the heart of the conflict with the Sinhalese. The Tamils are perceived as a danger to the Sinhalese identity, while they regard themselves as an oppressed people within the Sri Lankan state. A section of this community also provides logistical and financial support for their fellow Tamils who have taken up arms: it is no accident that they style themselves as **Tigers**, in stark contrast to the symbol of Sri Lanka, the lion.
For all that, the population of immigrant Tamils has suffered a steady decline in recent years (9.4 % in 1971, 5.5 % in 1981), either because they have returned to India, or because they have been absorbed into the ranks of Sri Lankan Tamils. Even so, the two communities hardly ever intermingle.
The low-caste, or "untouchable" origin of the immigrants alienates them in the eyes of the native Tamils, whose society is extremely hierarchical. Furthermore, the separatism claimed by the Eelam party scarcely offers much hope to a population stranded in the plantation region. Like the Sinhalese, the Tamils can be recognised by their language, **Tamil**, sustained by a literary tradition hundreds of years old, and by their religion, **Hinduism**, although around 20 % of them have long since been converted to Christianity.

A mischievous look from a passing train

J du Boisberranger / HEMISPHERES

The Veddahs – Gradually forced back to the eastern edges of the heart of the island, the Veddas make up the **aboriginal** component of the population, and are now gradually dying out. Absorbed into the Tamils of Batticaloa or the Sinhalese of Uva, there are no more than 300 people left speaking the language of their ancestors. They are, without any doubt, the legacy of one of the first colonisations of the island. The chronicles of the Indian world used to make reference to the *yakkha* (natural spirit) or *naga* (dragon) when referring to the peoples of Asian countries before the introduction of Indian influences. The Veddahs – whose name means "hunter" – survived colonisation from the continent by retreating into the highlands. Despite legendary claims surrounding their origins, there is nothing to suggest any attempt on the part of the Sinhalese kingdoms to wipe them out.

...and the peoples of history

Sri Lanka has also witnessed successive waves of immigrants after Ceylon became first an island trading-post on the spice route, then a British colony.

The Muslims – Whilst bound together by the **Sunnite form of Islam**, they had widely disparate origins. Communities of Arab merchants settled in the 8C and 9C in the eastern part of the Indian Ocean. The earliest reference to them in the history of the island comes from Beruwela, near Kalutara, which grew up around the cult of the tomb of a Muslim saint in 1204. These groups gradually settled and expanded by marrying into the local population.

Under British domination, the **Moors** (a term inherited from the Portuguese), Muslims who had been born on the island and spoke Tamil, were set apart from the **Malays**. The latter, who were concentrated around the port of Hambantota, and who number approximately 40 000 today, are the descendants of civilian and military employees exported by the Dutch from their Indonesian colonies. Unlike other Tamil-speaking Muslims, who also sometimes speak Sinhalese, they speak a **créole** with a strong Malaysian influence.

A family spirit

Despite the differences in their origins, the Muslims form a very close-knit community which expresses itself through a political party, the Sri Lanka Muslim Congress. They have been particularly active during the conflict, since the partition claimed by the Tamil separatists directly affects them: in fact, one third of the population in the east of the island is Muslim.

The Burghers – Once upon a time, this term was used to describe the **Europeans** – mainly the Portuguese and the Dutch – employed in the service of the East India Company or free to set up in business on their own. With the onset of British colonisation, in which they played an important auxiliary role, this distinction disappeared: the word Burgher began to be used to describe anyone with European ancestors. During the same period, they abandoned the language of Dutch in favour of **English** and monopolised the top posts in the colonial administration. With the gaining of independence, when Sinhalese replaced English as the official language, many of them chose exile, with Australia as a favourite destination. Today these heirs to the colonial past number about 35 000, and openly describe themselves as a community threatened with extinction. Their chief spokesman is the humorous writer, **Carl Müller**.

Religions

Having enjoyed a golden age in the pre-medieval period, Buddhism is still the dominant religion of Sri Lanka, practised by 69 % of the population. According to Article 9 of the Constitution, it is the State's duty to grant it priority and to protect it, at the same time guaranteeing freedom of worship to other religions. The remainder of the population is divided between Hinduism (15 %), mainly among the Tamils, Sunnite Islam (8 %) and Christianity (8 %).

The way of the Buddha

One of the paradoxes of Sri Lanka is the fact that it is simultaneously a preserver of the most orthodox form of Buddhism, the **Theravada**, yet responsible for leading it through profound changes since the end of the 19C in order to adapt it to the modern world. Sri Lanka has always been able to reconcile Theravada with other religious cults, an attitude that has resulted in the saying: "The Buddha for spiritual refuge, the gods for temporal help".

The three joys of Buddhism

"I take refuge in the Buddha, the Dharma, the Sangha", murmur the faithful seated at prayer on the square in front of the *dagobas*. This is not a creed but an enunciation of the three pillars of the Buddhist faith.

The way of the Buddha – **Siddharta Gautama** was born in the 6C BC into a noble family on the borders of present-day India and Nepal. His mother gave birth to him in a garden, supporting herself with a branch of a *sala tree* which is still regarded as sacred in Sri Lanka. The child was brought up according to his rank, but was confined to the palace because of a prophecy made at the time of his birth, according to which he would renounce the ways of the world. His only outings were the walks in the garden where he had been born. In the course of these walks he met four people who were to affect his destiny profoundly: an old man, a leper, a dead man and a monk. The first three were a terrible shock to the young man, whose privileged upbringing had protected him from reality. But the fourth person who appeared was to lead him down the path of renunciation. The encounter with the monk made up the prince's mind: he abandoned his wife and young son and left the palace. Having reached the borders of his father's kingdom, he cut off his long hair, took off his rich clothes and, dressed only in a few rags, set off on many years of **spiritual quest**. But all his endeavours failed to find an answer to the fundamental question that his four encounters had raised: what was the root of human suffering and what was the way to be freed from it? In the end, alone and abandoned by the handful of disciples who had followed him, he eventually found his way. Seated under a banyan tree, after a long night of meditation and wakefulness, he became **Buddha**, "the Enlightened One".

The Dharma, the Buddhist law – Buddha's teachings refer to individual morals and the fundamental questions of existence discovered during his Awakening. They are summarised in the **First Sermon** which he preached to his five disciples in the Park of the Gazelles near Benares. First he pointed to the fundamental and universal existence of pain which had driven him to renounce everything. Then he explained to them that if pain was spread universally, this was because of desire. Eternally dissatisfied, people are linked to their painful existence by desire, which leads them to be re-born again and again. In order for suffering to cease, desire must be suppressed. According to Buddha, this is possible for anyone who, like him, renounces any form of attachment and devotes himself to practising the eight virtues: the perfection of opinion and intention, of word and act, of means of subsistence and effort, and of attention and concentration. A difficult path, since concentrating on these forms of perfection can only be contemplated by men and women who withdraw from the world.

The Sangha – On hearing the First Sermon the five disciples decided to follow Buddhist doctrine. They were the first members of the community who meditated upon and spread Buddha's teachings: the **Sangha**. Buddha remained their spiritual leader until his death when, having reached absolute detachment, he entered the Great Extinction, the **Parinirvana**, freed from the long chain of cause and effect, from good and bad conduct called **karma** which drives people to be constantly re-born.

Some terms associated with Buddhism

Bo tree	Tree of the "Bodhi" (see below) under which Buddha was seated when he experienced "the Awakening".
Bodhi	Awakening, Illumination, root of the term Buddha, "the Enlightened One".
Bodhisattva	One whose essence is enlightenment, male or female holy figure of the Buddhist "Mahayana" (Greater Vehicle) pantheon.
Karma	Notion common to Buddhism and Hinduism, see p 54.
Mahayana	Broad way of deliverance proposed to all beings, by means of the virtuous example of the bodhisattvas. An early form of Buddhism which appeared, also called the Greater Vehicle.
Nirvana	"The Extinction", the cessation of pain and desire, which enables those who have achieved it to live in a state of complete serenity.
Parinirvana	"The Great Extinction" or "total nirvana", the end of the cycle of re-birth marked by the physical death of Buddha or a saint.
Theravada	Name given to primitive Buddhism. It is sometimes inappropriately referred to by the term "Smaller Vehicle".

Buddhism and Society

Monks and lay people – Buddha spent his life teaching, but left no written works, nor did he appoint a successor. Thus the mission of the *Sangha* was to pass on his doctrine. In the meantime, the community survived with the help of lay people, kings and merchants, who made gifts of food and land where the monks settled during the rainy season. Little by little, a **delicate equilibrium** was established between monks and lay people. The monks showed the true way and made progress, while the lay people, in meeting their needs, participated in a mission of collective protection. **Gifts** also guaranteed them merit. This modus operandi governing relations between monks and lay people still persists today in countries which, like Sri Lanka, draw their inspiration from the "Way of the Elders", the Theravada (inappropriately known as the "Smaller Vehicle").
The lay people visit the monastery in their parish at least once a month, and cater for most of the monks' daily needs, ranging from medicines and clothes to building work and repairs. Contrary to tradition, however, the monks now accept gifts in the form of money and they rarely need to go out to beg for food. There are also families in the parish who organise rotas to provide them with their daily meals. The gift of food to the *Sangha* is still regarded as an action worthy of great merit.

S Held

Women praying at the Temple of the Tooth

The congregations – There are more than 6 500 monasteries in the country housing a community of around 20 000 monks. They are divided into three main congregations *(nikaya)*, descended from a system which has evolved to ensure the continuation of the *Sangha* which has sometimes come under threat from other religions. In such cases an appeal is made to a congregation in another community of the Theravada which, since practising full ordination is one of its rules, re-establishes the orthodoxy. The **Siyam Nikaya** congregation which accounts for more than 50 % of the monks under the protection of the Malwatte and Asgiriya monasteries in Kandy, was founded by monks from Thailand who arrived in Ceylon in 1753, at the request of the king of Kandy. Its rival, **Amarapura Nikaya** (accounting for 30 % of the monks), was established by Sinhalese monks who had been ordained at Amarapura in Burma in 1802. Both congregations are prone to a certain amount of elitism, only granting full ordination to monks of high caste. This attitude led to the foundation of the third congregation - the **Ramanna Nikaya** (20 %), which favours a return to the ideal of poverty, founded by monks ordained in Burma in 1864. There is also an order of about 500 monks, the **vanavasin**, which places great importance on meditation as an austere ideal, with monasteries established well away from the other much older communities.

The daily life of the monks – A house, a *dagoba* and a bo tree, surrounded by a wall: it is so discreet in fact that a traveller could easily fail to notice that it is a monastery. Inside, a few monks – often no more than a dozen – devote their time to studying Buddhist texts, daily meditation and performing blessings at ceremonies financed by the lay population. The rules do not allow much time for household chores, washing or sweeping, but the monks are relieved from such duties by widowers or bachelors and young boys.

Unlike countries in South-East Asia which observe the Theravada, the **ordination** of monks in Sri Lanka is permanent. It marks renunciation, symbolised by the tonsure (shaving of the head) and the acceptance of the robe, and the departure to a life regulated by 227 articles of the *Vinaya*, including one establishing meal-

The habit makes the monk

Whatever his congregation, a monk must be tonsured and wear the clothes prescribed by the monastic rules, which are offered by the family when the monks are ordained. Around their legs, they wear a sarong ("antaravasaka") held in place with a leather belt, while the upper part of the body is wrapped in a piece of cloth worn over the left shoulder ("uttarasangha"). A voluminous toga, the "sanghati", which the monk wears outside the monastery, completes his wardrobe. It is not made from a single piece of fabric but from long bands of fabric sewn together, a reminder of the first communities in which each member made his own robe by sewing together rags and pieces of cloth that he had begged or collected. This patchwork was dyed fairly neutral shades of brown, colours that chemical dyes have transformed into saffron yellow, which has become the symbol of the Buddhist robe.

times: the first is taken at dawn, and the second and last before midday. It is difficult to understand what part a sense of vocation can possibly play in the mind of a boy of ten… especially when it is appreciated what an honour it is for the family to have a son admitted to one of the great congregations. However, monastic life isn't entirely confined within the monastery walls. The monks do travel on pilgrimages, staying at one of the monasteries in the network belonging to their congregation.

Changes and concessions to the modern world

Whatever congregation they belong to, monks are highly respected in Sinhalese society. In their presence, even a head of state must take up an inferior position, sit on a lower chair, for example. In public, they are always treated with the greatest respect.

Teaching – The monks of Sri Lanka have lost some of their pre-eminence in a domain which was once exclusively theirs: teaching. This phenomenon came about with the development of schools during the colonial period. At the same time, the spread of teaching in the English language gave a broad swathe of middle-class Sri Lankan society access to a certain amount of knowledge about **Buddhist doctrine**, which, hitherto, had been known exclusively to monks and a few scholars.

The Tripitaka – For a long time, the passing on of the doctrine depended on the memory of the disciples who had heard it. The need to set it down led to the holding of Buddhist **councils**, the first of which took place nearly half a century after the Buddha's death. Gradually, the precepts cited at these great assemblies were organised into three collections of **reference works**, called the "Three Baskets" or **Tripitaka**: the first concerns the rules governing monastic discipline *(Vinaya)*; the second the sermons and parables *(sûtra)*; the third contains philosophical commentaries *(Abhidharma)*.
The Tripitaka was communicated by word of mouth until the Council of Ceylon was held in the 1C BC. Its content, passed on by master to disciple, was learnt by heart, with commentary and explanations added as was felt necessary. The canon set down in writing after this council was recorded in the old Indian language called **pali**.

The increasing role of lay people – The first translations of these collections into modern languages were made within the framework of studies carried out by oriental scholars during the 19C, and they were translated into English before they were translated into Sinhalese. This movement is associated with an American, **Henry Steel Olcott** (1832-1907), founder of the Theosophical Society, whose ideas were actively supported by Anagarika **Dharmapala** ("the guardian of the

Law"), a Sinhalese who was never ordained as a monk, but who typified the increasingly important role played by lay people in Buddhism. Nowadays, lay people are on practically the same footing as monks as far as knowledge and everyday practice of Buddhism is concerned, all the more so since the latter are increasingly drifting towards the universities to study ancient languages or theology, rather than the monastic teaching structures.

An American in Kandy

The American HS Olcott arrived on the island on February 17, 1880 (a date that is still commemorated as "Olcott Day"). It was during his five-month stay that he founded the Theosophical Society. His institution, which imitated many aspects of Christian missions, was behind many initiatives which still exist today including the creation of a Buddhist flag, based on the colours of the haloes painted around Buddha in Ceylon (blue, yellow, red, white and pink), the establishing of a catechism, which is still taught in Sunday schools, and the declaration of Vesak as a national holiday.

Salvation by women?

Buddha had included women in his first congregation and although subordinate to monks in the hierarchy of the order, the **nuns** contributed to Buddhist life and spirituality until the 11C.

Then, for unknown reasons, the female *Sangha* was suppressed in Ceylon and in all areas following the Theravada. These days there are women in the congregations, but, in the absence of ordination, they remain at the edge of the *Sangha* and follow a less restrictive regime. More recently, however, the island is witnessing an attempt to restore the nuns' order. The plan to re-establish the "fourth wheel" of Buddhism (the three others being the layman, the lay woman and the bonze) has been instigated by the head of the great temple at Dambulla. In February 1998, he took 20 women to India to be ordained as **bikkhuni** on the holy site of Bodhgaya, where Buddha experienced the Enlightenment. Consecrated by ten bonzes of each sex, the nuns in turn presided over the full ordination of women in Sri Lanka. Condemned for heterodoxy by the male congregations on the island, and applauded by militants of equal rights for women, this initiative is an astonishing event in the world of the Theravada. Furthermore, in a country where monks have been seen driving about in luxury air-conditioned Toyotas, or listening to the latest hi-fi equipment, the return of women kindles a hope among the indignant lay population that the order will become usefully involved in missions associated with education and health-care on the island.

Hinduism

Only a few functioning Hindu temples remain as a reminder of the Indian presence in ancient times. At Chilaw or Trincomalee, the brahman priest in charge of the shrine will explain to visitors the story of how they were founded. Interestingly there is no history of competition with the great Buddhist shrines. In the eyes of Hindus, Buddhism was never more than a sort of avatar, an interpretation, or mutation of Hinduism, like all forms of thought born on Indian soil. Even today, Sri Lankan and Indian Tamils perpetuate the weighty legacy of this complex socio-religious system known as Hinduism. It translates into social divisions and ritual practices governed by fundamental notions.

The four keys of Hinduism

Karma	A series of good or bad acts, the sum of which, accumulated over successive lives, determines the conditions of rebirth.
Dharma	Moral and religious law decreeing the duties one must perform within a caste and laying down the rituals to be performed to honour the gods.
Samsara	Cycle of re-births or reincarnations which never ends except by obtaining deliverance.
Moksha	Deliverance from "samsara" which may be achieved by conforming to the "dharma", absolute devotion to a god ("bhakti"), or knowledge.

Hindu society – The division of Tamil society into castes is a social legacy. Old hymns relate how, after the explosion of the great original body, its mouth became the brahman, its arms formed a warrior *(kshatriya)*, its thighs became a craftsman and a merchant *(vaishiya)*, and its feet became a servant *(shudra)*. These four ancient divisions, called **varna** (colours), no longer have any real significance today. The structure is defined more by the **jati**, or socio-economic status. One does not enter a *jati*, one is born into it and this implies a certain number of obligations, including marriage within one's own caste. This system persists and keeps out of the caste all those whose jobs, which are regarded as being dirty and impure (road sweepers, cesspool workers, laundresses, cobblers, etc) make them untouchable. These distinctions deeply divide the Tamils of Jaffna, who claim lineage from high castes, from those in the centre of the island, who are descended from castes judged to be inferior.

Rites and religious worship – Old temples carved out of stone, the brightly-coloured *kovil* of the streets of Colombo, a modest rural shrine: everywhere worship is the same. Mainly the devotees worship **Shiva** and his wife – the goddess presented here in the form of the sweet **Parvati**, the terrible **Durga** or the terrifying **Kali** – or their offspring, **Ganesh** and his brother **Skanda**. Unlike other gods, who tend to be portrayed with all kinds of weapons and magical attributes, and sometimes with several arms expressing their divine power, Shiva is almost exclusively revered in the form of a simple block of stone of complex symbolism, the linga.

The ultimate act of worship is **puja**, a personal daily offering, which can also be public and ceremonial. Whatever the offering, whether it consists of garlands of flowers, puffed rice or ghee (which makes the statues black and shiny) it is placed at the feet of the statue, around the linga, while the worshippers murmur invocations. This worship is not addressed to the image but to the divine force or energy with which it was invested at the moment of its consecration, in the quest for a fusion with the spirits.

An elephant-god for the farmers

The pantheon of Sinhalese gods has changed with the passing of time, but the island has always been protected by four great patron divinities, assigned to the four points of the compass. Thus the north is under the protection of Vibhishana but, in practice, it is a god of the Hindu pantheon who is worshipped by the farmers in the Anuradhapura region, namely Ganesh, the son of Shiva, who is depicted with the head of an elephant. His is a very ancient cult dating from the time when Sinhalese and Tamils rubbed shoulders in the capital of Anuradhapura. A precious aid in overcoming obstacles, Ganesh is the god who ensures good harvests. Devotees improvise shrines, putting his image in places that he loves, such as rocky crevices or the maze of roots below banyan trees. If there has been a good harvest, they never fail to prepare sweetmeats, of which he is particularly fond.

The island gods

Buddhism has never eradicated previous or contemporary religious orders. It merely criticised their excesses if it seemed necessary. The best proof of this is in the presence of one or more temples consecrated to one of the god-protectors of the island within the wall of a Buddhist monastery. In addition to the Sinhalese pantheon there is the pantheon of the Hinduism professed by the Tamils. The borders between these two universes of belief are plain to see. They are evident in the architecture of the temples – the Sinhalese *devale* and the Tamil *kovil* – and in the rites that are performed on a daily basis, but the distinctions become blurred in certain practices and associated cults like that of the god Kataragama.

The language of offerings

The religious devotion of the Sri Lankans is expressed through **offerings** and **gifts**, but these gestures differ in nature, depending on whether they are addressed to the Buddha or to the gods. The faithful call upon the gods to help with all kinds of problems, from unemployment or the passing of an exam, to the conceiving of a child or a surgical operation, romantic problems or problems with the law…
The **devala**, dedicated to the most important gods on the island, exist in nearly all the towns and villages. Apart from the daily homage which is offered to them (such as lighting a coconut oil lamp), a veritable contract is entered into by the person invoking divine help: if you help me to accomplish what I want, I will return with a present or I will perform all kinds of penance and self-mortification in your name.

Offerings are made to **Buddha** in quite a different way. Their symbolic nature is a mark of homage to the memory of the dead master and a form of meditation on the four moral precepts of Buddhism: eloquent speech and kindly conduct, justice and generosity. At the entrance to the most holy shrines,

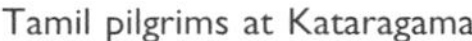

Tamil pilgrims at Kataragama

P Grielen

wrought-iron frames in the shape of a figleaf or a stupa are used as supports for the lighting of oil-lamps, the ephemeral flames of which serve to symbolise awareness of the fragility of life. The armfuls of water-lilies or lotus flowers strewn on the altars and squares of *dagobas* have the same symbolic meaning: like the beauty of a flower that inevitably withers, the human body also gradually changes.

The religious melting-pot of Kataragama

The great temple dedicated to the Kataragama, in the city which bears his name *(see p 311)*, is where the religions of the island meet and mingle. Their influence on each other is also evident here. Whether Buddhist, Hindu, Muslim or Christian, every family is sure to make at least one pilgrimage here. But in this place, the moral precepts of Buddhism or of the Jewish and Christian religions vanish, replaced by practices, exercised in a state of trance and ecstasy, which come directly from a deep and ancient form of religious devotion. Within this complex blend of creeds and practices, one attitude dominates: **bhakti**, or trusting and absolute devotion to the god of one's choice.

In Hinduism, it is manifested in the hymns chanted during the ceremonies, or by the offering of a coconut which is split with a sharp blow, as if it were a skull, in a gesture symbolising the abandonment of self into the hands of the god. In the worship of the god Shiva, this giving of oneself sometimes reaches a climax when it is expressed in a trance, making even the most spectacular acts of self-**mortification** possible. It was the Hindus who first introduced this devotional trend to the cult of Kataragama, and they have since been joined by Sri Lankans from every social class who come each summer. Christians make the journey to the temple on their knees. Muslims hang themselves from carts on hooks passing through their flesh. Buddhists march barefoot on glowing embers or walk for hours, singing and dancing, holding the *kavadi*, the mount of the god Kataragama, at arm's length.

The crescent and the cross

The Sri Lankan populations of both Muslims and Christians are the same (8 %), having been established or converted when Ceylon became a trading-post.

The Muslims

Mosques of every conceivable style are dotted throughout the different regions of the island, testifying to the expansion of the Muslim community since this faith was first introduced by Arab traders. Muslims are the only community who claim an identity based on their religion. They include a few Tamils, converted because they were of very low caste, or "untouchable", but very few Sinhalese. As **Sunnite Muslims**, they all observe Friday prayers, stopping all activity between 11am and 1pm. They also all follow the Islamic rituals regulating daily life such as the choice of a name for a baby by an imam 40 days after its birth, circumcision, abstinence from drinking alcohol and eating pork, and fasting during the months of Ramadan. They are divided between towns and the coast, and are actively involved in business, trade, (especially precious stones) and fishing. Adam's Peak (which owes its name to them), and the tombs of the holy men of Kataragama and Kalutara are their main **pilgrimage sites**. Their traditional festivals are inscribed in the Sri Lankan calendar and they play an important role in maintaining relations with the Arabian peninsula as well as with Indonesia and Malaysia.

The Christians

Christians form the final chapter in the story of the island's religions. The discovery, at Anuradhapura, of a bas-relief of a hand holding a cross may point to the presence of a community of Syrian Christians as early as the 5C or 6C, following the example of the west coast of India. But more than anything, it was the successive waves of European missionaries and colonists who contributed to the spread of Christianity, either by force or through conversion, by the various branches of the church in Europe: Roman Catholic, Baptist, Methodist and Anglican.

However, **Roman Catholicism** still predominates, the legacy of Portuguese-Goan proselytising in the 16C.
Although they are no more numerous than the Muslims, Christians feature in every social category of the island, from the poorest (the fishermen on the west coast) to the most influential (the middle classes of Colombo), and Christmas is a public holiday in the national calendar.

A wayside pietá

Y Keller

A CONSTELLATION OF FESTIVALS

The numerous festivals in the Sri Lankan calendar illustrate the religious diversity of the island. The patron saints of the churches on the west coast, the landmarks associated with the spread of Buddhism, the temples of the different gods of the island together with Hindu shrines weave a fabric of commemorative festivals which provide an opportunity for people to come together in large numbers.

The days of poya

The Buddha was born, experienced Enlightenment and died on a day with a full moon, with the result that, for Buddhists, each new full moon *(poya)* is a bit like Sunday in Christian countries, a holiday on which special ceremonies are held. On such a day, devotees go to the temple to make offerings (flowers, oil-lamps, etc) and listen to sermons and blessings performed by the monks.

The perahera, signature of religious festivals

An important Buddhist festival cannot take place without a *perahera*, a great parade of brightly-coloured elephants, dancers and drummers, but the scale and the splendour of the procession vary according to the temple to which the parade is dedicated. The **elephants**, richly caparisoned with brocades and batiks embroidered with gold and silver, symbolise the wealth and importance of the shrine. The **dancers** *(oli)* and **drummers** *(berava)* who accompany them are descended from family dynasties traditionally attached to the services of the temple and, curiously, are regarded as one of the lowest castes in Sinhalese society. The *perahera* of Kandy has become an event in its own right, being particularly popular on account of the dancers. Their legs enveloped in a white, pleated, voluminous sarong, and their chests and arms decorated with ornaments, their faces surmounted by an imposing silver diadem, they perform their dances to the rhythm of percussion instruments. Of ritual origin, their movements are dramatic, almost acrobatic, but, as in Indian classical dance, are all regulated by a code of gestures and positions.

As such the *perahera* is a **procession**, an organised demonstration conducted by the people responsible for the *devale*, the curators *(basnayaka nilame)* and priests *(kapu-rala)*, in which the faithful merely participate as spectators. According to tradition, it should take place the night before a day of *poya*, but the popularity of this wonderfully colourful spectacle means that nowadays the *perahera* is more likely to be held during the day. As for the largest *perahera* on the island (at Kandy, Kataragama and Dondra), which should traditionally take place in the month of Esala, they are increasingly being held at the next full moon of the following month *(see table)*.

Muslim festivals

Muslim festivals respect the **lunar calendar** of Islam and in this respect change from year to year *(see p 89)*. They only involve the Muslim community itself, since they take the form of special prayers held at the mosques and family celebrations. The three main festivals, which are public holidays for Muslims, are **Id ul-Kebir**, which commemorates the sacrifice of Abraham, **Milad un-Nabi**, the birthday of the Prophet, and **Id ul-Fitr** which marks the end of Ramadan.

S Held

All set for the "perahera"

The festivals held each month

The traditional Buddhist and Hindu religious calendars follow a **cycle associated with the moon and the sun** of twelve months, adding an extra month every two or three years. In this way, they always take place in the same season, with a difference of a few days from one year to the next. The year begins in spring (March-April).

Bak (March-April)	The traditional New Year, common to Buddhists and Hindus, has now been fixed on April 14. This is a family festival, an occasion to exchange presents around a traditional dish, "kiribat", rice cooked with milk, cut into diamond shapes. The Christian fishermen of the west coast celebrate the Passion at Easter and Good Friday.
Vesak (April-May)	The full moon of Vesak is the most important of the Buddhist festivals and the following day is also a public holiday. It commemorates the Birth, Enlightenment and Parinirvana of Buddha which took place on this day. Devotees go to the temple, offer gifts to the monks and listen to their sermons. Lamps made of clay or paper are lit in front of each house, and towns and villages have platforms decorated with scenes of the life of Buddha.
Poson (May-June)	The full moon of Poson commemorates the arrival of Mahinda and the introduction of Buddhism to the island, a time of important pilgrimages to Mihintale and Anuradhapura.
Esala (June-July)	The full moon of Esala celebrates the day when Buddha preached his first sermon. This is the important time of the "perahera" (elephant parades), organised at Kandy, Kataragama and Dondra.
Nikini (July-August)	The full moon of Nikini marks the start of the Buddhist period of fasting, a time of retreat for the monastic communities. The Hindu community celebrates the festival of Vel at Colombo. A cart carrying the spear (vel) of Kataragama is pulled from Pettah to Bambalapitiya.
Binara (August-September)	The full moon of Bigara celebrates the time when Buddha pronounced a sermon to the heaven of the Thirty Three gods.
Vap (September-October)	The full moon of Vap marks the end of the Buddhist period of fasting.
Ill (October-November)	Full moon of Ill. Deepavali, the Hindu festival of lights commemorates the return from exile of Rama, the hero of the Ramayana. Oil lamps are lit in each Tamil household.
Unduvap (November-December)	The full moon of Unduvap commemorates the coming of Sangamitta with the cutting from the Bodhi tree, a time of lustration ceremonies in all the courtyards ("bodhighara") in the country.
Duruthu (December-January)	The full moon of Duruthu is preceded by a "perahera" lasting several days at Kelaniya. For four days, Hindus celebrate Thaipongal, the traditional period of the changing of the season in the farming calandar. Duruthu marks the beginning of three months of pilgrimage to Adam's Peak
Nawam (January-February)	The full moon of Nawam is an occasion for a "perahera" at the Buddhist temple of Gangaramaya in Colombo.
Madin (February-March)	Maha Shiva Ratri is the great night of the god Shiva, which his devotees celebrate with chanting and acts of grace. It takes place in all the large temples on the island dedicated to Shiva.

DAILY LIFE

Despite the industrialisation policy adopted by successive governments, the vast majority of the Sri Lankan population works in agriculture. Work in the fields or in the fishermen's villages makes up the daily life of three-quarters of the island's inhabitants, while urban life is essentially concentrated in Colombo with its population of 2 million.

Sri Lanka of the fields

Life in the countryside reveals the most enchanting side of the Sri Lankan personality. The villagers are very hospitable and the air of equality and dignity is very different from the social tensions which haunt the city.

A simple, austere life

Life is often frugal and not always easy in the country. There are still many families living below the poverty line, working tiny plots of land. **Usury is common practice**, because more than a quarter of farmers do not own their land and have to give half the produce from the fields they farm to their sponsors. Monthly earnings average about US$90 when the monsoon is kind. At this level, every penny counts: enough has to be put aside for seed, fertiliser or renting agricultural machinery; enough must be produced to ensure a daily minimum ration of a kilo of rice for a family of four people. Many families count on a supplementary revenue by sending one of their members to work as a salaried employee in the plantations in the centre of the island, or by choosing to go and settle on one of the new areas of colonised land in the dry zone.

Winnowing the rice

P Haussherr

Dwelling in the countryside

Sri Lankan **villages** are very different from their European counterparts with their clusters of houses scattered in the countryside, tucked away in a garden or hidden behind a screen of bamboo. Two things usually betray the presence of a village: a bus stop, identifiable by its sign with its symbol of an ancient vehicle, and the presence of one or more shops which not only act as supply centres but also as places to meet and do business.

Small concrete houses, like the ones in the suburbs of Colombo, are found across the island, some more attractive than others. If travelling off the beaten track you will sometimes encounter more basic types of dwellings, simple huts standing on beaten earth or **adobe huts**. Like many other aspects of tradition, it is in the museums of Anuradhapura or Kalutara that you will rediscover what the traditional architecture in days gone by was like.

Since the standard of living does not always permit young people to build a new house for themselves, two or three generations often live under the same roof in rural areas.

Glimpses of life

The corner kade – Known as **kopi kade** or **te kade**, they are grocery shops where you can obtain betel leaves to chew, tea and biscuits, coconut oil for cooking, and kerosene for lamps (many villages do not have electricity). Everything is bought in small quantities, less out of thrift than a desire to come back the next day for the latest gossip!

What is more, everything can be bought on credit. The *mudalali*, the owner of the *kade*, carefully writes down in a notebook the small debts of a few pence which sometimes remain unpaid for years. A master of the game, he is resigned to this state of affairs and knows very well that it is useless to put pressure on his debtors, who would only desert his shop for another. A *kade* is only worth its salt if it also procures the latest novelties for its customers.

Betel

500 million people chew betel in Asia. The recipe for the mixture might vary a great deal, but the basic ingredients are always the same. Betel is the leaf or fruit of a type of pear tree. It contains an aromatic essential oil with a burning taste. The leaves are given a coating of slaked lime before being rolled round a crushed betel nut containing the tannins which turn saliva red. Chewing betel acts as a tonic, an antiseptic, a purifier and refreshes the breath. However it has lost its traditional value as a token of hospitality during ceremonies, a role to which only the museums now testify, with their exhibits of the pottery once used for preparing and presenting this tobacco substitute.

The **newspaper** is the pivot of social intercourse: the customers go over the births, marriages and deaths columns with a fine tooth-comb, or find subjects for debate such as politics and tax increases. When the news has been digested, the newspaper still serves as a tablecloth or as wrapping paper for tea leaves and sugar.

The market – The Sunday market, which generally takes place at the village crossroads, complements the *kade*. A visit to the market may prove disappointing to anyone in search of exotica because of the absence of craft products, but is full of interest for anyone wishing to know more about the Sri Lankans. Among the vegetable stalls are others selling manufactured products essential to everyday life, like clothes, cooking utensils, mirrors and bars of soap.

J du Boisberranger / HEMISPHERE

A brightly coloured market

Bath-time – Very few houses have running water so, like the *kade*, other sources of water play both a functional and social role in country life. As in most Asian countries, a bath is a **daily ritual**. Children swim and splash about, but adults rarely bathe in the water. They wash themselves with the aid of a scoop and sometimes a powdered-milk tin, first wetting their knees, then gradually working their way up to their hair which they rinse with buckets of water. The whole ritual is accompanied by a great soaping operation: the more suds there are, the cleaner they feel! Men take their bath sitting on their haunches, preferably in the morning or the evening, before or after their daily tasks. Women tie a light cotton cloth around their chests, which leaves their shoulders bare but stretches down to their ankles. They go to the well, the reservoir or an irrigation channel, at any time of the day, usually accompanied by their offspring. When they have had their bath, they begin washing clothes or washing the dishes, conducting lively conversations with their neighbours all the while.

Life in Colombo

For an island with only 18 million inhabitants, the metropolitan area of Colombo is huge. Originally a trading post, which then expanded around the port, it has inherited a variety of very different communities, divided between the legacy of the British colonial spirit and the Sri Lankan way of life. Despite its appalling traffic congestion, the disruption caused by the bombing, and polluted by the incessant stream of buses and *tuk-tuk*, the city still has fewer growth problems than most large cities in Asia.

The urban mosaic

In contrast to the egalitarian society of rural villages, in Colombo the rich rub shoulders with the poor. The Burghers, who are resolutely city dwellers, have settled in the opulent-looking residences of Cinnamon Gardens or in the area around Galle Face Green. They share these classy areas with members of Sinhalese high society who, in turn, have family ties and houses inland, near Kandy. The middle class, which includes many Tamils, lives in the suburbs in Dehiwala, to the southeast. To the north, on the road leading to the airport, are the workers' districts with their community housing projects. Shanty towns are rare, because the more impoverished have benefited from a **housing aid policy**, set up by the Premadasa government in the 1980s and still in operation today. Because a large part of the city-centre is occupied by offices, people tend to live on the outskirts of the city, and in a **house** rather than a block of flats. These houses are usually built of concrete, but some of them have the traditional tiled roofs which provide some respite from the sweltering heat throughout the year. The rather bare interior is intended to encourage maximum air circulation. The rooms have high ceilings and the windows have only a simple grille to keep out intruders. Protected by walls or an enclosure, the house preserves family intimacy, yet this does nothing to hamper the Sri Lankan propensity for building up a wide network of neighbourly relations. Another trait of a more Western way of life in the city is that it is rare to find more than two generations living under the same roof. In more well-to-do families, the circle extends to domestic servants who live-in and do everything. In more modest homes, the wife takes charge of the daily chores, while the husband's duty is to bring home the money.

Chitra, a cleaning lady in Beirut

It's 7am at Katunayake Airport. This is the time when the flights arrive from the Arab countries, and while there are few foreigners going through immigration, the queue of Sri Lankan nationals is getting longer by the minute. Nearly all of them are women and Chitra is one of them. Six months ago, she left Kalutara to fly to Beirut. Her two children are at secondary schools and her husband's salary is not enough to run the household. A friend put her in touch with an agency recruiting for jobs in countries in the Middle East which rely on Sri Lanka for their labour. Chitra has no qualifications and speaks hardly any English but easily found a job as a cleaning lady. With food and lodging provided by her employers, she has managed to save almost all her salary, a small fortune for Sri Lanka: she is happy and proud to be back.

City life

On weekdays, between 6.30am and 9.30am, the **traffic** heading from the outskirts to the city centre is appalling, despite the government's attempt at carefully scheduling the traffic with the aim of improving the situation. School begins at 7am to enable parents to drop off their children before heading off to their offices at about 9am, or to open up their businesses between 9am and 10am.

However, the inhabitants of Colombo seem to have a remarkable tolerance of city **stress**. Resigned as they are to the inevitability of traffic jams, they are equally relaxed in their approach to work, presumably to the detriment of their profit levels: in the middle of the morning or during the afternoon they always manage to make time for the vital tea break where they work. A moment of relaxation which has not been Westernised, since, as yet, there are no vending machines!

20 years old in Sri Lanka

Having undergone a spectacular three-fold increase, the birth rate has finally stabilised. Whatever ethnic group they belong to, women usually have two or three children: a real advantage for Sri Lanka, when its giant neighbour India has to cope with an average of more than four children per household. However, Sri Lanka remains a very young country: there are 5 million people under the age of 15 and 4 million aged between 15 and 20.

Education for all

Successive governments can be justifiably proud of having given top priority to **education**. Today, more than 90 % of the population can read and write and there are many young people, even in rural areas, who are pursuing secondary education.

Whether in the town or in the country, school is compulsory from the age of 6. Each morning, children must put on a **white uniform**: a shirt and trousers for boys, a shirt and pleated skirt for girls. Despite the heat, the shirt must be buttoned up to the neck and a tie or scarf must be worn, and girls even have to wear a petticoat since the skirts are deemed to be too transparent. Although schoolchildren in towns tend to wear shoes, children in rural areas often go to school barefoot.

After the morning roll-call, the day's lessons begin with a Buddhist, Muslim or Christian **prayer**, depending on the school and where it is located. There is a break every 40 minutes: the bell rings, announcing a change of subject and classroom. On rushing out as the lesson ends, the pupils then form orderly rows in pairs.

Two years before the final exams, the election of the school council takes place which has the responsibility of awarding the senior and most deserving pupils with prizes for achievement at a special presentation.

The school forms a micro-society inherited from the British colonial organisation in which **sport** plays a key part. The most important event is the inter-school cricket tournament. Each school has a team, a band of supporters and a flag. The most prestigious teams are those of the Royal College of Colombo and St Thomas's College in Mount Lavinia. During the tournaments, pupils at the colleges take time off to parade in trucks supporting their team, loudspeakers blaring and pennants flying.

When China dresses the schoolchildren

There is no feverish rush to the shops when term is about to begin. It is the State which supplies the metres of fabric which will be used to make shirts, trousers and skirts for its schoolchildren. Each year, the state education budget allocates US$30 million for school uniforms, textbooks, stationery and transport. Although Sri Lanka dresses the pupils, it does not provide the textiles for the school uniforms, only the labour. For some years now, it has been negotiating with the People's Republic of China to provide the material for its schoolchildren's uniforms. In 1999, China agreed to provide the 11 million metres needed for the uniforms of Sri Lankan schoolchildren in 2000 at a favourable price.

The disenchantment of youth

The young people of the island may be educated, but there are not many jobs. Only the service sector absorbs some of the young job-seekers, notably in tourism. But tourism has also had an adverse impact which has affected the young people of the southwest coast in particular: the influx of foreigners with high spending power has led to juvenile prostitution and with it, Aids and drug-addiction.

Many young adults are affected by **unemployment**, especially those from a rural background who account for 50 % of the unemployed. At best, wages are disappointing and the majority prefer to emigrate to Singapore, the United States or Germany. Better education and the difficulties in finding work are also behind a very unusual social phenomenon in Asia. Young people are waiting longer and longer to get married and relying for much longer on their parents. This mixture of intellectual emancipation and **material dependence**, added to uncertainty about the future, is one of the causes of the disenchantment of youth today.

Umbrella addicts

A legacy of the British, the umbrella is a vital accessory in Sri Lanka. It protects lay people and monks from the rain and the burning sun and, at the market, it marks the territory of the sellers. It is even large enough to shelter two people, provided they walk very close together! It has thus become a favourite refuge for lovers. At weekends and after lessons, in parks or on the promenades by the sea, umbrellas sprout like large black flowers, allowing a moment of intimacy away from prying eyes. What other solution is there in a society where most people live with their parents?

This helplessness has manifested itself on several occasions recently, in the form of young people being drawn towards the revolutionary ideas of extremist movements, which were heavily repressed in 1971 and in 1988-89. It also manifests itself in the **suicide rate**, for which Sri Lanka sadly holds the Asian record: 29 for every 100 000 inhabitants, well above the 17 per 100 000 in Japan.

Afternoon of recreation on the west coast

P Haussherr

The milestones of life

Although the temptation to follow Western ways has sometimes taken the edge off certain family rites, it has not entirely eradicated them. Family celebrations remain an occasion to reinforce links between members of the extended family, who are often scattered across the island for professional reasons. An important traditional figure, the **astrologer** continues to be the authority to consult to establish which days are auspicious or inauspicious for their celebrations.

Puberty

In more conservative Sinhalese families, the astrologer continues to play a role when young girls reach puberty. When they have their first period, their mother goes to consult an astrologer. The girl must remain confined to the house, without even washing, receiving visits only from female members of the family, until the propitious day which is calculated according to the astrological parameters of her birth. This confinement may last up to a week, at the end of which it is announced that she has reached puberty. Then a party is organised. All the relations are invited and shower the girl with jewellery and necklaces, in celebration of the fact that she is now able to marry.

Marriage

Prospective spouses have more and more say in their choice of partner, provided they have their parents'consent. Christian and Hindu weddings are celebrated in their place of worship, be it church or temple. Buddhist families organise the union of spouses at the house of their parents and in the presence of monks. During the ceremony, the bride and bridegroom are bound together by a piece of cotton tied to their little fingers, while the bonzes recite protective incantations, the power of which is such that it is said that the young bride will not fail to faint if, by mischance, she is not a virgin. In fact, **virginity** is a vital pre-requisite for most families and verifications are still made to establish whether the wedding has been duly consummated, even at a hotel.

Funerary rites

Despite a gradual erosion of traditional social values, the Sri Lankans continue to have great respect for their elders. Old people's homes are very rare and it is generally the children who look after their parents. In most communities it is the custom to **hold a wake over the body** of a dead member of the family for several days, a time when close relations come to pay their respects. During this period of mourning, the fire must not be lit.

In spite of the customs of the different religions – **cremation** for Buddhists and Hindus, **burial** for Christians and Muslims – it is more common to follow the wishes of the dead person. In the case of a cremation, the relations remain at the crematorium to receive the ashes and, according to the wishes of their dead relative, place them in an urn in the garden at home, at the cemetery or perhaps scatter them at the river mouth. The road leading to the cemetery is decorated with white flags, the traditional colour of mourning, black flags in Christian villages, or saffron yellow if a monk has died.

Do's and don'ts

Travelling in Sri Lanka can be very pleasant: the hospitality in rural areas and the fact that many towns have adopted Western ways have removed many of the social barriers. Sri Lankans are naturally sociable and friendly and they show a courteous tolerance of any *faux pas* committed by tourists, who are sometimes just in too much of a hurry.

How to mix with the locals

On the bus – Travelling by public transport is a good way of meeting local people. There are two types of bus, which enable you to travel everywhere, even to the smallest villages. On a comfortable, air-conditioned **Intercity Express**, you will have the freedom to chat and exchange addresses with your neighbour, albeit in a rather sterile atmosphere; whereas, in the ramshackle old **local buses** which stop everywhere you might be too squashed to make conversation, but you will be sampling a real slice of Sri Lankan life.

Mihintale Terminus

Midday. It's very hot and the terminus at Anuradhapura is almost deserted. An Intercity Express is parked in a corner, it's not leaving immediately. The driver has closed the door, switched on the AC and is having a siesta. The vehicle looks as if it is ready for the bus cemetery although no doubt the engine still works and this is the bus that serves Mihintale, 11km away. It will leave as soon as it is full, when all the seats are occupied, all the spaces stuffed with packages and baskets, with kids perched on makeshift seats, and the roof transformed into a surrealistic composition of bundles of cloth, boxes and bicycles. Finally a ghastly grinding noise signals that it is ready to depart, while a few students in immaculate uniforms, their books tucked under their arms, jump on at the last moment. The university is halfway along the route.

On a pilgrimage – For poorer families, setting off on a pilgrimage is both an act of piety and a form of tourism. **Adam's Peak** is the place to go, where one can meet Sri Lankans from every walk of life, in an environment combining reverence, religious respect and the cosy warmth of a family outing. A tourist labouring under the weight of his video equipment, an old Sinhalese woman dressed in her white sari, climbing slowly but with dignity up the hill, groups of boys and girls, out of breath but laughing: everyone is equal on the climb up the steps to the sacred peak.

In the guest-houses – One of the most pleasant things about travelling in Sri Lanka is its network of small guesthouses which are often more like a Bed and Breakfast. They are comfortable and it seems that, albeit for a few days only, you are part of **family life**. Most of the owners speak English and sometimes German. Having had a great deal of experience of the good and bad habits of foreign tourists, they have a whole host of practical advice at their fingertips which would be hard to find even in the best travel guide. All of which helps to make a stay in a guest-house a warm and very human experience.

Useful tips on behaviour

Long experience of tourism means that Sri Lankans are familiar with Western ways, but their courteous tolerance does not excuse the visitor from attitudes that can sometimes be regarded as shocking and polite silence may signify total disapproval. The rules of knowing how to behave are not difficult and mainly concern the spheres of politics and religion.

Greetings – The traditional form of greeting, *"ayubowan"*, is accompanied by a joining of the hands at chest level and a slight bow of the head. Do not forget that this is a Sinhalese, Buddhist greeting and will be of no use unless you know a person's language or religion. So, how does one strike up a conversation with a Sri Lankan? As you would in the West, very simply, according to their age, function and circumstances by saying *"hello"* or *"Good morning, Sir"*. And do not underestimate the effect of a smile. Another tip: no-one will ever say "I'm going" when they say goodbye to you, but always "I'm going and coming back", because it is regarded as impolite to leave someone.

Sociability – Although Sri Lankans are mostly sociable and open by nature it is useful to know how familiar one should be. Unless one is related, greetings between men and women are formal and affection is never shown in public. A man may shake your hand in greeting but it is rare for a woman to do so. In Sri Lankan society, modest bearing and a **reserved attitude** are still the most admired attributes in a woman. In appearance they may sometimes seem very Westernised, but they remain profoundly Asian, and discreet in their relations with one another.

Body language – Hail a bus by raising your hand but beckon to someone by waving your hand with the fingers pointing downwards. When making gestures use the index finger rather than the thumb. Finally, as in India, show approval by shaking the head from side to side, which would pass in the West for a sign of denial. This movement of the head is very contagious and, after a few days, you will surprise yourself by shaking your head yourself while you speak.

Dress – Dress codes are very simple in a country which has borrowed its costumes from abroad. The **sarong** worn by the men is of Malaysian origin, while the **sari** worn by some women is Indian, and skirts and trousers are very common. There is no point in disguising oneself in the hope of blending in with the population, but two rules should be respected: no slovenly or sloppy-looking clothes in general, nor low necklines or clothes that are tight-fitting or too short in the case of women. Apart from around places of worship, which are always treated with great respect, Sri Lankans are less prudish and more relaxed than their Indian neighbours: outside work, men often wear shorts and women reveal their calves and arms.

Footwear – As in many parts of Asia, removing your shoes when entering a holy place or someone's house becomes second nature. You get used to it very quickly if you wear simple shoes like flip-flops or sandals.

Meals – No-one will be offended by seeing you use a knife and fork – they will be given to you automatically – but you will be regarded with great esteem if you get used to eating with your fingers: only use the fingers of the **right hand** (not your whole hand!), plunge them bravely into your helping of rice and mop up the sauces accompanying it. Beware of meals where the alcohol flows freely: it is not that Sri Lankans don't drink alcohol but those who drink *toddy* or *arak* generally do so to excess.

Politics – Democratic tradition imposes certain obligations and Sri Lankans – the men in particular – have a passion for politics. This is coupled with an in-depth knowledge of the political situation, gleaned from numerous daily newspapers, radio and television. You may find yourself confronted with effusive outpourings by the person you are talking to on the social situation or what he would do if he were in the government. Beware: a polite, sympathetic silence is the best response in a context that is difficult to judge for outsiders. After all, they say that three Sri Lankans discussing politics will express four different opinions!

Religion – Whatever the religion, places of worship are always treated with great respect. You should enter only if decently dressed and having removed your shoes (except in churches). This respect also extends to religious images and, in Buddhism, to the **monks** who are revered by the faithful.

You may photograph a statue of the Buddha, provided you do not linger beside him or take a photograph of a bonze without his permission. The seats at the front are reserved for monks who take precedent even when confronted with a frail old lady.

When lay people address monks, you will notice that their attitude is full of **deference**, even to the point of prostrating themselves at their feet. Not as much is expected of you as a tourist, but only engage them in conversation if you are invited, especially if you are a woman. Do not forget that the vows of chastity and celibacy are part of the monastic rules, and that the only contact possible with women is when discussing questions on doctrine or the practice of meditation.

Ride on a tandem

Pérousse / HOA QUI

The flavours of the island

Sri Lankan cuisine echoes its history. Situated on the maritime trading routes of the Indian Ocean, it has borrowed all sorts of recipes, from *aluwa*, sugared semolina from the Arab world, to *dodol* (coconut milk caramel with palm syrup), *sathe* (thin strips of meat on skewers) and *sambol* from Malaysia. It has also incorporated the culinary traditions of the various peoples who have settled on the island over the centuries: Muslims sometimes prefer *biryani*, rice sautéed with spices, to local *rice and curry*; the Portuguese handed down new combinations of sugar and spices, such as the *bolo de amor*, a semolina cake with cashew nuts flavoured with cinnamon; *lamprais* was inherited from the *lomprijst* of the Dutch; as for the British, they left the island a flavour to which it will always be devoted: tea. Together with the countless variations of *rice and curry*, all this exotic fare blends into a unique and very rich cuisine. Eating in a restaurant can be disappointing because, in Sri Lankan culture, the only cuisine worthy of the name is prepared at home. However, hotel restaurants and small eating-houses often cater very well.

A bite to eat

Sri Lankan families enjoy getting together for elaborate meals prepared at festival time, but on a daily basis, eating remains an intimate experience whether in traditional restaurants – the dark interiors of which always surprise visitors – or on a sheet of newspaper bought at the corner *kade*. It's often a moment of self-indulgence, perhaps best expressed in the use of the fingers to separate some grains of rice, mix them with curry sauces, and add seasonings to make the fritters known as *papadam*. There is nothing ritualistic or religious involved, but in the eyes of Sri Lankans, it is the only way to fully enjoy the flavours of local cuisine. The most important meals are breakfast and dinner; during the rest of the day, people make do with a snack or light meal.

At breakfast

An English breakfast is served in all the hotels, with toast, eggs, tea or coffee, but you can also start the day with a flourish by trying out local specialities made with rice flour, which take so long to prepare that they are now seldom made at home. **Hoppers** *(appa)* resemble pancakes which have been leavened by incorporating palm beer *(toddy)*, mixed with coconut milk and fried in a special little pan. A good *hopper* should be thick, gooey in the middle and crispy at the edges. It is eaten with an egg, or a meat or fish curry, and the ubiquitous *sambol*, but people won't be shocked if you prefer to eat them with sugar or jam. **String hoppers** *(idiappa)*, little steamed nests of noodles, are eaten with the same accompaniments.

An assortment of curries...

Rice, always served in generous helpings, is a fundamental ingredient of every meal. It must be perfectly cooked, with grains neither too sticky nor too dry to be rolled in one's fingers.

Nourishing, but too insipid for Sri Lankan taste-buds, rice demands to be eaten with **curry**. This generic term conceals a whole host of different recipes incorporating vegetables, different meats and fish. Served on the table in little dishes placed around the bowl of rice, they make a colourful display which never fails to stimulate the appetite.

Palm-trees worth their weight in gold

The coconut could be the described as the symbolic fruit of the Indian Ocean. Its flesh, pressed into milk or dried and grated, blends delicately with the flavour of spices and mellows the fiery quality of chillies, while the liquid from young nuts, which are particularly abundant in the case of the King coconut, makes a refreshing drink. But the coconut palm that lines the beaches of Sri Lanka or the Maldives has even more to offer: its sap is either used fresh to make a cider-flavoured "toddy", or is fermented and distilled to make the golden drink called "arak", its wood is used for carpentry, its leaves for weaving and its graceful, slanting trunk provides shade over the silver sand.

Curry has nothing to do with the yellow powder sold in the West for livening up and colouring certain stews. It is a cunning mixture of **spices** and **seasonings**, freshly ground in a mortar, then thrown into coconut oil or boiling clarified butter *(ghee)* to bring out the flavour. All these spices grow on the island: coriander, fennel, cumin, cloves and cardamom, and turmeric root (Indian saffron, or a saffron substitute, which turns the food a golden yellow). These are combined with curry leaves, garlic, onions, citronella, ginger and fresh or powdered chillies. Sometimes the more acidic flavour of lime, tamarind pulp or vinegar is added. The final touch, typical of Sri Lankan cuisine, consists in simmering everything in **coconut milk**.

Sri Lankans love to eat very spicy food. If the combination of spices in the dish is not hot enough, they tuck into some **mallun** (a salad of shredded green leaves served cold having been cooked in water with onions and chillies) or **sambol**, a seasoning based on ground chilli pepper, salt, onion and dried fish, sometimes served with grated coconut *(pol sambol)*.

...and the dishes which accompany them

Such a festival of flavours almost puts the dishes that accompany them into second place, except for **vegetables**, which are present at every meal in a bewildering variety. Pink lentils are commonplace, but at the markets you can also find exotic gourds (*christophines* and *gombos*) and various kinds of leaves which are difficult to identify.

Chicken and goat *(mutton)* are the most popular **meats**, since pork and beef are rare and banned from the cuisine of two of the religious communities on the island; the first by Muslims and the second by Hindus. Sri Lankans are eating less and less meat, not for religious reasons but for reasons of hygiene, and the fact that the hot, humid climate is ill-suited to a diet containing a lot of meat.

Apart from the coastal resorts and tourist spots, Sri Lankans eat very little **fish**, since it is very expensive. Fishing is not commercially viable and has been badly affected by the current conflict *(see p 29)*. As for seafood, (langoustines, crabs, prawns, etc), these are much sought after and mainly sold for export. Tuna fish, bonito and shrimps are, however, used in the preparation of curries, and small dried fish are mixed with *sambol*.

Sweet food

The climate of the island is conducive to growing delicious **exotic fruits** such as papayas, pineapples, bananas and mangoes (in certain regions) which grow all year round. Others, like the mangosteen and the rambutan with its perfume of lychee, which ripen in July and August, are seasonal. This also applies to the jackfruit and the durian (which has a disgusting smell), two enormous fruits with delicate flesh which grow in bunches on the trunk of the tree.

There is an infinite variety of food based on rice flour, coconut milk and molasses *(jaggery)*, but they are rarely served as a **dessert**. Their elaborate preparation means that they are reserved for special occasions, but you will also find them being sold by itinerant merchants or in specialised shops. Certain foods are served either as sweets or savouries, like the New Year recipe called *kiribat*, a cake made with rice cooked in milk, cut into diamond shapes, or *string hoppers*. In the south of the country, they make a refreshing dessert by pouring curdled buffalo milk over a bowl of palm syrup *(kitul)*.

M Gotin / SCOPE

Kandy market: all the flavours of nature...

Drinks

Sri Lankans – men in particular – like their **beer**, both pale and dark, which they sip while nibbling snacks.

They are particularly fond of **toddy**, a palm beer which is drunk just after it has been collected, since it does not keep (and can only be found in places where it is collected). When it is distilled, it produces **arak**, the Sri Lankan answer to whisky, a golden liquid smelling of caramel. It is sold in bottles at a modest price in shops selling spirits, but is served in bars and some restaurants at exorbitant prices.

The **tea break** is a tradition in its own right and is universally popular, a moment to be savoured every day in every conceivable environment. With their meals, Sri Lankans generally drink **water**, or sometimes **fizzy drinks** or beer (except on *poya days*) and, at any time of day, **King coconut** water makes a deliciously refreshing drink.

HANDICRAFTS

Sri Lanka is blessed with a magnificent tradition of craftsmanship, which is expressed in a wide variety of spheres. The museums on the island are a good place to go to see what has been produced in the past, but you risk being sorely disappointed if you go shopping. A small survey of existing or past handicrafts follows.

Everyday objects

Some potters still make the range of **clay pots** used for cooking, which are gradually being replaced by light, unbreakable objects in aluminium. Their shapes are identical, and beautifully formed; there are pots for storing water, cooking rice, simmering curries, collecting coconut pulp, conserving palm sap or curdled buffalo milk. The wooden cooking utensils peculiar to Sri Lanka, have also been replaced by other materials. This applies to the indispensable coconut-pulp grater *(hiramane)*, on the handle of which the cook used to sit, the *string hoppers* press, based on the same principle as a garlic press, or the lovely engraved wooden moulds used to make *kiribat*, the New Year rice pudding cake, into flower or diamond shapes. Artisans still take advantage of the abundant variety of vegetable fibres to make **baskets** and **mats**. There is an enormous variety of baskets and one of the most delightful everyday objects is a small woven panel on which to hang ladles, made from half an empty coconut shell with a wooden handle.

Craftsmanship of courts and princes

Royal patronage was the inspiration behind the masterpieces of patience and virtuosity, evidence of skills which are no longer practised today, except in the spheres of **embossed silver** and **silver and gold plate**. At one time embossed silver was used to make tools for preparing betel, pill-boxes or jewellery boxes, and to cover religious books. In the field of silver and gold plate work, there are still extraordinary collections of little gold and silver chains, precious stones set in the shape of rosettes and filigree.

There are still a few craftsmen who know how to apply **lacquer** to wooden objects. Lacquer was once used to protect and decorate crockery, boxes and ceremonial weapons. The resin, which is applied in the form of rods onto a rotating object shaped by soft filaments using the thumb, results in charmingly colourful work. Finally, we must not forget to mention the craft that is now prohibited: the delicate skill of working **ivory**. The National Museum in Kandy has a wonderful collection of items fashioned in ivory, among them caskets made with carved ivory panels, miniscule statuettes, and pearls that have been completely carved with open-work.

Cult objects

The endowment of monasteries and temples also employed the skills of the craftsmen on the island. Nowadays, copperware manufacturers engrave **leather**, **pewter** and **silver** to make dishes for offerings, with scrolled edges, often of silver plate. They beat and assemble sheets of metal to erect the tall upright lamp surmounted by a bird, used by the Sinhalese for religious and family ceremonies. They also forge **iron** in volutes, or in the shape of a leaf of the Bo tree, as a support for the little clay oil-lamps used in the Buddhist faith.

The ritual theatrical performances of long ago have almost entirely disappeared, but one of their main accessories, the **mask**, has survived. Carved out of a very light wood, they are helping to keep this kind of sculpture alive. The carving is often vigorous and dramatic, with expressions emphasised by the use of colour. Nowadays mineral- or vegetable-based paints have been abandoned in favour of the smoothness of acrylic paints.

Colonial craftsmanship

The Portuguese, Dutch and British also contributed to the legacy of craftsmanship. They used traditional Sri Lankan materials to make jewellery, objects and furniture that were European in form. At the museums of Galle and Colombo, and in certain antique shops, look out for small objects made of tortoiseshell (combs, fans, spectacles), tobacco pouches in carved leather, caskets inlaid with ivory, ebony or porcupine quills. Colonial rule took advantage of local woodworking skills and the abundance of exotic species to have **furniture** made, now regarded as masterpieces in cabinet-making. The heavy, grandiose furniture of the Dutch period gave way to the lighter, more functional style made for the British, of which the most characteristic is a planter's cane armchair, with arms that extended so that the legs could be stretched out. Finally, the colonists also inspired new techniques, some of which are still in use, such as **batik**, the secret of which was brought by the Dutch from their colony in Java, and a special kind of **traditional lace** which the old ladies of Galle still know how to make.

The art of turning a pot

C Bourzat

LANGUAGES

There are three main languages spoken in Sri Lanka. **Sinhalese** is spoken by most of the people (74 %), while **Tamil** (8.5 %) is spoken in the north and east of the country. Finally, as in India, **English** (10 %) is the main language of communication of the educated middle classes and well-to-do families. Pronounced with a distinctive accent, it is a Sri Lankan version of English in its own right, full of expressions translated from Sinhalese, anglicisms and *faux amis*.
This linguistic co-existence can be observed on signposts and on banknotes. The Sinhalese script is a beautiful succession of arabesques and bubbles, while Tamil employs elegant angular letters and characters, dotted with punctuation marks.

Sinhalese

Sinhalese, or Sinhala, is the official language of Sri Lanka, used in public administration and in education. It belongs to the family of **Indo-European** languages, but underwent a different evolution to other languages in the group (Hindi, for example) from the 5C onwards. Its grammar and script were established in the 13C. Over the years the Sinhalese vocabulary has borrowed many terms from Pali and Sanskrit, the main media of Buddhist texts, as well as from Tamil and, from the 16C onwards, from Western languages particularly Portuguese, Dutch, and English. Here and there odd words betray these European influences, such as the Portuguese *mese* for table, *pan* for bread or *karatte* for barrow.

Tamil

Less than 10 % of the population use this language which is spoken by 60 million people in the world. It is mainly the official language of the State of Tamil Nadu and of the Territorial Union of Pondicherry in India. In Sri Lanka, where it is spoken by the Tamil minority, and by numerous Muslims, it was given the status of an **official language** in 1988.
Tamil belongs to the family of **Dravidian** languages of Southern India. Having remained virtually unchanged for 2 500 years, it has a rich profane and religious literary tradition. The Tamil script and alphabet were established in the 11C-12C.

Names and usage

There is a difference in the way names and terms of address are used in the Westernised towns and the more traditional countryside.
Contrary to the habits of the Tamils and Muslims, who state their identity beginning with their father's name, a complete Sinhalese name juxtaposes the name or names of origin (the village or sphere, or caste) to which they add the suffix "-ge", with the first name and then the family name. However, the modern world has simplified things. On visiting cards are featured only the first name and father's name, or the initials of the first two names followed by the family name.
In rural areas, names are of little importance. They are replaced by terms of address which denote the links within the community. Among people of the same generation, there will be a *"nanda"* (aunt) or a *"mama"* (uncle), an *"akka"* (older sister) or a *"nangi"*, (younger sister), an *"aiya"* (elder brother) or a *"malli"* (younger brother). *"Malli"* is also commonly used as a term of endearment between lovers.

P Haussherr

Public letter-writer

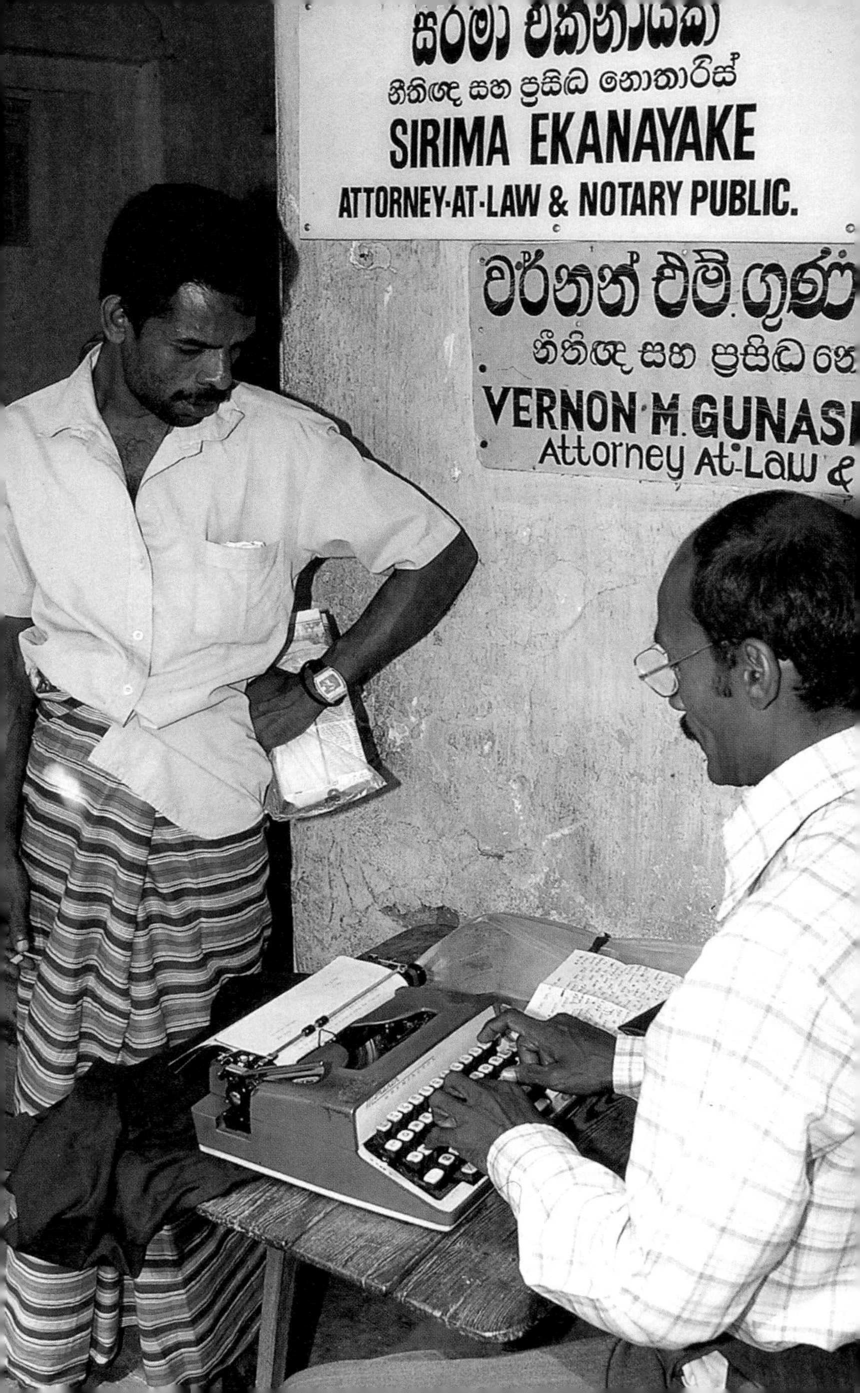
SIRIMA EKANAYAKE
ATTORNEY-AT-LAW & NOTARY PUBLIC.
VERNON M. GUNAS
Attorney At-Law &

Practical information

B Pérousse / HOA QUI

The market at Kandy

Before going

• Local Time

Sri Lanka is 6 hours ahead of Greenwich Mean Time (GMT) (and 5 hours in the summer) and 11 hours ahead of Eastern Standard Time (EST).

• How to call Sri Lanka

00 + 91 + the city code (without dialling 0) + the number you wish to call *(for city codes in Sri Lanka, see p 88)*.

• When to go

Keep in mind that whatever season you choose to visit Sri Lanka, heat and rain will be common. February and March are however the most pleasant months to visit.

Two monsoons intersect in Sri Lanka, each affecting half the island. When the southwest monsoon blows from May to September, the rain falls over the west, south and centre of the island. The "winter monsoon" which hits the north and the east lasts from December to February. During this time the sea is very rough and even dangerous.

For further information on the climate, consult: www.cnn.com/WEATHER/cities/world.html

Average temperatures in Sri Lanka

	Jan-Apr	May-Aug (min / max °C)	Sept-Dec
Colombo	22 / 30	24 / 30	22 / 29
West coast and north central	17 / 31	21 / 29	18 / 28
Centre	14 / 21	16 / 18	15 / 18
East coast	24 / 32	25 / 33	23 / 33

The sun rises between 5.30am and 6am and sets at about 5.30pm to 6pm year round. The main holidays on the island take place during the summer months. But be aware that if you plan to stay in the cities where they occur, the hotels are full and the rates are astronomical. November to March is a pleasant period to visit most of the island, but is also the main tourist season when rates and airfares are considerably higher.

• Packing list

Clothing

Bring light and informal clothes but be sure to always **dress appropriately**. Short skirts, shorts, and low-cut clothing are banned unless you are on the beach. A **light jumper** is also recommended for air-conditioned places and for the mountainous region in the centre where the altitude exceeds 1 500m (4 950ft). Day and night-time temperatures vary considerably and a jacket or jumper is essential if you plan to travel in the winter.

Bring comfortable shoes that are easy to slip off as you cannot enter religious places with them on (you may wear socks if your feet are tender). Hiking boots are advisable if you plan to go trekking (beware of leeches!).

Accessories

Certain small accessories can prove to be very useful, such as an alarm clock if you want to watch the sunrise; Band-Aids or adhesive tape to repair holes in mosquito nets; a small lock for your luggage, particularly if you plan to use local transport; a flashlight in the event of electrical shortage and, depending on your itinerary, a set of binoculars to better appreciate the views; a pocket knife to peel fruit and a flask for water. You may also want a sleeping bag if you are uncomfortable with the lack of bedding in local guesthouses, and earplugs if you are sensitive to noise.

Always carry a photocopy of your airline ticket and the first six pages of your passport, as well as photos of yourself. This will facilitate the process of replacing them if your documents are lost or stolen.

A trip for everyone

Before leaving home, consult your country's official advice to travellers or the Sri Lanka Consular Information Sheet (www.travel.state.gov/sri_lanka.html). Also see the note to readers, p 2.

Travelling with children

Sri Lankans love children so travelling with yours will open many doors. They can enter all sites and nature parks half-price. Many hotels and some guesthouses have rooms with three or four beds to accommodate entire families. Certain deluxe establishments also provide games rooms and babysitting services.

Women travelling alone

A woman travelling on her own should not encounter any particular problems but she will be harassed by a plethora of questions: *"Where do you come from? How old are you? Are you married? How many children?"* If you're single and childless, you can easily put a stop to the questions by showing a photo of a male friend and claim he's your husband and then one of your nephew…

On the other hand, some attacks have been reported at the beaches on the southern and western coasts. Avoid walking alone at night – young soldiers who have deserted will not hesitate to take advantage of the virtue of female travellers.

Disabled travellers

Unfortunately, there are few facilities available for disabled people. To fully enjoy your holiday, contact a tour operator to help you with the logistical organisation. For more details, partially blind people can contact the **Sri Lanka Federation of the Visually Handicapped**, 74 Church St, Colombo 2, ☎ and Fax(01) 43 77 68.

• Address book

Tourist Information Office

United Kingdom – Ceylon Tourist Board, Trade Centre, 22 Regent Street, London SW1Y, ☎ (020) 7930 2627, Fax(020) 7930 9070, srilanka@cerbernet.co.uk

USA – Ceylon Tourist Board, One World Trade Centre. Suite 4667, New York, NY 10048, ☎ (212) 432-7156, Fax(212) 524-9653, ctbusa@anlusa.com

Australia – Atutil Pty, Ltd, 39, Wintercorn Row, Werrington Downs NSW 2747 ☎ (02) 4730 3914, Fax(02) 621 6142.

Embassies and Consulates

United Kingdom – Sri Lanka High Commission, 13 Hyde Park Gardens, London W2 2LU, ☎ (020) 7262 1841, Fax(020) 7262 7970.

USA – Embassy of the Democratic Socialist Republic of Sri Lanka, 2148 Wyoming Avenue, NW, Washington DC, 20008, ☎ (202) 483-4025/26/27/28, Fax (202) 232-7181 or 483-8017, slembasy@clark.net, www.slembassy.org

New York – Mission of Sri Lanka, 630 3rd Ave., 20th Floor, New York, NY 10017, ☎ (212) 986-7040, Fax(212) 986-1838.

Los Angeles – Sri Lanka Consulate, 5371 Wilshire Blvd, Suite 201, Los Angeles, CA 90036, ☎ (323) 634-0479, Fax(323) 634-0581. www.angelfire.com-la2-slconsgenla

Canada – Haute Délégation, 333 Lauries Ave West, Suite 1204, Ottawa, Ontario KIP ICI. ☎ (613) 23 38 44 09.

Web Sites

Sri Lanka Web Server – www.lanka.net A general site with complete information and numerous links and chat rooms.

A Journey to Sri Lanka – www.srilanka-travel.com A mini travel guidebook with some practical information.

Sri Lanka Explorer – www.infolanka.com. Many links have been updated with other sites.

Sri Lanka Info Page – www.lacnet.org/srilanka/cult1.html

World Heritage Sites – www.cco.caltech.edu/-salmon/wh-srilanka.htm

WWW - Sri Lanka – www.lacnet.org/srilanka/sites.htm

Tourism in Sri Lanka – www.lsplk.com/tourism.htm

• Formalities

All formalities are listed for information only and are subject to change. Contact your local embassy at least one month before leaving home for the most up-to-date information.

Identity Cards

A valid **passport** is necessary to enter Sri Lanka. Nationals of the United Kingdom and Canada will automatically receive an entry visa for a maximum stay of 30 days upon arrival at the airport at no charge. Nationals of the USA and Australia will be given an entry visa for a maximum stay of 90 days upon arrival without any payment. If you plan to stay longer than 30 days, you must request a visa from the **Department of Emigration and Immigration**, Tower Building, Station Rd, Bambalapitiya, Colombo 4, ☎ (01) 43 63 53. Come prepared with your passport, your airline ticket with your return date, and traveller's cheques, cash or a credit card to prove that you have enough money to prolong your stay (approximately US$15 per day is needed). Nationals of the UK and Canada may extend their stay for up to 60 days.

Customs

Sri Lankan law allows for the **importation** of 1.5 litres of alcohol, 2 bottles of wine, 200 cigarettes or 50 cigars, as well as perfume and souvenirs of a value no greater than US$250. You must declare any amount more than US$10 000. Upon departure, you may **export** up to 3kg (6.6lbs) of tea as well as souvenirs and precious stones, whatever their total value, providing they were purchased with money changed officially (be aware of the excise tax imposed in your country). Cash of a value higher than 250 rupees (your remaining rupees must be reconverted before departure), antiques (objects and old books more than 50 years old), tea leaves, coconut palms, and hevea may not be taken out of the country.

Vaccination

No vaccination is required, but it is advisable to update your vaccinations against polio, diptheria, tetanus and hepatitis A and B. Sri Lanka has cases of malaria and is classified as zone 2. As malaria and prevention of this disease are constantly evolving, discuss details of your planned itinerary with your doctor at home for further information.

Driver's licence
If you plan to stay only a short time, your international driver's licence must be validated by the **Automobile Association of Ceylon**, 40 Sir Mahamed Macan Markar Maw, Colombo 3, (01) 42 15 28.

• Currency
Money
The monetary unit is the Sri Lankan **rupee**. *(Please note that although the international bank code is LKR, it will be simplified to R in this guide)*. The rupee is comprised of 100 **cents** and comes in notes of 10, 20, 50, 100, 200, 500 and 1 000Rs, printed in Singalese, Tamil, and English, and coins of 5, 10, 25, 50 cents and of 1, 2 and 5Rs. The current exchange rate at the time of publication is **US$1** equals **79.50Rs**.

Money exchange
It is a good idea to change money as soon as you arrive at the airport as the rates are better and you will not have to wait as long as in the exchange bureaux in town. You will need to show your passport for the transaction and hold on to the receipt that will allow you to change your rupees when you leave the country. You can change US dollars, sterling, French francs, and German marks in cash or in traveller's cheques in the hotels (lower rates due to commission on the exchange) and in the banks in larger towns. Plan ahead before leaving the larger cities and always ask for smaller notes as changing money elsewhere can prove to be difficult.

Traveller's cheques
Traveller's cheques are accepted in banks and the exchange rate may even be slightly more favourable than the rate for cash.

Credit cards
American Express and **Visa** are recognised by a growing number of hotels, tourist shops, and banks. Visa and **MasterCard** also allow you to take money out at the day's exchange rate in the larger banks in Anuradhapura, Colombo, Nuwara Eliya and Kandy. You will even find automatic cash dispensers (ATMs) open 24 hours a day in the capital and in Kandy. To avoid unpleasant surprises, consult your bank for its rates and commission before departure.

Spending money
If you prefer the comfort of large hotels, you would be better off contacting a tour operator in your country *(see p 85)* or on site *(see "Colombo", p 134)* because you will be able to benefit from discounted rates for this type of establishment. Almost all the hotels cited in this guide that cost more than US$65 a night belong to the country's larger travel agencies.

If you prefer small family-run guesthouses, you will find **double rooms** for $10-15, breakfast included, all over the country. Some even have triples or family-sized rooms to share. Most offer **meals** for between 150 and 200Rs (drinks are extra).

Public **transport** is very inexpensive. For example, a train ticket from Anuradhapura to Colombo (around 200km) costs between US$0.65 to US$3.50 depending on the class of service, and the price for a ticket on an air-conditioned express bus from Colombo to Trincomalee (257 km) is 100Rs. The yellow government-operated buses (called "normal bus") cost 5Rs for every 10 km.

Car rental with a chauffeur is a good compromise to allow you to organise your stops as you wish. The general rate is on average 15Rs for every kilometre, plus 150Rs per day for the chauffeur. Be aware that this rate does not include his accommodation and only some small hotels have drivers' quarters. If this isn't the case in the hotels you plan to stay in, you'll need to settle on the rate for his overnight stay.
Overall, a daily budget of US$50 per person will allow you to enjoy your holiday fully, staying in good hotels, eating in restaurants and hiring a car for your side trips. If you're on a tight budget, approximately US$15 will be enough to sleep in more modest accommodation, to dine in smaller restaurants, and use public transport.

• Booking in advance

Be aware that during the weekends, school holidays, and certain religious holidays or processions, hotels are filled with Sri Lankan tourists in the sacred cities (Anuradhapura, Kataragama, Kandy) and at some beach (Polhena) or mountain (Nuwara Eliya) resorts. In this case, a reservation is essential. It is not necessary the rest of the time, but can facilitate your journey as some hotel owners will pick you up at the station if you have booked in advance.

• Repatriation insurance

Consider taking out traveller's insurance before leaving home as this is the only way to obtain coverage throughout your trip. If you purchase your plane ticket or if your trip is organised by a tour operator, you will generally be offered an optional insurance policy that will reimburse you in case of trip cancellation, emergency care and repatriation, as well as a lump sum for theft or baggage damage. Otherwise, you can also contact companies at home that offer this type of insurance. First contact your credit card company as some will provide coverage abroad. Some insurance companies also offer this service.

• Gifts

To thank your hosts for their generous hospitality, you may want to bring along some small gifts from home as a token. In particular, anything that is foreign (postcards, T-shirts, perfume samples, etc). Photos of your country, especially if there's snow on the ground, always cause a sensation in this country where there is little change in season. Sri Lankans collect addresses tirelessly and are always looking for new pen pals. Leave yours and you will be sure to receive mail.

Getting there

• By air

As long as the problems in Sri Lanka prevent ferry connections with the Indian continent, airplanes are the only means of reaching the island. There are numerous scheduled flights to this small country located between south and southeast Asia. Direct flights from London take approximately 11 hours and involve at least one stop en route. Some companies that specialise in packages to Asia publish air rates in their brochures.

Scheduled flights

There are no direct flights from the USA or Canada to Sri Lanka. Srilanka Airlines offers direct flights from London several times a week. There are also flights with stopovers in various cities. Below is a list of some of the companies with regular flights to Colombo.

Srilanka Airlines – In the UK (0870) 5111 666, in the USA (1-800) 247-5265, in Canada (1-800) 837-5377.

Aeroflot – In the UK (020) 7491-1764, in the USA (1-888) 686-4949, in Canada (514) 288-2125.

Cathay Pacific – Reservations in Canada (1-800) 268-6868.

Gulf Air – In the UK (020) 7408 1717, in the USA (1-888) 359 4853.

Malaysian Airlines – Flights via Kuala Lumpur. In the UK ☎ (020) 7341-2020, in the USA ☎ (1-800) 552-9264, in Canada ☎ (416) 925-6670.

Pakistan International Airlines – In the UK ☎ (020) 8741 9376, in the USA (1-800) 221-2552, in Canada (1-800) 387-1355.

Royal Jordanian Airlines – In the UK (020) 7878-6300; in the USA and Canada (1-800) 755-6732

Singapore Airlines – In the USA (1-800) 742-3333.

Thai Air – Has flights via Bangkok. In the USA ☎ (1-800) 426-5204, in Canada ☎ (416) 971-5181, in Australia ☎ (1-300) 651-960.

Departing from another Asian country

Thai and Singapore Airlines fly daily to Europe and operate numerous flights between Bangkok, Singapore, and Colombo. India however offers a wider choice as Srilanka Airlines connects Madras (Chennai) to Colombo several times a day. Madras has connections to Europe on Lufthansa, KLM Royal Dutch Airlines, British Airways and Air India.

Reconfirmation

Don't forget to confirm your return flight at least 72 hours prior to leaving.

Airport

Bandaranaike International Airport is in Katunayake, 31km north of Colombo (airport code CMB). Airport tax is 500Rs when you leave Sri Lanka.

• By tour operator

Many tour operators include Sri Lanka in their brochures. The most common package is an à la carte tour, based on 2 people, in a chauffeur-driven car, with different hotel categories proposed depending on your budget. The package includes 4-5 day excursions around the island followed by a beach resort stay. Only operators specialising in Asia offer variations in the length of the stay (from 1 to 3 weeks) and the content (theme tours). Always compare quality and value before making your decision.

Generalists

Adore Travel – 1494 S Robertson Blvd, Suite 201, Los Angeles, CA 90035, ☎ (800) 236-7322 / (310) 859-8740, Fax(310) 859-8982, sales@adore-travel.com

Bhindi's Travel Inc – 18516 Pioneer Blvd, Suite 202, Artesia, CA 90701, ☎ (800) 949-FARE or (562) 402-7597, Fax(562) 402-7413

Upul's Travel Service – 1218 S Glendore Avenue, West Covina, CA 91790, ☎ (1-800) 918-9770 or (626) 918-9770, (323) 686-1616, Fax(626) 917-7827, utravel@lankapage.com

Kuoni Travel UK Ltd – Kuoni House, Dorking, Surrey, RH5 4AZ, ☎ (01233) 211 300, Fax(01306) 744 683

Saga Holidays Limited – The Saga Building, Enbrook Park, Sandgate High Street, Sandgate, Kent CT20 3SE, ☎ (0800) 414-383, Fax(0800)504555

Asia Specialists

Calverly Travel Ltd – 16 Lonsdale Gardens, Tunbridge Wells, Kent, ☎ (01892) 515 966, Fax (01892)521 500

Adventure and cultural travel

Ceylon Express International – 9524 Dumbreck Drive, Huntington Beach, CA 92646, ☎ (714) 964-6896, Fax(714) 968-4296, ceylon@pacbell.net www.tdesign.com/trisk/ceylon

Geographic Expeditions – 2627 Lombard Street, San Francisco, CA 94123, ☎ (1-800) 777-8183 or (415) 922-0448, info@geoex.com

Sita World Travel, Inc – 16250 Ventura Boulevard, Suite 300, Encino, CA 91436, ☎ (1-800)421-5643, Fax(818)990-9762, sitatours@sitatours.com, www.sitatours.com

Cox & Kings Travel Limited – Gordon House, 10 Greencoat Place, London SW1P 1PH, ☎ (01233) 211 401, coxandkings@bptts.co.uk

Oksana Adventure Travel – 98b Water Lane, Wilmslow, Cheshire SK9 5BB, ☎ (0870) 442 3303, Fax(0870) 442 3304

Travelbag – 15 Turk Street, Alton, Hampshire, GU34 1AG, ☎ (01420) 541 007, Fax(01420) 541 022, info@travelbag-adventures.com

World Spirit – 12 Vale Road, Altrincham, Cheshire, WA14 3AQ, ☎ / Fax(0161) 928 5768, worldspirit99@aol.com

See also the list of travel agencies located in Colombo, p 134.

The basics

• Address book

Tourist information

Tourist information offices are only available in Colombo and Kandy. While staff are helpful, you will only be able to obtain general brochures relating to the major sights on the island.

Embassies and consulates

See "Making the most of Colombo", p 133.

• Opening and closing times

The working week lasts 5 days. In addition to Saturdays and Sundays, nobody works on holidays and during the monthly full moon *(poya)*.

Banks

Banks are open Monday to Friday from 9am-1pm. However, in larger towns, some banks are open until 3pm and on Saturday mornings. All banks are closed every 30 June and 31 December (Bank holidays).

Post offices

Post offices are open from 8am-4.30pm during the week and until 12noon on Saturdays. In some of the tourist sites and beach resorts, post offices are open until 8 or 9pm as well as on Sunday mornings.

Shops
Shops are generally open Mondays to Saturdays from 9.30am-6 or 7pm.

Restaurants
Restaurants close early in the evening but you can eat at any hour during the day. Establishments that have a public bar licence can only serve alcohol from 11am-2pm and from 5-11pm.

Offices
Open Mondays to Fridays from 9am-4.30pm (however they are not reliable during siesta time between 1-4pm), and sometimes on Saturdays from 9.30am-1pm.

• Museums, monuments and archeological sites

Hours
Archeological sites are open daily from 7am-6pm. Most museums are open from 9am-5pm but close either Thursday or Friday (sometimes both).

Entrance fees
The larger archeological sites are managed by the **Central Cultural Fund** (212 / 1 Bauddhaloka Maw, Colombo 7, ☎ (01) 58 79 12. Offices in Anuradhapura, Polonnaruwa, Sigiriya and Kandy) which provides a **visitors pass** valid for 2 months for US$32.50 (payable in Rs according to the daily rate). The pass allows you to visit and photograph the following sites: Anuradhapura (with the exception of the Bodhi and Isurumuniya temples), Polonnaruwa, Sigiriya, Kandy (except Dent Temple), Nalanda, Ritigala and Medirigiriya. Dambulla and Avukana are not included on this pass. Be aware that with the exception of Anuradhapura, the pass is only valid for **one visit** to each site. You will be given a small booklet and each ticket will be removed at the entrance to the site. If you wish to return, you'll need to obtain an additional ticket for US$15 for Polonnaruwa and Sigiriya, US$12 for Kandy, US$8 for Medirigiriya, and US$5 for Nalanda and Ritigala.

Religious sites
Anyone can enter a religious site, regardless of their belief, providing that they are dressed appropriately with their shoulders and legs covered. Temples and monasteries do not always charge an entrance fee, but a donation is always welcome (never give money directly to the monks). If you wish to visit a Buddhist temple, ask for the key at the monastery (there is always one nearby), but avoid disturbing the monks during mealtime, between 11.30am-12.30pm. The daily offering of flowers, water and food to Buddha *(Buddha puja)* takes place at 6am, 11am, and 6.30pm and is the best time to visit. In the Hindu temples, ceremonies *(puja)* take place at 7am, 12pm, and 5pm.

Guides
Guides appointed by the Ceylon Tourist Board carry an official guide ID. You can hire them according to the language you need from the **Travel Information Centre** in Colombo ☎ (01) 43 70 59 or from the **National Tourist Guide Lecturers Association of Sri Lanka** (37 / 35 Temple Rd, Colombo 10, ☎ (01) 68 12 41). Their salary is based on what you pay them. Be sure to agree on an hourly rate before beginning the visit. Unfortunately, there is no official rate. This situation can prove to be embarrassing as many guides allow you to determine the rate depending on how much you appreciate their services. This is a cultural phenomenon. Insist therefore that in the West every service has a price, and don't hesitate to add a tip if your guide proves to be particularly competent.

• Post office

Although the postal service operates efficiently, it will take 8-15 days for a postcard to reach its destination. Sri Lankans have relatively little faith in the proper dispatching of letters or packages of value and favour aerograms instead – advice to take to heart. It is better to leave your mail directly at the post office instead of a post box where pick-up can prove to be haphazard. Poste restante is available at post offices (GPO) in the principal cities. All envelopes must be labelled as follows: surname in capital letters, first name, GPO, poste restante, city. Mail is generally held for up to 2 months.

• Telephone, fax and internet

Except in emergencies, avoid making phone calls from your hotel room as you will always be charged for at least 3 minutes and a hefty surcharge is added for service and taxes. All tourist centres have a **Communication Centre** where local or international calls are billed by computer according to the time used. Some agencies are open late in the evening and on Sundays. You will find phone booths that accept coins or cards everywhere, including at large archeological sites. There are 2 networks, **Lanka Pay Phone** (yellow phone booths) and **Metrocard** (red phone booths). You can purchase phone cards in shops that display red or yellow labels.

The Web has taken the island by storm, and more and more hotels communicate via e-mail or have their own website. To go on-line is another story: all communication goes via Colombo where the heavy traffic slows down access. Some telephone agencies in Kandy and Colombo will allow you to send e-mails. However, there is only one cyber café in the capital.

International calls

Telephone offices are the best place to call abroad. Check and see if your phone company covers service to Sri Lanka if you plan to use a calling / charge card.

Local calls

Phone numbers all have a city code which you don't need to dial when you are in the city. Mobile phones, administered by private companies, begin with a number between 071 and 079.

Dialling codes

To call Sri Lanka from the UK – dial 00 + 91 + city code (without 0) + phone number.

To call Sri Lanka from the US or Canada – dial 011 + 91 + city code (without 0) + phone number.

To call other countries from Sri Lanka – dial 00 + country code + area or city code + phone number.

Local codes

Anuradhapura 025
Badulla 055
Bandarawela 057
Bentota 034
Chilaw 032
Colombo 01
Dambulla 066
Galle 09
Haputale 057
Hikkaduwa 09
Kandy 08
Kurunegala 037
Matara 041
Negombo 031
Nuwara Eliya 052
Polonnaruwa 027
Ratnapura 045
Tangalle 047
Tissamaharama 047
Trincomalee 026

Rates
The rate to call to the United Kingdom, United States and Canada from Sri Lanka costs approximately US$0.90 to US$1.20 per minute.

Mobile phones
If you can't possibly leave yours at home, several companies offer a temporary service in Sri Lanka. The most dependable are **Celltel** (163 Union Place, Col 2, ☎ (01) 54 15 41) and **Dialog GSM** (475 Union Place, Col 2, ☎ (077) 67 86 78).

• Public holidays
Sri Lanka has a number of fixed public holidays, determined according to the universal calendar. In addition, there are holidays in different religious communities which change according to the lunar and solar calendars (Buddhist and Hindu) or lunar (Islamic).

Fixed public holidays
4 February Independence Day (1948).
13-14 April Avurudu, Sinhala and Tamil New Year.
1 May Labour Day.
22 May Day of the National Hero.
30 June Bank holiday.
25 December Christmas.
31 December Bank holiday.

Moveable public holidays
The **Ceylon Tourist Board** publishes an annual calendar of holidays that change each year. This calendar is available in its offices overseas or on the Internet: www.lanka.net/ctb/current-eve-info.html

The **monthly full moon** *(poya)* is comparable to "Sunday" for Buddhists, since Buddha was born, found Enlightenment, and died on the day of the full moon. They are therefore considered holidays by most communities. Try to get hold of a pocket calendar which indicates the full moon to pinpoint them.

Based on the lunar calendar, **Islamic holidays** are much more changeable. Those recognised as public holidays are:

Id ul-Kebir Commemoration of the sacrifice of Abraham and the beginning of the pilgrimages to Mecca (Hajji, 5 March 2001, 22 February 2002, 11 February 2003. This day is a holiday for Muslims only).
Milad un-Nabi The Prophet's birthday (3 June 2001, 23 May 2002).
Id ul-Fitr End of Ramadan (27 December 2000, 16 December 2001, 5 December 2002).

GETTING AROUND

The bus and railway networks are very extensive and you can go almost everywhere on the island by public transport. Once you have arrived safe and sound, three-wheeled motorbikes "tuk-tuks" or rented bicycles are available to cover short distances. The most comfortable (and safest as long as isolated terrorist attacks continue to target public transport) solution is to hire a chauffeur-driven car.

• By car

Car rentals

Chauffeur-driven car – All tour operators, hotels and most guesthouses offer this service. Rates are established according to your itinerary and the duration of your stay instead of by mileage. This system is not very expensive and even Sri Lankan families use it. The minivans in common use can hold up to six passengers and allow you to share the cost by the same number. Most drivers speak rudimentary English. Some also act as guides based on their knowledge of their country acquired after many years of practice. There is no standard rate but rather it is based on whether or not they own their own vehicle. Whatever you negotiate for a rate, be sure to give them a tip (plan on around 300Rs per day).

Self-drive car – This solution is more or less the same price as the preceding one, except with more headaches. Driving on the left is based more on habit than regulation, and there are no road signs off the main roads. Nevertheless, if you prefer to drive yourself, you can find car rental agencies in Colombo: **Avis**, Mackinnnons Travels Ltd, 4 Leyden Bastian Rd, Colombo 1, ☎ (01) 32 98 87; **Crown**, 60 / 02, Old Kesbewa Rd, Nugegoda, ☎ (074) 30 23 99; **Casons**, 583 / 1, 2nd Lane, Nawala Rd, Rajagiriya, ☎ (074) 40 50 70; and **Quickshaws**, 3 Kalinga Place, Jawatta Rd, Colombo 5, ☎ (01) 58 31 33.

Driving

Driving is on the left. Average speed is rarely more than 40 kph. In Colombo traffic is completely congested from 7.30am-9am and from 4.30pm-6pm. After 11pm traffic is practically non-existent in the large cities where police controls are deployed.

Road network

The roads are in rather poor condition, particularly beyond the built-up areas. Beyond the Negombo-Colombo-Kalutara metropolitan areas, Sri Lanka resembles an immense village where people and animals come and go on the roads without always being conscious of danger. The best roads have two lanes and are used by the Intercity buses which travel against the clock, overloaded lorries, and in the country, oxcarts or (occasionally) elephants.

In emergencies

One of the main reasons for having a chauffeur-driven car is that problems arising from minor incidents are usually settled by negotiation on the spot. In the event of a serious accident, the person or company who hired the vehicle will be liable.

• By train

Thanks to history and the British, Colombo is at the heart of the island's railway system and every city and town with a station can be reached from the capital. The four main lines are **Colombo-Matara** via Hikkaduwa and Galle, **Colombo-Badulla** via Kandy and across the mountain region, **Colombo-Vavuniya** via Anuradhapura, and **Colombo-Trincomalee** via Habarana.

Most trains are equipped with second class (cushioned seats and fans that function sporadically) and third class (wooden seats). As there is no reservation system, all seats are generally taken and people sit where they can, in the corridors or doorways. The best solution is to arrive at the train station 30 minutes prior to departure to buy your ticket. Then find a cooperative employee to help you find a seat. Only certain special trains allow you to reserve your seat, as early as 10 days in advance and as late as the day before your trip. These are the **express trains** that run between Colombo and *Badulla (Podi Menike, Udarata Menike, Night Mail, Night Express)*, with first class service, observation saloons and sleeping cars, and the Intercity Express Colombo-Kandy (first and second classes). Note that reservations are only possible from the original city of departure. You must go to the railway station to book and pick up your ticket. Special ticket offices are open during office hours or sometimes longer depending on traffic and timetables.

• By bus

All the major cities have a bus station. These are generally located near the railway station or at the foot of the clock-tower. There are no signs or information boards, but you will not have any trouble recognising the battalion of buses, coupled with the army of three-wheeled motorbikes. Destinations are indicated on the windscreen, most often in Singhalese. Ask one of the tuk-tuk drivers who often speak a few words of English. They can give you the best advice on the bus network, know absolutely everything about schedules and rates and will indicate the bus you need. Tickets may be purchased on board.
The difference between public service and private companies tends to disappear to make room for two other categories. The **Intercity Express** buses cover long distances, are comfortable and equipped with air-conditioning, operate continuously (and very quickly) between the two metropolitan areas. You can hop on to an Intercity Express bus if it passes through your destination but you will nonetheless most likely have to pay the total fare from its point of departure. The **CTB buses**, called "normal bus", are operated by the State. These yellow or red buses are often no more than a heap of metal and an engine but they travel to even the tiniest of villages and are very inexpensive. None of them will depart at a fixed time. They just leave when they are full.

• By tuk-tuk

You will find these three-wheeled motorbikes absolutely everywhere. In the cities and towns they will sometimes have a meter, but it will rarely work. In fact, the practice is to establish the fare of your journey before leaving according to the time and distance. The best procedure is to get information on the current rates before negotiating with the driver.

B. Gaisne

• Renting two-wheel vehicles

An agreeable and practical means of transportation in town, to visit a site or a surrounding area is the **bicycle**. You will easily be able to negotiate this service with the owners of your guesthouse or hotel staff who will be more than happy to rent you their own bike. Rates are approximately US$2 per day.

Motorbikes are also a pleasant way of exploring the region, but must be used carefully due to the chaotic traffic. Some guesthouses provide this service. Always remember to verify the condition of the engine before leaving. In case of mechanical problem, you will find small garages everywhere that are able to fix common breakdowns.

• Domestic flights

Due to instability in the northeeast of the island, domestic flights have been interrupted for security reasons. If and when the situation improves, the companies below have flights to Kandy, Galle, Kataragama, Nuwara Eliya, Polonnaruwa and Trincomalee. In Colombo, the domestic airport is **Ratmalana**, located south of the international airport, 20 minutes from the centre.

Ace Airways, 315 Vauxhall St, Col 2, ☎ (01) 32 45 86, Fax (01) 42 23 81.

CDE Helicopters, 140 Dawson St, Col 2, ☎ (01) 32 09 17, Fax (01) 42 22 24.

Lankair, 104 Nawala Narahenpita Rd, Col 5, ☎ (01) 58 07 42, Fax (01) 50 37 55.

Sky Cab, 294 1 / 1 Union Place, Col 2, ☎ (01) 33 31 04, Fax (01) 43 02 03.

• Organised tours and excursions

Travel agencies are more dense than the jungle in Ceylon. In addition to the dozens of large agencies dealing with many foreign tour operators, small businesses are growing. If you don't go to them, they'll come to you as soon as you arrive at the international airport. Be prepared for an onslaught of proposals, from a transfer to Colombo to a 10 day organised trip with chauffeur. Take a few business cards but wait to further examine the possibilities when you are more rested. *See also "Making the most of Colombo", p 134.*

BED AND BOARD

• Rates

Unless otherwise specified, the rates indicated in this guide are based on double occupancy with breakfast and taxes included (10 % in the guesthouses and 12.5 % in the hotels). In beach resorts, we have indicated high season rates (from November to March on the west coast). Expect to spend 30 to 50 % less during the low season.

• Various categories of accommodation

Thirty years of tourism have endowed Sri Lanka with a very wide range of types of accommodation. Close to the tourist sites and in the beach resorts, there are deluxe hotels providing the best of comfort and offering a multitude of activities. Although the middle or lower scale hotels show little interest, those travelling on a budget will find very satisfactory conditions in the many guesthouses on the island, coupled with the charm of staying with local people.

Hotels

There are few **mid-range hotels** (from US$25-50) that are of good value because the government taxes on hotels inflate the rates considerably. A guesthouse is a better option for this price range.

From the colonial period the island has inherited a network of **Rest Houses** which provide lodgings for civil servants away on business. Others have been built since Independence. Besides their attractive colonial style, the older ones were built on the most beautiful of sites. Managed by the Ministry of Tourism, these establishments charge excessive rates (from US$25-45) for very ordinary – and often very poor – service. It's a better idea to sample their atmosphere by having a meal or a drink. Booking centre in Colombo: **Ceylon Hotels Corporation**, 411 Galle Rd, Bambalapitiya, Col 4, ☎ (01) 50 34 97, Fax (01) 50 35 04.

The best hotels (US$50 and up) belong to the large hotel chains or to tour operators. The rates indicated in this guide are based on public rack rates. You will obtain much better conditions if you book through the intermediary of a tour operator in your country or on site. We have provided a list of the large tour operators in Sri Lanka. However, more modest but equally efficient companies are to be found in the *"Making the most of Colombo"* section.

Aitken Spence, 315 Vauxhall St, Col 2, ☎ (01) 34 51 12 / (074) 71 44 41, Fax (01) 43 63 82, ashmpvtl@slt.lk, www.aitkenspence.com

Connaissance de Ceylan, 58 Dudley Senanayake Maw, Col 8, Borella, ☎ (01) 69 46 25, Fax (01) 68 55 55.

Hem Tours, 75 Braybook Place, Col 2, ☎ (01) 30 00 01, Fax (01) 30 00 03, hemtours@sri.lanka.net

Jetwing, 46 / 26 Navam Maw, Col 2, ☎ (01) 34 57 00, Fax (01) 34 57 25, jetwing@sri.lanka.net, www.lanka.net/jetwing

Walkers Tours and **Keells Group**, 130 Glennie St, Col 2, ☎ (01) 32 75 40, Fax (01) 33 47 72.

Guesthouses

Guesthouses have all been built according to the same model – **functional** as opposed to charming. Guesthouses registered with the Tourist Board must be equipped with air-conditioning. It's the upkeep, of course, but also the **owners** who make the difference. These people can be mines of information and of valuable assistance in helping you organise your trip. Everything is possible when you have found a good guesthouse: ordering a bus or train ticket, shopping advice, organising transportation to sites difficult to access, and especially experiencing the hospitality and kindness of Sri Lankans.

A few hints for digging out a good address: visit the room and agree on the rate before settling in and ensure your choice by reading some of the comments written by previous guests in the visitor's book (you should immediately leave those which don't provide one).

Never leave your passport or your money in your room and always lock your luggage. Your hosts will not be to blame, yet all the comings and goings in their home can occasionally lead to theft. In more modest guesthouses or those frequented by backpackers (in Kataragama or Anuradhapura), bedding, towels, toilet paper and soap are not provided. Also note the presence of **Retiring Rooms** in the main train stations. These are basic rooms, equipped with a bed, shower or sink, and are primarily reserved for travellers who have tickets.

Hustlers

Tourism is an important source of revenue for Sri Lanka. It's a large piece of pie and it's only fair that everyone has his due part – from the large travel agencies to the modest family-run guesthouses. However, it also attracts loathsome parasites: hustlers. "Toutism" is a genuine institution. Individual travellers are their favourite prey; trains and buses their hunting ground. Their only objective is to extort money from you by any means. Often they will approach you in a friendly manner by boasting about having the least expensive and most charming guesthouse, from which they will receive half of the rate you pay. The only remedy is to choose your accommodation yourself from your guidebook or based on advice from other travellers and to go there by your own means – on foot or by asking the bus driver for the correct stop as the *tuk-tuk* drivers are often implacable hustlers. Be firm and never underestimate the power of their imagination. They are capable of convincing you that they are the owners of the guesthouse you have chosen, then explaining that it has burned down and then steering you towards an establishment managed by a "friend".

• Eating out

The choice of restaurants is very limited outside Colombo which, like all capital cities, offers a large variety of eating places. Going out to eat is a more common practice for tourists than for Sri Lankans. Families who travel are more apt to cook for themselves or to eat with the family they are visiting. During the day, a snack ("*short-eats*") will satisfy your hunger. This explains the fact that the best Sri Lankan cuisine is prepared at home. For this reason the guesthouses, where the lady of the house prepares the meals herself, are considered to serve the best meals on the island. It is not at all unusual to eat in one, even if you are not staying there.

In the hotels

The hotels prepare mostly **international cuisine** that lacks originality and consists of a choice of Eastern, Western, and Chinese menus. The first is a highly-seasoned local cuisine, where fresh spices are replaced by ready-made condiments. The spiciest version consists of meat, fish and vegetables in a devilled sauce, which is a type of spicy ketchup. The second menu consists of traditional international meals, such as spaghetti or steak and chips. The third is a Sri Lankan interpretation of Chinese food, such as noodles, stir-fried dishes, and soups. The main meals are served à la carte or buffet-style. Full English breakfasts are served with toast, scrambled or fried eggs, tea or coffee. You may also order a local breakfast consisting of hopper, string hopper and curry. The government **tax** (GST) of 12.5 % added to all meals and drinks makes the bill rather expensive.

In the guesthouses

Some guesthouses serve **high quality meals** and will provide you with the opportunity of tasting true Sri Lankan cuisine. Although the actual menus may seem repetitive, they mask the extraordinary diversity of the meals prepared with a mixture of spices. Instead of a simple rice and curry dish, you will be served a variety of curries, since at least three dishes of vegetables and one of meat or fish with a side dish of rice will be provided in very generous portions. Although in Sri Lanka seasoned always means very spicy, the chefs know how to adapt their dishes to suit the tastes of Westerners unaccustomed to the explosive sauces.

In restaurants

For the same reasons mentioned above, good restaurants are very rare. On the other hand, there are small, modest establishments, usually near the bus stations, that serve a **daily curry special**. Hygiene is questionable, the sauces are always spicy, and you will be able to determine the quality of the food by the number of customers who dine there. Curries are prepared in the morning so by lunchtime there will be a good choice of freshly prepared meals. By dinnertime the choice is more limited and meals are usually warmed up. You will find **Chinese restaurants** in most of the towns whereas on the coast the restaurants are adapted to an international tourist and the menus consist of fish and other seafood.

In the street

Although there are no food carts, you will find "*short-eats*" sold throughout the day in the "hotels" and bakeries: *rotties* (salty turnovers stuffed with seasoned vegetables and hard-boiled eggs), *patties* (vegetable fritters), *cutlets* (fried meatballs made with lentils and spices) and *vadai* (lentil fritters).

Drinks

You will find mineral water and **carbonated drinks** everywhere. The national brand, *Elephant*, and ginger beer are the most popular. The **local beer** is very good. Imported wine and alcohol are excessively expensive due to the taxes. The local whisky is **arak**, made from distilled palm leaf beer *(toddy)*. Alcohol cannot be served in any establishment during *poya*.

SPORTS AND PASTIMES

The large hotels provide equipment for practising a variety of sports. But the island's natural features with the sea and the mountains provide sufficient activities for everyone.

• Sports

Hiking

There are currently no organisations that arrange hikes on the island. However, there are numerous possibilities for people of all levels. In Nuwara Eliya, and particularly in Uva, you will find representatives with sufficient experience to provide you with useful advice. Climbing Adam's Peak, which is easily accessible if you take your time, is a fantastic experience. You will find several itineraries for hikes when you are there. These are well-documented in the **Trekkers' Guide to Sri Lanka**, published by Trekking Unlimited, Colombo, 1994.

Water sports

The water temperature, which ranges between 27°C and 29°C (80-84°F), is ideal for **swimming** but be careful at certain times of the year when the sea can be rough. The waves in Hikkaduwa and Midigama are great if you plan to **surf**. In the few areas protected by the coral reefs (Polhena, Hikkaduwa, Unawatuna), everyone can swim without risk and enjoy the spectacle of brightly coloured fish with proper snorkelling equipment. More experienced **scuba divers** will find good diving clubs at Hikkaduwa and Tangalle.

The day of the match

The cricket season runs from January to April and the most prominent cricket grounds are in Colombo, Kandy and Galle. Even if you don't join in with the mass of supporters, you will participate indirectly since match commentaries are broadcast over loudspeakers in villages, and restaurants equipped with televisions are packed.

Cricket

The game is a national passion. Sri Lanka is very proud that it doesn't have any professional players unlike its rivals India and Pakistan.

Golf

Sri Lanka has one of the most beautiful golf courses in all of Asia in Nuwara Eliya. Since it is managed by the town, you may learn or perfect your game for a very reasonable price.

• Night-life

Traditionally there is hardly any night-life in the "big village" of Sri Lanka. For security reasons, there is little activity and quotas are controlled by security forces in the large cities.

Cinemas and theatres

The Sri Lankan screen is dominated by films made locally or in India, but a number of Colombo cinemas show English-language films and there are occasional film shows at the British Council.

Concerts and dance performances

Several theatres in Kandy and large hotels throughout the country offer the chance to attend classical or traditional dance performances. The *perahera*, with its retinue of dancers in ceremonial costume, is spectacular, particularly in Kandy where the Esala procession is more of a performance than a religious event.

Shopping

Compared to its industrious neighbours in India and Thailand, Sri Lanka has a poor selection of handicrafts. Its craftsmanship is repetitive and lacks originality and creativity. This has not always been the case, on the contrary, and the collection at the National Museum of Kandy displays an expertise that has since been lost, or at least forgotten. The decline in tourism during the difficult years of internal conflict is one of the causes of the disappearance of traditional handicrafts. Hopefully they will make a comeback once tourism returns en masse. For the moment, only elephant enthusiasts will find their treasures. The elephant, being the national symbol, is worked into all materials (from exotic wood to batik pillowcases) and all sizes (from amulets to coffee tables).

• What's on offer

Antiques

In principle, exporting antiques is strictly controlled. It is forbidden to leave the country with any object more than 50 years old. If you are an antique shopper, seek out the prosperous and highly respected antique dealers in Kandy or Colombo. They will take the responsibility of getting you a certificate to authorise exportation. The most interesting objects are the **jewellery** and **betel serving dishes**. The latter includes all sorts of boxes and nutcrackers in the most fanciful shapes.

Metalwork

Repoussé, which consists of moulding a sheet of metal on an elastic support, is the most widespread technique. This is used to manufacture ceremonial or **decorative dishes** (tea service or trays) and **religious objects** (oil-lamps on stands). The silver is shaped in a filigree pattern to make jewellery. You can find items made of old silver pawned at jewellery shops in Kandy or Colombo and sold according to their weight.

Carved wood

This secular tradition in Sri Lanka is practised mainly in two fields: doorframes, the leafs and lintels on doors, carved in bas-relief and **theatre masks**. The theatre masks have become obsolete but sculpted and painted masks of Kolam or the Sanni demons make up an unlimited repertory of tourist souvenirs. Before

B. Gaisne

buying one, have a look at the collection found in the museums in Colombo, Ambalangoda or Koggala. The sculptors also create a variety of statues as well as lavishly decorated furniture.

Basketry

Bamboo strips, cane lianas, and sheets of pandanus, rush and palm leaves are the primary materials used to weave **mats** and **baskets**. The shops along the road between Colombo and Kandy, near the villages of Bataliya and Weweldeniya, offer a large selection. The small hemstitched diamond-shaped mats are typically Sri Lankan. They are used to arrange the ladles, sculpted from half of a coconut shell.

Spices and tea

Cinnamon sticks, nutmeg, curcuma or tumeric (Indian saffron), cardamom seeds and cloves represent the scented souvenirs of Ceylon. As such, these spices are sold in the tourist shops wrapped in small packets of plastic. If you wish to spice up your kitchen, buy them in the **market**, but don't buy large quantities because they go stale quickly and lose their enticing fragrance. You will have numerous occasions to buy tea in the higher altitude areas but this is a purchase you can wait to make until the end of your trip at the airport tea shop.

Precious stones

Shopping for precious stones is reserved for the experts. Do not waste your time with this costly acquisition if you don't know anything about them. The criteria for quality of a gem is as scientific as it is subjective. The most reputed precious stones on the island are the clear blue **sapphires** (as well as white, pink, violet, yellow or green sapphires) and **rubies**, which are rarer. Some of them take on a crystalline shape which gives them a starlike reflection. Other stones in descending order according to their hardness are: alexandrite, tiger's eye, aquamarines, topaz, garnet, quartz, amethyst, tourmaline, and moonstone. In all cases, shop only in authorised shops and take your time before buying. It is also possible to obtain free expertise on stones through the **State Gem Corporation**, 310 Galle Rd, in Colombo. Open Monday to Friday, 9am-12.30pm / 1.30pm-4.30pm.

Textiles and clothing

It is now quite difficult to find traditional weaving in Sri Lanka *(see "Making the most of Colombo", p 138)*. You can however easily find inexpensive sportswear. Batik cottons are made into all sorts of items (from household linen to clothing).

• Where to shop

What to buy where

The state-run stores, **Laksala**, display the entire range of handicrafts – in other words, not much. You can nevertheless get a good idea of the prices around the island. These shops can be found in Colombo, Galle and Kandy. The Kandy shop, located on Peradeniya Rd, has the largest selection. The main beach resorts also have numerous souvenir shops.

Hotel shops

With the exception of the rare deluxe establishments in Colombo, hotel shops are deceptive and you will only find necessity items you may have forgotten to pack (such as toothbrushes and mystery novels) as well as the inevitable shop selling precious stones.

• Bartering

It is almost impossible to avoid the "unauthorised" tax imposed on tourists – commission. With the exception of state-operated stores, prices are never displayed and bartering is essential.

• Dispatching your purchases

You can ship your purchases home via the postal service without any risk or give this responsibility to the shops that offer this service (particularly antique dealers and furniture stores).

Health and safety

• Precautions

As in many countries around the world, you will limit your risks of catching a disease if you observe basic rules of hygiene.

Sun

The first rule is to protect yourself from the sun and heat in order to prevent any risk of **sunstroke** or **dehydration**. Go out in the sun progressively and always wear a hat, sunglasses and suntan lotion, even if the sky is cloudy. It is also important to drink lots of liquid frequently.

Stomach problems

The change in food and climate often causes **intestinal problems** for many travellers. These are more annoying than dangerous.

In any case, you can easily cure yourself by eating white rice and drinking lots of salty vegetable broth and by taking an anti-diarrhoea pill and upset-stomach medication.

As a precaution, never drink tap water that has not been boiled or purified beforehand. Always wash your hands before and after each meal, peel fruit and raw vegetables before eating them and don't eat meat or fish unless they are well-cooked.

Mosquitoes

Sri Lanka does have cases of **malaria**, but the risks vary according to the region and the seasons. In any case, good disease prevention begins with protection against mosquito bites as it is also common to get other diseases through them such as **dengue fever**, endemic in Sri Lanka, for which there is no preventive treatment. Use a good dose of repellant, wear trousers, long-sleeved shirts, and closed shoes when evening comes. Check that your mosquito net is in good condition or burn mosquito coils. It is also advisable to avoid wearing dark colours and perfume. For anti-malaria pills, consult a doctor specialising in tropical diseases before leaving home

AIDS

As Sri Lanka is not immune to AIDS, don't forget to protect yourself and carry condoms and disposable syringes.

• Medical kit

Don't forget to bring a sufficient supply of medicine if you have a particular prescription. Also plan to bring aspirin, antiseptic, antibiotics, anti-diarrhoea pills, and upset-stomach medication, nasal decongestant, plasters and sterile bandages, an analgesic, water-purifying pills, pills for motion sickness, mosquito repellent, suntan lotion and eye drops. More adventurous travellers should also bring sterile syringes for emergency injections, anti-inflammatory lotion, and athlete's foot powder. And finally, don't forget commonly-used

items such as razors, shaving cream, tampons and sanitary towels, contraceptives, condoms, contact lens solution, and an extra pair of contact lenses or glasses.
Be sure to get advice from your doctor before leaving home or to contact your local international travel medical service for information.

• Health services

Although there are good doctors available, hospital facilities outside Colombo and Kandy are inadequate. To avoid all serious problems, we strongly advise taking out repatriation health insurance (*see p 84*). Don't forget to always carry a card stating your blood type and the address and phone number of your insurance company.

Emergencies

When you arrive you can ask the owner of your guesthouse to suggest a local doctor or ask the hotel you are staying at to find one for you. In case of a more serious problem, contact your embassy to provide you with a list of doctors and establishments capable of giving you the best care.

Hospitals

Only the hospitals in Colombo and Kandy have modern facilities and efficient emergency care. Elsewhere you will find only clinics that are able to deal with common problems.

Pharmacies

There is a pharmacy in Colombo open 24 hours a day, 7 days a week (*see p 133*). You can also get medicine in Kandy and Nuwara Eliya.

Traditional medicine

Two types of medicine prevail in Sri Lanka: Western medicine and traditional medicine, based on the use of plants. Called Ayurveda, the "knowledge of life", it is derived from nature, plants or animals, and incorporates traditional recipes used by peasants, hunters and shepherds. This medicine not only focuses on the body, but also on the patient's personality: from his relationship with his natural environment, time and the cosmos, to his psychic state, from the depths of his subconscious. An effective use of pharmacopoeia ensues, consisting of diet and massage to re-establish a biological equilibrium to eliminate stress and bad food habits. Ayurvedic medicine is long term. Western travellers, used to a completely different system, should not expect miracles. You can benefit from its soothing effects in the spas located in some of the larger hotels or at the beach resorts.

From A to Z

• Drinking water

You must not drink tap water, but you can easily find bottled mineral water. Bring chloride tablets if you plan to visit more isolated areas.

• Electricity

Although 220 volts is generally used, it is nonetheless recommended to check the voltage before plugging in your appliance. Wall plugs have three pins so you may need to have an adapter, depending on the outlet in your country. A flashlight may be useful in the event of power cuts and if you plan to visit caves.

• Laundry service

Many hotels and some guesthouses offer laundry service. Leave your laundry in the morning and it will be ready that evening.

• Newspapers

Ceylon Daily News, *Evening Observer* and *The Island* are the three daily newspapers available in English. On Sundays, you can also find six weekly papers in English: *Sunday Observer*, *Sunday Island*, *The Sunday Times*, *The Sunday Leader*, *Weekend Express* and *Midweek Mirror*.

• Photography

You will easily find inexpensive standard **film** (100 ASA) in all the large tourist areas. If you need high sensitivity film (50, 400, 1000 ASA), bring a sufficient supply from home. **Film development** is inexpensive and is high quality in Colombo.

With the exception of monks who may show some reluctance, Sri Lankans love to be photographed. Keep in mind that they may however ask for a tip. To show respect, always ask permission before taking a picture of someone and don't insist if you are refused! You will also make them very happy if you send them the photo you have taken.

• Radio and television

Other than the national *Sri Lanka Broadcasting Corporation (SLBC)*, several private radio stations have FM programmes in English, such as *Yes FM* (24 hours a day, 7 days a week), *TNL Radio* (6am to midnight daily), *FM 99* (6am to midnight daily) and *ABC Network*.

There are two national TV channels: *Rupavahini* and *Independent Television Network (ITN)*, and four cable channels: *MTV*, *Sirasa TV TNL*, *ETV* and *Swarnavahini*. Many programmes are in English.

• Safety

To avoid **theft**, it is wise to respect some basic rules of safety. Never leave your baggage unattended and watch it carefully in **public areas**, particularly when travelling by bus or train. Also close your luggage with a small lock. Leave your documents and valuable items in the hotel safe-deposit boxes and keep a copy of your passport on you. Keep your money hidden in a money belt.

The conflict between the Sri Lankan government and the Tamil Tigers started 15 years ago and continues today. It is strongly recommended not to visit the north, east and the extreme southeast of the island. The conflict manifests itself everywhere else **as endemic terrorism**, particularly in Colombo which is the main target.

• Smoking

Only men smoke in Sri Lanka and few are heavy smokers. You can find cigarettes easily, including in the village *kade* where you can even buy them individually. A packet of the local brand costs about 110Rs. It is forbidden to smoke at religious sites and in public places.

• Tipping / gratuities

Most hotels and restaurants include a 10 % service charge on the bill. As in many countries, the practice of tipping is widespread for hotel staff, guides, chauffeurs, porters, etc.

• Units of measurement

Sri Lanka follows the metric system. Distances are generally stated in kilometres on the roads, however people will often refer to distance in miles (1km = 0.62 miles).

Distances in this guide are given in kilometres. As a rule of thumb, one kilometre is five-eighths of a mile: 5 miles is therefore about 8 kilometres, 10 miles is about 16 kilometres and 20 miles is about 32 kilometres.

Consult the table below for other useful metric equivalents:

Degrees Celsius	35°	30°	25°	20°	15°	10°	5°	0°	-5°	-10°
Degrees Fahrenheit	95°	86°	77°	68°	59°	50°	41°	32°	23°	15°

1 centimetre (cm) = 0.4 inch
1 metre (m) = 3.3 feet
1 metre (m) = 1.09 yards
1 litre = 1.06 quart
1 litre = 0.22 gallon

• Weather

Weather reports are announced daily on TV, in the newspapers and on English radio stations.

LOOK AND LEARN

• Archeology

ASIAN EDUCATIONAL SERVICE, ***The Great Temples of India, Ceylon, and Burma***, South Asia Books, 1988.
POLE, John, ***Stone Implements***, Laurier Books, Ltd, 2000.

• History

KELLY, Robert C, EWING, Debra, DOYLE, Stanton, YOUNGBLOOD, Denise (editors), ***Country Review: Sri Lanka***, Commercial Data International, 1998.
SIVANANDAN, Ambalavaner, ***When Memory Dies***, Dufour Editions. The history of 20C Sri Lanka from a socialist point of view.
DE SILVA, Chandra Richard, ***Sri Lanka A History***, South Asia Books, 1997.
VENKATACHALAM, MS, ***Genocide in Sri Lanka***, South Asia Books, 1987.

• Literature

GUNESEKERA, Romesh, ***Monkfish Moon***, New Press, 1993. Short stories that present a poignant picture of Sri Lanka and its people.
GURUGE, Ananda WP, ***Free at Last in Paradise: A Historical Novel on Sri Lanka***, Buy Books on the web.com, 1998. A fictional autobiography that delves into the social, political, religious, and cultural evolutions of modern Sri Lanka.
ONDAATJE, Michael, ***Anil's Ghost***, Knopf, 2000. Set during the civil war, when a native Sri Lankan returns to her homeland as part of an international human rights mission.
SELVADURAI, Shyam, ***Cinnamon Gardens***, Harcourt Brace Trade, 2000. The story of two people who try to escape the tyranny of parents and mentors and to achieve inner freedom.

• Poetry

AMIRTHANAYAGAM, Indran, ***The Elephants of Reckoning***, Hanging Loose Press, 1993.

• Religion and society

CALDWELL, Bruce, ***Marriage in Sri Lanka; A Century of Change***, South Asia Books, 1999.

KARIYAWASAM, AGS, ***Buddhist Ceremonies and Rituals of Sri Lanka***, Vipassana Research Publications, 1995.

RATNATUNGA, Manel, ***Best Loved Folk Tales of Sri Lanka***, South Asia Books, 1999.

SEKHERA, Kalalelle, ***Early Buddhist Saghas and Viharas in Sri Lanka (up to 4th century AD)***, Rishi Publications, 1998. This book traces the mythological and physical history of Sri Lanka with a focus on the Buddhist monasteries.

SENEVIRATNE, HL, ***The Work of Kings: The New Buddhism in Sri Lanka***, University of Chicago Press, 2000. A look at the turbulent modern history and sociology of the Sri Lankan Buddhist monkhood.

WELBON, Guy, ***Religious Festivals in South India and Sri Lanka***, South Asia Books, 1982.

WICKREMERATHNE, Ananda, ***Buddhism and Ethnicity in Sri Lanka: A Historical Analysis***, South Asia Books, 1995.

• Maps

Sri Lanka, 1/450 000, Nelles Maps.

Glossary

GLOSSARY

Three languages are spoken in Sri Lanka: Sinhalese, which represents the largest number of speakers, Tamil, spoken by the Tamil minority and a large percentage of Muslims, and English.

• Pronunciation

Neither Tamil nor Sinhalese have letters that are difficult to pronounce but you will quickly discover that it is easy to elide syllables. Transcribed into the Latin alphabet, some words seem disproportionately long. Once you pronounce them, they make up brief expressions from which long vowels emerge in a burst of rolled "r"s.

Common expressions

	Singalese	**Tamil**
greeting	ayubowan	vanakkam
hello (to a man)	mahatmaya	aiya
hello (to a woman)	nona mahatmaya	thirumadhi
please	karunakara	thayavu seithu
thank you	es-thu-thi	nandri
thank you very much	bohoma es-thu-thi	miga nandri
yes	ov	ahm
no	na-tha (nay-hay)	illai
maybe	venna puluvan	sila way lai

agreed	meka hondai	ithuru seri
OK	kamak na	paruvai illai
excuse me	samavenna	manniyungal
I don't speak Sinhalese/Tamil	mama sinhala katha	ennaku tamil
do you speak English?	obata ingreese kata karanna puluvan da?	ungalukku angilam pesa mudiyuma?
I don't understand	mata thayrennay nehe	anakku vilangavillai
Basic conversation		
what's your name?	obeh nameh monawada?	ungal payar enna?
my name is...	mage nama...	ennudaya payar...
how are you?	kohamada sahpa sahnipa?	ehppadi sugam?
I'm alright	sanee-pen innava	nalla sugam
I'm not alright	sanee-pa na-tha	sugamillai
where are you from?	oba vah-sa-ya karannay kohayda?	neengal engay val gi reergal?
I'm from...	mama vasaya karannay...	naan... ill val-gi rain
how old are you?	obeh vayase kee ya da?	ungal vayasu eth-thanai?
I'm... years old	magay vayasu avurudu...	en vayadu...
are you married?	oba we-va-ha ve-la-da?	ungalukku pillai gal irukku rargalah?
Time		
what time is it?	welaawa kiiyadha?	taim yenna aagudungal?
now	dang	ippoh
today	atha	indru
yesterday	iye	naetru
tomorrow	heta	nalai
morning	ude	kalai
afternoon	dawal	pitpagal
evening	sawasa	malai
night	raya	iravu
day	damasa	naal
Monday	sanduda	thinkat kilamai
Tuesday	angaharuwada	sevai kilamai
Wednesday	badhada	puthan kilamai
Thursday	brahaspathinda	viyalak kilamai
Friday	sikurada	velli kilamai
Saturday	senasurada	sanik kilamai
Sunday	irrida	gnatruk kilamai
Common adjectives		
closed	wahala	moodu
open	arala	thira
hot	rasnai	ushnamana
cold	sithai	kulir
dirty	apirisudui	alukku
clean	sudda	suththam
Getting around, visiting		
where is...?	koheda...?	...enge?
next to	langa	arugil

on the right	dakunata	valathu kai pakkam
on the left	wamata	idathu kai pakkam
in front of	anith-patta	edire
straight ahead	kelin yanna	naerakapogavum
village	gama	kiramam
city	nuwara, nagaraja	nagaram, paddanam
path	adi para	ottai adi pathai
road	maha para	pirithana veethi
street	mawatha, vidiya, para	veethi
market	market eka	angaadi
museum	katu-ge	
post office	tapal kanthoruwa	thabal kanthor
bank	bankuwa	bank
monastery	arama	
Buddhist / Hindu temple	pansala	kovil
church	palliya	vetha kovil
mosque	muslim palliya	palli vasal
river	ganga / oya	kulam, aaru / aruvi aaru lake
water reservoir	wewa	kulam
beach	wali, werala	manat-karai
mountain	kanda	malai
forest	kaleva	vanam
Transport		
bus	bas	bas
bus station	stesemata / bas stand	bas stand
train	kochiya	treyin
railway station	dumryapola	treyin steshan, nilayam
At the hotel		
hotel	hotalaeya, thanayama	vaadi veedu
room	kamaraya	arai
fan	fan	katotra sathanam
mosquito net	maduru delak	kosu valai
At the restaurant		
restaurant	kamata / apana sala / hotel	sapathu
eat	kama	unavu
drink	bima	kudi
the menu please	menu eka penwanna	thayavu seithu thin-pandangal
the bill please	karunakara bila gaynna	bill kondu varungal
very good	hari honthai	miga nallathu
rice and curry	elavalu bath	saadam saambaar
water	wathura	thannir
coffee	copi	coffee
tea	the	theyilai
bread	pan	pan
spice	mris	karam
no spice please	miris nathuwa	karam vendam

pepper	gammiris	milagu
salt	lunu	uppu
cane sugar	hakuru	vellam
egg	biththara	muttai
fish	malu	min
shrimp	isso	iral
meat	mus	iraichchi
chicken	kukulmas	koli
rice	buth	arisi
fruit	palathuru	palam
banana	keselkan	valaippalam
coconut	pol	thenkai
(fresh) coconut	kurumba	pachcha niramulla thengai
mango	amba	mangai
papaya	papol	pappa palam
pineapple	annasi	annasi
vegetables	elawalu	kai kari vagaigal
Shopping		
how much does this cost?	may kay gana kee yada?	ithan vilai enna?
it's too expensive	ah vadi neda	kooda vilai thanay
that costs 50Rs	rupial panahai	athan vilaiompathu rupa
Numbers		
1	eka	ontru
2	deka	erantru
3	thuna	moontru
4	hathara	nangu
5	paha	ainthu
6	haya	aru
7	hatha	aelu
8	ata	ettu
9	namaya	onpathu
10	dahaya	pattu
20	wissai	erupathu
30	thihai	muppathu
40	hathalihai	natpathu
50	panahai	mpathu
100	sihiya	nooru
200	desiyai	irunooru
1000	dahai	aiyuram
2000	dedahai	iranda iuram
Emergencies		
I'm sick	mata saneepa ne-he	parmasi
doctor	dosthara	darktarai
hospital	rohala	aspathri
pharmacy	bet sappuwa	marundu kadai
police	policiya	police ilaka

Exploring Sri Lanka

B Pérousse / HOA QUI

View across the tea plantations

Itineraries for visitors

To draw up a standard itinerary which will not be dependent on the length of your stay poses something of a challenge. Some travellers may prefer visiting archeological sites or hiking, others may choose to stay longer in one of the island's resorts...

We have, however, put together four itineraries which you can adapt to suit the length of your stay, your personal interests, your means of transport and whatever takes your fancy.

10-day itinerary

This short itinerary takes in the principal sights of the island and can be extended with a trip to the coast.

Colombo★ – Anuradhapura★★★ – Dambulla★★ – Sigiriya★★★ – Kandy★★ – Nuwara Eliya – Galle★★ – Mount Lavinia★

18-day itinerary

An itinerary which focuses on the west coast, the royal cities and the wild landscapes of the heart of the island.

Colombo★ – Marawila★ – Chilaw – Panduwas Nuwara★ – Yapahuwa★★ – Anuradhapura★★★ – Polonnaruwa★★★ – Sigiriya★★★ – Dambulla★★ – Kandy★★ – Nuwara Eliya – Adam's Peak★★ – Ratnapura★ – Sinharaja★★ – Uda Walawe★★ – Unawatuna★ – Galle★★

18-day itinerary

This itinerary, which includes the island's most famous sights as well as some lesser-known ones, also takes in much of the Uva province and the southeast.

Colombo★ – Kurunegala – Ridi Vihara★★ – Dambulla★★ – Anuradhapura★★★ – Polonnaruwa★★★ – Sigiriya★★★ – Kandy★★ – Badulla★ – Ella★★ – Haputale★ – Horton Plains★★★ – Buduruvegala★★ – Kataragama★★ – Tissamaharama★ – Yala★★ – Tangalle★ – Galle★★ – Bentota★

22-day itinerary

This is the complete programme, including both cultural and "natural" attractions, which takes in all the different facets of the island, from the principal archeological sites to the beaches of the south coast, visiting the plantations in the centre of the island and the wild animal reserves on the way.

Colombo★ – Negombo – Pinnewala★★ – Kurunegala – Anuradhapura★★★ – Mihintale★★ – Polonnaruwa★★★ – Medirigiriya★★ – Sigiriya★★★ – Dambulla★★ – Kandy★★ – Bandarawela – Horton Plains★★★ – Uda Walawe★★ – Kataragama★★ – Yala★★ – Tangalle★ – Mount Lavinia★

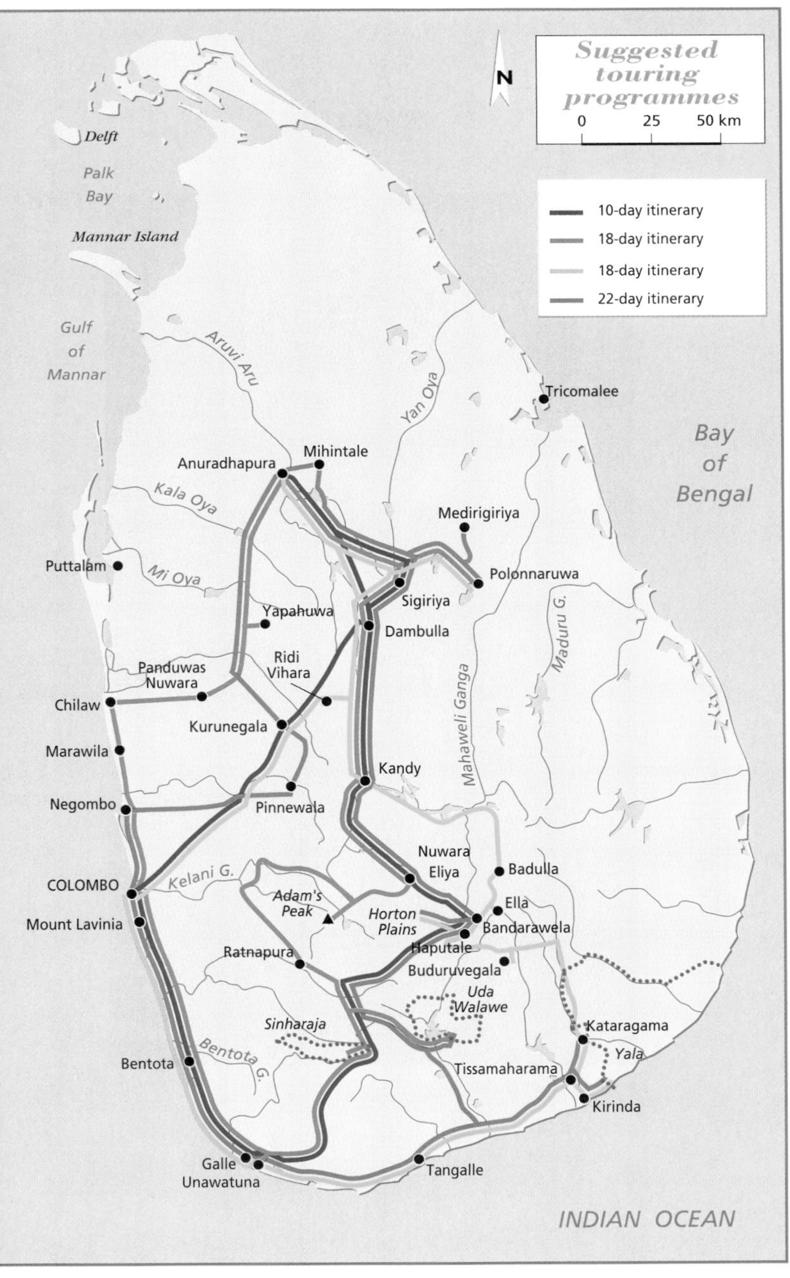
N
Suggested touring programmes
0
25
50 km
10-day itinerary
18-day itinerary
18-day itinerary
22-day itinerary
Delft
Palk Bay
Mannar Island
Gulf of Mannar
Aruvi Aru
Yan Oya
Tricomalee
Bay of Bengal
Mihintale
Anuradhapura
Kala Oya
Medirigiriya
Puttalam
Mi Oya
Polonnaruwa
Sigiriya
Maduru G.
Yapahuwa
Dambulla
Ridi Vihara
Panduwas Nuwara
Chilaw
Kurunegala
Mahaweli Ganga
Marawila
Kandy
Negombo
Pinnewala
Nuwara Eliya
Badulla
COLOMBO
Kelani G.
Adam's Peak
Ella
Horton Plains
Bandarawela
Mount Lavinia
Haputale
Ratnapura
Buduruvegala
Uda Walawe
Sinharaja
Kataragama
Yala
Bentota
Bentota G.
Tissamaharama
Kirinda
Galle
Unawatuna
Tangalle
INDIAN OCEAN

J du Boisberranger / HEMISPHERES

A narrow ribbon of sand…

COLOMBO AND THE WEST COAST

A narrow ribbon of sand, backed by grey-blue palm trees from which some pink-tiled roofs emerge: this is the image of the west coast greeting visitors to the island arriving by air.

Colombo, the capital, is not exactly in the centre of the region, but with its adjoining port being the economic pivot of the island, it exerts a strong influence. This conurbation stretches for 70km from Negombo to Kalutara, in a series of built-up areas which have never really become a metropolis.

To the north, the coastline is broken up by lagoons and mangrove swamps and studded with fishing villages: in the evening the catamarans, with their tobacco-coloured sails, can be seen coming ashore against a background of mosques, temples and churches. This remarkable landscape also includes views of the palm-tree forests, strung with cables, where the *malafoutiers* perform their acrobatics, like tightrope walkers.

To the south, one of the island's oldest roads runs along the narrow coastal strip, connecting Colombo to Galle. A railway line accompanies it, laid out through the ocean's sandy fringe. The road and railway form a tangible border between two worlds: the coastal region, with its hotels, its palm-trees casting their oblique shadows, its seaside restaurants and occasional colonial villas; and the interior of the island, with its tropical woodland, dotted with ricefields and ponds, furrowed with irrigation channels, where life follows the rhythm of the growing seasons *(see regional map p 143)*.

COLOMBO★

Capital
Pop 650 000, 2 million in the metropolitan region
116km from Galle and Kandy, 206km from Anuradhapura
Climate – hot and humid all year round

Not to be missed
Breakfast on the top floor of the Grand Oriental, the port of Colombo below you.
The bronze masterpieces in the National Museum.
Sunday amid the Buddhist fervour of Kelaniya.

And remember...
Allow a whole day for a tour of the city.
Colombo is a convenient point of access, but has few places of interest.
A better place to stay is the resort of Mount Lavinia.

Adjoining its artificial harbour developed by the British, but not really looking out towards the sea, Colombo is a capital with an identity crisis. Symbolic of the crisis is the empty shell of the Presidential Secretariat, this Victorian building dwarfed by the twin skyscrapers of the Treasury and the Bank of Ceylon. Created by the great maritime trading route to the East Indies and expanding at the same time as Bombay on the Arabian Sea, this city with the Portuguese name is still the economic nerve centre of the nation, though affairs of state are nowadays conducted from the town of Sri Jayawardhanapura.
However, as a target for terrorists, Colombo struggles to translate this dream of good government into reality. Streets are closed to traffic, pavements are out of bounds to pedestrians and police barriers restrict city life, dividing the town up into a series of enclaves kept under close surveillance. Prevented from using routes that have been blocked, traffic is very congested. Particularly in the light of the current unrest there is no necessity to stay here, as the international airport is actually nearer to Negombo beach, and the Bambalapitiya commercial centre is only a 30-minute train journey from the resort of Mount Lavinia. Tourists in a hurry can make their own minds up about whether or not to visit this stricken city, symbol of a nation in crisis.

The Kelani Trading Post

Compared to the ancient Sinhalese royal cities, the capital of Sri Lanka is in its formative phase, its fate determined by economic interests rather than politics. Called **Kalan-totta**, "the Kelani ferry", by the Sinhalese, it became **Kalambu** under the Muslim merchants in the Middle Ages and a strategic port of call between the Arabian peninsula and the Malayan world. In 1948, the discovery of a maritime route between Europe and the East Indies via the Cape of Good Hope put an end to the Arab monopoly in the spice trade between Europe and the Orient. With the opening of the East Indies route, Kalambu became an important link in the chain of trading posts spread out along this lucrative spice route, between Goa and the Far Eastern ports of Malacca in Malaysia and Macao on the Sea of China. In 1517, the Portuguese obtained authorisation from Parakramabahu VII, the king of Kotte, to set up a trading post to the south of the Kelani estuary, which was an important centre in the trade of ivory and pearls. Kalambu thus became **Colombo** and is still known today by the name given to it by the Portuguese. The trading post was soon protected by a fort and placed under the jurisdiction of the Viceroy of Goa. Apart from the rock in Gordon Garden, a *perao* (milestone), a boundary marker of 1610 bearing the Portuguese coat of arms, nothing survives from this Lusitanian period.

At the centre of the spice war

In the 16C, the battle for the spice trading monopoly in Europe brought the Iberian peninsula into conflict with the English and the Dutch; control of the spice trade became a rich prize in the struggle between the Catholic Habsburgs and the Protestant nations.

On 2 April 1595, the first Dutch expedition, financed by rich merchants and led by **Cornelis Van Houtman**, left Amsterdam in four of the ships known in the Netherlands as *indiamen*. Sailing east via the Cape of Good Hope, they reached Sumatra and Java in 1596. Having defied the power of Portugal the fleet returned to Amsterdam on 4 August 1597.

In 1601, **the Dutch** secretly negotiated an alliance with the king of Kandy against the Portuguese, and the following year saw the creation of the great capitalist company which would arm the Batavian vessels: the V.O.C. (Vereenigde Oostindische Compagnie). This company made Batavia – the future Jakarta – the new epicentre of the spice route. Colombo fell to the Dutch after a siege lasting seven months in 1656. A new fort replaced the Portuguese one, to the south of the harbour.

With the advent of the Dutch, the European occupation of Ceylon became more systematic. A route was established between Colombo and the port of Galle at the southern tip of the island. To the north, a canal was built, linked by the network of lagoons, to form a continuous aquatic corridor from Negombo to Puttalam. Colombo therefore became the bridgehead in the island's river and sea trade, struggling to balance its destiny, with its western face turned towards the rest of the world, while the ancient royal Sinhalese kingdom continued to withdraw into itself in Kandy, in the island's interior.

The Secretariat overlooked by the modern world

Y Keller

From port to port

At the start of the 19C, the colonial administration harnessed together the ports of Galle and the still embryonic Colombo to take on the triple role of administrative centre, principal port of the island and centre of trade and finance. In 1815, the British took control of the kingdom of Kandy, gaining access to the highlands where conditions favoured the cultivation of high-yielding crops, and this was an important factor in the fate of the island. The creation of a road in 1830, then the Colombo-Kandy railway in 1867, also helped to influence the English governors' choice in favour of Colombo. During his visit in 1875, the Prince of Wales laid the first stone of a 1 264m breakwater, built into the extended natural promontory which had protected the harbour until then. These developments, together with two new sea walls to the north and northeast, were completed in 1899, giving the new capital a 256ha harbour.

Changes in the balance of economic power at the end of the 18C, however, shifted in favour of England. Ruler of Bengal and Calcutta since 1757, and of Penang, on the Malaysian coast, since 1786, the English were to eclipse the Dutch position in Ceylon. Between 1795 and 1796, the **British fleet** seized the strategic ports of the island, the new occupants benefiting from the administrative organisation that their predecessors had set up.

The workings of the colonial machinery

In the 19C, Ceylon ceased to be merely an island of cinnamon and cardamom, and like Malaysia and Indonesia, witnessed the development of extensive crop cultivation, with crops from both the ancient and the modern worlds: **coffee** (1840) and **hevea** (1900), the first shoots of which were cultivated in the gardens of Henaratgoda, near Colombo, as well as **tea** (1880), brought from the British plantations of Assam, then from China.

Financial empires were founded on the profits from these estates, as well as the coconut-palm area to the northeast of Colombo, where the Ceylonese upper middle classes invested their savings in copra, molasses and alcoholic beverages (*toddy* and *arak*).

Colombo's current appearance largely dates back to the British regime. The old Dutch fort was dismantled and replaced by English or Italian **neo-Renaissance buildings**, the style fashionable in Victorian England, henceforth occupied by the colonial administration and the head offices of the principal companies. In 1869, the opening of the Suez canal led to a flood of new settlers heading for possession of the British Raj. Colombo, 26 to 28 days by sea from London, was one of these destinations.

Grandiose buildings and tea warehouses stretched the length of Union Place as far as Victoria Park, a green space in this tropical British city, to which the Archeological Survey department donated a magnificent **Palladian-style** museum in 1877. Around the Park, the municipal authorities restrained the exuberance of the former Dutch plantation of the Cinnamon Gardens, the shaded alleys lined with the opulent villas belonging to the Sinhalese upper class and freemen. Finally, to the far south along the coast, Kollupitiya and Bambalapitiya, linked to the Fort by train, housed the employees of the City banks and shops.

At the start of the 20C, the town was one of the reassuring microcosms of colonial Europe, described by the French journalist Charles Müller at the time of his voyage to the East Indies in 1924: "I am going to explore the city, which resembles all the great ports of the world. It is like describing Le Havre or Genoa… Trams, policemen, department stores, arc lights, this is Colombo. The Indian quarter is without interest. The whole town is Europeanised to the highest degree, so much so, that for the first time in five months, I have seen drunkards." (Charles Müller, *Cinq mois aux Indes – De Bombay à Colombo*, H Floury, Paris, 1924). This really says it all.

Modelled on Asia's Tiger Economies

The island's independence in 1948 in no way lessened the pre-eminence of Colombo – in fact, the opposite was the case, to such an extent that the capital could be said to be abnormally large: 80 % of the island's industry and almost all its administrative offices are concentrated here.

The current appearance of the city owes much to **J R Jayawardene**, Prime Minister from 1977 to 1987. **Katunayake**, one of the first free trade zones to be developed on the island and founded on the clothing industry, is situated to the north of Kelani, near the international airport. The glass and steel towers that have sprung up amongst the colonial buildings in the Fort district seem to have come straight from Singapore, the economic model for Sri Lanka at the end of the 1980s. The modernisation of the port since 1985 has made it one of the best in southern Asia, with a current capacity of 3 000 ships a year. Certain administrative services have been transferred to **Sri Jayawardhanapura**, or Kotte, the former seat of power, today forming the eastern suburb of Colombo. A Parliament building in the austere, elegant style of Kandy, built by the architect **Geoffrey Bawa**, was inaugurated there in 1984. Its cost (US$43 million) testifies to the ambitions of the government. As a metaphor for the insularity of Sri Lanka, (it is built on a man-made island in the Lake of Diyawanna), its architecture betrays the sentiment of a Sinhalese identity besieged by the uprising of the Tamil separatist movement. Had the latter not just provoked the pogroms of July 1983 that reduced the central market of Pettah to ashes? Or is this the reflection of what continues to be the demographic reality of Colombo, whose population consists of 40 % Sinhalese, to 50 % Tamil and 10 % Muslim? At the beginning of the 21C, the Tamil question weighs heavily on everyday life in the capital. 1994 was the year of the bombs: four exploded in the city centre that year. And in the face of what has become endemic terrorism the deployment of security measures has become a necessity in the city.

The 15 districts of Colombo

Colombo is organised into numbered postal districts (1 to 15).

Among the sights to see, only the Fort (Colombo 1) and the Pettah (Colombo 11) lend themselves to being visited on foot, although the whole of the north-west section of the Fort district, around the *chaitya* elevated on stilts and Gordon Garden, is sometimes subject to restrictions. It is not impossible to walk around Slave Island and the shores of the west arm of Beira Lake, in the direction of the National Museum (about 30min), but it can be quite demanding: the road is congested with traffic, walls of sandbags in front of the banks and military buildings, have turned the place into a permanent obstacle race, and the shores of the lake are certainly not designed for the walker. Those feeling nostalgic for colonial Colombo might think of turning back towards the famous promenade of Galle Face Green, but its great lawns have not been maintained for a very long time. As for strolling idly through the shady streets of Cinnamon Gardens (Colombo 7), in search of architectural curiosities among the luxury villas, the barriers blocking access to the houses of the local VIPs transform the stroll into a depressing labyrinth.

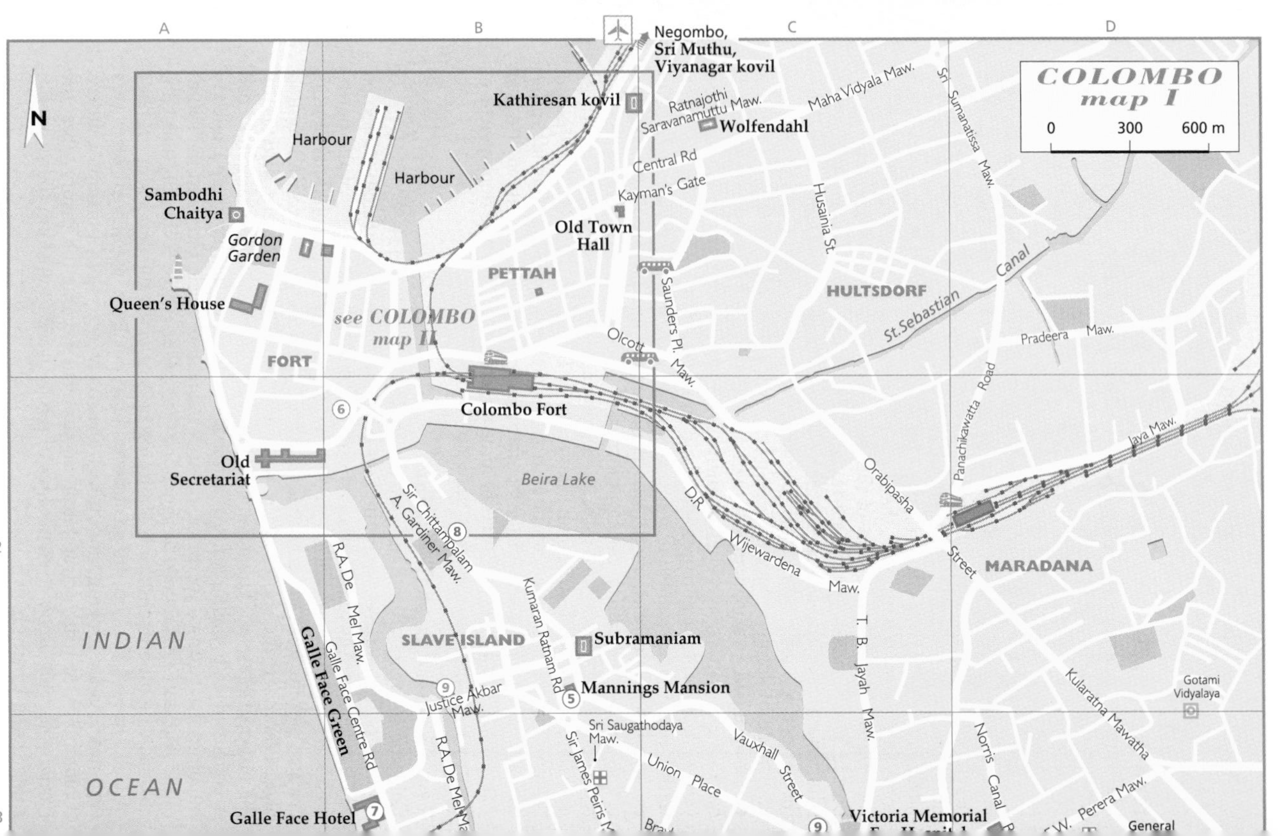
COLOMBO
map I
0
300
600 m
A
B
C
D
1
2
3
N
Negombo,
Sri Muthu,
Viyanagar kovil
Kathiresan kovil
Wolfendahl
Harbour
Harbour
Sambodhi
Chaitya
Gordon
Garden
Old Town
Hall
PETTAH
Queen's House
see COLOMBO
map II
FORT
Colombo Fort
Old
Secretariat
Beira Lake
HULTSDORF
MARADANA
SLAVE ISLAND
Subramaniam
Mannings Mansion
Galle Face Green
Galle Face Hotel
Victoria Memorial
Gotami
Vidyalaya
INDIAN
OCEAN
Ratnajothi
Saravanamuttu Maw.
Maha Vidyala Maw.
Sri Sumanatissa Maw.
Central Rd
Kayman's Gate
Husainia St.
Saunders Pl. Maw.
Olcott
St.Sebastian
Canal
Pradeera Maw.
Panchikawatta Road
Jaya Maw.
Orabipasha
Street
D.R. Wijewardena Maw.
T. B. Jayah Maw.
Kularatna Mawatha
Norris Canal
Perera Maw.
General
Sir Chittampalam
A. Gardiner Maw.
R.A. De Mel Maw.
Galle Face Centre Rd
Justice Akbar Maw.
Kumaran Ratnam Rd
Sri Saugathodaya Maw.
Sir James Peiris M
Vauxhall Street
Union Place
R.A. De Mel Ma
5
6
7
8
9
9

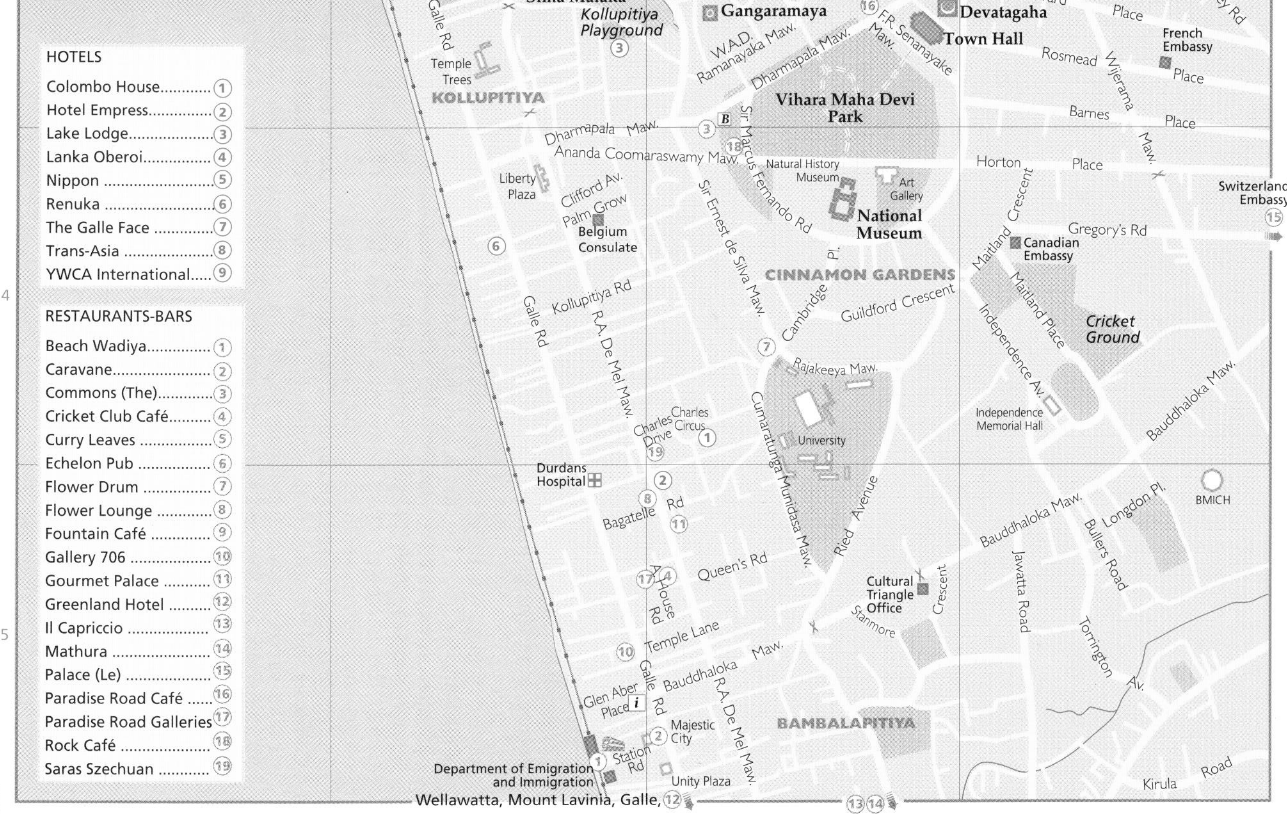
HOTELS
Colombo House 1
Hotel Empress 2
Lake Lodge 3
Lanka Oberoi 4
Nippon 5
Renuka 6
The Galle Face 7
Trans-Asia 8
YWCA International 9
RESTAURANTS-BARS
Beach Wadiya 1
Caravane 2
Commons (The) 3
Cricket Club Café 4
Curry Leaves 5
Echelon Pub 6
Flower Drum 7
Flower Lounge 8
Fountain Café 9
Gallery 706 10
Gourmet Palace 11
Greenland Hotel 12
Il Capriccio 13
Mathura 14
Palace (Le) 15
Paradise Road Café 16
Paradise Road Galleries 17
Rock Café 18
Saras Szechuan 19
Kollupitiya Playground
Gangaramaya
Devatagaha
Town Hall
French Embassy
Rosmead Place
Wijerama Maw.
Barnes Place
Horton Place
Temple Trees
KOLLUPITIYA
W.A.D. Ramanayaka Maw.
Dharmapala Maw.
F.R. Senanayake Maw.
Vihara Maha Devi Park
Ananda Coomaraswamy Maw.
Sir Marcus Fernando Rd
Natural History Museum
Art Gallery
National Museum
Liberty Plaza
Clifford Av.
Palm Grow
Belgium Consulate
Sir Ernest de Silva Maw.
Switzerland Embassy
Gregory's Rd
Canadian Embassy
Maitland Crescent
Maitland Place
CINNAMON GARDENS
Galle Rd
Kollupitiya Rd
R.A. De Mel Maw.
Cambridge Pl.
Guildford Crescent
Cricket Ground
Independence Av.
Rajakeeya Maw.
Independence Memorial Hall
Charles Drive
Charles Circus
University
Baudhaloka Maw.
Durdans Hospital
Bagatelle Rd
Cumaratunga Munidasa Maw.
Ried Avenue
BMICH
Longdon Pl.
Bullers Road
Jawatta Road
Queen's Rd
A. House Rd
Cultural Triangle Office
Crescent
Stanmore
Temple Lane
Torrington Av.
Glen Aber Place
Bauddhaloka Maw.
BAMBALAPITIYA
Majestic City
Station Rd
Department of Emigration and Immigration
Unity Plaza
Kirula Road
Wellawatta, Mount Lavinia, Galle,

Tour

Allow one day.

One day in Colombo will make the capital's congestion problems self-evident. Traffic flows freely only between 1.30pm and 3.30pm, when workers are still at their desks. The rest of the time, the jams are unimaginable and vehicles sometimes remain at a standstill for over an hour. Only air-conditioning can render the ordeal bearable, and the *tuk-tuk* claims to be the only vehicle capable of avoiding the snarl-ups.

The district of Pettah* (Map II B1-2)

Allow one morning and choose the right day: the museum is closed on Friday, and the shops in the Pettah on Sundays. The Pettah, from the Tamil *pettai*, "outside the walls", was set up by the English to accommodate the bazaar, thereby perpetuating the art of doing business Indian, Muslim or Malay-style. The district itself is nothing special, having suffered greatly during the anti-Tamil pogroms of Black July. Except on Sundays, the crowds are so dense that it is impossible to get there by car, and even the *tuk-tuk* have difficulty negotiating their way between the hawkers pulling carts heavily laden with their oddly assorted wares, ranging from old engine parts to bags of rice, boxes of electronic games or lengths of coloured nylon. The Pettah is in fact a huge supermarket, a continuous succession of small shops selling identical products, in a deafening hubbub.

Begin your visit at the **Colombo Fort*** railway station which is not without a certain charm; this long Victorian building has hardly changed since the island's railway network was created in the 19C. Along Olcott Maw, there is a permanent bazaar, with leather goods, alarm clocks, ties and holy images on sale. The stalls line the pavements and you have to elbow your way through, but by the time you reach the junction with 1st Cross Street, you will be ready to negotiate the Pettah.

Turning into Prince Street, it is easy to pick out the façade, fronted by a white portico, of the **Dutch Period Museum****: it is the only building without a sign *(95 Prince St 9am-5pm; closed Friday. Entrance fee. Allow 1hr)*. In the 1750s this austere building was the residence of the Dutch governors and its architecture alone merits a detour. The first floor of the main body of the building looks out onto a courtyard which is a haven in the suffocating heat of the Pettah. All the fittings (doors, shutters and the staircase leading up to this floor) are of the period. The collections housed inside evoke the way of life of the Dutch in the tropics and their relationship with the Kandyan court.
The entrance hall retraces the history of the founding of the **Dutch East India Company** and the arrival of the Dutch in this part of the world. It leads into a corridor which separates two rooms. In one, the pomp and splendour of the Kandyan court are illustrated by the costumes and jewels of the *perahera* dancers of the Temple of the Tooth, the carved ivory casks, the repoussé silver betel sets and the lacquered covers for manuscripts written on palm leaves. In the other room, luxury items belonging to the Dutch, and manufactured in Europe or in their Asian trading posts, are displayed in an imposing European-style dresser, made from local timber: on show are tortoiseshell chignon combs and everyday items in ivory, made in Ceylon, blue and white porcelain from China and crystal imported from Europe. In one window, dummies are dressed in 17C colonial costume, identical in every detail, despite the island's climate, to those worn by their compatriots in Amsterdam.

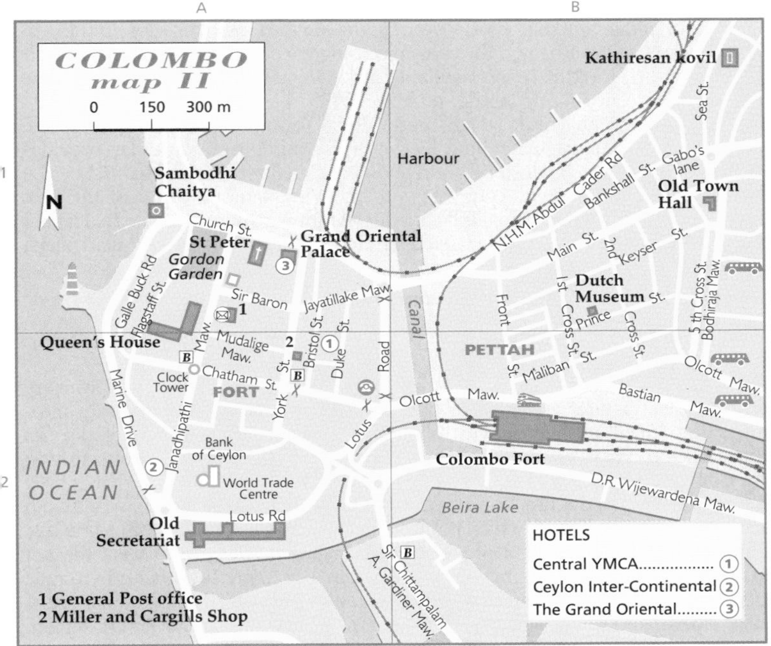

In addition to the dresser, there are displays of some sumptuous examples of the work of the local furniture-makers who could adapt to the standards and customs of their European clients: they include ebony writing desks with secret compartments, chests for pistols and clothing. The **furniture collection★★**, the jewel of this museum, continues on this floor. A few copies of letters between the governors and the Kandyan court and maps of the fortified Dutch ports (the originals are in the library of the Colombo National Museum) are also on display here. In one of the buildings around the courtyard are some **tombstones** from the former Dutch cemetery in the Pettah, all marked with symbols of the skull-and-crossbones and the hourglass.

On leaving the museum, turn left, then turn into 2nd Cross St. Follow as far as N H M Abdul Cader Rd.

N H M Abdul Cader Road is where the wholesale dealers in **dried fish** hang out. The variety of fish on display is tremendous: look out for the famous fish of the Maldives which sometimes accompanies *sambol*.

Then head back towards Gabo's Lane, where the aromas are more pleasant: sandal-wood shavings, herbs used in local medicine, essential oils with antique-style labels, all emanating from the **pharmacopoeial market**.

Sea Street, the most Tamil of the streets of the Pettah, is lined with little **jewellers** shops selling the gold jewellery that women traditionally adorn themselves with. It is also the area of the highest concentration of **kovil** Hindus in the city. The **Kathiresan** and the **Sri Muthu Viyanagar** are easily recognised by their **gopuram**, the carved porches decorated with a kaleidoscopic pantheon of heroes and gods.

By way of total contrast, head towards the eastern extremity of Ratnajothi Saravanamuttu Mawatha and the most imposing of the Protestant churches built on the island by the Dutch. **Wolfendahl**, the "Valley of the Wolves", is an austere building with a neo-Doric façade, built in 1749.
Then make your way back along Central Road towards Kayman's Gate where the **Old Town Hall** originally built by the British administration today provides shelter for a market. Its austerity, still showing signs of being influenced by the rigours of the Dutch style, contrasts with the Victorian splendour of the Fort district. The building was finally deemed to be unworthy of the colonial capital and was replaced by the neo-classical edifice which stands near Vihara Maha Devi park.

If you still have the energy after negotiating your way through the crowds in the Pettah, you could go on to explore the Fort district.

The Fort District* (Map II A1-2)

The bombing attacks of the 1990s and the presence of government Ministry buildings in this area have led to the deployment of draconian security measures and killed off the activity of this former British financial district. Its appearance today is more that of a hybrid curiosity of Victorian architecture in the tropics.
Begin your visit at the junction of York Street and Chatham Street, with its red and white brick buildings which could have been taken straight from some district of London. The old **Miller and Cargills department stores*** were the last word in modernism when they were opened in 1902 and 1906, with hydraulic lifts and electric fans. Products of the import-export trade of the colonial years, these firms were both founded by families of planters from the Kandy region. The first shops specialised in importing wines from Australia, porcelain from China and household electric goods of the time. Then came the tea-traders, who created a sort of tropical women's Friendly Association, with ladies' ready-to-wear clothing and a gentlemen's tailoring department, as well as anything that a well-run European household might require like curtains and lighting, imported alcoholic beverages and groceries.

Head back up York St for 200m, until you come to the discreet façade of a former colonial palace, now the Grand Oriental Hotel.

Public access to the port is currently prohibited and it is hard to believe that the nerve-centre of Colombo lies at the end of this street now blocked off by fencing. And yet, this was the grand entrance to the city seen by travellers at the time of the East Indies packet-boat. After disembarking, they would go down this avenue guarded by the imposing **Grand Oriental Hotel**, under the impassive gaze of a white marble statue of Queen Victoria, brought from London in 1897 and erected on the other side of the street. Since then, Victoria has been resited in Gordon Garden, and the Grand Oriental is a sorry shadow of its former glory. Two thirds of the 154 rooms that the palace comprised at the start of the 20C currently accommodate the civil service. For a long time now, its famous exotic garden, where people would come to listen to the music of the hotel orchestra on Saturday evenings, has been nothing but a memory. Its top-floor restaurant, however, offers a unique view over the port and the old customs building. The food served here is not the best in Colombo, but take advantage of the view while you have a tea break and watch the ballet performed by the cargo-boats.

Main Street, no longer the picture of tranquillity...

MBROS
140
AIRMOD
RAMBROS
Rekha
150
MINOLTAA
TRADE
CENTRE
152
Moon
Star
TAILORS
16-8331

Turn right on leaving the old hotel; you are now in **Church Street**, dominated at the far end by a curious concrete structure which calls to mind a flying saucer. This is the **Sambodhi Chaitya**, a votive *dagoba* erected during the 1980s with donations given by the port employees.

Church Street gets its name from the Anglican Church of **St Peter**, located on the site of a former residence of the Dutch governors. The nave is nothing other than its reception hall, converted to a place of worship from 1804 onwards and consecrated in 1821.

Further along is **Gordon Garden**, given to the town by the governor of the same name in 1890, on the occasion of Queen Victoria's Jubilee. The proximity of the Ministry of Defence makes it a sensitive area, and these days the public garden is closed to visitors. It borders what was **Queen's House**, today Janadhipathi Medura, a residence built in 1856 for the British governors. Standing guard is a bronze statue of one of the most prestigious governors, Sir Edward Barnes, who was Governor from 1820 to 1822 and from 1824 to 1831.
Opposite, the **General Post Office*** (GPO) is an imposing white edifice, built in English Renaissance style.

Make your way down Janadhipathi Maw. This avenue rejoins the esplanade of Galle Face Green.

Galle Face Green and Slave Island (Map I B2-3)

The former billets of the British officers of the Indian army and its great seafront lawn, designed as a place for the cavalry to exercise, extended the Fort district to the south. Between 1856 and 1859, the municipal authorities maintained a promenade there along the lines of the Maidan in Calcutta and the Esplanade in Bombay: this was **Galle Face Green**, where Colombo high society came to stroll and show off their finery, against a backdrop of the neo-classical façades of the Colombo Club and the Galle Face Hotel. Now a shadow of its former self, it has been a long time since the esplanade was "green" in anything but name only. The towers of the Taj Samudra Hotel have replaced the buildings of the Colombo Club and its lawn, now nothing more than a bare strip of earth stretching down to the sea. The façade of the **Galle Face Hotel*** and its white colonnade is all that survives, the Victorian terrace of the **Presidential Secretariat***, the former Parliament building, now dominated by the glass and steel skyscrapers of the World Trade Centre and the Bank of Ceylon. This sector was seriously damaged in 1997, by a bomb which targeted the Treasury.

To the east of this promenade lies one of the branches of **Lake Beira**, once a stretch of putrid water which was only cleaned up in the early 20C. A rowing club is based there and its members can be seen passing back and forth in the late afternoon.

The day goes by at Galle Face Green

Even though Galle Face Green is bare, it is one of the few open spaces in Colombo where you can relax and which has not been closed off with wire fencing and security barriers. Like anywhere on the island, life on the esplanade starts at dawn, between 5am and 6am. That is when the joggers can be seen pounding the Green, talking politics and business as they run. If the weather is good and a slight sea breeze is blowing, a few kite-flyers might turn up. As noon approaches and the temperature rises, only the odd tourist will brave the heat. The esplanade only really comes to life on Friday and Saturday evenings when the youth of Colombo take over, music blaring from their radios. This is also when the kiosks selling kebabs and doughnuts ("vadai") open up.

R Holzbachova-P Bénet

The charming Galle Face Hotel

Justice Akbar Street, with its Victorian façades painted in pastel colours, connects Galle Face Green to Slave Island. On Kumaran Ratnam Road the **Mannings Mansion** survives, a gallery built on cast-iron pillars, occupied by the Nippon Hotel since the early 20C. Nearby, an alley leads to the *gopuram* of the **Temple of Subramaniam***, one of the most extraordinary in Colombo, the Indian garrison's place of worship during the British occupation. Although the district was taken over by the European and Ceylonese business middle classes during the British period, **Slave Island** has kept the name which links it to the Dutch occupation. It was in this area, separated from the fort by a branch of Lake Beira, that the slaves who worked for the Dutch families were confined every night.

Going down Sir James Peiris Mawatha, you rejoin Lake Beira, on the banks of which is situated the Buddhist temple of **Sima Malaka****, designed by the great Sri Lankan architect of the 1980s, Geoffrey Bawa. Its original design plays on elements taken from traditional Sinhalese architecture (the Bo tree enclosure, stone threshold in the shape of a half moon and guardstones), framing an openwork structure in wood. It is attached to the **Gangaramaya** monastery in Sri Jinaratna Road, the setting for an important *perahera* in February every year.

You are only some 500m from Vihara Maha Devi Park, but the area you pass through is rather uninspiring.

Cinnamon Gardens (Map I C3-4)

The former cinnamon plantation has evolved into an upmarket residential district, where the University and the majority of the embassies are now based in the old colonial mansions along the beautiful shaded avenues. To the northeast, the **Town Hall*** was built in 1927, in the neo-classical style of the Capitol in Washington. De Soysa Circus, more commonly known in Colombo as Lipton Circus (the depots of the famous tea company are situated there), has several monuments of note, such as the **Devatagaha Mosque***, with its red and white façade, and the **Victoria Memorial Eye Hospital**, built in 1903 in Indo-Muslim style, as typified by the colonial architecture of Bombay. But worthy of a visit above anything else is **Vihara Maha Devi Park***, formerly Victoria Park, which marked the boundary between the business quarter and the Cinnamon Gardens during the British period. Both names refer to a queen: Vihara Maha Devi was the royal title of the mother of King Duttugemunu, the unifying ruler of the area who is glorified in legends *(see Tissamaharama p 306)*.

Enter the park by way of Ananda Coomaraswamy Maw, the Green Path which divides it into two sections: nature and relaxation in the northern half, culture in the southern half. This route takes you past the Library.

The British created a **Botanical Garden** in this park, a conservatory for tropical species. It is still in existence, but in a sorry state of neglect, although a few specimens can be identified from the notices. In a society unwilling to accept pre-marital contact and marriages that have not been arranged by the family, in a city without a real haven of peace to retreat to, this garden has become the refuge of lovers who, with no woodland to hide in, embrace half-hidden beneath big black umbrellas. At weekends, it is the turn of the middle classes to flock to the amusement park, which was developed by President Premadesa. Also of interest are the **elephants** from the Gangarama Temple, chained up in the enclosure of the park during the day to graze at their leisure, and taken back to their houses every evening at around 5pm.

As you make your way towards the museum, you pass between the Natural History Museum (an exhibition of various animal and botanical specimens, precious stones and geology) and the Art Gallery (temporary exhibitions of contemporary art).

The National Museum** (Map I C4)

South of the park; access also from Sir Marcus Fernando Rd where the post office and left luggage office are located. Open 9am-5pm; closed Friday. Entrance fee. Allow 1hr30min.

This elegant white colonnaded building, built by the English architect James Smither, was inaugurated in 1877 by the governor William Gregory. The museum is in a permanent state of reorganisation and the way in which the collections are displayed is both dated and chaotic to such an extent that it is possible to miss its crowning exhibit, the Bronze Gallery. Directions are not clear and you have to go through the room of games and toys to get to it! On the ground floor, the entrance hall has an educational bias with the **Introduction to the Evolution of the Image of Buddha**. It begins with what historians call the aniconic period, when Buddha was represented by nothing more than a group of symbols: the *chaitya* (stupa or *dagoba*), the symbol for his entry into Nirvana, the tree and the triumphal throne for his accession to Enlightenment *(Bodhi)*, and the sacred prints *(sri pada)* for his immaterial presence. The side rooms contain a rather uninspiring display of terracotta pottery.

On either side of the staircase leading up to the first floor, there are some images of **Hindu Gods**, including a stele from Polonnaruwa (12C), sculpted with a Vishnu with four arms and an imposing image of the goddess Durga.

The **Mask Collection***** begins on the landing and continues on this floor, in the room on the right, starting with the **Sanni** (diseased demons). Note Prince Maha Kola, who became leader of this demonic cohort in order to revenge the unjust killing of his mother. His diadem is made up of eight interwoven snakes, from which he would make germ-bearing devils. The satirical undercurrent of the **Kolam** (masked drama) lies at the origin of the caricature masks, which featured policemen, soldiers with their faces covered in wounds crawling with worms, Dutchmen with moustache, side-burns and top hat, or Muslim traders. Only a fine slit below the eye-sockets allowed the actors to see through the masks.

C Bowman / SCOPE

Traditional mask

Along with the masks, the great gallery on this floor has a series of themed displays dedicated to the **Traditions of the Island**; among the items on display are wicker-work baskets used for transport and storage, cooking utensils, local medicines, and oil-lamps used by Buddhists. Continuing along the right-hand side of the gallery, you come to the passage leading to the **Art Gallery**. Displayed here are reproductions of the complete collection of paintings from Sigiriya and those from other sites. On the left are games, flags and banners carried during royal processions, weapons attributed to the various *devala* and the ex-voto offerings left in their temples, and accessories and costumes from traditional dances that are no longer performed. Further along is the **Children's Museum**, a room dedicated to games and toys, under the surrealistic protection of the skeleton of a whale! Look out for the entrance to the Bronze Gallery.

Theatrical Masks

Now marketed as souvenirs for tourists, these masks were once linked to forms of ritual dance, no longer in existence. One of these took the form of an exorcism: it consisted of summoning the "Sanni" demons responsible for disease, then winning them over with offerings, before sending them back to their realm. They are represented by masked dancers, and their demoniacal characters breathe life into the masks, each portraying one of their individually spectacular attributes. Of an equally ritualised nature, the "Kolam" is a dance performed by villagers; it is a lively portrayal of the ills affecting society, such as the inevitable bribery of government officials, and always with a moral perspective. Watched over by a royal couple, portrayed by two impressively-crowned masks, the dance ends with a parable taken from Buddha's previous lives.

The first section of the **Bronze Gallery***** contains a display of **Hindu bronzes** which originally came from the Polonnaruwa *devala*.

The majority of the statuettes are connected with the cult of Shiva. Note in particular a statuette depicting him as **Nataraja*****, the king of the Dance (11-12C), with a minute effigy of the goddess of the Ganges entwined in his hair, her hands clasped in prayer. The bronze-smiths also made images of the worshippers, singing hymns while beating the rhythm on cymbals, along with **Parvati***, his wife. She also personified Shiva's energy, as represented in the portrayal of her idealised beauty, slender figure, curvaceous bosom and serene face (11C bronze).

Various **items of goldplate** mark the end of this section and the beginning of the Buddhist bronzes. The collection includes the marvellous **ear-ring** originally from the citadel of Sigiriya (5-6C), composed of a profusion of gold foliage

coming out of an amethyst drop. An elephant, ridden by a couple and mounted on a support extended by a chain, is the hydrostatic reservoir of an **oil lamp****, discovered in the relic room of a 12C *dagoba*. **Seven gold plaques**, carved in imitation of sheets of palm-leaf manuscripts, are inscribed with a Buddhist text in Sanskrit, a discovery made during excavations of the Jetavana in Anuradhapura.
The **Buddhist Bronzes** begin with statuettes relating to the "Greater Vehicle" school of Buddhism, portraying *bodhisattvas* (sages) of both sexes. A **silver Tara** (female bodhisattva) dating from 9-10C, originally from Kurunegala, is seated in meditation. Her hollow eye-sockets and chignon were originally encrusted with jewels. A group of small bronze pieces (9C), their delicately-chiselled features unchanged by their malachite patina, represent some of the great *bodhisattvas*: **Vajrapani**, the Bearer of the symbol of purification and wisdom, and **Avalokiteshvara*****, whose chignon contains a miniature seated Buddha. Two effigies of the latter (8-9C) are seated in the so-called royal relaxation position, one knee bent up, one foot on the ground. The gilded bronze, discovered near Anuradhapura, is one of the sculptural masterpieces of the island. The suppleness of the figure's position is marvellous, emphasised by the flowing drape of the sarong and the stole around the shoulders. The hair, a profusion of curls gathered up into a chignon, has lost its precious stone studs, but the eyes are still encrusted with crystals.
The gallery ends with some **bronze statues of Buddha**, all seated in a position of meditation, apart from the first and the last. The latter, cast in the 8C, comes from Kurunegala, and its face is as solemnly static as the drape of the robe is fluid. Among the effigies in *samadhi* which follow, the **Buddha teaching*** from Badulla (6C) is exceptional for its size (54 cm) and its technique. The casting, using a lost-wax process with a clay centre, has produced a hollow statue, which can be seen through perforations in the torso and abdomen, produced with a layer of ultra-thin metal. Canonical texts prescribed the principles of this process. The last of the seated Buddhas, in gilded bronze, was made in 18C, and the robe, with its rippling pleats, is characteristic of this later period. The **Buddha standing**, discovered near Anuradhapura and dating from 9C, is the last piece in the gallery. The crystal eyes gaze at the visitor, while the right hand suggests the gesture of appeasement *(abhaya mudra)*. The figure's anatomy is emphasised by the flowing drape of the monastic clothing.

Mobile images

Buddhist or Hindu, the metal images were not intended to be worshipped in the most sacred places. They were destined for ritual processions around the temple, or even through the streets of the town. On these occasions, they were not displayed as they are seen today, but were ornately dressed and adorned with jewels, and their bases were designed to be fitted onto wooden carts.

This peaceful interlude ends here but if you wish to see Colombo at its liveliest, take a "tuk-tuk" as far as Station Rd, in the Bambalapitiya district. You also get the train from there if you are staying in Mount Lavinia.

Bambalapitiya

With the Fort district being out of bounds, the focus of life in Colombo has shifted to **Majestic City** (commonly known as MC) in Bambalapitiya. Opened some fifteen years ago, this shopping centre attracts every section of the population. The Kentucky Fried Chicken and the Food Court, a self-service restaurant with dishes from all over the world, are never empty. On Saturday afternoons, young people meet there for promotional concerts organised by the big brand names. The Legend, a fifth-floor bar, takes over in the evening. Saturday is also a day of frenzied shopping, in MC as well as in Liberty Plaza and along the heaving pavements of Galle Road.

The area around Colombo

Mount Lavinia Beach*

See map p 139. 12km south of Colombo. Trains run from Colombo Fort, as well as from the various stations at intervals along Galle Rd. Buses are not recommended due to traffic congestion.

Stretching to the west of Galle Road, Mount Lavinia is a pleasant residential district in the suburbs of Colombo, and its beach is the most popular with the inhabitants of the capital at weekends. It owes its popularity as a resort to the prestige of **Mount Lavinia House**, the British governor's residence, which gave this small section of the coast its name, and which became a hotel in 1877. Although of a modest nature, the conglomeration which has grown around this rather grand building provides alternative accommodation which is cheaper and more tranquil. The beach is neither long nor wide, but is much more attractive than the one at Negombo, despite the patches of oil visible at low tide. The skyscrapers of the Fort district in Colombo can be clearly seen to the north. The sun setting over the Indian Ocean is particularly beautiful.

For the love of a dancing-girl?
The Mount Lavinia residence is associated with the memory of Sir Edward Barnes, the benevolent governor responsible for the King's Pavilion in Kandy and the Grand Hotel in Nuwara Eliya. There is a long-standing tradition that it was named Lavinia in honour of his wife... except that she was never called Lavinia! In fact, the name predates Barnes' acquisition of the residence, and is shrouded in the secret love affair between Sir Thomas Maitland, governor of the island at the start of the 19C, and a half-caste dancing-girl called Lovina. Rumour has it that during the building of the Colombo to Galle railway – which passes very close to the present-day hotel – a tunnel was discovered. The dancer supposedly used the tunnel for trysts with her lover who left Ceylon in 1811, and whose residence, Mount Lavinia, remained empty until the arrival of Barnes. The mystery remains, but Lovina and Lavinia are not so very different from one another...

Kelaniya*

13km northeast of Colombo, taking the road that forks right off the Colombo-Kandy highway. Bus n° 99 departs from Kollupitiya station, n° 235 departs from the Pettah.

The Raja Mahaviharaya* is an active Buddhist temple which is one of the sixteen great centres of Buddhism in Sri Lanka which are associated with Buddha's travels on the island. It is believed that it was here that he preached his doctrine to an assembly of serpent-kings *(nagaraja)*. The place is imbued with an atmosphere of religious fervour, especially on Sundays when large numbers of worshippers come here from Colombo and the rest of the island, laying swathes of lotus flowers around the great white **dagoba**, lighting rows of oil lamps, or queueing to sprinkle the base of the tree of Enlightenment with purifying water. The buildings were pillaged by the Portuguese in 1555, then closed to religious worship until the reign of Kirti Sri Rajasinha of Kandy (1747-82), and were only restored in the course of two campaigns, one in 1767, another in 1851.

Detail from a frieze of dwarfs, Kelaniya

In addition to the great *dagoba*, on the site of the throne where Buddha is believed to have preached, there is also a **Temple with three naves**, built in the style of the Polonnaruwa sanctuaries. It takes the form of a huge gallery which encompassed the image hall erected in the 19C. Restoration work was funded by the generous Mrs Helena Wijewardhane, a benefactress who had the temple restored to its former glory between 1888 and 1927. The central nave is decorated with scenes from Buddha's previous lives, executed in Kandyan style on a red or black background. The gigantic effigy of a *nagaraja* recalls the legendary origins of the site. On the walls of the left nave, around a large reclining Buddha, there is a procession of disciples bearing lotus-flowers, and *bodhisattvas* carrying swords. The **Paintings** in the three chapels and those in the nave on the left have equally traditional subjects (the life of Buddha and the introduction of Buddhism to the island), but are radically different in style: they consist of large-scale works depicting people in a Chinese-inspired setting, painted in a style that is both realistic and mellow. The work of the artist Solias Mendis between 1932 and 1946, they are famous throughout the world and mark a completely new departure in religious painting. In the left nave, a reliquary *dagoba* is on display for the faithful to worship.

Henaratgoda Botanical Gardens

In Gampaha, on the north bank of the Midita River, 34km northeast of Colombo and 26km from Negombo. It is possible to get there by train via the station at Gampaha. Vehicular access to avenues. Open every day, 7.30am-5pm. Entrance fee.

These gardens, albeit smaller (14.5ha) and less well maintained than their counterparts in Peradeniya, mark a turning point in the pioneering history of rubber cultivation on the island. In 1876, the Royal Botanic Gardens at Kew sent some hevea seeds here, brought back from the Amazon region by Sir Henry Wickham. Nowadays, this important landmark cuts a rather sorry figure; from February to March, however, the avenues of the park are worth visiting for the spectacular flowering trees.

Making the most of Colombo

Coming and going

By air – The ***Bandaranaike*** international airport is at Katunayake, 31km to the north of Colombo and 8km south of Negombo, ☎ (01) 25 28 61.

On arrival: You will be able to purchase items from the duty free shops after going through immigration, and the bureaux de change are open at all hours, following arrivals of international flights. As you enter the airport itself, be prepared for the barrage of services being offered, ranging from transfers to Colombo to ten-day chauffeur-driven organised tours! There is nothing to stop you from taking business cards from these people, but wait until your head has cleared before making any decisions. Left-luggage offices (60Rs per day) can be found in the Arrivals hall, where there is also a hotel reservation desk open 24 hours a day, ☎ (01) 45 24 17.

On departure: the majority of flights to the West take off during the night or early in the morning. Security procedures prior to check-in can take a long time and it is recommended that you arrive 2hr in advance. Confirm the departure time of your flight by calling ☎ (01) 25 28 61 and expect to pay 500Rs airport tax. You can convert your rupees on presentation of a currency exchange receipt and your passport.

To / from Colombo and Negombo: Buses go the bus station situated on the far side of the car park, between 6am and 10pm, arriving at Bastian Maw in Colombo (30min-1hr15min) and the bus station in Negombo (30min). Expect to pay 6.5Rs for the bus, and 25Rs for an Intercity Express.

In the airport foyer at the exit to the terminal, there is a "prepaid taxis" kiosk, offering flexible and comfortable travel at reasonable prices (expect to pay about 300Rs to go to Negombo, and about twice as much to Colombo). ***Airport Express***, 340 / 11, DR Wijewardena Maw, Col 10, ☎ (075) 33 66 99, is an efficient taxi company specialising in airport transfers. Finally, it is worth knowing that many guesthouses will come and pick you up (including those in Galle and Kandy!), provided that this has been agreed when you made your reservation by letter, fax or e-mail.

By train – The influence of the British and historical developments have made Colombo the central terminus of the island's railway network: from the capital you can get to any town which has a train service. The principal station is ***Colombo Fort***, on the edge of the Pettah bazaar district (Map II B2). Information from Railway Tourist Information Centre, Fort Railway Station, Col 1, ☎ (01) 43 58 38. Reservations for Intercity Express trains at ticket desks in Colombo Fort, open 8.30am-3.30pm, ☎ (01) 43 29 08 or 43 42 15. Some trains, however, leave from ***Maradana*** station (Map I D2).

The four main railway lines are: Colombo-Matara via Hikkaduwa and Galle, Colombo-Badulla (only a few trains make the detour to Kandy) via Nuwara Eliya, Colombo-Vavuniya via Anuradhapura, and Colombo-Trincomalee via Habarana. Secondary lines also connect the capital to Puttalam via Negombo (14 trains per day between 4.30am-8.20pm, departing from Colombo Fort, 35min-1hr40min).

Trains departing daily from Colombo Fort to ***Badulla*** (9hr15min-10hr50min) include: the Podi Menike at 5.55am (observation saloon), the Udarata Menike at 9.45am (observation saloon), Night Mail at 7.40pm (couchettes in 1st and 2nd class) and the Night Express at 10pm (couchettes in 1st class). To ***Kandy*** (2hr30min-3hr30min): the Intercity Express at 7am (observation saloon), at 10.45am, 12.45pm, 3.35pm (observation saloon) and at 4.50pm. To ***Matara*** (3hr30min-4hr30min): train n° 40 at 9am, the Rajarata Rajini at 2pm and the Ruhunu Kumari at 4.15pm. To ***Anuradhapura*** (4hr50min): the Yaldevi via Vavuniya at 5.45am, and the Rajarata Rajini at 2.05pm. To ***Trincomalee*** (7hr50): train n° 81 at 6.10am. To ***Matara*** (4hr20min): train n° 50 at 7.15am, departing from Maradana station.

By bus – Travelling out of Colombo is easier by train than by bus, especially if you are at the start of your tour and are

Colombo

not yet accustomed to the level of chaos in Sri Lankan bus stations. The three bus stations are in the Pettah district, between 200m-400m from the Fort railway station. Broadly speaking, the services they offer can be categorised as follows: ***Bastian Mawatha*** (Map II B2) and ***Olcott Mawatha (CTB)*** (Map II B1-2) for "Intercity" and long-distance buses between the major towns of the island. The first of these is privately-owned, the second is national…or semi-national. Buses from ***Saunders Place*** (People's Park) (Map II B1) serve medium-distance destinations including the area between Puttalam and Ratnapura. If you have to travel by bus, you will find that there are frequent departures to the main towns between 6am-10pm. In any case, there are no timetables – buses leave only when they are full!

Getting your bearings

See "The 15 districts of Colombo", p 117.

Travelling around

By bus – This is without doubt the cheapest form of transport. At the bus-stop, check that you are going in the right direction by enquiring of the teeming mass of regular travellers as they make for one of the regular service buses or the numerous minibuses (un-numbered).

By taxi – An air-conditioned taxi is an investment: they are relatively cheap and will be greatly appreciated in a traffic-jam. They can be found outside all the larger hotels or by calling the free-phone radio-taxi services: ***Cool Kangaroo*** (red taxis), 91 Galle Rd, Col 4, ☎ (01) 50 28 88 / 50 15 02 or ***GNTC*** (dark blue taxis), 811 / 1, Sirimavo Bandaranaike Maw, Col 14, ☎ (01) 68 86 88. You will have to pay 28Rs for the first kilometre, after which the price is 24Rs / km, whatever the length of the journey. They can also be hired by the day or the half-day.

By three-wheeler – Called "bajaj", "tuk-tuk" or "three-wheelers", these vehicles are the only ones that can beat the traffic-jams. They are a practical means for covering moderate distances around the city, as long as you do not mind the pollution and missing out on the best views of the passing scenery. You also need to have nerves of steel and make sure you fix the price before you set off (as an indication, allow 60-70Rs for the trip from the Pettah to Slave Island).

Address book

Tourist information – The ***Ceylon Tourist Board***, 80 Galle Rd, Col 3 (Map I B3), ☎ (01) 43 70 59, Fax (01) 43 79 53, ctb@dm-sri.lanka.net and its branch office, the ***Tourist Information Centre***, 41 Glen Aber Place, Col 4 (Map I B5), ☎ (01) 58 65 85 / 58 95 86, are open Monday-Friday, 9am-4.45pm; Saturday, 9am-12.30pm. Limited information available, apart from some tourist maps of the more well-known attractions.

To make a booking for a bungalow in one of the National Parks, contact the ***Department of Wildlife Conservation***, 18 Gregory's Rd, Col 7 (Map I D4), ☎ (01) 69 42 41, and for all information and bookings for Sinharaja Forest, contact the ***Forest Department***, Rajamalwatte Rd, Battaramulla (in the outskirts), ☎ (01) 56 66 31.

The pass for the Cultural Triangle can be purchased from the ***Cultural Triangle Office***, 212 / 1 Bauddhaloka Maw, Col 7 (Map I C5), ☎ (01) 50 07 33 / 58 79 12, which also has a book-shop selling numerous publications about the various sites.

Bank / Currency exchange – When changing money, avoid using the hotel exchange desks, which charge commission, and use the bureaux de change concentrated in the Fort district.

Bank of Ceylon, York St, Col 1 (Map II A2), ☎ (01) 42 27 30. Open 9am-6pm; Saturday and Sunday, 9am-4pm. Cash withdrawals with Visa card.

Hatton National Bank, 16 Janadhipathi Maw, Col 1 (Map II A2), ☎ (01) 42 14 66. Open 9am-6pm; Saturday 9am-5pm, Sunday 9am-12noon. Withdrawals possible with Visa card.

People's Bank, Sir Chittampalam A Gardiner Maw, Col 2 (Map II B2), ☎ (01) 32 78 41. Tuesday-Friday 3.30pm-7pm, Saturday 9am-1.30pm.

Sampath Bank Ltd, 55 DR Wijewardena Maw, Col 10 (Map II B2), ☎ (01) 44 82 91. 9am-6pm; closed at weekends.
Hong Kong & Shanghai Bank, 24 Sir Baron Jayatillake Maw, Col1 (Map II A1), ☎ (01) 32 54 35; another branch at 38 Galle Rd, Wellawatta, Col 6. 24hr automatic cash dispensers. Visa card accepted.
American Express, 104 Dharmapala Maw, Col 7 (Map I C3), ☎ (01) 68 12 15. 9am-5pm, Saturday 9.30am-12.30pm; closed Sunday.

Main Post Office – ***GPO*** (General Post Office), Janadhipathi Maw, Col 1 (Map II A1), ☎ (01) 69 11 11. Open every day. Stamps sold 24hr a day; poste restante service from 8am-5pm (☎(01) 32 62 03); special-issue stamps sold, 9am-3pm; registered mail service, 8am-4pm.

Telephone – The ***GPO*** has direct-dial phone-card booths and an operator-connection office (Monday-Friday, 9am-3pm). If this is closed, try the ***Central Telegraph Office (CTO)***, Duke St, Col 1 (Map II A2), ☎ (01) 32 62 67, or one of the many private agencies situated in the Fort district, the Pettah or the commercial section of Galle Rd.

Internet – You can get on-line in the "business centres" of the large hotels, even if you are not a resident (charged per 30min). ***Internet Café***, 479 Galle Rd, Col 4, is at present the island's only cyber-café. (Open daily 10am-9pm).

Health – All the large hotels have a 24hr medical service, which is in principle reserved for their guests.
Colombo General Hospital, EW Perera Maw, Col 8 (Map I D3), ☎ (01) 69 11 11 / 42 22 22 / 69 22 22, has a round-the-clock emergency service, but this is not an attractive option. You would do better to go to one of the many private (and more costly) establishments where you will find English-speaking interpreters, such as ***Nawaloka Hospitals Ltd***, 23 Sri Saugathodaya Maw, Col 2, ☎ (01) 54 62 58, or ***Durdans Hospital***, Kollupitiya, Col 3 (Map I B5), ☎ (01) 57 52 05, or ***Asiri Hospital Ltd***, 141 Kirula Rd, Col 5, ☎ (01) 50 06 08.
Osu Sala, De Soysa Circus, ☎ (01) 69 47 16. State-run pharmacy. Open 24hr a day.
Medi-Calls, 26 Clifford Ave, Col 3, ☎ (01) 57 54 75. Ambulances and home medical care.
Siddhalepa Ayurveda Hospitals, 106 A Templer's Rd, Mount Lavinia. Traditional medicine.
A & A International Opticians, 100 Bullers Rd, Col 4, ☎ (01) 59 54 13. Open every day. Glasses, contact lenses and accessories.

Diplomatic Services – ***British High Commission***, 190 Galle Road, Kollupitiya (P.O. Box 1433), Colombo 3, ☎ (1) 43 73 36.
Australian High Commission, 3 Cambridge Place, Colombo 7, ☎ (01) 69 87 67, austcom@sri.lanka.net
Canadian High Commission, 6 Gregory's Rd, Col 7 (Map I D4), ☎ (01) 69 58 41.
Indian High Commission, 36-38 Galle Rd, Col 3 (Map I B3), ☎ (01) 42 16 05.
Maldives High Commission, 23 Kaviratne Place, Pamankade, ☎ (01) 58 67 62.
New Zealand Consulate, c/o Aitken Spence & Co Ltd, PO Box 5, Colombo, ☎ (01) 32 78 61.
United States Embassy, 210 Galle Road, Colombo 3, ☎ (01) 44 80 07.

Airlines – ***Air France***, Galle Face Hotel Shopping Complex, Col 3, ☎ (01) 32 76 05, Fax (01) 43 60 26.
Air Lanka, 37 York St, Col 1, ☎ (01) 073 55 55 (to reconfirm flights, ☎ (01) 073 55 00), www.airlanka.com
Air Maldives, 81 York St, Col 1, ☎ (01) 34 22 91. ***AOM***, 323 Union Place, Col 2, ☎ (01) 43 55 97, Fax (01) 44 79 78. ***British Airways***, Trans-Asia Hotel, 115 Sir Chittampalam A Gardiner Maw, Col 2, ☎ (01) 32 02 31. ***Emirates***, Hemas House, 75 Braybrooke Place, Col 2, ☎ (01) 44 07 09, Fax (01) 44 79 06. ***Gulf Air***, 11 York St, Col 1, ☎ (01) 43 46 62, www.gulfairco.com ***Indian Airlines***, Bristol Complex, 4 Bristol St, Col 1, ☎ (01) 32 31 36. ***KLM***, 29 Braybrooke St, Col 2, ☎ (01) 43 97 47. ***Kuwait Airways***, Cargills Building, 30 Sir Baron Jayatillake Maw, Col 1, ☎ (01) 44 55 31, Fax (01) 44 99 80. ***Lufthansa***, 61 EML Building, 2nd floor,

WAD Ramanayaka, Col 2, ☎ (01) 30 27 92, Fax (01) 30 05 05. ***Pakistan International Airlines***, 342 Galle Rd, Col 3, ☎ (01) 57 34 75. ***Quantas***, Trans-Asia Hotel, 115 Sir Chittampalam A Gardiner Maw, Col 2, ☎ (01) 34 84 90, Fax (01) 44 79 06. ***Royal Jordanian Airlines***, 40 A Cumaratunga Munidasa Maw. (Thunstan Rd), Col 3, ☎ (01) 30 16 21, Fax (01) 30 16 20. ***Singapore Airlines***, 323 Vauxhall St, Col 2, ☎ (01) 30 07 57, Fax (01) 30 07 69. ***Tarom***, 18 / 1 York St., Col 1, ☎ (01) 44 85 93. ***Thai Airways International***, Ceylon Inter-Continental Hotel, 48 Janadhipathi Maw, Col 1, ☎ (01) 43 88 94.

Cultural centres – ***British Council***, 49 Alfred House Gardens (PO Box 753), Col 3, ☎ (01) 58 11 71. Various organisations providing information or selling items relating to Buddhism, with information about centres for meditation: ***International Buddhist Research and Information Centre*** (Sasana Sevaka Society), 380 / 9, Sarana Rd (on the corner of Bauddhaloka Maw), Col 7, ☎ (01) 68 93 88; ***Buddhist Cultural Centre***, 125 Anderson Rd, Nedimala, Dehiwala, ☎ (01) 72 62 34, Fax (01) 73 67 37, www2.lanka.net/bbc ***International Buddhist Library***, Buddhist Books and Information Centre, Sri Sambuddhaloka Viharaya, Lotus Rd (opposite the Hilton Hotel), Col 1, ☎ (01) 43 55 32.

Travel agencies – They are as thick underfoot as the jungle in Ceylon! Besides the ten or so major agencies mainly dealing with foreign tour operators, there is a proliferation of smaller establishments. If you do not go to them, they will come to you as soon as you arrive at the airport! A very small sample of these independent operators:

ACME Lanka, Sales Gallery of the Trans-Asia Hotel, ☎ (01) 54 42 00, Fax (01) 33 26 73, acmesl@sri.lanka.net Tours to suit your interests and your wallet.

Lanka Voyages, n° 108 1 / 1 Stanley Thilakarathne Maw, Nugegoda (Kotte district), ☎ (01) 82 73 76 / (071) 73 38 76, Fax (01) 85 24 68. M Vijitha Dassanaike will help you organise a reasonably priced itinerary.

Rail Tours, Fort Railway Station (to the right of the entrance), Col 11, ☎ (01) 44 00 48 / (072) 22 24 49. You could also contact the very helpful manager, WA Linton Wanniarachchi, in Kandy, ☎ and Fax (08) 23 23 43. His drivers know the minor roads of the interior like the back of their hand.

Paradise Holidays, 160 / 2 Bauddhaloka Maw, Col 4, ☎ (01) 59 10 94, Fax (01) 50 21 10.

Visas – If you are staying for more than 30 days, you must make an application for a visa to the ***Department of Emigration and Immigration***, Tower Building, Bambalapitiya Station Rd, Col 4, ☎ (01) 43 63 53. You will need your passport, air-ticket, as well as travellers cheques, currency or bank card, to prove that you have sufficient means to extend your stay (about US$11 per day). The cost of the visa, payable only in Sri Lankan rupees, varies according to nationality but the average in 1999 was about 2000Rs.

Security – ***Police***, ☎ (01) 43 33 42.

Where to stay

The absence of choice and the prices charged by the hotels are good reasons for not staying too long in the capital. You will get better value for money in Negombo or Mount Lavinia.

• In the Fort district and the Pettah (Map II)

Under US$10

Central YMCA, 39 Bristol St, opposite the Miller and Cargills shops, ☎ (01) 32 52 52 – 22rm. Basic hotel, close to the stations for the cheapest night's stay in Colombo. Couples admitted. The four rooms with bathroom are respectable, but the others are very basic and the communal bathroom is not always clean. Library. Restaurant in building next door.

From US$50 to US$70

The Grand Oriental Hotel, 2 York St, Col 1, ☎ (01) 32 03 91, Fax (01) 44 76 40 – 62rm. CC Colombo's old palace has not followed in the footsteps of its counterpart, the Taj in Bombay. The hotel now only runs a third of the rooms, and these do not have a great deal of character, with furnishings in light wood and tiny bathrooms with no more than a trickle of hot water. The single rooms are the size of a broom-cupboard. More worthy of note is the hotel restaurant, the Harbour Room, which overlooks the port, but be prepared for the exceptionally slow service there. Ground floor bar closes at 10pm.

From US$70 to US$150

Ceylon Inter-Continental, 48 Janadhipathi Maw, ☎ (01) 42 12 21, Fax (01) 44 73 26, colombo@inter-conti.com – 250rm. This five-star veteran from the 1970s provides all-round luxury with no surprises: three restaurants, one of which is outdoor and serves seafood, a pizzeria, two bars, a sauna, exercise room and a few shops.

• **On Slave Island** (Map I)

From US$15 to US$30

Nippon Hotel, 123 Kumaran Ratnam Rd, Col 2, ☎ (01) 43 18 87, Fax (01) 33 26 03 – 32rm. Panelled walls, great wooden doors and uniformed bellboys give this nearly 100-year old establishment lots of style. Whilst a little dilapidated, the bathrooms and bedrooms are still very acceptable, as long as you avoid the ones with a balcony overlooking the very busy street. Supplement for air-conditioning.

YWCA International, 393 Union Place, ☎ (01) 42 31 43 – 18rm. This vast Dutch-colonial style residence with its large garden offers accommodation in simple, clean rooms and also accepts couples. You can also read or chat on the veranda. Very friendly welcome.

From US$70 to US$150

Trans-Asia Hotel, 115 Sir Chittampalam A Gardiner Maw, ☎ (01) 54 42 00, Fax (01) 44 81 84, tah_asia@sri.lanka.net, www.transasiahotel.com – 358rm. Although vast, this is the best of the luxury hotels. At the rear of the hotel there is a lush garden and a near Olympic size swimming pool, while the north wing has a view of Lake Beira. Jacuzzi, sauna, hammam, massages, leisure club, volleyball and squash court, shopping gallery. The three restaurants have an excellent standard of Indo-Sri Lankan, Chinese and French cuisine, and there are delicious themed buffets in the "coffee-shop".

• **In Kollupitiya** (Map I)

From US$8 to US$15

Lake Lodge, 20 Alvis Terrace, near the Kollupitiya sports ground, ☎ (01) 32 64 43, Fax (01) 43 49 97 – 16rm. Near Lake Beira (watch out for the mosquitoes), this guesthouse with its family atmosphere has clean rooms, but few windows, and two small terraces where guests can have a drink or eat their meals. It is possible to hire a chauffeur-driven vehicle here for the remainder of your journey. Supplement for air-conditioning.

From US$15 to US$30

Colombo House, 26 Charles Circus, ☎ (01) 57 49 00, Fax (01) 57 49 01 – 4rm. An imposing 1930s mansion, with the additional attraction of a beautiful garden, in a quiet residential district. The rooms, although simply furnished, do have mosquito nets and are very large, impeccably clean and have balconies. Breakfast and meals (mixed cuisine) on request, but there are plenty of restaurants in the vicinity. Supplement for air-conditioning.

Hotel Empress, 383 RA De Mel Maw, ☎ (01) 57 49 30 / (071) 77 33 63, Fax (01) 57 49 31, heasong@sitnet.lk – 20rm. Not attractive in appearance, but functional and well-situated, this hotel offers good value for money, although the rooms are a bit gloomy. Restaurant with Korean specialities.

From US$50 to US$70

Renuka Hotel, 328 Galle Rd, ☎ (01) 57 35 98, Fax (01) 57 41 37, renukaht@panlanka.net – 80rm. These two twin buildings have all the requisite amenities you would expect in this price range, with very comfortable rooms, two restaurants, including the Palmyrah, which serves delicious Sri Lankan curries, plus a swimming pool and secluded patio at a lower level, down towards the sea.

The Galle Face Hotel, 2 Kollupitiya Rd, ☎ (01) 54 10 10, Fax (01) 54 10 72 – 78rm. The reception area, with its white arches and dark-wood furnishings, the colonnaded veranda of the sea-front restaurant and the open bar on the shore have lots of atmosphere. The bedrooms, however, are not all of the same standard, the air-conditioning is unreliable and some of the bathrooms are showing signs of wear and tear; look before checking-in to your room. One wing looks out onto Galle Face Green, the other overlooks the sea.

From US$70 to US$150

Lanka Oberoi, 77 Steuart Place, ☎ (01) 43 74 37, Fax (01) 44 92 80, lkoberoi.bc@netgate.mega.lk – 600rm. TV CC Looking down over the presidential residence, Temple Trees, this large hotel has some architectural peculiarities, with a reception area the size of a ball-room and, at different levels, wooden galleries overhanging small interior areas. A good range of amenities: two restaurants, one with Indian specialities (compulsory in Taj hotel chain), a coffee-shop, a bar open until 1am, discotheque, leisure club, shops. Designed with a business clientele in mind.

Eating out

You will not find the best of Sri Lankan cuisine in Colombo, but if exploring the Fort district or the Pettah, this is the place to find a cut-price "rice and curry": this is the common fare at most of this area's "hotels", which are actually restaurants. However, as in all self-respecting capital cities, Colombo has a wide variety of international cuisine (especially Chinese, particularly in Colombo 3). It is also worth knowing that for US$7 to US$10 (not including drinks) you can fill up at the buffets in the ***Galadari*** or the ***Trans-Asia*** hotels, which vary every day. For atmosphere, try ***The Verandah***, the restaurant in the Galle Face hotel.

US$2.50 to US$5

Caravane, 435 R A De Mel Maw, Col 3, Alexandra Place, Col 7, Havelock Rd, Col 6, and Majestic City. Pastries, Viennese bread and buns, cakes and all kinds of rolls filled with garlic butter or spicy vegetables.

Fountain Café, 1 Justice Akbar Maw, Col 2, ☎ (01) 32 64 55. Pastries, filled rolls and sandwiches to eat in or take away. Some Sri Lankan and Eastern dishes.

Greenlands Hotel, 3-A Shrubberry Gardens, Galle Rd, in one of the alleys leading down to the sea, Col 4, ☎ (01) 58 55 92. Indian vegetarian "thali" dishes for next-to-nothing. Also acts as an agency for IDD, fax and photocopying.

Orient, Kumaran Ratnam Rd, Col 2, ☎ (01) 43 18 87. The restaurant in the Nippon Hotel is famous for its Indonesian cuisine ("sate" and "nasi goreng"), its Chinese food and its reasonably priced "rice and curry".

US$8 to US$15

Beach Wadiya, 2 Station Ave, Wellawatta, near the station, ☎ (01) 58 85 68 / (074) 51 44 77. Here you can sample all types of shellfish and fish in season, prepared to your liking, with your feet in the sand and your head in the stars.

Curry Leaves, 66 W A Silva Maw, Col 6, ☎ (01) 58 02 23. Great Indian cuisine, "veg" and "non veg", in quiet surroundings.

Flower Drum, 26 Cumaratunga Munidasa Maw (Thunstan Rd), on the corner of Sir Ernest De Silva Maw, Col 3, ☎ (01) 57 42 16, and ***Flower Lounge***, 18 Bagatelle Rd, Col 3, ☎ (01) 59 30 32. The mild flavours of Cantonese cuisine share the impressive menu with more fiery Szechuan dishes. Size of portions served varies according to your appetite.

Gourmet Palace, 399A, RA De Mel Maw, Col 3, ☎ (01) 59 67 00. A mixture of Thai and Chinese cuisine, served in a homely atmosphere, with a variety of delicious vegetarian dishes.

Il Capriccio, 29 De Fonseka Rd, Col 5, ☎ (01) 58 46 63. Open 7pm-11pm; closed Sunday and "poya" days. Introduced by German tourists, Italian food is becoming increasingly popular. No pizzas, but all the flavours of Italian cuisine with produce made on the premises or imported from Italy.

Le Palace, 79 Gregory's Rd, near the crossroads with Kinsey Rd, Col 7, ☎ (01) 69 59 20, Fax (01) 69 47 98. Open every day, 7am-11pm. Innovative French cuisine adapted for this climate, in a colonial Dutch building. French bakery and confectionery shop, open every day 7am-7pm.

Mathura, 185 Havelock Rd, Col 5, ☎ (01) 58 29 09. Wide range of Indian "thali" dishes, mild Gujarat-style or hot,

Tamil Nadu-style: "poril" (potatoes fried in massala), "raita" (a mixture of tomatoes, onions, cucumber and yoghurt), "poori" (vegetable fritters), "dhal" (spicy pink lentil soup), with pickles and chutney.

Paradise Road Café, 213 Dharmapala Maw, Col 7, ☎ (01) 68 60 43. Light lunches served in pleasant surroundings, located in a lovely colonial building, opposite the Town Hall.

Paradise Road Galleries, 2 Alfred House Rd, Col 3, ☎ (01) 58 21 62. Open every day 10am-11pm. A large patio-restaurant, an exhibition gallery and small shops selling objets d'art and clothes have been opened inside what was formerly the office of the architect Geoffrey Bawa, now a beautiful house complete with courtyard and impluvium. Serves good Italian food: a place to eat and be seen…

Saras Szechuan, 450 RA De Mel Maw, Col 3, ☎ (01) 57 52 26. At the end of a garden planted with bamboo, serving Indian and Chinese dishes (no pork or beef) in a gloomy room, in the great tradition of vegetarian restaurants in the East Indies!

Having a drink

Colombo boasts a number of places which, whilst not wildly exotic, are pleasant enough.

Cafés and bars – ***Cricket Club Café***, 34 Queen's Rd, Col 3, ☎ (01) 50 13 84. Open 11am-1am. The interior is completely dedicated to cricket (trophies, TVs and a giant screen for repeat showings of matches), but you can also have a quiet drink on the veranda of this colonial villa. A meeting place for English speakers. Also serves ice-creams, sandwiches and salads. ***Echelon Pub***, Colombo Hilton Hotel, ☎ (01) 54 46 44. 11am-1am. A real English pub, authentic in every detail but one... the draught beer is cold! ***Gallery 706***, 706 Galle Rd, next to the Barefoot shop, Col 3, ☎ (01) 58 93 05. Café, exhibitions of photographs and contemporary paintings, in a restored colonial residence. ***Rock Café***, 41 Ananda Coomaraswamy Maw (Green Path), Col 3. Yoko Ono salads, Paul McCartney hamburgers, Bette Midler ice-creams, all served beneath the gaze of rock and pop stars from all over the world, to the beat of their music, with TV screenings of concerts. ***The Commons***, 74 A Dharmapala Maw, Col 7, ☎ (01) 57 43 84. Open 11am-11pm. "Espresso" coffee and fruit juice served in a convivial setting, with works by young artists on display.

Discotheques – The best of these are in the large hotels: ***Cascades*** (Lanka Oberoi), a pub from 4pm-8pm, then a disco until 2am; ***Colombo 2000*** (Galadari) has live music performed by groups every evening; ***Little Hut*** (Mount Lavinia Hotel) is only open at weekends; ***The Library*** (Trans-Asia) is an amazing place, sectioned off with mirrors and bookshelves, open only to members and hotel residents; finally, the ***Legend*** (on the 5th floor of Majestic City) is very popular with the youth of Colombo, with a bar open 6pm-9.30pm.

Entertainment

Feast days / Festivals – Two important "peraheras" take place each year in Colombo and the surrounding area: the first, on the "poya" day in February, with dancers and elephants, takes place at the Gangaramaya monastery, near Lake Beira; the second, the Kelaniya "perahera", around the time of the full moon in January, is the second most colourful on the island, after the one which takes place in Kandy.

In June-July, the Tamil community celebrates Vel in honour of Kataragama (Subramaniam in Tamil), with a festival lasting several days, culminating in a procession with the god's chariot, from the temples in Sea St to the two "kovils", situated on Galle Rd in Bambalapitiya.

What to buy

It is no use expecting to find a window display of the island's handicrafts in Colombo. It is no better than anywhere else. However, there are some excellent antique dealers as well as a few shops selling original pieces.

Antiques – *Serendib Gallery*, 36 1/1 Rosmead Place, Col 7, ☎ (01) 69 74 67. Open every day 9am-6pm. The ultimate... a veritable museum specialising in statues of Buddha, antique bronzes, terracotta pottery, porcelain and coins. Organises exhibitions. ***Treasure House***, 133 Kotte Rd, Col 8, ☎ (01) 69 67 54. Something for everybody, from rare pieces to curiosities, to suit all budgets. ***Villa Saffron***, 4 Chandra Wettasinghe Maw, Nawala, south of Parliament Rd, ☎ (072) 28 09 81. The whole house is furnished with antiques, some restored, some not, but all for sale.

Shops – *Barefoot*, 704 Galle Rd, level with the crossroads with Temple Lane, Col 3, ☎ (01) 58 93 05, Fax (01) 57 69 36, barefoot@eureka.lk Cotton fabrics or woven silks and cottons made up in every conceivable way, from bed-covers to sarongs, including tablecloths, napkins and soft toys. Very popular with expatriates. ***Eco House***, 249 Park Rd, Col 5, ☎ (01) 50 13 03. Back to nature with linen and cotton shirts (vegetable dyes only!), beeswax candles, sun-baked pottery, recycled paper, essential oils and sticks of incense. ***Lanka Hands Handicraft & Gift Centre***, 135 Bauddhaloka Maw, Col 4, ☎ (074) 51 23 11. High quality products: carved wood, silver, jewellery, tea, spices. Ask for your parcel to be gift-wrapped – it will be done with style. ***Paradise Road Promenade***, 213 Dharmapala Maw, Col 7, ☎ (01) 68 60 43. Stationery, hand-painted ceramics, metal trays exquisitely engraved. A second boutique is located in the shopping gallery of the Trans-Asia Hotel. ***Ranfer's Tea and Spices***, 32 R A De Mel Maw, Col 4. A good selection of attractively presented teas (tastings possible).

Precious stones – An expert will look at your purchases free of charge and provide a valuation certificate at the ***National Department Gem and Jewellery Authority***, 310 Galle Rd, Col 3.

Clothes – The two "temples" to cotton clothing at rock-bottom prices are ***Cotton Collection***, in Majestic City and at 40 Sir Ernest de Silva Maw, Col 7 and ***Odel Unlimited***, 5 Alexandra Place, Col 7.

Books – *Barefoot Book Shop*, 704 Galle Rd, Col 3, ☎ (01) 58 93 05. A bookshop affiliated with the textile shop of the same name. Wide range of publications, with emphasis on Sri Lankan literature in English. Also publishes original postcards. ***Lake House Book Shop***, 100 Sir Chittampalam A Gardiner Maw, Col 2, ☎ (01) 43 21 05. One of the largest bookshops in Colombo, attached to a publishing business. You will find everything that has been published about the island or any other subject.

Making the most of Mount Lavinia

Where to stay

Considered to be a place of sin, Mount Lavinia is where lovers spend illicit weekends, hidden from the prying eyes of the prudish Sri Lankans. Moral considerations aside, this is useful information: hotel rooms can be in short supply from Friday night onwards. With the exception of the luxurious, and therefore pricey, Mount Lavinia, the hotels have little to recommend them and are nearly all situated alongside the railway track! However, some of the guesthouses offer good value for money. Most only cater for breakfast, but there are plenty of restaurants. Make your mind up to stay here rather than in Negombo for your last night on the island. It is only 46km from the airport and there are several organisations that can arrange transfers (US$12-US$20).

Under US$10

Aquamarine Tourist Inn, 6 Vihara Rd, near the corner of Station Rd, ☎ (01) 72 38 06 – 5rm. Very near Mount Lavinia's tiny railway station, this is a quiet and impeccably clean guesthouse, with bathrooms worthy of a special mention. You can even have morning tea served in your room.

Jayan's Mount Resort, 6 Liliyan Ave, ☎ (074) 20 40 65 – 8rm. Large rooms with very high ceilings (unfortunately reducing the efficiency of the fan).

Lak Mahal's Inn, 8 Vihara Rd, ☎ Fax (01) 73 48 48 – 6rm. The walls and floors could do with a fresh coat of paint, but the rooms look out onto a small area of garden. Price apart, there is little else to say, except that you can have dinner here and the friendly owner can organise transport to the airport for a modest sum. He also rents out his attractively furnished house.

From US$10 to US$15

Ocean View Tour Inn, 34 / 4 De Saram Rd, ☎ (01) 73 84 00 – 23rm. Contrary to its name, the view from the hotel is not of the ocean, but of the railway! Rooms are dark, but acceptable, with small, rather dilapidated, bathrooms.

Ratna Inn, 8 Barnes Ave, ☎ (01) 71 66 53, Fax (01) 73 24 93 – 10rm. A very pretty colonial house, impeccably maintained by a welcoming proprietor. The rooms off the landing are serviceable (immaculate bed linen, mosquito net, shower cubicle) and have a balcony. Supplement for air-conditioning. Airport transfers. Excellent value for money.

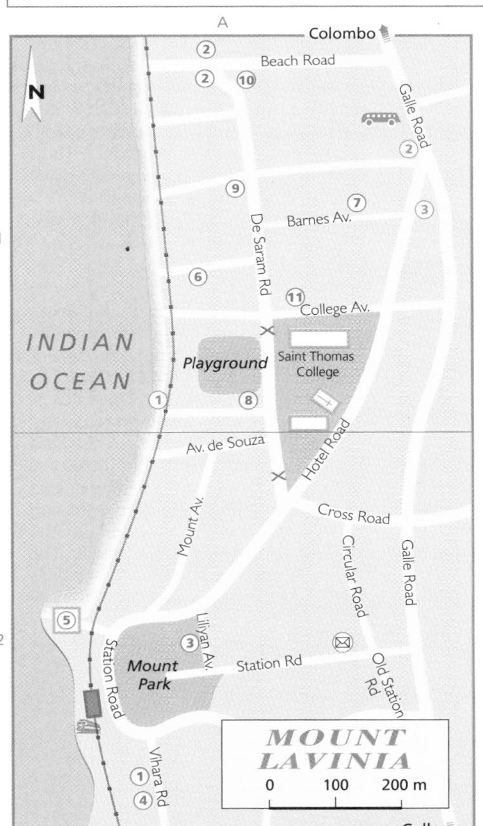

HOTELS

- Aquamarine Tourist Inn... 1
- Haus Chandra et Carrington Villa.................. 2
- Jayan's Mount Resort........ 3
- Lak Mahal's Inn.................. 4
- Mount Lavinia 5
- Ocean View Tour Inn......... 6
- Ratna Inn........................... 7
- Rivi Ras............................... 8
- Sea Breaze 9
- Sunray Beach Vilas............ 10
- Tropic Inn........................... 11

RESTAURANTS

- Langousterie (La)................ 1
- Lion Pub............................. 2
- Mount Palace...................... 3

Sunray Beach Vilas (M Shanti Perera), 3 De Saram Rd, on the corner of Beach Rd, ☎ (01) 71 62 72 – 3rm. A guesthouse which is well run by a charming and attentive couple. Although sharing the accommodation with the owners, you can come and go as you like and each room has its own independent access through the garden. An odd assortment of furniture and the bathrooms are rather tatty, but the address is worth remembering.

From US$15 to US$30

Rivi Ras, 55 / 2 De Saram Rd, ☎ (01) 71 77 31 – 33rm. Curious brick bungalows, with two storeys and colonnades. Large, spotlessly clean rooms with mosquito nets, bathrooms with bath-tubs and hot water. Bar.

Sea Breeze Hotel, 22 / 5A De Saram Rd, ☎ (01) 71 40 17, Fax (01) 73 30 77 – 15rm. This is one of the hotels built alongside the railway. The rooms are clean, but small and not very attractive. The rooms without air-conditioning are slightly better. Dark, badly-ventilated restaurant.

Tropic Inn, 6 College Ave, ☎ (01) 73 86 53, Fax (01) 34 46 57 – 16rm. A small hotel without much character, but quiet and well-run. Bedrooms have mosquito nets, and the bathroom is tiled. Supplement for air-conditioning.

From US$30 to US$50

Haus Chandra and ***Carrington Villa***, 37 Beach Rd, ☎ (01) 73 27 55 / (072) 24 25 70, Fax (01) 73 31 73 – 38rm. CC Two hotels built to the same design, on either side of the street. The rather noisy foyer leads off to the bedrooms, which are stacked on top of one another, rather like a stage set. Having said that, they are comfortable, with occasional little touches of art deco. The restaurant terrace that overlooks the complex is a pleasant place to have dinner and the food is good. As an added attraction, guests also have free access to the swimming pool at the "University Hotel", 50m away.

From US$70 to US$150

Mount Lavinia Hotel, at the end of Hotel Rd, ☎ (01) 71 52 21, Fax (01) 73 82 28, lavinia@srilanka.net – 275rm. TV CC On a promontory looking down over the sea, the old palace still cuts a fine figure, watched over by bellboys in a livery of shorts and tropical helmet, as worn here since 1823! The rooms are of varying quality: fairly standard, but the rooms in the Sea Garden wing have balconies overlooking the sea; in the Bay View wing, they are luxuriously furnished and carpeted; and in the governor's (Barnes) wing, they are decorated with antique furniture, have high ceilings (but no air-conditioning) and parquet flooring. Swimming pool on the sea terrace, with a pleasant restaurant alongside it. Three other restaurants serve seafood, themed menus and Oriental specialities. Two bars, a shopping gallery and a discotheque at weekends.

EATING OUT

Apart from the restaurants in the Mount Lavinia Hotel, there are no "gastronomic" locations in this suburb of Colombo. For reasonable prices, try the ***Lion Pub*** (on the corner of Galle Rd and Hotel Rd) or the ***Mount Palace Restaurant*** (in Hotel Rd, level with Barnes Ave): the food is not very original, but the quality is good. Of all the straw-hut restaurants on the beach, ***La Langousterie*** (at the end of the street running alongside the Rivi Ras Hotel) has a good seafood menu. The terrace of the ***Haus Chandra*** hotel has wonderful views and its seafood restaurant leads down to the beach.

The west coast★

From Negombo to Puttalam

119km round trip starting from Colombo
Accommodation in Negombo, Marawila, Chilaw or Puttalam
See map p 143

Not to be missed
The church in Marawila.
The fish-markets in Chilaw and Negombo.
The evening "puja" at the temple in Munneswaram.

And remember...
Head for the wild and beautiful beach at Marawila, rather than the practical but dirty resort of Negombo.

Once beyond the suburbs to the north of Colombo, you enter the coastal region with its vestiges of occupation by the Portuguese missionaries from the 16C onwards. Some small Buddhist temples and a few mosques can still be found, but there are far more **Catholic churches**, especially to the north of Negombo. However, none have survived from the era of the Portuguese trading posts: as symbols of the Counter-Reformation, buildings with baroque façades were systematically destroyed by the Dutch Reformation. But at every crossroads, inside their glass-fronted niches, are familiar figures: St Francis, perhaps St Christopher carrying the baby Jesus, or maybe St Sebastian pierced with arrows, or the Pietà with Mary mourning the dead Christ, watching over the passing traffic *(see illustration p 57)*.

Pretty colonial villas testify to another aspect of the history of this coastline: they were the houses of the Sinhalese dignitaries, who prospered whilst the British were in power thanks to the coconut trade. With the exception of Negombo, there is not much in the way of tourist development along this coast and the main source of income is still **traditional fishing** from catamarans.

The long walk of Joseph Vaz

In 1540, the Portuguese settled in Puttalam, building a church there that became the epicentre of activity for Franciscan missionaries, joined soon afterwards by Dominicans, then by Jesuits who came from Goa. Their claim to fame was the conversion of a Kandyan prince who was christened Don Juan and who reigned over the Sinhalese realm as a Christian monarch from 1542 to 1597.

In 1642, the Dutch established the Reform Church and forced the Catholic priests into exile but despite their efforts, they never succeeded in eradicating Catholicism. One of the great figures of the time was **Father Joseph Vaz**, originally from Goa, whose travels and repeated imprisonment made him immensely popular with the island's Catholic community. Over a five-year period in the 1690s, he travelled all over Ceylon on foot converting many to Catholicism. During a visit to Kandy, he was put in prison, but spent his two years in jail learning Sinhalese. At the time of his release, an epidemic had just been declared, so he opened hospices to take in and care for the sick. In 1696, he was declared vicar-general of Ceylon by the Bishop of Cochin. He died in 1711, after 24 years of missionary activities. His zeal was a strong factor in reinforcing Catholicism on the island.

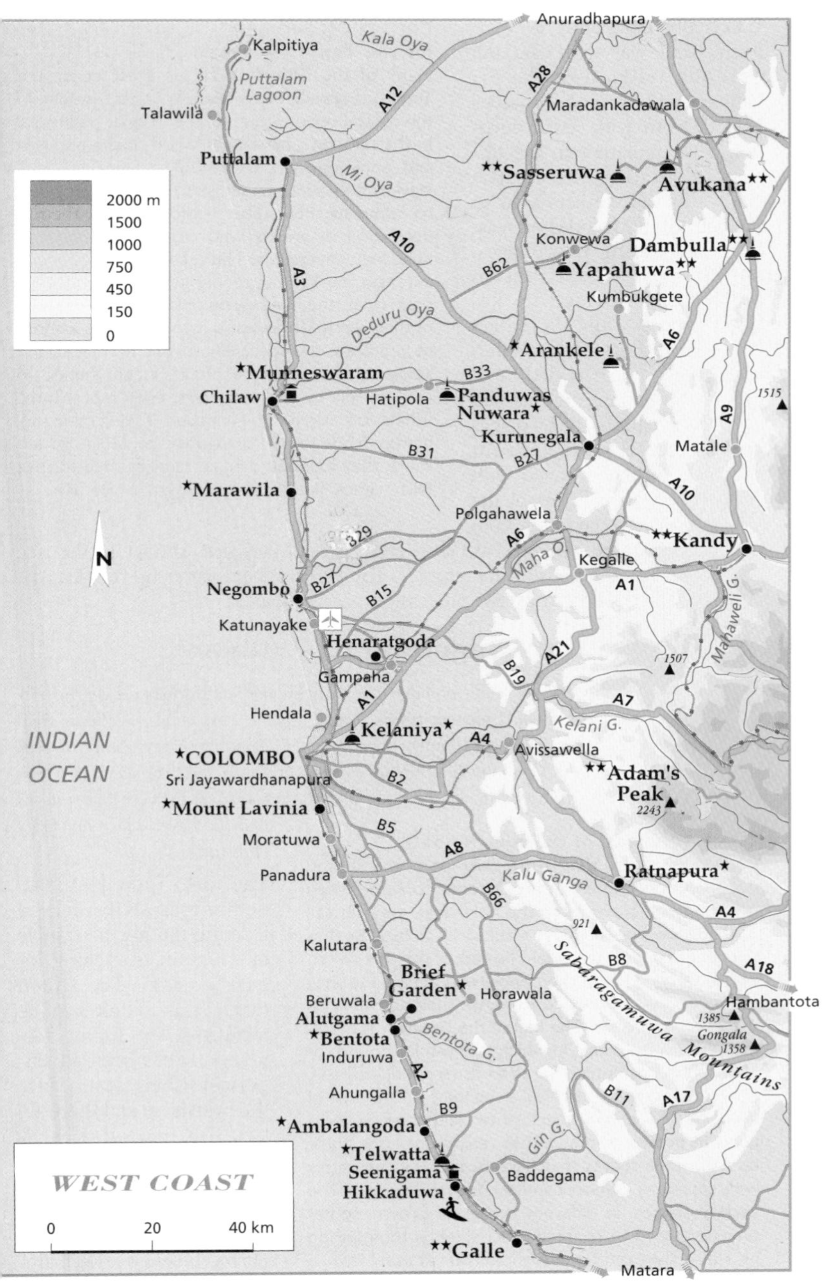

Anuradhapura
Kalpitiya
Kala Oya
Puttalam Lagoon
Talawila
A12
A28
Maradankadawala
Puttalam
Mi Oya
★★Sasseruwa
Avukana★★
2000 m
1500
1000
750
450
150
0
A10
Konwewa
Dambulla★★
B62
Yapahuwa★★
A3
Kumbukgete
Deduru Oya
A6
★Arankele
★Munneswaram
B33
Chilaw
Hatipola
Panduwas Nuwara★
1515
A9
Kurunegala
Matale
B31
B27
★Marawila
A10
Polgahawela
B29
A6
★★Kandy
N
Maha O.
Kegalle
Negombo
B27
B15
A1
Katunayake
Mahaweli G.
Henaratgoda
1507
B19
A21
Gampaha
A1
A7
Hendala
Kelani G.
Kelaniya★
INDIAN OCEAN
A4
★COLOMBO
Avissawella
Sri Jayawardhanapura
B2
★★Adam's Peak
2243
★Mount Lavinia
B5
Moratuwa
A8
Panadura
Kalu Ganga
Ratnapura★
B66
A4
921
Kalutara
B8
Sabaragamuwa Mountains
A18
Brief Garden★
Horawala
Hambantota
Beruwala
1385
Alutgama
Gongala
★Bentota
1358
Bentota G.
Induruwa
A2
Ahungalla
B11
A17
B9
★Ambalangoda
Gin G.
★Telwatta
Seenigama
Baddegama
Hikkaduwa
WEST COAST
0
20
40 km
★★Galle
Matara

Catholic feast days

In the same way as in Goa, the Catholic religion of the Sri Lankan coastal region combines Latin fervour with Asian devotion. Ever apparent in the images decorating the church walls and the trinkets sold to the faithful, it explodes on feast days and during pilgrimages. During Holy Week, Passion plays are performed in Negombo; on 26 July, St Anne's Day, crowds flock to the church in Talawila which is dedicated to her. Processions are inspired by Hindu rituals: holy places are decorated with coconut arches, villages are paved with palm-leaves, the effigies of the Virgin Mary and the saints, covered with jasmine garlands, are showered with puffed rice, similar to the rice consecrated by the gods in the temples. The faithful then gather up this manna, which has been blessed by the procession passing over it.

Portuguese surnames for the Tamil fishermen

Many of the fisherfolk of the west coast are Tamils, originally of the Karava caste who live in the coastal region, south of the Mannar peninsula. In the mid-16C, having got word of the miracles and conversions performed by Saint Francis-Xavier, they sent messengers to him begging him to come to them. The missionary sent them a delegation of priests who rapidly made several hundred conversions. The success of Catholicism amongst the Karava people incited the wrath of their ruler, the Hindu king of Jaffna, who had 600 of these early Christians put to death. He wanted to eradicate the spreading of this new faith, but achieved the opposite effect: strengthened in their beliefs by these martyrs, even more Tamil fishing-folk asked to be baptised. Taking their surnames from their Portuguese or Goan godfathers, they founded the first families on Sri Lanka with names like Perera, de Soysa, or de Silva.

From Negombo to Puttalam

■ **Negombo –** *37km north of Colombo. The railway and bus stations are on the outskirts, on the road into town. Frequent trains from Colombo Fort between 4.30am-8pm (journey takes from 35min to 1hr40min). Private and CTB buses, every 15min, depart Saunders Place Station in Colombo (journey takes 1hr-1hr30min, buses crowded at weekends). Less frequent departures in the direction of Puttalam. Travel between the stations and the Lewis Place hotels by "tuk-tuk".*

The town (pop 140 000) occupies a strip of land forming the northern edge of a lagoon, stretching for nearly 15km. The Dutch dug a canal to link it to the mouth of the Kelani *(see p 114)*. It has been an important fishing centre since the British era and there are two **fish markets*** every day, except Sundays. From 6am, the large catches (tuna, small sharks) are sold on the small island of Duwa, linked to the main-

The brown sails of the oruwa boats

Ten hours at sea: that is the daily lot of the shrimp and bonito fishermen. From October to April, when the monsoon blows from the northeast, they set sail in their "oruwa" boats, a traditional pirogue with a type of dug-out or pirogue. The rest of the year, when the wind blows from the opposite direction and they cannot go to sea, they concentrate their activities on the rivers and lakes. The hull of the "oruwa" is a hollowed-out tree-trunk, in which two planks, bound together using palm-tree fibres to form a funnel-shape, provide storage for the fish, depending on the size of the catch. From a distance, their sails seem to be a uniform brown colour, but in reality, they are made up from four sheets that have been dyed separately with tree-bark essences and then sewn together. The vertical stripes, in different shades of brown, sometimes so faded as to be almost white, is the method by which they can be recognised out at sea.

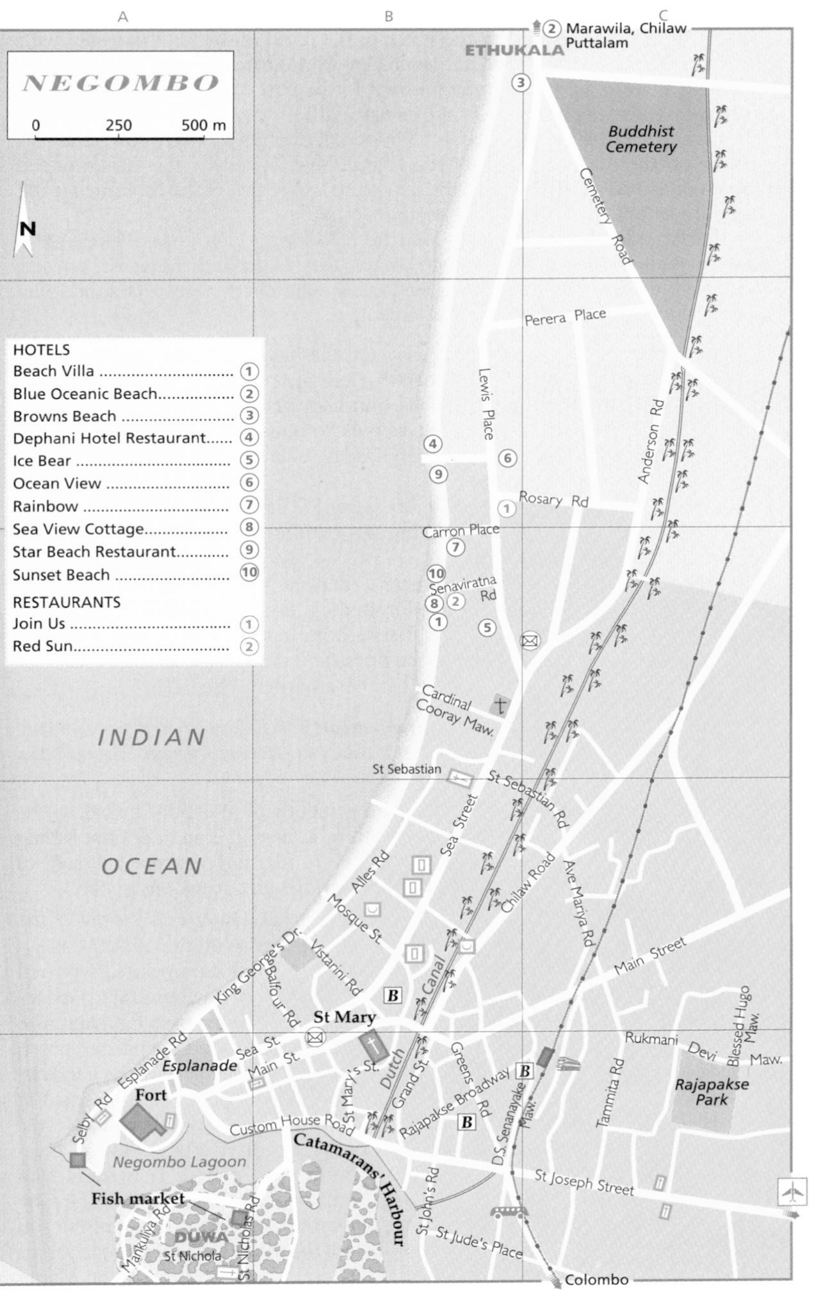

NEGOMBO
0 250 500 m
N
A
B
C
HOTELS
Beach Villa 1
Blue Oceanic Beach................. 2
Browns Beach 3
Dephani Hotel Restaurant...... 4
Ice Bear 5
Ocean View 6
Rainbow 7
Sea View Cottage................... 8
Star Beach Restaurant........... 9
Sunset Beach 10
RESTAURANTS
Join Us 1
Red Sun.................................. 2
INDIAN
OCEAN
2 Marawila, Chilaw Puttalam
ETHUKALA
Buddhist Cemetery
Cemetery Road
Perera Place
Lewis Place
Anderson Rd
Rosary Rd
Carron Place
Senaviratna Rd
Cardinal Cooray Maw.
St Sebastian
St Sebastian Rd
Sea Street
Alles Rd
Mosque St.
Chilaw Road
Ave Mariya Rd
Main Street
King George's Dr.
Vistarini Rd
Balfour Rd
Canal
St Mary
Sea St.
Main St.
Esplanade Rd
Esplanade
Fort
Selby Rd
Dutch
St Mary's St.
Grand St.
Greens Rd
Rajapakse Broadway
D.S. Senanayake Maw.
Rukmani Devi Maw.
Blessed Hugo Maw.
Rajapakse Park
Tammita Rd
Custom House Road
Catamarans' Harbour
Negombo Lagoon
Fish market
Mankuliya Rd
St Nicholas Rd
DUWA
St Nichola
St John's Rd
St Jude's Place
St Joseph Street
Colombo

land by two bridges. By 10am, the beach to the north of the fort is covered with small fish and shrimps. The **fort** is an ancient Portuguese bastion that the Dutch extended to form a fortified outer harbour to the port of Colombo. Nothing remains of it today except the eastern gateway, with the clock tower over it (1698). The harbour, where the *oruwa* boats are moored, extends between Duwa and Negombo on the northern bank of the lagoon, overlooked by the façade of the church of **St Mary** (1874-1922): the departure and return of the fishermen is the main attraction.

On the far side of the cemetery, 3km from the fort along Lewis Place, is the **seaside resort**. The beach, however, is not very clean and the waves are not conducive to swimming. *From Negombo, it is possible to get to the archeological sites of the Cultural Triangle via Kurunegala* *(see p 164)*.

■ **Marawila*** – *20km north of Negombo.* On the road that leads from the small town to the deserted beach is a **church***. Dedicated to Mary, it is an imposing building of basilican proportions. Five hundred metres further on, there is an old **Catholic cemetery**: the oratory was built to house a figure of Christ on the cross which was found in the sea. Every Friday, worshippers assemble here and light oil lamps.

Still unspoilt, the **beach**** is the most beautiful on this stretch of the coast, although the size of the breakers discourages bathing for much of the year, even between July and December.

A legacy from the Dutch presence there, Marawila is still an important **centre for batik**. This process was introduced from the Indonesian colonies to be developed as a product for export. Today, batiks from Marawila are sold in the main tourist centres. Perhaps surprisingly the prices and designs (cushion covers, 70s-style dresses, and caps) are the same here as anywhere else.

■ **Chilaw** – *12km north of Marawila. Trains depart from Colombo Fort at 6am, 2.45pm, 6.20pm, 6.55pm and 8.30pm (3hr journey). Private and CTB buses depart from Saunders Place bus station in Colombo.*

Chilaw (pronounced "Chilao") straddles the mouth of a lagoon, linked to the lagoons of Mundal and Puttalam to the north by a canal. It is an important fishing port and a large **fish market*** is held here every morning, (except Sunday), in the market building on the other side of the bridge that spans the lagoon.

The temple of Munneswaram** *(2km away, on the road to Kurunegala)* is one of the four great temples dedicated to Shiva still in active service on Sri Lanka *(A puja is held there every day at 7am, 12am and 5pm)*. Within an enclosure painted with red and white stripes are some rare and beautiful (although heavily restored) examples of **medieval Hindu statues**. Tradition attributes the temple's foundation to the legendary times of Ramayana. The rear of the sanctuary and the pillared porch *(mandapa)* fronting the cella (the holy of holies) bear the hallmarks of the Pandyas, who ruled in the very south of India from the 12C-14C (the two fish, carved in bas-relief on the ceiling of the porch, were in fact their emblem). As you leave the *mandapa* and head along the external wall of the sanctuary in a clockwise direction, you will come across some statues from the same period. They stand with their backs against the recess, gleaming from the butter with which they are anointed by the priests officiating during *puja* services. A seated statue of the god Shiva, his hair untied, instructs the wise-men of the forest in mastering the senses and tramples on the personification of Ignorance. This is Dakshina, the Master who explains that acquiring knowledge is also a means of deliverance from the cycle of rebirth. Past a recess containing a linga, there is a statue of the goddess Durga with ferocious teeth, sitting upon a demon buffalo that she has defeated, brandishing weapons in her multiple arms. Finally, a statue of the serene god Vishnu, his four arms holding the magic symbols: the conch shell, the club, the wheel and the lotus flower.

If you are travelling in a vehicle, continue beyond Chilaw to the east to get to the ancient capital of Panduwas Nuwara (34km) (see p 165). From here, you can head for Kurunegala (37km), a possible stopover (see p 169).

The image of Shiva, the wild and ascetic god

Every detail of the image of Shiva opposes and complements that of Vishnu. While the latter is crowned with a tiara and his loins are girded with pleated cloth, Shiva's mane of hair sports a "sadhu" in which a crescent moon shines and his nakedness is covered by an animal skin. While Vishnu reclines on the serpent Ananta and dreams of the world, Shiva breathes rhythm and life into creation in a savage dance. Vishnu has his avatars (incarnations), Shiva has his forms: he is in turn the wise husband at the side of Parvati, or a yogi meditating under a tree, or a fierce warrior battling against demons. His home is on Mount Kailash in the Himalayas, but he prefers the nomadic life of an ascetic, alongside the hermits of the forest, or among the ghouls in the cemeteries, his face smeared with ash.

■ **Puttalam** – *50km north of Chilaw. Trains depart from Colombo Fort at 4.30am, 8.25am and 5.35pm (journey takes 4hr-4hr30min).* At the side of an enormous **lagoon**, this small town has a few places to stay, but not much to see. There are several military bases in this region, which borders on the North province, and until further notice visitors are not admitted to the **Wilpattu** reserve, which is closed for security reasons. It is however still possible to get to Anuradhapura, 74km north-east of Puttalam.

The "oruwa" coming ashore

Y Keller

Making the most of the West Coast

Address book

• In Negombo

Banks and services are located in the centre of Negombo town, 3km south of the tourist resort (expect to pay about 50Rs to get there by "tuk-tuk"), but you can find everthing that you need along Lewis Place: telephone agencies, bureaux de change, photographic shops, mineral water and post cards.

Bank / Currency exchange – The ***Bank of Ceylon*** has two branches: one opposite the railway station, on the corner of D S Senanayake Maw and Rajapakse Broadway (B-C5), the second on Main St, opposite St Mary's church (B4).

Post office / Telephone – ***GPO***, Main St, level with St Mary's church (B4-5). Small post office at the lower end of Lewis Place (C3).

Where to stay

• In Negombo

The hoteliers in Negombo benefit from the town's proximity to the international airport and rarely make much effort to offer top-class accommodation. There are some pleasant guesthouses located in the few tourist ghettos and some small hotels, which are among the least attractive on the island. Why stay in Negombo, then? Because it is a very convenient location if your flight arrives or departs in the middle of the night. Because, as in Mount Lavinia, you can find some decent places to stay which are significantly less expensive than in Colombo. And finally, because some of the enterprising guesthouse owners can be of valuable assistance in organising the remainder of your trip. The small hotels and guesthouses are located at the southern end of Lewis Place. To the north, along Ethukala beach, there is a group of larger establishments, more popular with large groups of tourists.

Under US$10

Ocean View Guesthouse (W J J Thamel), 104 Lewis Place, ☎ (031) 386 89 – 6rm. It is not in the idyllic "ocean view" location that its name suggests, as the guesthouse is not situated on the right side for the beach. The rooms are simple and clean (mosquito nets, cold water). The owner is a good source of information and can help you organise your trip.

From US$10 to US$15

Beach Villa Guesthouse (Mr D Nissanka), 3 / 2 Senaviratna Rd, ☎ (031) 228 33, Fax (031) 341 34 – 14rm. One of the best value guesthouses in this category. The ground floor rooms are a bit gloomy, but, from the first floor upwards, you get a sea view. The bathrooms, complete with shower cubicle, are kept clean. The restaurant menu has a seafood bias. Finally, something very much in its favour, the owner is a guide: he has information on excursions in the area and can also organise itineraries for touring the island by car (with driver).

Dephani Hotel Restaurant (Mrs Wini Fernando), 189 / 15 Lewis Place, ☎ (031) 343 59, Fax (031) 382 51 – 14rm. This white maisonnette, hidden away at the end of a small street which runs at a right angle to Lewis Place, has clean rooms, beds with mosquito nets and bathrooms with cold water. Meals are eaten on a terrace which opens onto a lush little garden. It is such a good place to stay that it is impossible to get a room here without a reservation from October to March.

Rainbow Hotel, 3 Carron Place, ☎ (031) 220 82 – 8rm. A modest, quiet hotel, set back from Lewis Place, in a small street leading to the beach. Its spacious rooms overlook an attractive garden and the beds have mosquito nets. Shower with cold water.

Star Beach Restaurant and Guesthouse, 83 / 3 Lewis Place, ☎ (031) 226 06 – 15rm. A dingy and characterless establishment which can serve as a fall-back while waiting for a vacancy in the Dephani (immediately opposite). It has the same amenities, but in a less attractive setting. Its only advantage is its association with the Golden Star Beach Hotel which allows you use of the swimming pool there (the hotel itself is to be avoided, it really is awful).

From US$15 to US$30

Sea View Cottage, 5 Senaviratna Rd, ☎(031) 359 05 – 4rm. A warm atmosphere in this beach-front guesthouse. Huge breakfasts and delicious Sri Lankan meals are served in the family dining room. The rooms are acceptable, although they could do with a lick of paint, and there is hot water in the shower.

From US$30 to US$40

Ice Bear Guesthouse, 103 / 2 Lewis Place, ☎ and Fax (031) 338 62 – 6rm. White bungalows with patios, in a sprawling tropical garden. The rooms, with black marble floors, are all prettily furnished with old wooden furniture, batik bedcovers, marionettes and lace curtains made in Galle. Hot water and refrigerator. Some slightly less expensive rooms. Very reasonably priced food, including a special "shark" menu. The guesthouse also offers boat-trips, ayurvedic treatments and discounts for luxury hotels in Colombo.

Sunset Beach Hotel (Jetwing), 5 Carron Place, ☎ (031) 223 50, Fax (074) 87 06 23 – 36rm. Rooms are large, spotlessly clean, light and very comfortable, all with double bed, cane chairs and private balcony with sea view. Beach-front restaurant and swimming pool. Some slightly less expensive rooms.

From US$40 to US$70

Blue Oceanic Beach Hotel (Jetwing), Ethukala, ☎ (01) 34 57 00, Fax (01) 34 57 29 – 92rm. Light, spacious rooms in a three-storeyed building overlooking the sea. Pleasant restaurant. Beach huts and deckchairs on the beach.

Brown's Beach Hotel (Aitken Spence), 175 Lewis Place, ☎ (031) 220 32, Fax (031) 243 03 – 140rm One of the first hotels to be opened in Negombo, Brown's Beach specialises in longer stays. Extensive facilities including sports sessions in the pool, cultural activities and buffet meals with a menu that is changed every day. The hotel is spread out along an unspoiled and well-maintained beach, and an elegant arcaded gallery takes you from your room to the restaurant. Whilst a little impersonal the rooms have large bay windows opening onto a balcony with a view. Two restaurants, two bars, leisure club, children's play area, boutiques.

• In Marawila

From US$15 to US$30

Aquarius Beach Club, Beach Rd, 2km from the centre of Marawila, ☎(032) 548 88, Fax (078) 605 55, aquarius@sri.lanka.net, www.sportreise.de – 50rm. Behind an imposing white portal, a lush tropical garden stretches along Marawila beach. The 17 rooms (with air-conditioning) are housed in bungalows, spread out like a little village. Founded to promote German-Sri Lankan sporting exchanges, this holiday club is not in the least exclusive. Table tennis, beach sports, basketball, physiotherapy and ayurvedic massages are available.

Sanmali Beach Hotel, Beach Rd, 500m north of the previous entry, ☎(032) 547 66, Fax (032) 547 68 – 20rm. A little characterless, but perfectly acceptable, this two-storeyed hotel also gives guests access to the Marawila beach. Rather on the small side, with heavy blue curtains, the rooms do have the advantage of a beautiful view and bathrooms with hot water. Overlooking the beach, the dining room seems a bit like an aquarium behind its bay windows. A good stand-by, and slightly less expensive, if the Aquarius is full.

• In Chilaw

From US$7 to US$15

Rest House, on the coast, at the end of the road that runs through the town, ☎(032) 222 99 – 17rm. The rooms might not be spotlessly clean but the food is very good. Seafood bias. No beach at this location.

• **In Puttalam**

From US$7 to US$15

Senatilake Guest Inn and Restaurant, 81 / A Kurunegala Rd, ☎ (032) 654 03, Fax (032) 652 99 – 7rm. Acceptable accommodation with serviceable rooms (hot water). Avoid those that overlook the very busy street. Good Sri Lankan cuisine.

EATING OUT

• **In Negombo**

There are plenty of restaurants along Lewis Place, affording a change of scene if not a change of menu. Indeed, every menu invariably has a choice of Chinese stir-fry cuisine, fish and seafood, according to availability, as well as the ubiquitous curries. Expect to pay from US$3 for fish, to US$10 for grilled prawns. But beware! The restaurants remain, but owners come and go and their names can change from one year to the next. Good food can also be had in some of the guesthouses, notably ***Ice Bear***, ***Sea View Cottage*** and ***Beach Villa***.

Under US$7

Join us, 103 Lewis Place, opposite the green stucco façade of the Golden Star Hotel. Very reasonable prices. Sri Lankan breakfasts also served.

Red Sun, Senaviratna Rd, under a straw roof, in a small street running down to the sea. Menu typically caters for every eventuality: from breakfast to lobster Thermidor with Chinese noodles thrown in.

Silva's Beach, 16 Porutota Rd, Ethukala, ☎(031) 794 08. Generous portions of grilled fish. Value for money.

ENTERTAINMENT

Excursions – The sea can be dangerous along this coast so swimming is not always possible. In Negombo, however, you can organise a trip out to sea or join a fishing expedition on board an "oruwa" (ask for information at your hotel or negotiate directly with the fishermen), or you can hire a bicycle (hire agencies on Lewis Place). There are organised boat-trips on the Dutch-built canals between Negombo and the Pegasus Reef Hotel (20km away, south of the airport).

Swimming pools – The large hotels located to the north in Lewis Place and in Ethukala open their pools to non-residents (expect to pay about US$1.50 per person).

Feast days / Festivals – ***The Fishermens' Festival*** and celebration of Holy Week, which is in July in Negombo, complete with organised boat races.

Maha Shiva Rathri: Munneswaram, an important pilgrimage centre for the worship of Shiva, comes alive during the festival dedicated to Shiva in January-February.

WHAT TO BUY

Local specialities – Models of the "oruwa" and sea-shell products sold by the fishermen along the beaches.

In Marawila, several batik workshops have showrooms, open daily. Try ***Eric Batiks***, Chilaw Rd, ☎ (032) 540 54.

The beach coast
From Alutgama to Hikkaduwa

46km round trip including the beach resorts of the southwest
Map p 143

Not to be missed
A trip to the Brief Garden or along the Bentota River.

And remember...
Hop on to one of the many buses that travel between Colombo and Galle, and get off wherever you like.

The coastal stretch between Colombo and Galle is the most densely populated region on the island and it will seem as if you are travelling through one enormous village that stretches for miles and miles.
North of the Bentota River, the coastline is badly eroded and the beach is non-existent. A few decent hotels nonetheless offer luxury accommodation, but you can only stay there as part of an organised package holiday or tour. To enjoy the real beaches and more reasonable prices, you have to go further south. You might find more German than English spoken there, but then again, it was the Germans who were the first to discover Sri Lanka's beaches.
Whereas there will be a few things to remind you that you are in still in Sri Lanka, it is not in this region that you will see the island at its best: the beach coast is entirely dedicated to tourism which was first introduced to the area in the 1960s.

■ **Alutgama and Bentota**★ – *61km south of Colombo.* The bridge spanning the mouth of the River Bentota connects the two towns. Alutgama, to the north, is a small town with no history but which benefits from railway and bus stations. Bentota, to the south, is a seaside resort which has been completely taken over by the developers, whose most recent achievement is a 200-room luxury hotel run by the Indian Taj hotel chain. To find a beautiful unspoilt beach, you have to travel further south towards Induruwa. Use Bentota as a base for expeditions into the interior.

The River Bentota★ is navigable by boat for 13km. *(Enquire at the Rainbow Boat service, at the entrance to the bridge, south side, ☎ (034) 753 83. 6hr return cruise-trips on motor-boats, with visits to riverside villages. Expect to pay about US$20 per person, including lunch. Boat hire, about US$30 for 3hr).* Upstream the river forms a lagoon, an aquatic maze dotted with small islands and fringed with mangrove swamps. This forest on the water is the permanent home of herons, cormorants, eagles and king-fishers, as well as some predators, such as crocodiles and Bengali water monitors.

Brief Garden★ is a 2ha tropical garden, with terraces looking down over the surrounding rice-fields and coffee plantations. *(10km east on the road to Horawala. Check that your driver knows the road, as it is very badly sign-*

The intoxication of the heights
As you travel the length of the coastline, you will see that the areas wooded with coconut-palms are strung with cables. They do not supply electricity to the villages, but are used as walkways by the men who gather sap, the *malafoutiers*. With their sarongs rolled up to their thighs, a knife and a container fastened to their belts, they climb like cats, more than 10m off the ground, to collect the precious "toddy". This beer made from the coconut palms is drunk cold, or is distilled to make the local whisky, "arak", which is very popular with the Sri Lankans.

P Haussherr

All a question of balance

posted. If you are making the expedition by bicycle, ask for directions to "Bawa Garden". Open every day, 8am-5pm. Entrance charge). An artist and literary figure, Bewis Bawa (who died in 1992) began designing the landscape around his home in 1929 and continued working on it for the next 60 years. The originality of his thinking lies in his use of local species (philodendrons, hibiscus, bougainvilleas, anthuriums and fifty or more varieties of fern) in a setting which is Japanese or Italian by turn. This becomes apparent as soon as you enter the park, where the gate is guarded by laughing fauns. An avenue leads up towards the house, which contains works by Bawa and his artist friends, around which the four garden areas are arranged. The cascading ornamental ponds, set between two rows of bamboo canes, are a masterly exercise in perspective. An enormous lawn goes down towards a paved area in the shape of a half-moon, forming a terrace above the rice-fields. An exotic garden, with its Japanese-style wooden bridge and its Italian-style stone statues, has mossy ponds hidden under large ferns. A circular expanse of water reflects a screen of giant bamboo canes. Paths link and give rhythm to these areas with their subtle combinations of carpets of dieffenbachias, crowned with clumps of shrubs such as crotons or dracaenas, beneath the intertwined creepers.

■ **Ambalangoda**★ – *83km from Colombo.* Ambalangoda is a quiet holiday destination; it is not a seaside resort, but more of a little town by the sea. It is also the home of one of the masked dances of Sri Lanka, the **Kolam** *(see p 127)*. By the end of the 1950s this form of theatre was obsolete but a few families in Ambalangoda have carried on carving the very colourful wooden masks.

The Mask Museum★★ *(417 Main St, on the corner of the main road to Colombo)* is housed on the ground floor of the workshop belonging to the Wijesooriya family. The presentation is remarkably good, with explanatory notices in English, with some of the 120 masks made by its craftsmen on display. There is a list of the characters of the Kolam and also of the characters of the Sanni exorcism ritual *(see p 127)*. The Wijesooriya workshop is just one of many with other mask-carvers having opened shops in the town *(Try Southlands Masks, 353 Main St)*.

■ **Hikkaduwa** – *See Map p 159.* *95km from Colombo.* This resort has many things to recommend it: its sandy beach which stretches for miles, the coral reef which is good for diving and affords some protection to the bathing area and the surfing, among the best on the island. Hikkaduwa has become so popular that today there are dozens of hotels and guesthouses, built in serried rows to the south of the bus station, only thinning out 2km further away, along Narigama beach. If your idea of a holiday involves crowds, busy restaurants and every conceivable kind of shop, you will like Hikkaduwa; if not, give it a wide berth.

Created in 1988, the **Coral Sanctuary** lies level with the Coral Sands Hotel, a few hundred metres from the shore. The water is not very deep, so you can swim out to the reef, but there is also a flotilla of eighty glass-bottomed boats allowing you to observe the fish and turtles without getting wet *(for hire from the hotels and restaurants, boats depart from south of the Poseidon diving club)*.

The coral forest on fire

For corals to live, the sea has to be very warm (from 21 to 23°C), but not too hot! At the beginning of 1998 and in the aftermath of El Niño, the temperature of the water rose as high as 30°C on the coasts of the Indian Ocean. A great number of corals died as a result, leaving behind only their white calcified skeleton. The multicoloured reefs have yet to regain their former glory, but diving here is nonetheless immensely pleasurable. The death of the corals has in fact led to a proliferation of algae and there are greater numbers of colourful feeder-fish here than ever before!

The temple of Seenigama *(2km north along the coast road)* is a curiosity given that **Devol**, the god to whom it is dedicated, is evil by nature. The sanctuary is built on a small rocky island, about 100m from the shore, and can only be reached by boat *(fishing-boats moored along the coast)*. Those seeking vengeance go there to invoke the power of Devol. The supplications are carried out by the priest: grinding grain in a mortar or smashing a water container, he begs the god to break the limbs of the enemy, scatter his family and destroy his house.

Totagamu Maharaja Vihara* (Telwatta Monastery) *(3km north of the previous entry. A sign, on the right, indicates the road to take, 200m on the other side of the railway)* was founded in 12C and enjoyed a golden age three centuries later as the home of the renowned Totagamuva Sri Rahula. A monk who was famous for his poetic talents (he is even acknowledged as the writer of some profane poems celebrating the beauty of women and the glory of the rulers) and for his exorcism skills, he drew crowds of pilgrims. A modern statue stands in his memory at the entrance to the monastery, which, like most of the religious establishments along the coast, was destroyed when the Portuguese arrived in the 16C and was not rebuilt until work began in 1805. The vestibule paintings which date from this period are housed in a small **hall of images**. The larger gallery, built in the mid 19C, begins with a double *makara torana*: note the finely painted ladies on the tympanum. Along the walls, paintings on a red background depict a multitude of different characters. Note the women with long hair, their loins girded with sarongs embroidered with flowers.

South of Hikkaduwa, beyond Thirangama, the main road to Galle (15km) passes through a series of fishing villages, mangrove swamps and lagoons.

Making the most of Alutgama and Bentota

Coming and going

By train – The express trains on the Colombo-Matara line stop at Alutgama, where you can get a bus or a "tuk-tuk" to Bentota.

Address book

Bank / Currency exchange – *Bank of Ceylon*, on the square before the Susantha Guesthouse, on the road in to Bentota. Monday-Friday, 9am-2.30pm. Cash withdrawals with Visa card.

Post office / Telephone – Post Office next to the Bank of Ceylon. Monday-Saturday, 8am-5pm.

Where to stay and eating out

There are some small hotels in Alutgama, to the north of River Bentota, along Manju Sri Maw. The rooms are clean but suffer the inconvenience of being situated alongside the very busy main road from Colombo to Galle. The centre of Bentota, around the small railway station, leads to the beach. The majority of the hotels there are large tourist complexes with pools, with every kind of activity on offer (expect to pay more than US$70 for a room). Further south, along the road to Induruwa, there are a few establishments, colonial in style: some more successful in this respect than others.

From US$10 to US$15

Susantha's Hotel, Resort Rd, to the north of Bentota, ☎ and Fax (034) 753 24 – 18rm. The only good accommodation in this category. A well-run guesthouse with garden, on the edge of the beach. Rooms are a little gloomy, but with good facilities including canopied beds, mosquito nets and tiled bathroom. The food is highly rated.

From US$15 to US$30

Hemadan Tourist Guesthouse, 25A River Ave, next to the Terrena Lodge, ☎ (034) 753 20 – 11rm. Decent rooms (mosquito nets, hot water), with balconies overlooking the river that has to be crossed by boat to get to the beach.

Terrena Lodge, Manju Sri Maw, near the bridge, Alutgama, ☎ (034) 750 01 – 5rm. This hotel offers good value for money, with large, airy bedrooms, a terrace and a lawn going down to the river, along with excellent food. Just one bad point: the hotel is next to the noisy road to Galle.

From US$40 to US$80

Club Villa, 138 / 15 Galle Rd, access through an alleyway, 1.5km south of Bentota, ☎ and Fax (034) 753 12 – 16rm. CC There is nothing about this place that brings to mind a seaside hotel. The old colonial villa only has 16 rooms and its attraction lies in the sheer volume of space on offer: huge rooms with little courtyards or duplex suites, with refined colonial furnishings, a large garden stretching towards the beach (the little train goes to Matara), an open-air restaurant serving delicious Italian food. An exceptional place.

Villa Walauwa (Keells), Galle Rd, Warahena, 2km south of Bentota, ☎(034) 753 72, Fax (034) 753 95 – 20rm. CC A villa with a garden, but not on the beach. Enormous rooms, elegantly furnished. Supplement for air-conditioning. Attractive patio restaurant and a bar.

Over US$80

The Villa, 138 / 18-22 Galle Rd, ☎(034) 753 11, Fax (072) 301 02 – 15rm. CC A neighbour of the Club Villa, this late-19C residence is much more luxurious, and the rooms are more like suites, furnished with antiques.

• **In Induruwa**

A deserted beach, 5km south of Bentota.

From US$15 to US$30

Emerald Bay Hotel, Induruwa, ☎ (034) 753 63 – 24rm. CC Friendly and unpretentious, this hotel is situated beside a large beach which borders the mangrove swamp. Functional rooms with hot water in the bathrooms. The complex has a bit of an ocean liner feel to it, with its kidney-shaped swimming pool underneath the building.

Alutgama and Bentota

Making the most of Ambalangoda

Coming and going

By train – The ***Railway Station*** is on Galle Rd. Ambalangoda is situated on the Colombo-Matara railway line, but not many trains stop at its small station. It is better to get off in Hikkaduwa and travel from there by bus.

By bus – The ***Bus Station*** is also situated on Galle Rd.

Address book

Bank / Currency exchange – The ***People's Bank*** has a branch on Galle Rd.

Where to stay and eating out

A perfect stopover for travellers on a budget, with quiet guesthouses 3min from the sea. They are all in the town, which lies between Galle Rd and the beach.

Under US$7

Terence da Silva, n° 58 / 2 Sea Beach Rd, ☎ (09) 588 17 – 2rm. Rooms with mosquito nets are in a bungalow, at the bottom of the garden of a large white house run by a friendly young woman. Meals on request.

From US$7 to US$15

Shangrela Beach Resort, 38 Sea Beach Rd, ☎ (09) 583 42 – 8rm. A large seaside villa, very 1950s in style, owned by a pleasant and enterprising retired couple. The rooms are very clean (mosquito nets). Three others, with shared bathroom, are rented out for less than US$7.

Sumudu Tourist Guesthouse (E. Ranjith de Silva), 418 Main St, ☎(09) 588 32 – 6rm. A charming old house, surrounded by a large, well-maintained garden. Good food and huge breakfasts.

From US$15 to US$30

Famedons Inn, 95 / A Sea Beach Rd, ☎ (09) 598 88 – 5rm. Large, spotlessly clean rooms (mosquito nets), in a modern house on the sea front. Direct access to the beach. Plans for an Ayurvedic centre.

• In Ahungalla

A large palm-grove 5km north of Ambalangoda.

From US$70 to US$140

Triton Hotel (Aitken Spence), ☎ (09) 640 41, Fax (09) 640 46, www.aitkenspence.com/triton – 160rm. Total luxury in a secluded hotel in magical surroundings: a palm-forest, a large hall with pillars and an enormous pool that seems to merge with the sea. The rooms are very comfortable, and the hotel has many lovely features, such as the patio gardens, the library that looks down over the pool and the sea, or the restaurant with the breeze coming from the sea. Worth seeing, even if you cannot stay there.

Making the most of Hikkaduwa

Coming and going

By train – The ***Railway Station*** is situated to the north of town, at the crossroads of Galle Rd and Baddegama Rd (A1). Ten express trains daily, in both directions, between Colombo and Matara. Colombo (2hr30min), Galle (30min), Matara (from 2hr-2hr30min). For Kandy (5hr30min) and Anuradhapura (7hr), it is easier to go via Colombo.

By bus – The ***Bus Station*** is near the railway station (A1). Very good bus service to Colombo (from 2hr-2hr30min) via Ambalangoda, Induruwa and Alutgama, and to Galle (30min).

Address book

Bank / Currency exchange – Branches of the ***Bank of Ceylon*** near the railway station (A1) and of the ***People's Bank*** opposite the Coral Sands Hotel (A1).

Bureaux de change on Galle Rd, near the Blue Corals Hotel and level with the Refresh restaurant.

Post office / Telephone – Opposite the railway station (A1). Monday-Saturday, 8am-7pm, Sunday 8am-10am.

Security – A victim of its own success, Hikkaduwa has become a centre for delinquents. Its attractions are a draw for the unemployed and for the young army deserters who can find nothing better to do than lay siege to the virtue of female tourists as night falls on the beaches. The old tradition of smoking marijuana has unfortunately been overtaken by hard drugs, such as cocaine and heroin, with their associated problems of addiction and the dealer networks. Finally, the lack of distinction for some tourists between a holiday destination and a place for total indulgence has contributed to the development of prostitution, including that of children. There is a ***Police Station*** on the road in to town, opposite the Hikkaduwa Beach Hotel.

Where to stay

This resort now takes in four beaches: Hikkaduwa, Wewala, Narigama and Thirangama. Hikkaduwa beach proper only begins to the south of the Coral Sands Hotel, and it is completely eroded in places. Hotel development is so dense here that many hotels are long buildings with several floors, built end-on to the sea: only the rooms at this end have a sea view. The area south of Hikkaduwa is the most pleasant and least crowded. Wewala, level with the Surfing Beach guesthouse, is where the surfers gather but the beach there is very narrow. Narigama starts where the beach-huts begin and is the widest section of a beach which is dirty in parts with no shade.

Under US$7

El Dorado Tourist Guesthouse, Milla Rd, Wewala, ☎ (09) 770 91 – 8rm. A well-run Sri Lankan guesthouse, in a clean, modern house (mosquito nets and tiled bathrooms) 250m from the beach. Bicycles for hire.

Elephant Garden Beach Resort, Galle Rd, Thirangama, south of Thiranagama Beach – 5rm. An open-air café on the beach for a Swiss Family Robinson-style holiday. Three wooden cabins with a tiny bathroom (sea water shower). Avoid the two rather indifferent rooms with communal bathroom inside the owner's house.

Miga Villa Tourist Garden (A B Jayasundara), Galle Rd, Wewala, ☎ and Fax (09) 770 92 – 12rm. The rooms are ordinary, but respectable, providing you get one on the first floor. One disadvantage however: the garden of the villa is strangely sandwiched between the main road to Galle and the railway. The dining room is elaborately furnished with drapes and lanterns in a heavy mid Victorian style.

Thiranagama Beach Hotel, Galle Rd, Thirangama (three houses to the south of Ocean View Cottage), ☎ (074) 38 31 97 – 8rm. A respectable, basic guesthouse, with a little lawn leading to the sea with not even the slightest bit of shade. Two rooms with a view.

From US$10 to US$15

Bird Lake Lodge, Panthana, 3km along the road to Baddegama, then along 1km of track through a coffee plantation; it is possible to get there by "tuk-tuk" from Hikkaduwa bus station, ☎ (09) 770 18 – 10rm. A delightful place to stay, in a tropical grove set back from the coast. Enjoy the birds singing while listening to the sound of the waves on the shore of the lake, or from the balcony of your light and airy room (mosquito nets). You can enjoy walks in the spacious 2.5ha grounds, sunrise over the lake, and there are canoes and catamarans for moonlit picnics and bicycles for hire if you want to get back to the bustle of Hikkaduwa.

Paradiso Hotel (L Wijegoonaratna), 406 Galle Rd, opposite the Francis Hotel, Wewala, ☎ (074) 38 31 25 / ☎ and Fax (09) 776 54 – 18rm. Although built end-on to the beach and therefore with no sea view, this hotel offers comfortable accommodation. The rooms, local in style, are a bit on the dark side but are attractively furnished (mosquito nets). One of the two restaurants leads onto a small area of beach.

The Tandem Guesthouse, 465 Galle Rd, Wewala, ☎ and Fax (09) 771 03 / ☎(074) 38 30 19 – 9rm. One of the older guesthouses in Hikkaduwa, quiet and well designed, although not on the beach. The rooms are very clean (mosquito net canopies and tiled bathrooms) and are situated in a one-storey building with a garden.

From US$15 to US$30

Blue Ocean Villa, 420 Galle Rd, Hikkaduwa, ☎ (09) 775 66 – 8rm. A very clean, simple guesthouse, with a small area of garden leading to the beach. Large rooms with tiled floors.

Blue Note Hotel, 424 Galle Rd, level with the Hikkaduwa exit sign, ☎ and Fax (09) 770 16, bluenote@eureka.lk – 9rm. Bungalows in an airy setting leading to a very pleasant section of the beach. Good accommodation, even if the welcome is a little unfriendly.

Golden Beach Hotel, 869-873 Galle Rd, Thirangama, ☎ (09) 763 13 – 5rm. The tone of this villa is set by the entrance hall, furnished in traditional style with various collector's items. Beachside garden. Functional, clean bathrooms. A little too close, however, to the main road to Galle.

Nippon Villa, 412D Galle Rd, Hikkaduwa, ☎ (074) 38 30 95, Fax (09) 771 03 – 23rm. This hotel, built end-on to the beach like many others, has the advantage, however, of rooms which overlook a patio garden (two with sea views). Some rare touches of individuality, with corner-baths and small interior garden areas. Torch-lit dinners served on an outdoor terrace. Bar, billiards and TV room.

Ranmal Hotel (Ajith de Silva), Galle Rd, Narigama, ☎ and Fax (09) 771 14 – 15rm. Only four of the rooms, which are very comfortable, on garden-level, with bay window, mosquito nets, bathtub and hot water, are in this price range. This hotel, has rooms in all price ranges.

Sansibar Garden, Galle Rd, Thirangama, ☎(09) 770 81 – 6rm. A very simple guesthouse, in the middle of a garden beside the sea. The beach is unspoilt. Decent rooms with balconies overlooking the garden and hot water.

Ocean View Cottage, Galle Rd, Thirangama, ☎(09) 772 37 – 3rm. The bedrooms and bathrooms are enormous, with rattan furniture and a small lounge. Beachside garden.

From US$30 to US$40

Blue Corals Hotel, 332 Galle Rd, Hikkaduwa, ☎ and Fax (09) 776 79, blue_cor@sri.lanka.net – 50rm. The façade onto the street is hideous, but the interior contains a pleasant surprise: it opens onto a garden which is at beach-level. Protected by the coral reef, safe paddling can be enjoyed by all on this section of beach. Enormous, light bedrooms, with spotless bathrooms, hot water and sea views. The only disadvantage is that the corridors are very noisy due to the proximity of the main road to Galle.

Coral Sands Hotel, 326 Galle Rd, Hikkaduwa, ☎(09) 775 13, Fax (09) 774 36 – 30rm. Normal standards of comfort (hot water) in a building end-on to the beach, but with rooms that run across it to provide a view of the sea or of the swimming-pool. Solarium and diving club.

Suit Lanka Hotel, Galle Rd, Thirangama, 50m from the Elephant Garden Beach Resort, ☎ and Fax (09) 771 36 – 9rm. A Japanese-style bridge leads into this stylish hotel which has a small swimming-pool surrounded by frescoed walls. Rooms furnished in a slightly heavy style, but all overlook the sea. Large bathrooms (hot water).

Eating out

In Narigama, the ***Why Not Rock Café*** and the ***Pop Star Beach Restaurant*** are the first in an continuous succession of cheap sea-front restaurants, built on stilts and topped with a palm-roof. German-Italian cuisine, Chinese and seafood dishes are the main trends on the menus. The restaurants at the Coral Gardens Hotel, the only 4-star establishment in the resort, offer a better choice, albeit at a cost, but you can pay by credit card.

Refresh, 384 Galle Rd, Hikkaduwa, ☎ (09) 778 10. Excellent restaurant for fish and seafood, catering for all tastes. A very pleasant place during the heat of the day.

Mama's, 338 Galle Rd, Hikkaduwa, ☎ (09) 771 37. Modest, but pleasant because of its seafront location. Hires out diving equipment and arranges glass-bottomed boat trips.

Abba's, Waulagoda Rd, a small street running inland, opposite the Coral Reef Beach Hotel. Cuisine for young travellers at any time of the day.

Hotel Francis, Galle Rd, opposite the Paradiso Hotel, Hikkaduwa, ☎ (09) 770 19. It does not let rooms, but does have an impressive menu. Unfortunately situated beside the main road.

Sukhawati, Galle Rd, opposite the Sansibar Garden, Thirangama, ☎ (074) 38 30 62. Chinese stir-fry dishes and delicious, healthy, vegetarian dishes are served here. The restaurant also acts as an office for an Ayurvedic clinic.

Entertainment

Nautical activities – *Diving*: Hikkaduwa offers interesting dives from November to March, catering for all levels. Masks, snorkels and flippers can be hired from several shops on Galle Rd, as well as from the three good schools which cater for all types of underwater exploration, at depths of between 0 and 40m, including children: ***Poseidon Diving Station***, next to the Hikkaduwa Beach Hotel, ☎ (09) 772 94, Fax (075) 45 08 18, poseidon@visual.lk ***Aqua Tours Dive Centre***, next to the Coral Reef Beach Hotel, ☎ (09) 77 197, Fax (09) 774 53; ***International Diving School***, Coral Sands Hotel, ☎ (09) 774 36, Fax (09) 771 03.

Surfing: Surfboards can be hired from the shops and guesthouses on the "surfing spot" section of the beach, between Narigama and Hikkaduwa.

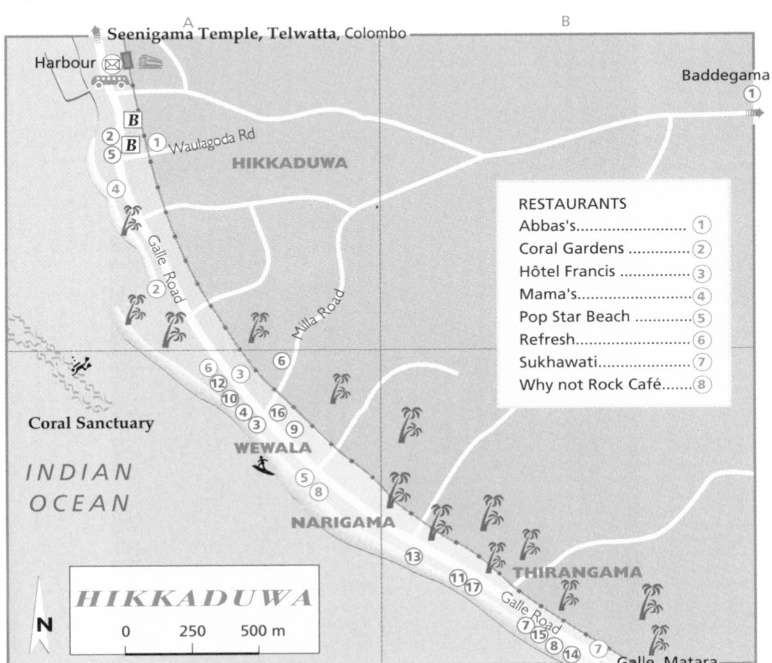

HOTELS

Bird Lake Lodge	1	Elephant Garden Beach Resort	7	Paradiso	12
Blue Corals	2	Golden Beach	8	Ranmal	13
Blue Note	3	Miga Villa Tourist Garden	9	Sansibar Garden	14
Blue Ocean Villa	4	Nippon Villa	10	Suit Lanka	15
Coral Sands	5	Ocean View	11	The Tandem	16
El Dorado Tourist	6			Thiranagama Beach	17

R Holzbachova-P Bénet

The hanging gardens of Sigiriya

THE ANCIENT KINGDOMS

Delineated by two rivers – the Mahaweli which flows into the sea near Trincomalee and the Deduru Oya which flows towards Chilaw, the Rajarata ("Country of the Kings") forms a triangle containing three great capitals: ancient Anuradhapura, medieval Polonnaruwa and Kandy, the refuge of royal power in modern times.

A feature of the great north-central plain are the unusual, smooth outcrops of granite left by some geological cataclysm. These monoliths lie dotted here and there in the green ocean of the jungle or on the chessboard of rice-fields: eroded by the rain, they look like chess pieces abandoned during a game between giants. Thick vegetation grows around their bases concealing the caverns where anchorites used to come to meditate, far away from prying eyes. As winter comes to an end, the crevices collect rainwater, dotted, like Impressionist paintings, with lotus flowers and water lilies but the water eventually evaporates with the torrid months of the dry season. Was it these wild, forbidding rocks, arranged like gigantic milestones, which attracted the kings of Ceylon? They must have done, because as soon as Buddhism was introduced to the island, they started to build mountains of bricks here as high as the pyramids of Giza by way of homage. They were also used as reliquaries. Today, Rajarata is a fascinating rendezvous with history, the extraordinary landscape being just one of its attractions.

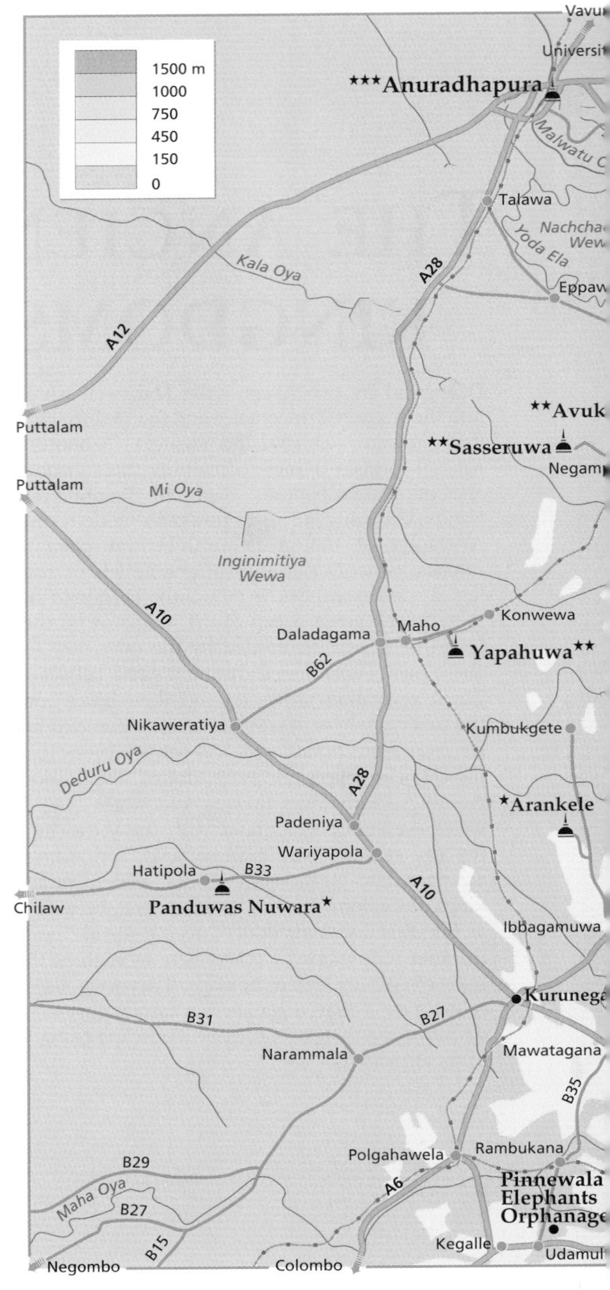
1500 m
1000
750
450
150
0
Anuradhapura
Malwatu
Talawa
Nachcha
Yoda Ela
Eppaw
Kala Oya
A28
A12
Puttalam
Avuk
Sasseruwa
Negam
Puttalam
Mi Oya
Inginimitiya
Wewa
A10
Konwewa
Maho
Daladagama
Yapahuwa
B62
Nikaweratiya
Kumbukgete
Deduru Oya
A28
Arankele
Padeniya
Wariyapola
Hatipola
B33
Chilaw
Panduwas Nuwara
A10
Ibbagamuwa
Kurunega
B31
B27
Narammala
Mawatagana
B35
B29
Polgahawela
Rambukana
Maha Oya
A6
Pinnewala
Elephants
Orphanage
B27
B15
Kegalle
Negombo
Colombo
Udamul

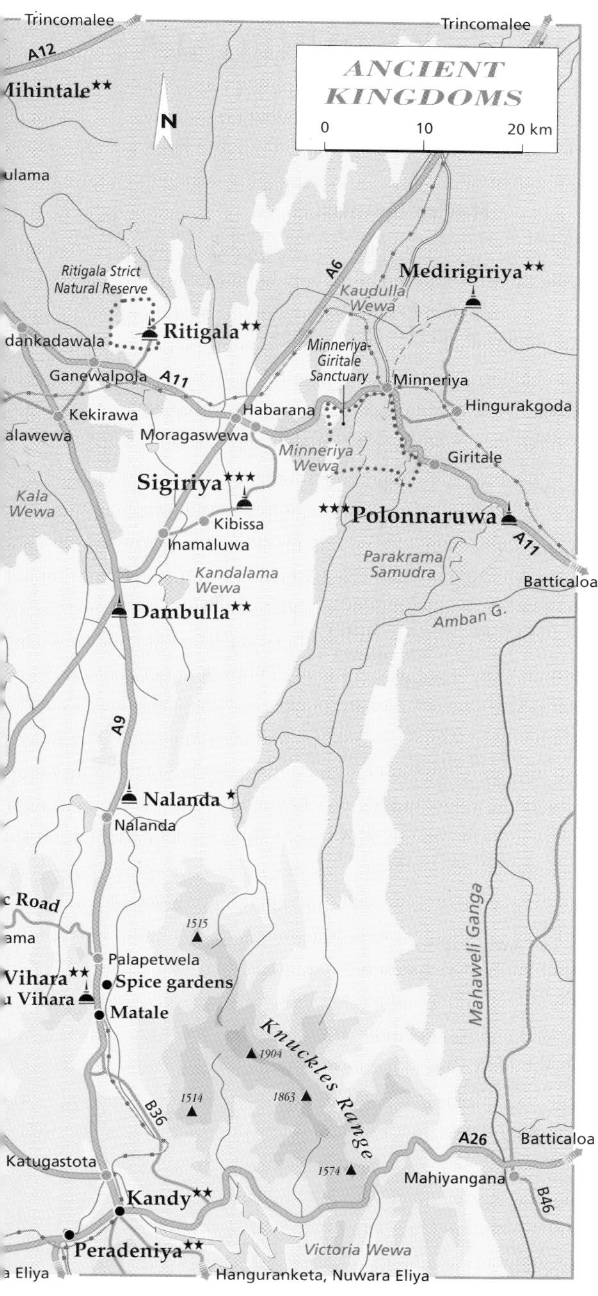

ANCIENT KINGDOMS
0
10
20 km
N
Trincomalee
Trincomalee
A12
Mihintale★★
Ritigala Strict Natural Reserve
Ritigala★★
Ganewalpola
A11
Kekirawa
Habarana
Moragaswewa
A6
Medirigiriya★★
Kaudulla Wewa
Minneriya-Giritale Sanctuary
Minneriya
Hingurakgoda
Minneriya Wewa
Giritale
Sigiriya★★★
Kala Wewa
Kibissa
Inamaluwa
★★★Polonnaruwa
A11
Parakrama Samudra
Batticaloa
Kandalama Wewa
Dambulla★★
Amban G.
A9
Nalanda★
Nalanda
1515
Palapetwela
Spice gardens
Matale
Knuckles Range
1904
1863
1514
B36
1574
Mahaweli Ganga
A26
Batticaloa
Katugastota
Mahiyangana
B46
Kandy★★
Peradeniya★★
Victoria Wewa
Hanguranketa, Nuwara Eliya

AROUND KURUNEGALA

THE ITINERANT CAPITALS

207km circuit from Kurunegala to Anuradhapura – 1 day
116km circuit from Kurunegala to Dambulla – half a day
Map p 162-163

Not to be missed

All the stops on these itineraries are worth a detour: if you are hesitating about which route to take, you could visit the sites of the Cultural Triangle by one route and come back by another.

And remember...

A vehicle is vital for visiting these sites.

At the junction of the roads leading inland from the coast (from Colombo and Puttalam) and the roads from the Cultural Triangle (from Kandy, Dambulla, Anuradhapura), Kurunegala is a good starting point for visiting some of the country's most famous sites via a variety of scenic routes. With very little tourism and deep in the countryside, these temples, citadels and ancient capitals are just waiting to be visited.

A nomadic power

The fall of Polonnaruwa in 1235 marked the beginning of a period of political instability which was to last until the foundation of the Kingdom of Kandy at the end of the 16C. This period of Ceylon's history is a long chapter of short-lived capitals: **Dambadeniya** (1236-72), **Yapahuwa** (1272-84), **Polonnaruwa** (1284-93), **Kurunegala** (1293-1341), **Gampola** (1341-1408), **Rayigama** (1408-15), and **Kotte** (1415-1597). Their names remain, but of the cities there is no longer any trace. Their existence, from the late 13C, was the result of a decisive turn in the history of the island: the desertion of the north-central plain and the abandoning of its ingenious irrigation system. It was at this time that the population moved gradually towards the more humid western part of the island, near the trading-posts where Muslim sailors had developed trade (at Dambadeniya, Kurunegala and Kotte), or withdrew to the shelter of the mountains in the centre of the island (Gampola, then Kandy). This exodus was accompanied by a rift between the Sinhalese and Tamil communities, the latter withdrawing to the **Jaffna** peninsula in the far north of the island, where it established an independent Tamil kingdom from the 14C to the 16C.

Clock-towers in Sri Lanka

There is not a town in Sri Lanka that does not have a clock-tower standing at its main crossroads. The one at Kurunegala dates back to the colonial period: built in grey stone in an austere Tudor style, it doubles as a war memorial to the soldiers who died on European battlefields in the 1914-18 war. But most of these clock-towers are not a British legacy. It was Prime Minister J R Jayawardene who was responsible for erecting them in many towns on the island. As you travel around, check how many of them are actually showing the right time; very few are and this has no effect whatsoever on the punctuality of the buses, despite the fact that the bus station is often nearby. On the other hand they provide the perfect place for putting out flags during political campaigns!

■ **Kurunegala** – Situated 93km from Colombo, but only 42km from the international airport, Kurunegala is also good for finding your feet on the island. Since nothing remains of the time when it was a royal capital there are, however, few points of interest. To the north of this decidedly modern, business-like town, the large reservoir surrounded by rocks of curious shapes is a pleasant place to stop.

On the road to Anuradhapura

The roads leading to the ancient capital pass through countryside that has changed little over the centuries. You may encounter a convoy of bullock-carts transporting fodder. You will certainly see some rare examples of adobe houses buried under magnificent thatched roofs, a traditional form of architecture that has been largely swept away by the increasing use of concrete.

Leave Kurunegala on the Anuradhapura road. At Wariyapola, turn left towards Chilaw. On entering the town of Hatipola, turn left at the "Ministry of Housing and Construction" sign: the site extends for 2km and covers an area of 160ha to the south of the road. A guide may be useful for locating the various monuments. Apply at the museum, situated 2km further on down the Chilaw road, opposite the college.

▪ **Panduwas Nuwara*** – With its moat, palace, monasteries and even a small reservoir which is now dry, this ancient city is a miniature Polonnaruwa which will particularly interest those with a passion for ruins. In a countryside setting, the site is still being excavated, adding to its charm. The city was begun in the early 12C, during the wars of succession which ravaged the island for more than 40 years upon the death of Vijaya Bahu. One of the pretenders, **Parakrama the Great,** made Dakkhinadesa ("Country of the South") his fief, and Panduwas Nuwara his capital. In effect it served as a testing ground for the great masterpiece of building that Parakrama Bahu was to undertake at Polonnaruwa.

Having passed the ruins of a brick **dagoba**, you emerge in the moat of an **enclosure wall** faced with bricks. Behind it lies the **royal palace complex**. It consists of a succession of ascending terraces, with facilities such as a large dining room and a vast latrine complex. On the right hand side, the small hypostyle building was used for the sermons of the Buddhist congregation. On the left, twin **pools*** with half-moon paving belonged to the ancient harem. At the entrance to the highest terrace, which served as an audience hall, Nissamka Malla, the prolific interpreter of the works of Parakramabahu, left an inscription commemorating his visit during a dance performance.

To the south, two **monasteries*** adjoined the enclosure wall of the palace. There are still some ruined *dagobas*, some sculpted stair treads showing a *hamsa* procession, some *poyage* and some baths, with pools and latrines.

An **adobe house** stands nearby. It is still inhabited by a family of potters who make traditional water jars. First they are put onto the potter's wheel and formed into something resembling a big moneybox with thick sides. It is left to dry, then filled with rags and given its final shape by the use of a bat. The house itself is a testimonial to a type of architecture that is gradually being replaced by brick, white-painted buildings roofed with tiles.

Continuing further south, you will come to a functioning **monastery**. In 1977, an elegant structure in the Kandyan style was added to the pavilion within its walls. It was once thought that it had been one of the "strongboxes" for the relic of the Tooth which travelled all over the island when its safety was threatened, but there is nothing to confirm this theory. At the edge of the temple is an empty **pool**, the stone wall of which is shaded by Banyan trees.

Make time to visit the museum when you have explored the site. The excavations, which have been going on since 1998, have unearthed a few interesting artefacts, such as the ends of tiles moulded in the shape of animals, small bronze votive objects, utensils from the royal kitchens or pieces of stucco decoration from the palace.

Return to the Anuradhapura road. Fifty-seven km north of Kurunegala, at the Daladagama junction, turn right and continue through Maho. Six kilometres further on, turn right again and cross the railway line: the site of Yapahuwa is 3km further on. The landscape is extraordinary, scattered with granite outcrops sprouting out of lush green vegetation.

▪ **Yapahuwa**** – Perched on a hill that is difficult to negotiate, the fortress of Yapahuwa *(entry charge)* is a relic from the troubled times of the late 13C. The complex is protected by two concentric walls which are joined at the base of the rock. Today flocks of animals graze among the scattered ruins, one of which is a strange little **temple**. According to tradition (rather than archeological fact), this was one of the "strongbox" temples built to safeguard the sacred Tooth relic in the capital. Despite its impressive position, Yapahuwa fell into the hands of a Pandya king from Southern India, who stole the relic and sent it to his capital at Madurai. Parakramabahu III succeeded in negotiating its return in about 1287.

Below the rock, a small **museum*** *(8am-5.45pm, closed Thursday)* has some exhibits on display. There is a collection of fragments of ceramics from China, a country with which Ceylon enjoyed diplomatic relations to the extent that a mission from Kublai Khan was received at Yapahuwa in 1282. Some fine **relief sculptures in granite** are of Hindu rather than Buddhist inspiration: the god Vishnu holds a withered lotus flower in one of his four hands, and wears a sarong knotted in spirals around his loins. The goddess Kali is depicted with her hair standing on end.

Behind the museum, a small **sanctuary** hidden in a mass of tumbled rock was decorated with frescoes in about 1720, during the Kandyan period. Having been badly damaged by the smoke from oil lamps, only ghostly silhouettes of kings, praying gods and processions are visible.

The path to the bottom of the staircase which climbs steeply up towards the second wall, passes through a functioning monastery. At the top of the steps there is a magnificently carved **cruciform gateway***** which dominates the plain below. Two stone **lions** guard the gateway, the base of which is decorated with a relief depicting dancers and tambourine players. The **view** which stretches away to far-off hills poking through the sea of palm-trees, is just as spectacular as the view from the rock fortresses of Dambulla or Sigiriya. A path winds up towards the natural platform of the summit which stands at 300m.

Return to the junction at Daladagama, and turn right towards Anuradhapura.

The lion staircase at Yapahuwa

From Kurunegala to Dambulla★★

The direct route from Kurunegala to Dambulla is very pleasant. The road surface is excellent, the route is shaded by tall trees and lined by stalls selling fresh fruit. However, one only has to turn off the road to be immersed once more in open countryside. At the end of a road with rice-fields on either side, where women work side by side dressed in their traditional *chitha*, the hermitage of Arankele is tucked into the edge of a forest. The Silver Temple of Ridigama stands on a mountainous escarpment, with fine views of the blue outline of the Knuckles Range.

Leave Kurunegala on the Dambulla road. After Ibbagamuwa (12km), turn left towards Madagalla. 9km further on, a sign on the left points the way to Arankele (3km).

▪ **Arankele★** – Founded in the 6C by an austere sect of monks from the forest, the **monastery** of Arankele is still a place of retreat today. It is the seat of one of the 162 monasteries of the **Aranya Senasana** congregation, which numbers only about 500 monks, known as the **vanavasin**. Unlike most monasteries on the island, its spiritual activity is more geared to meditation than the study of canonical texts. Its activities start at 5am and end at 10pm, when the monks go to bed. Their day is punctuated by the sound of a wooden bell which announces mealtimes, alms, sermons, meditation sessions, sweeping the courtyard and reading. The *vanavasin* do not visit the town unless they require medical treatment or are needed at the bedside of an ailing relative.

Behind the modern monastery, a perfectly straight, stone-paved meditation walk sets off into the nearby forest, where pious country folk gather for picnics. It leads to a clearing containing the ruins of the old hermitage, imposing structures with **terraces for meditation★** and ablutions pools, similar to the hermitages at Ritigala *(see p 187)*. A perpendicular path climbs up to the top of a hill, where there is a marvellous view over the forest and the surrounding rice-fields.

Return to the Dambulla road. 3km further on, fork right, then right again after 5km (there is no sign). Having crossed a river, you enter Ridigama. Turn left on the other side of the village, cross the riverbed (impossible in heavy rain): the monastery is 2km further on.

▪ **Ridi Vihara★★** (the Silver Temple) was founded by King Dutugemunu above a silver-ore deposit. The original site is hidden behind a small monastery *(ask one of the five monks for the key)*. The temple is approached via a rocky balcony, where there is a small 11C Hindu temple, the **Varakha Valandu Vihara★★**, which was converted into a Buddhist sanctuary during the Kandyan period. The cella is carved out of a granite block, and has a hypostyle porch in pure Dravidian style.

Half carved out of the rock and half built of stone, **Ridi Vihara★★** is preceded by a long, stark whitewashed hall, and by a courtyard surrounded by two superimposed sanctuaries. In the vestibule of the lower one, a carved ivory plaque has miraculously escaped vandalism, although, in 1998, others like it were spirited away. The bodies of five graceful women are linked together to form a medallion. Two heavy teak doors open onto the cave containing figures of Buddha, sculpted in the Anuradhapura period, under a rocky ceiling painted with lotus flowers. Along the left-hand wall, another Buddha figure reclines on the strangest of platforms. It is decorated with some fine 17C **Delft tiles** depicting stories from Dutch folklore and scenes from the life of Christ.

The upper temple was built during the Kandyan period. A door framed in stone opens onto the cella where the Buddha meditates under very elaborately decorated arcading. The frescoes on the walls painted in panels are particularly fine, together with the ones of the throne of the statue. Particularly striking is the composite intertwined figure of an elephant and a bull. A chest is lacquered with a golden-yellow foliage motif featuring female creatures. Female figures also decorate a small sanctuary nearby. Its façade has a fresco showing nine maidens forming the silhouette of an elephant. On the door, female torsos emerge from volutes of plants. The decoration of the interior, executed in the 18C, is still incomplete.

Retrace your steps. After Ridigama, take the small road on the right which rejoins the Kandy-Dambulla road at Palapetwela (25km). It climbs in a series of hairpin bends uphill towards a cocoa plantation, providing dramatic views over the terraces of rice-fields. At Palapetwela, you may choose whether to go to Kandy via Alu Vihara (see p 211), or to Dambulla via the Nalanda Temple (see p 210).

Making the most of Kurunegala

Coming and going

By train – The ***railway station*** lies to the south of the town, on the road to Kandy. It is situated on the Colombo-Anuradhapura line, but most of the trains that stop here are local trains. This impractical mode of transport is best avoided.

By bus – The ***bus station*** is near the clock tower, on the Colombo-Dambulla road. There are regular buses for certain destinations in the Cultural Triangle: Dambulla (90min), Anuradhapura (3hr), Kandy (1hr), and Negombo (2hr).

By car – This is the only practical way of following these itineraries. Negotiate car-hire at ***Diva Dahara*** (see below) or ask at your guesthouse if you are coming from Dambulla or Anuradhapura. Roughly, you should be able to negotiate each itinerary for approximately 1 500Rs per vehicle.

Where to stay / Eating out

Under US$10

Madonna Inn, 44 North Lake Rd, 1.5km from the bus terminus, ☎ (037) 232 76 – 5rm. A large house near the lake has rather old, well-appointed rooms kept cool by the shutters. An atmosphere reminiscent of a "colonial siesta in the tropics". Good quality-price ratio.

From US$15 to US$30

Diva Dahara, 7 North Lake Rd, 2km from the bus terminus, ☎(037) 234 52 – 2rm. TV CC All modern comforts at a price which defies competition. The restaurant is excellent and meals can be taken on a terrace overlooking the lake. 20 more rooms are planned. The hotel can send someone to meet you at the international airport.

Kandyanne Reaf Hotel, 344-350 Kandy Rd, 1km from the clock tower, just outside the town on the road to Kandy, ☎ (037) 242 18, Fax (037) 245 41, athgirir@eureka.lk – 52 rm. TV CC The hotel is so well designed and furnished that it is easy to forget the nearby road and enjoy its enormous rooms. However it is a pity that its large bay windows overlook the reception area.

Anuradhapura★★★

North-Central Province – Pop 99 000 – Alt 453m
101km from Polonnaruwa, 138km from Kandy and 206km from Colombo

Not to be missed
Exploring the Abhayagiriya complex on foot or by bike.
The hermitage forest of Ritigala.
Sampling the delicate flesh of the fish of Nuwara wewa.

And remember...
Hire a bike to explore the archeological park.
Take a picnic if spending all day on site, because there are only biscuits and lemonade for sale.
After 10am be careful not to burn the soles of your feet on the red-hot granite.

Set between the walls of its two huge *wewa* (tanks) of precious water, Anuradhapura is the site of the longest sequence of Sinhalese history: 15 centuries of continuous occupation and dozens of monarchs.
Since 1980, UNESCO has been financing the clear up operation around its columns and pagodas which were engulfed by the jungle for nearly 1 000 years. Dressed in white and barefoot, the pilgrims visit the immaculate *dagobas* of the holy city. Their footsteps follow the map of holy places to be honoured by their offerings: they leave an armful of purple water lilies at the foot of the peristyle of Thuparama, some fragrant frangipani flowers on the area in front of the Ruvanveliseya, they light oil-lamps at the entrance to the temple of the bo tree, and tie flags at the enclosure of the Buddha in *samadhi*. Soldiers dressed in khaki and wearing boots guard the gate of the town, behind low earth walls where grass has long since taken over. The unstable north is not far away.

Chronicles and men

The history of the ancient city of Anuradhapura is very well documented, thanks to an abundance of literary sources and correspondence on archeological findings. Two great chronicles, the *Mahavamsa* and the *Cûlavamsa*, were compiled by monks at the beginning of the 6C AD. A wonderful mixture of historical facts, mythological themes, and Buddhist ideology, they provide a description of the whole succession of great builder-kings in the island's history.

The Sons of the Lion

A legend tells the story of the arrival on the island of the **Sinhala**, Indo-European colonists who called themselves the Sons of the Lion (*Sinhala*, the origin of the modern word Sinhalese), on the same day as the Buddha's death (in 483 BC). Their ruler, Vijaya, was recognised as the first king of the island and the capital was established at **Tambapanni** ("Leaf of Copper"), which the Greeks called **Taprobane**.
In the late 5C BC, one of Vijaya's successors transferred the capital to Anuradhapura, which was to remain the seat of royalty for more than a millennium. The history of the "city of Anuradha" was an eventful one, with princes obsessed with murdering their fathers or their siblings, palace quarrels, poisoner-queens, influential monks and the permanent threat from the kingdoms of Southern India. The permanence of the site was also due to economic factors.

In the shade of the bo tree

S. Held

The capital was not far from the main ports of the island, which had been established in the northeast and northwest in Antiquity, but, more particularly, it was in the centre of the rice-producing area in the heart of the island, irrigated thanks to an ambitious hydraulic programme controlled by the State. It has been established that, during the first centuries AD, the produce from this irrigated agricultural land could feed a city of 123 000 inhabitants. Royal inscriptions confirm the very rational organisation of the distribution of water. A complex bureaucracy was responsible for its maintenance. Taxes were levied on the use of reservoirs, ensuring the funds for their maintenance, but also the pay of the workers employed on royal building projects. Anuradhapura was abandoned temporarily on several occasions. It was then abandoned indefinitely after it was sacked and burned by **Chola** Tamils in 993. The power of the Sinhalese kings was re-established at Polonnaruwa.

The conversion of a hunter

In the 3C BC, **Devanampiya Tissa**, the sixteenth king mentioned in the chronicles, was on the best of terms with **Asoka**, founder of a Buddhist empire in India and the instigator of the first missions of preachers to the furthest parts of his land. The mission that landed on the island one warm May evening in 250BC was led by the emperor's son, **Thera Mahinda**. The chronicles prefer to tell that Mahinda and his four companions arrived through the air and landed on Mount Missaka (now Mihintale), where Devanampiya Tissa was setting off on a hunting expedition. He gave the mission a warm welcome and, having heard his first sermon, he and his followers embraced the Buddhist doctrine.

For seven days, Mahinda preached at Anuradhapura, before an increasingly large crowd. The king gave the Buddhist community a park to the south of his palace. This is the origin of the founding of the first monastery in Ceylon. The historical link between the Sinhalese kings and the monastic community has never been broken throughout the island's history. The royal families ensured the protection of the monks who, as guarantors of a doctrine that had been adopted on a national scale, sanctioned any drift towards absolute power.

Three monasteries for one town

The **Mahavihara** and its sister monastery in the Mihintale hills reigned for a long time over the monastic life of the island. In 89 BC, this hegemony wavered with the foundation of a new monastery, **Abhayagiriya**. The rivalry between the two establishments was such that it was ended by setting down Buddhist law, hitherto transmitted orally, in writing *(see Alu Vihara p 211)*. During the reign of Mahasena (274-301 AD), Abhayagiriya triumphed: the king dissolved Mahavihara and built a third monastery, **Jetavanarama**, with the rubble. The old monastic establishment was finally taken over by Mahasena's successor, but the rift between Mahavihara and Abhayagiriya lasted more than 1 000 years, until Parakrama Bahu reconciled them in the 13C.

The giants of Anuradhapura

The huge dimensions of the "dagobas" of the first Anuradhapura period confirm the strong hold that Buddhism had at that time on the Sinhalese sovereigns. The Mahathûpa of Duttu Gemunu (167-137 BC), known to tradition as the Ruvanveliseya (Ratnamali chaitya), was 54m high. The Abhayagiriya "dagoba", founded by Vattagamani in the 1C BC, is a mountain of bricks 70m high with a circumference at the base of 93m. The Jetavana "dagoba", the largest of them all, was equally tall, but reached a height of 160m when it was rebuilt by Mahasena at the end of the 3C.

Receiving relics

Still under royal patronage, the first religious monuments to the new doctrine were erected. These were not temples or images, but gigantic reliquaries, called *dagobas*, which were destined to receive the relics of the body of the Buddha or of his most important disciples, notably Mahinda. The **Thuparama** was the first of them. With the passing of the centuries, Ceylon became the main depository for these holy relics, the arrival of which was consecrated by the building of a new *dagoba*. Today it is impossible to know what these buildings originally looked like, since they were all maintained and enlarged by the monarchs of the island, up to the Kandyan period.

The art of living in a community

In the 4C, Abhayagiriya sheltered a Chinese monk called Faxian who had stopped in Ceylon on a journey which had the aim of studying Buddhist doctrine, from China to the valley of the Ganges, and from the Bay of Bengal to Indonesia. In his journal, *Memoir of the Buddhist kingdoms*, he gives a detailed account of his stay in Anuradhapura. The capital and the surrounding area housed 10 000 monks (5 000 at Abhayagiriya, 3 000 at Mahavihara and 2 000 at Mihintale). The subsistence of these important communities, the rules of which forbade any secular activity, was provided by **farming villages** near the *wewa*, which were attached to them by royal endowment. Since their food and lodging were provided, the monks were able to devote themselves not only to the study of the teachings of Buddha, but also to philosophy, astronomy, mathematics, architecture and other subjects in vogue in the ancient world *(see also "The Island's Artistic Heritage" p 33)*.

Unesco at work

When the French traveller and novelist Pierre Loti visited Ceylon, in December 1899, Anuradhapura was no longer in a state of abandon. Growing interest in the archeology of the island had resulted in the founding of the **Archeological Survey of Ceylon** in 1891. Under the direction of H C P Bell, archeologists uncovered the past of the island at Anuradhapura and Polonnaruwa. This immense enterprise gradually extended to other sites and continued after Ceylon gained independence, winning recognition from international authorities on archeology. The importance of the work inspired the largest enterprise undertaken by UNESCO: the **"Cultural Triangle" project**, consisting of six sites situated in the three ancient valleys and the surrounding area. For fifteen years, from 1980 until 1995, it involved local and foreign expertise, and was financed by international aid. The colossi of Anuradhapura are without a doubt one of the greatest challenges: even today, the domes of the *dagobas* of Jetavana and Abhayagiriya are still being patiently restored.

Pierre Loti at Anuradhapura

"One casts one's eyes all around, as from the topmast of a ship one observes the monotonous circle of the sea, and nothing human is to be seen anywhere. Only trees, trees and more trees, the tops of which succeed each other, magnificent and equal; a swell of trees, which continues as far as the eye can see in far-off places unmarked by any milestones. (...) However, very strange, wooded hills, green like the forest, but with contours that are far too regular, in the form of pyramids or domes, emerge here and there, isolated above the uniform expanse of foliage. And there are the towers of ancient temples, the gigantic dagobas, built two hundred years before the birth of Christ. The forest has not been able to destroy them, but has enveloped them in its green shroud, gradually overwhelming them with its earth, its roots, its scrub, its creepers and its monkeys." (Pierre Loti).

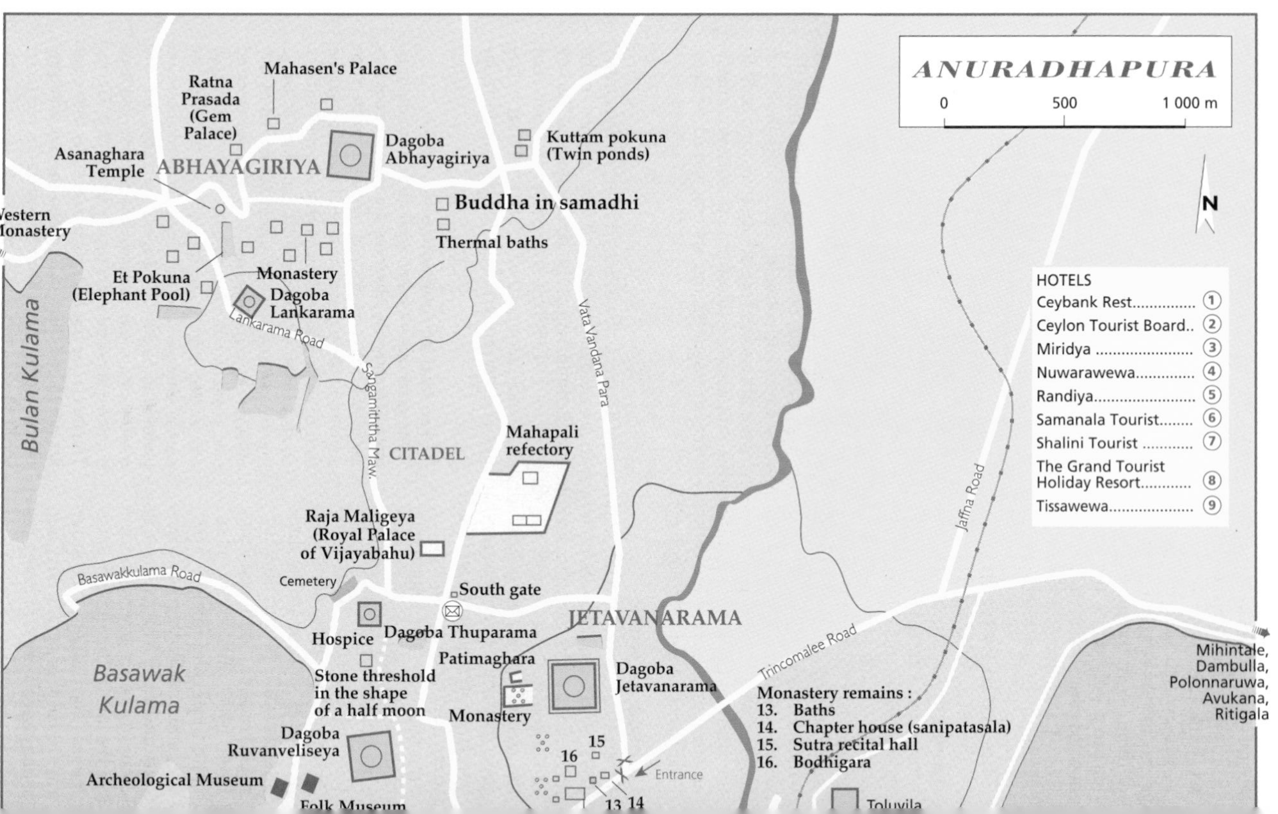
ANURADHAPURA
0
500
1 000 m
N
HOTELS
Ceybank Rest. ①
Ceylon Tourist Board ②
Miridya ③
Nuwarawewa ④
Randiya ⑤
Samanala Tourist ⑥
Shalini Tourist ⑦
The Grand Tourist Holiday Resort ⑧
Tissawewa ⑨
Mahasen's Palace
Ratna Prasada (Gem Palace)
Asanaghara Temple
ABHAYAGIRIYA
Dagoba Abhayagiriya
Kuttam pokuna (Twin ponds)
Buddha in samadhi
Thermal baths
Western Monastery
Et Pokuna (Elephant Pool)
Monastery
Dagoba Lankarama
Lankarama Road
Bulan Kulama
Sangamiththa Maw.
Vata Vandana Para
CITADEL
Mahapali refectory
Jaffna Road
Raja Maligeya (Royal Palace of Vijayabahu)
Basawakkulama Road
Cemetery
South gate
JETAVANARAMA
Hospice
Dagoba Thuparama
Patimaghara
Trincomalee Road
Basawak Kulama
Stone threshold in the shape of a half moon
Monastery
Dagoba Jetavanarama
Monastery remains :
13. Baths
14. Chapter house (sanipatasala)
15. Sutra recital hall
16. Bodhigara
Mihintale, Dambulla, Polonnaruwa, Avukana, Ritigala
Dagoba Ruvanveliseya
15
16
Entrance
Archeological Museum
Folk Museum
13
14
Toluvila

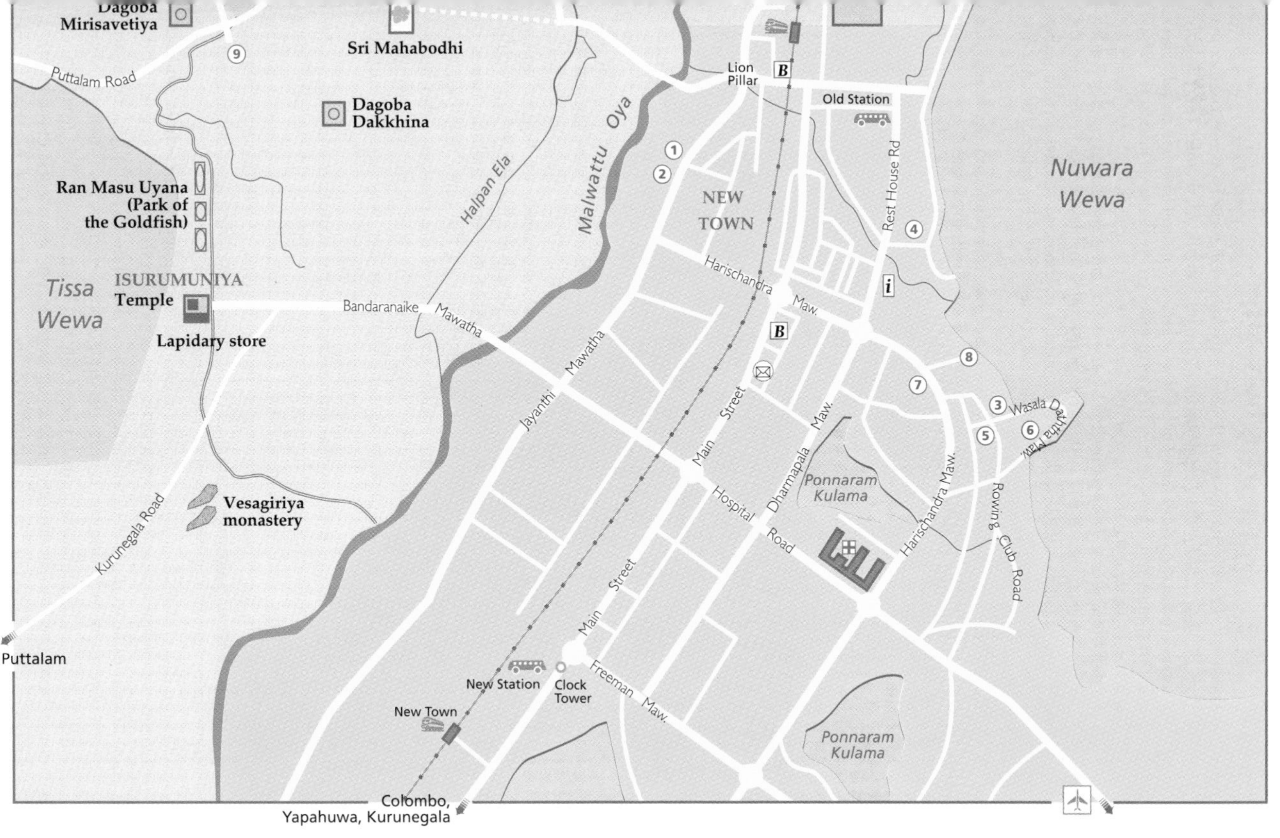
Dagoba Mirisavetiya
Sri Mahabodhi
Puttalam Road
Lion Pillar
Old Station
Dagoba Dakkhina
Malwattu Oya
Rest House Rd
Nuwara Wewa
Ran Masu Uyana (Park of the Goldfish)
Halpan Ela
NEW TOWN
Harischandra Maw.
Tissa Wewa
ISURUMUNIYA Temple
Lapidary store
Bandaranaike Mawatha
Jayanthi Mawatha
Main Street
Dharmapala Maw.
Wasala Daththa Maw.
Ponnaram Kulama
Hospital Road
Harischandra Maw.
Rowing Club Road
Vesagiriya monastery
Kurunegala Road
Puttalam
Main Street
New Station
Clock Tower
Freeman Maw.
New Town
Ponnaram Kulama
Colombo, Yapahuwa, Kurunegala

The holy city

The perimeter of the holy city has been the object of draconian security measures since the gunfight of 14 May 1985 in the Temple of the Tree, resulting in 45 victims. There is now only one access to the site (daily 7am-6pm, entry tickets or Cultural Triangle round ticket) and the fact that many roads have been closed means that a long detour is necessary. Allow at least a day for visiting the site, especially if you are travelling by bike. Entry to the site is included in the Cultural Triangle multiple-entry ticket, but a supplement is charged for visiting certain monuments. If you wish to return the following day, apply to the Cultural Triangle office situated on the first floor of the museum at Jetavanarama, which will stamp your ticket or round ticket, which can normally only be used once. The order of the description of the various sites takes traffic restrictions into account.

Start your visit at the Jetavanarama complex, situated just beyond the security barriers at the entrance to the site. Its remarkable museum is an excellent introduction.

Jetavanarama***

Every day, on lawns that would make a cricket pitch blanch with envy, battalions of women bend down to collect the cigarette butts and litter from around the foundations that have been excavated by the UNESCO programme since 1981. The last of the great monasteries to be built in the capital, Jetavanarama is a very complete example of classical monastic architecture. Culminating in a height of 120m, it is visible from miles around, and its gigantic **dagoba** is forever being cleared of weeds. It is the third-highest ancient monument in the world, after the two pyramids at Giza. It took 24 years and 10 million bricks to build this artificial hill in the 3C. Amongst other relics, it contains the alms bowl and belt of Buddha. The section to the north of the *dagoba* is currently being excavated.

The Museum of Jetavana** *(daily 8am-5pm. Allow 30min)* is housed in the old British town hall of Anuradhapura (1902), a white building in neo-Classical style topped with an inverted lotus flower. All the exhibits, which are splendidly displayed, come from the complex. **Sculptures and bas-reliefs** are housed in the left-hand wing. Two of the cases contain some small marble reliefs and sculptures in the round, strongly influenced by Indian art: they include heads of Buddha dating from the 5C, as well as *salabhanjika* ("the ones that break the branch of the *sala tree*"), from the Indian tradition of the nymphs who inhabited the tree with long leaves under which Buddha was born. A beautifully flowing marble bas-relief depicts Queen Maya on her way to the Lumbini gardens.

The section devoted to **ornamental and architectural sculptures** includes a jar of abundance *(punkalasa)* and figures guarding the effigy of the serpent king *(nagaraja)*. At the end of the room, two sandstone heads of bodhisattvas (the male on the left, the female on the right) frame the base of a Buddha meditating. The **fragments of paintings**, panels depicting *hamsa* evolving amid lotus flowers, come from one of the buttresses of the *dagoba* (4C-6C).

Beyond the entrance, a room is furnished with displays of **precious objects**. Dozens of crystal pearls, garnets, amethysts, jade from China and cornelian from Southern India were used to make jewellery or ornaments for clothes. Bone and ivory objects include domino combs decorated with engravings. There are some small items cut from natural bluish glass (silicate) from Ratnapura. Other objects come from the Roman Empire including intaglio cut from rock crystal with a Greek profile. The hair "implants" of Buddha, made of various materials, show the role played by inlay (buckles, eyes) for statues. Earrings in the form of bottle-caps have been sculpted into the spiral of a shell; a minuscule gold ornament (8mm) is in the shape of a jasmine flower.

The right-hand wing houses exhibits of **utilitarian pottery**. Bricks were the building material par excellence in the ancient cities of Ceylon, and capable of sustaining much greater weights than their present-day counterparts. They were laid without using mortar but were bound with a heavy clay.

Having been excavated since 1981, the remains of the **monastery** lie between the museum and the gigantic *dagoba*. As you leave the museum, on the left, there is a **bath** area with a pool, septic tank and latrines. Beyond them, the columns standing on the terrace denote the **chapter house**, where philosophical discussions were held, and the **hall for the recitation of Buddhist texts** (behind the pool), which can be recognised by its small central room.

Opposite, on the other side of the museum, there is a complex consisting of four terraces arranged around a vast central **esplanade**, a feature common to most of the Anuradhapura monasteries and the organisation of which doubtless represented the wisdom and the Four Noble Truths of Buddhism. Nearby, a large **well** with steps made it possible to go down to fetch drinking water. Continuing towards the *dagoba*, note the imposing **balustrade****, built of monoliths assembled with mortice and tenon joints, imitating wooden architecture, and based on the great Buddhist sites of India. It formed the **bodhighara**, the enclosure of the bo tree. In front of it stood two monumental statues of Buddha, of which only the feet remain.

Stele of a cobra-king (nagaraja)

B Brillion

When you reach the gigantic *dagoba*, on the left of the terrace there is a **monastic residence** of which the stairway remains. Its **ramps** are carved in the form of a *makara*, a mythical animal borrowed from the Indian bestiary. Finally, two monoliths 9m high framing a door indicate a **patimaghara** (temple of the image). The roof has disappeared, but the thickness of the walls suggests that it was vaulted. Behind it, the **three pools** built of brick were part of the area's drainage system. They made it possible to decant rainwater before taking it towards the channel running alongside the enclosure wall and were also used for irrigation.

Head back to the road that runs north of Jetavanarama, turn left towards the south gate, then right at the crossroads (see map).

The Citadel

Little remains of the administrative heart of the city. The **Raja Maligeya** (Royal Palace of Vijayabahu)* was the residence of the sovereigns of Polonnaruwa whenever they visited the holy city. It was built using material from earlier buildings. The flight of steps leading to the terrace is guarded by two dwarves from the retinue of Kubera (the protector of wealth), one wearing a conch on his head as a symbol of wealth, the other a lotus flower symbolising prosperity. A little further on, on the right, the ruins of a 6C *gedige* (temple), overgrown with vegetation, have been identified as one of the fortified temples, present on several sites on the island, in which the Tooth of Buddha was concealed. It was situated in the enclosure wall of the little **Mahapali monastery and refectory** of which a well survives, together with the refectory and a huge stone rice-trough.

Continue in the same direction. Abhayagiriya is situated on the far north of the site.

Abhayagiriya***

It is worth devoting two hours to visiting this huge monastery, the rival of Mahavihara. It comprises some of the most famous ruins in Anuradhapura and its monastic residence, scattered in undergrowth to the south of the road, is full of surprises and tiny masterpieces of sculpture.

Dug out of the granite bedrock, the **Kuttam pokuna** (Twin ponds)** were built by two sovereigns in the 4C and 6C. In 1985, heavy rain filled the two pools, which are 43m long, 23m wide and 6m deep, to the brim. On one side, an inspection hole made it possible to control the level of the water, which first filled the upper rim of the pools, then ran away through a natural filter system.

The Buddha in samadhi*** *(leave your shoes on the brick ledge around the base of the statue)* is a classic example of early Sinhalese Buddhist statuary (4C). It was originally one of a group of four statues that would have been seated around a Bo tree (the base of one of them is visible opposite). The whole group was protected by a dome supported by columns. The surviving statue is particularly revered and pilgrims hang votive banners on the grilles which surround it. In the 1950s, Pandit Nehru came to meditate at the foot of this statue with its serene, peaceful face.
50m further south, a small **healing bath** complex has recently been excavated. On the edge of the pool, marks show where the piles of plants used in the various essences were stacked.

The **dagoba****, which is still being restored, was enlarged during the reign of **Gaja Bahu I** (112-134) so that it had a diameter and a height of 100m. On each side of the staircase leading to the terrace, statues of the dwarves **Shankha** (the Conch) and **Padma** (the Lotus flower) are invoked by the owners of precious-stone mines in the area of Ratnapura. The *dagoba* of Abhayagiriya is the first example of the use of *vahalkada*. These masonry blocks, which lie at the four cardinal points, fulfilled the dual function of buttresses to balance the mass of bricks comprising the dagoba and altars for offerings. Their high- and bas-reliefs in gneiss are some of the earliest examples of Sinhalese sculpture.

To the north of the road, the **Mahasen's Palace**, nicknamed the "Queen's Pavilion", is in fact a 7C temple, of which only the five rectangular terraces survive. Their bases were built with enormous granite monoliths, which were undoubtedly manoeuvred into place using lifting machines with treadwheels. The sculpted **moonstone threshold?** in front of the central terrace is the most famous in Anuradhapura.

The Ratna Prasada (Gem Palace)★★ is an 8C *poyage*, the floors of which (no longer extant) were supported by monolithic columns sunk up to a third of their height below ground level. Its staircase is guarded by one of the finest *nagaraja* in Anuradhapura. The cobra-king is framed by an arch depicting couples, symbols of the senses, ending in mouths of *makara* (mythical beasts) swallowing elephants, symbols of power.

The secret of moonstones

Although their function seems to have been to purify the feet before entering a sacred or royal place, there are infinite interpretations of the symbols sculpted on the thresholds with semi-circular steps. Seeming to emerge from under the steps, they show the visible half of a universe composed of figures in concentric circles. Tongues of fire form the first circle, followed by four friezes of walking animals (elephants, horses and bulls), then a garland of flowers and, finally, "hamsas" (bar-headed geese) carrying a bouquet of three flowers in their beaks. A withered lotus flower occupies the centre. Is the circle of flames a symbol of the fire of desire which consumes us during our lives or does it represent the cosmic, eternal fire? Are the four friezes of animals the four stages of life, the four cardinal points or the mounts of the gods of India?

To the south of the *dagoba* lie the **monastic residences**. Innumerable terraces, hypostyle rooms, flights of steps, baths and even a glazed tile factory are scattered in the undergrowth. The **refectory**★, with its rice-offerings trough dug out of a 15m-long monolith, gives an idea of the size of the community. A nearby pool ensured the water supply.

To the west, the **Ath pokuna**★★ (Elephant Pool) is a huge bath dug out of the bedrock, 150m long and 50m wide. The **Asanaghara** temple was hidden under a road built at the time of the British colony. Dating from the 3C BC, it has a sculpted paving stone depicting a *siri pada* and a sandstone statue of Buddha. Nearby stands a small temple, the ceiling slabs of which, supported by pilasters, are sculpted to imitate wooden coffers.

The Lankarama dagoba marks the southern boundary of the Abhayagiriya complex. Built by King **Walagamba** in 89 BC, it was restored in 1872. The columns encircling it show that it was a *vatadage*.

Before proceeding with your visit of the holy complex, you could go and visit the western monasteries, situated 2km from the Abhayagiriya dagoba. Take the road that follows the northern edge of the Bulan kulama. This is a lovely excursion at sunset, when the silhouettes of the Ruvanveliseya and Mirisavetiya "dagobas" rise up in the distance.

The western monasteries

There are neither *dagobas* nor temples in this complex, which stretched to the edge of the city, because these monasteries were built according to the rules of the most austere of the Buddhist congregations, the **Pansukulika**, the monks "in the tattered robe" or monks of the forest. In the early 8C, this sect grew up in reaction to the sumptuous way of life of the great royal monasteries. Their wish to return to the most ancient prescriptions was plain to see from their clothes, made from rags or shreds of clothing collected from the dust. Cultivating extreme deprivation, they preferred retreat and isolation in the jungle to the tumult of the cities.

Contempt for gold

The sumptuousness of the urinals in the baths of the three austere forest monasteries is only apparently a paradox. When the sculptured decoration is figurative, it depicts symbols of wealth, such as a profusion of gems or the residence of Kubera, the guardian of treasure. This shows the contempt with which the Pansukulika, who practised extreme privation, held material possessions, on which they could urinate as often as they liked, thanks to this device combining as it did both symbolism and functionality.

The architecture of their monasteries placed the emphasis on meditation, to the detriment of the cult. The focus of the complex is a pair of terraces (*padhanaghara*), built on an imposing masonry substructure, in the centre of a pool which, at Anuradhapura, was partially dug out of the bedrock. Built on an east-west axis, they are connected by a stone bridge. To the east of this structure are some of the remains of the monks' cells, or *kutis*. The baths lay to the west. They include a sumptuously decorated urinal.

Retrace your steps and rejoin Lankarama Rd which leads to the monuments of Mahavihara.

Mahavihara**

Allow 2hr for this part of the site which can be visited entirely on foot. Smoking is forbidden within the holy precinct and shoulders and knees should be kept covered. You will inevitably be pestered by people selling postcards or flowers (at much higher prices than those charged to pilgrims) as well as by kids collecting "school pens".

Today it is difficult to understand the plan of the "Great Monastery" or "Great Buddhist Temple", but the buildings that were attached to it are regarded by Buddhist pilgrims as the most sacred part of Anuradhapura. You cannot help but notice the pilgrims, hearing them in prayer, and learning something about their rites.

Founded in 276 BC to house a clavicle of Buddha, the **Thuparama dagoba**** is the oldest reliquary monument in Anuradhapura. In the 1C AD, King Wasaba protected it with a dome supported by granite columns arranged in concentric circles. This is the prototype of a Buddhist monument that is only found in Ceylon: the **thupaghara**, the "stupa house", called **vatadage** in Sinhalese. All that is left today are the rows of columns around the *dagoba*. Beside the staircase leading to the square, guarded by two cobra-kings, a pool enables the many pilgrims to wash the flowers they have brought as offerings.

Proceed south, along a path cutting across an area that has been partially cleared, towards the gigantic silhouette of the Ruvanveliseya.

In the middle of the ruins, which have been cleared of vegetation, there is a modern grille. It protects a **moonstone threshold?**, sculpted with a honeysuckle-tendril motif. The risers of the steps depict peaceful metaphors: a panther with a gazelle, a mongoose with a cobra, below bouquets of stylised trees.

The jasmine of Mahinda

The city of Anuradhapura includes eight large sites ("ata masthana") dear to the hearts of Sinhalese pilgrims: the Bo tree, the palace of Airain and the six "dagobas" – Ruvanveliseya, Mirisavetiya, Thuparama, Lankarama, Abhayagiriya and Jetavana. According to legend, they were erected in places set down by Thera Mahinda. The holy man threw a jasmine flower offered by King Devanampiya Tissa up into the air. Its petals fluttered to the ground defining the layout of the future sites of eight great monuments in the holy city. According to tradition when Buddha made three journeys to the island, he is supposed to have stopped to meditate in these holy places.

You will come to a road (closed to traffic) where stalls sell cool drinks, biscuits and camera film. After passing the modern monastic university, you reach the point of access to the Ruvanveliseya "dagoba". Leave your shoes with the custodian, giving a small tip. Bags are checked before entering the square.

Nowadays, this 100m-high stupa is called the **Ruvanveliseya****. It was the masterpiece of Dutugemunu, who began building it in 161 BC, but died before it was completed. It is the most revered of the *dagobas* in the holy city: every four years its dome is whitewashed and pilgrims meditate in silence on its square, where several **oratories** commemorate the sovereigns who built and later embellished the building.

To the right of the steps providing access, the glass-covered statue is supposed to represent Dutugemunu. A modern statue of his mother, Queen Vihara Maha Devi *(see Around Tissamaharama p 306)* has been erected opposite it. If you continue in the clockwise direction, you will come across a chapel dedicated to the four predecessors of the historical Buddha, to Buddha himself, and to the future Buddha, Maitreya, who wears a tiara and holds a lotus flower in his hand. These ancient statues were found in pieces and were reconstructed. The paving of the square is punctuated with *padapittika*, slabs decorated with a pair of footprints marking the places for practising meditation. On the northeast side, a pool contains the whitewash which is applied every four years, by painters abseiling down the length of the dome.

A paved road connects the Ruvanveliseya *dagoba* to the Sri Mahabodhi temple. On each side of it stand the ruins of the buildings associated with the Mahavihara, including the **Loha Pasada** (Brazen Palace). According to chronicles, King Devanampiya Tissa built a residence of nine storeys, each with 100 rooms, the roof of which was covered with bronze tiles. Sadly it was destroyed by fire. Subsequent reconstructions were less ambitious: in the 12C, when the Brazen Palace was taken over by Parakramabahu, it only had five floors. The Tamil invasions and incursions by Malaysian pirates in the 13C gradually diminished its splendour and only a few of the original 1 600 columns survive. The wooden pavilion was a gift from the Indian government.

A focal point of Buddhist worship, the **Sri Mahabodhi*** (Temple of the Great Enlightenment) built around the *Bodhi* tree, was maintained and rebuilt over years. *(The tree enclosure is closed daily from 11am to 3pm. Entry charge. Shoes must be removed and there are security checks)*. At the entrance, a large panel displays Thera Mahinda's warning to King Devanampiya Tissa: "Sire, the birds that soar in the sky and the animals that roam in the jungle have an equal right to live and go where they wish in this country. Also, your domain is primarily the domain of the people and all the creatures that live in it. You are merely the administrator". Together with the cult of relics, the tree cult

The tree cult

When Buddhism was introduced to Ceylon, Sangamitta, Mahinda's sister, was charged with bringing cuttings from the Banyan under which Buddha had achieved Enlightenment. Planted in Anuradhapura and several other places on the island, these Bo trees reconciled a traditional cult of spirits, trees, rivers, and rocks with the veneration due to the doctrine of the Master. Even today, the tree of Sri Mahabodhi is revered as the witness of a decisive event in the spiritual journey of Buddha and, more prosaically, invoked to make wishes come true. The sacred Bo tree is cared for by the Management of the Botanical Gardens and it is protected by the army.

is the most ancient manifestation of Buddhist worship, during times when any representation of the Lord Buddha was taboo. In context, the Indian fig evokes for the devotee the Enlightenment, the *Bodhi*, that is the attainment of the state of Buddha.

Before leaving the archeological park, you can make a detour to visit the museum and the old lodge of Tissa wewa.

The billets of the colonial administration occupied a large part of the archeological site. The excavation of the holy city swept most of it away. Apart from the former *Town Hall* which now houses the Jetavanarama museum, there remain the offices of the Department of Archaeology and its annexes, and an old lodge, the Tissa wewa Rest House.

The Archaeological Museum *(daily, 9am-5pm)* is a depository of statues, architectural sculptures and steles displayed without any information whatsoever. However, it is pleasant to wander around it, because some of the statues are masterpieces.

The Folk Museum* *(9am-5pm; closed Thursday and Friday. Entrance fee)* is devoted to country life and craftsmanship. Objects evoking the religious life include a diagram showing how a monk's robe should be worn. Bundles of *ola palm* manuscripts and their styluses emphasise the importance played by the monasteries in teaching. A collection of utensils represents various spheres: cooking, medicine and hunting. On the first floor, the reconstruction of an adobe rice store with a thatched roof is surrounded by crude implements used in slash and burn cultivation.

Not far away is the **Tissa wewa** built under Devanampiya Tissa. Its primary aim was ritual. It served as a ritual bath in which to baptise the king during the coronation rites and water was taken from here to wash the Bo tree at the Sri Mahabodhi temple. It was enlarged in the 5C, and today is still a precious stretch of water for farmers in the surrounding region.
On its northeastern shore, the **Mirisavetiya dagoba** was the first monument to be erected by King Duttu Gemunu after the reconquest of Anuradhapura *(see Around Tissamaharama p 306)*. He had embedded a spear in the ground here with a sacred relic attached to it. Since no one could pull out the weapon of victory, it was decided to build this reliquary, which was entirely reconstructed between 1991 and 1993.

The southern sites

Allow 2hr, preferably towards the end of the day, at sunset, or early in the morning.

Outside the perimeter of the holy city, more ruins served by another road lie at the southern edge of Anuradhapura. Security is tighter here, since this is open countryside...

At the end of the road leading to the Isurumuniya temple, take the path heading north beside the irrigation channel.

Ran Masu Uyana (Park of the Goldfish)**, built in the 6C as pleasure gardens for the royal family, shows the same concern for the harmonious reconciliation of nature and architecture as the water gardens at Sigiriya. The proximity of the Tissa wewa ensured the supply of water, which was forced through an aqueduct and brought here by means of a series of channels and waterfalls to three ponds. They were built beside some granite outcrops which have been incorporated into the ensemble thanks to their very low-relief sculptures, depicting a group of elephants playing among lotus leaves. Water no longer flows through the ponds, but the setting with the rice-fields surrounding is idyllic.

The small rock sanctuary of **Isurumuniya*** was founded by Devanampiya Tissa to mark the occasion of the ordination of 500 nobles *(Daily, 7am-7pm. Entrance fee. Shoes must be removed on entering the courtyard)*. The temple was rebuilt at the beginning of the 20C and houses modern statues, including a reclining Buddha. It stands above a pool dug out of the bedrock, the wall of which bears sculptures in very low relief (they are best lit by the early morning sun): a group of elephants bathing, a groom and his horse. Steps cut into the stone climb up the granite retaining wall next to it. This rare hill provides views of the silhouettes of Mirisavetiya, Ruvanveliseya and Jetavana, against the background of the Mihintale hills. To the left of the site entrance, a pavilion houses a **collection of bas-reliefs** found in the southern foundations. All the figures are depicted in a very flowing, elegant style, possibly influenced by contemporary Indian statuary. The absence of any context or inscription makes it impossible to interpret them, but this has not stopped them being given nicknames. The "Royal Family" may well be a depiction of a divine couple, potrayed and adorned like sovereigns. The famous relief known as "The Lovers" may be the duo of a bodhisattva and his consort. In the centre of the hall, a stone throne has the form of a lion with a curly mane, with a perforated tail that doubles as a parasol holder.

Follow the road south for about 100m, as far as the group of rocks on the right hand side of the road.

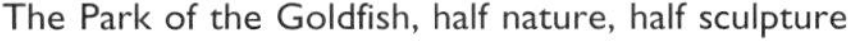

The Park of the Goldfish, half nature, half sculpture

C Bourzat

Three outcrops of granite were the starting point for the building of the monastery of **Vesagiriya***, started in the 3C BC, but it was Kasyapa, who built Sigiriya, and his daughters who developed the complex, adding various buildings. On this half natural, half constructed site, there is a spirit similar to that at Sigiriya: an astonishing sense of observation of the landscape, in which man's intervention traces harmonious counterpoints. There are few remains, but the flights of steps cut into the bedrock, zigzagging among the chaos of the rocks, the fantastic imbalance of the latter and the bases of flights of steps guarded by cobra-kings combine to make a most unusual landscape.

Around Anuradhapura**

Exploring the area around Anuradhapura is a wonderful opportunity to get to know the countryside of the central north, where life still depends on the precious water in the pools and channels built by the kings of long ago.

Mihintale**

11 km east of Anuradhapura. Can be reached by bus from the New Station terminus. If you are travelling by bike, beware of the false plateau between Anuradhapura and Mihintale. At the entrance to the town, a road on the right leads towards the hills: 200m further on, a flight of 1 840 granite steps sets off up the hillside. If you have motor transport, a road zigzags up the hill to the Sinha pokuna. Compulsory donation at the entrance to the esplanade of the Ambasthala "dagoba" where smoking is prohibited. Allow 2hr.

As the setting of the meeting between King Devanampiya Tissa and Thera Mahinda, the Mihintale hills are of enormous spiritual significance to Sinhalese Buddhists: this was where the first Buddhist sermon on the island was preached, the first conversion of a long line of kings took place, and the springboard for the spread of Buddhism in Ceylon. Over the centuries, monasteries were established here, right up to the present time.

To the right of the road leading towards the hills, a curious **stone sarcophagus** has been exposed, pointing to the function of the surrounding ruins. This is one of the many hospitals with which the monasteries were associated. The "sarcophaghi" were medicinal baths in which patients were treated for skin diseases, by immersing them in a mixture of oils and plants with therapeutic properties. The various utensils found on the site are housed in the small **museum** *(8am-5pm; closed Thursday)*, on the opposite side of the road. It is worth a brief visit because there is an example of a **reliquary chamber**, usually sealed inside the mass of the stupa, from a *dagoba* near Kantaka chaitya. Its three superimposed compartments represent the three worlds of the Buddhist cosmogony: the sky, the earth and the underground universe. The paintings which decorate it, simple sketches in red and black lines, date from the 8C and depict the *Lokapala*, the divine guardians of the cardinal points. According to the same convention as the Damsels of Sigiriya, they are cut off half-way down their bodies by the clouds from which they are emerging.

Do not be put off by the number of steps: they are in shade and there are many resting points. Stalls on the way up sell cold drinks and itinerant salesmen provide mangoes and flowers for offerings. After a few steps, take the stairway that goes off to the right of the main staircase.

P Haussherr

Mihintale: the power of flowers

The **Kantaka chaitya**** has the oldest examples of stone buttresses (1C). The corner pilasters are decorated with exceptional bas-reliefs depicting cobra-kings, elephants, foliage, and so on. On the west side, an altar has been carved with a pair of footprints, a characteristic feature of ancient cults.

Go down the stairs opposite the others. They lead to a road near a pool.

The **Sinha pokuna** (Lion Pool)* is a small pool next to the rock, surmounted by the sculpture of a lion rampant. There are sculpted friezes of lions, human figures and dancers around its edge. It was fed by pipes with water from the Naga pokuna higher up.

The remains of a **monastery** extend into the continuation of the road, bounded on one side by a wall of Cyclopean dimensions. Signs make it possible to locate the main buildings: the room for reciting sutras and its central throne surrounded by a peristyle, and the refectory with its large rice-trough. On the terrace overlooking the wall, the entrance to a relic chamber is framed by two tall steles covered with inscriptions.

Follow the staircase which leads up from the second terrace of the monastery. Half-way up, opposite a tea stall, take the path to the right.

The **Naga pokuna** (Cobra Pool)**, thus named because it is guarded by a rock carving of a many-headed cobra, lies under a natural rocky crevice. From the promontory next to the pool, there is a splendid view of the plain of Anuradhapura, recognisable by its gigantic *dagobas*.

Following the same path, you come to another staircase. It descends towards a valley sheltering a few ruins, including a small room of the image. From here, a very steep staircase leads up to the **Et Vihara**, a ruined temple on the summit of the highest hill from which there is an exceptional view.

Behind the room of the image in the valley, another staircase climbs gently up towards a granite ridge with rock-cut steps leading to the **Mahaseya** (Mango-tree Dagoba)*, one of the monuments that pilgrims come here to worship. The mango-tree is the symbol of Mihintale because Mahinda preached his first sermon under such a tree.

The plateau, with palm-trees casting their shadows over the white sand, stretches out below the enormous granite block supporting the dagoba. *(Entrance fee. Shoes should be removed)*. The trees conceal the little **Ambasthala dagoba****, an ancient *vatadage* surrounded by headless statues of Buddha and other ancient effigies. In the southwest corner of the esplanade, a group of modern statues in a rock sanctuary portrays the meeting between Devanampiya Tissa and Mahinda.

A climb up the steep peak to the east is rewarded by a dramatic view of the plain below. On the same side, a path winds through the small functioning monastery and leads to **Mahinda's cave**. Here and there, in rocky crevices, anonymous hands have slipped images and figurines of Ganesh, who is particularly revered in this region.

Return down the monumental staircase which leads straight to the platform of the Ambasthala "dagoba" at the bottom of the hill.

On the road to Polonnaruwa**

Reservoirs thronged with birds and bordered by villages and cultivated land gradually give way to a wilder, drier landscape where only cotton grows. The villages become scarcer and are sometimes only a few months old, sheltering Muslim refugees from the Jaffna peninsula. This is the road leading to giant statues of Buddha, colossi of stone carved into the walls of two cliffs.

Leave Anuradhapura on the Mihintale road. After 7km, turn right towards Maradankadawala. As you drive along, you will notice the "dagobas" of Mirisavetiya and Jetavana, silhouetted behind Nuwara wewa. After 40km, turn off this road onto the road for Kalawewa, one of the great reservoirs which enable this dry region to live and where the country folk bathe in the morning. The site is 10km further on, its location marked by a small car park and drinks stalls on a bend.

■ **Avukana**** – The "Sun-eater", so named because it faces east, is invisible from the road despite its height. A gentle slope leads up towards the site. *(Entrance fee. Shoes should be removed.)* On the right, a small rocky mass with a trident embedded in it is covered with images of Ganesh, the protector of the holy sites in the region of the reservoirs. At the top of the ramp, a **Bo tree** is decorated with votive ribbons in front of the giant Buddha. His image was carved out of the rock and stands 13m high, a technically daring achievement which forced the sculptors to take some precautions: his back and right elbow have not been separated from their rock support. Standing on an upturned lotus flower, he holds his cloak in one hand and raises the other in blessing. Despite the fact that its creation was attributed to King Dathusena (453-477), it now seems that these statues, erected in several places on the island (the most famous are at Polonnaruwa), are not earlier than the 8C-9C. In any case, they met new requirements in terms of religious practice, replacing the vogue of the *dagobas* and the chapels housing smaller statues with these imposing visions of the Master of the Law, offered for the worship of lay people.

Continue towards the village of Avukana (1km). Turn left at the crossroads. Soon afterwards there is a sign to Reshvihara, the local name for Sasseruwa. It is then better to rely on the driver's expertise since certain sections of the road are not asphalted, many junctions are not signposted and villages are few and far between. The total distance is 15km, but allow 1hr, bearing in mind the state of the road. Donation welcome.

■ **Sasseruwa**** – Off the beaten track and rarely visited, this site in its wild setting seems a real retreat from the everyday world: gentle curves of granite outcrops stretch as far as the eye can see, there are few trees but they provide plenty of shade. At the entrance to the valley, apply to the tiny **Reshvihara monastery** to obtain the key that opens the gate to the **rock statue** of Sasseruwa.

The statue stands at the top of a flight of steps under a cliff. According to tradition, King Dathusena commissioned this statue from a group of sculptors from India. But, while work was in progress, the rock proved to be unreliable (long cracks can still be seen on the torso) with the result that the statue was left uncompleted and the project transferred to Avukana. Tradition tells that the rock-cut monastery below the granite monoliths, to which the surrounding caves belong, was founded in the 3C by King Devanampiya Tissa, in the earliest period of Buddhism on the island. Some were restored during the Kandyan period, like Dambulla, and still bear traces of their pictorial decoration, as well as seated or reclining statues wrapped in pleated or flowing robes.

Return to Kekirawa to reach the Anuradhapura road. From here it is possible to go back south to Dambulla (19km) or head northeast to the hermitages of Ritigala (15km) which stretch to the edge of the protected reserve of the same name. Access to the site is 5km to the east of Ganewalpola, at the start of a track carved by the rains and the local elephants. The Archaeology Department bungalow is 6km further on, after which there is a further 2km of very rough track.

■ **The hermitages of Ritigala**** – *Daily, 9am-4pm. Entrance fee or ticket included in the Cultural Triangle multiple-entry ticket. Allow 90min. It is very important to be out of the site before 4pm because of the wild elephants.*

Thick jungle dotted with giant mango-trees with shiny leaves, kapok trees with tentacle-like roots, ebonies with their deeply-grooved trunks, higgledy-piggledy rocks where an infinite number of streams flow and disappear… The strange site of Ritigala was chosen by a monastic community which established itself in the caves from the 3C BC. Today, the visible remains are those of a settlement of *Pansukulikas*, the monastic congregation which practised meditation in total austerity, preferring the wild environment of the forest to the company of people in the towns *(see "Monasteries of the West" above)*. Ritigala is the most perfect expression of this choice and unites all the architectural demands of this sect which spread during the 8C and 9C.

A paved path following a stream winds up through the forest, serving a series of half-natural, half-built terraces, occupied by the foundations of the **monastery buildings**. One of the first is a hospital with a central pool and grinding stones where the ingredients used in pharmacology were prepared. A little further on, there is a double platform served by a footbath, a characteristic feature of the forest monasteries. On one of its sides, a path between two steles was used to practise a severe form of meditation, without any support other than these two standing stones. Two other sets of foundations of the same type have been excavated. Further on, the site ends in a cul-de-sac at the edge of the reserve.

Go back to the Habarana road, and then follow the main road in the direction of Polonnaruwa or Dambulla.

Making the most of Anuradhapura

Coming and going

By train – The railway station is quite far out of the centre, 1km north of the modern town, on the edge of the archeological park. It is served by "tuk-tuks". You are advised to take the train only to get back to Colombo: for any other destination, the Intercity bus is far preferable. The most practical and the busiest service is the n° 86 Rajarata Rajini at 5.05am, which stops at Colombo Fort (4hr50min) and continues to Matara (9hr). Turn up 30min before departure to be sure of getting a seat. There are three other trains daily to the capital, leaving at 9.20am, 2.30pm and 11pm. It is possible to spend the night in a "retiring room", on the first floor of the station: adequate rooms and ancient bathrooms are available for US$2 per person.

By bus – Most destinations are served from the ***Old Station*** (Parama Stand), either from the actual bus terminus, or from the road which heads south. There are frequent departures between 7am and 9.30pm, for Colombo (4.30hr), Kandy via Dambulla (3hr) and Dambulla (1hr). A bus for Polonnaruwa (3hr, no AC or express service) leaves every 45min from ***New Station***, on Main St, to the south of the town.

Getting around

The site is much too extensive to be covered on foot. Car and "tuk-tuk" drivers offer an overview of the site lasting three or four hours for about US$7. Their route includes the monastery of Jetavana, the palace of Vijaya Bahu, the Twin Pools, the Buddha in "samadhi", the Abhayagiriya "dagoba", Mahasena Palace, Lankarama, Thuparama, the sanctuary of Sri Mahabodhi and Isurumuniya. If you want to see more and spend more time on the site, a bike is the best means of transport. Bikes can be hired for about US$1 a day. Cars can also be hired for US$6 per half-day. You can also take advantage of the services of a guide from the Tourist Board: they await their customers at the entrance to the site, between 7.30am and 4pm.

Address book

Tourist Office – There are plans to open an information office at the entrance to the Ceylon Tourist Board Rest House. The ***Tourist Information Centre*** situated on Dharmapala Maw is completely useless.

Banks / Currency exchange – ***Hatton National Bank***, 30 Mathripala Senanayake Maw (Monday-Friday 9am-3pm. Visa and MasterCard), and ***Bank of Ceylon***, Super Great Branch, Main St (MasterCard).

Where to stay

It's best to avoid coming to Anuradhapura at the weekend because, except for a few guesthouses which only take foreign guests, the hotels tend to be occupied by pilgrims from all over the island. The hotels near the holy site, the Ceybank Rest House, the Ceylon Tourist Board and the Tissawewa Rest House do not serve alcohol.

From US$8 to US$15

Ceylon Tourist Board Rest House, Jayanthi Maw, ☎ (025) 221 88; book from Colombo, (01) 44 78 45 – 37rm. 5ha of garden, next to the holy city, this hotel was built to cater for Sri Lankan tourists. Excellent quality-price ratio, on account of its functionality rather than its charm.

Samanala Tourist Guesthouse (V U Bandula), 4N / 2 Wasala Daththa Maw, ☎ (072) 62 13 84 – 4rm. Simple and impeccably clean, the rooms overlook a charming central patio. Two of them have a view over the lake. The cooking is good, especially the fried fish from the Nuwara wewa.

Shalini Tourist Rest & Guesthouse (Harsha Gunasekera), 41 / 388 Harischandra Maw, ☎ / Fax (025) 224 25 – 8rm. You may choose between rooms with or without hot water. Rooms with hot water are large but rather gloomy, overlooking the dining room, while the small rooms without hot water have more charm, being located in bungalows in the garden. Dishes from various cuisines are served here, but the local dishes are excellent. Free transfer to station provided.

The Grand Tourist Holiday Resort (Damian Perera), 4B2 Lake Rd, Harischandra Maw, ☎(025) 351 73 – 4rm. Very large rooms with mosquito-nets and spotlessly clean bathrooms. Meals may be taken on the veranda, facing the Nuwara wewa, with the Mihintale hills in the distance. You may admire the sunrise at breakfast, but bring an insect repellent to dinner.

From US$15 to US$30

Ceybank Rest (Ceylon Bank Rest House), Jayanthi Maw, ☎ (025) 355 20; book from Colombo, ☎ (01) 44 78 45 – 20rm. This concrete building next to the holy precinct has large, clean, functional rooms (mosquito nets and cold water). Its restaurant serves a varied cuisine, freshly prepared (count on waiting 45min once dinner has been ordered). This is a good place to stay, but it is impossible to find a room at the weekend, when the Bank of Ceylon employees come here on pilgrimage.

Randiya, Rowing Club Rd, ☎ (025) 228 68 – 10rm. The hotel looks pleasant with its white-washed walls, and its pergola, its red tiles and little garden, but although impeccably clean (mosquito nets), the bedrooms are a bit disappointing.

Tissawewa Rest House, to the west of the archeological park, ☎ (025) 222 99, Fax (025) 232 65; book from Colombo: Quickshaws Ltd., 3 Kalinga Place, Col. 5, (01) 58 29 95, Fax (01) 58 76 13, quiktur@lankacom.net – 25rm. CC Opened in 1907 under the name of Grand Hotel, this old lodge of the functionaries of the British Crown has experienced various fortunes. Today it is a residence full of charm, surrounded by a garden with monkeys and situated next to the holy city. Parquet floors in bedrooms. Colonnaded veranda and terrace with period furniture.

Over US$30

Miridya Hotel, Rowing Club Rd, ☎ (025) 221 12, Fax (025) 225 19 – 36rm. CC The charm of the place lies in its luxuriant and maze-like garden, with benches where guests can enjoy the sunset, and the birds in the morning. The rooms are functional, some have balconies, others have a bath. Small swimming pool, shop / bookshop and dining-room open onto the garden.

Nuwarawewa Rest House, ☎(025) 225 65, Fax (025) 232 65; book from Colombo: Quickshaws Ltd, 3 Kalinga Place, Col 5, ☎ (01) 58 29 95, Fax (01) 58 76 13, quiktur@lankacom.net – 70rm. CC This old lodge has been enlarged several times and its rooms vary considerably. The best (comfortable, views over the countryside or the garden) rub shoulders with the worst (terrible plumbing and noisy AC systems).

• At Mihintale

From US$30 to US$45

Mihintale Hotel (Ceylon Hotels Corporation) on the edge of the town, ☎ (025) 665 99 – 17rm. Like all hotels managed by the state, this one is much too expensive for the services it provides. However it is pleasantly set among the hills which are especially attractive at dawn or at sunset.

Eating out

Several of the hotels have good restaurants. ***Shalini***, ***Samanala*** and ***The Grand*** serve delicious local cuisine, spiced according to your taste. Be sure to book as places are rare. Reckon on US$4 for a full meal, without drinks. Do not forget to sample the fish from the Nuwara wewa, but beware, it is only good when fried. There is no restaurant on the site. You can buy cold drinks and biscuits near the Twin Pools, the Abhayagiriya and Ruvanveliseya dagobas and near the Mahabodhi Temple.

Other things to do

Swimming – Swimming is possible in Nuwara wewa.

Feasts and Festivals – ***Festival of Ruvanveliseya*** and of the Mihintale hills on the "poya" day of the month of Poson (June). This is one of the great Buddhist gatherings and tens of thousands of pilgrims flock to it.

New Rice Festival, in May-June, after the first monsoon rains. Farmers carry the new rice in a procession into the sacred heart of the city.

Nanu Mura Mangalliya, the day of "poya" in April. Lustrations and offerings of garlands of flowers in the enclosure of the Tree of Enlightenment.

POLONNARUWA★★★

North Central Province – Pop 106 000
Influenced by the climate of the east coast:
intermittent rain in January and February.
68km from Dambulla, 104km from Anuradhapura
and 140km from Kandy

Not to be missed

The figures of dwarves, the processions of animals or sacred carts, animating the monuments of Polonnaruwa.
The restrained atmosphere of Medirigiriya.

And remember...

Visit Polonnaruwa by bike if you want to see everything because the site is very extensive and the ticket is only valid for one day.

Polonnaruwa grew up when the European cathedrals were being built. Its temples and palaces, the ruins of which are scattered over several square kilometres, on the east bank of a huge *wewa* (tank), are almost all the achievement of one king, **Parakramabahu** (1153-86), the most prestigious of the island's sovereigns. At the same time, Polonnaruwa symbolises both the Renaissance of the Sinhalese civilisation born at Anuradhapura and its dying flame. In fact, in the late 12C, the monarchy fell into a long decline, while the island suffered raids at the hands of Malaysian pirates and was torn by civil wars between pretenders to the Sinhalese throne. The jungle then gradually engulfed the medieval capital until the beginning of the 20C. Since then, generations of archeologists have been excavating the city of Parakramabahu, revealing his work as a builder but also exposing the porous rock to the torrential downpours of the rainy season. After a century of archeology, the question must be asked: is the opening up of the site not also condemning it? Does the royal city not risk dissolving like a dream?

A medieval capital

The Tamil century – For a hundred years before it became the symbol of the Sinhalese Renaissance, Polonnaruwa was the seat of power under Tamils from the mainland. In the 10C, two seats of power were established in the south of India: the Pandya of Madurai and the Cholas of Tanjore. Thanks to their formidable fleet, the Cholas gradually established their dominion over the whole Indian Ocean. In 993, their sovereign **Rajaraja I** (985-1012) made only one incursion into Ceylon, a strategic stopping place on the route of the straits of Malaysia. Anuradhapura was put to the sack and burned and the Tamil monarchy installed a viceroy in a city which had once served as a holiday residence for the Sinhalese kings, Polonnaruwa. This was a strategic choice because it enabled them to control the crossing of the Mahaweli Ganga, a dozen kilometres to the southeast. On the other side of the river lay the Ruhunu, where the princes of Ceylon had sought refuge. The presence of the Chola tolled the death knell of the power of the Buddhist monasteries: as followers of Shiva, they erected magnificent temples on the island and cast bronze statues honouring various aspects of the god. Absolute royal power replaced the social equilibrium based on collaboration between the monarchy and the monastic communities. A large part of the irrigation network fell into disrepair. However, the attitude of the occupying force was not always hostile: near Trincomalee, the Buddhist sanctuary of Velgam Vihara was rebuilt under the patronage of the Chola.

The Sinhalese re-conquest – In the middle of the 11C, the Sinhalese princes of Ruhunu finally found a federating force in the person of **Vijayabahu I** (1055-1110). Having built up power again at Kataragama *(see p 311)*, this king formed alliances with Burma and Indonesia to challenge the seaborne empire of the Chola in the Indian Ocean. Weakened, the Tamil conquerors withdrew and Vijayabahu was crowned king in the holy city of Anuradhapura in 1073, keeping Polonnaruwa as his capital. The old order had been ruined and the country had to be rebuilt. The task facing him was enormous, and Vijayabahu, the first sovereign of Ceylon to mint coins bearing his name, re-established institutions rather than founding new ones. One exception was the **Atadage**, the first Temple of the Tooth in Polonnaruwa, erected to house this relic which was so inextricably linked to Sinhalese royalty. But, on his death, the island descended once more into chaos, and was plagued for 40 years by a war of succession between three rival principalities.

The cult of the tooth

The tooth of Buddha, which is still revered in Kandy today, is the most famous of his relics. Brought to the kingdom of Anuradhapura in the 4C AD, it was never buried in the brick centre of a "dagoba", but was jealously guarded in temples specially built for the purpose in successive capitals. The Dalada Maligawa at Kandy was the last to be built (see p 218).

Conqueror and builder – Parakramabahu (1153-86), prince of Dakkhinadesa *(see Panduwas Nuwara p 165)*, succeeded in pacifying the country and putting the finishing touches to the work of Vijayabahu. Once the country had been reunited, he embarked on the most ambitious irrigation programme ever undertaken in Ceylon. "Not a single drop of rain must reach the ocean without having first been used to benefit mankind", he declared in one of the numerous inscriptions left by him. The chronicles portray him as a lover of water sports and attribute to him the building or restoration of 165 dams, 136 large and 2 376 small reservoirs, and 3 910 canals. The largest pool is the one he had built for Polonnaruwa, the capital where his palace was located together with numerous new monasteries, generously endowed by him and his queens. Two older reservoirs were united to form the **Parakrama Samudra** (Sea of Parakrama), covering 2 400ha, fed by a dam and a diversion canal from the Amban Ganga, a tributary of the Mahaweli. No reservoir of this size was ever built again until Ceylon became independent.

It was also necessary to breathe new life into the *Sangha*, which had been considerably weakened by the Chola occupation. In this context, he achieved the impossible by merging the dissident Buddhist sects of Abhayagiriya and Jetavanarama with the **Mahavihara**, the oldest congregation on the island, thus putting an end to a schism that had lasted for 13 centuries *(see insert p 172)*. The event is described in a long inscription at the Gal Vihara in Polonnaruwa.

But the Renaissance brought with it the seeds of decline, because 30 years of material, political and religious reconstruction had weighed heavily on the people of the island. The reign of **Nissamka Malla** (1187-96) was its last respite. This monarch travelled the length and breadth of the kingdom he had inherited, leaving a considerable number of inscriptions at the places he visited.

The dark period – In 1214, a new threat loomed over the exhausted country: the Malaysian pirate **Magha** and his thousands of mercenaries pillaged and burned everything they found in their way for 40 years. Hidden in their invincible fortresses, the Sinhalese princes were reduced to appealing to their old enemies the Pandya and the Chola of Southern India to eradicate the Malaysian scourge. But this was the end of the Golden Age.

The Archaeological Park

Daily, 7am-6pm. Allow a minimum of half a day. There is only one entrance to the Archaeological Park, where the ticket or Cultural Triangle round ticket can be purchased. Eight kilometres separate the royal palace of Parakramabahu from the temple of Tivanka, the most southerly monument, but the most important ruins are concentrated within about 4km between the Citadel and the Gal Vihara. The buildings are described in the order in which they can be visited, starting at the south gate and working towards the exit to the north, near Alahena Pirivena. A bike is the ideal way to visit the site. Cold drinks, coconut slices and postcards are on sale near the Kumara Pokuna, the Sacred Quadrangle, the Rankot Vihara and the Gal Vihara.

This great medieval city of Ceylon, the ruins of which are scattered over 15sqkm, has retained something of its mystery. Here and there, cows graze amid mounds covered with vegetation which may conceal small stupas, Bengal lizards swim in the channels of the ancient water supply system, and giant trees conceal temples inhabited by statues.

The walled city

The city was protected by a double rampart with ditches on the north side, while the Parakrama Samudra provided defence on the west side and the river formed a natural moat to the east. A wall subdivided the city into two districts: the servants and the royal guard lived in the southern part, next to the Citadel, while the religious buildings lay to the north.

The Citadel

Within its double line of walls, the Citadel sheltered secular buildings linked to the exercise of power.

The *Culavamsa* describes the **Parakramabahu's Palace*** (Vejayanta Pasada) as having seven floors and a thousand rooms at the height of its splendour. Whether this is true or not – the chronicles liked to give royal buildings this number of floors – the rows of loopholes in its thick walls suggest three levels, confirmed on the inside by the presence of holes where beams supporting the floor above were inserted. Preceded by a square to the east, the façade is supported by buttresses alternating with timber pillars, a substantial and necessary form of construction for its high walls. The entrance arch, which gapes open today, was once closed by a wooden door. It opens onto a hypostyle room, possibly used for audiences, of which only the stone bases of the columns remain. To the east of the palace, a high terrace is all that remains of the **Council Chamber**** (Rajaveshiabhujanga) of Parakramabahu. The stone base is engraved with some perfectly preserved **bas-relief friezes****, among them a procession of placid, life-like elephants, seated lions posing majestically, and a frenzied dance of *gana*. On the north side, there are two **threshold moonstones** with decorative friezes, while a flight of steps bordered by two *makara* leads up to the platform where two octagonal granite **columns*** are still standing. Each one is delicately engraved with figures of dwarves, lotus petals and flowers, and vases of plenty.

A passage in the ramparts of the Citadel leads to the **Bathing Pool** (Kumara pokuna), all that remains of the water gardens which once adorned the royal palace. The water from the huge tank flows into the nearby canal through gargoyles in the form of *makara*.

Follow the dirt track heading north which leads to the main buildings.

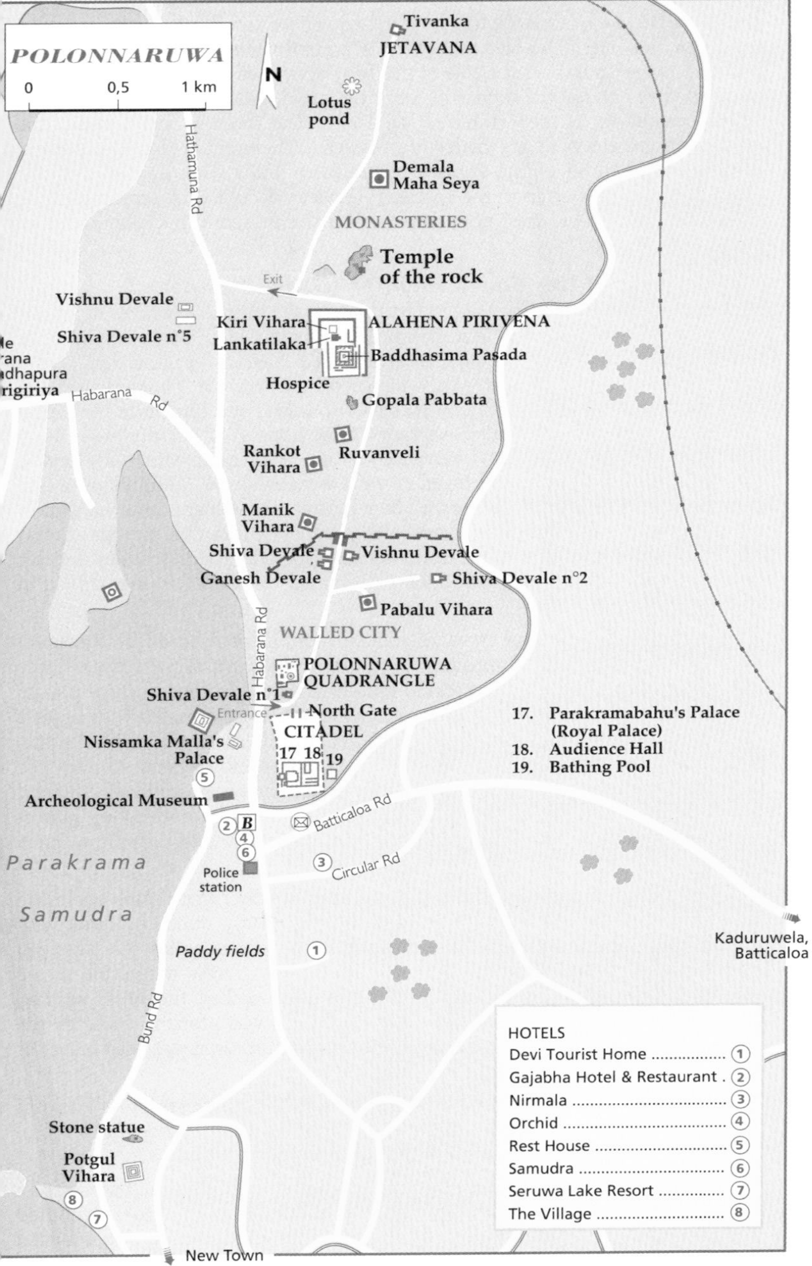
POLONNARUWA
0
0,5
1 km
N
Tivanka
JETAVANA
Lotus pond
Hathamuna Rd
Demala Maha Seya
MONASTERIES
Temple of the rock
Exit
Vishnu Devale
Shiva Devale n°5
Kiri Vihara
Lankatilaka
ALAHENA PIRIVENA
Baddhasima Pasada
Hospice
Habarana Rd
Gopala Pabbata
Rankot Vihara
Ruvanveli
Manik Vihara
Shiva Devale
Vishnu Devale
Ganesh Devale
Shiva Devale n°2
Pabalu Vihara
Habarana Rd
WALLED CITY
POLONNARUWA QUADRANGLE
Shiva Devale n°1
Entrance
North Gate
CITADEL
17 18 19
Nissamka Malla's Palace
17. Parakramabahu's Palace (Royal Palace)
18. Audience Hall
19. Bathing Pool
Archeological Museum
Batticaloa Rd
Circular Rd
Police station
Parakrama Samudra
Paddy fields
Kaduruwela, Batticaloa
Bund Rd
Stone statue
Potgul Vihara
New Town
HOTELS
Devi Tourist Home 1
Gajabha Hotel & Restaurant . 2
Nirmala 3
Orchid 4
Rest House 5
Samudra 6
Seruwa Lake Resort 7
The Village 8

The Shiva Devale n° 1* is the first building you encounter heading north *(remove shoes before entering)*. The fact that there is a Hindu temple within the city of Buddhist kings underlines the role of the Tamils, even in times of peace. Valiant warriors, they entered the service of the royal guard, indeed guarded such prestigious sanctuaries as the Temple of the Tooth. The roof has disappeared, but its massive granite walls are perfectly preserved. The architectural features are reminiscent of those of the Pandya of Southern India: they include regular pilasters gracing the exterior, the spaces in-between occupied by sensuous gods. Some fine Shivaite bronzes, now displayed in the museum in Colombo, were found here *(see p 127)*.

The terrace of the Tooth Relic*** (Dalada Maluwa)

Sometimes referred to as the Sacred Quadrangle, the terrace is where the buildings were sited which were used to house the relic which was the symbol of power of the Sinhalese kings *(signs make it possible to identify the buildings)*.
Entering it on the south side, you will see on the left, the **Thuparama***, the external walls of which consist of a pattern of pilasters and miniature buildings. This is one of the three large *patimaghara* (image houses) of Polonnaruwa. They constitute the most original innovation of medieval architecture in Ceylon because, instead of being held together with raw clay, as at Anuradhapura, the stuccoed bricks are fixed together with lime mortar. These high, solid walls made it possible to build a barrel vault over the entrance corridor. A passage *(closed)* built inside the walls leads to the upper terrace. The only room contains nothing but the brick core of a seated Buddha surrounded by other Buddhas carved in stone.

On the right, the **Vatadage***** is an ancient monument restored by Nissamka Malla in a harmonious composition of volumes. Its heart is the ruined dome of a stupa watched over by four seated Buddhas, facing the four cardinal points. These **statues**** have the unique characteristic of being portrayed with neither curls in their hair nor folds in their clothes. A circular screen of bricks surrounds the complex. Around the edge is a gallery of columns which once supported the roof protecting the building, linked by a balustrade ornamented with a four-petalled flower motif. Four steps, guarded by **cobra-king guardstones****, lead down to the lower terrace (the finest couple guard the north steps).

On the western side of the quadrangle, the small, badly-ruined brick enclosure wall once surrounded a **Bo tree** *(bodhighara)*. Beyond it is another cloister with a stone balustrade. It surrounds a number of columns of an almost Art Nouveau sensuousness; coiling skywards like lotus stems, they grace a minuscule *dagoba* with a truncated top. This elegant little ensemble, called the **Nissamkalata Mandapa**** and attributed to King Nissamka Malla, was probably built for the chanting of protective religious texts. The small central stupa was used to house the relic during the ceremonies.

Between the Nissamkalata and the Vatadage, a small, square structure encloses a decorated **statue** which faces the reliquary monument. It is thought to represent either King Parakramabahu or a *bodhisattva*.

The two buildings standing side by side on the north side of the terrace were both models for the Temple of the Tooth at Kandy. The **Atadage***, attributed to King Vijayabahu, is the earlier of the two. With its seated Buddha, situated at the end of a columned room, it has all the attributes of an image house. Notice the staircase in the hypostyle vestibule: it leads up to a floor where the precious relic was probably kept. A stele on the left-hand side of the temple has reminders of the supervisory role of a regiment of Tamils. The pillars of the porch are delicately carved with tendrils, the interlacing of which forms decorated medallions.

The nearby **Hatadage****, surrounded by a brick and stone wall, is much more impressive. According to an inscription on the porch, Nissamka Malla claims to have built it, but it seems more likely that the construction of this strongbox temple was the work of Parakramabahu, who had taken the Tooth relic back from the lords of Ruhunu.

Beside the east wall, there is a short inscription on a huge stone lying in the grass. On the **Gal Pota*** (Stone book), King Nissamka Malla extols his military feats and his relations with other countries. It also reveals that this block of granite, 8m long by 4m wide, weighing 25 tonnes, was dragged here from Medirigiriya *(see p 201)*. Behind it, the **uposatha ghara**, or chapter house, has a single column like the ones in the Nissamkalata mandapa. It stands beside the **Sat Mahal Prasada** (Palace of Seven Storeys), a sort of ziggurat which was possibly a short-lived variation of a stupa, reminiscent of Chinese or Nepalese pagodas.

Walk down the monumental staircase from the terrace to the main road. After 200m, take the path on the right.

The Pabalu Vihara* is a small stupa on a triple terrace in a glade in a delightful woodland setting. Its reliquary chamber has yielded objects dating from the end of the Anuradhapura period, which are now displayed at the local museum. The building was erected by Rupavati, one of Parakrama Bahu's queens. Four image houses and four secondary oratories form a crown around its brick dome. This is an innovative feature of the Polonnaruwa period. The statues of these chapels are very fragmented and without a doubt constitute a re-use of material from the Anuradhapura period.

At the end of the lane, the **Shiva Devale n° 2**** is still in use. The Hindu community here worship Shiva in the form of a linga. This solidly built stone shrine with its harmonious proportions dates from the time when the Chola reigned in Polonnaruwa. Founded by one of Rajaraja I's wives, it is the oldest monument on the site.

Go back to the main road.

Before leaving the walled city by the north gate, you pass three small temples situated on either side of the road. The one on the right is dedicated to **Vishnu**, the ones on the left to **Shiva** and **Ganesh**.

The monasteries outside the walls**

Just as he had done at Anuradhapura, Parakramabahu complemented the citadel of secular power with a city of monasteries. The most important ones lie to the north. Only the smaller Potgul Vihara lies to the south, outside the perimeter of the park.

Beyond the north gate, the road crosses an incompletely excavated and still wooded part of the **Manik Vihara***. This monastery was built in two separate periods: from the 8C-9C, when Polonnaruwa was merely a satellite of Anuradhapura, then continued in the 12C and 13C. The gaping centre of its ruined **stupa**** reveals the secret hiding-place of its reliquary. Terracotta plaques moulded with a symbolic lion decorate the base of the building. You can spend hours walking in the undergrowth, which is full of surprises. You will no doubt come across one of the flagstones lying on the ground, with traces of wear in the centre. When the monastery was abandoned, these were used as grinding mills by the Vedda aboriginals. Some Bengal monitor lizards live beside the canal which supplied the town with water in the Middle Ages. In the remains of the two image houses, the Buddhas, carved in a crystalline limestone, look as if they are waiting for something.

A stream marks the boundary with the monastic complex of Rankot Vihara.

The badly ruined remains of **Rankot Vihara** lie to the south of the **Ruvanveli*** stupa. It is quite small compared to the giants at Anuradhapura but, with a height of 54m, is the largest at Polonnaruwa. Founded in the 12C by one of the queens of Parakramabahu, it was completed by Nissamka Malla, who had himself portrayed on an inscription, admiring the building work. A survey has revealed the existence within the dome of a solid central cube, surrounded by a layer of bricks. The four *vahalkada*, the buttresses invented to support the stupas at Anuradhapura, each house a chapel dedicated to the gods protecting the four cardinal points and are flanked by oratories. There are only plastic Buddhas inside, but this does not dissuade pilgrims from laying flowers as a sign of veneration.

Follow the paved path heading north, towards Kiri Vihara.

On the right, the granite blocks of **Gopala Pabbata** (Hill of the Herdsmen) conceal a cave, the entrance to which is masked by a curtain of aerial roots from a Banyan tree. According to an inscription, a community of anchorites settled here in the 2C BC.

The cella of Lankatilaka

Valdin / DIAF

The Alahena Pirivena** (Monastery of the Cremations)

This monastery owes its name to the fact that it was founded by Parakrama Bahu on the site of an ancient cemetery. A large part of the 80ha covered by the complex, which housed up to a thousand monks, has been excavated thanks to funds from UNESCO. By following the lane to the north, on the left, you will see a **hospice**, the foundations of which are built around an atrium. A medicinal garden and a pool are to be found close by.

Further on, to the right, the **Baddhasima Pasada*** is an imposing structure with a central platform. This room was used for reciting the common rules of discipline of the *vinaya*, on *poya* nights. There was a **reliquary** in the centre of the terrace around which sat four monks on stone thrones. The eight stones marking the edge of the complex suggest that its use was reserved strictly for the monks. On the west side there is a stepped **pool** in the shape of an inverted pyramid.

To the west, stairs lead down to a lower level, where a **chapter house** can be distinguished by a double row of stones. Curiously, the threshold stone is a simple rectangular flagstone and not a traditional moonstone. It lies below the two temples of Alahena Pirivena: Lankatilaka and Kiri Vihara.

The Lankatilaka** (Glory of Lanka) is a vertical *gedige* 46m high, with brick walls reinforced by vertical granite supports. A barrel vault hangs over the now headless 13m-high Buddha. The **statue** stands beside a screen wall, forming a narrow, corbelled vaulted passage. On each side of the front room, 17 pillars support a wooden platform. The outside walls are decorated with large stucco compositions featuring **gods in chariots** riding through the air.

Parakramabahu had **Kiri Vihara** built in honour of his wife Bhaddhavati. The nearby **stupa**, which is smaller and probably intended for another queen, includes three superimposed reliquary chambers. It stands on a tall base with **gargoyles**** beautifully carved in the shape of *makara*.

The Temple of the Rock*** (Gal Vihara)

The Temple of the Rock belonged to the northern monastery *(Uttararama)*, another building founded by Parakrama Bahu. Its four **rock-cut Buddhas** are the high point of Ceylonese medieval carving *(the statues are best seen in the morning light)*. The first, deep in meditation, is seated on a throne engraved with lions and *vajra*, symbols of esoteric Buddhism. A halo of celestial palaces, where miniature Buddhas in *samadhi* are seated, hangs above his head, suspended by a *makara torana*.

The nearby chapel was closed by grilles in 1993 to protect it from damage. Suddenly the colourful harmony of the murals adorning its side walls becomes apparent in the gloom. The Master is seated at the back of this stone chapel under a parasol, like a king, flanked by bearers with fly-swats and the protector gods Brahma and Vishnu.

The next giant statue, which is 7m high, standing up and slightly hunched, his arms folded, has been interpreted in many different ways, none of which is certain. Although his clothing is unquestionably that of Buddha, there is nothing conventional about his attitude, but neither is Sakyamuni usually depicted in this sensual pose *(see illustration p 35)*.

At his feet, the 14m-long body of the last statue reclines as he enters the peace of *Parinirvana*. The serene expression on his face idealises this final moment, while a slight depression in the pillow adds a touch of realism. Although the interpretation of this Buddhist tetralogy is uncertain, its general layout is clear. It was a semi-rock-cut **image house** like the ones seen in the rest of the island. The associated structure (brick and timber framework) has long since disappeared.

The imposing semi-spherical mass on the right-hand side of the track leading north is not a hill, but an uncleared stupa. According to the chronicles, it was supposed to have risen to a height of 200m, exceeding that of all the other reliquary monuments on the island. But Parakrama Bahu left the building of this

Masterpieces in peril

The dark veins that form waves on the four statues at Gal Vihara add to their beauty, but betray what is threatening them: rain-water which filters down through the layers and is slowly eating away the stone. This danger, which affects a large part of the site, is the reason for the erection, in 1994, of a hideous awning, the only possible protection against the elements.

Mahathupa, "the Great Stupa" unfinished. The mass of bricks was built by Tamil prisoners of war, hence its nickname, **Demala Maha Seya**, the "Great Stupa of the Tamils". A path provides access to the platform on the top where there is a splendid view at sunset.

The Jetavana monastery

Only a few scattered ruins of this monastery survive. Its image house, the **Tivanka Pilimage****, was excavated during the colonial period. In 1885, the archeologist SM Burrows drove a tunnel into the interior of the monument, which was still submerged by earth and vegetation, and discovered a series of **paintings** executed on the inside of the nave in the second half of the 12C. At that time, they were in a perfect state of preservation, but their sudden exposure to the light rapidly changed the colours which, at the beginning of the 20C, were already difficult to see. A certain amount of guesswork is involved when looking at this unique example of medieval painting in Ceylon (copies are displayed in the National Museum in Colombo). The best preserved paintings occupy the left-hand wall of the entrance corridor, just in front of the cella: a celestial vision of gods with gentle smiles, their heads crowned with tiaras, their bodies bedecked with every conceivable kind of jewel. As in the other two *pilimage* at Polonnaruwa, there is a staircase in the left-hand wall, an ambulatory around the cella and a side exit in the north wall. The barrel vault of the vestibule was restored in 1989: the structure of the cella in 1988. It protects the brick core of a **statue**, standing on a granite base in the shape of a lotus flower, the right knee slightly flexed, giving a triple flexion to the body. This movement, called *tribangha* in Pali, has given its surname to the temple: *tribhanga* became *tivanka*. The outside walls are decorated with an entertaining bevy of dwarves: one turns away from the others, one reveals his posterior and, in a corner, a woman displays her ample bosom.

About 100m further south, the **Lotus bath*** was one of the monastery's eight pools; the scalloped rim forming the shape of a lotus flower.

Go back towards the Alahena Pirivena monastery and take the road leading towards the exit.

Outside the Archaeological Park, 100m from the exit, the **Shiva Devale n° 5*** is another temple dedicated to Vishnu. This is the largest of them and most of the bronzes displayed in the museum come from here. Inside, a linga is still wedged in a *yoni* (engraved flagstone symbolising the female organ).

The east bank of the Parakrama Samudra

A road running along the top of the river embankment makes it simple to visit the sites scattered from north to south, outside the archeological area. The rice fields irrigated by the Parakrama Samudra conceal a number of remains which have not yet been excavated.

The remains of the **Palace of Nissamka Malla*** are situated on a promontory jutting out into the lake, on the right-hand side of the road. This is an ideal place to watch the sunset over the Parakrama Samudra. The pillars of the **Council chamber***, based on the model of the one built by Parakramabahu, bear inscriptions assigning places to dignitaries on each side of the royal throne, which has the shape of a lion. They give a very precise picture of the kingdom's administrative structure and its various ministers: of justice, trade, education, defence and charitable works. A curious building without any windows, called the **mausoleum**, stands beside the **audience chamber**, of which only the walls remain. It may possibly represent Mount Meru, the axis of the world according to the Buddhist cosmogony.

The Archaeological Museum**

Daily, 7am-6pm. Entrance fee, included in Cultural Triangle multiple entry ticket on sale at the museum. Allow 90min. Photography prohibited.

Opened in 1998, this museum provides an excellent introduction to the site. There are not many objects on display, but there are numerous maps and scale models of the monuments at Polonnaruwa which give a very precise idea of what the city must have been like. Most of the information is in English.

Room 1 concentrates on the **first period** of occupation of the site, from 500-300BC (see scale model of the complex).
Room 2 is devoted to the **Citadel** and contains a scale model including the seven floors of the Palace of Parakrama Bahu as described in the chronicles, various statues from the palace, and carpentry tools (hammers, nails, and door handles).
Room 3 is particularly devoted to the complex of the **terrace of the Tooth Relic**, and has a hypothetical reconstruction of the **Vatadage**. Fragments of ritual pottery are engraved with good-luck motifs, also encountered in ornamental sculpture, such as the vase of plenty or the swastika. In the centre of the room, the elegant **statue of the bodhisattva** is reduced to its simplest form. Other objects on display are associated with the worship of relics: oil lamps, a stone reliquary shrine, a pottery support carried by lions, and reliquaries in semi-precious stones from the Pabalu Vihara. The **statue of Vishnu** comes from the oratory near the north gate.

The Council Chamber in the Palace of Nissamka Malla

S Held

Room 4 introduces the three large **monastic complexes** which occupy the area north and south of the walled city. There is a scale model of the Baddhasima Pasada, with the twelve storeys attributed to it in the chronicles. Another model shows what the hospital of the Alahena Pirivena was like: exhibits include surgical instruments (scalpel, pincers, forceps), as well as scales and mortars for preparing medicinal compounds.

In Room 5 there are some very fine **statues**** from the monasteries around the edge of the walled city (Gal Vihara, Jetavanarama and Potgul Vihara). In the centre is a Buddha in *samadhi* (8C-9C) dressed in a smooth robe.

The last room contains a collection of **Hindu statues**, in bronze or stone, from various temples erected on the site between the 11C and 13C. Most of them refer to Shivaite iconography with a predominance of **Shiva Vatuka**, a terrifying portrayal of the god, with bulging eyes, his hair standing on end, and lips drawn back to reveal his prominent canines, an image sometimes used to guard Buddhist sanctuaries in the Middle Ages. There are superb examples of **Shiva king of the dance***** cast in bronze in the 12C, and of **Parvati**, his slender wife, carved in granite, dating from the 11C.

Potgul Vihara* (Library Monastery)

This group of buildings lies to the east of the road, 2.5km from the museum. The site has only been partly excavated by the Archaeology Department and it is obvious that ancient structures underlie the hillocks that seem to be part of the countryside.

The rock-cut image** of the Potgul Vihara retains its aura of mystery. According to tradition, this bearded giant holding either a book or possibly a yoke of kingship is King **Parakrama Bahu**. The simplicity of his attire and his curly hair gathered in a bun have suggested to certain archeologists that this is a Shivaite hermit: others interpret it as a Buddhist ascetic. Whatever it may be, this august figure has fallen victim to the unfortunate methods used to protect the statues of Polonnaruwa from the elements: ugly metal scaffolding.

The monastery as such was surrounded by a wall. In the centre are the remains of a library *(potgul)*, to which it owes its name. The massive brick terrace has gargoyles which also serve as a support. The thickness of the walls of the entrance corridor suggests the existence of a vault, which has disappeared, together with the dome which once crowned the central circular room. Here and there, traces of paint are all that remain of the murals which once decorated the building. The water gardens which once lay to the west are buried beneath the embankment road built by the British.

On the road to Medirigiriya**

47.5km. Allow half a day.

It is worth spending an extra night at Polonnaruwa or close by in order to make this excursion. It is not entirely unfeasible by public transport but the tiresome bus changes involved will prevent you from enjoying the pastoral charm of the tiny road that winds its way across the countryside.

Leave Polonnaruwa by the Habarana road. After 13km, you will come to the lake of **Giritale**, built in the 7C as part of a regional irrigation plan. A few hotels mean that the area has potential as a delightful holiday place, immersed in the natural landscape.

Nine kilometres further on, **Minneriya** is a huge water tank of 3 000ha, built in the 4C by King Mahasena, the builder of the Jetavana *dagoba* at Anuradhapura. The region is home to wild elephants and, during the dry season, *(April-August)*, you will certainly catch a glimpse of them, perhaps at night in the car headlights. Otherwise, ask your hotel to arrange an outing with a 4x4 vehicle to the lake of Kaudulla, 26km north of Minneriya, where hundreds of elephants assemble to drink.

Leave the Habarana road and follow signs to Hingurakgoda. This is the prettiest part of the route. The road runs alongside an irrigation canal shaded by ancient trees, across which wooden bridges have been built to provide access to the villages on the other side. *When you come to the village of Medirigiriya, 20.5km from Minneriya, there is a sign to the Vatadage, situated 3km further on.*

Medirigiriya**

Medirigiriya has a sort of end-of-the-world feel about it and is a peaceful allegory of Buddhist spirituality. A white house accommodates the pilgrims who come here to visit the sacred site. Men and women dressed in white meditate alone under the banyan trees. A depression in the rock collects rainwater, providing the perfect habitat for spotless lotus flowers to grow. The remains of this holy site, built by the kings of Polonnaruwa, lie beside a monumental street, within a wall that follows the lie of the land. Three Buddhas stand against the wall of one of the image houses. In another, only the brick couch that once supported a reclining Buddha remains.

The **vatadage*****, surrounded by a balustrade imitating a wooden barrier, has three concentric circles of columns: one circle has octagonal shafts topped with seated lions, while the other two have capitals supported by dwarfs. Four Buddhas meditate for eternity at the cardinal points of the central stupa. The vatadage was built before the transfer of the capital to Polonnaruwa and dates from the construction of a temple in the 2C. The holy city reached its apogee in the 8C when the *vatadage* was built. Under the Chola, Medirigiriya became a satellite of Polonnaruwa. Parakrama Bahu and Nissamka Malla were responsible for building its finest monuments.

Making the most of Polonnaruwa

COMING AND GOING

Polonnaruwa is a cul-de-sac. The bus terminus and train station are at Kaduruwela, 5km east of the Parakrama Samudra, on the Batticaloa road.

By train – There are two trains daily to Colombo: an express at 8.30am (a 6hr journey) and a small mail train (9hr) at 6.30pm.

By bus – On arrival, you may ask to get off at Giritale, at the entrance to the archeological site, or at the crossroads of the Habarana and Batticaloa roads, near the police station, where there are also some hotels. When you leave, however, catch the bus at Kaduruwela if you want to get a seat. There are plenty of buses to Colombo (6hr) and Kandy (5hr), via Habarana (90min) and Dambulla (2hr30min). If travelling to Anuradhapura, it is better to go first to Habarana (43km), where ordinary and "Intercity" buses leave every 30min. For Sigiriya, change at Dambulla, where there are frequent bus services in the morning.

By car – Polonnaruwa is not very practical in terms of public transport. A car with a driver may facilitate the continuation of your journey. Several hotels offer this possibility. Estimate roughly US$20 to go to Kandy and Anuradhapura, US$30 to the international airport at Colombo and US$25 to go to Sigiriya and Dambulla and back in a day.

Getting around

By bike – Bikes can be hired from the Samudra hotel for about US$1 per day. You can also hire the services of a guide at the Rest House or the museum (estimate between 300Rs and 500Rs for a tour of between 2hr and 4hr).

Address book

Bank / Currency exchange – *Ceylan Bank*, on the corner of Circular Rd, near the Gajabha hotel. Monday-Friday 9am-3pm, Saturday 9am-12pm.

Post office / Telephone – *GPO*, Batticaloa Rd, 200m from the police station, towards Kaduruwela. Monday-Friday 9.30am-5pm.

Where to stay / Eating out

Polonnaruwa itself does not have a great range of accommodation because all the tourists with a vehicle only spend half a day here, and prefer to stay around Habarana, Dambulla or Giritale. There are a few hotels on the edge of the archeological site, and some others scattered around the modern town: that is all you have to choose from. There are no restaurants to speak of but some of the hotels have an adequate restaurant.

• In Polonnaruwa

Under US$7

Devi Tourist Home (Raheem Johoran), New Town Rd, 10min on foot from the police station and 1.5km from the bus stop, ☎ (027) 231 81 – 3rm. This smart little house in a residential area is spotlessly clean (mosquito nets), so that one can excuse the very small bathrooms. Good home cooking.

Orchid Guesthouse (D A Sooriyaarachchi), 70 Habarana Rd, access by passage between two shops, ☎ (027) 237 20, Fax (027) 237 21 – 8rm. Two categories of accommodation: the cheaper, rather gloomy rooms are situated in the house of the proprietor who has built another house at the end of the garden to accommodate his guests. The rooms are impeccably clean and the bathrooms modern. TV lounge and music available. Possible to hire car with driver.

Samudra Tourist Guesthouse (Ajantha Jayasinghe), Habarana Rd, ☎ (027) 228 17 – 7rm. You will receive a warm welcome here from a considerate young couple who will also help you to explore the area. They have even had a reference map of the area painted on the side of their house. The rooms (mosquito nets) are very clean and all have a balcony facing the garden. Agent for the hire of bikes, motorcycles and cars with a driver.

From US$7 to US$15

Gajabha Hotel & Restaurant, Kuruppu Garden, Lake Bund, ☎ (027) 223 94 – 17rm. A rather old hotel with small rooms (mosquito nets) and pre-historic bathrooms (cold water), but you will receive a warm welcome and the situation, just below the dam, opposite the museum, is ideal. The meals, served in the garden, are delicious and very reasonably priced. Bikes for hire and transfer available to Kaduruwela for a small sum.

Nirmala Guesthouse (N A Sooriyaarachchi), Circular Rd, ☎ (027) 230 40, Fax (027) 237 21 – 8rm. Basic rooms with clean, tiled bathrooms, situated in the house of the proprietor or in a separate building. Good local cooking.

Over US$30

Polonnaruwa Rest House, near the museum, by the Parakrama Samudra, ☎ (027) 222 99 – 10rm. Its situation is as idyllic as its service is appalling. In fact, only Room N° 1, where Queen Elizabeth stayed in 1954, is worth the investment (ship's cabin style with a terrace overlooking

Parakrama Samudra). No criticism of the rooms in general, except that the price is excessive for rooms with cold showers.

Seruwa Lake Resort (Ceylon Hotels Corporation), New Town, ☎(027) 224 11 – 28rm. A building with two floors, reached by a catwalk has rooms with mosquito nets and a small balcony overlooking the lake. Pleasant bar.

The Village, New Town, ☎(027) 224 05; book from Colombo: Harisons Hotel Ltd, 137 Main St, Col 11, ☎(01) 54 11 98, Fax (01) 54 11 99 – 36rm. Fairly pleasant brick bungalows or rooms opening onto the central patio of the main building. Rather a gloomy motel ambience, but it has hot water in the bathrooms and a very small swimming pool. Sri Lankan cooking.

• **In Giritale**

Some comfortable establishments have been built on the shores of the lake but the Royal Lotus and the Deers Park are too big to enable guests to enjoy the peaceful nature of the place.

From US$7 to US$15

Homage Hotel, Polonnaruwa Rd, on the edge of Giritale, ☎(027) 462 57; book from Colombo: Channel Hotels Ltd, 115A Duttu Gemunu St, Kohuwela, Dehiwela, ☎(01) 82 50 14 – 16rm. A simple, clean hotel, with an immense garden, at the crossroads where the Polonnaruwa road enters Giritale (bus stop). Its rooms have the essentials and the local cuisine is excellent.

From US$30 to US$45

Giritale Hotel, this is the third hotel, after the Royal Lotus and the Deers Park, ☎(027) 463 11, Fax (027) 460 86 – 42rm. An exceptional price-quality ratio at this hotel which has huge rooms – 35 of them with a view – painted in soft colours, as well as a restaurant, bar and swimming pool on the terrace above the lake. Bathrooms have hot water and guests are asked not to waste it. Massage and herbal baths available.

Other things to do

Feasts and festivals – ***Maha Shiva Ratri*** in the Shiva Devale n° 2, late February-early March. The old Chola temple is decorated with flowers, coconuts and palms, while the Tamil crowd in their best clothes chant hymns in honour of the god.

Water sports – Swimming and canoeing on the Parakrama Samudra (estimate US$3 for about 90min, arrange through the hotel). Also possible to hire boats on Lake Giritale (about US$5 for 1hr).

Shopping guide – ***Dhammika Wood Carving & Furniture Shop***, Bendiwewa, on the way out of Polonnaruwa on the Habarana road. Tourist shop selling wood carvings where you can see how the objects on sale are made.

THE CAVE TEMPLES★★★

SIGIRIYA AND DAMBULLA

North-Central Province – Sites are 19km apart
66km from Anuradhapura, 68km from Polonnaruwa and 72km from Kandy

Not to be missed

The pools and the rock fortress of Sigiriya, one of the oldest gardens in the world.
The life of Buddha portrayed on the wall of the Temple of the Great Kings of Dambulla.

And remember...

Make the ascent up to Sigiriya in the morning, as soon as the site opens.
Take a pocket torch to illuminate the paintings at Dambulla.
Avoid weekends and Sri Lankan public holidays.

Sigiriya and Dambulla: these are the names of two rocks perched above the Central Northern plain, each with an unusual history. They both served as refuges for a king, one hiding his shame at Sigiriya, the other fleeing his invaded capital for Dambulla. Today, these two sites are the most popular attractions on the island for Sri Lankan and foreign visitors alike, who brave the roughly-hewn steps to admire their treasures and, in particular, their paintings. On the cliff of Sigiriya, a group of large-breasted young girls holds a silent conversation, a piece of a puzzle which has never been deciphered. In the caves at Dambulla, various painters have portrayed the life of the Buddha and Buddhism on the island. The former are profane, the others more pious images, but all of them inspire the same sentiment in those who look at them: that they are participating in a colourful, universal dream.
The rock citadels are not only a cultural "must" but also a marvellous place to stop, with magnificent views of the wild landscape in this region. Visitors staying in the vicinity will soon begin to understand something of the rhythm of life in the jungle: the vibrating wings of insects and the croaking of frogs and toads fill the Sri Lankan night, until the birdsong begins at daybreak.

The hanging palace of Sigiriya★★★

Allow 2hr.

Daily 6am-7pm. Entrance fee, included in the Cultural Triangle round ticket. Tickets may be purchased at the Rest House and the round ticket at the Cultural Triangle office (3km from the site entrance). The site can only be reached via the west gate, 1.5km from the Rest House. Take the path opposite the gate, then turn left along the moat. The ideal solution is to stay nearby and then visit the site in the morning when it is quiet and still cool. Groups of visitors flock in from 9am onwards and are forced to queue at the more vertiginous, difficult places. Visiting the park also introduces visitors to the botany of the area: small signs identify the various types of trees.

Patricide to suicide

The king must have been in a curious state of mind to prefer this eagle's eyrie to the comforts of the city of Anuradhapura: but in the 5C, fear and remorse persuaded **Kasyapa** to establish himself in this citadel in the middle of the jungle. As King **Dhatusena's** elder son, he let himself be persuaded by the spiteful words of a cousin and deposed his father in order to take his place. As if this was not enough, his cousin, who had since become a general, told him that the old prisoner king had great riches. When Kasyapa confronted him about this, Dathusena invited his son to the shores of the Kala wewa, which he had had built to collect the precious water, and told him that this was all his wealth. Feeling swindled, Kasyapa ordered the evil cousin to kill Dhatusena, whom he walled up alive. But the new king, who had sought refuge at Sigiriya, had a brother, Mugalan, who raised an army to avenge his father. The citadel was impregnable, but he summoned his patricidal brother to come and face him on the battlefield, near Kurunegala. Kasyapa's men deserted him to re-join Mugalan's ranks. Left alone, he committed suicide, cutting his throat.

The rock citadel

Buddhist anchorites had been established in the region since the 3C BC, long before Kasyapa sought refuge on the rock of Sigiriya, but the extent of this royal enterprise is astonishing. Kasyapa the usurper reigned for 18 years, from 477 to 495, and devoted seven of those years to building his citadel. Abandoned after little more than ten years of occupation when Kasyapa committed suicide, it was "re-discovered" by **H Forbes** in 1831. Sigiriya, the "Lion Rock", is both a fortified capital, a palace with gardens and a monastery, all built on an unusual site that harmoniously combined a defensive stronghold with the comforts of royal life. In this respect, the architects of the 5C excelled themselves and laid out one of the most beautiful gardens ever conceived, marrying the symmetry of pavilions and pools with extraordinary rock forms, sculpted by nature, distributing the water of the reservoirs in cascades, rivers and jets of water. The whole site, with its fortifications, moats and gardens, covers an area of more than 100ha.

Tour of the site

Opposite the west gate, the **Archaeological Museum** *(8am-5pm; closed Thursday)* houses some architectural engravings confirming the existence of Buddhist communities before the arrival of Kasyapa, as well as two bricks from the 5C which have preserved the footprints of a man and a dog. The clay tiles and pipes of Sigiriya are stored in the pools! In 1967, vandals covered the portraits of the Damsels with green paint: photographs record the incident.

The area between the moats and the base of the rock was entirely devoted to the pleasure of the sovereign. Beyond the wall is a huge **garden*****, symmetrically arranged on two rising terraces on either side of the 160m-long avenue which rises towards the rock.

The first garden is that of the **pavilions** and **pools**. The excavation of the area (notice the old ground level which corresponds to the bank at the bottom of the trees) brought to light a whole network of terraces, courtyards, stretches of water of various depths and passages decorated with marble or pebbles. This complex was altered in the 10C-12C, during the Polonnaruwa period. On the right of the central avenue, the large square pool is served by four paths that once led to a central pavilion.

The second terrace aligns the **elegant perspective** of a French-style garden, with stretches of water fed by a complex system of channels, using the principle of inter-linked containers. The underground supply system still works and the pressure created by the narrowing of the pipes forced the water up through the holes in the stones. Look out for these small fountains after heavy rain.

On the third terrace, the landscape gardeners of the 5C traced the sinuous course of a river winding among the rock outcrops. On the right is a large platform surrounded by a ditch: at one time it supported a building (purpose unknown) that has since disappeared. On the left of the fourth terrace, an enormous block of granite lies next to an octagonal pool.

Further over is the **large rockery** situated at the foot of the rock. This garden makes brilliant use of the labyrinth of rocks, caves and rocky outcrops, working its way among them with a series of low brick walls which bank up the earth behind. It is here, in this chaos of minerals, that one of the secrets of the citadel is hidden: a passage under two blocks of stone resting against each other (notice on the left, below the overhang, traces of a painting of a female body.)

The citadel, which stands 180m above the plain, is sometimes interpreted as a replica of the residence of Kubera Vessavana, the god of wealth, ruler of the north and sovereign of the *yakkha*. The ascent is steep, but there are steps, terraces and walkways where one can pause for breath.

The first flight of steps ends under the rock that forms the gallery of the Damsels. A platform and a spiral staircase make it possible to climb up to admire the damsels (tickets are checked again at the entrance).

Only 21 **Damsels***** survive in the long painted gallery, which can be likened to a decorative wallpaper which once adorned the rock of Sigiriya up to the beginning of the Lion Staircase. Only the top half of their bodies are portrayed and it is probable that the lower half of the body was intentionally concealed by mist or clouds, to give the idea of creatures flying through the sky. They are undoubtedly not portraits but are part of a **vast composition** with a narrative purpose and are either symbolic or decorative. The women of the court, with their hairstyles and jewellery, portrayed according to the canons of beauty of the time, may have posed as models. The graceful gestures of the hands and the exchange of glances hint at a mysterious aura of complicity among these Damsels, masterly pieces in a puzzle of royal symbolism which will probably never be deciphered. Other fragments of paintings survive among the shelters of the rock garden which resembles a series of decorated pavilions at the base of the rock.

As you make your way down the spiral staircase, look out for the entrance to a gallery backing onto the rock wall decorated by the famous paintings above. This is the **Mirror Wall**, built in brick, but thus named because of the smooth coating of its inner surface. Between the 6C and 13C, the softness of the stucco prompted various visitors to write their impressions of the mysterious Damsels in **magnificent verses**. These admirers, not all of whom are anonymous, almost certainly include some of the monks who occupied the site after royalty had moved out.

Speak to me of love...

Some 700 of the literary graffiti on the Mirror Wall have been translated: "I, Lord Sangapala, wrote this verse / We spoke to them without receiving any response / These women of the mountain did not even deign to flutter their eyelids at us"; "Sweet young maiden against the mountainside, whose teeth are like gems, whose eyes shine like the lotus flower, let your heart pour out its feelings for me"; "Women such as you and the hearts of men, surrender yourselves, bodies trembling with desire"; "Their bodies shine, like the moon floating in the cool breeze"...

M Gotin / SCOPE

The mysterious conversation between the damsels of Sigiriya

The Mirror Wall ends in a terrace *(drinks stall, expensive but welcome)*, where the paws of a colossal brick lion, which once framed the bottom of the staircase, are all that is left of the **Lion Platform**** which led to the palace of Kasyapa. This last flight of steps, cut into the granite, leads to a **platform** (1.5ha) occupied by the actual palace *(in May-June, be careful of the strong winds which buffet the exposed platform)*. Up here, the only really spectacular remaining feature is the pool gouged out of the bedrock, but the **view***** over the gardens, the Sigiriya ponds and the jungle beneath the rocky outcrops is worth the vertigo.

Go back down the same way. Once past the Mirror Wall, take the other staircase (not the one you came up before). This brings you back to the rockery, but this time on the south face of the rock.

After the palace was abandoned in the 5C or 6C, the base of the rocky escarpment and the gardens were converted into a monastic complex. Several rock shelters were converted into temples. Look out for the **audience hall***, a rocky platform which juts out in mid-air, the floor and throne of which have been carved out of the rock. Below, a rocky projection forms the silhouette of the head of an angry cobra. Below this Cobra Hood Cave are the remains of some ornamental paintings (tendrils and medallions) with traces of red and green.

The path leads gently down towards the exit, where there are stalls selling refreshments.

The cave temple of Dambulla★★

Allow 1hr.

Daily 6am-7pm. Access to the rock temple is about 3km south of the clock-tower in Dambulla. A modern concrete temple marks the entrance at the foot of the rock. Tickets can be purchased here. Since the monastic authorities have made a separate entrance for foreign tourists, the latter cannot mingle with the pilgrims who make the ascent from another point further south. These two worlds do not meet until they reach the top, on the esplanade which leads to the caves. The rock stands 150m above the plain. Allow 10min for the fairly easy ascent, up steps cut out of the rock. En route are stalls selling wood carvings, reproduction antiques, T-shirts and postcards. Shoes must be removed at the top. Shoulders and knees should be covered when entering the temple. A torch is vital. Photography is not permitted inside the caves.

According to archeologists, cults were celebrated in the caves at Dambulla long before Buddhism was introduced to the island, but legend links their destiny to that of the arrival of the doctrine. According to the *Mahavamsa*, when Devanampiya Tissa embraced the doctrine as a result of his encounter with Mahinda, a bamboo forest miraculously sprouted in front of the caves. Later on, they served as a refuge for King **Vattagamani Abhaya** (89-77 BC) who had fled Anuradhapura when it was overthrown by Tamil invaders. He endowed the site to which he owed his safety and gave it to the *Sangha* (community of Buddhist monks). In the 12C, the very prolific **Nissamka Malla** of Polonnaruwa (1187-96) transformed this austere place of meditation into a fairytale world of gold and silver, which the *Mahavamsa* described as **Swarna Giriguhava** (Golden Caves). Today, nothing remains of the later periods. The wooden, stone or brick statues have been covered with so many coats of paint that it is no longer possible to date them. As for the profusion of paintings which adorn the smallest crevice, like a brocade coloured with vermilion and ochre, they date back to the great works of **Kirti Sri Rajasinha** of Kandy (1747-82), the Tamil prince who became a great patron of Buddhist art. His patronage was responsible for almost all the 6 000sqm of rock paintings. A site of key importance for Buddhism, Dambulla is also a national symbol. At the fall of the kingdom of Kandy, there was an uprising amongst the monks which resulted in the enthronement of a monarch here in 1848. Suppressed by the colonial army, the revolt was short-lived.

The golden temples

The ascent ends on a **paved courtyard** with a Bo tree. Clinging to the rock, this terrace has a marvellous view of the plain as far as the citadel of Sigiriya. A cloister gallery daubed with lime seems to disappear into the long cleft in the rock. Behind it are the caves of Dambulla. They were part of a deep, half-natural, half man-made cave, divided into temples by partitions. The first four caves are decorated with paintings dating from building and restoration work carried out under the patronage of King Kirti Sri Rajasinha. The fifth was restored under the auspices of a local figure in 1915.

Cave 1, the **Devaraja Vihara**★ (Temple of the Lord of the Gods), is entered through an archway between two bearers of fly-swats. Reclining on its side, along the rock wall from which it is separated, a 14m-long Buddha rests in the eternal sleep of *Parinirvana*. His body has the multi-coloured halo typical of the Kandyan school, while his disciples stand against the wall, holding water lilies. At the Master's feet, two of them hide their face in their hands as a sign of sorrow. A small blue-painted chapel nearby is dedicated to the protector god Kataragama.

The Maharaja Vihara*** (Temple of the Great Kings) is the second cave and the largest of them all, 52m long and 23m deep. It is attributed to **Vattagamani Abhaya**. It was altered several times over the centuries before being completely restored in the 18C. Access is through two doors, the main one of which *(on the left)* opens onto the statue of Buddha, with the bodhisattva Maitreya, the god Natha, and two other seated buddhas. At the back, against the rock wall, are the guardians Saman and Vishnu, accompanied by painted effigies of Kataragama and Ganesh. On the right, the *dagoba* with eight seated buddhas has been gouged out of the rock. The buddha lying against the entrance wall dates only from the 19C. Bathed in light diffused by the begging bowls on the ground the paintings covering the ceiling have a surreal quality about them. The narrative cycle starts from a point in the corner to the left of the main statue. A panel divided into registers, at the level of the seated Buddha, tells the story of events in the **life of Buddha***** before the Enlightenment: you will recognise the dream announcing his birth to his mother, Queen Maya, by the white elephant near the door of the pavilion in which she is resting; then comes the Great Departure and the assaults by Mara (the depiction of his attempt to seduce his daughters, with their bare breasts and their hips swelling beneath the pleats of their sarongs, is the most remarkable). The sequence of the Seven Weeks after the Enlightenment is illustrated on the overhang of the *dagoba*; the *naga* Mucilinda protects the Master in meditation by enveloping his body. On one side, a rocky overhang forms a natural alcove over which a statue of King Nissamka Malla watches. Its walls portray the important stages in the **spread of Buddhism to Ceylon**, among them the conversion of Devanampiya Tissa, the building of the great *dagoba* reliquaries of Anuradhapura, and the fight between Duttugemunu and Elara.

In one corner of the cave, a container collects flowing water. It is attributed with miraculous properties because it flows all the year round, even during the dry season.

The temples of Dambulla

The Maha Alut Vihara* (The New Temple), opens with a *makara torana* in the Kandyan style and is separated from the previous cave by a stone wall. The **statue of King Kirti Sri Rajasinha**, dressed in courtly robes, his hands folded, stands at the entrance, and his court of dignitaries are painted behind him. On the ceiling, seated in a pavilion with columns culminating in lotus flowers, Buddha preaches to two gatherings: his disciples and the gods. The **Buddha in samadhi***, seated against the far wall, under an exuberant *makara torana*, and the **reclining Buddha*** by the left wall are particularly remarkable. Both have been carved out of the granite of which the cave is composed.

The last two caves, which are very small, are less interesting. There is a small stupa on the floor of the **Pacchima Vihara** (West Temple), where the statues of Vishnu and Saman, behind their curtains, watch over the meditating Buddhas. In the **Devana Alut Vihara** (Second New Temple), Buddha rests among his seated followers.

From Dambulla to Kandy

72km – Allow 2hr30min.

The road that connects Dambulla and Kandy is excellent. If you are travelling by car, go the long way round and take in the small stone temple where Buddhist doctrine was written down for the first time. The road that goes back to Kurunegala (56km) is similarly dotted with remains *(see p 168)*.

Leave Dambulla by the road leading to Kandy. After about 20km, a track on the left leads to a temple (1km).

■ **Nalanda Gedige*** – *Entrance fee, but included in the Cultural Triangle round ticket.* The only Buddhist temple to be built in stone and in the purest style of the Hindu temples of Southern India, this *gedige* is shrouded in mystery. No buildings, apart from the ruins of a small stupa, provide any information about the monastery which once stood here. Only an inscription dates the building to the 10C. Today it is reached by a track lined with the remains of sculpted ramps, that has been built across the lake. Until the late 1970s, the temple was surrounded by rice-fields, but the building of a dam as part of the Mahaweli project flooded this area. The *gedige* was dismantled and rebuilt, stone by stone, on the hill where it stands today.

The structure of the temple is pure **Dravidian**, with a horseshoe shaped roof, the south tympanum of which features a statue of a basking Kubera. The custodians of the site will not fail to show you the explicit depiction of eroticism engraved on the south side of the base. Unusual on the island, such depictions are nevertheless common in Indian shrines. The cella, which is open to the west, was preceded by a hypostyle porch, the pillars of which, decorated with ornamental bas-reliefs, can still be seen. Inside, on each side of the restored Buddha, there is an extraordinary, fragmented pantheon which adds to the air of mystery. When cooled by the breeze from the lake, the site is idyllic.

Go back to the Kandy road. Seventeen kilometres further on, you pass through the town of Palapetwela. Continue on the A9. Alternatively, to the right, there is also a minor road with hairpin bends, which climbs up through the terraced rice-fields towards the cocoa plantations and eventually rejoins the Dambulla-Kurunegala road. It also leads to the Silver Temple of Ridigama (see p 168).

After Palapetwela, the houses on either side of the road advertise **Spice Gardens**, or *Batik workshops*: you are entering the area of the famous spice gardens. Here you can find out (in almost every language) everything there is to know about the various plants and spices that are grown here and their culinary or medicinal applications. The area is particularly well known for its essential oils that are made here and sold all over the island: panaceas for migraine, cough syrup, dental powder, acne cream, etc.

Continue as far as Alu Vihara, situated 2km before Matale.

■ **Alu Vihara** (Temple of the Ashes) – This complex has great significance for the Buddhist world. Buddha spent his life teaching, but left nothing written down. The preservation of his doctrine was therefore entrusted to the memory of the disciples who had listened to him. The need to set it down permanently was the reason behind the Buddhist councils, the first of which was held in India in the 6C BC. The Buddhist doctrine was divided into three parts, known as the Three Baskets *(Tripitaka)*, which were still handed down orally. The fourth council took place in Ceylon, at the end of which the *Tripitaka* was finally written down, in Pali, in the scriptorium of the Alu Vihara monastery. This **precious library** was partially destroyed when the British quelled the revolt of the monks of Dambulla in 1848. An association is patiently reconstructing it on sheets of talipot palm. If you offer a donation, they will give you a demonstration.

Writing on palm-leaves

The long leaves of the talipot were the papyrus of Ceylon. The palm leaves are cut into strips, dried, then polished by rubbing them against bamboo. The writing is engraved with a stylus, then rubbed with carbon powder thinned down with coconut oil. Finally, the surface is cleaned with ground rice which soaks up the excess, leaving only the engraved text black.

Nothing remains of the semi-rock temple built in the 1C BC. The main **cave** houses a reclining Buddha and its walls are decorated with modern paintings. The paintings in the vestibule portray hell with sadistic complacency. Beware, sinners, for you risk being mutilated, carved up, burned alive, impaled, torn apart or disembowelled!

2km further on, you enter the small town of Matale. Hindu temples and mosques show that the inhabitants are mainly Tamil, descendants of the labourers imported by the British to work in the plantations. Kandy is 26km away.

Making the most of Sigiriya and Dambulla

COMING AND GOING

By train – Habarana, on the Colombo-Trincomalee line, is the nearest railway station for visiting Sigiriya (24km) and Dambulla (25km). Buses run to Dambulla every 30min. However, only two trains a day stop at this station, on the line from Trincomalee or from Polonnaruwa.

By bus – The bus is by far the most practical solution and also the fastest. Whatever your point of departure or your next destination, you are strongly advised to go first to Dambulla, which has two bus terminals. The first, located below the clock tower, has regular services to the south of the island: Colombo (5hr), Kandy (2hr) and Kurunegala (1hr). The second, situated on the edge of the town on the Habarana road, provides regular services to Anuradhapura (1hr), Sigiriya (30min), Trincomalee (4hr, and many road-blocks en route) and Polonnaruwa (2hr30min). There are services every 20min between Dambulla and Sigiriya. Buses stop at the Rest House, opposite the site entrance.

By car – If you are travelling by car, a short cut cross-country means that it is possible to get from Polonnaruwa to Sigiriya, without going to Habarana. To do this, leave the road at Moragaswewa, 41km north of Polonnaruwa: Sigiriya lies 13km along this road.

Address book

Banks / Currency exchange – ***Hatton Bank***, opposite the bus terminus on Habarana Rd, at Dambulla.

Post office / Telephone – Post offices at Sigiriya and Dambulla.

Where to stay

At the epicentre of the Cultural Triangle, the area has been singled out for development of some luxurious tourist resorts. Some are "tourist factories", while others, built deep in the landscape, are pleasant places to spend a holiday. There is plenty to do if you decide to stay three or four days depending on your budget: special buffets, folk performances, Ayurveda massage parlours, rides on elephants, in ox-carts, jeeps or on horseback, bird-watching itineraries (there are at least 50 species here, including a kind of falcon in the dry area). All the sites in the Cultural Triangle are situated within a radius of less than 100km from Dambulla: Anuradhapura (66km), Polonnaruwa (68km), Kandy (72km) and Kurunegala (56km).

• In Sigiriya

Since the government's archeology department has declared that the sector to the south of the citadel is to be excavated, this part of the village, where the cheaper hotels are situated, is likely to disappear. The choice is thus considerably restricted. Travellers on a lower budget will have to try Inamaluwa.

From US$30 to US$40

Sigiriya Rest House, opposite the site entrance, ☎ (066) 234 84 – 17rm. The price of rooms is totally unjustified, but this is still a pleasant place to come for breakfast or a cup of tea. Veranda, opposite the rock.

From US$40 to US$70

Sigiriya Hotel, in the forest, on the southeast edge of the site, ☎ (066) 849 31, Fax (066) 848 11, sigiriya@slt.lk – 80rm. CC Benefiting from the same surroundings, but much more successfully than its neighbour, the Village, the hotel has the advantage of a view of the rock. Very large, comfortable rooms.

Sigiriya Village, in the forest, on the southeast side of the site, ☎ (066) 849 31, Fax (066) 848 11 – 120rm. CC Bungalows dotted around the luxuriant garden but lacking atmosphere. Restaurant. Disappointing.

• In Inamaluwa

10km from Dambulla and 9km from Sigiriya, at the crossroads of the Habarana-Dambulla and Sigiriya roads. The hotels, advertised by signs, are near the road.

From US$10 to US$15

Ancient Villa, Galakotuwa, Kibissa, 2km from the crossroads and 7km from Sigiriya, ☎ (072) 62 78 54, Fax (066) 845 28 – 3rm. The ideal place for nature lovers. Bungalows with balconies are scattered in an area planted with trees, on the edge of the jungle. Good cooking. The owner has a "tuk-tuk" (three-wheeler). The best address in this area.

Eden Garden, Sigiriya Rd, Inamaluwa, 100m from the crossroads, ☎ (066) 846 35, Fax (066) 845 28 – 18rm. CC A pleasant setting with comfortable rooms (hot water). Very warm welcome. Possible to hire car with driver. Swimming pool.

Inamaluwa Inn, Sigiriya Rd, Inamaluwa, 1km from the crossroads, ☎ (066) 845 33 / (072) 66 94 72 – 5rm. Rooms with the bare essentials, overlooking a veranda – good for relaxing in the shade. The restaurant is on the gloomy side.

• In Dambulla

From US$15 to US$30

Dambulla Rest House, at the foot of the cave temple, on the other side of the road, ☎ (066) 847 99 – 4rm. Although reasonably clean, its rooms with painted concrete walls are nothing special (tiled bathrooms with cold water), although it is well situated. Poor restaurant and service.

Gimanhala Transit Hotel, 754 Anuradhapura Rd, opposite the caves, north of the town centre. ☎ (066) 848 64 / (072) 22 51 43, Fax (066) 848 17 – 10rm. Rooms regularly given a coat of fresh paint and bathrooms with hot water. Local cooking with restaurant overlooking the small swimming pool. Only one disadvantage: too close to the road.

• At Kandalama

From US$70 to US$85

Kandalama Hotel (Aitken Spence), on the south shore, access along 6km of very bad track, ☎ (066) 234 75, Fax (066) 234 82 – 162rm. TV CC. Hanging gardens blend with the surrounding jungle. Built of metal, granite and huge glass windows. One of the restaurants, accessed by a bridge, is situated in a cave. Swimming pool, spectacularly positioned above Lake Kandalama.

The Culture Club (Connaissance de Ceylan), on the northern shore, 12km from Dambulla, ☎ (066) 318 22, Fax (066) 319 32 – 92rm. CC A hotel village devoted to the cultural and natural side of island traditions. The bungalows are built like rural adobe houses, their doors painted like those of small temples. An ideal holiday place on the shores of Lake Kandalama. Note the Ayurveda treatment centre.

• In Habarana

15km from Sigiriya and 25km from Dambulla.

From US$10 to US$15

Habarana Rest House, opposite the bus-stop, on the Dambulla road, ☎ (066) 700 03; book from Colombo: Ceylon Hotels Corporation, 411 Galle Rd, Col 4, ☎ (01) 50 35 58, Fax (01) 50 35 04 – 4rm. This old British colonial lodge is not without charm. Good facilities, but too near the road. Only if there is nowhere else.

From US$15 to US$30

Acme Transit Hotel (Asoka Bandara Abeysinghe), 1km from the centre of the Polonnaruwa road, ☎(066) 700 16 – 4rm. The comfort of AC in a small but airy house, only a stone's throw from the bus terminus. Local cooking at modest prices.

From US$40 to US$70

The Village (Keells), behind The Lodge, near the Habarana reservoir, ☎ (066) 700 46, Fax (066) 700 47 – 106rm. TV CC Could be described as "rustic luxury", with its clusters of squat, tiled bungalows spread over 12ha of forest.

From US$70 to US$85

The Lodge (Keells), 1km from the centre, on the Dambulla road, ☎ (066) 700 12, Fax (066) 700 72 – 150rm. TV CC Massive, but well thought-out, this complex offers bungalows (tastefully furnished) in 9ha of parkland. Waiters in traditional costume serve in the restaurant, which overlooks a huge swimming pool. Bar, massage and sauna.

Eating out

• In Dambulla

Under US$7

On the road between Matale and Kandy. ***JC's Village***, 175 Kapuwatta, 2km from the caves, ☎ (066) 844 11. Excellent Western or local cuisine, served on a shady veranda overlooking the garden. Two rooms in bungalows: but prices inflated. ***Rangiri Restaurant*** (Saman's), 44th Mile Post, Matale Rd, 500m from the caves, ☎ (066) 844 12. An impressive selection of curries, delicious at lunchtime but rather disappointing when heated up at dinner. With its tea-room and antiques, has unusual charm.

• In Habarana

Under US$7

Rukmali Rest, Polonnaruwa Rd, Sigiriya junction, Moragaswewa, 2km from Habarana, ☎ (066) 700 59. A blaze of colour and a cornucopia of curries.

Other things to do

Elephant rides are the attraction of this area. All the large hotels organise them. You can also approach the pachyderm owners directly, on the edge of Habarana on the Dambulla road. Estimate US$15 per person for an hour's ride.

Kandy★★

Central Province – Pop 105 000
Alt 488m – Mild climate all year round
73km from Nuwara Eliya, 116km from Colombo and 138km from Anuradhapura

Not to be missed
The "puja" in the morning at the Temple of the Tooth.
The sombre elegance of the "devala", almost devoid of tourists.

And remember...
Watch out for fake gems (in the shops),
false bargains (tea and spices), and other rip-off merchants.

On the edge of the old country "of the mountains" *(kanda)*, Kandy was the last capital of the Sinhalese monarchy and a testament to the kings as aesthetes in their choice of location: a ridge of mountains, the dense jungle that borders the gardens, tea and rice fields, the artificial lake to reflect the sky, the arc of the royal city skirting the water's edge. This royal city is also a **holy city**. Ever since it was founded in the 16C, it has housed one of the most sacred relics of Buddhism, a tooth of Buddha, collected from his funeral pyre. Every day, at dawn, midday and dusk, the reliquary containing the relic is venerated to the sound of drums. A depository of the last vestiges of Sinhalese royalty, a focal point of worship for Buddhists all over the world and a great centre of monastic tradition, Kandy is still a **capital city**, despite the creation of Colombo. It is the custom for the heads of state of Sri Lanka to organise important official ceremonies here and it is here that they come to make their inaugural speech. This combination of symbols made it a target for the LTTE (Liberation Tigers of Tamil Eelam) who were responsible for the bomb that went off here on 25 January 1998. Security measures around the sacred enclosure have since been tightened up. But Kandy was quick to regain its confidence: its great annual festival, the parade in the month of Esala in honour of the tooth of Buddha, took place as usual that same summer. More than Colombo, it is at Kandy, half city, half country, that visitors can experience both everyday Ceylon and the Ceylon of festival and ceremony.

The last capital of the kings of Lanka

The shifting sands of power – In the 13C, the fall of Polonnaruwa, which had by then been the capital for five centuries, weakened the power of the Sinhalese royal family. While a Tamil royal family had established itself in the north, in the Jaffna peninsula, the Sinhalese royal family had built and abandoned as many as ten capitals in the southwest. They eventually established themselves at Kotte, not far from the modern city of Colombo, moving nearer the west coast and its maritime trade. Also attracted by the maritime trade, the **Portuguese** of Goa settled on the coast of the "cinnamon isle" in 1505, moving their seat of power to Kotte and then Jaffna. Then in 1590 the Sinhalese withdrew to Kandy, one of the cities built during the period of itinerant power, in the heart of the mountains of the southwest.

A natural fortress – Up in the mountainous bastion of Kandy, which had become **Maha Nuwara**, "the Great City", the Sinhalese monarchs reconstructed the splendour of royalty for more than two centuries. The choice of the site proved to be a good one, since neither the Portuguese, nor the Dutch who came after them with the highly lucrative spice trade succeeded in conquering the last independent kingdom of Ceylon.

But the shock waves from the European wars had repercussions even in Southern Asia, and with the occupation of the Low Countries by France, England annexed Ceylon in 1796. Without doubt, these new masters of the island would not have been able to bring down the kingdom of Kandy if the latter had not been undermined by court intrigues. In fact, the royal house had been linked to the **Nayak aristocracy**, descendants of the last Hindu kingdom on the mainland, Vijayanagar. Nayak princesses married Sinhalese kings, so that, in 1739, when one of the sovereigns passed on the crown to his wife's brother, the Nayaks, now converted to Buddhism, mounted the throne of Kandy. This is the origin of the factions which divided the throne of Kandy at the end of the 18C, when the old Sinhalese aristocracy came into conflict with the nobles of the Dravidian princes.

A tooth of wisdom

In the 13C, the venerable Dharmakirti composed a poem that related the legend of the tooth of Buddha. Like the relics transported by the Crusaders in the Middle Ages, it played the role of a talisman for the Sinhalese kingdoms. A guarantee of royal sovereignty, it fell into the hands of the Portuguese in 1560. The Buddhist kingdom of Burma offered to redeem the relic from them but principle proved stronger than profit: the tooth was crushed publicly in a mortar and dispersed on the coast of Goa. This, however, did not account for the miraculous nature of the relic of Buddha. Some time afterwards the Buddhist world learned that the Portuguese had merely used a vulgar copy of the sacred relic and that the tooth was still in the possession of the kings of Kandy.

Twilight of a kingdom – In 1789, **Sri Vikrama Rajasinha** became king of Kandy. He was to be its last. It was he who gave the city the face we see today. He had a dam built to contain the waters of a tributary of the Mahaweli and to create a pleasure lake, with a royal park, baths, and small island for escaping the summer heat. In the palace, near the Temple of the Tooth, he built an octagonal tower on which to appear to the people of Kandy. In politics, he showed himself to be strong enough to thwart British ambitions: in March 1800, the legation led by General McDowall was obliged to retreat to the frontiers of the realm; in June 1803, the troops of Major Davie were massacred on the banks

Kandy nestling in its verdant setting

C Bowman / SCOPE

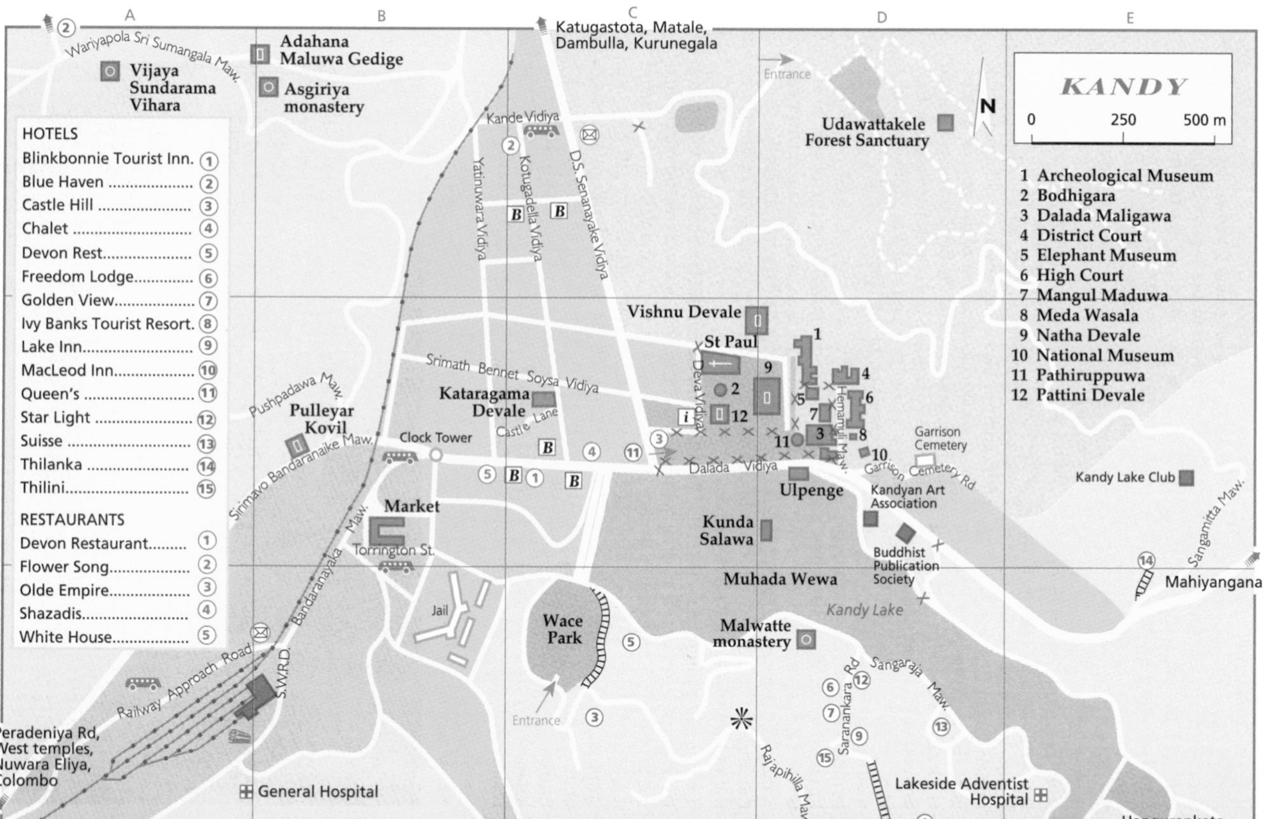
KANDY
0 250 500 m
1 Archeological Museum
2 Bodhigara
3 Dalada Maligawa
4 District Court
5 Elephant Museum
6 High Court
7 Mangul Maduwa
8 Meda Wasala
9 Natha Devale
10 National Museum
11 Pathiruppuwa
12 Pattini Devale
HOTELS
Blinkbonnie Tourist Inn. 1
Blue Haven 2
Castle Hill 3
Chalet 4
Devon Rest 5
Freedom Lodge 6
Golden View 7
Ivy Banks Tourist Resort. 8
Lake Inn 9
MacLeod Inn 10
Queen's 11
Star Light 12
Suisse 13
Thilanka 14
Thilini 15
RESTAURANTS
Devon Restaurant 1
Flower Song 2
Olde Empire 3
Shazadis 4
White House 5
Udawattakele Forest Sanctuary
Katugastota, Matale, Dambulla, Kurunegala
Vijaya Sundarama Vihara
Adahana Maluwa Gedige
Asgiriya monastery
Vishnu Devale
St Paul
Kataragama Devale
Pulleyar Kovil
Market
Clock Tower
Jail
Wace Park
Kunda Salawa
Muhada Wewa
Malwatte monastery
Ulpenge
Kandy Lake
Kandy Lake Club
Kandyan Art Association
Buddhist Publication Society
Garrison Cemetery
Lakeside Adventist Hospital
General Hospital
Mahiyangana
Peradeniya Rd, West temples, Nuwara Eliya, Colombo
Wariyapola Sri Sumangala Maw.
D.S. Senanayake Vidiya
Kotugadella Vidiya
Yatinuwara Vidiya
Kande Vidiya
Srimath Bennet Soysa Vidiya
Castle Lane
Deva Vidiya
Dalada Vidiya
Hemamuli Maw.
Garrison Cemetery Rd
Sangamitta Maw.
Sangaraja Maw.
Saranankara Rd
Rajapihilla Maw
Torrington St.
S.W.R.D. Bandaranayaka Maw.
Sirimavo Bandaranaike Maw.
Pushpadawa Maw.
Railway Approach Road
Entrance

of the Mahaweli. However, Sri Vikrama Rajasinha was far from being a popular king: his **expensive building projects** in Kandy weighed heavily on the population, and the Sinhalese aristocracy took the popular discontent to heart. Also, when Great Britain finally succeeded in taking over the kingdom in 1815, when Vikrama Rajasinha was deported to the country of his Nayak ancestors, in the Fortress of Vellore in Tamil Nadu (in southern India), the Kandyan nobility officially dismissed their king, entrusting his lands to British sovereignty. This extraordinary meeting took place in the audience hall of the royal palace, one of the last achievements of the deposed king.

Tour of the city

Allow one day.

The **lake** of Kandy is an ideal point of reference. It was created by the last King of Ceylon and so well does it blend into its surroundings that you would think it were natural. On its northern shore lie the old royal palace and its religious buildings, the white walls of which stand out against the forest of Udawattakele with the precision of an architect's drawing. On the south side, it hugs the hills of the residential quarter, where the better hotels are situated. Now that the **Dalada Vidiya** has been closed to motor vehicles, the traffic on the southern shore is much more congested, making the walk around the lake (4km) a less pleasant experience because of the pollution. However, short cruises on the lake on small motorboats leave from the jetty, to the west. To the northwest, the city is built around the commercial centre of the White House, the market and the clock tower. It is possible to visit the most important monuments in half a day. As for strolling through the town or walking in the hills, take as long as you like.

The Temple of the Tooth and the royal buildings** (D2)

Daily 5.30am-4pm. Entrance fee, not included in the Cultural Triangle ticket. Photography charge. Since the bomb attack in 1998, only two of the three daily "pujas" are open to the public: between 6am and 7am and between 10am and 11am. Ideally, come to the first, the second being very crowded with tourists. The perimeter of the Temple of the Tooth is now subjected to draconian security measures. The only point of access is on the esplanade, opposite the Queen's Hotel. Visitors must be correctly dressed, their legs covered (sarongs can be hired to the left of the entrance) and bags are checked. Leave your shoes to the right of the temple, by the railings. Take note! You will not be allowed to come back out of the same entrance. To collect your shoes, you must walk around the temple boundary.

Until Kandy was taken over by the British, the relic of the Tooth was the centre of attention. The chapel was situated within the precincts of the palace, some parts of which are still standing, now converted into offices and museums. The temple is still managed by the *diyawadana nilame*, the lay curator elected by the high priests, who is also in charge of the calendar of ceremonies.

The procession in the month of Esala

Established in the 18C by King Kirti Sri Rajasinha, this procession revives the pomp of the Sinhalese kingdoms of old: there are elephants caparisoned with brocade, gold and silver, spear and banner bearers, yak-tail fly-swats and precious palanquins, dancers and acrobats. This splendour pays homage to the relic of Buddha of which Kandy is the custodian. For six nights, there are five "perahera", four of which represent the divine protectors of Buddhism and of the city, the fifth, headed by a master elephant with long tusks, is consecrated to the Tooth (only a replica is now carried in the procession for security reasons). On the seventh night, the palanquins ("randoli") of the participants in the "devala" come to assemble at the five columns and the "perahera" reaches its final climax.

The present **Dalada Maligawa**★★ (Palace of the relic of the Tooth) was built between 1687 and 1707, with further work being carried out between 1747 and 1782. Like all buildings destined to house the precious relic, it is a veritable strongbox. The structures visible from the outside comprise an impressive stone rampart enclosing the actual temple, which stands two storeys high on a platform in the centre of a courtyard. This enclosure wall and the octagonal tower in front of the entrance gate date from the time of the last king of Ceylon.

The Pathiruppuwa★ (Octagonal Tower) was originally the platform for the royal appearances built by Sri Vikrama Rajasinha in the early 19C. These days it has a new role, because it is from here that the new heads of State come to make their first official speech.

A flight of steps leads up to the entrance of the palace, opening onto a **monumental porch** flanked by two guardian statues. A corridor leads to the covered courtyard of the temple built by King Narendrasinha (1707-39). In the old **image house** of Buddha, on the ground floor of the building, are treasures that have been proffered by the kings and dignitaries of Kandy. The door, which is always kept closed, is masked by a curtain embroidered with a *dagoba*, the threshold in the traditional half-moon shape. Stone columns with capitals in the form of a lotus flower support a canopy, the **caissons**★★ of which are adorned with decorative compositions: there are interlaced human and animal figures, as well as figures clasping lotus flowers. Opposite the temple, a pavilion with columns shelters the drummers during the daily ceremonies.

A staircase leads to the **upper gallery** of the courtyard, which is closed off by shutters. It is connected to the first floor of the temple by a small bridge. There, behind a gilt railing, the **golden reliquary** in the form of a *dagoba* rests on a silver table. It contains a nest of six more boxes: the famous tooth, which is rarely on view, lies inside the smallest one. Three keys are needed to open the portal: one is kept by the *diyawadana nilame*, the other two by the superiors of the monasteries of Malwatte and Asgiriya. Whether visible or invisible, the holy relic is very dear to the hearts of Buddhists. As the stream of tourists moves along, the women in particular pause momentarily, getting down on their knees in the shade cast by the shutters. Others lay flowers on the table, almost invisible under the colourful array of offerings.

The building that occupies the side of the courtyard opposite the entrance is an **image house** built in 1956. Inside, a series of panels relates the episodes from the history of the relic up to the openings organised by the British Governor Edward Barnes in the hope that the miraculous powers of the Tooth would put an end to a long period of drought. This is the current exit of the Dalada Maligawa. It opens onto the **Meda Wasala** (Princesses' Apartments), one of the 18 buildings and pavilions which comprised the royal palace in the late 18C. The others have not survived.

Turn left out of the exit and walk around the temple to get to the **Elephant Museum** (*Daily, 9am-5pm. Entrance fee.*) which is situated next to the Archaeological Museum. This is a veritable mausoleum, housing the embalmed remains of **Maligawa**, the patriarch of the elephants of Kandy, who died in 1988 aged 84. The venerable pachyderm, whose responsibility it was to carry the relic of the Tooth in the procession held in the month of Esala, was honoured with a state funeral.

Head back towards the Temple of the Tooth and turn right to collect your shoes. You are very near the museum, situated on the corner of Garrison Cemetery Rd and Hemamuli Maw.

On the shore of the lake, the **Ulpenge*** (Bathing Pavilion) was converted into a library by the British and is now the police superintendent's office. This elegant building, surrounded by a peristyle on two levels, completes the female quarters of the palace and is the reason behind the creation of the lake: the pleasure of the sovereign and his harem, for which the **Kunda Salawa** had been built, on an island in the middle of the water. The British prosaically replaced it with a powder magazine, which was destroyed in the 1960s.

Since it was closed to motor traffic, **Dalada Vidiya** has become the great pedestrian thoroughfare between the commercial centre of the town and the offices which were established in the colonial period near the royal complex. At rush hour, a constant stream of civil servants, briefcase in hand, together with schoolchildren in uniform flows along beside the railings of the Temple of the Tooth.

The National Museum** *(9am-5pm; closed Fridays and Saturdays. Entrance fee, but included in the Cultural Triangle round ticket. Allow 1hr. Bags must be left at the entrance)* is housed in the **Palle Wasala** (Queen's Palace)**, built in the last third of the 18C. The pomp of the Kandyan court was expressed through a collection of artistic objects which reflect a level of skill that has been practically abandoned by craftsmen today *(the tour starts on the left of the entrance, then works round clockwise)*. The first section is devoted to the **textiles** and **jewellery**** worn by the women and dignitaries of the court: there are ladies' blouses embroidered with gold thread, cotton with woven geometric patterns or stamped with wooden moulds, as well as muslin garments with gold brocade worn by the nobility on important occasions.
The **crockery** in the royal kitchens gives an idea of the refined nature of the objects used in the royal household: it includes presses made of rice pulp, carved wooden coconut graters, skimmers with carved handles depicting rows of animals or human figures, and ladles made with half a lacquered or carved coconut. The small copper plates with stands *(serak kale)* served as "plates" for the nobility and the clergy.
The gallery opening out onto the courtyard exhibits some **old palm manuscripts****, together with the instruments that were used for writing. The central pavilion contains some magnificent **window frames**** and some door frames carved with *makara torana*. There are also some **ceremonial weapons**, and examples of insignia and ritual objects used in the *devala* and during the *perahera*. The two last rooms contain **ivory carvings**** and **watercolours** by European artists, providing a chronicle of Kandy in the 19C.
Turn right out of the museum: this short street is lined by the most important remains of the old royal complex.

The Mangul Maduwa* (Audience hall) lies on the north side of the Dalada Maligawa. This is where the Kandyan nobles ratified the transfer of the kingdom to the British Crown in 1815. This hypostyle room with carved wooden pillars was built (but not completed) by the last king of Kandy. During the visit of the Prince of Wales in 1875, it was extended using columns from the Meda Wasala. Despite the handover in 1815, the hall has remained a venue for important official ceremonies. This is where the celebrations of the 50th anniversary of independence were supposed to have been held, in the presence of Prince Charles, before the bomb attack of 25 January 1998. Badly damaged, Mangul Maduwa has been undergoing major restoration work. It is closed to the public for an unspecified period.

On the other side of the street, the **High Court** occupies the old Kachcheri (seat of the colonial administration); it has a neo-classical façade.

At the end of the street is the **District Court** with its carved wooden columns. This pavilion used to be part of the royal women's quarters. Today, it houses the sessions of the court which are completely open to the public since the building is open on one side. Neither photography nor the taking of notes is permitted.

Housed in the nearby royal palace, the **Archeological Museum** is a much more peaceful place *(9am-5pm; closed Friday)*. Inside, the ordinary council chamber of the last kings of Kandy is decorated with stucco reliefs, featuring royal symbols: fly-swat bearers, lions and *hamsa* (bar-headed geese). The museum contains various architectural stone, brick and wood fragments, but without any information as to their origin. They include the original wooden caissons of the Temple of the Tooth. Looking out over the moat, the palace's façade is stamped with the emblems of the sun and the moon, which were also emblems of Kandyan royalty.

The Devala** (Temples of the gods) (C-D2)

You can visit the temples after the royal palace, because the Vishnu Devale is right next to it. There is another entrance from Deva Vidiya, near the Cultural Triangle office. Do not forget to remove your shoes before entering the holy precincts.

Kandy lies under the protection of four great gods, just as the four cardinal points of the island are guarded by four gods: the east by Vishnu, (Upulvan), the south by Kataragama, the west by Saman and the north by Vibhishana. However, at Kandy, the last two are replaced by Natha and the goddess Pattini. All four are summoned during the Esala procession. The shrines dedicated to Buddhist gods are called *devale* (plural *devala*) in order to distinguish them from the temples of the Hindu religion *(kovil)*. They are always very crowded and are illuminated on *poya* days.

The Vishnu Devale** was built in 1748 to house an idol with magic properties, formerly venerated at Dondra *(see p 297)*. It has a porch decorated with old paintings. A staircase leads up to the **dig-ge**, the "long house" where the drummers stand during the *puja* and the faithful lay their offerings of flowers on small plates. Another flight of steps leads to the shrine. The accessories used for the processions (palanquins, umbrellas, banners) are displayed along the length of the walls of the nave. An oratory on the left is dedicated to Dedimunda, general of Vishnu's armies. Behind it stands a Bo tree, which is certainly older than the temple, and the stone on which coconuts are broken as a sign of devotion, in the Hindu way. The whole complex, which is arranged on three terraces, is surrounded by a wall.

The tour continues with a visit to the temple situated on the other side of the street.

Built in the 14C, the **Natha Devale**** is the oldest building in Kandy. Inside the enclosure wall, which is entered by a delightful porch with a pinnacle, stand a Natha Vihara and the Natha

The origin of the "perahera" of Kandy

For the Kandyans, the Vishnu Devale is the "Maha Devale" (Great Temple), underlining the importance of this god. In fact, until the 18C, it was this god, and not the relic of the Tooth, who was the object of the great procession in the month of Esala. The purpose of this "perahera" was to ensure the prosperity and fertility of the kingdom. Its structure was altered in the time of Kirti Sri Rajasinha (1747-82). On the advice of Thai monks, the king integrated the relic of the Tooth into the procession and gave it priority. Vishnu thus passed into third place in the procession of Esala, behind Natha, the most Buddhist of the gods of Kandy.

B Brillion

The entrance to the Natha Devale

Devale, the oldest part built of stone, with a roof on three different levels, surmounted by a small stupa. Natha is very important in the pantheon of the city. The sovereigns of Kandy had to come to his temple to be enthroned when they received their titles and the royal gold sword. From the time of Sri Vijaya Rajasinha until the fall of the kingdom in 1815, all the kings were Tamils who had converted to Buddhism. Their allegiance to Natha, a god of purely Buddhist origin, thus took on a political sense of devotion to the religion of the Sinhalese. Despite its importance, the temple is less frequented by devotees. Natha, a god of deep spirituality, remains plunged in meditation, detached from the affairs of the world: there is no point in asking him to resolve everyday problems.

Leave by the west door of the Natha Devale and go round to the Pattini Devale nearby.

The Pattini Devale is a simple building with some carved panelling dating from the Kandyan period. The statue of the goddess is invisible, hidden by a large curtain on which her effigy is portrayed. On either side, the small chapels are dedicated to her servant **Mari-amman** and **Kali**.

The fate of a bracelet

The origins of the goddess Pattini lie in the south of India, from where her cult was introduced to Ceylon in the 2C. As an orphan, with a gold ankle bracelet her only possession, she was taken in by a merchant. When she grew up, she married Prince Kovalan but he was to leave her for a courtesan and his extravagant ways also reduced him to poverty. He begged the faithful Pattini to take him back and she did, even giving up her gold bracelet as a guarantee. But when a similar jewel was stolen from the queen Kovalan was assumed to be the thief and was put to death without a trial. Pattini rushed to the palace to denounce the injustice. Her imprecations were so vehement that the gods intervened on his behalf to explain that with his death her husband had redeemed himself from his errant ways in a former life. Now free, he would come to look for her in a flying chariot and take her to heaven. So Pattini made it to heaven to be venerated by the kings and their people for her goodness.

In a highly ecumenical form of co-habitation, the enclosure of Pattini Devale stands right next to a **bodhighara** (Bo tree enclosure), where votive flags flutter, and the brick tower of the English church of **St Paul** (1846). The Anglican liturgy is celebrated here every day, to the sound of an organ centuries old accompanied by the rhythm of Kandyan drums.

This complex stands by Deva Vidiya, the old area of the royal stables, today occupied by **notaries' clerks**. At tea-time, you will find them gathered in the shade of the Olde Empire dining-room. The small square planted with trees beside this old colonial establishment is a favourite place for crows, which provide a cacophony at sunrise and sunset. At the corner of D S Senanayake and Dalada Vidiya stands the **Queen's Hotel**⋆, an old British palace built in place of the residence of an important Kandyan family. The city-centre, which stretches away in the chessboard of streets beyond it, is also British in terms of its architecture, but not at all in terms of atmosphere: every façade has become a shop-front.

The city centre (B-C2)

Enter the city along Srimath Bennet Soysa Vidiya and take the first street on the left.

Between a shirt shop and a winding lane stands a **gate**⋆ decorated with coloured statues. This is the entrance to the **Kataragama Devale**, the shrine dedicated to the fourth god of the quartet protecting the city. Kataragama has the wind astern *(see p 311)* and his temple is by far the most frequented, throughout the day. It is also the only one organised for leaving shoes. It has nothing of the Sinhalese *devale* but all the characteristics of a Tamil *kovil*. The shrine is looked after not by a *kapu-rala* but by a brahman, wearing the insignia of his caste: the string of dual birth and the hair tied up in a bun. In the holy of holies, golden jewels can be seen through a window, proof of the sincerity of the god: there are gifts for services rendered and wishes granted. The devotees also pray to **Kali**, **Ganesh**, or the nine stellar gods on the oratories that form a cloister around the *devale*.

On leaving the temple, head for Castle Lane, the little street full of **ironmongers** and **tinsmiths' workshops**. It comes out below Yatinuwara Vidiya, where the **jewellers' shops** are concentrated and the wealthy come to indulge their passion for gold and precious stones. Look out for the ladies dressed in white saris, which only the Kandyans wear, with a length of fabric pleated and draped over the hip. The façade of the old commercial centre of the **White House** dominates this quarter which is both bourgeois and domestic, the seat of banks and those venerable institutions which are the British-style tea-rooms, where one can nibble at sandwiches and savoury delicacies.

Curtain!

The Sinhalese regard the devala as the house of the gods, kept by officials called "kapu-rala" who feed, wash and perfume the gods and keep the temples clean. In general, the holy of holies is always closed or invisible, to preserve its purity. Only the "kapu-rala" has the right to penetrate it. More often, it is hidden by a curtain of the appropriate colour for the god: red for Kataragama, blue for Vishnu, yellow and white for Saman, sometimes yellow, sometimes white for Natha and Pattini. Occasionally there is a painting of the god on it. The cella contains the image, or a symbol of the god, and his ornaments: the ankle bracelet of Pattini, the bow and arrows of Saman, and the spear of Kataragama.

Walk along Dalada Vidiya to the clock tower.

Deva Vidiya, the street of the lawyers

A.B.WEERASEKARA
C.DOOLWELA
S.KEKULANDARA
N.B.D.WETTEWA
S.ABEYSUNDARA
C.B.ELANGASINHA
Licenced Surveyors
විජය වික්‍රමරත්න
WIJAYA WICKRAMARATNE
KRAMA RANASINGHE
DE SILVA & DE SILVA
P.MAPALAGAMA
PROCTOR S.C.& NOTARY PUBLIC

The clock tower soars over the food **market**: very familiar vegetables (carrots and cauliflowers) from the market gardens of Nuwara Eliya lie next to the more exotic fruits from the west coast or Matale. All the **spices** required for a *massala* can be found here, particularly the dried red chillies, so highly prized throughout the island, either piled up or ground to powder. The fact the tea is sold loose here is a reminder that Kandy is situated on the edge of the most prestigious tea plantations.

S W R D Bandaranayaka Mawatha links the usual bustling crowd at the bus terminus and the square of the **old colonial station**. There are shops selling suitcases and souvenirs, to a background cacophony of film music and the shrilling of alarm clocks. At the beginning of Sirimavo Bandaranaike Mawatha, on the other side of the railway, the **Pulleyar Kovil***, dedicated to Ganesh, the god with the head of an elephant, is the most popular with the Tamil community who came to live here when the large tea plantations were created.

The monasteries

Like Anuradhapura, the ancestor of the royal capitals of Ceylon, Kandy became a centre for large monastic complexes like Malwatte, on the south shore of the lake, and Asgiriya, on the hills that dominate the city to the north. Both were generously endowed by sovereigns and their ministers. In the reign of Kirti Sri Rajasinha, they welcomed the monastic congregation "purified" by the ordination of Thai *Sangha (Siyam Nikaya)*. Immense institutions, they constituted cities in their own right within the city, the saffron-robed population of which performed the activities of the order. The noise of the town disappeared within the maze of courtyards swept by the young monks every morning, or in the wooden galleries spanning the spotless façades.

Providing an architectural counterpoint to the Temple of the Tooth with their imposing octagonal tower, the buildings of the **Malwatte monastery*** (D3), the aptly-named "Flower Garden", scale the hillside which is dotted with woodland paths. Built in the 16C to accommodate a delegation of monks from Burma, this is one of the largest monastic establishments in Kandy: 375 monks live there today. Its **poyage**** (assembly hall) was decorated in the 18C with elegant Kandyan columns supporting a ceiling with painted caissons. It is still used for monastic executive council meetings and the annual ordination ceremonies. The whole complex is an architectural museum in its own right, maintained each year thanks to the donations of Buddhists from all over the world. In 1995, a small **museum** *(Daily 8am-8pm, donations welcome)* was set up in the old *vihara* in which beams supported by wooden columns alternate with small impluvium courtyards. It contains pieces of furniture and monastic possessions offered by the monarchs.

Walk along the shore, heading east, as far as the beginning of Saranankara Rd, a small road leading up towards the hills. At the top, a flight of steps leads up to the panoramic Rajapihilla Maw opposite the McLeod Inn.

Rajapihilla Mawatha has one of the best **views**** of the lake and the royal city. If you follow it (heading west) you come to the entrance to **Wace Park** (Royal Park) (C3), built by Sri Vikrama Rajasinha, dominating the lake. Near a garishly decorated pool, there is a souvenir of Lord Mountbatten: the cannon bequeathed to the city in memory of his stay there as commander of the Allied Fleet in 1944-45.

Go back to the clock tower and follow Pushpadawa Maw, then Wariyapola Sri Sumangala Maw. The Asgiriya Monastery is 1.5km northwest of the centre.

The founding of the **Asgiriya Monastery** (B1) dates from the 14C. All the sovereigns of Kandy contributed to its image houses. The **Adahana Maluwa Gedige* (Gedige of the terrace of royal cremations)** (B1) is the oldest. Built in the late 15C, it has the same austere elegance as Natha Devale. During the Esala *perahera*, the reliquary of the Tooth is placed here on the last night of the festival, in honour of the mother of King Kirti Sri Rajasinha, whose body was cremated in the monastery. Today nothing remains of the royal burials, because those that escaped pillage were destroyed during the building of the Kandy-Matale railway line in 1878-1980.

500m to the west, continuing along Wariyapola Sri Sumangala Maw, there is another monastery.

The Vijaya Sundarama Vihara** (A1) is a small complex of rustic charm, which was separated from the complex of Asgiriya Mahavihara when the road was widened in the late 18C. Two **image houses** stand above the impeccably raked sand of the courtyard. The largest was commissioned by the last sovereign of Kandy. A carved stone Buddha reclines here, his head on a pillow decorated with lotus flowers. At his side, the offerings tables, which are incredibly long, are each hewn from a single piece of wood. The beams and caissons of the ceiling are a veritable parterre of flowers and tendrils. Commander Vijayasundarama made a gift of the room next door, where his portrait hangs, holding a bouquet of flowers, to one side of the door. The monastery also houses a copy of the reliquary of the Tooth, made by a monk in the 1950s.

The Forestry Reserve of Udawattakele** (D1) *(Daily, 7am-5pm. Entrance fee. Access via road that winds steeply uphill from Deva Vidiya. Vehicles prohibited; reference map at start of walk)* extends along the hills to the east of the Asgiriya monastery. Created in 1938, it is a green space of more than 100ha. This walk is not to be missed, especially early in the morning, when the forest, with its aura of miracles and legends, resounds to birdsong. The network of footpaths passes through luxuriant vegetation, populated with monkeys, monitor lizards… and leeches after the rain! This almost virgin forest was used as the setting for a remake of Tarzan, with Bo Derek in the role of Jane.

Making the most of Kandy

Coming and going

Choosing your means of transport depends a great deal on your next destination. For the sites of the north (Dambulla, Polonnaruwa and Anuradhapura), the bus is the simplest and most comfortable solution, because trains have to go via Colombo. For the mountains, the train is preferable, and some of them have a panoramic "observation saloon", which is ideal given the spectacular scenery. If you go to Adam's Peak, the nearest station is Hatton; and for Nuwara Eliya, Nanu Oya is the nearest; both are on the Badulla line.

By train – The ***railway station*** lies on the west side of town (A-B3). The ticket office for making reservations on the Intercity Express is open daily from 5.30am to 5.30pm. The main daily trains include: two services to Badulla, one at 8.15am (7hr45min), via Hatton (3hr), Nanu Oya (4hr) and Haputale (6hr), with an observation saloon (book), the second at 11.10pm (9hr30min), with couchettes in 1st and 2nd class (book); three trains to Colombo Fort: two Intercity Expresses at 6.30am and 3pm (2hr30min), with an "observation saloon" (must be booked), and a mail train at 10am (3hr).

By bus – Buses serving the Kandy and Matale area leave from the ***Torrington St Bus Stand***, near the market (B2-3), or from the ***Clock Tower Bus Stand***, on the square below the clock tower (B2). There are buses on the hour and every half hour to Colombo (2hr30min-3hr), Hatton (2hr30min), Nuwara Eliya (3hr), Kataragama (9hr), Dambulla (2hr), Sigiriya (2hr45min), Polonnaruwa (3hr) and Anuradhapura (3hr). CTB and private coaches leave from the ***Good Shed Bus Station***, behind the railway station (A3). Departures every hour for Colombo (2hr30min-3hr) and Nuwara Eliya (3hr). Buses for other destinations are less frequent. Buses to Kurunegala and Kegalle leave from a bus stop situated higher up on Railway Approach Rd, near the post office (C2).

Getting around

It is easy to explore Kandy on foot. If you get tired of going up and down between the centre and your hotel, you will easily be able to find a "tuk-tuk" (three-wheeler) to take you (they often wait near the clock tower). Although they will take you further afield they will rarely wait for you and cannot be relied upon to bring you back. Sample a bit of colonial nostalgia by catching one of the two double-decker buses which run all day around the city. If you want to hire a taxi for a day, apply to ***Savoy Confort***, ☎ (08) 23 33 22 (vehicles equipped with meter and tariffs negotiable for a long journey).

Address Book

Tourist Office – ***Ceylon Tourist Board Office***, 3 Deva Vidiya, opposite the Central Cultural Fund (C2), ☎(08) 22 26 61. Monday-Friday 9am-1pm / 1.30pm-4.45pm. ***Central Cultural Fund***, Deva Vidiya, by the wall of the Pattini Devale (A3). Daily 8am-5pm. The Cultural Triangle round ticket may be purchased here, also certain publications.

Banks / Currency exchange – There are three banks on the short stretch of Dalada Vidiya west of the Queen's Hotel (C2): ***Bank of Ceylon***, 8.30am-2.30pm from Monday to Friday, 8.30am-1.30pm on Saturday; Visa accepted. ***Hatton Bank***, 9am-3pm from Monday to Friday. ***People's Bank***, 9am-3.30pm from Monday to Friday, 9am-1pm on Saturday. ***Hong Kong & Shanghai Bank***, Kotugadella Vidiya, 9am-2.30pm from Monday to Friday; automatic cash-point with Visa, open 24hr (C1).

Post office / Telephone – ***GPO***, opposite the railway station (B3). Small post offices on Deva Vidiya (near the Olde Empire) and to the north of the town, on the corner of Kande and Senanayake Vidiya (C1).

To call abroad, it is best to use the small agencies offering STD connections. On Peradeniya Rd, on the outskirts of the town, some have e-mail facilities. ***Matsui Communications***, 3A Deva Vidiya, beside the Olde Empire, open until 10pm.

Health – ***Lakeside Adventist Hospital***, 40 Sri Sangaraja Maw (E3), ☎ (08) 22 34 66. Kandy ***General Hospital*** (A3), ☎ (08) 22 22 61.

Where to stay

The most pleasant hotels and guest-houses are located in the hills surrounding the town. Choose your accommodation according to the length of your stay; some have a peaceful atmosphere but are very far out, others are handier for visiting the town-centre but have less charm. However, the very wide range of accommodation, from guesthouses to luxury hotels, is affected by the Esala festivities, during which prices shoot up and rooms are hard to find without prior reservation. Most places have hot running water in the bathroom, but the mildness of the climate in Kandy means that air-conditioning is not vital. Beware of the on-going war among "tuk-tuk" drivers, who are real rogues, and of certain hotel proprietors. It is advisable to telephone and book to be sure of a room wherever you choose to stay.

Under US$10

Blinkbonnie Tourist Inn, 69 Rajapihilla Maw, ☎ (08) 22 20 07 – 9rm. Small, very clean rooms, all with view, and tiny bathrooms, with or without hot water. Good local cooking.

Blue Haven (WA Linton Wanniarachchi), 30 / 2 Poorna Lane, ☎ (074) 47 09 06, Fax (08) 23 23 43

– 5rm. Rather far out, but situated in a wonderfully peaceful residential district (there is a short-cut across the hill leading down to the town-centre), this hotel is spotlessly clean. Delicious home cooking. The proprietor is the manager of the Rail Tours agency in Colombo and will help you to organise your journey.

Star Light Guesthouse (Mr H M Wijekoon), 15 / A Saranankara Rd, ☎ (08) 23 35 73 – 5rm. An old Kandyan family gives its guests a warm welcome and has rooms with mosquito nets and very clean bathrooms. Good family cooking. A good base from which to explore the region because the proprietor owns two "tuk-tuks" and his driver friends will charge a reasonable rate.

Thilini Guesthouse (Lakshman Wijesekera), 60 Saranankara Rd (advertised by a red sign "Thilini no60"), ☎ (08) 22 49 75 – 2rm. Although the bedrooms are delightful, the bathrooms are rather shabby. The owner is a chef and the cooking is excellent, his wife is an English teacher. Both will look after you well. The elephant's tooth set in the threshold of the house is supposed to bring good luck.

From US$10 to US$15

Golden View, 46 Saranankara Rd, ☎ (074) 47 19 22 – 5rm. Small pleasant hotel with a good Chinese restaurant and an Ayurvedic (sauna and massage) centre.

Ivy Banks Tourist Resort, 68 Rajapihilla Maw, beyond the Chalet Hotel, ☎ (08) 22 24 67 – 4rm This brick house, with a pleasant veranda overlooking the lawn, has a marvellous view of Kandy, the lake and the Knuckles, and has reasonably-priced rooms. Be careful as there are three Ivy Banks guesthouses in town; the main one, situated at the end of the lake, right on the road, is to be avoided at all costs.

Lake Inn, 43 Saranankara Rd, ☎ (08) 22 22 08 – 6rm. Rooms with mosquito nets and private balcony. Safe available.

MacLeod Inn, 65 Rajapihilla Maw, ☎ (08) 22 28 32 – 6rm. Very simple rooms, two of which have a view of the lake. The dining-room has a large balcony, where one can enjoy the view and sit and chat in the evening.

From US$15 to US$30

Devon Rest, 4E Sangaraja Maw, ☎ and Fax (08) 23 23 92 / (074) 47 25 10 – 10rm. A basic, functional establishment with a good price-quality ratio if you go for the rooms with a view of the lake, bathrooms and hot water. Very pleasant staff. Good restaurant serves international cuisine.

Freedom Lodge, 30 Saranankara Rd, ☎ (08) 22 35 06 / (074) 47 15 89 – 3rm. Family accommodation, in a house with garden. The rooms are perfect and the breakfasts plentiful, but the prices are too high.

From US$25 to US$35

Castle Hill Guesthouse, 22 Rajapihilla Maw, ☎ and Fax (08) 22 43 76 – 3rm. A house in the style of a 1930s liner, with a huge lawn and an unimpeded view of the lake. Everything is vast, peaceful and bright. A guesthouse with style.

Queen's Hotel, 4 Dalada Vidiya, ☎ (08) 22 28 13, Fax (08) 23 20 79 – 54rm. TV CC The facilities listed refer to the 27 rooms in the east wing because this old establishment of 1838 has undergone a gradual face-lift. The rooms in the west wing have not changed since the British colonial period, and have large fans and antique plumbing. They are, however, much quieter. Strangely, all the rooms cost the same. Better to enjoy the old-fashioned charm of the Queen's by having a dip in its pool (charge for non-residents) or by having a drink in its splendid bar.

From US$40 to US$70

Thilanka Hotel, 3 Sangamitta Maw, ☎ (08) 23 24 29, Fax (08) 22 54 97, thihtl@sri.lanka.net – 80rm. TV CC Only the 35 rooms in the modern wing, with balconies and views of the lake, benefit from all the comforts listed, since the rooms in the old wing, albeit only a little cheaper, are dark and noisy because of the proximity of the kitchens. Small swimming pool with terrace overlooking the lake and the town, pleasant bar and a few shops. Good price-quality ratio for its category, but the food could be better.

Chalet Hotel, 32 Frederick E de Silva Maw, ☎ and Fax (08) 23 45 71; book from Colombo: 284 Vauxhall St, Col 2, ☎ (01) 33 23 51, Fax (01) 33 23 48 – 28rm. People looking for something a bit different will be delighted by this hotel with its façades and walls painted with naive frescoes, its antiques and bohemian ambience. Small library, pleasant bar, elaborately furnished restaurant and a pretty garden with a view of the Knuckles Range.

Suisse Hotel, Sangaraja Maw, ☎ (08) 22 26 37, Fax (08) 23 20 83 – 96rm This palace dating from the late 1930s was the headquarters of Lord Mountbatten when he commanded the Allied Fleet in 1944-45. Everything is on a grand scale: the rooms, the corridors, the restaurant and the panelled bar. Pleasant swimming pool with terrace, and impressive view over the lake, open to non-residents. Billiards, shops.

• In Alupothuwela

19km north of Kandy, on the road from Wattegama to Ukuwela.

From US$15 to US$25

Grassmere Holiday Home (Mrs W M Jayawardene), access by very steep 500m ramp, ☎(078) 66 83 29 – 3rm. This large planter's house, with its huge rooms and family photographs on the walls, has a wonderful terrace garden, beside a small waterfall. Traditional Sri Lankan cuisine.

• In Elkaduwa

23km north of Kandy.

From US$70 to US$85

Hunas Falls (Mr Jetwing), ☎ (08) 47 64 02 / (071) 236 30, Fax (071) 351 34 – 31rm. An exceptional position and a very British atmosphere in this fairly modern hotel, built above the Hunas falls which cascade down through the huge tea plantation of Hunasgeriya. Plenty for sport enthusiasts. Library, bar and billiards table. Playroom and baby-sitters available for small children. Ayurvedic baths and massage.

• In Yahalatenna

15km northwest of Kandy on the Kurunegala road, turn left at the Barigama junction.

From US$40 to US$70

Tree of Life, Barigama, Werellagama, ☎ (08) 49 97 67, Fax (08) 49 97 11 – 38rm. This hotel offers zen-style luxury with a choice between rooms in small brick houses opening onto a patio or others close to the swimming pool overlooking the surrounding tea plantations. Pleasant Ayurvedic massage pavilion. Billiards, disco at the weekend; mountain bikes for hire.

• In Katugastota

5km north of Kandy.

More than US$100

Mahaweli Reach Hotel, on the right bank of the Mahaweli, ☎ (074) 47 27 27, Fax (08) 23 20 68, mareach@slt.lk; book from Kandy: 35 P B A Weerakoon Maw, PO Box 78 – 115rm. A large hotel that plays on the sombre elegance of Kandyan architecture. Huge swimming pool by the river, with a bar. Table-tennis and billiards. The restaurant is the best one in Kandy.

• In Pinnewala

There are numerous small hotels and guest-houses on the road leading to the Elephant Orphanage. The places mentioned are situated on the road leading to the elephant bath.

From US$10 to US$15

Green Land Guest House (JM Ratnayake), ☎(035) 656 68 – 2rm. This very simple guesthouse has a spice and medicinal herb garden and is set in very pretty surroundings.

Hotel Elephant View, ☎ (035) 652 92 / (078) 61 08 65, eleview@sitnet.lk – 4rm. First and foremost, this is a jewellers and a restaurant, pleasantly arranged around a patio. Its rooms have all mod cons and an unbeatable price-quality ratio.

Eating out

No restaurant takes pride of place in Kandy but there are some places serving decent meals or take-away food. As for hotel restaurants, the ***Kong-de-ling*** (at the Queen's Hotel), ☎ (08) 23 30 26, serves authentic Shanghai cuisine, while the Chalet Hotel has a pleasant setting (Western cuisine) and the Mahaweli Reach has special buffets and a varied menu. The dining rooms at the ***Thilini*** and ***Star Light*** guesthouses serve excellent local dishes at very moderate prices.

From US$5 to US$10

DJ's Restaurant, 26 / 1 Devani Rajasinha Maw, ☎ (08) 22 57 38. Rather far out, 5km west of the town centre, but it offers a rare opportunity to sample the delicacies of Sri Lankan cuisine.

Devon Restaurant, 11 Dalada Vidiya, ☎ (08) 22 45 37. This restaurant serves local cuisine and Chinese-style seafood.

Flower Song, 137 Kotugadella Vidiya, ☎ (08) 22 36 28. Chinese cuisine: generous portions.

Olde Empire, 21 Deva Vidiya, ☎ (08) 22 42 84. A place of unusual charm, perfect for brunch after watching the early-morning "puja" at the Temple of the Tooth.

Shazadis, 42 Dalada Vidiya, ☎ (08) 22 25 75. Spotlessly clean and very cheap. Serves a variety of food. Eat in or take away.

White House, Dalada Vidiya, next to the Devon. Frequented by Kandyan families and Sri Lankan tourists, this restaurant is the most popular one in town. Serves all sorts of dishes.

Having a drink

Bars – Muffled, colonial atmosphere at the ***Queen's*** bar.

Entertainment – Kandy is the only town in the country that offers performances of traditional dance, executed by the dancers who perform the "perahera". A chance not to be missed, because although these performances are aimed at tourists we should be grateful that they exist at all and the choreography is superb. Tickets are sold at the tourist office and in the hotels and guest-houses.

Kandy Lake Club, Sangamitta Maw, near the Thilanka hotel. Daily, 6-7pm.

Kandyan Art Association & Cultural Centre, Sangaraja Maw. Daily at 5.45pm.

Other things to do

Swimming pools – The small pools at the ***Queen's*** and the ***Suisse*** hotels and at the ***Thilanka*** (exceptional location) are open to non-residents at a modest charge.

Feasts & festivals – The "perahera" of the Tooth takes place during the ten days before the full moon of the month of Esala (July-August) when a procession of caparisoned elephants makes its way through the streets of Kandy. The festival ends on the tenth day: after the purification ritual, the huge parade of elephants makes its way around the city for the last time. It has become a spectacle in its own right, which is watched from seating set up for the occasion; but the seats are expensive and tickets difficult to obtain. There is another "perahera" at the end of August, around the western temples.

Shopping guide

Kandy has an impressive concentration of souvenir shops (precious stones, masks, exotic wooden elephants, batik fabrics, etc). Don't shop in the town centre though: head for the shops on Peradeniya Rd, on the outskirts of the town, on the road to Colombo. Compare prices and be very careful if you buy precious stones. For expensive purchases or shipping back home, ensure that the establishment is approved by the Tourist Board.

Market – Pyramids of fruit and vegetables, perfumes, spices… it is worth visiting for these alone. But no bargains.

Crafts – Craftsmen carve wood and cast bronze (oil-lamps) near the temples of Gadaladeniya and Embekke.

Antiques – ***Darshana Lanka Art***, 923 Peradeniya Rd, ☎ (08) 22 25 72. Antique craft products and jewellery.

Prema Brothers, 757 Peradeniya Rd, ☎ (08) 23 26 95. Founded in 1910 and constantly expanding, this reputable business has remarkable collections of antiques at very reasonable prices.

Waruna Antiques, 761 Peradeniya Rd, ☎ (08) 22 02 66. Housed in an old, restored Kandyan house.

At the end of Yatinuwara Road are a handful of jewellers selling old silver and bronze objects (betel boxes, water pipes) and jewels.

Bookshops – ***Buddhist Publication Society***, near the National Museum, ☎ (08) 22 36 79. Monday-Friday 9am-4pm, Saturday 8.30am-12noon. Library, bookshop and a mine of information about Buddhist doctrine. For English publications, consult ***K V G De Silva***, 86 DS Senanayake Vidiya, and ***Vijitha Yapa***, 9 Kotugadella Vidiya for the foreign press.

Around Kandy

Map p 231

Not to be missed

Strolling round the gardens of Peradeniya.
The small Kandyan temples dotted around the countryside.
Watching the baby elephants of Pinnewala having a meal.

And remember...

Allow half a day for each excursion.
A "tuk-tuk" is better than a car,
but ensure that the driver knows the destination.
Be careful: roads are often in poor condition due to heavy rain.

Studying plants in the botanical gardens or visiting ancient temples in the countryside: there are plenty of reasons to prolong your stay... if you can't bear to leave Kandy.

The small Kandyan temples*

A vehicle is vital. In any case, apply to the monastery to have the buildings opened. No ticket but donations gratefully accepted.

The Kandyan period witnessed the building of large numbers of small temples and there are now more than 200 in the region, dating from the 18C or early 19C. Because many of them are difficult to reach we have only made a few suggestions. Most of them are the work of that highly prolific king of Kandy, Kirti Sri Rajasinha (1747-82). Treasures of the past, they lie in a circle north of the town: a luxuriant suburb, where the houses are few and far between, dotted along an intricate network of small roads... defying even the best sense of direction.

Leave Kandy on the road heading for Mahiyangana, to the east, then turn left towards Madawela. The first monastery is 2km away.

The Gangarama Viharaya* is a small temple-monastery built by Kirti Sri Rajasinha on the sandy banks of the Mahaweli. Its image house is a very homogeneous example of late 18C Kandyan art. Inside stands an imposing statue of Buddha, 8m tall. The side walls relate the tribulations of the Siddharta in panels which should be read from the bottom up and from left to right. The painters have combined the restrictions of narrative with concern for decoration, so that the empty spaces between the figures are filled with flowers and bouquets.

Continue in the same direction crossing the Mahaweli at the Lewella bridge.

Two kilometres further on, the shrine of **Degaldoruwa*** lies under an overhanging block of granite. The room where Buddha rests under enormous painted lotus leaves has been made from a rock shelter, and is preceded by a drumming hall and a hypostyle antechamber. The wall separating the antechamber from the image house is painted with five panels depicting the former lives of Buddha (outer façade), the Seven Weeks after the Enlightenment and the Sixteen Pilgrimage Sites (inner façade). The hinges on the doors are inlaid with silver. On the ceiling of the shrine, there is a spectacular portrayal of the **fight with the demon Mara****. Buddha sits unperturbed under the tree of Enlightenment, a multi-coloured cloud irradiating from him, appealing to the world to testify

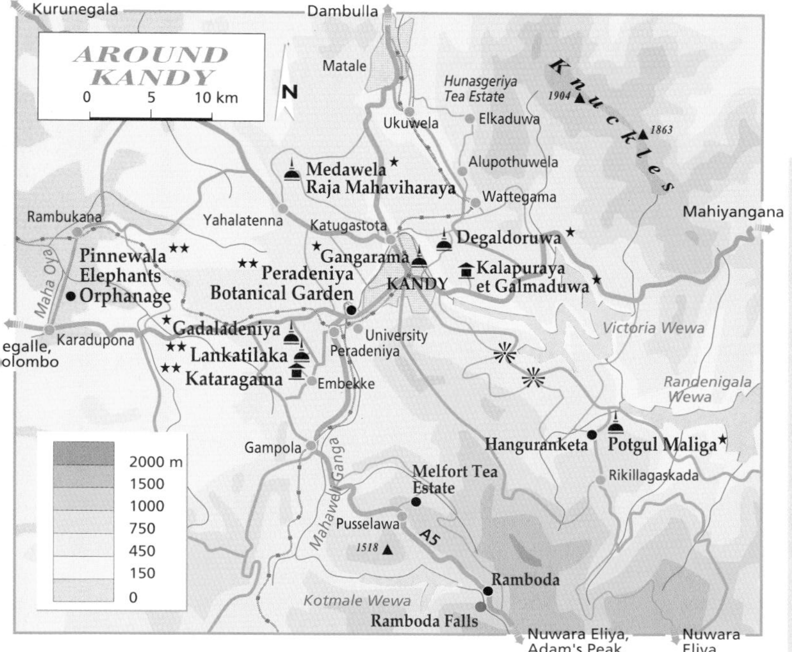

against Mara. The latter appears in female form holding a cornucopia on her throne. On the left of the Buddha, with several arms and riding an elephant, Mara leads his armies into battle. On his right, the demon is thrown off his mount. These paintings are one of the finest expressions of Kandyan art. They date from 1771-86 and the names of the artists are known: one was associated with the studio of Ridi Vihara *(see p 168)*, the other with the workshop of Dambulla *(see p 208)*. The pillow on which Buddha's head rests is inlaid with a huge amethyst. The monks will tell you that the painters worked by the light from this huge stone.

Go back to the Mahiyangana road. Five kilometres from Kandy, fork left for Kalapuraya (1.5km).

Kalapuraya is a craft village, set up by the state to try to preserve the handicrafts that blossomed under the royal patronage of Kandy. This is a rare opportunity to see artisans at work because there are 100 houses where artisans work embossing silver, casting bronze with the *cire perdue* technique, carving wood and making batik fabrics. Their creations are sold in the Laksala shops. In the village, the **Galmaduwa Gedige** is an architectural curiosity. An imposing base of carefully cut stones forms a cloister surrounding the shrine. The shrine itself has a stone pyramid on the top, reminiscent of the *gopuram* of southern India. Left unfinished by Kirti Sri Rajasinha, this *gedige* was never used as a temple and its function remains a mystery. It was not until restoration was completed in 1967 that an image house was created inside.

Go back towards Kandy and follow signs for Matale. At Katugastota (5km to the north), take the minor road on the left which follows the Pinga Oya. Medawela is 12km further on.

The Raja Mahaviharaya* of Medawela is a small monastery built next to a hill surrounded by groves of croton trees. On the upper terrace there is a **tampita vihara** (image house on piles), a characteristic feature of Kandyan architecture. The interior is tiny (3.5 x 1.5m), but decorated with a complete and perfectly preserved iconographic series. A recent Buddha sits under a *makara torana* with a background of flowers evoking the tree of Enlightenment. Processions of disciples, a frieze of stylised clouds floating above their heads, converge on the Master along the side walls. On either side of the door, the minister who executed the works in the reign of Kirti Sri Rajasinha is depicted along with the monk elect.

If you have a vehicle, you could continue with the following itinerary. Otherwise, return to Kandy and catch a bus at the Torrington St bus station.

The Botanical Gardens of Peradeniya**

Six and a half kilometres west of Kandy on the road to Colombo; buses No 652 and 724 from Torrington St Daily 8am-5pm. Entrance fee. Allow 2hr; guided tour available; reference map at the entrance. Flowering season between January and April.

Situated in a loop of the Mahaweli, the site of the gardens of Peradeniya was a seat of power between 1371 and 1377, during the time of the itinerant capitals. Nothing remains from this period. King Kirti Sri Rajasinha created the gardens and later came to live here. The British made them into the Royal Botanical Gardens in 1821. There are 4 000 tropical species, either indigenous or imported, 2 000 of which are varieties of tree: the site occupies 60ha of land.

In the **Spice Garden**** *(access along a path to the right of the entrance)* are centuries-old nutmeg trees, cinnamon trees, cardamoms, vanilla and clove trees so highly prized in medieval Europe.

A *Tabubbiya seratifoliya* with yellow flowers and a jacaranda mark the **Orchid House***** which contains 450 hybrid species. In their natural state, these epiphytes grow on trees in the jungle and require a humidity level of 85%. They all have flowers with six petals, the sixth serving as a platform for the insects which pollinate them.

The mania for spices

When he returned to Venice, Marco Polo stopped in Java, then in Ceylon, the riches of which he described in his book "Il Milione": pepper, nutmeg, nard (a herb similar to valerian, used as flavouring), galanga (a rhizome with a peppery flavour, belonging to the ginger family), cubeb (a sort of pepper tree, used for medicinal purposes) and cloves. The Western craving for spices had begun as early as the 13C, and people would go to great lengths to obtain these highly desirable commodities. Then pharmacopoeia took over from cooking, and spices, consumed in the form of preserved fruits and cunning powders, provided a remedy for every conceivable affliction.

At the entrance to the **Flower Garden** stands a 160-year-old **durian**, some **giant bougainvilleas** which flower all the year round, and a species of dwarf palm whose bright red trunk has earned it the name of "lipstick tree". At the corner of the path of the **Palmyra palms** *(Borassus flabellifer)*, giant almond trees from Java display their spectacular tentacle-like roots near a group of *Cicus*, fossil trees from Australia. The **cabbage palms from Panama** *(Roystonia oleracea)*, which line another path along with ancient mahoganies, owe their name to the fact that when young, the plants are a delicacy: when boiled, they can be made into a salad with a cabbage taste. The **royal palm of Cuba** *(Roystonia regia)* is called the "bottle tree" because of the shape of the young trees.

The Great Crown* is formed by commemorative trees planted by important public figures: the *Saraca* with beautiful yellow flowers was planted by Yuri Gagarin (1961), the *Bauhinia* with white flowers by Indira Gandhi (1967), the *Amherstia nobilis* by Lord Mountbatten (1947), etc.

Giant bamboo from Burma line the edges of **River Drive**, which follows the Mahaweli. This species grows very quickly, reaching its maximum height, 3m, in three months.

On the **Great Lawn**, the fronds of a 140-year-old **ficus benjamina**** cover an area of almost 1900sqm. On the south side, Monument Road is lined with a species of palm native to the Seychelles; its bi-lobed nuts have an amusingly suggestive shape.

The **South Garden** includes a **Medicinal Herb Garden** (medicinal plants used in Ayurvedic medicine) and a **Students' Garden**, where plants are presented in their botanical families.

The southern part of the gardens *(on the other side of the road)* is occupied by the campus of the **University of Peradeniya**, the largest in the country (6 500 students). It is open to the public, with the same luxuriant profusion of plants as in the Botanical Gardens.

You will have no problem visiting the western temples if you have a vehicle: Gadaladeniya Viharaya is only 11km away from Kandy and 4.5km from the Botanical Gardens. Otherwise, follow the order of the itinerary below combining the bus service and walking.

The temples west of Kandy**

Buses leave Torrington St for Embekke (18km). The other temples occupy an area of 5km from south to north, cutting across the rice-fields. The last one, Gadaladeniya, is 1km beyond the Pilimatalawa junction, on the road to Colombo, or you could hail one of the many buses which pass by.

The building of these temples dates from the period of Gampola (1341-1408), one of the itinerant capitals which preceded Kandy. They are spectacularly situated since they occupy the top of a small chain of rocky promontories on the edge of a valley carpeted with rice-fields.

500m from the village of Embekke, you enter the **Kataragama Devale**** *(entry charge)* through a **gate**** with carved wooden pillars, which have worn smooth with the passing of time. The shrine dedicated to the god is preceded by a **digge*****, with its veritable forest of columns. They are surrounded by panels which form small engraved tablets: they depict real or fantastic animals, scenes of mourning and combat, dancers and musicians. According to tradition, they come from the old council chamber of Gampola. Some of them were restored during a restoration programme conducted in 1948. An appeal was made to the sculptors of the area who were descended from the craftsmen who worked for the royal court. Their shops often stand beside the western temples. At the far end of the shrine, the customary statue of Kataragama is hidden behind a curtain.

One and a half kilometres further north, the **Lankatilaka Viharaya**** dominates the rice-fields from a granite plateau *(access by rock-cut steps or by a road which comes out on the platform. No entry fee, but leave a donation)*. An inscription in Pali,

engraved in the rock, dates the foundation of this temple to 1344. Its exterior architecture belongs to the tradition of the great *gedige* of Polonnaruwa, but its ground plan is unusual. You enter the image house of Buddha from the east. The stuccoed brick statue of the Master, whose robe is finely pleated and folded in the usual way, is typical of Kandyan art, the throne standing under an imposing vault, with traces of 18C paintings. This chapel is surrounded by a vestibule which is entered from the hypostyle room situated on the opposite side of the building, on the west side. Oratories dedicated to the great protector gods of the island are incorporated in the stonework. The Lankatilaka temple is thus a skilful combination of an image house and a *devale* in one building. An 18C inscription reveals that the temple once had four storeys which were reached by a staircase inside the wall. Now ruined, the two upper floors have been replaced by a wooden roof.

Four kilometres to the north, the **Gadaladeniya Viharaya*** is a small complex built on a granite escarpment *(entrance fee)*. At the entrance, its *dagoba*, the **Vijayotpaya****, is in fact a temple, the central stone mass of which is confined by four small chapels housing a statue of Buddha. This cruciform plan is crowned by five small *dagoba*, which are protected by a roof supported by pillars. The **main shrine**** shows a marked influence from Southern India: the cella, where Buddha sits under the *makara torana*, is preceded by a corridor and a hypostyle porch, by which it is connected to a second temple dedicated to Upulvan. The profile of the cornices is Dravidian and is reminiscent of the Hindu art of Vijayanagar. The stonework of the steps and the pillars which frame the entrance is carved with delicate figures of dancers, drummers and gods.

The following place can be visited on the way back to Colombo.

The Elephants Orphanage at Pinnewala**

Situated 38km west of Kandy, on the banks of the Maha Oya. If you go by bus (a tedious journey and not very practical), take the bus for Kegalle, get off at the Karadupona junction, and catch another bus in the direction of Rambukana. By train (more practical), get off at Rambukana, on the Colombo line, and catch a bus or a "tuk-tuk" to the orphanage (10min). Daily 7am-6pm. Entrance fee.

This institution, which is part of the National Zoological Gardens, was created in 1976 to look after baby elephants which had been abandoned by the herd (following the death of their mother, for example). Nowadays the centre concentrates on studying the behaviour of its 63 elephants. Every day, the huge babies born at Pinnewala are fed by bottle (*feeding times open to the public at 9.15am, 1.15pm and 5.15pm*). Feeding-time is followed by a bath in the river for the whole herd. Despite appearances, elephants have very sensitive skin; it becomes chapped with the heat, increasing the risk of parasites. The adults work, helping to clear the site and transport food.

They are chained up at night because they are so used to humans that they would not hesitate to satisfy their hunger by raiding the larder of a nearby house. This situation of their dependence on humans is a mixed blessing. Left to themselves, the elephants of Pinnewala are incapable of procuring food and water.

Bath-time at the Pinnewala Elephants Orphanage

Around Kandy

C Goupi / SCOPE

The tea harvest at Cardamon Hills

THE HEART OF THE ISLAND

Sri Lanka's mountains form the heart of the island. The "roof" of Ceylon culminates at 2 524m with Mount Piduru Talagala which dominates Nuwara Eliya. To the west, the massif of Adam's Peak is where four of Sri Lanka's largest rivers have their source: the Mahaweli, the Kalu, the Kelani and the Walawe. To the east, the Uva mountains form a balcony suspended 1 000m above the coastal lowlands. For a long time the refuge of aborigines who lived from hunting, gathering and slash and burn agriculture, the central highlands never really became populated until the arid area was abandoned upon the fall of Polonnaruwa (13C) and the Europeans began to settle on the coast in the 16C. As a result, the highlands have preserved many rural traditions. But in the 19C, British capital was invested in the mountains and converted them into an immense garden. The king of the crops was coffee and thousands of hectares were wrenched from the jungle thanks to the patient work of elephants. To bring in labour, and transport the harvest from the plantations to the ports on the coast, a new network of roads and railways opened up this natural fortress to the outside world. Then the plantations were given over to tea which resulted in further changes to the landscape. For hundreds of miles, the hilltops are carpeted with perfectly trimmed bushes, like box hedges in a formal garden. Only a few patches of land escaped the complete metamorphosis of the heart of the island: the forest of Sinharaja, the Horton Plains and the south flank of Adam's Peak still have an abundant wildlife.

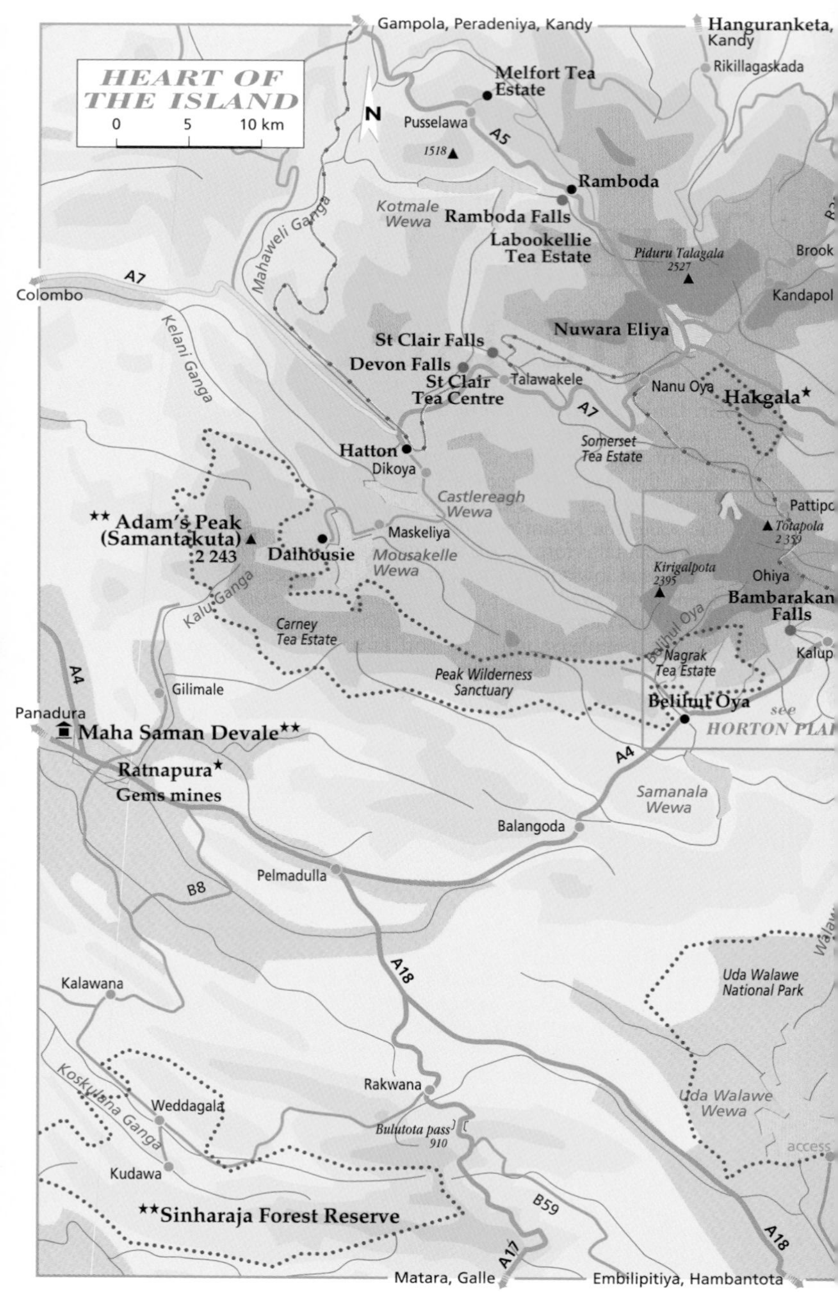
HEART OF THE ISLAND
0 5 10 km
N
Gampola, Peradeniya, Kandy
Hanguranketa, Kandy
Rikillagaskada
Melfort Tea Estate
Pusselawa
A5
1518
Ramboda
Ramboda Falls
Kotmale Wewa
Mahaweli Ganga
Labookellie Tea Estate
Piduru Talagala 2527
Brook
Kandapol
A7
Colombo
Kelani Ganga
Nuwara Eliya
St Clair Falls
Devon Falls
St Clair Tea Centre
Talawakele
Nanu Oya
Hakgala
A7
Somerset Tea Estate
Hatton
Dikoya
Castlereagh Wewa
Pattipo
Totapola 2 359
Adam's Peak (Samantakuta) 2 243
Dalhousie
Maskeliya
Mousakelle Wewa
Kirigalpota 2395
Ohiya
Bambarakan Falls
Kalu Ganga
Carney Tea Estate
Belihul Oya
Nagrak Tea Estate
Kalup
A4
Gilimale
Peak Wilderness Sanctuary
Belihul Oya
see HORTON PLA
Panadura
Maha Saman Devale
Ratnapura
Gems mines
A4
Samanala Wewa
Balangoda
Pelmadulla
B8
A18
Uda Walawe National Park
Kalawana
Koskulana Ganga
Weddagala
Rakwana
Uda Walawe Wewa
Bulutota pass 910
access
Kudawa
Sinharaja Forest Reserve
B59
A17
A18
Matara, Galle
Embilipitiya, Hambantota

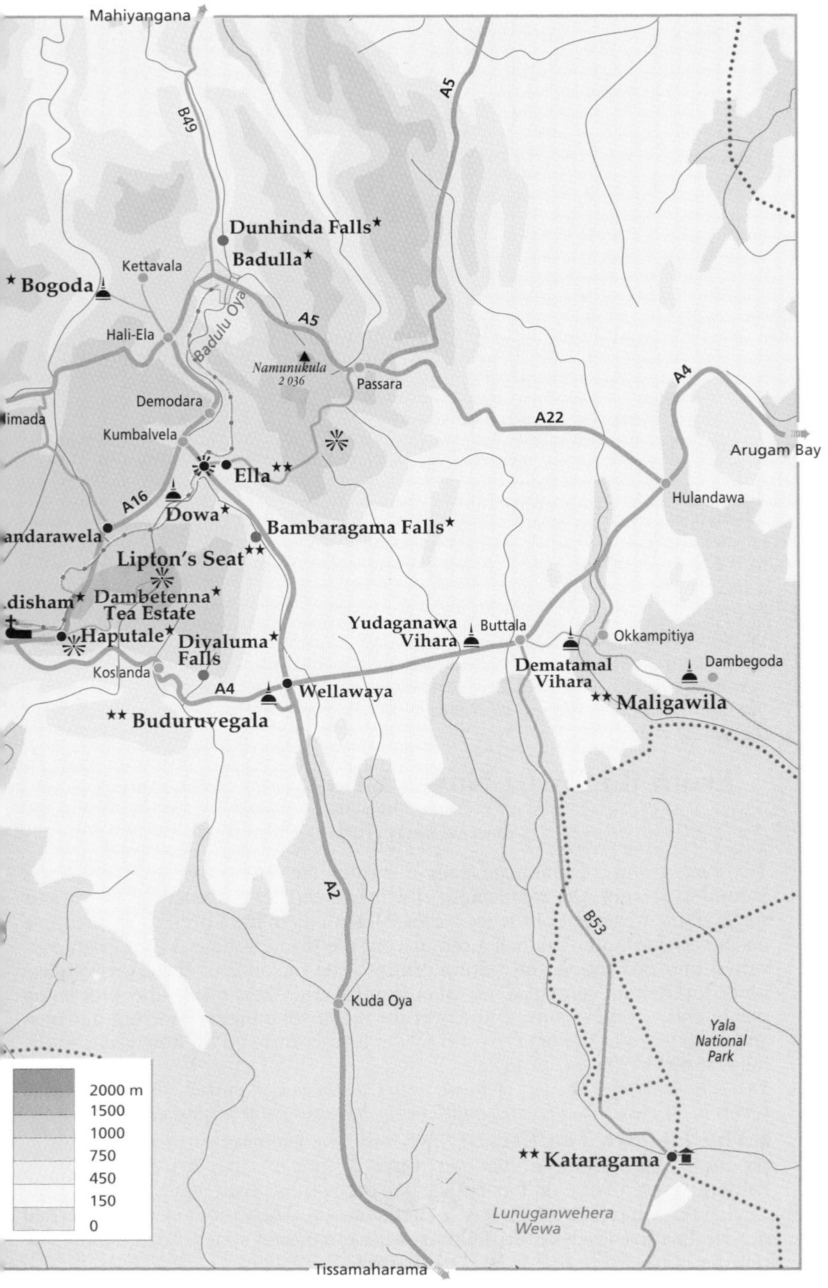
Mahiyangana
A5
B49
Dunhinda Falls★
Badulla★
Kettavala
★ Bogoda
Badulu Oya
A5
Hali-Ela
Namunukula
2 036
Passara
A4
Demodara
imada
A22
Kumbalvela
Arugam Bay
Ella★★
Hulandawa
A16
Dowa★
andarawela
Bambaragama Falls★
Lipton's Seat★★
disham★
Dambetenna★
Tea Estate
Haputale★
Diyaluma★
Falls
Yudaganawa
Vihara
Buttala
Okkampitiya
Dematamal
Vihara
Dambegoda
Koslanda
A4
Wellawaya
★★ Maligawila
★★ Buduruvegala
A2
B53
Kuda Oya
Yala
National
Park
2000 m
1500
1000
750
450
150
0
★★ Kataragama
Lunuganwehera
Wewa
Tissamaharama

The tea gardens

From Kandy to Adam's Peak

Central Province – Map p 238-239
142km circuit via Ramboda or 176km via Hanguranketa
Allow three days to cover the most interesting routes, visit Nuwara Eliya, and climb Adam's Peak

Not to be missed

Visit a tea factory to discover the secrets of black tea, and wander among the surrounding tea plantations.
The perfect shadow of Adam's Peak, cast over the mountains or the clouds at sunrise.
Play billiards at the Hill Club, or golf at the Nuwara Eliya golf course.

And remember...

Avoid staying in Nuwara Eliya in April: there are too many people and water is scarce.
Don't attempt to scale Adam's Peak on a "poya" weekend, during the pilgrimage season (January to April).

Situated at the edge of the highlands, Kandy provides access to the great tea garden of Ceylon. Entirely shaped by the plantation economy, this land is home to the great *tea estates*. They govern the organisation of social space according to a fixed model. On the slopes, the tea factories, offices, warehouses, employees' houses *(lines)* are at the heart of the estate with the bungalows belonging to the plantation managers set somewhat apart. But this carefully constructed landscape is far from monotonous, because the mountains and valleys form broad perspectives dotted with rushing torrents, waterfalls or a swirling mist. The plantations stretch right up to Adam's Peak, the sacred mountain that dominates the whole island.

From Kandy to Nuwara Eliya via Ramboda**

73km. Allow 3hr.
Numerous buses ply this route.

The main groups of buildings along this route are the **estates**, each organised around its **factory**, the architecture of which is entirely governed by the various stages of the treatment of the tea leaves. Most of them have been using the same machinery for more than half a century but the planters' houses have been converted into promotion and tasting centres. The majority of these estates have tours for visitors, provided no photographs are taken inside the processing plants: this is your chance to discover the secrets of a brew conceived in China and introduced to the whole world by the British, or to go for long walks in the hills tended by the tea pickers.

Take the Peradeniya Rd out of Kandy. After the botanical gardens, fork left towards Gampola. At Pusselawa (41km), a track on the left leads to the Melfort plantation.

▪ **The Melfort Tea Estate** *(Daily 9am-5pm. Entrance free)*, covering 250ha, produces 220 tonnes of tea per year. A tour of the factory includes a demonstration of the different stages of processing involved in making black Ceylon tea, which has a high level of fermentation. The various stages are carried out on the three levels of the building, with a trap-door system ensuring the safe transfer of the tea from one level to another.

S Frances / HEMISPHERES

British heritage: the "factory"

■ Fifteen kilometres further on, the town of **Ramboda** stands at an altitude of 960m, above a wide wild valley into which the **Falls** of the same name cascade *(on the right-hand side of the road)*. On the other side of the town, a stele commemorates the building of the very first **Anglican church** on the island, which was dedicated to St John the Evangelist in 1850.

Continue along the same road for 6km, to the Labookellie tea plantation.

■ **Labookellie Tea Estate**, the highest plantation on the island, employs 6 000 people to farm its 540ha of tea bushes *(Daily 9am-5pm. Tours every hour. Tea-tasting and shop in very chic showroom)*.

Along the 11km of road to Nuwara Eliya, the countryside is a succession of hilltops entirely covered with tea bushes. The rare spaces in between are exploited by market gardens and nurseries which sell their modest and colourful products on stalls at the side of the road.

From Kandy to Nuwara Eliya via Hanguranketa★★

113km. Allow half a day.

The little road to Hanguranketa is a wilder and quieter way of reaching Nuwara Eliya, provided you have a vehicle. On the way up to the outskirts of this mountain town, there are no tea bushes, but fields in layered perspective, no estates, but little villages built along a single road lined with grocers and tobacco shops. Meeting another vehicle can be quite stressful on the narrow strip of tarmac with its series of hairpin bends, but it rarely happens (it is a good idea not to break down!). More importantly, the road is closed at night, from 6pm until 6am, to protect the lakes of the Victoria and Randenigala dams from terrorist attacks, and stray motorists from passing wild elephants.

Leave Kandy on the road leading to Hanguranketa and Rikillagaskada. Before long you reach Lake Victoria, a vast reservoir built on the course of the Mahaweli River in 1989, which you leave by a little road lined with giant acacias leading towards the abandoned citadel of Hanguranketa (33km from Kandy).

▪ **Hanguranketa –** During the Portuguese occupation in the 17C, this city served as a refuge for King Rajasinha II who hid the Tooth, symbol of his power, here. The palace was burned down during a British expedition in 1803. All that is left of the royal palace are a few ruins of the *devale* and a Buddhist temple. Apply to the working monastery *(at the edge of the town, on the left hand side of the road)* to visit the **Potgul Maliga Vihara**** opposite, at the end of a long lawn which has been converted into a basketball court. At the entrance, an imposing pink building houses the **library** *(potgul)* which contains illuminated sheets of palm manuscript, kept in beautiful engraved copper or silver covers. Behind it, the **image house** is unusual. It consists of two side-rooms opening onto the outside on either side of the central nave with one opening, at the end of which there is a small room. With its small *dagoba*, it is supposed to have housed the **Tooth Relic** when the sovereign sought refuge in Hanguranketa. Its walls are guarded by the gods of the four cardinal points, surrounded by their armies. In front of it is a room occupied by statues of Buddha and an antechamber where rows of paintings depict the former lives of the Master. In the room on the left, a stuccoed wooden Buddha rests under the protection of Vishnu. The paintings on the ceiling are highly imaginative: they show two Atlas figures, wearing 18C wigs, supporting a sun with a halo of *hamsa* (bar-headed geese), their necks intertwined. The moon is surrounded by bare-breasted women and by gods forming a chain. On the wall of the other room, to the right of the Buddha in *samadhi*, Duttugemunu is depicted fighting Elara. On the ceiling, the paintings portray the sermons which Sakyamuni preached to the gods and to men, as well as the stellar gods of the *poya* days, depicted with animal heads. A restoration programme conducted in 1996 has succeeded in reviving all the freshness of these murals executed in the 18C.

6km further on, at Rikillagaskada (bus service from Kandy), is the turning for Nuwara Eliya.

A delightful mountain road overlooks the cultivated terraces, separated in places by small waterfalls. As you climb up towards the mists of Nuwara Eliya, the terraced rice-fields give way to a harsher, wilder landscape. By the time you reach **Brookside**, it is cooler and the first tea plantations come into view. At **Kandapola** (58km after Hanguranketa), a track climbs for 4km towards **Tea Factory**, a hotel in a converted tea-processing plant, in the heart of the Hethersett plantation. You are no more than 16km from Nuwara Eliya.

▪ Nuwara Eliya

Alt 1 880m. Allow 2hr.

With its cold winters, its drizzle and fog in spring, and the heavy rain followed by storms between May and August, the British, who discovered this site in 1819, felt quite at home in the Nuwara Eliya (pronounced "Nioorayliya") basin. It became one of several hill stations which dotted the colonial empires of the tropics, a sanatorium where those afflicted could come

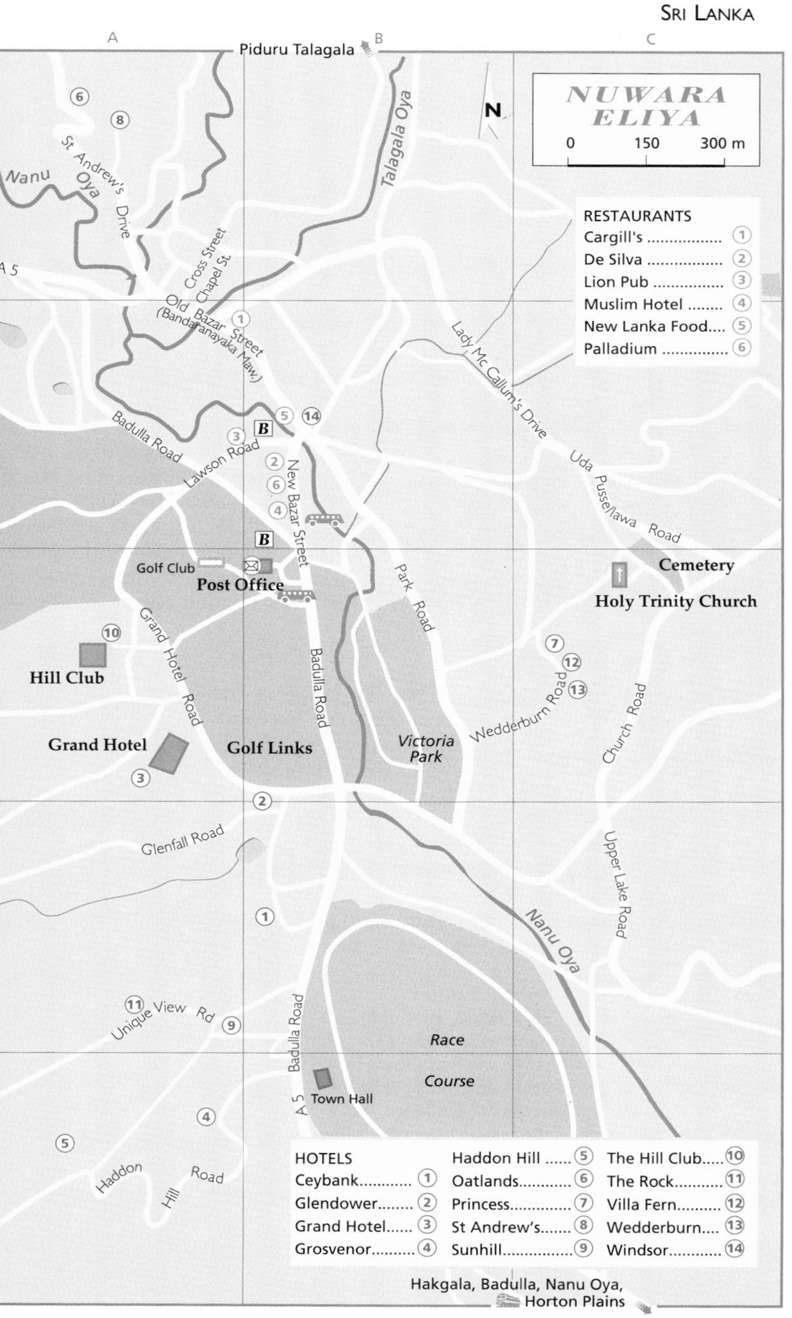
A
B
C
Piduru Talagala
NUWARA ELIYA
N
0
150
300 m
RESTAURANTS
Cargill's 1
De Silva 2
Lion Pub 3
Muslim Hotel 4
New Lanka Food.... 5
Palladium 6
Nanu Oya
St Andrew's Drive
Talagala Oya
A 5
Cross Street
Chapel St.
Old Bazar Street
(Bandaranayaka Maw.)
Lady Mc Callum's Drive
Badulla Road
Lawson Road
New Bazar Street
Uda Pussellawa Road
Park Road
Cemetery
Holy Trinity Church
Golf Club
Post Office
Hill Club
Grand Hotel Road
Badulla Road
Wedderburn Road
Church Road
Grand Hotel
Golf Links
Victoria Park
Glenfall Road
Upper Lake Road
Nanu Oya
Unique View Rd
Badulla Road
Race
Course
A 5
Town Hall
Haddon Hill Road
HOTELS
Ceybank............ 1
Glendower........ 2
Grand Hotel...... 3
Grosvenor.......... 4
Haddon Hill 5
Oatlands............ 6
Princess.............. 7
St Andrew's....... 8
Sunhill................ 9
The Hill Club..... 10
The Rock........... 11
Villa Fern.......... 12
Wedderburn.... 13
Windsor............ 14
Hakgala, Badulla, Nanu Oya,
Horton Plains

to recuperate from ailments contracted in the furnace of the coast. Its inauguration was consecrated by the governor **Edward Barnes** when he had a house built here in the mid-19C, but the real father of Nuwara Eliya was **Samuel Baker**, who was subsequently to discover the source of the Nile, who brought calves, cows, hunting dogs, chickens and seedlings here from England. Since then, the station has always been the island's market gardening centre. Nuwara Eliya was to become very British, with its half-timbered Tudor-style houses complete with inglenook fireplaces, its billiard tables for rainy days, its golf course for drizzly days, its rivers for fishing, its lake for canoeing and its race-course for staging the Derby.

Today, the former British mountain resort has become a favourite haunt of the middle classes of the island who come to stay here in April. This is the great season of tennis and golf tournaments, and horse-races, where tradition insists that one comes to be seen. But these days Nuwara Eliya has lost much of its appeal: **Lake Gregory** has silted up, **Victoria Park** is poorly maintained, and the TV antenna on the top of **Piduru Talagala** now prevents walkers from reaching the island's highest point (2 524m). What's more, Nuwara Eliya offers little in the way of walking. Drivers, guides and some hotel owners will strongly recommend you visit **Horton Plains★★★** 32km away *(see p 260)*. So take Nuwara Eliya for what it has become, a practical stopping place thanks to its many places to stay, a good starting-point from which to escape to Adam's Peak or the Uva Mountains, travelling on one of the most beautiful railway routes on the island.

Tour of the town

To explore Nuwara Eliya's colonial past, begin with a stroll through the few surviving arcades in Old Bazar Street, a shopping street with no great charm these days, then head round the corner towards the delightful little **post office★** with its pink brick walls. Continue towards the 18-hole **golf course**, the largest in Sri Lanka and the oldest course in Asia, and climb up to the **Hill Club★** which you will recognise by its grey stone façade reminiscent of a Scottish manor house. This is a very British-style club, founded in 1876, and a social environment that is very difficult to penetrate. However, you can use the bar and restaurant by paying a temporary membership fee of US$10.

From here, follow Grand Hotel Road south, past the golf course and Victoria Park to rejoin Wedderburn Road, where there are some rather quaint **planters' houses**, some of which have been turned into guest-houses.

Finally, don't forget to have a look at the little **cemetery** next to **Holy Trinity Church** where the epitaphs on the tombstones provide a chronicle of days gone by: soldiers and planters, dead by 30 or 40 through disease, or colonials who retired to the pleasant coolness of these heights and lived until they were over 80.

The demise of an elephant hunter

The tombs at Nuwara Eliya include that of Major Rogers, who was assistant to the governor of Badulla from 1834 until 1845. He was caught by a storm during a tour of inspection at Haputale, on 7 June 1845, and ran for cover at the lodge. As he looked outside to see if the rain had stopped, lightning rent the sky. The iron in his wet shoes attracted the lightning and he was struck down. He was only 41, but during his 12 years in Badulla he had shot 1 200 elephants during hunting parties. Was this punishment sent from heaven perhaps? Rumour has it that his tomb has twice been struck by lightning.

The Botanical Gardens of Hakgala*

9km southeast of Nuwara Eliya, on the Welimada road. Can be reached by bus. If you are staying in Nuwara Eliya in April or in August-September, go and visit the botanical gardens at Hakgala *(Daily 7.30am-5pm)*, because that is the season of the **roses** for which it is so famous. The road passes the market gardens on the outskirts of Nuwara Eliya, the legacy of Samuel Baker, now cultivated by the Tamil population, large numbers of whom live in this area. In front of small mosques and brightly coloured temples, women in brilliant saris shop for cabbages, potatoes, carrots and radishes. The Hakgala gardens are situated on the side of the mountain of the same name which is 1 707m high, its peak formed by a great bare rock. Hakgala means the "rock of the jaw" which legend associates with the monkey general Hanuman. He is supposed to have transported a whole mountain covered with medicinal plants through the air in his jaw. Pieces of it fell out here and there, some here at Hakgala and others at Rumassala near Galle. Created in 1861 to introduce **cinchong** from Peru (which produces the quinine essential for treating malaria), the gardens were gradually made into a pleasure garden by the Nock family. If the roses aren't in bloom, console yourselves with the amazing **ferns**, including the tree fern, a plant fossil which still grows in Horton Plains. On a clear day you can see the rolling Uva hills from the gardens.

From Nuwara Eliya to Adam's Peak

69km. Allow 2hr.

All the roads out of Nuwara Eliya pass tea plantations. The road to Hatton winds down through the **Somerset Tea Estate**.

■ Twenty-six kilometres beyond Nuwara Eliya, after Talawakele, to the right of the road in the background, you will see the double cascade of the **St Clair Falls**, 73m high. Two kilometres further on, the **St Clair Tea Centre** *(Daily 9am-5pm. Tea-tasting and shop)* has been cleverly built above a steep drop, with fine views of the valley below and its two waterfalls: the **St Clair Falls** on the right and the **Devon Falls** on the left.

The further you get from Nuwara Eliya, the drier the landscape becomes; the first silhouettes of eucalyptus appear, sometimes in solitary isolation but otherwise in groves, together with outcrops of crystalline limestone. After 12km, just before Hatton, the magnificent pyramid of Adam's Peak looms into view.

■ Hatton is a small town bustling with life. The only urban centre for miles around in a region dotted with hamlets inhabited by workers from the tea plantations, it is dominated by the great Hindu temple of **Sri Manniyar Pillai**.

Seven kilometres from Hatton, the bungalows of Lower Glencairn and Upper Glencairn are a pleasant place to stay and a perfect base for expeditions to Adam's Peak.

Beyond the **Moussakele** dam *(security check)*, is **Dalhousie**, a town surrounded by tea estates which transforms itself into a pilgrimage site once a year: here you are at the foot of one of the paths up to the summit.

▪ Adam's Peak★★

Culminating at 2 243m, Adam's Peak isn't the highest mountain in the island, but its perfect, conical silhouette endows it with a majestic quality.

An ecumenical holy mountain

In the eyes of all the religious communities of the island, this is a holy mountain because of the mysterious footprint in a slab of rock at its summit. For Hindus, it is **Sivanolipatha Malai**, the "Mountain of Shiva's footprint", for Muslims **Adam Malai**, "Adam's Mountain". According to the latter, when Adam was chased out of the Garden of Eden, he stopped on this mountain, where he remained standing on one leg in penitence until his sins were forgiven. This belief was commonly held among Arab traders in the 11C and Ibn Battuta from Tangier made a pilgrimage here in the 14C. To Sinhalese Buddhists, the footprint is known as **Sri Pada**, and was made by the left foot of Buddha during his third journey to the island, at the request of the god Saman, who also lives in the mountain. Although discovered in the 1C, it did not become an important pilgrimage site until the Polonnaruwa period: Parakramabahu built a shrine here and his successor, Nissamka Malla, made the journey to the top. Marco Polo described this place of worship in his book *Il Milione*: "Now it is true that, on this island, there is a very large, high mountain, the rocks of which are so steep that I swear they are impossible to climb. Now on this mountain there are many large, heavy metal chains to enable people to climb it. And they say that on the top of the mountain there is a monument to Adam, our first father. The Saracens, at least, say that it is the tomb of Adam, but the Idol Worshippers (Buddhists) say that it is the monument of Sagamoni Burcan (Sakyamuni Buddha)".

The "Mecca" of Sri Lanka

Nowadays, a long flight of **4 500 steps**, cut or built into the bedrock, enables pilgrims to make the ascent, weather permitting, between February and April. For three months, the path to the summit is just a long series of shops selling tea and sweets, caps to protect pilgrims' heads from the icy wind on the top, religious images and alarm clocks, against a background of loudspeakers pouring out blessings.

At weekends and on days of the full moon during the pilgrimage season, up to 20 000 people ranging from 7 to 77 make their way up the narrow path leading to the summit. They climb in groups, rarely on their own. The more fortunate hire a vehicle as far as Dalhousie and spend part of the night there. Others begin the climb as soon as they get off the bus. They sleep on their mats, spread out under one of the shelters built along the path, or on the platform at the top. Those making the pilgrimage for the first time follow the instructions of the **nade gura**, a veteran who has already made the ascent at least three times and knows the rules. And this despite the saying: "He who has never made the ascent is mad, and he who makes the ascent a second time is even madder". Everyone takes care to have their journey blessed by a monk who ties a piece of cotton thread around their wrist. They are laden with bags, containing bottles of coconut oil and terracotta lamps, which they light along the way as prayers.

Adam's Peak, a mountain of piety

Right at the top, on the tiny platform, the pilgrims take it in turns to ring the **bell** of the temple of the holy footprint. The footprint itself, which is said to have been inlaid with a blue sapphire by a king in ancient times, is invisible, hidden under a stone slab for protection. There is even a letterbox where pilgrims can post a letter *(daily collection at 1pm)* announcing that they have fulfilled this vow of pilgrimage dear to all the inhabitants of the island. On the railing surrounding the platform, thousands of votive flags flutter in the morning wind. In May, everything disappears and the deserted summit becomes peaceful, mysterious and wild again.

The pilgrimage season is the best time to mingle with the Sri Lankans making the ascent, although peak days should be avoided. Every year there are fatal accidents (people falling at narrow places or overcome by the heat).

The ascent of Adam's Peak

Seven kilometres, between 4 or 5km of which are very steep. Allow 3hr at a gentle pace. If you leave Dalhousie at about 2am, you will reach the last tea-shop before the summit (sign 10min from the top) just before sunrise (between 6am and 6.30am). In doing so you will be able to wait for sunrise out of the wind, because the platform is buffeted all the year round by an icy blast. Don't forget to take a torch with you, as well as an anorak and a jumper.

The cobbled path climbs gently to the **makara torana** which marks the beginning of the holy precinct. Nearby, devotees purify themselves in the waters of the **Kelani Ganga** before starting the ascent.

The path is easy to follow up to the **Peace Pagoda**, built at the foot of the mountain by Japanese Buddhists. The first steps begin just beyond it, becoming gradually steeper with altitude. The bushes beside the path are strewn with long tangles of white thread unrolled by women as a sign of piety. The best time to make the ascent is at night. The temperature is cool, the tea-shops provide sustenance when necessary and you can negotiate the rocky path by the light of the pocket torches which shine all the way up the slope (don't forget to bring yours). Don't miss sunrise. When the sun appears, you will see the **shadow of the summit**, a perfectly formed triangle, cast on the hills at the foot of the mountain, or on the clouds which encircle the mountain. The hardest bit is yet to come: the descent! Take the steps gently to minimise the strain on your leg muscles *(and a muscle relaxant balm is a good idea after such a huge effort)*.

There is another much longer, more difficult but less crowded path (15km, 2 000m of ascent), which descends to **Gilimale**, on the opposite side of the mountain. You can go down by this route provided you arrange for a vehicle to wait for you at the bottom, because this difficult, more challenging route is poorly served by public transport.

Making the most of Kandy to Adam's Peak

COMING AND GOING

By train – Some of the stops on this circuit are served by the Colombo-Badulla line, which is as winding as it is magnificent. There are three trains daily in both directions. Bear in mind that none of them go via Kandy. On leaving Colombo Fort, allow 6hr for the journey to Hatton, and 7hr-8hr to Nanu Oya (6km southwest of Nuwara Eliya). From Badulla, allow 3hr30min for the journey to Nanu Oya, and 4hr30min to Hatton.

By bus – The region is also served by a very good bus service.

• **In Nuwara Eliya**

Bus terminus in the town-centre, on the edge of the town and opposite Victoria Park. Buses leave every hour (until late afternoon) for Hatton (from 2hr to 3hr), Kandy (3hr) and Colombo (6hr). There are buses every 30min for Badulla (from 2hr to 3hr). For other towns in the Uva Mountains (Haputale, Bandarawela), you must change at Welimada (1hr), on the way to Badulla. There is one service a day to Matara (from 6hr to 8hr, leaving in the morning). Buses and "tuk-tuks" provide a service to Nanu Oya station.

• **In Hatton and Dalhousie**

During the pilgrimage season (December-January) it is easy to reach Dalhousie. Buses leaving Colombo, Kandy, Nuwara Eliya and Badulla stop at Hatton or Maskeliya (10km away from Dalhousie), then others provide a shuttle service to Dalhousie. The journey from Hatton to Dalhousie (29km) takes 2hr and seats are hard to find. On "poya" days, you feel you may literally suffocate! During the rest of the year, you can actually breathe and sit down… but connections are not very frequent.

Address book

There are no large towns on this route apart from Nuwara Eliya, to which all the addresses given refer.

Bank / Currency exchange – ***Bank of Ceylon***, 41 Bristol St (B2). Monday 9am-1pm, Tuesday-Friday 9am-1.30pm. Cash withdrawal possible with Visa. ***Hatton National Bank***, near the post office (B2). Monday-Friday 9am-4pm, Saturday 9.30am-1pm. Cash withdrawal possible with MasterCard.

Post office / Telephone – ***GPO***, opposite the main bus terminus (B3). Monday-Saturday 7am-9pm, Sunday 8am-8pm. To telephone, try ***Salika***, Old Bazar Rd (north of Cargills shop). Daily 8am-9pm.

Health – ***Cargills***, Kandy Rd, has a range of pharmaceutical products.

Where to stay

• **In Nuwara Eliya**

Nuwara Eliya is a holiday resort. The choice of accommodation is, therefore, particularly important, especially as it rains quite frequently. Do not trust the odd cheap guesthouse, because they tend to be inadequately maintained. The nights are cold, indeed icy in winter; ensure that you have hot water (and that it actually works) and enough blankets in guesthouses which do not have heating or open fires. Since air-conditioning is pointless in this area, the symbol ▤ has been used to denote the provision of heating in the rooms.

Finally, you should be aware that Nuwara Eliya suffers from a serious shortage of water at the end of the dry season (April) and in August, and certain establishments remain entirely without. Beware of inflated prices in April-May (Vesak holidays).

From US$10 to US$15

Princess Guesthouse, 12 Wedderburn Rd, ☎ (052) 224 62 – 7rm. ✗ A charming guesthouse with fireplaces in the bedrooms (supplement for lighting the fire). Water heated by electricity. A pity that the dining-room is rather gloomy.

Grosvenor Hotel, Haddon Hill Rd, ☎ (052) 223 07 – 12rm. ✗ A recently renovated house, around 100 years old. A corridor with coconut matting and earthenware jars leads to spacious rooms with spotlessly clean bathrooms (heating). Restaurant rather gloomy. TV room. Good price-quality ratio.

From US$15 to US$30

Wedderburn Rest, Wedderburn Rd, near Princess Guesthouse, ☎ (052) 223 95 – 7rm. ▤ TV ✗ This modern, immaculate guesthouse offers excellent service. Parquet floors and wood panelling in the house and ebony furniture in the rooms. Sadam Hussein, its friendly owner also has rooms at Villa Fern, a delightful colonial residence situated a few doors away.

Sunhill Hotel, 18 Unique View Rd, ☎ (052) 228 78 / (071) 726 67, Fax (052) 237 70 – 4rm. ▤ TV ✗ A small, well-situated hotel. The standard rooms, which are functional, spotlessly clean and have a small balcony, are better value than the de-luxe rooms. Hot water from solar heating. Panoramic restaurant on fourth floor serves excellent local (on request) or Chinese cuisine.

Oatlands (Mrs Doreen Wickramasuriya), St Andrew's Drive, ☎ (052) 225 72 – 16rm. A charming place, full of souvenirs from its 50 years of existence. Large rooms with wash-basin, sharing two bathrooms. Family dining room. TV and library available in the cosy living-room.

Haddon Hill Hotel, 24 / 3 Haddon Hill Rd, the last house on the way up to Single Tree Hill, ☎ (052) 232 27 – 12rm. A small, perfect place to stay, up above Nuwara Eliya, in a pastoral setting. Excellent hospitality.

Glendower Hotel, 5 Grand Hotel Rd, ☎ (052) 225 01, Fax (052) 227 49 – 9rm. CC A recently built, half-timbered house in the style of the planters' residences, on the edge of a vast lawn where you can have tea. The rooms are very comfortable and there are even small lounges with comfy armchairs for rainy days. The restaurant serves excellent Cantonese cuisine.

From US$30 to US$40

Ceybank Rest House, Badulla Rd, ☎ (052) 230 53; book from Colombo, ☎ (01) 44 78 45 (vital at weekends) – 20rm. CC This old house formerly belonged to a British civil servant and has great charm, with its waxed parquet floors and faience-tiled fireplaces, but it somehow lacks warmth. The rooms, which have high ceilings, are simple and clean. Bar and local cuisine at fair prices.

The Rock, 60 Unique View Rd, ☎ (052) 231 96 – 10rm. CC Large hall with colonial-style furniture where an open fire is lit every evening. Superb view from the windows of the dining-room. Large, very comfortable rooms. Chinese or local cuisine at reasonable prices.

Windsor Hotel, Kandy Rd, ☎ (052) 225 54, Fax (052) 228 89 – 50rm. CC Large rooms with parquet floors and colonial-style furniture, arranged around a patio enhanced by an indoor garden. Cake shop and pub outside.

From US$40 to US$70

The Hill Club, by the golf-course, ☎ (052) 226 53, Fax (052) 226 54 – 36rm. TV CC One almost expects to meet ghosts in this Scottish-style manor! Rooms have elegant English furniture and electric logs in the fireplace (but be careful, the 18 rooms at the back of the building have no view). Library where guests can sink into deep leather armchairs. Billiard room with muffled atmosphere and restaurant with exposed beams (men are required to wear a tie). Utterly British atmosphere with one recent concession: the bar now serves women!

Grand Hotel, by the golf course, ☎ (052) 228 81; book from Colombo, ☎ (01) 34 37 20, Fax (01) 43 45 24 – 183rm. TV CC Behind its imposing half-timbered colonial-style façade, long panelled corridors with parquet floors lead to rooms with a cosy atmosphere. Only the rooms in the new wing (66rm) are fully equipped. Opt for the new restaurant (Western cuisine). Pub with pleasant atmosphere and billiards room.

St Andrew's Hotel (Jetwing), 10 St Andrew's Drive, ☎ (052) 224 45, Fax (052) 231 53 – 52rm. TV CC An old colonial-style guesthouse renovated with great taste: aura of British elegance with grey stone, huge lawn, restaurant with muffled atmosphere, small cosy lounges for reading or having tea, and comfortable rooms with 19C furniture.

• In Kandapola

16km northeast of Nuwara Eliya.

From US$70 to US$85

The Tea Factory (Aitken Spence), ☎ (052) 236 00, Fax (052) 220 26 – 57rm. TV CC Situated in an unusual location, a traditional tea factory. Has cosy rooms overlooking the tea plantation. The restaurant, offers excellent cuisine. Bars, gym and English library.

• In Ramboda

17km north of Nuwara Eliya, on the road to Kandy.

From US$15 to US$30

Ramboda Falls, Rock Fall Estate, 76 Nuwara Eliya Rd, below the road, just before Ramboda coming from Kandy, ☎ (052) 596 53, Fax (052) 595 82 – 5rm. CC A very pleasant place to stay, in the middle of the tea plantations, by a waterfall forming a small natural swimming-pool. The rooms, which are large and spotlessly clean, look out onto the Ramboda Falls. Bathrooms with hot water. Cooking indifferent.

• In Dikoya

7km from Hatton on the road to Dalhousie.

Under US$15

Upper Glencairn Bungalow, reached by a track (poor condition) going uphill to the left of the main road, ☎ (051) 223 48 – 5rm. An old planter's house dating from 1903, with endless corridors, waxed floors, fine fireplaces, 1930s furniture and a pleasant garden, all set in the middle of the plantations, right out in the country. Hot water and electricity sometimes erratic. Excursion to Adam's Peak for 1 500Rs.

• In Dalhousie

Despite the seasonal influx of pilgrims, Dalhousie has no tourist infrastructure. When travelling, Sri Lankans tend to make do with a simple shelter where they unroll their mats and blankets, and they bring their own cooking equipment. Avoid the few (rather dirty) hotels in favour of the small family guesthouses which have the advantage of being right at the bottom of the path leading to the top. Adam's Peak is a sacred area, therefore the sale and consumption of alcohol is prohibited.

Under US$10

Green House, 20m to the left of the path to the top – 4rm. Its international cuisine has earned it the approval of the travelling fraternity. The rooms are reasonable but the communal bathroom leaves something to be desired.

Yellow House, to the left of the start of the path to the top, under a giant mango tree – 3rm. A rather quaint house with a delightful little garden. Cold water in the spotlessly clean bathrooms, but the owner will allow you to use his hot water to soothe your aches and pains. Delicious local cuisine and fresh vegetables from the garden.

EATING OUT

• In Nuwara Eliya

Some restaurants in the town-centre, on New Bazar St: the ***Palladium*** serves the best "rice and curry". If it is closed, try the ***New Lanka Food***, on Old Bazar St. ***De Silva*** serves some international dishes and snacks at reasonable prices. For breakfast, go to the ***Muslim Hotel*** (Gold Leaf sign), at the end of New Bazar St, near the bus terminus: they serve "string hoppers" prepared fresh every morning (try them filled with coconut or molasses). The ***Lion Pub***, Lawson St, by the Bank of Ceylon, has excellent draught beer (pale and dark) and a few snacks, but unfortunately closes at 9pm. As for the restaurants of hotels and guesthouses, try the one at the ***Grand Hotel***. The one at the ***Hill Club*** will leave you with humorous rather than gastronomic memories. Stiff service and terrible cooking. There is excellent cuisine in the little ***Sunhill***, and Cantonese flavours at the restaurant of the ***Glendower***.

OTHER THINGS TO DO

Excursions – In the absence of any official tourist organisation, good and bad guides abound in Nuwara Eliya. As elsewhere, guesthouse owners are extremely helpful when it comes to organising excursions in the area. For your information, ***Mr V P Selvam*** knows Horton Plains like the back of his hand. Contact him at the Sunhill or at ☎ (072) 61 72 83.

Outdoor pursuits – ***Golf***: whether you are a beginner or an expert, the 18-hole course at Nuwara Eliya is magnificent. Special lessons are available for beginners. Fees and hire very reasonable. The entry fee is 300Rs a day, plus a 50Rs temporary membership fee.

Horse-riding: horses and ponies may be hired for trekking. Apply to the racecourse.

SHOPPING

Local specialities – Attractive packages of tea are on sale at the factories. The average price per kilo is 300Rs and varies slightly according to the type.

If wondering what flavour to choose, the large leaves of ***Flower Pekoe*** or ***Flower Broken Orange Pekoe*** make a light tea. The small leaves of ***Broken Orange Pekoe*** or ***Broken Orange Pekoe Fannings*** release a stronger aroma.

RATNAPURA★
THE FOREST OF SINHARAJA★★

Sabaragamuwa Province – Pop 109 000
74km from Embilipitiya, 90km from Haputale and 100km from Colombo
Map p 238-239

Not to be missed

The temple of the god Saman, at the foot of Adam's Peak.
The woodland paths of Sinharaja.
The mineshafts along the gem belt.
Herbal beauty treatments and a massage at the Hotel Kalawati in Ratnapura.

And remember...

Don't buy precious stones from street sellers.
Protect your feet and calves from leeches in the tropical humidity of Sinharaja.

At the very western edge of Adam's Peak, swimming in the sweltering tropical heat, lies Ratnapura, immersed in lush vegetation. The Sinharaja reserve, the sole survivor of Sri Lanka's tropical forest, lies about 50km to the south. These foothills of the mountainous region are too low for growing tea, and where the vegetation has been cleared, it is to make way for rows of hevea trees, with their spindly trunks. The hevea is the current choice of the planters in the great garden of Ceylon.
The name Ratnapura still conjures up images from the past: it means the "City of Gems", a reputation founded on the countless deposits, rich with sapphires and zircons, which run across the gem belt to the east of the town, on the way to Ganegama. It is an interesting stopping place, surrounded by a wondrous mineral and plant world, natural treasures which constituted the wealth of the island's kingdoms when merchants came from overseas in search of rubies and ebony.

Tour of Ratnapura★

Allow a whole morning. Can be done by "tuk-tuk".

The Ratnapura Gem Bureau Museum★ *(Potgul Vihara Maw, 1.5km southwest of the centre, on the left bank of the Kalu Ganga,* ☎ (045) 224 69. Daily 9am-4.30pm. No charge. Beware, Ratnapura is full of "Gemmological Museums" which are all shops selling precious stones) is the first museum of gemmology to have been founded in Sri Lanka (1960), with the aim of studying gems and the cutting of stones. This private institution is a testament to its creator, **Purandara Sri Bhadra Marapana**, a highly skilled gemmologist with an erudite and original personality, and a passion for the traditional arts of the island.

The display cases in the mineralogy section contain an impressive number of gems mined in Sri Lanka and the rest of the world. The sheer variety and quality of certain stones will delight stone enthusiasts. Other visitors may prefer the art galleries which display works of rare artistic skill: pieces of silver filigree or embossed work (including the very New Age creations of Purandara Sri Bhadra himself), marquetry, ivory and musical instruments. All show a level of craftsmanship which today's artisans seem to have lost. If you wish to know what the Sinhalese gods look like, one gallery contains their portraits, with the attributes and animal mascots of some of the 250 gods worshipped on the island.

Head back towards the town-centre, as far as the junction of Senanayake Maw and Zaviya Maw.

The gem market* is held here every day, between 6am and 2pm. There are no shops or stalls, just men with their hands in their pockets! They might indeed have some real bargains in their pockets... but you should not buy unless you know what you are doing. The stones sold on the street are in their raw state and come from the mines in the area: sapphires, zircons, tourmalines and tigers' eyes from Pelmadulla, spinels from Balangoda. Most of the sellers are miners from the gem belt and come here to sell the "surplus", the quality of which is judged to be insufficient for the stone-cutters. Their work means that they know a great deal about the stones and gem enthusiasts will be delighted by the minerals with unusual crystals which have been discovered by chance during the sifting process. However, ignore the sellers of "precious stones" (only rubies, sapphires, emeralds and diamonds belong to this category and the latter are not found in Sri Lanka). The colours emanating from the stones in their matchboxes lined with cotton wool are, at best, synthetic.

If you are interested in fossils and palaeontology, make a detour to the **National Museum** *(1.5km from the centre, on the edge of the town on the road to Colombo. 9am-5pm; closed Thursday and Friday. Entrance fee)*. Otherwise, go up to the **Rest House** for a cup of tea: this is an old British guesthouse magnificently situated on a hill with a view over the whole town.

With its long whitewashed walls, dark wooden pillars and pink tiles, the **Maha Saman Devale**** *(4km west of the centre, on the road to Panadura)* is as austere as it is majestic. The building was erected in the reign of Rajasinha II (1634-84), on the site of a shrine founded in the 13C. The latter was entirely destroyed by the Portuguese when they temporarily invaded the region. Under Dutch domination, the province of Sabaragamuwa passed once more under the control of the kings of Kandy who restored and maintained this holy site.

In the Sinhalese pantheon, Saman is the god who protects the West. His origins remain a mystery to historians, but in the eyes of his Buddhist devotees, he is the god who lives on the mountain of **Samantakuta** (another name for Adam's Peak) and who met Buddha during his journey to Ceylon. He is sometimes depicted holding a bow and arrow. More often he has the traits of a benevolent king, accompanied by a white elephant and portrayed in front of his mountain. So why did they erect a temple to the god of the most revered summit on the island on the outskirts of Ratnapura? Undoubtedly because the sides of the holy mountain were too steep and the top too small for such an enterprise. But Ratnapura is also the starting-point for the classic pilgrimage to Adam's Peak, by the most difficult route, which leads up from Gilimale and the **Carney Tea Estate**. And finally because, during the rainy season, when the muddy roads make the journey impossible, the faithful can come here to make their supplications to the benevolent god Saman.

At the top of the monumental staircase, the temple of the god, oriented towards the east and Adam's Peak, is visited throughout the year. In the room where Saman is hidden behind a curtain, votive flags wave gently from the ceiling as the devotees murmur their prayers. With its painted doors and long elephants' tusks, the decoration is worthy of a throne room. Outside on the esplanade surrounding the chapel, oil lamps on delicate wrought-iron stands burn for Saman and the other deities who accompany him: the goddess **Pattini**, to whom a small temple is dedicated, and **Suniyan**, who is worshipped in a copper oratory on the esplanade. This god of terrifying power, his body and head enveloped by venomous cobras, brandishing a flaming pot in his bare hand, is invoked so that the malevolent hordes will not spread disease. Behind the wooden doors, painted with delicate fusions of women and flowers, a Buddha surrounded by his retinue of disciples looks down on this divine order.

Around Ratnapura

The luxuriant natural landscape of Ratnapura is a foretaste of that of Sinharaja, a ribbon of tropical forest about 20km long, designated by UNESCO as a World Heritage Biosphere Site in 1989. The walking routes marked by the Forest Department provide a magnificent opportunity to penetrate the universe inhabited by these giant trees and to drink in the saturated atmosphere emanating from the earth.

Sinharaja, the Emerald Forest★★

Situated 60km south of Ratnapura. Buses go as far as Kalawana, where you must change for Weddagala. Then it is another 6km (appalling road) to the bungalows of the Forest Department at Kudawa, on the banks of the Koskulana Ganga. If you opt for the bus, you have no choice but to cover this stretch on foot, because there is no public transport to Kudawa. A less restricting solution is to hire a jeep in Ratnapura (this is the only vehicle that can cope with the last few kilometres), a service that can be arranged through the hotels and guest-houses. Estimate 1 500Rs there and back. Entrance fee 250Rs per person. Walkers must be accompanied by a guide (only 4 of the 11 rangers speak English). Estimate between 100Rs and 200Rs depending on which path you choose. Cameras and videos are prohibited. Accommodation available. Best time to visit: from December to the beginning of April (good for birds) and in August-September. Risk of showers in the afternoon, except between the end of December and the end of February.

Sinharaja consists of 4 475ha of tropical rainforest at an altitude ranging between 200m and 1 300m. Here, unlike other parks on the island, no vehicle is allowed to disturb the natural environment. It is covered on foot, on two **paths** which penetrate the canopy of vegetation *(Mulawella path: 6.5km between 3hr and 4hr; Sinhagala path: 14km, between 8hr and 10hr)*. A third path, which is accessible to everyone, links Kudawa to the research station *(5km loop)*. The annual rainfall of 2 500mm (maximum in May-July, then from October to December) means that the level of humidity is very high. Protect your feet and legs, because leeches thrive in the damp vegetation.

Noah's Ark of the planet Earth

The tropical rainforest is one of the richest ecosystems on the planet. Called sempervirentes, because they are always green, these biospheres are divided between the inter-tropical part of South America, Southeast Asia, Australia and Africa. Over the centuries, the unusual conditions that exist in these areas – a temperature that varies little, between 18°C and 32°C, regular, heavy rainfall, and an identical climate over a large area – have favoured the emergence of an incredible level of plant and animal biodiversity. Although tropical rainforests only occupy 7% of the earth's land-surface, they harbour half the earth's species: scientists currently estimate that there are about 100 million species, of which only 10% have so far been recorded. Despite a policy of protection orchestrated at international level, the exploitation of their resources leads each year to the disappearance of 133 000sqkm of rainforest, an area the size of Greece.

Look out for the tall shafts of the common orchid, the large clumps of the giant cardamom, the creepers of the wild pepper or ginger plant, troops of red-faced monkeys and, perhaps, a flock of blue magpies. Out of the 3 620 animal species recorded in Sri Lanka, 99 % live in Sinharaja. But the real stars of the forest are its **trees**, the growing cycle of which differs from their counterparts in temperate latitudes. They grow very slowly and their trunks increase by 0.5mm to 1mm a year. By the time they reach a diameter of 50cm or 1m, they may be 500 or even 1 000 years old. They grow to a great height: they may have trunks with an average length of between 35m and 40m, even as much as 50m in the case of the largest, without any knots. Because of this, and their unusual colours, ranging from red to purple or black, these species have always been sought after.

You will almost certainly come across the inhabitants of the local **villages**, whose way of life has changed little over the centuries. Sinharaja is fairly typical of a new policy in biosphere conservation. Around the virgin forest, the domain of botanists and zoologists, there is a circle of 22 villages which use the resources at the forest's edge: rattan creepers, fuel resins or gum, as well as plants for medicinal purposes and food. Around their traditional adobe huts, with roofs made of natural fibres or leaves, the inhabitants cultivate sweet potatoes and manioc, the breadfruit tree and the jackfruit.

On the road to Haputale★★

If you are coming to the end of your journey, Ratnapura is a pleasant, practical place to stay, since it is only 100km from Colombo. To continue your journey, there are two possible routes to Pelmadulla (19km east). The southern route heads off towards the coast, towards Matara via the Bulutota Pass (alt 1 500m), or to Hambantota via the Uda Walawe elephant reserve. The eastern route follows the edge of the Peak Wilderness Sanctuary and enters the Uva Province at Haputale (90km).

Shortly after crossing the Kalu Ganga, you will notice some rudimentary shacks and forests of poles by the side of the road. They mark the position of the **mineshafts** of the **gem belt**, which runs for 15km east of Ratnapura. The mines are centuries old, and there are few concessions to modernity in the methods of extraction. They depend on the existence of **gem-bearing gravel** *(illam)*, alluvial deposits along watercourses with a high concentration of gems. The shafts, which are simply shored up with beams, are sunk to a depth of 15m. Nearby, a pool helps the filtration process. After two months, it is flushed with water to remove the particles of clay. The bed of the nearby river, a tributary of the Kalu Ganga, is also dredged using long wooden rakes. The mines are leased and managed by an entrepreneur who provides the material and organises the recruitment of the workforce. Another intermediary negotiates the mining rights with the **State Gems Corporation**. They share the best of the production with the owner of the land, leaving the surplus for the paid workers who sell it at the market in Ratnapura.

Patience and all the time in the world...

F Rhodes

From Balangoda, 45km beyond Ratnapura, the road begins to climb, heading up the mountainous range of the Uva. Fourteen kilometres on, it enters Belihul Oya.

From stones to flashes

No less than 25 varieties of gem lie in the depths of the earth and in the riverbeds of Sri Lanka. Once upon a time, their sparkling colours decorated Buddhist reliquaries, enhanced the beauty of women, or lay in the coffers of princes. Even today, men and women like to own and wear even the simplest ring, inlaid with one of the stones of the island: the blood red of the ruby, the pale blue of the sapphire, the vermilion of the garnet, the pale yellow of the topaz, the deep mauve of the aquamarine, the pearly white of the moonstone, or the bright amber of the zircon.

■ **Belihul Oya** is named after the river which flows through it. It cascades in a torrent past the Rest House and forms a pool further down where one can paddle *(except at weekends, when it is too busy)*. Belihul Oya is situated at the foot of the mountains. To the northeast, there is a gap, framed by the mountains of Paraviangalai and Ellamana. To the north, **World's End** on Horton Plains forms its edge, perched at an altitude of 2 000m, high above the tea plantations. Serious walkers can hike to **Horton Plains★★★** *(see p 260)* from Belihul Oya. An old path, which is still used by workers from the plantations for fetching supplies, starts at the Rest House and climbs 1 500m through the **Nagrak Tea Estate**, up to World's End *(13km, about a 6hr walk)*.

Beyond Belihul Oya, the road climbs up to Haputale (31km).

Making the most of Ratnapura

Coming and going

By bus – The ***bus termini*** are situated in the town-centre, in the middle (near the clock tower and the post office) and at the end (below the Rest House) of Senanayake Maw. There are Intercity Express services between Ratnapura and Colombo (3hr), Hambantota (4hr) Matara (4hr) and Nuwara Eliya (5hr) via Hatton. For Belihul Oya and Haputale, the Intercity Express buses running between Colombo and Badulla stop at Ratnapura, but are often full... You can always catch a yellow bus.

Address book

Banks / Currency exchange – ***Bank of Ceylon***, Dharmapala Maw (opposite the Nilani Lodge Hotel). Monday 9am-1pm, Tuesday-Friday 9am-1.30pm.

Post – The post office is in the square with the clock tower. Monday-Friday 9.30am-5pm.

Where to stay

Under US$10

Ratna Gems Halt, 153 / 5 Outer Circular Rd, 1km north of the centre, on the road that passes below the Rest House; access via a very steep staircase which starts at the guest-house sign, ☎ (045) 257 45 – 3rm. This basic guesthouse may not be the Ritz but it's clean. The rooms, which have mosquito nets, are located in a separate building, above the house of the owners. Meals on request.

From US$10 to US$15

Kalawati, Polhengoda, 2km northeast of the centre, ☎ (045) 224 65 18rm. ✕ A large, airy house opening onto a luxuriant garden, with a gallery decorated with old Sri Lankan paintings, furniture and curios worked by the owner. Restaurant pleasantly ventilated. By paying a 100Rs supplement, you can have one of the huge rooms overlooking the garden. Wonderful place for aromatherapy beauty treatments or massage with essential oils.

Darshana Inn, 68 / 5 Rest House Rd, below the Rest House, ☎ (045) 226 74 – 4rm. Perfectly adequate but rather gloomy rooms, arranged around a large central area. Pretty view over the town and meals at reasonable prices. Guests who like to go to bed early may be disturbed by the noise from the small bar.

From US$15 to US$30

Rest House, Rest House Rd, on the hill above the bus terminus, ☎ (045) 222 99 – 10rm. Like other "Rest Houses" on the island, the one at Ratnapura is magnificently situated in a large colonial-style house with lots of character, but is poor value for money. The rooms are in serious need of a coat of paint and the bathrooms are not always clean (cold water). Better to come here for lunch to enjoy the view, because the cooking is OK and the prices reasonable.

From US$30 to US40

Ratnaloka Tour Inn, Kosagala, Kahangama (7km, beyond the Saman Devale), ☎ (045) 300 17, Fax (045) 224 55, ratnaloka@eureka.lk; wwww.eureka.lk/ratnaloka – 54rm. Very comfortable, in the middle of a hevea plantation. Although rather far out, it is ideal for tour groups. In the evening, the restaurant serves a Sri Lankan buffet.

• In Sinharaja

The accommodation at Sinharaja is managed by the ***Forest Department of Colombo*** (see p 132). You must come in person to book, produce your passport, and pay cash in advance. The basic tariff is 220Rs per night in a dormitory. You may hire pillows and sheets on the spot and use the electricity for 30Rs an hour. As in the Department of Wildlife reserves, you must bring your own provisions, which the resident staff will prepare for you.

• In Belihul Oya

From US$15 to US$30

River View, at the beginning of Belihul Oya coming from Ratnapura, ☎ (071) 77 47 75 – 10rm. You enter through the restaurant on the roadside, which dominates the Belihul Oya and has delicious buffets and barbecues. The bungalows are quiet, set in a garden further down the hill (hot water). Swimming possible in the river. The establishment organises excursions several days a week, with transport, camping, meals and entry tickets to national parks for about US$15 per person per day. A good base for exploring the area.

From US$30 to US$40

Belihul Oya Rest House (Ceylon Hotels Corporation), to the left of the bridge over the Belihul Oya, ☎ (045) 875 99 – 8rm. A very pleasant place for lunch, on the banks of the Belihul Oya (except at weekends when it's very busy), but nothing can justify such high prices. Unless the ten bungalows being built at the time of our visit are a success. Watch this space…

Eating out

At Ratnapura, the ***Sanara Restaurant***, 141 Ethulram Rd (1km northeast of the town-centre), is set in a beautiful garden and has good Thai and Chinese cuisine.

The ***River View*** at Belihul Oya hold barbecues and the helpings are generous.

Other things to do

Feasts & festivals – Great "perahera" with procession of elephants to the ***Maha Saman Devale*** for the full moon of the month of Esala (at the same time as the festivals at Kandy and Kataragama).

Haputale★
Horton Plains★★★

Uva Province – Alt 1 430m
Average annual temperature 21°C, but nights are cold in winter
57km from Nuwara Eliya, 90km from Ratnapura and 190km from Colombo

Not to be missed
The view from Lipton's Seat and its huge tea garden.
Dawn over Horton Plains and daybreak at World's End.

And remember...
Do not take short cuts or paths that are not marked if you are walking alone.
Be prepared for the cold and rain: the climate in the mountains is very changeable.

It may be the unhurried pace of daily life here. Or the warmth of its little guest-houses. Or possibly its simplicity, devoid of the Victorian affectations of Nuwara Eliya. You don't feel like a tourist in Haputale, you feel at home. That is the secret of this place, set in one of the gaps of the Uva mountains: a section of mountains suddenly clears revealing a panorama of lowlands stretching as far as the southernmost tip of the island. It is also within easy reach by train or coach of a wide range of walks in its extraordinary and highly diverse land-scapes, where pickers can be seen at work harvesting Uva, the tea most prized by connoisseurs. Haputale isn't just worth a detour: it's worth staying here for its own sake.

Haputale★

Allow 2hr.

Situated where the railway crosses the Colombo-Badulla road, Haputale is one of the small towns where the workers from the surrounding tea estates come to buy their supplies. It's also a favourite stop for travellers.
Each morning until 11am, there is an open-air **vegetable market** down by the station and the only shopping street. The stalls are mostly manned by men sitting under black umbrellas with their old-fashioned scales. Housewives carefully inspect the green cabbages, which lie beside jackfruits, aubergines, gombos, bunches of bananas and pyramids of onions. Other stalls sell fabrics by the metre, pots and pans, soap and toothpaste, calendars and posters of pop-stars. Apart from this lively interlude in daily life, peace reigns at Haputale, spectacularly located on the southern escarpment of the mountainous region. The village is poised more than 1 000m above the rolling hills which stretch away towards the coast. The **changeable climate** of the mountains of Haputale adds to the beauty of the place. On a clear day, you can see the salt marshes of Hambantota to the southeast. When the rain falls over the ridges planted with mist-covered pines and the fog rolls into the lowlands below it, the village seems to float above a sea of cloud.

Around Haputale

The area around Haputale, which is well served by buses and trains, has plenty of scope for enjoyable half-day outings, depending on the type of transport.

Adisham*

3km from Haputale. Open on Saturday and Sunday, 9am-12.30pm / 1.30pm-4.30pm.
Adisham is a Benedictine monastery situated on the edge of the bird reserve of Tangamalai *(closed to visitors)*. It can easily be reached on foot *(about 30min)* by the road leaving the centre of the village, which follows the railway for a while, then winds across a tea plantation. The Benedictine order acquired this residence in the 1960s. Despite its austere appearance, which seems to have destined it to be a retreat, Adisham, named after a village in Kent, was built by a British planter, **Sir Thomas Lister Villiers**, in 1931. It's an imposing grey-stone building, with mullioned windows and a roof of tiles of teak shingles from Burma, and still contains some of the belongings of its first owner. With their fireplaces, watercolours painted by Lady Villiers, a few photographs and family portraits, the rooms conjure up colonial family life as it was in Ceylon. The mouldings are of plaster of Paris, but the wallpaper, which has barely faded at all, the library and the heavy desk were brought from England. Visitors are not allowed to enter the monastery, but once beyond the planter's apartments, they may walk in the **rose garden** and the orchard. The fruit is used to make syrups and jams, which are sold in the shop by the entrance.

Lipton's Seat**

16km northeast of Haputale. The finest **view** from the mountains of Haputale over the southern lowlands is from the **Dambetenna Tea Estate***, 9km to the northeast *(the road is a dead end, but the plantation can be reached by bus from Haputale)*. The path running along the escarpment is a delight. Tea bushes and curious blocks of stone form a sort of Japanese garden, interrupted here and there by clumps of pines, the silvery trunks of eucalyptus trees, or jacarandas hung with bunches of blue flowers. The route is dotted with Hindu temples of various sizes and their bold colours carve a path to a small cemetery overhanging the valley, on the edge of the plantation.

Three kilometres away from Haputale, **Green Field** *(on the left-hand side of the road)* is a medium-sized but highly diversified plantation, which is holding its own despite the legacy of the large 19C tea estates. The tea factory is open to the public *(for an appointment ring ☎* (057) 682 01) and its products are for sale. At Dambetenna, there is no road, but a track (not suitable for vehicles) which winds its way up through the tea plantation to the **Agarapatena Tea Estate** *(if you have a vehicle, ask for permission to take the track to the entrance to the plantation)*. Seven kilometres further on, you come to **Lipton's Seat**, the favourite haunt of Ceylon's most famous planter, who used to come here to enjoy the view of the land he owned and the panorama of the island.

Diyaluma Falls*

About 30km east of Haputale. For an outing combining walking and swimming, visit the Diyaluma Falls, on the road to Wellawaya, southeast of Haputale. Take the bus to Koslanda. Here you leave the Wellawaya road and continue on foot along the flat path to the left past the People's Bank. Two hundred metres beyond a deserted Hindu temple, there is a path on the right which emerges at some natural pools situated above the falls *(7km, about 90min easy walk)*. Rather than retracing your steps, head back down the very steep path which leads down among the rocks with the waterfall on your left to a small latex factory. It is situated about 10min on foot from the Wellawaya road. From the bottom, you will be able to see the double waterfall in all its glory (170m). Hail a bus to return to Haputale or continue to Wellawaya, but remember that the last one goes past at about 5pm. The walk in the opposite direction is not recommended because the path up beside the waterfall is very steep.

You are now near Buduruvegala (see p 270).

Horton Plains***

From Haputale, catch the first train (at about 8am, a 40min journey) to the station of Ohiya. When you get there, walk alongside the railway for a few hundred metres. Before the tunnel, a steep path leads off on the left (the first 10min of the climb are quite tricky). At the top, follow the track on the left in the direction of the Far Inn, which stands at the entrance to the reserve (a total of 7km and about 2hr climb). Entrance fee (815Rs). Leaving from Belihul Oya, hire a 4x4 to reach Kalupahana, pass the Bambarakanda Falls and drive up the gravel track following the ridge through the tea plantations of West Haputale. From there, a track leads to Anderson Lodge, 2km from the Far Inn. Numara Eliya is also a good place from which to visit Horton Plains and the road to it from there is excellent.

A wild landscape

Buffeted by the wind, the Horton Plains highlands include some of the island's most spectacular landscapes, with stretches of grassland and forest, giant ferns, trees clawing at the clouds, and peat-rimmed lakes. They are a classic destination for keen walkers, using Haputale as their base.

This strange, wild, almost melancholy landscape was discovered by the planter **Thomas Farr** who named it after **Sir Robert Wilmot Horton**, who was governor of the island from 1831 until 1837.

Overlooked by the Kirigalpota mountains, the second highest range on the island (2 395m), Horton Plains forms the western edge of the Haputale range, poised high above the Ruhunu lowlands. Buffeted by the wind and too high (between 1 800m and 2 160m) for farming, these vast highland prairies *(patna)* do not permit any kind of serious crop cultivation and have escaped the intensive exploitation of the centre of the island. However, their clean rivers full of fish are a great attraction for the planters living in Nuwara Eliya, who come here to catch carp and trout. Today, 30sqkm of Horton Plains is protected by the Wildlife Conservation Department.

The vegetation gradually turns to gold as the dry season progresses. In October, it is covered with little deep-blue flowers (*Aristea eckloni* and *Exacum bleu*), while, in April and May, the purple rhododendron flowers are in bloom. Only a few animal species have elected to live on the plains, but, early in the morning, you have a good chance of seeing **sambar** *(Rusa unicolor)*, which come here in small groups to graze, or types of deer (*Muntiacus malabaricus* and *Moschiola memmina*). The main predator here is the leopard, the largest of which are 2m long. You can sometimes hear them roaring as night falls.

Walking on Horton Plains

Starting at the Far Inn, a not particularly demanding circular walk of about twelve kilometres provides the chance to see some of the area's natural curiosities *(allow 3hr)*.

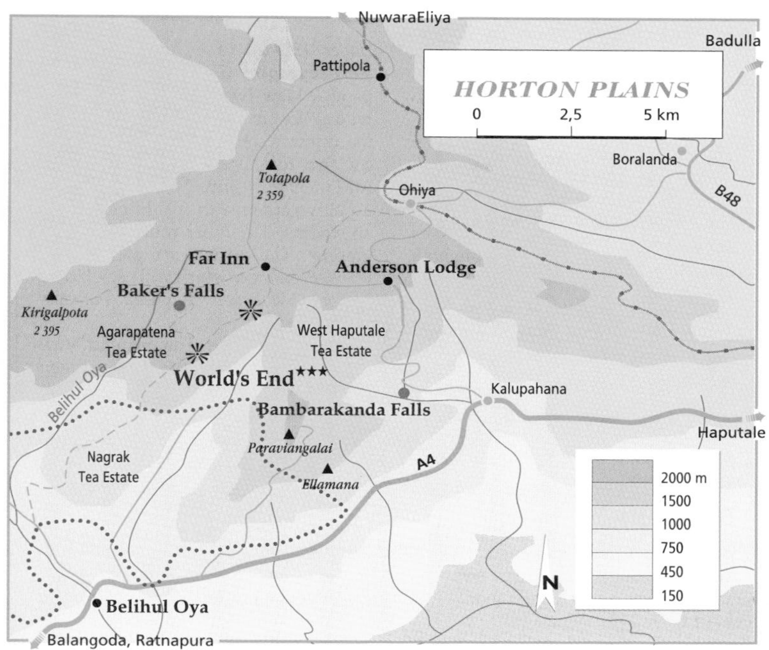

The path crosses the plain, then follows a dry riverbed with purple pebbles to **World's End★★★**, the steep edge of the plains which plummets down to the **Nagrak Tea Estate**, 800m below. The path then sets off across an area to the north scattered with streams and tarns, leading to **Baker's Falls** and the Belihul Oya rushing down between the tree-ferns. The river has its source in the foothills of Totapola (2 359m) and forms small pools where wild trout lurk in the shallows. From Baker's Falls, it is an easy walk back to the Far Inn, 2km to the northeast.

From here, continue to Anderson Lodge (3km to the east), one of the Department of Wildlife bungalows, where a track winds down to Ohiya station (8km). On Sundays, there is a shuttle bus service between the station and the Far Inn. But be careful coming back: don't miss the last train for Haputale which leaves at about 4.30pm. Remember to check the timetable when you arrive at Ohiya.

Making the most of Haputale and its surroundings

Coming and going

By train – Haputale lies on the Colombo-Badulla line. The small ***railway station*** is in the centre of the town and most of the guest houses can be reached on foot. There are three trains daily to Bandarawela (30min), Ella (1hr) and Badulla (2hr), as well as to Ohiya (40min), Nanu Oya (2hr30min) and Colombo (from 7hr30min to 10hr). Note that none of the trains go via Kandy.

By bus – The ***bus termini*** are central and close together, located at the junction of the main road and the road to Bandarawela. Note that, because Haputale is not at the end of a line, you are likely to have trouble finding a seat. If you are going to the Uva area, the best plan is to go to the neighbouring town of Bandarawela (10km), which is served by numerous bus services throughout the day. If your destination is Nuwara Eliya, take the train, because you will have to change buses at Welimada (1hr). To get back to the south and the coast, go to the bus terminus at Wellawaya (90min). Each morning a bus leaves for Matara (7hr) via Hambantota and Tangalle.

The bus service to Colombo (6hr) goes via Ratnapura.

By car – Guest house owners will be able to assist you in organising your departure from Haputale, particularly if you are heading for the coast. As a rough guide, transport to Tangalle should cost about US$30 per vehicle.

Address book

Banks / Currency exchange – *Bank of Ceylon*, Colombo Rd, 300m from the centre on the road to Bandarawela, by the post office and the Queen's Rest Inn. Monday-Friday, 9am-1pm. Cash and traveller's cheques exchanged.

Post office / Telephone – Colombo Rd, near the Bank of Ceylon. Monday-Friday 9.30am-4.30pm. Telecommunications office at the crossroads of the main street and the road to Bandarawela. Daily 8.30am-8pm.

Where to stay

• In Haputale

Provided it lasts, Haputale holds the record for good value accommodation with rooms available at very reasonable prices. Owners are good for advice about the local area. The guesthouses can easily be reached on foot, all lying within a radius of 100m to 200m from the bus and railway stations. The altitude means that AC is not necessary.

Under US$10

Amarasinghe Guesthouse, Thampapillai Maw (walk west following the railway for about 150m and, opposite the primary school, go down the steps on the left), ☎ (057) 681 75 / (071) 659 05 – 5rm. 🚿 ✕ No view, but a pretty garden with two bright, pleasant rooms. The other rooms are more gloomy. The owners are planning to open seven more which will each have a balcony. Meals are very cheap, but variable in quality.

Bawa Guesthouse, Thampapillai Maw (white house above the Amarasinghe guest-house), ☎ (057) 682 60 – 3rm. 🚿 ✕ A modern, very well-kept house overlooking the valley (hot water). Good family cooking and lots of helpful advice for walkers. If the weather is bad, find out about the gems from the owner, who is a stone-cutter.

Cuesta Inn, Temple Rd, on the edge of Haputale, on the road leading to Adisham monastery, ☎ (057) 680 97 – 5rm. 🚿 ✕ A dream of a guesthouse for the price. The rooms, which are bright and clean, all have a balcony overlooking the tea plantations and pine forests. Unlike other guesthouses which use electricity, the hot water here is heated by solar panels. Good tasty home-cooking and large helpings. It has a "Golden Book" which is a mine of information in every language and the owners themselves are an inexhaustible source of information about the local area, which they love dearly. They will pick you up from the station.

Highcliffe Rest Inn & Restaurant, by the market, opposite the Old Rest House, ☎ (057) 681 25 – 6rm. 🚿 ✕ The rooms are spotlessly clean (mosquito nets) and the furnishings not lacking in charm. The bathrooms are gloomier, but they have hot showers. The house is right by the railway, but fortunately trains are few and far between.

From US$10 to US$15

Queen's Rest Inn, Bandarawela Rd, 300m from the centre on the Bandarawela road, between the Bank of

Ceylon and the post office – 6rm. 🚿 ✕ Clean, rather dark rooms (mosquito nets and hot water), and a terrace with a wonderful view over the valley and the town of Haputale. TV room for rainy days and meals at very reasonable prices.

Sri Lak View Holiday Inn, 48 Sherwood Rd, below the bus station and the road to Colombo, ☎ (057) 680 96 – 6rm. 🚿 ✕ Set on the edge of the escarpment of Haputale, where the view drops down to the lowlands, this fairly new establishment is spectacularly located. The rooms are pleasant and the bathrooms have hot water. The owners plan to add two rooms in cottages.

• In Horton Plains

If you are travelling with a sleeping bag, you could stay on the plateau (apply to the rangers who will give you a bed in their barracks: basic accommodation at a negotiable price) or in the surrounding tea plantations where the bungalows occasionally rent out beds. ***Anderson Lodge*** can accommodate between 6 and 8 people and has showers, but belongs to the Wildlife Conservation Department which means you must book through their office in Colombo (see p 132). It is also very expensive (about US$20 per person, not including meals). Take food or a picnic with you when visiting this wilderness, but take your rubbish away with you, because the litter bins on the plateau are constantly emptied by the wind.

EXCURSIONS

If it seems too complicated to organise a walk in the Uva province using public transport, bear in mind that most of the guesthouses are able to arrange a vehicle with a driver. As a rough guide, a trip to Horton Plains should cost about US$20 for the day, and the circuit which takes in the Diyaluma Falls – Ella Gap – Dowa Temple – Bandarawela costs US$25 for a day's outing.

The view from Haputale

R Holzbachova-P Bénet

THE HIGH UVA★★

FROM BADULLA TO WELLAWAYA

Uva Province – Map p 238-239
Alt between 600m and 1 200m – Monsoon from November to mid-January
49km circuit from Badulla to Bandarawela, 35km circuit from Ella to Wellawaya
Allow three days, with stops at Bandarawela and Ella

Not to be missed
The little wooden bridge at Bogoda.
Tea at the Rest House, opposite Ella Gap.
The cliff at Buduruvegala.
The giant statues in the forest of Marawila.
The train journey from Nuwara Eliya or Haputale to Badulla.

And remember...
Try to go in the season after the rains when the landscape is a lush green and the waterfalls are spectacular.

Mountains account for one quarter of Uva Province, the remainder comprising lowlands which stretch away to the south and east of the island. Until 1985, it was the route to the mythical beach of Arugam Bay, that great meeting-place of surfers and travellers, but today the conflict with the Tamil Tigers has closed this route to the east coast.

The mountainous part includes some of the most spectacular scenery on the island, because it forms the edge of the highlands, a steep escarpment, with breathtaking views from Haputale or Ella Gap. Ideally, you should travel on foot, following the paths used every day by the schoolchildren in white uniforms, villagers and workers from the tea estates. Invisible from the road, their tiny villages cling to rocky outcrops, concealed by a curtain of bamboo or a row of arecas. Unbroken countryside awaits you everywhere you turn here in the High Uva. At the foot of the giant escarpment, great works were carried out in honour of Buddha by the ancient kings of the island, now hidden in the jungle. This is a journey that takes in the invigorating air of the mountains of the High Uva as well as the mysteries of the giant statues down below.

At the heart of the Kingdom of Ravana

The **Ramayana**, an Indian epic known all over Asia, tells the story of the **Rama** March, a war waged by a prince to win back his wife Sita who had been abducted by **Ravana**, the king of Lanka. In the long story related by the Indian poets, Rama is a valiant knight, unjustly exiled by his father, Ravana is a lecherous, cruel demon, and Sita a model and virtuous wife…

And what if the same story had been told by a Ceylonese poet? He would have said that the magical landscape of the Uva mountains was the dwelling place of Ravana, the erudite sovereign and musician, whose power stretched far beyond the island. He had a sister, Surpanakha, who, being madly in love with Rama, tried to seduce the Indian prince. In response, the young man and his brother Lakshmana cruelly mutilated her by cutting off her nose and ears. Did such humiliation not demand vengeance? So Surpanakha went to see Ravana. But instead of arousing his hatred, she aroused her brother's desire by describing the incomparable beauty of **Sita**, Rama's wife. Ravana was unable to resist such temptation: the wise monarch became a mad king, devoured by passion. He carried off the beautiful woman in his magic chariot, which had the power to fly through the air, and took her to a cave by a waterfall in the cool Uva mountains. Each day, he visited her by means of a network of underground passages running across the countryside. He gave her gifts of the most sumptuous jewels, perfumes and stones, and all the riches of his island. His brother, the wise astrologist Vibhishana, tried in vain to bring him back to his senses. But the bashful lover was to bring about his own ruin. Rama raised an army and marched on the island. Hanuman, his faithful monkey general, built a road connecting the easternmost point of the mainland to Lanka. The epic battle took place at Welimada, in the north of the Uva province. Ravana was killed, his brother, Vibhishana, was proclaimed king of Lanka, and Sita was restored to Rama. But, in the end, no-one knows what the princess thought about the charms of the island.

A rebellious province

The Uva region is associated with the history of the ancient kingdoms of Ceylon. In the late 16C, the local chiefs swore allegiance to the king of Kandy. Neither the Portuguese nor the Dutch ever succeeded in taking the Uva mountains. The Portuguese suffered a crushing defeat there in 1630, about twelve kilometres from the Ella Gap: their cannon, rendered useless by the rain, were unable to prevent them being encircled by the Sinhalese armies, who massacred the troops of Constantine of Sanivalle. With the submission of Kandy to the British in 1815, the Uva region was administered from the Central province. Two years later, it was the focus of a **revolt** against the colonial administration. The movement to restore the Sinhalese monarchy, supported by the Buddhist *Sanghas*, was conceived around a pretender to the throne in Kataragama. It took the British army a year to quell the rebellion, at the cost of such massive destruction that the region did not recover until the beginning of the 20C.

The tea line

1867 saw the inauguration of the **railway** linking Colombo to Kandy and the arrival of the first locomotives caused a sensation. The train was christened the Iron Yakkha and women were not allowed to see the spectacle on the grounds that the movement of its pistons was obscene! The expansion of the tea plantations in the mountainous region led to the extension of the line to Badulla, the capital of the Uva region, thus opening up a route through 240km of the most beautiful scenery in the world.

The ascent starts at Rambukana. At the end of the first tunnel, the railway clings to the side of the mountain, offering breathtaking views of the first foothills, dominated by the unusual silhouette of Bible Rock. After Gampola, the train enters the most spectacular section of the route, climbing to an altitude of 1 860m on a track dotted with tunnels (no fewer than 47!) and metal bridges strung across rivers. Before it arrives in Badulla, it performs a final acrobatic feat as it descends. As it leaves Demodara, it circles the mountain, disappears briefly into a tunnel and reappears 30m below the station to continue its journey to Badulla.

A rural ride...

If you take the train to Badulla, you might be surprised to see that it never passes through any towns, travelling through landscape so wild that it feels as if this is the first time a train has passed this way. When the train stops (which is very frequently) you can even hear birdsong. Only a few stations grace the side of the tracks. And what delightful stations! They are all testimonials to the triumph of industrial architecture at the turn of the century, with white-painted bricks, cast-iron columns that look as though they belong in the nave of a church, gables with wrought-iron rosettes, the old woodwork of the ticket offices and information boards. There isn't a single corner that doesn't have something of interest.

From Badulla to Bandarawela

49km. Allow 1 day.

■ **Badulla*** – Nestling in a loop of the Badulu Oya, the capital of the Uva is the only town worthy of the name in the whole province. However, it is not a very pleasant place to stay: at 600m it is encircled by the surrounding mountains, baking in a constant heat haze. The British made it an administrative centre, which at first depended on Kandy, then a capital in its own right when Uva Province was re-established in 1886. But unlike the towns in the mountainous region that have grown up on the back of the tea plantations, Badulla has ancient origins linked to the spread of Buddhism on the island.
At the south side of the city lies the **Mutiyangana Viharaya***, a large Buddhist shrine visited by many pilgrims. Having been honoured by a visit from the historical Buddha at one time, it is one of the sixteen holy places on the island. Since the 4C BC, its spotless, elegant *dagoba* has housed a relic from the jaw of the Master. The whole complex is a haven of peace, dominating the rice-fields beside the river.

To the north of the sacred site there is a maze of streets lined with shops. The **Kataragama devale*** stands at the centre *(enter on the east side from Lower St)*. Cows sometimes graze along the path leading up to the **gate** with its carved wooden columns and capitals in the shape of drooping wilted flowers. Above the elaborately carved door is a good luck motif of the goddess Lakshmi in the company of two elephants. The long *puja* drums are stored in the little room in front of the god's resting place, closed off by a coloured and extraordinary *makara torana*. Around the exterior, **paintings** depict the procession of a *perahera*, their colours now faded. The temple, which is little frequented except during the Kataragama festival, has the elegant stamp of Kandyan shrines. The peacefulness here provides a contrast to the bustle of Post Office Road, which runs along beside its northern wall, where a covered market echoes the cacophony of the bus termini nearby.

Seven kilometres to the north, on the road to Mahiyangana, are the **Dunhinda Falls***, a very popular place with Sri Lankan tourists *(frequent bus service from the bus terminus)*. The path leading to it starts opposite the coach park *(2km, allow 1hr there and back)*. The stalls, which run along the length of the path and are sometimes closed on weekdays, sell framed pictures of landscapes, mysterious pharmacopoeia ingredients, tea and cold drinks. The path descends steeply (the rocks are sometimes slippery) towards the natural pool formed by the waterfall as it pours down a narrow gap. A good time to see it is mid-afternoon when the path is in shade and the light produces iridescent reflections.

Leave Badulla on the Haputale road. Drive through the village of Hali-Ela (6km), and take the road on the right to Kettavala. Eight kilometres further on, at the Jagula junction, look out for the sign saying "Bogoda bridge 2.7km" pointing along a rough track going downhill to the left. It ends in a cul-de-sac, in front of a shop seemingly standing in the middle of nowhere. You are at Bogoda.

■ **Bogoda**** – Formerly situated on the road between Kandy and Mahiyangana, Bogoda is now a place where peace and quiet is rarely disturbed. A cobbled street interspersed with steps descends towards the Gallanda Oya which cascades down onto the granite rocks below. A small **monastery*** stands on the edge of the valley *(ask for the key to continue the tour)*. Endowed by King Sri Vikrama Rajasinha in the 18C, it is built in the purest Kandyan style.

A flight of stairs continues to a small **rock-cut temple*** below. Its foundation is associated with the wanderings of Vattagamani Abhaya (89-77 BC) when Anuradhapura was occupied by a Dravidian army *(see "Dambulla" p 208)*. He is supposed to have found refuge in this area and commissioned the 18m-long statue of the Buddha which lies in the shrine. The natural tunnel in the rock on one side of the temple is said to be the beginning of an underground passage which links up with the secret network running under the Uva, but the smell of bats is enough to dissuade anyone from further exploration.

In front of the shrine, a covered **wooden bridge**** resting on solid piles spans the gorge of the Gallanda Oya. Built in the 18C, it is unique because of its pink-tiled roof supported by elegant columns. The old road continues on the other side and disappears gradually into the countryside.

Retrace your steps to Hali Ela and continue in the direction of Haputale. The road runs across hills planted with tea or overlooking rice-fields. Thirteen kilometres further on you pass the junction at Kumbalvela and the road which leads to Ella. Two kilometres further on, on the left-hand side of the road, a white-painted fence surrounds the precinct of the small temple of Dowa.

■ **Dowa*** – The Dowa valley is a place full of atmosphere which was chosen to found a Buddhist retreat in the 3C BC. Pilgrims journeying through the region never fail to stop here. Having passed through a gateway modelled on one belonging to a Portuguese church, you find yourself on the esplanade of the small monastery, guardian of the sacred place *(ask for the key)*. Near the Bo tree enclosure, a flight of steps leads down to the valley with the Badulla River on one side.

The temple*, which was altered during the Kandyan period, is tucked under an enormous rock at the foot of the cliff, on which the rock-cut statue of the Buddha remains unfinished. In front of it are two rooms, the first decorated with scenes depicting the former lives of Buddha, the second with images of Buddha in *samadhi*, surrounded by a painted procession of disciples. In the actual cave, two Buddhas rest under the protection of the gods Vishnu and Kataragama. A passage extends like a labyrinth to other rooms, their walls decorated with recent paintings depicting the life of Sakyamuni and the vicissitudes of the spread of Buddhism in the island. They end in a rock shelter which protects a small *dagoba* guarded by the statue of a cobra. According to tradition, the stone wall at the end of the shelter conceals a tunnel, dug by Ravana, leading to his retreat at the falls of Ravanella.

6km from Dowa, the road leads down to the large town of Bandarawela.

■ **Bandarawela** – At the junction of several roads passing through the Uva and at an altitude of 1 230m, the commercial centre of this small town stretches out along Welimada Road in a series of bends. The residential area extends over the hills planted with pines and orchards, carpeted with tea bushes and market gardens. Like Nuwara Eliya (although it enjoys a much milder climate) the town has charm and still has a few vestiges from the colonial period, including its **railway station** and its **post office**. On top of the natural promontory which dominates the centre is the elegant **Bandarawela Hotel**, an old British club which was converted into a hotel in 1904. Opposite, a small, well-stocked supermarket is housed in what used to be a branch of **Cargills**, a well-known chain of shops.

At this point in the itinerary, you can choose whether to stay at Bandarawela, continue to Haputale (11km), or return to the Kumbalvela junction (7km) to spend the night at Ella (3km beyond the junction) and proceed with your exploration of the Uva.

From Ella to Maligawila

94km. Allow 2 days, including one to walk around Ella.

■ **Ella**★★ – The village of Ella has one of the most spectacular **views** in the Uva. Coming from the north, the road follows the foothills covered with thick woodland which totally obscures the view. From the village, the way seems barred by an apparently impassable valley, but you soon come across a ravine with a rushing stream. All at once there is an extraordinary sight, a precipice plunging 900m into the abyss. Framed by the cliff of the rock of Ravana and a wooded ridge, this is the **Ella Gap**★★, giving a breathtaking view over 100km of the rolling hills which stretch into the distance and eventually disappear into the pale line of the Indian Ocean. The Rest House and the guest houses built on the edge of the village on the Wellawaya road are excellent observation points. As at Haputale, a stay at Ella is good for recharging the batteries and for walking in the surrounding area.

There are other fine views of the lowlands around Ella, especially from Passara (25km east). Although not well known, they are no less spectacular, but you will need to hire a 4x4 and a guide who knows the area well. *(see the "Making the most of..." section p 275).*

■ The road which runs down beyond the Rest House leads to the simple **Kataragama oratory**, which stands beside a pretty lookout platform with a wonderful view over the valley. One kilometre lower down, a stream flows under the road and cascades down the hillside in a waterfall. Now leave the main road and take the road leading up to the right. After 500m, you will reach a small temple built in the 19C on a medieval site. From here, a very difficult path *(ask someone to accompany you)* leads to **Ravana's cave** on the left. Whether or not it was, as legend has it, the cave where the king kept the beautiful Sita captive, it has certainly been used as a shelter by humans for at least 21 000 years: human remains and artefacts dating this far back have been found here.

■ On the other side of the hill are the **Bambaragama Falls**★, sometimes called the Ravanella Falls. They disappear into a gap, descend the cliff for 8m, then flow under a bridge lower down into the valley *(best seen in the afternoon for the light, and sometimes dry in the dry season).*

Ella Falls

P Haussherr

■ Also on the Wellawaya road, 6km from the Ella junction, there is a sign for "Kurugama Falls 3km". Head in this direction, then take the dirt track which goes up steeply to the right. Five kilometres further on, your efforts will be rewarded when you come to the **Kanda Vihara** (Mountain Temple), an ancient rock hermitage where an anchorite monk still lives.

■ The road to the south plunges into the gap, the slopes of which are planted with acacias and mango trees. At **Wellawaya** (35km beyond Ella), the mountain barrier is left behind and you enter the Ruhunu plain. There is no reason to go to Wellawaya except its large bus terminus *(situated on the edge of the town)*, but the area around the town has many sites associated with the island's history, all in a magnificent natural setting. To visit them it's best to have a vehicle, which the owners of the guest houses at Ella will help to organise. One day is sufficient to visit them all.

The A2 goes to Hambantota on the south coast. After 5km, a track leads off on the right into a landscape of pools which attract many birds. It finishes 4km further on at the doors of a small monastery which looks after the site of Buduruvegala.

■ **Buduruvegala**** – *Entrance fee.* The "Rock of the Buddha", a granite escarpment with the outline of an elephant lying down, appears at the end of a woodland path *(best seen in the morning for the light)*. Chronicles make no mention of the site, despite the fact that this is the largest group of rock figures on the island. Around a 15m-high **Buddha**, which is almost identical to the uncompleted giant statue at Dowa, two groups of people have been carved out of the stone. They are all wearing tiaras and are lavishly decorated with jewellery, according to the convention established by Mahayana Buddhism for depicting bodhisattvas. On the left, **Avalokitesvara** (the most important bodhisattva) occupies the centre of the scene. You can still see traces of his stuccoed robe, and the image of Buddha in meditation, identifiable by the way in which his hair is tied in a knot. The woman in a slightly hunched-over pose, with a vase in her right hand, is possibly **Tara**, the companion of the large bodhisattva. No one can identify the man holding a sword.
On the other side, the second group has been executed with great attention to detail. Only the figure on the right can be identified, thanks to the symbol in his left hand: he is **Vajrapani**. These statues retain their aura of mystery, but were probably carved in the 8C-10C, when rock-cut statues were much in vogue.

The venerable gentleman who looks after the **monastery** is a friendly sort who will show you his archive of photographs of Buddhist sites all over the world and will tell you about the benefits of meditation. This place is ideal for it: beautifully serene, the natural environment surrounding the stretches of water is in perfect harmony with the monastery and the men in saffron-coloured robes.

Head back towards Wellawaya and turn onto the Maligawila road, to the east. It is scattered with remains associated with the deeds of Duttugemunu, the conqueror of Ruhunu (see *"Tissamaharama" p000**). Fifteen kilometres Wellawaya, a track heads off to the left towards the Yudaganawa Vihara (2.5km).*

■ **Yudaganawa Vihara** – These ruins at the edge of a forest have recently been excavated. The tour starts with the **Culangani Vihara**, a small 12C monastery, consisting of a small brick *dagoba*, an image house and a Bo tree enclo-

The giant Buddha of Maligawila

sure, scattered in the undergrowth. Two hundred metres beyond it, among the remains of an enclosure wall, a path leads to an 18C **Kandyan temple**. The paintings which adorn the interior are rustic in style and full of vigour. The temple stands below the steps leading up to the terrace of a **dagoba** which would have been enormous had it been completed. But the site has an even more ancient history, because Yudaganawa was the site of the battle between Duttugemunu and his brother Sadhatissa in the 2C BC, a battle commemorated by an earlier group of Buddhist monuments, of which there is no longer any trace.

Return to the road to Buttala which you pass through after 2km. Turn right at the only crossroads in the town, then left. Look out for signs to Maligawila. After 7km, on a bend, the wall surrounding the Dematamal Vihara can be seen in splendid isolation in the middle of a chessboard of rice-fields.

■ **Dematamal Vihara** – As at Yudaganawa, the origins of the site go back to the time of Duttugemunu (it was founded by his brother), but there are still some remains dating from the Polonnaruwa period. A recent donation has made it possible to rebuild the image house, around a 12C **Buddha**** standing next to two new companions.

Continue along the same road: Maligawila is 11km further on (there are direct buses from Wellawaya, but they do not stop at the monuments described below).

■ **Maligawila**** – Unusually located against a backdrop of a majestic forest, this place is greatly revered. The forest path leading to it from the road ends, 200m further on, in a track through huge trees hung with creepers and inhabited by troops of monkeys. It links two giant statues carved out of crystalline limestone *(photography not permitted)*. Both of them lay in pieces on the floor of the jungle until 1991, when they were reconstructed by the Department of Archaeology. They belong to a huge religious complex which includes terraces and monumental gates, as well as a council chamber which, according to chronicles, is supposed to have been a royal foundation dating from the 7C.
The path on the left leads to a **Buddha**** more than 10m high. He stands in the posture, frequent in Ceylon, of *abhaya mudra*, his left hand holding a fold of his robe to his shoulder. Despite its size, the statue has been carved with great care. In particular, note the regularity of the pleating of his robe and the tight curls of his hair. He stands in the middle of the remains of a *gedige*, the steps of which are guarded by two *naga* (cobra-kings).
The path on the right leads to a huge statue of a bodhisattva, identified as **Avalokitesvara**** thanks to the statue of the seated Buddha. He is placed on a terrace with five steps, now protected by a pyramid-shaped roof supported by concrete pillars. A flicker of a smile plays on the face of this graceful statue. With his two hands, the bodhisattva makes the questioning gesture *(vitarka mudra)*; a lotus blossoms on his shoulder. Below the terrace, a square pier bears an inscription dating from the 10C. It tells of the sovereign and his actions to support the *Sangha* and lays down the rules of monastic administration. It stands near the ruins of a monastery.
With Maligawila being on the edge of the area controlled by the Tamil Tigers there are soldiers on patrol.

You can return to Wellawaya by a more direct route. It lies further south than the one you took to get here and runs through a hevea plantation before returning you to Buttala. At the end of your visit, you can either return to Ella or continue south. There are buses to Kataragama (55km) and Tissamaharama (59km) which leave from the Wellawaya bus terminus.

Making the most of Badulla

Coming and going

By train – The ***railway station*** lies 1km south of the town-centre and 500m from the Mutiyangana temple, on the other side of the Badulu Oya. There are six trains daily between Badulla and Colombo (between 10hr and 11hr).

By bus – The ***bus terminus*** is right in the centre, below the clock tower, at the junction of the roads from Bandarawela, Mahiyangana and Passara. There are frequent services to neighbouring towns in the upper Uva. Buses leave every 30min for Nuwara Eliya (2hr) and every two hours for Kandy (5hr) and Wellawaya (2hr), where you can then catch buses heading south. Intercity Express buses run a service to Colombo (between 6hr30min and 7hr).

By car – All the guesthouses are able to organise transport with a driver to explore the area or reach your next destination. As a rough guide, it should cost between US$20 and US$25 to reach Tangalle.

Address book

Banks / Currency exchange – ***Bank of Ceylon***, Bank Rd, 100m from the Mutiyangana Viharaya.

Post office – The post office is situated in the north wall of the Kataragama devale, opposite the market.

Where to stay

The capital of the Uva does not represent value for money, despite its popularity with Sri Lankan tourists. One explains the other because the island's inhabitants do not use the same criteria for accommodation: they pay very little for basic services, or stay with friends or relatives. The addresses below are only recommended as last resorts.

From US$10 to US$15

Badulla New Tourist Inn, 1km from the centre on Mahiyangana Rd, ☎ (055) 234 23 – 30rm. Situated alongside the very noisy Mahiyangana Road, this hotel and the rooms are rather uninspiring. But the owner also rents out 5 rooms (2 of which share a bathroom) in a house set further back on the other side of the road. They have mosquito nets and are very clean. Meals are served only in the hotel, and the cooking is good.

Badulla Rest House, at the junction of Bandarawela Rd and Mahiyangana Rd, ☎ (055) 222 99 – 17rm. The hotel is situated right in the centre, at the noisiest crossroads in town. The rooms have the advantage of overlooking a courtyard at the back planted with giant bougainvilleas, but are still noisy. The bathrooms are gloomy but clean (cold water only).

Dunhinda Falls Inn, Bandaranayaka Maw, 1km from the centre and 50m to the left of the road to the falls, ☎ (055) 230 28 / (072) 22 75 59, Fax (055) 236 91 – 12rm. A concrete building, but everything is clean and quiet. The rooms have mosquito nets and the bathrooms have hot water. International cuisine.

Dunhinda Sisila, 2.5km north of the falls, on the road to Mahiyangana, ☎ (055) 313 02 – 5rm. At the confluence of the Dunhinda and Badulu Oya rivers where you can paddle. The rooms are clean (mosquito nets) but dark, and the bathrooms are adequate. Good Sri Lankan cooking.

From US$15 to US$30

Green Woods Holiday Inn, 301 Bandarawela Rd, on the edge of the town on the Bandarawela road, ☎ (055) 313 58 – 80rm. In a two-storey building below the road (very busy). Decent rooms but the bathrooms are tiny. The four rooms on the first floor have pleasant views.

Eating out

As elsewhere, the family cooking in the guesthouses is often the best bet: a good reason to consult the visitor's book before checking in. The ***Rest House***, which is very central, serves decent "rice and curry", at moderate prices.

Other things to do

Feasts & festivals – *The Buddhist festival of Vesak*, at the Mutiyangana temple, is the occasion for a "perahera" with dancers, drummers and caparisoned elephants.

Festival of Kataragama for the full moon of Esala (July-August). Great "perahera" at the Kataragama devale, with dancers, elephants, torches, firecrackers and walking on red-hot embers.

Making the most of Bandarawela

Where to stay / Eating out

Under US$10

Mount View Holiday Inn, 35 / 2 Welimada Rd (access opposite the Anglican church), ☎ (057) 22 56 11 – 6rm. A two-storey concrete building in an uninspiring location, but facing the mountains. The rooms are basic, bathrooms tiny (cold water).

From US$10 to US$15

Caps Holiday Inn (Mr Amarakoon), 21 Welimada Rd, ☎ (057) 311 15 – 4rm. The owners' house is an attractive colonial villa. The rooms, without much character, but clean, are located in a modern building on a lower level, and have a small balcony overlooking the garden and the valley. Only two of the bath cubicles have hot water.

Sandella Holiday Inn, (Mr Amarakoon), 50 / 5 Welimada Rd, ☎ (057) 225 93 – 9rm. Good value for money, with light, functional rooms (hot water). The pleasant restaurant overlooks the neighbouring sportsground.

From US$15 to US$30

Ventnor, 23 Welimada Rd, next to the Caps Holiday Inn, ☎ (057) 225 11 – 4rm. A charming colonial residence in an attractive garden, but near the very busy Welimada Rd. Very spacious, carpeted rooms, and bathrooms with hot water. The dining room, in the centre of the building, is a little gloomy.

From US$30 to US$45

Bandarawela Hotel (Aitken Spence), 14 Welimada Rd, in the centre, ☎ (057) 225 01, Fax (057) 228 34 – 36rm. CC The restoration of this old lodge combines colonial charm with modern facilities. The rooms are located on two levels around an airy courtyard decorated with potted plants. They have been tastefully decorated (Liberty fabrics, metal-framed beds and dressing tables, antique-style washbasins). Well-equipped bathrooms. Beautiful lounge graced with old prints and photos and large leather armchairs. The restaurant offers good Western-style cuisine in a quiet atmosphere with attentive service.

Other things to do

Excursions – Walks in the mountains, through the plantations and the villages are the main attractions. Information is available from the guesthouses and you can also get some good ideas from ***Woodlands Network***, 30 / 6 Esplanade Rd, ☎ (057) 227 35, Fax (057) 227 12, haas@personal.is.lk Open Monday-Friday 8am-4.30pm. This women's networking association is concerned with all aspects of the region's culture and is attempting to develop services for individual travellers. You can obtain information on Uva, ideas for excursions, names of contacts, as well as useful details of self-catering accommodation and rooms to let in the homes of the local people.

Making the most of Ella

Coming and going

By train – The ***Railway Station*** is at the northern end of the village.

By bus – There is no ***Bus Station*** in Ella: ask for "Ella Gap junction", at the crossroads of the Wellawaya and Passara roads. When you leave, remember that the southbound Intercity Express buses do not officially stop here. Guesthouse managers may offer to book a seat for you, but be on your guard, as some of them charge an exorbitant fee for this service. Depending on your next destination, the best solution is to stop a CTB bus for Bandarawela or Wellawaya (services are frequent during the morning).

Address book

Post office / Telephone – The post office is located at the start of Police Station Rd, the first road on the left to the south of the station.

Where to stay / Eating out

Guesthouses in Ella compete fiercely for custom and each train or bus which arrives is greeted by a feverish deployment of hotel touts. Fortunately, all establishments are located up in the high part of the village, along the main road between the station and the Rest House, and are accessible on foot. Make your own choice and do not hesitate to consult the visitors' book for comments before making up your mind: some proprietors have earned the unfortunate reputation of being complete rogues!

Under US$10

Forest Paradise Guest Home, behind the Primary School, 100m above the road to Namunukula, ☎ (057) 235 07 – 4rm. ⁋ ✕ Set apart from the other guesthouses which compete for the view over the Ella Gap. Guests have free access to the beautiful garden. Comfortable rooms with canopied four-poster beds, mosquito nets, and Western-style bathrooms with hot water. Generous breakfasts and weekly barbecues.

Mount View Inn (Mr Sisira Kumara Jayasooriya), above Ella Gap Junction, ☎ (057) 232 92 – 3rm. ⁋ ✕ A modern house with good facilities (mosquito nets and hot water), where the friendly welcome makes up for the lack of view. Small terrace. Excellent breakfasts.

From US$10 to US$15

Beauty Mount Tourist Inn, down from the road to Wellawaya, on the opposite side of a river spanned by a footbridge – 3rm. ⁋ ✕ Respectable accommodation with rooms leading onto an interior hall, with hot water in the bathrooms. The food is good, especially the "special rice and curry". Its garden is a haven for birds every morning.

Hill Top Guesthouse (Mrs Swarna), access via a very steep 60m path, above Ella Gap Junction, ☎ (057) 300 80 – 4rm. ⁋ ✕ Lacks character, but has good facilities. The veranda, at the rear of the building, overlooks Ella Gap. Clean, airy rooms, spotless bathrooms (hot water on request). Information available about walks in the area.

Lizzie Villa (Mrs M S Rodrigo), in the northern part of the village, access via a woodland track, to the left off the Wellawaya road, ☎ (057) 232 43 – 7rm. ⁋ ✕ With one of the more enterprising guesthouse owners in Ella, this large, peaceful house surrounded by fruit-trees and spices (ask the owner for a tour) has simple, clean rooms. Meals are served on the veranda (international cuisine). There are also three rooms to let for less than US$10 with shared bathroom. Telephone with IDD connection.

Rawana Holiday Resort (Kumara Jayawickrama), access via a staircase, on the right off the Wellawaya road, ☎ (072) 66 40 94 – 4rm. ⁋ ✕ The rooms are clean and simple, and the verandah is very pleasant. The food is respectable, if a little bland.

Rock View (Mrs Warnasooriya), on the right off the Wellawaya road, next to the Rawana Holiday Resort, ☎ (057) 226 61 – 4rm. This colonial style house has a certain elegance and the terrace looks out over one of the rock faces of the Ella Gap. The rooms are enormous (no mosquito nets), but the bathrooms leave something to be desired… as does the food.

Tea Garden, next to the Rawana Holiday Resort (connected directly to one another by a passage), ☎ (057) 229 15 – 6rm. This establishment has considerable advantages, including the best view over the Ella Gap which it shares with the Rest House. The rooms open onto a veranda with climbing plants. Like the weed-infested tea garden below, the place suffers somewhat from neglect. Meals (small portions) served on crockery which is none too clean.

From US$15 to US$30

Country Comfort Inn, Police Station Rd, to the north of the village, opposite the sportsground, ☎ (057) 231 32 / (01) 71 63 49 – 8rm. An airy, peaceful and comfortable guesthouse, in the style of the planters' houses, with tiled floors and windows with cast-iron features. Good restaurant serving international cuisine.

Ravana Heights (Jith and Indu), Ella-Wellawaya Rd, further on from the Rest House, level with the 27km milestone, ☎ (057) 311 82 / (077) 30 95 42 / (01)57 74 11 – 3rm. The guesthouse of your dreams. The rooms are large and have excellent facilities (hot water), the dining-room, with huge bay windows all the way around it, has views over the countryside or of an interior garden, and the veranda looks over the Ravana rock. Wonderful Sri Lankan food, adapted to more sensitive Western palates, but only available to guests of the establishment. The crowning glory is the incomparable hospitality of Jith and Indu who are devoted to looking after their guests. Depending on your level of fitness and your interests, Jith leads walks through the villages, the plantations or the mountains for a very reasonable price.

Ella Rest House (Ceylon Hotels Corp), to the south of the village, access via a road leading up to the right off the Wellawaya road, ☎ (057) 226 36 – 4rm. CC Work was in progress when we visited, as the old lodge is to be demolished to make way for a modern wing with ten rooms with good facilities (telephone, television) and balconies overlooking the Gap. Watch this space. The terrace which overhangs the Ella Gap has a spectacular view which you can enjoy while having a cup of tea or a meal… and you will have plenty of time, as the service here is proverbially slow.

OTHER THINGS TO DO

Excursions – *JP* (Janaka Piyadarshana) is an English-speaking guide, originally from Wellawaya. He organises a very comprehensive tour of the Uva, which includes the Ravana Falls, an introduction to the agricultural economy of the region, the Diyaluma Falls, the Buduruvegala site and treks lasting 2-3hr through the Wellassa jungle, around Wellawaya. Contact him via the ***Forest Paradise Guest Home***, or by telephone on ☎ (057) 230 57 / (072) 65 88 23, or by e-mail: jungle.patch@usa.net

Making the most of Wellawaya

Coming and going

By bus – The station at Wellawaya has bus links with all the towns of the High Uva and is an ideal departure point if you are travelling on towards the south coast. Departures until 4pm for Wirawila (1hr), Hambantota (2hr), Tangalle (3hr30min), Matara (4hr30min) and Galle (6hr). Some buses connect with services to Kataragama (90min-2hr) and Tissamaharama (1hr). If not, head for Wirawila (1hr), on the Hambantota road, where you will find buses to Tissa (8km away) and Kataragama (23km).

Where to stay, Eating out

From US$7 to US$15

Saranga Holiday Inn, 37 Ella Rd (old road to Ella), ☎ (055) 748 91 – 6rm. Some way from the noisy town, this establishment looks pleasant enough from the outside, but its rather characterless rooms leave a lot to be desired and are infested with mosquitos. Cold water only. Repair work in progress, but this is the only accommodation of an acceptable standard in Wellawaya.

C Bourzat

P Haussherr

Fishing with nets on the south coast

THE SOUTH COAST

The south coast entered the fray of maritime trade well before the west coast. The natural harbours of Galle and Matara, still used by large ships on the route for the Straits of Malacca, were well protected from the monsoon. From west to east, you can experience the way in which the Sri Lankan climate gradually changes from the humid area with its palm forests to the arid area with its sparse scrubland. This is the Ruhunu, the counterpoint of the "Land of the Kings" in the north of the island. Land clearance and irrigation with the aid of reservoirs made it possible for centres of civilisation to develop here in ancient times. The region also served as the base for the Sinhalese reconquest in the 2C BC, when the usurpers from the south of India claimed the throne of Anuradhapura.

History and the blending of different cultures have forged a particular identity in the south, which will be evident to the discerning traveller at different levels. People here like eating brown rice, with its flavour of hazelnuts, and *kitul*, curdled buffalo's milk with palm syrup. The earthenware pots of this Sri Lankan version of mozzarella can be seen hanging in front of the shops dotted along the route heading east beyond Dondra. The coast has the wildest beaches, much less cluttered by tourism than their counterparts on the west coast, and, morning and evening, the fishing villages on the coast are awash with colour when the men gather to heave their nets onto the sand.

Finally, what was once the refuge of kings now provides shelter for wild animals: elephants, sambars and leopards, which are protected species at Uda Walawe and at Yala, one of the largest nature reserves on the island.

Galle★★

And the surrounding area

Southern Province – Pop 97 000
45km from Matara and 116km from Colombo
Map p 280

Not to be missed

Houses with verandas in the old streets of Galle.
Watching the fishermen on the coast when evening falls.
Scenes from Buddha's life in the murals at Purvarama.

And remember...

Make the most of the coolest hours of the day for a stroll around the old town of Galle.
At Unawatuna, stay in the village rather than near the beach.

On Sundays, people crowd on to the ramparts of the town: lovers kiss under large umbrellas, the saffron robes of the bonzes flap in the wind, and children run about laughing. However, there is no great Buddhist monarch nor any miraculous relic in the pages of the history of Galle. The town was one of the links in the chain of trading posts along the spice route, a stopover between the Malabar coast and the Straits of Malacca, where Arab dhows, Portuguese galleons and Dutch East Indiamen would tie up with their cargoes of cinnamon, mother-of-pearl and tor-

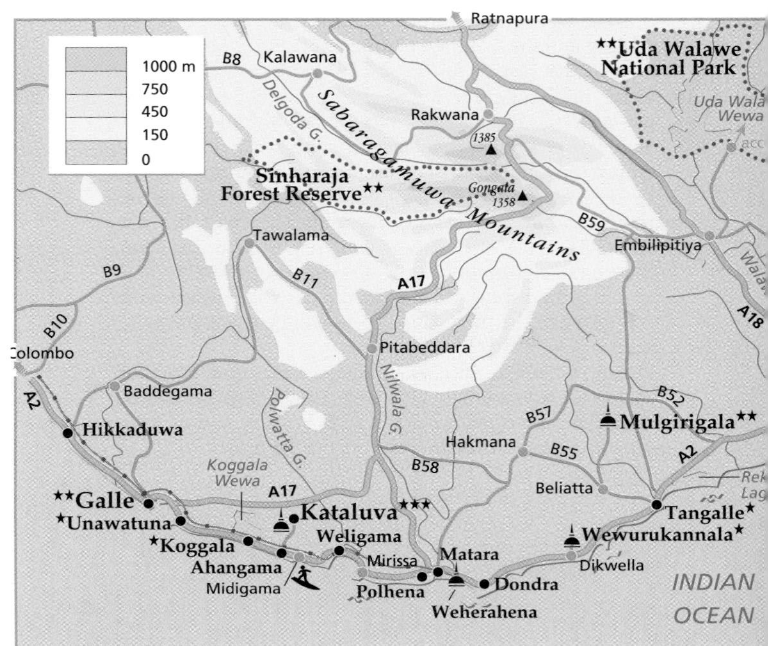

toiseshell, or citronella oil. Under the shadow of its ramparts, time seems to have stood still in this small town and there are no modern buildings to spoil your nostalgic reveries. Strolling out in the sea breeze you can almost smell the aroma of spices from long ago. The air of timelessness is really the main attraction and there are few places of interest although it is worth catching a bus or a *tuk-tuk* to get to the beaches and surrounding area which are little frequented by visitors.

Memories beneath the waves

Despite the wind and the waves which have beaten against their walls for four centuries, the ramparts of the fort of Galle are still an impressive sight. The Portuguese discovered this harbour in 1505 when they were pursuing an Arab fleet escaping towards the Maldives. Being deeper and much better protected than the ports on the west coast, it was one of the first Portuguese trading-posts on the island, and from 1589, was guarded by the fort of Santa Cruz. Its history runs parallel to that of Colombo: in 1640, it fell into the hands of the Dutch, who strengthened its defences and created the present fort district. Then came the British. Under their influence, Galle might have become the capital but for one reason: the railway line linking Colombo, one of the island's main ports, to Kandy, the new area of the plantations.

The history of the town can be seen in its buildings, which were designated a World Heritage Site in 1992. Since then, an international team of archeologists has been looking at its maritime past and exploring the twenty or so wrecks in the area, some of which date from the time of the Arab traders of the 10C. The most spectacular are the wrecks of the Dutch East Indiamen. The **Avondster** ran aground on the sandbanks just outside the harbour On 2 July 1659. The **Hercules** broke up on reefs off the island of Gibet in 1661 when a rope became entangled with the rudder. The objects found on board have helped to reconstruct the daily life of the crews: their cargoes tell us about the trade they conducted, their cannon about the inevitable battles which accompanied it. These underwater memories of the port of Galle are to be the focus of a permanent exhibition at the Maritime Museum.

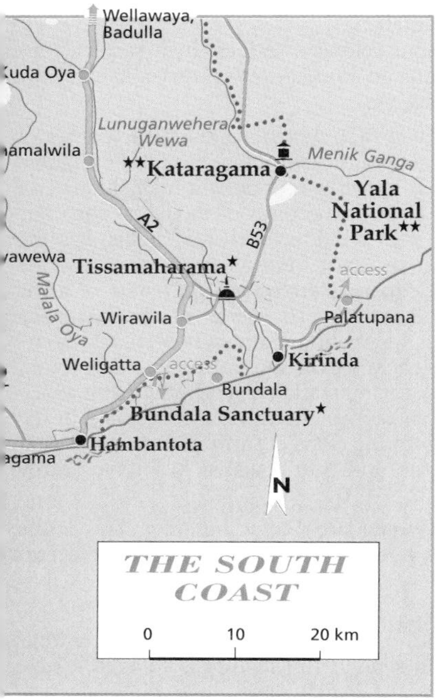

The three families of Islam

Islam only took hold on the island with the communities who already practised this religion. Having come here within the framework of commercial enterprise and the trading-posts, their involvement in the fields of trade and fishing along the coast continued. During the British period, the **Moors** (a term inherited from the Portuguese), Muslims born on the island who spoke Tamil, were to be distinguished from the **Malays**.

At the heart of the Moorish community was a distinction between the descendants of the Arabs, who had settled along the south coast, and the descendants of Indian origin converted to Islam, who were originally from the east coast of India and had settled in the east of the island. The latter were concentrated around the port of Hambantota, and were descended both from exiled princes and from the labour force brought here by the Dutch from their Indonesian colonies.

Tour of the fort**

Allow half a day to stroll round the fort.

The old town**

Begin your tour at the Main Gate and head along Church St which follows the line of the eastern ramparts.

The National Museum*(B3) (*9am-5pm; closed Sunday and Monday. Entrance fee. Allow 30min*) is housed in a rather austere building which once belonged to the **New Oriental Hotel*** nearby. Earlier still it was the quarters of the officers of the Dutch garrison. The collections would form an interesting chronicle of Dutch colonisation, if the exhibits were accompanied by more focused explanations. The first room is devoted to a legacy from Northern Europe, which became a Galle speciality: **lace**. The patterns are based on jasmine tendrils, chrysanthemums or lotus flowers, geometric motifs, or flowers with the form of letters of the Sinhalese alphabet. One case contains small objects made out of **tortoise-shell**, another speciality of the town in days gone by: among them are combs, spectacle frames, pill-boxes and fans.
In the second room, the imposing **Dutch cabinets*** contain porcelain pipes with their tobacco pouches, Portuguese swords, faience from Delft, blue and white porcelain from China and jars from Martaban.
The objects on display in the third room belonged to local high society: they include embossed silver betel sets, lacquered wooden plates, carved ivory, jewellery boxes inlaid with porcupine quills, etc.

The Dutch **Groote Kerk**** (Great Church) (B3), which stands at the corner of Middle Street and Church Street, occupies the site of a former Portuguese Capuchin monastery. It was built in 1775 thanks to a donation by the wife of the governor Casperus De Jong, in thanks for the birth of their first son. The bare interior, which is illuminated by high windows with lead lights, has the sombreness of a typical Reformed church. Apart from its **organ case** and the dark wooden **pulpit**, the white marble **funerary steles** and the **coats of arms** on the wooden panel are its only decoration. The **arms of the governor Abraham Samlandt****, crowned by a representation of his shirt, skull and hourglass (highlighting his vainglorious existence) are the most elaborate to be found in Sri Lanka. His name is associated with the repression of a large uprising which broke out in 1760. Look out for the tombstones which are incorporated in the floor. Those in the churchyard come from the cemetery which once stood next to the church and was dismantled by the British to make room for the nearby post office.

Further down Church Street is an imposing neo-Gothic building. This is the Anglican church of **All Saints** (B3), consecrated in 1871, on the site of a former courthouse.

If you continue into Church Cross Street, at the end of the road you will come across a **traditional Galle façade***, with a veranda sporting wooden columns running the length of the building. This style of architecture is a Dutch legacy. Known as *istoppuwa* in Sinhalese (from the Dutch *stoep*), this colonnade per-

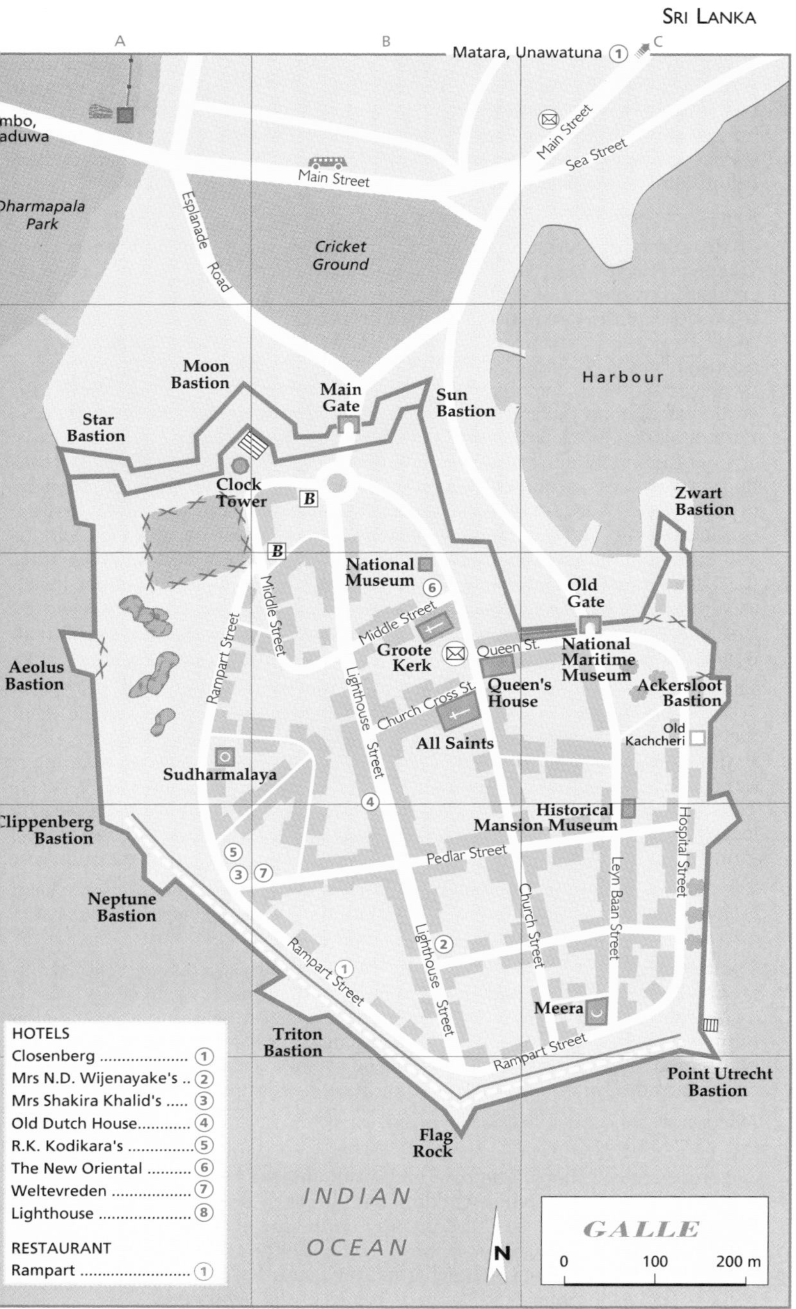

A
B
C
Matara, Unawatuna ①
mbo,
aduwa
Dharmapala
Park
Main Street
Main Street
Sea Street
Esplanade Road
Cricket
Ground
Harbour
Moon
Bastion
Main
Gate
Sun
Bastion
Star
Bastion
Clock
Tower
B
B
Zwart
Bastion
National
Museum
Old
Gate
Middle Street
Middle Street
Rampart Street
Groote
Kerk
Queen St.
National
Maritime
Museum
Aeolus
Bastion
Lighthouse Street
Church Cross St.
Queen's
House
Ackersloot
Bastion
Old
Kachcheri
All Saints
Sudharmalaya
Historical
Mansion Museum
Clippenberg
Bastion
Pedlar Street
Hospital Street
Leyn Baan Street
Church Street
Neptune
Bastion
Lighthouse Street
Rampart Street
Meera
Triton
Bastion
Rampart Street
Point Utrecht
Bastion
Flag
Rock
HOTELS
Closenberg ①
Mrs N.D. Wijenayake's ②
Mrs Shakira Khalid's ③
Old Dutch House ④
R.K. Kodikara's ⑤
The New Oriental ⑥
Weltevreden ⑦
Lighthouse ⑧
RESTAURANT
Rampart ①
INDIAN
OCEAN
N
GALLE
0
100
200 m

mitted the inhabitants to conduct their lives in the shade and, at the same time, protected the interior of the house from the heat. Nothing has really changed today: with the locals staying in the shade, Galle is almost deserted during the hottest hours of the day, apart from tourists on the ramparts. There are still several variations on the *istoppuwa* theme, notably No48 and the two houses before Mrs Wijayanake's guest house.

Retrace your steps and head along Queen St.

At the corner of Queen Street and Church Street stands the fine residence of **Queen's House**⋆ (B3). Its façade, which dates from 1683, bears a cockerel emblem, the symbol of Galle under the Dutch. This was based on the misinterpretation of the town's name by the Europeans. For them, Galle, pronounced "gaul" in English, came from the Latin "gallus" (cock), while in Sinhalese, pronounced "gaala", it meant a defensive wall. The building housed the offices of the governor of the Dutch garrison, before becoming the residence of the British governors when in Galle. It was eventually sold to the company Walker & Sons.
Further along Queen Street is the **Old Gate** (C3), emblazoned with the coat of arms of the Dutch East India Company (VOC), which led to the old port. It was built in the oldest section of the fortifications. The **Zwart Bastion** (Black Bastion) (C2) stands to its left, on the site of the Santa Cruz bastion, which guarded the entrance to the harbour in the time of the Portuguese (occupied by various administrative services, not open to the public). The next bastion, **Ackersloot** (C3), dates from 1789. It owes its name to the birthplace of De Coster, the Dutch captain who seized Galle from the Portuguese. The harbour is overlooked by two long buildings which were used as warehouses by the Dutch. One of them houses the Maritime Museum.

The presentation of the exhibits in the **National Maritime Museum** (C3) (*9am-5pm; closed Friday and Saturday. Entrance fee. Allow 30min*) is poor, but the main themes are the coastal economy (fishing) and maritime trade in former times. In the section devoted to marine flora and fauna, coral is the focus of an interesting display (*see "A chain of atolls" p 324*).
There are a few scale models of the different kinds of outrigger canoes used by local fishermen, along with models of some of the ships that plied the sea routes, from Dutch East Indiamen to British clippers, the vessels used to transport tea.

When leaving the museum, turn into Leyn Baan St which runs alongside a square shaded by acacia and banyan trees. At No 30, the Olanda shop has an imposing Galle façade with a wooden veranda. The Historical Mansion Museum occupies No 31-39.

The Historical Mansion Museum⋆ (C4) (*Daily 9am-6pm. No charge*) is housed in an 18C **Dutch residence**, which has been almost entirely restored by its present owner. Its collections are a varied, if not surreal, assortment of objects, ranging from betel sets, cheese-graters and sewing machines to telephones and letter-boxes from Galle! The shop selling precious stones at the exit reveals the main purpose of the "museum", however you have to admire the owner's initiative.

After leaving the museum, head along Leyn Baan St.

The far end of Leyn Baan Street is the old Muslim quarter, with a few jewellers and stone-cutters' shops. The road ends at the **Meera mosque**⋆ (C4), built just below the ramparts. A white building with a porch framed by two towers, it looks like a church and was built in 1909 on the site of a Portuguese cathedral. Opposite it, the Galle **lighthouse** was built in 1940 on **Point Utrecht Bastion** (C4-5). It overlooks a small beach (not very clean) where children come to paddle. The walk around the ramparts begins at the lighthouse.

B. Pérousse/HOA QUI

Sunday crowds on the ramparts at Galle...

The walk around the ramparts*

The southernmost point of the whole island, **Flag Rock** (B5) has pretty views over the tiled roofs of Lighthouse Street. During the British period (1848), this was the site of the old Galle lighthouse which, until the telegraph post was put here in 1858, served as a relay station for carrier pigeons, bringing mail from Europe by the Indian Mail packet. Its modern name is a reminder of the time when it was a signalling office under the Dutch.

Around this time, a windmill was erected on the **Triton Bastion** (B4) which pumped sea water up to spray the town's dusty streets (they were asphalted under the British).

From the **Neptune Bastion** and its neighbour the Clippenberg **Bastion** (A4) there is a good view of the inside of the fort. In the foreground, the Buddhist **Sudharmalaya Temple** (A3), recognisable by its white stupa, was built on the site of a Portuguese church in 1889. You can see the red-brick apse of All Saints Church in the background.

Because it is a military zone, the **Aeolus Bastion** (A3) is closed to the public. The last part of the ramparts can be reached by walking round at road level. Near the **clock-tower** (A2), built in 1881 thanks to a public donation in memory of a philanthropist Burgher of Galle, steps lead up again to the fortifications.

The line of defence guarded by the **Star**, **Moon** and **Sun Bastions*** (A-B2) was built by the Portuguese. The Dutch doubled the defences by building an inner rampart and gave the bastions their current names. These impressive fortifications were built with grey granite, brought by ships which used it as ballast. Like the rest of the fortifications, they were built by slave labour. The enterprise dates from the time of the Dutch governor Petrus Vuyst (1726-29), who had such a reputation for cruelty that he was recalled to Jakarta where he was executed for all the tortures he had inflicted. Below, the cricket ground occupies the site of the racecourse, built by the British on reclaimed land in the 19C. They also built **Main Gate**, thereby changing the appearance of the old maritime fort forever.

From Galle to Weligama*

28km. Allow half a day.

Numerous buses run between Galle and Matara making it possible to reach Unawatuna, the sights of Koggala, and Weligama, a protected cove brimming with fish.

Take the road to Matara. Unawatuna station is 5km from Galle. You can reach it by "tuk-tuk" or by bus. Be specific about whether you are going to Yaddehimulla or to the south of the bay.

■ **Unawatuna** – *See map p 294.* To the east of the bay of Galle lies the **Rumassala*** promontory, a habitat for plants with medicinal properties. Protected by the waves and lying next to a hill covered with vegetation, Unawatuna has become the **beach** for travellers on a low budget, an alternative to the trappings of Hikkaduwa, but these days it is seriously threatened by erosion as straw huts and beach huts have sprouted like mushrooms! However, it is still a marvellous place for a holiday if you choose to stay up the hill, in the village of **Yaddehimulla**, and head for the sea in the deserted inlets of Jungle Beach. The coral reef of Buona Vista will delight diving and snorkelling enthusiasts alike.

The legend of Rumassala

According to the legend, the rock of Rumassala is a fragment of the mountain that the monkey general Hanuman carried through the air to Lakshmana, Rama's brother, who had been injured by a poisoned arrow during a battle against King Ravana. Only four plants that grew in the Himalayas could cure him. The botanist Hanuman hurried off to collect them, but lacking the courage of his convictions, decided to bring back the whole mountain to save his hero, and some pieces of it fell off as he flew over the island. On the southeast side of the promontory, there is also a small sandy cove with a Polynesian-sounding name, Unawatuna, meaning "something has fallen".

Continue along the coast road to Koggala (10km beyond Unawatuna).

■ **Koggala** – The coral beach of Koggala has disappeared behind the soulless blocks of its hotels (including one with 200 rooms and 1km in length). Part of its lake is a military zone which, during the war in the Pacific, the Royal Air Force used as a seaplane base, and the rest of the town is a freeport. However, Koggala is worth a visit for its museum of popular art, housed in the residence of the Sri Lankan writer Martin Wikramasinghe.

Martin Wikramasinghe Folk Museum** *(North of the railway, opposite the Horizon Club, just before the Koggala bus-stop. Daily 9am-5pm. Entrance fee).*
Housed in a modern, well-appointed building (explanations in Sinhalese and English), the collections assembled by the writer give an insight into daily life in Sri Lanka in days gone by.
On the first floor, **Buddhism** and its *bhikkhu* (monks): a wooden basin used for dyeing their robes saffron-yellow, begging-bowls and holy-water sprinklers, palm fans with carved handles made of highly-prized wood or ivory *(vatapata)*, and old models of umbrellas made with palm-leaves. **Daily life in the country** is evoked by the cow-hide sandals worn when clearing the land, basketwork or bamboo rice measures, and wooden cow-bells. Then there is a section devoted to **fishing** with hoop nets, nets and fish-traps. After the very comprehensive collection of **Kolam masks**** *(see insert p 127)*, a second room contains **domestic objects**: betel sets, with limestone boxes in the form of fruit or flowers, anthropomorphic nutcrackers; cooking utensils, with the indispensable coconut-grater used for making *sambol*, including a version with a stool incorporated. Brooches for saris, ankle

Red saliva

In Asia, 500 million people chew betel nut. In Sri Lanka, it is sold on street corners by cigarette salesmen. However, it has lost its traditional value as a gauge of hospitality at the heart of rites of passage, such as weddings or funerals. Only museum displays testify to its role, through the dishes and utensils used in its preparation and presentation. The betel nut is the leaf or fruit of a species of pear tree which contains an aromatic essential oil with a spicy flavour. Daubed with a little lime, it is wrapped around a crushed areca palm nut. This is what contains the tannins which colour the saliva red.

bracelets, hairpins and porcupine-spine boxes conclude the display. Outside are some carriages and hand-drawn vehicles.

The writer's house stands at the end of the huge lawn. This wonderful 18C residence is the only one surviving in this small village, because the inhabitants had to evacuate the area in 24 hours when the air base was established. Personal objects and photographs trace the life of this man, author of numerous works on folklore and an active politician, who advocated a Socialist approach, drawing on the practice of meditation.

Continue in the direction of Matara. 3km from Koggala bus terminus, there is a sign pointing to the left. The monastery is 3km away.

■ **The Purvarama monastery of Kataluva***** – The monastery was built in the 1840s, at the height of the colonial period. The image house is one of the jewels of **Buddhist painting** in Ceylon, as much for the diversity of the subjects, which were painted in extravagant detail in the early 1880s, as for the strictly pedagogical nature of the organisation of these stories and fables. The cella, with its statues of Buddha placed under the protection of Vishnu and Kataragama, has a pair of *makara torana*, with a medallion depicting Queen Victoria. Between the two doors are depictions of two creatures which are half-human and half-bird. They symbolise absolute fidelity, their union being indestructible, despite reputedly already having lasted 1 000 years. The exterior of the wall surrounding the cella is painted with the succession of the Twenty-four Previous Lives of Buddha (the *Suvisi Vivarana* or Twenty-four Annunciations), crowned with an almond-tree in flower which is worshipped by the future Sakyamuni in various incarnations. The most interesting paintings are those in the panels on the outside wall of the ambulatory, the base of which is decorated with terrifying scenes of hell. The entrance wall relates the story of the **tribulations of Prince Vessantara**. The story begins in the top left-hand corner and zigzags back and forth, ending at the bottom right-hand corner. The long painted bands are treated like theatre scenery where the architecture of the

The long and unhappy story of Patacara

The beautiful and noble Patacara lost her heart to a man from a lower caste. The lovers fled and found refuge in a forest, where their two sons were born. Thinking that the birth of the boys would appease the wrath of her parents, she decided to visit them. But on the way there, her husband was bitten by a snake and her two sons also died, the eldest washed away by the strong current of a river and the youngest taken by a bird of prey. When she finally reached her parents' palace it had gone up in flames and she was forced to stand by helplessly and watch the destruction of her whole family. Mad with grief, she tore her hair, rent her clothes, and wandered around bare without any concern for the rest of the world. One day, she arrived at the place where Buddha was expounding his doctrine. She was shouted down by the crowd but the Master's compassion for her sad fate soon put a stop to the jeering. Patacara found solace in Buddha's teachings and became a nun.

building is part of the decor (balconies, doors, arches, and rooms separated by columns) and accessories (doors, oil lamps and ewers). The bottom left-hand corner depicts the **tragic story of Patacara**.

In the ten kilometres which separate Koggala from Weligama, the road passes through some of the most interesting sections of the coastline. Only a few small rocky coves have been developed into seaside resorts and these remain low profile. Midigama, a beach the size of a handkerchief, is a popular meeting-place for surfers, because apart from Hikkaduwa, it is the only place on the coast to go surfing and the sites in the east remain difficult to reach.

■ **Ahangama** – In the hotels and guest-houses of Ahangama or Mirissa *(4km east of Weligama)*, it is not uncommon to find guests who come every year to enjoy the peace and quiet of this short stretch of coastline, far away from the noisy beach resorts of the west.
The rest of the coast has remained the domain of **fishermen**. The water is so full of fish that they only have to cast their nets 100m from the shore. These large nets, called *madel*, are still made of *coir*, the coconut fibre that has the advantage of not spoiling the catch. Morning and evening, the spectacle of the fishermen at work is a daily ritual: up to their waists in water, they then gather to heave their nets up onto the beach. The fish (mainly bonitos) are sold at markets in the surrounding area *(Tuesday and Friday at Weligama, Wednesday at Koggala and Midigama, Thursday and Sunday at Ahangama, and Saturday at Midigama)*.
The fishermen of Ahangama are perpetuating a tradition that is unique to Sri Lanka, the origin of which is unknown. The west side of the cove is planted with a **forest of wooden stilts**, the positions of which are handed down from father to son. At daybreak and in the late afternoon, they swim to their perch and climb onto it, then stand with their feet resting on a single crossbar to fish with a simple line and hook. In this uncomfortable position, the fishermen earn a good livelihood. Although there is no shortage of fish here, the setting is so photogenic (particularly at sunset) that they also earn tips for photographs from passing tourists.

■ **Weligama** – This is the only fishing town of any size. It has a long, deserted beach stretching the length of a 2km bay. Very close to the shore lies the small private island of **Taprobane**. In the 1930s it was bought by an exiled Frenchman, the Count of Mauny, who built a house here surrounded by a tropical garden.
Take the road heading inland from the coast and cross the railway line. On the other side, opposite the sports ground, there is a small square. It contains a **megalith** carved with a face, in the tradition of the giant rock-cut figures of the 8C-10C *(see also "Buduruvegala" p 270)*. Popular tradition has identified it as **Kusta Raja**, the "leper king" who was miraculously cured by the milk from a coconut. His tiara, decorated with two meditating Buddhas, his jewellery and the questioning gesture means that he could possibly be identified as a bodhisattva of the Greater Vehicle. Below it, the mossy tomb of a Christian missionary dates from the late 18C.

Weligama has a wide enough range of accommodation to make it worth a stop. Otherwise you can head for Mirissa beach (4km). If you go on to Matara (15km), avoid staying in this capital city of Southern Province: it is dirty and dusty, and the heat is suffocating. A more pleasant option is the small beach at Polhena to the west, which is very popular with Sri Lankan families.

The right light.
TOYOTA
5132

Making the most of Galle

Coming and going

Galle can easily be reached by train but the nearby seaside resorts are only served by slow local trains. You can easily reach the beaches by bus, many of which ply the route between Galle and Matara.

By train – The railway station is on the edge of the town on the road to Colombo. (A1). There are ten daily express trains in each direction between Colombo (3hr) and Matara (between 2hr30min and 3hr).

By bus – Galle bus terminus is situated in Main St, opposite the cricket ground (B1). Every day there are numerous buses to Colombo (3hr), Hikkaduwa (30min), Unawatuna (20min), Matara (1hr), Tangalle (2hr) and Hambantota (3hr30min). Less frequent services run to Tissamaharama (4hr15min) and Wellawaya (5hr30min), at the bottom of the highlands.

Address book

Banks / Changing money – Branches of the ***Bank of Ceylon*** in Lighthouse St. (B2) and of the ***People's Bank*** in Middle St (B2-3).

Post / Telephone – *GPO*, Main St (C1). There is also a post office in the Fort, in Church St, next to the Groote Kerk (B3). You will find photocopying and communications facilities in Lighthouse St, near the junction with Middle St.

Where to stay

Despite its charm, Galle is not teeming with attractions that will occupy you for days on end. However, its reputable guesthouses, run by friendly staff and its old, colonial-style hotels may induce you to extend your stay.

You would be well advised to book a room in advance and to ask the owner of the guesthouse to come and meet you at the station. Otherwise, your dream could easily turn into a nightmare: the town is full of smooth-talking rogues. Do not let yourself be persuaded to be invited for a meal with the family of someone you have just met: if your finances do not extend to paying the invalidity pension of your new "friend's" mother, or his young sister's school fees, your companion may become threatening. The same advice goes for Unawatuna which has the same reputation as Hikkaduwa. Finally, remember that if a "tuk-tuk" driver offers to take you for a ridiculous sum, or for free, to a different guesthouse from the one you had in mind, it is likely that he will be getting a commission of up to 100 % of what it will cost you to stay the night. Enough said...

Under US$10

Old Dutch House, 46 Lighthouse St, ☎ (09) 223 70, Fax (09) 320 45 – 8rm. The rooms, named after various Dutch governors, are arranged alongside an internal patio. The bedding is spotlessly clean, the bathrooms are tiled, but does the concern for authenticity justify the fact that the walls are in such a bad state?

RK Kodikara's Guesthouse (Beatrice House), 29 Rampart St (no sign), ☎ (09) 223 51 – 4rm. A large white house with a garden, standing opposite the ramparts. Respectable rooms. Its owner, who is pleasant and articulate, knows the area very well.

Weltevreden Hotel, 104 Pedlar St, ☎ (09) 226 50 – 4rm. A charming owner, very cheap rooms with good facilities, a patio covered with plants... however the walls could do with a coat of paint.

From US$10 to US$15

Mrs ND Wijenayake's Guesthouse (Beach Haven), 65 Lighthouse St, ☎ (09) 346 63 – 6rm. The rooms on the first floor, with mosquito nets on the four-poster beds, large bathrooms and AC (supplement), are the most pleasant. Also serves good local cuisine.

Mrs Shakira Khalid's Guesthouse, 106 Pedlar St, ☎ (09) 349 07 – 3rm. Everything is so beautifully kept that it is hard to believe that this has been a guest house for 20 years. Large rooms overlook a small patio-garden where peace reigns. It is also an opportunity to sample real Galle cooking: here, the "rice and curry" is probably of Portuguese inspiration, crossed with Indo-Pakistani flavours and the traditional Muslim touch.

From US$30 to US$40

Closenberg Hotel, Megalle (3km east of Galle), ☎ (09) 322 41 – 21rm. This villa with its charming setting is of historical importance because it was built by a British captain on the site of the Klosenburg, a small Dutch fort that had fallen into disrepair. A garden terrace looks right down onto the bay and its fishing villages. Its restaurant, which serves delicious Sri Lankan cuisine, is decorated with rocks hollowed out to accommodate aquariums or planted with ferns. Sixteen of the rooms, situated in a new wing built in a sombre, colonial style, face the east and the sea, while the other five, with their old-fashioned shutters, have an aura of the past.

The New Oriental Hotel, 10 Church St, ☎ (09) 345 91, Fax (09) 220 59 – 35rm. Even if you don't want to stay here, come and have a drink beneath the fans on its veranda overlooking the ramparts. Tiny swimming pool in a delightful enclosed garden and old billiards table. Parquet floors and old furniture add to the charm of its rooms. Old-fashioned bathrooms (hot water).

Over US$70

Lighthouse Hotel (Jetwing), Dadella, 2.5km along the road to Colombo, ☎ (09) 237 44, Fax (09) 240 21, e-mail: lighthhousehotel@lanka.com.lk – 60rm. TV This stone, concrete and wooden building built to resemble a lighthouse is reached by a spectacular spiral staircase. It has two restaurants, one of which overlooks an impluvium, a bar with a panoramic view over the beautiful coast and an idyllic beach, decorated like a garden. Everywhere there is attention to detail, even in the bedrooms where the furniture has a beautiful matt finish. The luxury more than justifies the price.

Eating out

The cooking at ***Mrs Shakira Khalid***'s guest-house and the **Closenberg** is worth a detour, provided, in the case of the latter, that you avoid lunchtime, which is devoted to buffets for passing tour groups.

Under US$10

Rampart Hotel, 31 Rampart St, ☎ (074) 38 01 03. An old Dutch hospital has been converted into a gem shop and a restaurant. The meals are rather expensive but the shady terrace facing the Triton Bastion is a pleasant spot.

Shopping

Laksala, 30 Hospital St, ☎ (09) 343 33 Daily 9am-6pm; closed Friday between 12.30pm and 1.45pm. For once, this State-run shop offers a bit more than the ubiquitous craft products for tourists: from antique ceramics and jewellery to delightful objects from the colonial period.

A R M Cassim, 57 Leyn Baan St. Cassim makes silver jewellery designed by his wife. The result is original, with or without gems.

Historical Mansion, 31-39 Leyn Baan St. Daily 9am-6pm. The gem shop is registered by the State and profits go towards running the museum.

Olanda, 30 Leyn Baan St. Daily 10.30am-6pm. Housed in an old residence, with walls painted orange and blue with a sponge-effect finish, this shop sells antique china, imitation colonial-style furniture and ecologically-friendly craft products.

Making the most of Unawatuna

COMING AND GOING

By bus – There is no bus terminus at the little village of Unawatuna. When you get there, ask the driver to stop at the end of Yaddehimulla Rd. When you leave, go back to the same place and hail one of the numerous buses running between Galle and Matara. Even if you are coming from Galle, you are advised to take the bus as the "tuk-tuk" drivers here are real rogues: they will even offer you a free ride in order to take you to the guesthouse of their own choice.

ADDRESS BOOK

Post / Telephone – Post office in Matara Rd (B1). Small telephone communications agencies in Yaddehimulla Rd, between the Happy Banana and the Three Fishes.

WHERE TO STAY

The beach at Unawatuna is small and overcrowded. To find acceptable accommodation, avoid the area between the road to Galle and the Three Fishes guesthouse where there is a concentration of ugly buildings with suspect bathrooms and sea water showers. What's more, the place is very noisy because of the nightlife in the restaurants and the prices are too high. The best solution is to stay in the nearby village of Yaddehimulla: peace is guaranteed here, and there are rooms to suit every budget. Beyond the Heaven on Earth guesthouse some of the locals charge between US$3-US$5 a night for a bed. Several of them only rent out rooms by the week. South of the Unawatuna beach, at Dahawella (1.5km) and Talpe (2km), some small hotels have been built on a slope: swimming possible thanks to the reef which protects it.

• **At Unawatuna**

Under US$5

Blue Horizon, Yaddehimulla Rd – 5rm. Very clean rooms (with mosquito nets) in a modern house belonging to a grocer.

Upul, Yaddehimulla Rd – 6rm. Variable rooms, for under US$3, or cottage with bathroom.

From US$5 to US$10

Heaven on Earth (Bandu Palliyaguru), Yaddehimulla Rd, ☎ (09) 345 88 – 2rm. A cottage nestling in a tangle of vegetation, a haven of shade in the hottest hours of the day. The rooms are small, but customised. Two other larger rooms with a pleasant shared bathroom, cost under US$5. Good home-cooking includes "rice and curry". A good place to stay within a 30min walk from Jungle Beach.

Weliwatta Guesthouse, Yaddehimulla Rd, ☎ (09) 428 91, Fax (09) 227 47, gakd.uoc@mail.cmb.ac.lk – 5rm. Very simple large rooms are arranged around the central room of a family house built in the 1920s. If you don't stay here, come for a meal, because the owner changes the menus every day, and has no less than eight different kinds of "sambol". Taxi service (estimate US$30 to the international airport).

From US$10 to US$15.

Rock House (Markus Dias), Yaddehimulla Rd, ☎ (09) 249 48 – 12rm. Situated below the rocky escarpment of Rumassala where birds and monkeys gather in the morning, this guesthouse is run by two brothers. You are spoilt for choice between huge rooms with a lounge area, fridge and storage space for longer stays, or simpler but perfectly adequate rooms. It plans to open a restaurant.

Village Inn, Yaddehimulla Rd, ☎ (09) 253 75 – 15rm. A peaceful setting for this hotel which offers a room with a balcony or bungalows. The rooms are clean, the bathrooms variable. Generous breakfasts with jam "hoppers".

From US$15 to US$30

Point de Galle, Mihiripena, Talpe, ☎ (09) 832 06, Fax (09) 343 60, bindu@slt.lk – 12rm. Large ordinary rooms in a small building overlooking the beach protected by a coral reef. Good cooking and very attentive staff.

Secret Garden, Yaddehimulla Rd, ☎ (09) 418 57 – 2rm. Tucked away in an enclosed garden, this guesthouse belongs to the owner of the Three Fishes just opposite. For the same price, you can stay in a colonial villa, furnished with taste and with modern comforts. The showers have cold water but the bathrooms are magnificent.

The Strand (Asoka Weerasinghe), Yaddehimulla Rd, ☎ and Fax (09) 243 58, strand@sri.lanka.net – 5rm. Open 18 years. This house dates from the 1920s when the site was selected for building second homes for the inhabitants of Galle and was one of the first to be built at Unawatuna. Enclosed veranda opening onto a wonderful garden. The rooms, one of which is split-level, are designed for long stays and have independent access. Original in having its own website (pages.hotbot.com/biz/strand) from which it procures 60 % of its business. A place for a week's stay and an ideal retreat in the village of Yaddehimulla.

Three Fishes, Yaddehimulla Rd, ☎ (09) 418 57 – 5rm. Owned by the Hotel Closenberg in Galle (rooms may be booked from there), this guesthouse has the attraction of colonial charm, right by the sea. This may not justify the prices, because the bathrooms are very ordinary and the showers are cold. Avoid the single rooms, which are in a bungalow in the garden, and share an outside shower.

Sea View, last place before the point, ☎ (09) 243 76, Fax (09) 243 49 – 21rm. Try to stay in one of the five rooms on the first floor, which are a joy and have large balconies over the garden. Taxi agency, excursions, motorbike hire and IDD telephone connections.

Sri Gemunu Guesthouse, Dahawella, ☎ (09) 837 88 / (074) 38 00 78, Fax (09) 832 02 – 18rm. Small, pleasant hotel, with a lawn running down to the beach. Three price categories: cheap rooms in the old wing, acceptable but dark; medium-priced rooms with cold showers on the first floor of the new wing; rooms on the second floor are more expensive since they have balconies overlooking the sea, attractive pale wooden furniture and hot water. Minibuses can be hired to visit the island, also bike hire, airport transfers, boat trips and diving.

From US$30 to US$40

The Dream House, Yaddehimulla Rd, ☎ (074) 38 15 41, Fax (074) 38 12 12 – 5rm. A colonial house completely overhauled with the comfort of modern tourists in mind: parquet floors, wrought-iron beds, hot water, and so on. The ground floor, on the same level as the garden, is very pleasant, with sofas, cushions and small separate tables. Italo-Sri Lankan cuisine, with products imported directly from Italy.

• In Ahangama

From US$15 to US$30

Club Lanka Hotel, ☎ (09) 832 96, Fax (09) 833 61 – 6rm. CC Small unpretentious seaside hotel, where everything is impeccably clean.

• In Midigama

20km from Galle and 18km from Matara.

Under US$10

Hilten's Beach Resort, Midigama, level with the 139km milestone, ☎ (041) 501 56 – 6rm. Adequate rooms (mosquito nets), although dark and with very small toilets. Restaurant opens onto a small terrace garden above the beach.

From US$15 to US$30

Villa Gaetano, on the road to Ahangama, level with the Goviyapana railway bridge, ☎ (074) 38 09 47, Fax (074) 98 32 34 – 8rm. A villa built on two levels next to a beach the size of a handkerchief. But, lying only a few metres from the shore, the little island is perfect for a picnic or playing at Robinson Crusoe. Perfectly clean (the sheets are changed every two days), gargantuan breakfasts and cooking that caters for individual tastes. Cleaning service and medical assistance available. Car with driver can be hired at very reasonable rates. Fishing outings can be arranged.

Eating out

Some of the guesthouses have excellent cooking, which non-residents may take advantage of provided they book. ***Upul Restaurant*** is one of the first straw huts to the west of the beach. Beer and alcoholic drinks, mashed potatoes, spaghetti, steaks, squid, banana crêpes and fruit fritters.

Happy Banana, on the east side of the beach, ☎ (09) 242 70 / (077) 90 15 15. Situated on the widest part of the beach, it has a long room hung with Chinese lanterns. Ideal for watching the fishing catamarans over breakfast. Good seafood at a reasonable price.

Other things to do

Excursions – Bike and motor-bike hire at Sea View Hotel. The distances are short and the roads are flat.

Diving – Diving equipment can be hired at the straw huts on the beach, where there is also a diving school (at the far end of the beach, near the Buddhist temple).

Shopping

The shops are on Strand Rd, between the junction with the Galle road and the Strand Hotel. You will find the usual things on sale: precious stones, batik fabrics and wooden masks.

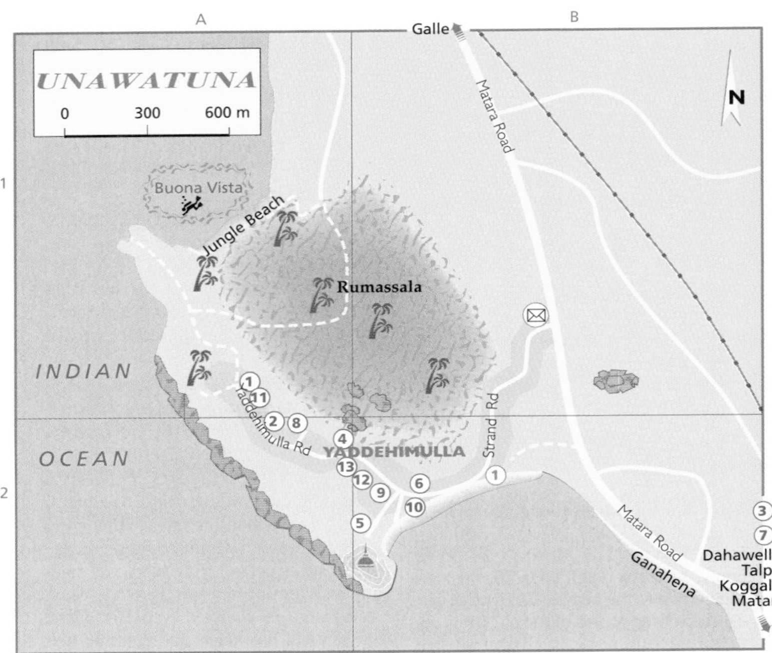

HOTELS

Blue Horizon........(1)	Sea View................(5)	The Strand.............(9)	Weliwatta ....(13)
Heaven on Earth.(2)	Secret Garden........(6)	Three Fishes...........(10)	
Point de Galle......(3)	Sri Gemunu ....(7)	Upul.......................(11)	RESTAURANT
Rock House..........(4)	The Dream House..(8)	Village Inn............(12)	Happy Banana.....(1)

Making the most of Weligama

Coming and going

By bus – There is no bus terminus but there is a bus stop in Matara Road which serves the whole town.

Where to stay

• In Weligama

Note that only the places built on the point southwest of Weligama are free from the noise due to the proximity of the road and the railway line.

Under US$10

Green Peace Inn (KKA Lakshman), Matara Rd, Palana, at the east end of Weligama – 5rm. Modern and very clean, this hotel has rooms at guest-house prices, in pleasant surroundings. Meals are served in the rooms pending the building of a restaurant.

Ruhunu Guesthouse, 12 Hettiweediya, beside the village, opposite the village playground, ☎ (041) 550 28 – 3rm. This guesthouse built in the local style, on the same level as part of the garden, has huge, functional, clean rooms and bathrooms. A good place for authentic Sri Lankan cooking.

Sam's Holiday Cabanas (Tony D Samaraweera), 484 New By Pass Rd – 5rm. The clean, dark rooms are not, in fact, in "cabanas", but in rows in a concrete block. Very hospitable host, but the restaurant is stuffy. It does not overlook the beach and the road is right outside.

From US$10 to US$15

Chez Frank, 158 Kapparatota Rd, ☎ (041) 505 84 – 5rm. Neat, fresh-looking, well-kept rooms with mosquito nets, opening onto an attractive garden. The guesthouse is situated on the calmer side of the bay, but the sea is always fairly rough.

From US$15 to US$30

Crystal Villa Hotel, Galle Rd, Palena, 1km along the Matara road, ☎ (041) 506 35 – 6rm. CC There is a choice of huge, very comfortable rooms with a large balcony overlooking the small swimming pool in the middle of the lawn, or more expensive large bungalows with luxurious rooms where the bathrooms are fitted with open-air showers. Only two drawbacks: meals are expensive and are based around Western cuisine, and between November and March the hotel will only accept guests on a half-board basis (prices US$10 higher).

• In Mirissa

27km from Galle and 11km from Matara, Mirissa forms a fairly sheltered bay, protected to the east by a rocky reef, but the sea is rough. The beach owes its rapid development to the Paradise Beach Club, which is overcrowded and a victim of its own success. Unfortunately there is virtually no competition.

From US$10 to US$15

Central Beach Inn (Nimal Senarathna), Galle Rd, ☎ (041) 516 99 – 8rm. You can choose between six rooms of average comfort situated in a block next to the beach, and two more spacious bungalows. International cuisine (crêpes and squid) at the restaurant which is a straw shack on the beach.

Mirissa Beach Inn, Galle Rd, ☎ (041) 504 10, Fax (041) 501 15 – 5rm. In a garden by the sea, permanent bungalows with rather shabby paintwork, or cheaper and more pleasant wooden "cabanas", with tiled bathrooms.

Ocean Moon, Galle Rd, ☎ (041) 509 59 – 5rm. Rooms for less than US$10 in the owner's house, nearer the road than the beach, and bungalows with very large rooms facing the sea which cost a little more.

From US$15 to US$30

Paradise Beach Club, 140 Gunasiri Mahime Maw, ☎ and Fax (041) 503 80 – 37rm. CC Travel guides have made the reputation of this establishment but success has turned the head of its owner. The bungalows are lovely, but clustered together on a patch of land that has become too cramped. If the ones by the sea are full, he will accommodate you 100m away in an untidy garden. The cooking is good, but they only accept guests paying half-board with a fixed menu between November 15 and May 15. This system tends to over-inflate prices.

THE WILD COAST★
FROM MATARA TO HAMBANTOTA

Southern Province
75km circuit along the coast
Map p 280-281

Not to be missed

The cave temples of Mulgirigala, the Dambulla of the south.
The ritual of the laying of turtle eggs on the Rekawa lagoon.
The coral reef at Polhena and its multi-coloured fish.
The herds of elephants at Uda Walawe.

And remember...

Polhena and Tangalle are the best places to stop on this itinerary.

End of the line, all change! Since the time of the British, Matara has been the terminus for trains coming along the coast. In the centre of Southern Province, the town marks the division between two different sections of coastline. After Dondra Head, the seemingly endless village stretching along the shore finally peters out. The coconut-palm belt comes to an end and sugar cane, kapok and manioc replace the rice-fields inland. On the other side of the Walawe River, the tropical farmland disappears and the cultivation of crops is only possible with irrigation. This is the southeast corner of the dry area of the island. The land near the coast is so low-lying that it is flooded with the salty waters of the lagoons, the *kalapuwa*, with only a few thorny bushes dotted here and there on the strips of sand.

■ **Matara** – *45km from Galle.* The deep estuary of the **Nilwala Ganga**, the haunt of crocodiles, has shaped the port and town of Matara. The port was developed by the Dutch as an extension to the port of Galle at the time of the cinnamon trade in the 18C. Nestling in the tongue of land separating the river from the ocean, the town was fortified during the same period.
The road follows the line of the beach (unappealing due to the lack of shade) but the **fort** district, with its narrow shady streets, lined with houses that belonged to planters and local dignitaries, and its low ramparts are charming. Next to an unusual and picturesque **mosque**, is a bridge that spans the estuary. On the right bank, the Dutch built a small redoubt in the form of a six-pointed star called **Star Fort**. Its gate bears the arms of Baron Van Eck, who was governor of the island in about 1760. Inside the fortification is the **Museum of Ancient Paintings** *(9am-5pm; closed Thursday)*, which is not a museum of old paintings, but a collection of copies of the pictorial heritage of the island, from prehistoric times until the 19C.
On the other side of the street, a modern Buddhist temple stands very ecumenically next to a Tuscan-style church. The complex, together with the inevitable cricket ground, lies at the edge of the modern town which extends along Galle Road (Dharmapala Mawatha). At the east end of this avenue, **Sri Madura** *(2 Dharmapala Maw,* ☎ (041) 215 86) has been a musical instrument factory for several generations and specialises in drums (they make 15 different varieties!). Cow- and goat-skins as well as bulls' stomachs are stretched with the aid of cords or copper straps across bases made from coconut palms, bamboo, mango and jackfruit trees.

The architectural sights on Galle Road complete the tour of the town. The façade of the **Broadway cinema** conjures up the buildings along Nice's famous Promenade des Anglais, while the nearby **Galle Oriental Bakery** occupies a colonial-style house with scalloped canopies. At the west end of Matara is the **old market hall**, which was built as a cloister with columns. It has been restored, but sadly, abandoned by the market.

Situated 3km from the town centre, in the suburbs southwest of Matara, **Polhena** is a residential suburb with a village atmosphere. Its small beach, which is protected by a coral reef, is a great attraction at weekends. It is popular with families whose children can learn to dive and paddle in safety in these calm, shallow waters.
If you are staying in the area and enjoy the more flamboyant excesses of modern Buddhist art, there are two magnificent examples near Dondra and Dikwella, on the road to Tangalle. These two towns are served by the buses running between Matara and Hambantota, but getting to the actual sites may prove to be more complicated. The guest houses at Polhena will help you to organise a vehicle to visit them.

Take the Hambantota (A2) road to the junction at Medhawatta (4km) and turn right. After a few hundred metres, a sign on the left points in the direction of the temple (1km).

■ **The Buddhist temple of Weherahena** – A meditating Buddha, 39m high, overlooks the pools and a long esplanade. It conceals a crypt 600m long *(can be reached from below the esplanade)*. It was built in granite in the late 18C, but its stone walls hide 20 000 scenes depicting the portraits of donors at the entrance, followed by episodes from the life of Buddha. This corridor leads to a chapel built just below the giant statue. A window looks down into a room situated below his feet, where a relic in a casket is displayed for worship. This building is part of a monastery occupied by 60 monks, 45 of whom are novices.

Return to the main road and follow signs for Hambantota. You will soon come across some buildings, as sombre as the ones in the Kandyan monasteries, set on the hills overlooking the sea. This is the University of Ruhunu, built by Geoffrey Bawa.

■ **Dondra** – 5km from Matara, a concrete copy of the Buddha of Avukana stands at the entrance to Dondra, situated at the southernmost tip of the island. Dedicated to the worship of Vishnu the ancient **Devi Nuwara**, the "city of the god" was a great religious centre. The Muslim traveller Ibn Battuta, who visited this coast in the 14C on his way back from a pilgrimage to Adam's Peak, reported that 1 000 Brahmans and 500 dancers served the *devale*, the gold statue of which had eyes inlaid with rubies. In 1588, the Portuguese general Thomas De Souza had the temple destroyed and built a church on the same site. Devi Nuwara never regained its former splendour, because the kings of Kandy attracted more attention to the Vishnu Devale in their city.
By the late 19C, the temple at Dondra was reduced to just an oratory and the **shrine** you see today was only built in the first half of the 20C. In 1980, however, the government declared Dondra a holy city, and organised major restoration projects at the state's expense. Since then, the *perahera* of Devi Nuwara, which takes place at the same time of year as the one in Kandy, has become one of the most colourful in Sri Lanka.
Dondra Head has the tallest **lighthouse** on the island. Along with the one at Galle it is the most important beacon on the south coast.

Continue in the direction of Hambantota. 17km after Matara, just before Dikwella, take the small road on the left. It leads to Wewurukannala, situated 2km further on.

■ **The Wewurukannala temple-monastery**★ – The complex is dominated by a **statue of Buddha** in *samadhi* 50m high, cast in concrete between 1966 and 1969 *(it is possible to climb up the building at the back)*. The complex was founded in the Kandyan period (c1750). There is still a small image house decorated with paintings which have been restored by the Department of Archeology, but unfortunately these are difficult to see behind the dirty glass. The main **image house**, built in the late 19C is preceded by a doorway emblazoned with the coat of arms of the British crown, supported by two lions, next to that of the royal house of Kandy (a crown above an elephant carrying a *dagoba*). The interior is pure kitsch. The scenes from the life of Buddha are depicted here in the form of very life-like, painted plaster statues. The *makara torana* opening onto the room where the Buddha in Parinirvana lies, is really over the top, with its monstrous faces spitting out foliage dotted with creatures that are part flower, part woman, surrounded by flying cherubim. Below the giant Buddha, a corridor illustrates all the horrors of hell in a series of pedagogical scenes: the vices are depicted in the upper panels, the corresponding tortures in the lower ones.

Head back to the A2 and continue in the direction of Hambantota (33km from Matara).

■ **Tangalle**★ – *See plan p 304.* Tangalle, pronounced "Tangaule" in English, but "Tangalla" in Sinhalese, is a fishing village. The sea is rough, the beaches are superb and the guest houses numerous. To the south, the coast becomes a succession of little bays: to the north, the beaches of **Medaketiya**★★ and **Medilla**, where you can hunt for shells, stretch for several kilometres along the edge of the **Rekawa lagoon**★★.

Rekawa is one of the places where turtles come to lay their eggs and, since 1996, has been protected by the **Turtle Conservation Project** *(can only be reached by "tuk-tuk" or 4x4 because the road is in a terrible state. At the Netolpitiya crossroads, 6km from Tangalle on the Hambantota road, turn right. The TCP office is 3km away,* ☎ and Fax (047) 405 81, turtle@panlanka.net Entrance fee). This non-governmental organisation is quite distinct from the **turtle hatcheries** established on the south-west coast in accordance with the legislation passed in 1972 protecting the species. Instead of collecting the eggs when they are about to hatch, and looking after the baby tortoises for a few days, the TCP protects the actual nesting sites without any intervention apart from discouraging predators. There is a visitor centre, which provides a magnificent opportunity to watch this ritual, inscribed for millions of years in the genetic heritage of sea tur-

The memory of a turtle...

Five of the seven species of sea turtles living in the world come to lay their eggs on the beaches of Sri Lanka. When the 120 or so eggs in each nest hatch (fathered by several males), the baby turtles set off on their perilous journey across the sand, at the mercy of a host of predators. But they have to make this journey, because this is how they engrave on their memory, the image of the beach where they were born, and to which they return as adults, 20 or 30 years later, to lay their own eggs. They have enough natural reserves to survive for five days, the time it takes to swim to where they will grow up. Each day lost could prove to be fatal, sapping the baby turtle's strength as it pursues its journey into the Indian Ocean.

The beach at Tangalle

tles. Turtles lay their eggs (when they also hatch) at night between 8pm and midnight. The best time to go is between January and July when an average of 17 turtles a day come onto the shore at Rekawa. They come in smaller numbers during the rest of the year.

Follow signs for Beliatta, then head for Mulgirigala (21km north of Tangalle). Accessible by bus if you change at Beliatta.

▪ **Mulgirigala**★★ – *Entrance fee. Local English-speaking guide.* The **cave temples** on the hill at Mulgirigala are the jewel among the art treasures spread out along the south coast, characterised by a profusion of detail and rich decoration, which spread during the 18C at the same time as the Kandyan school. According to an inscription on the site, the monastery was founded in the 3C BC. It underwent a true renaissance thanks to the venerable Vatara Goda Dhammapali (who died in 1878), under the patronage of King Kirti Sri Rajasinha of Kandy. In 1926, the Englishman George Turnour discovered a grammar in Pali and a commentary on the *Mahavamsa* in its important collection of *ola palm* manuscripts (written on tallipot leaves), which resulted in the first translation of this chronicle of the Sinhalese kingdoms.

The image houses are arranged on three terraces connected by stairs. On the first one, the **Padumaharahat Viharaya** stands under a rock shelter. Personifications of the twelve planets are painted on the ceiling. The wall beside the entrance illustrates the **Thela Patta Jataka**, a very popular story in Sri Lanka, which tells how an ogress succeeded in eating five young people by making them succumb to the five senses. The painters have depicted them using a classic narrative convention: a first room with a profusion of flowers, their scent awaking the sense of smell; a second in which musical instruments can be heard; a third decorated with precious objects stimulates the sense of sight; a fourth where mouth-watering foods appeal to the sense of taste; and finally a couple entwined in the fifth room evokes the sense of touch.

On the second terrace is another **reclining Buddha** in a room decorated with some rather sentimental paintings. **Four temples** stand on the third esplanade, from where you can see the beach at Tangalle. It was in the first temple that the manuscripts, now housed in the monastery situated at the bottom of the hill, were discovered. Paintings executed in the 18C decorate the walls of the antechamber and the frame of the door is carved with an unusual pineapple-leaf motif with frolicking squirrels. On the façade of the shrine nearby stand stucco statues of the gods who protect the four cardinal points of the island. Next to it, a pool dug out of the rock carries an inscription bearing the ancient name of the site, Muhungiri, "the Rock that can be seen from the sea". At the end of the temple of the Cobra, the wooden door painted with a snake is always closed. According to tradition, a cobra that had been locked up in there by a monk is still alive. Near the staircase leading up to the last terrace, where there is a small **stupa** and a Bo tree enclosure, there is a *sala* tree. Buddhists regard its fleshy, delicately-coloured flowers as the image of a *dagoba* surrounded by devotees and protected by the hood of a cobra (they bloom from November to January).

Head back to the road for Hambantota (75km de Matara).

▪ **Hambantota** – A bay sheltered by low red cliffs, canoes and colourful fishing-boats hauled up onto the beach: this is what you see of this **fishing town** from the terrace of the Rest House. A particular feature of the town is that it is inhabited by Malaysian Muslims who work on the saltpans just east of the town. Nothing else in Hambantota merits a visit although Embilipitiya (51km) is easily accessible, by the "Japanese road" which leaves the coast 5km west of the town. Situated 19km from the Uda Walawe elephant reserve, Embilipitiya has some accommodation and buses which serve the national park.

■ **Uda Walawe National Park★★** – *Daily 6am-6pm, ticket offices close at 5pm. Entrance fee (US$20 per person) including entry for passengers and vehicle and the services of a ranger (compulsory). Jeeps with a driver can be hired on the spot (approximately US$20 for 3hr). Mineral water and fizzy drinks are sold opposite the entrance to the park.*

Opened in 1980, Uda Walawe is one of Sri Lanka's most recently created parks. It was established in an area that was already a natural habitat for elephants. Forty kilometres away as the crow flies, Pannamure was the last *kraal* (a trapping enclosure for capturing wild elephants) on the island. It was closed in 1950 following the scandal of the killing of a wild elephant. The creation of the reservoir from the Rivere Walawe for irrigation provided a huge watering place for the elephants and made the project viable. The best time to watch the herds of wild elephants is between January and March and between August and October, preferably in the afternoon.

The saltpans at Hambantota

B Pérousse / HOA QUI

Making the most of Matara

Coming and going

By train – The ***railway station*** is situated to the north of the town centre. There are five daily trains between Matara and Colombo (4hr), via Galle (80min) et Hikkaduwa (2hr).

By bus – *The bus terminus* is below the east rampart of the fort. There are numerous buses for Galle (1hr) and Colombo (between 4hr and 5hr), Tangalle (1hr) and Hambantota (2hr). Some buses also serve Wellawaya (4hr30min) via Wirawila, and Kataragama (4hr) via Tissamaharama (3hr). Intercity Express buses leave for Ratnapura (4hr) by the Bulutota pass.

Address book

Banks / Currency exchange – It is possible to change money at the ***Hatton Bank*** (Dharmapala Maw) and the ***Bank of Ceylon*** (Kumaratunga Maw), both of which are located at the Star Fort junction.

Post office / Telephone – The post office is in the fort, near the bus terminus, to the right of the bridge which crosses the Nilwala Ganga.

Where to stay

Matara does not have the appeal of Galle; it is better to stay in Polhena. In any case, avoid the few hotels on the coast at the east end of the town, not far from the bus terminus: the road is noisy, the area is dirty and there isn't a patch of shade.

Under US$10

Old Dutch Mansion, 6 Wilfred Gunasekera Maw, Fort, ☎ (041) 227 98, (01) 72 31 70, Fax (01) 73 22 71 – 4rm. If you like the idea of staying in a historic place with a colonial spirit, here is a pretty white house in the residential quarter of the old fort. The rooms have no character but are spotlessly clean (cold water and mosquito nets) and the patios are decorated with lots of potted plants.

• In Polhena

The beach at Polhena is very busy at weekends. The hotels at Polhena, which are functional but rather uninspiring, are really designed for the local clientele.

From US$10 to US$15

Sunny Lanka Guesthouse & Restaurant, 93 Polhena Rd, ☎ (041) 235 04 – 5rm. Well run with charming owner, this guesthouse is good value for money. Generous helpings and super-fresh seafood. Bikes and diving equipment for hire.

TK Guesthouse, 116 / 1 Polhena Beach Rd, ☎ (041) 226 03 – 11rm. Large, clean, tiled rooms (mosquito nets) with clean bathroom. The owner is full of good advice and the cooking is prepared according to personal tastes. One hundred metres from the beach. Bikes for hire. Excellent value for money.

Eating out

Galle Oriental Bakery, Dharmapala Maw (next to the Broadway cinema), is the kind of place that Sri Lankans like. This marvellous bakery makes fresh filled rolls and sandwiches and serves good, cheap, simple "rice and curry".

Other things to do

Diving – Polhena and its superb coral reefs is an excellent site for diving, the haunt of an array of colourful fish. Ask Titus at the ***TK Guesthouse*** to take you out (two hours for US$5 including goggles, snorkel and flippers). Be careful as heatstroke is a real risk after 3pm!

Feasts & festivals *Perahera of Weherahena* at the full moon in November.

Perahera of Dondra at the full moon of the end of July / beginning of August.

Making the most of Tangalle

COMING AND GOING

By bus – The ***bus terminus*** is situated in the town-centre, equidistant from the bays to the south and the beaches to the north, which can be reached by "tuk-tuk". Frequent buses to Matara (1hr), Hambantota (75min) and Colombo (5hr, morning departure). There are some services to Wellawaya and Kataragama, via Tissamaharama.

ADDRESS BOOK

Post office / Telephone – The post office is in Main Road, 500m south of the bus terminus. Monday-Friday 8am-5pm.

WHERE TO STAY

Tangalle offers a vast choice of guest-houses for travellers on a low budget which line the beach at Medaketiya. Sunbathe rather than swim, because the strength of the waves and the ground swell make swimming dangerous. Avoid the bays near the port and the Rest House which are very dirty. Beware! Most of the establishments have no telephone and the numbers given are the private numbers of the owners.

Under US$10

Ibis Guesthouse, 27 Medaketiya Rd, Medilla – 2rm. Basic rooms with shared bathroom, but the owner will shortly be building three bungalows with bathrooms, which will be let for under US$15.

Shanika Beach Inn & Restaurant, 69 Medaketiya Rd – 6rm. Neither beach nor garden, a great deal of concrete and spartan rooms, but the kindness of the owners and the quality of the food compensate for this, in addition to which the prices are reasonable.

From US$10 to US$15

Ganesh Garden Beach Cabanas, Medilla, ☎(047) 406 65 – 3rm. Young, relaxed atmosphere and a very good restaurant overlooking the beach (giant barbecues and reggae disco every week). Well-maintained bungalows in a rather neglected garden. Possibility of airport transfers (about US$40).

Gayana Guesthouse & Restaurant (Padma), 96 Medaketiya Beach, ☎ (047) 406 59, Fax (047) 404 77 – 10rm. A pleasant guest-house because of its beach-side location. The rooms are large and clean although lacking in character, with small bathrooms. The restaurant is good. IDD telephone connections.

Green Jewel Cabanas, west of the Rekawa lagoon – 7rm. Rooms in a concrete building, with balcony overlooking the sea, or in more pleasant, small wooden bungalows. The restaurant on the beach serves good food, generous portions. The hotel organises trips around the lagoon in a motor catamaran.

Kingfisher, 91 Vijaya Rd, Medaketiya, ☎ (047) 408 17 – 4rm. Highly recommended for its cuisine and the owner's wife will prepare whatever you wish on the spot. The place is very well kept but the rooms seem curiously shabby for a hotel opened in 1999.

Panorama Rock Café & Palm Beach Resort (Ananda Wijethunga), Medilla, ☎ (047) 404 58 – 3rm. Rather a long name for a restaurant serving grilled food by the sea with its three rustic but well-equipped bungalows (mosquito nets).

Villa Araliya, Medilla, ☎ and Fax (047) 404 01 – 2rm. All the charm and character of a colonial-style residence, nestling in an enclosed garden. The rooms, which are ventilated in the tradional way by a space below the roof, are furnished with tasteful antique furniture. Delicious Sri Lankan cooking.

From US$30 to US$40

Nature Resort, 2km along the road to Hambantota, follow a track for 1.5km; if it rains, it can only be reached by boat, ☎ and Fax (047) 408 44; booking from Colombo: 467 High Level Rd, Delkanda, Nugegoda, ☎ and Fax (01) 81 22 55 – 11rm. CC The comfort of modern bungalows with AC or fans, and the pleasure of a swimming-pool in a wild, natural habitat on the coast: huge beach at Medaketiya where the turtles come to lay their eggs and the Tangalle lagoon, home to all sorts of birds. Delicious cooking blending the flavour of seafood with a host of different vegetables. Boat trips (no engine) on the lagoon.

Palm Paradise Cabanas, Goyambokka, 3km southwest of the bus terminus. ☎(47) 408 42, Fax (047) 403 38, secol@sri.lanka.net – 20rm. An idyllic setting with pretty wooden bungalows on piles, scattered in a palm grove running down towards a bay complete with reefs. Unfortunately, from November to March, accommodation is only available on a half-board basis and the cooking is variable.

Eating out

Tourists are well catered for in Tangalle. There is not a single guesthouse that does not offer fried squid, grilled fish or lobster accompanied by chips and salad. Beware! Not all of them have the space to accommodate non-residents. The most popular are the ones at Medaketiya, at the junction of Medaketiya Road and Wijaya Road: ***Gayana*** serves food on the beach, behind the guest house; ***Saman's Travellers Nest*** offers a menu of grilled seafood and Chinese cuisine at reasonable prices; the nearby ***Shanika Beach*** has the advantage of preparing the same products in the local way – in curry; further north, the ***Panorama Rock Café*** prepares fish and chicken barbecues on the beach. You can eat anywhere for between US$5 and US$10, unless you have lobster (price varies depending on the season).

Other things to do

Diving – Diving is available at Tangalle. Apply to ***Let's Dive*** (Neetha and Walter Michel), near the Nature Resort, ☎ (047) 408 44, Fax (047) 404 01. Diving school, diving equipment for hire, courses, diving trips.

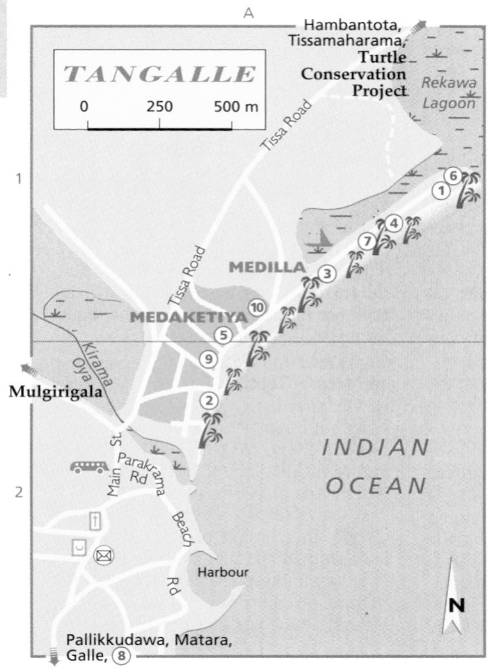

HOTELS

Ganesh Garden Beach Cabanas........ ①
Gayana........ ②
Green Jewel Cabanas........ ③
Ibis........ ④
Kingfisher........ ⑤
Nature Resort........ ⑥
Panorama Rock Café et Palm Beach Resort........ ⑦
Palm Paradise Cabanas........ ⑧
Shanika Beach Inn........ ⑨
Villa Araliya........ ⑩

Making the most of Hambantota

Coming and going

By bus – The small bus terminus is situated in the centre of the town, at the junction of the Galle and Tissamaharama roads. It is served by buses running between Galle or Matara and Kataragama or Wellawaya. Some Intercity Express buses run to Ratnapura (4hr), via Embilipitiya, on the road to the Uda Walawe reserve.

Address book

Banks / Currency exchange – *Bank of Ceylon*, near the Rest House, in the area of the promontory that dominates the town to the southwest.

Where to stay / Eating out

Despite the number of places including the word "beach" in their name, Hambantota is not a seaside resort: the sea is very rough and there is no beach. If you are on a low budget, it might be better to head for Tissamaharama (27km) which is not situated by the sea but on the shores of a lake.

Under US$10

Joy Guesthouse, Colombo Rd, on the outskirts of town on the Galle road, ☎ (047) 203 28 – 7rm. Basic, but adequate rooms (mosquito nets, but no bedding) in a little house with a veranda overlooking the garden. Only serves breakfast. Only in an emergency.

From US$15 to US$30

Rest House, on a small promontory southwest of the town, ☎ and Fax (047) 202 99 – 14rm. Impressively situated right above the bay of Hambantota and spotlessly clean, this guest house has huge rooms with wooden furniture, but without mosquito nets or hot water. Excellent freshly prepared local cooking.

From US$40 to US$70

The Oasis, Sisilasagama, 7km along the road to Matara, ☎ (047) 206 51 – 50rm. TV CC In a fantastically wild environment on a beach although the sea is very rough. The hotel has every comfort you could wish for and organises excursions in 4x4 vehicles to Uda Walawe and Bundala.

Making the most of Embilipitiya

Where to stay

• In Embilipitiya

51km from Hambantota, Embilipitiya is a good place to stay near the Uda Walawe reserve. You can also organise an excursion in a 4x4 vehicle to Rakwana (45 km), one of the access points to the Sinharaja forest.

From US$10 to US$15

Sarathchandra Tourist Guesthouse, Pallegama, 100m from the clock-tower and the bus terminus, ☎(047) 301 38, Fax (047) 301 65 – 14rm. Built in the Sri Lankan style, with six rather sombre bungalows (mosquito nets, cold water in a garden at the back, and large, spotlessly clean rooms (hot water) in the main building. Its public bar is rather noisy at weekends. Local cuisine and excursions in 4x4 vehicles to the reserves of Uda Walawe and Sinharaja at very reasonable prices.

From US$15 to US$30

Centauria Tourist Hotel, New Town, 1.5km east of the centre, ☎(047) 305 14 – 35rm. CC Mainly used by groups visiting Uda Walawe, the hotel is pleasantly situated in a large garden with a view over Lake Chandrika. The rooms are huge and clean, but lacking in character, and the bathrooms are tiny (hot water).

• In Uda Walawe

The Wildlife Department rents out bungalows inside the reserve. Although less popular than Yala, the booking procedure is rather complicated *(see detailed explanation on Yala p 310)*. It is also possible to camp here, provided you obtain permission from and book with the Wildlife Department in Colombo *(see p 132)*.

Around Tissamaharama★★

Southern Province
88km from Ella, 104km from Matara and 264km from Colombo
Hot climate (27°C) – Rainy season from November to January
Map p 307

Not to be missed
The bewitching ceremony of the evening "puja",
in the Maha Devale shrine in Kataragama.

And remember...
Devote a whole day to the wildlife of Yala.

Irrigated by the Tissa wewa, Tissamaharama (known as Tissa) is an oasis in the heart of the arid Ruhunu plain. A giant *dagoba* in immaculate condition, a few pillars and Buddhist statues scattered among the rice-fields make up just a few pieces of the jigsaw puzzle of the civilisation that flourished here for twelve centuries, until the year 1000 AD. There are other traces scattered throughout the enormous natural wildlife sanctuary of Yala. These days, Yala along with the Bundala bird sanctuary, is the main contributor to the tourist economy in Tissamaharama. Every day, convoys of 4x4 vehicles wind their way along the tracks of the park to observe its herds of elephants and, hopefully, a few panthers. For the Buddhists of Ceylon, the great stupa of Tissa, founded by the kings of the Ruhunu, is a stopping place on the pilgrimage route to Kataragama, the most ecumenical holy town of the island.

The story of Duttugemunu

In the early days of the Buddhist kingdom of Anuradhapura, the reign of the Sinhalese kings was under threat throughout the island. At the end of the 3C BC, the throne was taken by a conqueror of Dravidian origin, **Elara** (c204-161) and the Sinhalese pretenders, Kelani Tissa and Kavan Tissa, took refuge further south: the former in Kelaniya, near Colombo, and the latter to the south-east, in the Ruhunu.

Chronicles claim the eldest son of Kavan Tissa as the hero of the Buddhist reconquest. His quest to overthrow Elara was to bring him into conflict first with his father, who feared for his son's life, and later with his brother. So he came to be called **Duttugemunu**, "Gemunu the Unworthy". He recruited ten knights with magical powers, who could uproot trees or travel enormous distances in a day. Each of them was asked to find and train ten officers who, in turn, had to train ten soldiers. Little by little his army grew to a total of 11 110, but even with this many men, he was unable to surround the immense city of Anuradhapura. The city was eventually brought down by means of a stratagem devised by Vihara Maha Devi, the prince's mother. In front of the capital city's gates, the Sinhalese erected a fortified city, enclosed within several concentric earth ramparts, which forced the Tamils into attacking rather than defending. Elara's army was crushed and Duttugemunu triumphed over the king in single combat mounted on an elephant.

A lost civilisation

Duttugemunu's conquest highlights the importance of the Ruhunu in the ancient history of Ceylon. Like the dry region of Anuradhapura at the time, this arid zone benefited from an extensive network of reservoirs, built for irrigation purposes. Throughout the Yala park, there are countless relics which bear witness to a flour-

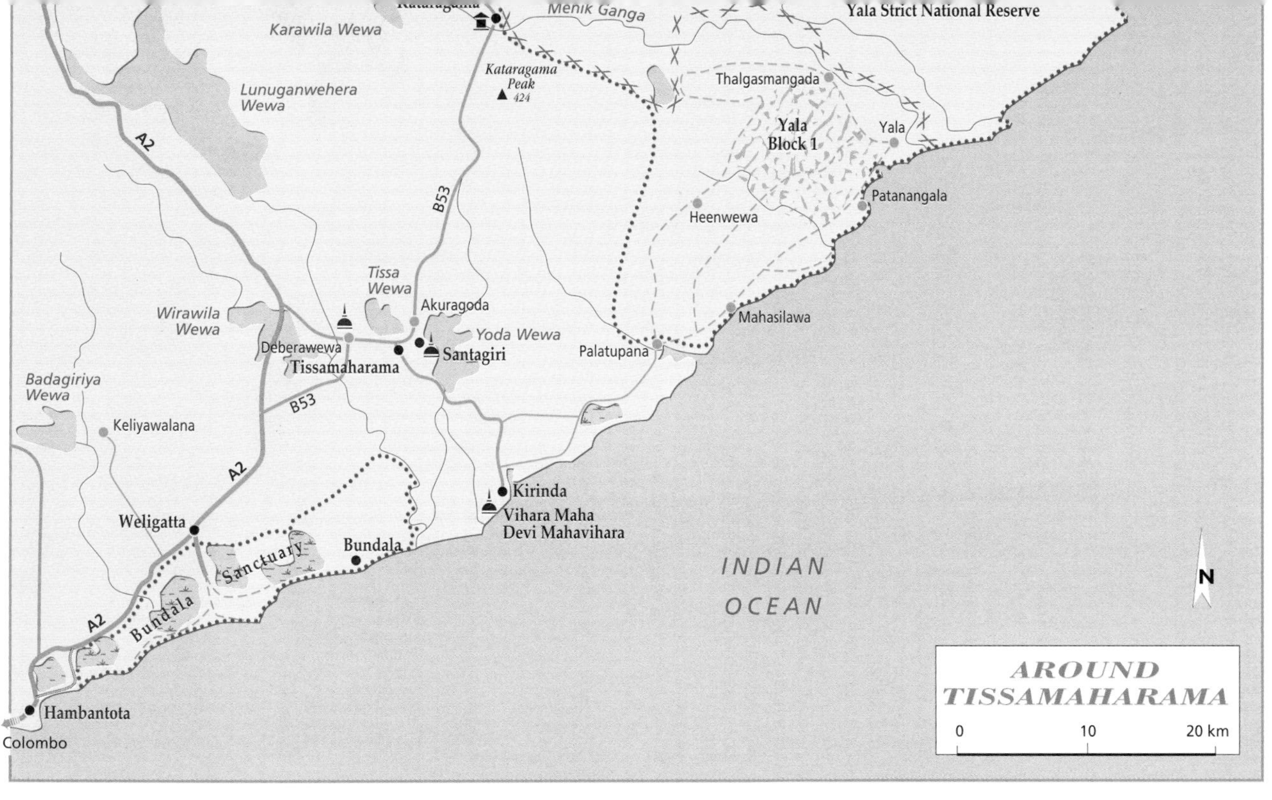
Menik Ganga
Yala Strict National Reserve
Karawila Wewa
Kataragama Peak
424
Thalgasmangada
Lunuganwehera Wewa
A2
Yala
Yala Block 1
B53
Patanangala
Heenwewa
Tissa Wewa
Akuragoda
Wirawila Wewa
Yoda Wewa
Mahasilawa
Deberawewa
Santagiri
Palatupana
Tissamaharama
Badagiriya Wewa
B53
Keliyawalana
A2
Kirinda
Vihara Maha Devi Mahavihara
Weligatta
Bundala
Sanctuary
INDIAN OCEAN
N
A2
Bundala
AROUND TISSAMAHARAMA
0
10
20 km
Hambantota
Colombo

ishing Buddhist civilisation in the south, with some monasteries housing as many as a thousand monks. However, around the 10C, the population dwindled, the irrigation system that ensured the region's survival was abandoned, and its buildings were gradually overgrown by vegetation. The southern Ruhunu remained cut off from the rest of the island until 1900, when the British administration made Yala into a hunting reservation, later to become a National Park in 1938.

Tissamaharama*

There is little trace of the ancient capital of the Ruhunu, but the shores of the lake and the rice-fields make a lovely setting for a pleasant bicycle ride *(for hire from hotels and guest houses. Ride takes about 2hr, best undertaken at sunrise or sunset when it is cooler and the light is better)*.

Majestically situated in splended isolation in the middle of the rice-fields, the **Santagiri dagoba***, or Mahathupa, has been completely restored thanks to donations from the locals. Its impressive dimensions evoke those of its cousins in Anuradhapura. Moreover, it was founded by Kavan Tissa, the father of Duttugemunu, who was also responsible for the Ruvanveliseya stupa *(access via the Kataragama highway, between the modern town of Tissa and the Rest House)*.

A road runs along the top of the southern embankment of the **Tissa wewa**, which was dug out a generation after its namesake in Anuradhapura and which is a sanctuary for migrating birds. On its eastern shore lies a palm-grove, which conceals further vestiges of ancient Tissa. The forest of stone pillars, near **Yatala Vihara**, is all that remains of a chapter room. As for the *dagoba*, its base is supported by elephants' forequarters. Further west, the trunks of the palm-trees surrounding the **Manik Vihara*** make it into a natural *gedige*. These monuments date from 2C BC, before Duttugemunu's conquest.

The pleasures of bathing in the waters of the Yala wildlife park

Around Tissamaharama★★

The area around Tissa offers greatly contrasting landscapes. Around the great Yoda wewa, the flat countryside is dotted with rice-fields frequented by herons and pelicans (the rice of this region is renowned in Ceylon). But further afield you enter a different landscape where brushwood and thorny plants grow around the *kalapuwa*, the salt lagoons which are a feature of Yala and Bundala.

The Bundala Park★

Turn left at the Weligatta crossroads, 16km along the road to Hambantota. The park entrance is 2km further on. Open every day, 6.30am-6.30pm. Entrance fee (US$6) includes vehicle permit and obligatory guide. There is no bus service, so you will have to hire a vehicle in Tissamaharama. A 4x4 jeep is not absolutely necessary, but some sections of the road are likely to be in poor condition.

This bird sanctuary is to be found among the salt lagoons, which are also a haven to aquatic fauna. Between September and March, when the monsoon blows from the northeast, the indigenous population of wader-birds is increased by the arrival of migrating birds, including pink flamingoes. This is the best time of year to visit the reserve. If you want to watch the birds, come between 6.30am and 9am. Towards late afternoon, between 4pm and 7pm, the crocodiles begin to hunt and the elephants come to drink on the shores of the lagoons.

Kirinda

12km south of Tissa. Bus service every 30min between the two towns.

Off the coastline of this fishing village lie the Great and the Little Basses, the red sandstone reefs where several boats have run aground. Were it not used as a rubbish dump Kirinda might be a pretty beach. An enormous granite monolith

P Haussherr

Ceylon's Iphigenia

King Kelani Tissa of Kelaniya held his mentor in great esteem and adored his wife, but both were compromised in a plot hatched by the king's brother. He therefore had his counsellor thrown into boiling oil and his wife into the sea. This angered the gods, who unleashed a tempest which soon threatened to engulf the entire kingdom. The king consulted advisers. He learned from one priest that if his only daughter agreed to be sacrificed to the raging waves, then this would calm the sea. The princess consented, and dressed up in her finery, set sail in a golden vessel. Scarcely had she set out to sea than the tempest ceased. The gods propelled her gently towards the shores of the Ruhunu, where the sleeping princess was found by fishermen, who informed King Kavan Tissa. Passionately in love with her, he made her his queen, Vihara Maha Devi, the future mother of Gemunu.

stranded on the shore is crowned with a small **dagoba*** shaded by frangipani trees, with the statue of a king bowing before it. The ruler had the building constructed in homage to his queen, Vihara Maha Devi, the mother of the future Duttugemunu. Further on, an oratory dedicated to Kataragama looks down over the sea.

Yala National Park**

Access at the Palatupana entry point, 21.5km southeast of Tissa. There is no bus service, so it is necessary to hire a 4x4 jeep, which is easily arranged in Tissamaharama where it is the main commercial activity. Most drivers offer half-day excursions (about US$25). Do not hesitate to negotiate a tariff for a full day, beginning at dawn, because Yala really is worth the effort and you will greatly increase your chances of seeing the wild animals if you have a chance to linger. A gravel road crosses Block 1, the only one open to visitors, for 17km; the complete circuit covers approximately 55km. Entrance fee: US$10 per person and US$1.50 per vehicle. It is compulsory to be accompanied by a member of the Wildlife Department staff. Do not get out of vehicles inside the park. Small museum at the entrance with various species displayed. Open every day, 5.30am-6.30pm.

A former hunting reservation, which was transformed into a natural park in 1938, Yala combines four numbered areas (blocks) and a zone offering special protection, covering an area of 1 570sqkm in the south-east of the island. Currently, 392 elephants, several of which are tuskers (elephants with tusks, of which there are none in Uda Walawe), and 120 spotted panthers live in these wild expanses. These are the most popular of Yala's natural spectacles, the former as they go for their bath at sunset, and the latter as they laze about

H Choimet

An elephant has an enormous appetite

An adult elephant spends about 18hr a day looking for food. Its daily ration is 160-200kg of fodder, but it wastes much more than it eats. It drinks proportionately very little, as 90-130 litres of liquid is all that it needs. By day, its chosen habitat is the forest, which it leaves in the evening for the savannah. Despite appearances, it never destroys trees, only cutting off young leaves, twigs and end branches, gathering fruit or picking up windfalls. It never attacks the bark of a tree except during periods of drought.

on the rocks. The park also contains other species of mammals: wild buffaloes, *sambhurs*, musk deer, black bears, macaques and jackals. April, May and June are the best months for seeing the elephants; November and December for bird watching.

Kataragama★★

15km north of Tissa. This site has a bus station, situated opposite the entrance, inside the sacred enclosure, and is connected to all the major towns of the island.

Kataragama is the most ecumenical of Sri Lanka's holy places. Inside an enclosure, around a temple dedicated to its namesake god, there stand various Hindu shrines, a church, two mosques and a large *dagoba*. It has been a centre for worship and pilgrimage for more than 2 000 years, with numbers visiting varying throughout the ages.

The cult of the god Kataragama – Kataragama is one of the four great protective divinities of the Sinhalese. To the Tamils, he is **Murugan**, or **Subramaniam**, other names for **Skanda**, the son of Shiva and the brother of Ganesh. Both religions have legends recounting how the god came to the island to fight the Asura, the enemies of the gods. While there, he fell in love with **Valli Amma**, the daughter of a hunter, who he made his second wife. As such, Kataragama is worshipped in two forms, as an ardent warrior and as a lover. In the present complex, his spear has been placed in the sanctuary and there is a temple dedicated to Valli Amma. Once a year, at the time of the new moon in July-August, their marriage is celebrated with processions and offerings.

At the end of the Kandyan period, the worship of Kataragama gradually fell out of favour with the Sinhalese, who reproached the warrior god for not having prevented the Tamil princes from acceding to the throne of Kandy. The case against him was further strengthened when the British took over the kingdom in 1815. Abandoned by the Buddhists, the cult was revived by the Tamils who arrived on the island in tens of thousands to work in the plantations: in fact, isn't Murugan, the young god mounted on a peacock, the most popular god in Southern India? The absence of roads suitable for vehicles, however, made the pilgrimage a difficult one. The construction of a road to Tissamaharama in 1949 resurrected Kataragama as a place of worship... for the Sinhalese! This renewed interest was in fact connected to a restoration programme for the great Buddhist monuments, of which the *dagoba* Kiri Vihara in Kataragama was one. From then on, the god was honoured as the one who had assisted King Duttugemunu in his victory. His status as a warrior who triumphs over obstacles was adapted to suit the mores of the day. Nowadays, the Maha Devale is frequently visited by middle-class businessmen, dealers in precious stones, and politicians.

The festival of Kataragama – The town is the setting for the most sumptuous of all the religious festivals of Sri Lanka, especially so because of the thousands of pilgrims of all faiths who gather at the temple. Some of them, in a tradition which is more Hindu than Buddhist, subject themselves to mortifications such as laying out on the sand scorched by the sun, or hanging themselves from hooks attached through their skin. Most spectacular are the pilgrims whose faith is such that they can walk on live coals without trembling (and without getting burnt!). The celebrations finish with a *perahera*.

The site – The attraction of the place is its atmosphere rather than its architecture. Buddhists come to meditate on the square in front of the **Kiri Vihara** *dagoba*. The Muslims come to pray at the **Masjad ul-Khizr** mosque. But they all assemble, together with the Hindu Tamils, in the courtyard of the **Maha Devale**, the "great temple" of Kataragama, an amazingly small and simple building, the interior of which is decorated with a profusion of lamps and elephant tusks. Two shrines adjoin it, one to Buddha, the other to his brother Ganesh. *(The whole area, from the Maha Devale to the Kiri Vihara, which towers over the temple enclosure at the end of a 700m-long alley, must be visited barefoot: take your shoes off and put them in a plastic bag).*

Two *puja* ceremonies take place every day, at 11am and at 7pm. The evening ceremony is a special time to be in the sanctuary. The ritual takes place by torch-light to the sound of drums and trumpets: the faithful come to break coconuts, an elephant kneels down before the shrines, there are old women in traditional costume and lamps flickering in front of the wall-hanging of the god…

In front of the sacred area – a large wooded park surrounded by a fence – there are stalls selling *puja vatti*, the plates for offerings, filled principally with fruit. The monuments are on the other bank of the **Manik Ganga**, in which it is customary for the pilgrims to purify themselves. They line up in the avenue that runs parallel to the river. Near to the temple enclosure, a **museum** is dedicated to the various gods of Sri Lanka, their associated symbols, some objects of worship and ex-voto offerings.

Making the most of Tissamaharama

Coming and going

By bus – Tissa is not really a village, but rather a crossroads to the south of the Tissa wewa, on the road that goes to Yala: the coach station can be found there (Main St). Frequent service to Colombo (journey takes 6hr), via Hambantota (1hr), Matara (3hr) and Galle (4hr). For Uva province and the mountain region, regular departures to Wellawaya (59km to the north), where you can easily get buses to Badulla and Nuwara Eliya. Frequent connections to Kataragama. On arrival, find out which block your guesthouse is located in: if you are staying in Deberawewa, ask for the "clock-tower" stop in this village; for Akuragoda, get off in Tissa. Travel between bus stops by "tuk-tuk".

Address book

• In Tissamaharama

Bank / Currency exchange – *Bank of Ceylon*, Main St, 100m from the coach station.

Post office / Telephone – Post office on the way out of Tissa, on the Yala road.

• In Kataragama

Bank / Currency exchange – *People's Bank* and ***Bank of Ceylon*** on Tissamaharama Rd.

Where to stay

There are few guesthouses in Tissa itself. The two main areas for accommodation are Akuragoda (1.5km to the north on the road to Kataragama) and Deberawewa (4.5km to the northwest). All the guesthouses can organise safaris to Yala.

• In Tissamaharama

US$10 to US$15

Happy Cottage, Akuragoda, 1km from the Rest House, access on the left off the Kataragama road, ☎ (047) 370 85 – 7rm. The rooms and bathrooms are spacious and clean. Excellent value for money.

Hôtel Tissa Guesthouse, Main St, near the coach station, ☎ (047) 371 04 – 5rm. The rooms are acceptable and have shuttered doors; interesting excursions to Yala.

Regina Holiday Home (A Rathubaduge), Deberawewa, near the Tissamaharama hospital, ☎ (047) 371 59 – 7rm. Rooms with light, pretty furnishings. A quiet and very pleasant setting. Barbecued seafood and fish at very reasonable prices. Bicycles for hire (US$1 per day).

Sakura Guesthouse & Restaurant (K De Silva), Swarna, Deberawewa, near the hospital, ☎ (047) 371 98 – 5rm.

The rooms vary in standard, but generous hospitality is guaranteed.

Tissa Inn (Ganesha Siriwardena), Wellawaya Rd, Deberawewa, (047) 372 33, Fax (047) 370 80, tissainn@cga.lk – 6rm. This small hotel on the Colombo road has quiet rooms with mosquito nets and cold shower. Sri Lankan meals.

Austria Lanka, Akuragoda, Kataragama Rd, (047) 376 48 – 7rm. Acceptable hotel with a garden, set back from the road, but balconies with a view of a wall!

Vikum Lodge, Akuragoda, 1km from the Rest House, access on the left off the Kataragama road, (047) 375 85 – 10rm. Near the lake, this family guesthouse is very well maintained. Restaurant very pleasant. Peaceful at night.

From US$15 to US$30

Priyankara, Akuragoda, Kataragama Rd, (047) 372 06, Fax (047) 373 26 – 26rm. cc The only hotel worthy of the name to be found in Tissa. Rooms with balconies overlooking the rice-fields. Attentive service.

• In Kirinda

Under US$10

Suduweli, 1km north of the beach, near the crossroads on the Yala road – 3rm. Two rooms and one bungalow in the garden. Pretty colonial furniture. Motorbikes and cycles available. The owners also have a 4x4 jeep.

• In Yala Park

Mahasilawa and ***Patanangala*** (on the coast), ***Heenwewa*** (inland) and ***Thalgasmangada*** (on the banks of Manik Ganga) are the four areas for accommodation in Block 1 of Yala Park. These bungalows can accommodate 4 to 6 people, and have a shower room, but no electricity (kerosene lamps for the evening). A cook prepares the provisions that you need to take with you. The bungalows are owned by the State, and civil servants have priority when booking. The rest of the time, they are grabbed by Sri Lankans. However, you can try booking accommodation in Yala through a travel agency *(see p 134)*. Expect to pay about US$20 per person, per night.

From US$45 to US$70

Yala Safari Beach Hotel (Jetwing), south-east of Palatupana, access via a track, (047) 390 75, Fax (047) 204 71 – 63rm. cc The rooms, on a level with the lagoon-side beach, are furnished in "safari tent" style. A small sheltered cove for swimming.

• In Kataragama

Very cheap accommodation. It is impossible to get a room here in January-February (pilgrimage season), during the summer festival and at weekends.

Under US$10

Bank of Ceylon Pilgrims Rest, Tissamaharama Rd, opposite the Bank of Ceylon, (047) 352 29 – 20rm. Large, clean rooms and bathrooms. Ask for an upper floor room: views of the sacred Kataragama Mountain.

Leisure Inn, first guesthouse on the way in to town coming from Tissamaharama, (047) 353 48 – 5rm. An attractive small hotel with a central patio. No mosquito nets, but spotless bathrooms. Inexpensive Sri Lankan food.

Rest House, Kataragama, (047) 352 27 – 5rm. Well situated near the entrance to the site, the only Rest House in Sri Lanka which does not charge the earth. Large rooms. Meals are included: based on vegetarian cuisine.

Eating out

From US$7 to US$15

Refresh, Akuragoda, Kataragama Rd, opposite the Rest House, (047) 373 57 cc A variety of good quality cuisine served in a pleasant setting.

Other things to do

Excursions – Organising a safari to Yala from Tissa is very easy: competition is fierce and prices are about the same everywhere. ***Ajith Safari Jeep Tours*** charges US$25 per vehicle per half-day (mornings, 5.30am-10am, or evenings, 3pm-7pm). Contact the agency at the Tissa Inn guesthouse or (047) 375 57 / (071) 644 17, Fax (047) 370 80.

Feast days / Festivals – ***The Katarągama festival*** on the day of the full moon in the month of Esala.

Géopress/EXPLORER

THE EAST COAST

During the 1970s, the Ministry of Tourism gambled everything on backing the east as an alternative location for beach-lovers to retreat to when the west coast was at the mercy of the summer monsoon. At the time, the mixed population of Tamils (43 %), Muslims (32 %) and Sinhalese (25 %) co-existed quite happily. However, in 1983, the death of thirteen Sri Lankan soldiers in an ambush orchestrated by Tamil separatists unleashed a wave of violent racist acts. In their hundreds and thousands, the Tamils fled from the pogroms launched by Sinhalese mobs, or enrolled in the Tamil Tigers. Since then, the conflict has followed its dramatic course, with campaigns conducted by the Sri Lankan army and terrorist reprisals. Caught in the crossfire of this bitter battle between the country's army and the separatist rebels, the resulting civilian refugees live in makeshift camps. Since the military took control of Trincomalee in 1992, the east has been partially opened up, but the road that connects the town to the rest of the island is a fragile link. To the north and to the south, tensions are still evident and acts of violence continue. In the separatist plan drawn up by the LTTE, the East and North Provinces would form an independent state, conferring control of 60 % of the country's coast to Eelam, the Tamil nation. The Muslims are opposed to this partition, as it would place them in a minority situation. Pockets of jungle controlled by the Tigers, villages constantly menaced with reprisals by suicide commando raids: the east remains the hidden and distressing face of the paradise of Ceylon.

Trincomalee

Eastern Province – Pop 91 000
85km from Habarana, 106km from Anuradhapura, 257km from Colombo

And remember...
If you visit Trincomalee, it is at your own risk.
The Sri Lankan government accepts no responsibility
for attacks on foreign tourists in this region.

Calm reigns in the old port of the kingdom of Kandy. A return to calm, however, does not mean a return to normal life even though Trincomalee is the only sector of the Northern Provinces where the army has sufficient control for there to be train and bus links with the rest of the country. Suddenly, the town has become an important transit point for the inhabitants of the Jaffna peninsula, which is reached by ferry. The number of travellers has increased since the Jayasekuru ("Operation Sure Victory") campaign was launched by the Sri Lankan army in 1997 to re-open the 76km stretch of road between Vavuniya and Kilinochchi. The operation ended in failure in September 1998 with heavy losses having been sustained on both sides (between 1 200 and 1 500 Sri Lankan army soldiers were killed). Since then Trincomalee has been the only route to the north. The hotels are packed, with people crammed in their rooms waiting for the permit which will allow them to continue their journey.

A town in slow motion

The institution of a 6pm curfew transforms Trincomalee into a ghost town every evening. During the day, everything runs in slow motion and there are not many people on the streets. Every morning, opposite the old stadium – these days nothing more than wasteland strewn with rubbish and plastic bags – a small number of fishing boats sell their catch. It doesn't take long with everything being snapped up by the hotel owners. The main market, along Konesar Road, to the east of the town, is mostly patronised by the residents of Trincomalee. For those living in the surrounding villages, the journey into town is no easy undertaking: they have to endure endless military road-blocks, produce their documents each time, have their bags and merchandise searched...

The main attraction is the cinema. Various establishments show the latest releases recorded in Madras in the Tamil language, but they are rarely full: in spite of security checks on the way in, there is still the fear that a bomb may have been planted.

A population taken hostage

The magnificent harbour in Trincomalee is deserted. Only the ferries and steamships which make the crossing to the Jaffna peninsula are moored there. Despite the military presence, people still fear a further terrorist strike. In September 1999, the Tigers sank a boat with 300 passengers on board. The acts of terrorism, carried out by the LTTE against a Tamil-majority civilian population, might appear inconsistent, but the terrorists are implacable in their attitude: anyone who submits to or acknowledges the authority of the government is a renegade punishable by death. There has been a crackdown on the Tamil leaders who are negotiating with the government of Chandrika Bandaranaike, but ordinary people who have had no choice but to negotiate with the armed forces on matters of transport or business are also regarded with suspicion. It is this fear, mixed with weariness, that pervades Trincomalee. The town has been plunged into what appears to be a hopeless state of waiting: waiting for the control which has been regained in the region to be followed by a political solution which would bring an end to the suffering of the people, who are psychologically being held hostage.

Trincomalee

It only takes a few hours to tour the town on foot.

The air of desolation that pervades Trincomalee is all the more striking because of its superb location. The town is situated on a narrow strip of land which stretches out into the Indian Ocean. To the east, the rocky Swami promontory plunges down into the sea, while to the west, the land curves away to embrace one of the largest natural harbours in the world.

Like all the maritime settlements on the island, Trinco has passed in succession through the hands of the Portuguese, the Dutch, and finally the British, who came here in 1795 from their footholds in what is now Malaysia. Five hundred metres to the south of the bus station stands the old gate of **Fort Frederick** *(security check at the entrance, where you have to leave cameras)*. Built by the Dutch in 1676, it is now graced by the British lion and unicorn, added in 1803 when it was given its present name in honour of Frederick, Duke of York.
These days the interior is a military zone: the old **Kachcheri** (headquarters of the colonial administration) and **Wellington House** are surrounded by barbed wire and army huts have sprung up here and there, under the giant banyan trees.

Entry to the fort is permitted because, at the far end, where the **Swami Rock** (The Rock of the Lord) drops down 100m to the sea, there is a *kovil* which is still in use, the **Tirukoneswaram**. Like Munneswaram near Chilaw, it is one of the most revered temples to Shiva on the island. The antiquities have long since disappeared, as the Portuguese destroyed the ancient place of worship, which was not rebuilt until the 1960s. Only the linga of the god remains, retrieved from the waters of the Indian Ocean by divers. Numerous other *kovils* are scattered around the town. The most popular is the **Kandaswami** temple, dedicated to Kali *(near the New Silverstar)*. Many worshippers assemble in its hypostyle hall, to the sound of trumpets and drums, during the three daily *pujas (7am, 12noon and 7pm)*.

Unlike the fort, the extraordinary natural harbour of the deserted **port** is a wretched spectacle. It forms a bay so broad that it encompasses a 53km stretch of the coast, riven with smaller inlets and dotted with small islands. Curiously, this port, which was active during the period of Kandyan rule, was under-exploited during the colonial era. During the Second World War it sheltered the allied naval forces. When the Royal Navy departed, a few years after independence, the port of Trinco went to sleep. Today, it represents an important stake in the conflict between Sri Lanka and the Tamil separatists. The former would like it to become the outlet for the developing regions of the lower Mahaweli. The latter dream of making it the capital of Eelam. Along the breakwater mole, young boys hunt for crabs and shellfish among the rocks. At the northern exit to the town, crows circle over the noxious rubbish tip which runs alongside the Uppuveli road.

Around Trincomalee

Nilaveli

16km north of Trincomalee. Access by bus or by "tuk-tuk". You should be aware that the sea here is at the mercy of the monsoon from the northeast from December-March, and jellyfish from the end of July.

Nilaveli used to be a dream seaside resort. Now it is nothing but a harbour at the end of the road (endless security checks). The journey from Trinco takes about 60-90min: the buses stop at five roadblocks at which all passengers must get off, their papers checked and their bags searched. All along the road, the opulent façades of villas, are riddled with bullet holes.

The region is populated by Tamil refugees, who have returned from the camps in Southern India where they had been based since 1995. They are largely dependent on the Integrated Food Security Project which issues them with rations of rice, financed by Western nations (mainly Germany). A few scratch a living from fishing; the majority from the onions which they cultivate in the sandy soil of the state allotments. The remainder of the economy consists of small commercial enterprises.

Nilaveli's **Beach** is deserted, and sea eagles circle above in search of prey. The hospitality of the people is all the more touching considering their extreme deprivation. Here, however, in contrast to the beach resorts of the west coast, they are not after your money. You might also come across people collecting shells, who sell what they collect to visitors staying in the guesthouses on Nilaveli Beach. Should you be interested, the fishermen will take you by catamaran to **Pigeon Island**, or to the tranquil waters of the **lagoon** which lap the beach to the northwest.

The hot springs of Kanniyai

8km northwest of Trincomalee. Access by "tuk-tuk". The springs are still popular with local holiday-makers. At the entrance to the site, a temple which is dedicated to Shiva is riddled with bullet holes, but that does not seem to deter people from taking the waters. Laughing and fully clothed, they crowd around the seven wells constructed on the thermal spring, splashing themselves from head to toe with the hot water (about 30°C).

Making the most of Trincomalee

Coming and going

By train – *The railway station* is on the way into town from the north, near the road to Uppuveli and Nilaveli. One train departs daily for Colombo Fort at 10.30am (journey takes 8hr). However, you should be aware that timetables can be disrupted by security checks. Regular travellers prefer the Intercity Express buses, which are faster despite the numerous security controls.

By bus – *The bus terminus* is in the town centre, to the north of the old stadium. Long-distance services depart in the morning: Intercity Express bus for Anuradhapura (3hr) and Colombo (6hr30min-7hr), via Habarana (2hr30min). The service to Batticaloa (138km to the south) no longer runs, the road being badly damaged by hurricanes and poorly maintained.

By car – Although access is permitted by the army allowing the bus services to run, you will not find a driver from outside the area willing to take you to Trincomalee: insurance cover excludes this area, and the Sinhalese are frightened of the Tamils, while Tamils living elsewhere are frightened of the Tigers.

ADDRESS BOOK

Bank / Currency exchange – *Bank of Ceylon*, Inner Harbour Rd, opposite the ferry departure point.

Post office / Telephone – *GPO*, Kachcheri Rd, near the New Silverstar. Various card-telephone booths in town. The ***Sundralingham Lodge*** has an IDD connection facility.

WHERE TO STAY

It is impossible to get accommodation in Trincomalee without a prior reservation.

• In Trincomalee

Under US$5

Sundralingham Lodge (formerly Votre Maison), 45 Green Rd, ☎ (026) 202 88 – 16rm. Set around a courtyard, with one communal bathroom. IDD telephone.

From US$5 to US$10

New Silverstar, 27 College St, ☎ (026) 223 48 – 8rm. A pleasant guesthouse; you have to book at least two weeks in advance. Incense coils available. Good food.

From US$10 to US$15

Rest House, 317 Dockyard Rd, opposite the Urban Council, ☎ (026) 222 99 / 225 62; reservation service in Colombo: ☎ (01) 91 03 56, Fax (01) 69 45 02 – 10rm. Fairly well maintained (mosquito nets). Prices do not discriminate against foreign tourists.

Seven Islands Hotel & Park (formerly Welcome Hotel), Orr's Hill Lower Rd, ☎ (026) 229 09 – 7rm. Hastily restored with a lick of paint, this place used to be a colonial lodge, magnificently situated on the port in Trincomalee.

The Villa, Orr's Hill Lower Rd, ☎ (026) 206 52 – 5rm. Poor value for money but pleasant restaurant.

• In Uppuveli

3km from the bus station, on the way out of town on the Nilaveli road. Not very clean, nor very attractive, but accessible on foot and provides a stopgap if you arrive too late to get to Nilaveli.

Under US$10

New Sea Lord, on Uppuveli beach – 4rm. Only four rooms in anything like reasonable condition. Food prepared on request.

• In Nilaveli

Between the 9th and 12th milestones, there used to be a seaside resort, of which all that remains are the establishments listed. Situated on the beach, they are linked to the main road running 1km to the west by tracks suitable for motor vehicles. A minibus shuttle service runs every 30min to the bus station in Trincomalee, but ceases to operate after 4pm.

From US$10 to US$15

Shahira Hotel, 10th Mile post, ☎ (026) 322 24; reservation service in Colombo: 436, Dematagoda Rd, Col 9, ☎ (01) 68 57 30, Fax (01) 69 45 02 – 17rm. Very well run. Rooms (with mosquito nets). Good local food.

From US$15 to US$20

Nilaveli Beach Hotel, 11th Mile post, ☎ (026) 220 71, Fax (026) 322 97, tangerinetours@eureka.lk, www.tangerinetours.com – 70rm. CC The luxury of this hotel, situated at the extreme northern end of Nilaveli beach, is almost out of place here, but it is showy rather than genuine. Excursions to Pigeon Island (675Rs). They will pick you up from Trincomalee station.

EATING OUT

Apart from the Seven Island hotel, none of the restaurants in Trincomalee come highly recommended.

OTHER THINGS TO DO

Feast days / Festivals – *Maha Shiva Ratri* is celebrated at the end of February-beginning of March in the temple on Fort Frederick point.

THE MALDIVES

Official name: Republic of Maldives
Area: 298 sqkm (1190 islands, 220 of which are inhabited)
Population: approximately 300 000
Capital: Male'
Currency: rufiyaa (MVR)

Setting the scene

E Valentin

Gangehi, a gem set in coral

A CHAIN OF ATOLLS

A veritable string of coral beads, the Maldives archipelago is one of the jewels of the Indian Ocean. Set in the eastern part of the ocean, about 650km south-west of Sri Lanka and 500km south of India, the 26 atolls which make up this island State stretch over 850km from north to south, but only 130km from east to west. These 1 190 low-lying islands – most of them are less than two metres above sea level – mark the centre of a chain of now submerged volcanoes, which stretches up to the Indian Lakshadweep Islands in the north and down to the British Chagos Archipelago in the southern hemisphere.

The coral archipelago

Originating from the Divehi word *atholhu*, **atoll** is almost certainly the only Maldivian word to be used throughout the world. It designates a ring of small islands linked to each other by a barely submerged barrier reef enclosing a lagoon with natural channels through which the waters flow into the ocean. Varying in shape, atolls follow the contours of old underwater volcanoes, now carpeted with coral formations which can reach a depth of around 30m at their centre.

A marine jungle

Coral is not a plant, as its form may lead one to believe, but the calcareous exoskeleton of marine animals, polyps (of the anthozoan class of marine coelenterates), which live in communities of several million individuals. **1 200 species** can be found in the Maldives, most of which live between the surface of the water and 30m below, although some, such as black corals, can grow at a depth of over 100m. In order to exist, they require highly oxygenated warm water, clear enough to enable the sun's rays to filter through. Most of the polyps live inside calcareous tubes, which grow between 2mm and 3cm per year, depending on the species. Living together in colonies, they appear in a great variety of shapes, such as plates, balls, rocks, cauliflowers, antlers, etc. During the daytime, only their external skeletons are visible, since these brightly coloured little animals only put out their tentacles to feed on plankton at night, turning these underwater fields into a kaleidoscope of multicoloured flowers in shades of yellow, orange, red and purple.

Some fish, such as the parrotfish, which has an actual beak, break this external envelope to feed on the polyps and discharge the calcium carbonate in the form of very fine, perfectly clean sand, like so many tiny white bones. It is this sand which gives the lagoons of the Maldives their turquoise green colour.

Uncertain origins

Charles Darwin was the first to describe **atoll formation**, in 1842. According to his theory, which was accepted by numerous scientists, the process of formation begins with the build-up of coral colonies along a partially submerged volcano. When the volcanic activity decreases, the original volcano slowly crumbles away under the effects of erosion, leaving the coral to continue its tireless climb towards the surface and the light. Several thousands or millions of years later, the central mountain completely disappears, leaving only the **barrier reef** to bear witness to its former existence.

Other studies credit a different theory, according to which atolls are the exposed part of a chain of underwater mountains.

SHELLFISH AND CORALS

The birth of an island

Currents, tides and variations in sea level are continually shaping these coral formations. Over thousands of years, part of the coral, reduced to dust by the waves or gnawed away by reef fish, is transformed into immaculately white sand. This accumulates in the shallow waters of the atoll, covering the seafloor and leading to the creation of **lagoons**. At low tide, the wind sweeps this sand into imperceptible dunes, which gradually form sandbanks and remain above water.

Seeds and coconuts, brought by migrating birds or the currents, wash ashore and easily take root thanks to the hot and humid climate (after a month in salt water, a coconut can actually start to grow as soon as it is "planted"). Gradually a small island starts to emerge and develop, unless it is submerged by the tides again. Most islands are formed in this way along the atoll's outer barrier reef and are elongated in shape, facing out onto the ocean on one side and into the atoll itself on the other. Other islands, often round in shape, come into being as a result of internal coral formations. The oldest ones are covered in **dense vegetation** of coconut palms, screw pines and tamarinds and, thanks to the flora and to the humus generated by it, have gradually managed to retain a thin layer of rainwater between the surface sand and the coral foundation. This fragile groundwater in turn enables vegetation to grow.

A living process to be respected

The Maldives have not yet completed their cycle of formation. As you travel around the islands, you will discover bare sandbanks, tiny islands with hardly any trees, and reefs which bear the promise of new islands to come within a few thousand years. But you will also come across islands which are slowly being eroded and carried away by the currents.

In order for the process of formation and regeneration to continue, it is absolutely essential to **protect the coral** from both pollution and physical attack. The government has therefore banned divers from touching the coral and boats are not allowed to drop anchor on it. The treatment of wastewater has become a top priority. Washing powder, fertiliser, household waste and even the waves caused by passing motorboats, which are unfortunately ever increasing in number, all harm this extremely fragile environment.

A new Atlantis?

Will the Maldives sink one day like the legendary city of Atlantis? According to some specialists, the rising sea level poses a threat to the small Maldive Islands, which are presently less than two metres above sea level. But this does not mean that the archipelago is doomed; with coral growth averaging between 1 and 3cm per year, the Maldives are also "rising". The increase in water temperature due to climatic changes (including the warm El Niño current) is already responsible for damaging some species of corals, but these are growing again and some are proving to be extremely resistant.

A changeable climate

The Maldives have an **equatorial** climate characterised by constant humidity and high temperatures ranging between 26°C and 30°C. However, the islands are subject to high winds accompanied by showers or **tropical storms**, which can last from a few hours to a few days, and can occur at any time of year.

Although we only distinguish between two main seasons in the Maldives, the summer monsoon and the winter monsoon – wrongly known as the wet and dry seasons – the Maldivians distinguish between 24, or 27 if we take the intermediary seasons into account. Each of these *nakaiy* lasts an average of around two weeks and has distinct characteristics according to whether or not it is windy, rainy or dry, and good for certain types of fishing, planting or harvesting. The climate is in fact very changeable, with rainy periods occurring during the winter monsoon and dry periods during the summer monsoon. The rainiest *nakaiy* are *Mula* and *Furuhalha* (10 December-5 January), *Dhinasha* (1-15 February), *Reyva* (25 March-10 April), *Buranu* (end of April), *Kheti* and *Roanu* (5 May-15 June), *Funoas* (1 -15 July), *Uthura* (5-20 September) and *Hey* (15-30 October).

Underwater gardens

D Noirot / HOA QUI

FLORA AND FAUNA

The flora of the Maldives, which is of the tropical and equatorial type, has n° particular specificity and is the same as on the other islands in the Indian Ocean. The wealth of the archipelago lies much more in its marine fauna, one of the most abundant in the world. *See also the illustrations on p 332-333.*

Exotic flavours and fragrances

With their sandy, poor and infertile soil, you might not think that the Maldive Islands had the right conditions for developing a very rich flora. However, by adapting to the local constraints, gradually some of the islands began to develop lush vegetation and some food crops.

It is not without reason that the **coconut palm** is the emblem of the Maldives. It is an impressively productive resource: the Maldivians eat the flesh of the coconut, drink its milk, use it for cooking and in traditional medicine; the wood is used in the construction of buildings and boats, the coir for weaving mats and ropes, and the leaves for making roofs and partitions. It is of such great importance that the Maldivians always judge the wealth of an island by the number of its coconut palms, and if someone cuts one down, they are obliged by law to plant another one immediately.

Although agricultural crops are rather poor and limited to a few vegetables, cereals and tubers, you will be able to enjoy a variety of succulent **tropical fruit** here, such as bananas, papayas, mangoes, watermelons and pineapples. This is also an ideal opportunity to try the fruit of the breadfruit and tamarind trees. There is no shortage of **flowers** either and you will be amazed by the beautiful hibiscus, frangipani, marsh mallows, bougainvillaea, and various kinds of arborescent shrubs, including screw pines, white *scaevola*, *tournefortia*, some bamboos and various mangrove formations in the largest and most humid island villages.

Fruits of the sun

E Valentin

Scant island fauna

The island fauna is far from being as rich as the marine fauna but, if you look carefully, you will see that the ground is crawling with all sorts of **crabs**, including the **hermit crab**. In your bungalow, you are bound to spot the inevitable **gecko**, a little lizard with an astonishing call, and suction pads on the ends of its legs. You have nothing to fear from these creatures; they are not at all dangerous and feed on mosquitoes, ants and every other undesirable insect. The islands are also home to bats of a rather impressive size – but don't worry, they are completely harmless and share the gecko's taste in food.

Over one hundred different species of bird live in the Maldives, but most of them are migratory. You may well come across a solitary **heron** (there are 13 known species) on the shore, standing motionless on one leg on the lookout for shellfish and small fish.

The only two kinds of terrestrial **snake** which exist in the archipelago are not poisonous, and like the small species of local frog, they are only to be found on the larger islands where agriculture is practised.

The crocodile packs its trunk

The story goes that at the beginning of the 1980s, the villagers of one of the northern islands were rather surprised one morning to find a crocodile on their beach. Still clinging to the trunk of a coconut palm and drained of its strength, the animal, like the tree, had been torn from Kerala on the Indian coast during a storm and had drifted 500km to the Maldives before being washed ashore. Fact or fiction? History does bear witness to such "voyages" by animals which, in the same way as the seeds, came to "populate" the Maldives. But nobody knows what became of the crocodile.

Creatures of the sea

Millions, maybe even billions of creatures frequent the waters of the Maldives. The marine life here is one of the richest in the world. Since underwater fishing is strictly prohibited, the sea creatures are relatively trusting and it is possible to get very close to them.

A rainbow of colours

A mask and snorkel are all you will need to begin your discovery of a fascinating world inhabited by a multitude of brightly coloured **reef fish**. Some of them live in groups, such as the yellow- and black-striped pyjamafish, triggerfish and jacks. They move around in shoals and will fearlessly brush past you, barely making an effort to get out of your way. Others live in pairs, such as damselfish, longfin bannerfish, angelfish and butterflyfish. Near the surface, you will come face to face with barracudas, snappers, emperorfish, fusiliers, groupers, wrasses and parrotfish, as well as scorpionfish, soldierfish, cardinalfish, hawkfish, boxfish and porcupinefish. At the heart of a **sea anemone**, you may catch a glimpse of a family of clownfish, which lives there and protects it. You might even spot an octopus lurking between two corals.

During your underwater outings, you will also encounter **sponges** (there are around one hundred species in the Maldives), starfish, sea urchins, sea fans and holothurians. These "sea cucumbers" are actually large worms, which swallow sand and feed on the minuscule organisms which live in it, before discharging it again in pristine condition. You are almost certain to pass a solitary **stingray**, which will swim around you, intrigued, or a family of manta rays, gigantic

Pratt-Pries / DIAF

The prodigious coconut palm

underwater "birds" which weigh several tonnes and can span up to 8m; you will be able to observe their silent and fascinatingly beautiful flight as they glide by gracefully in the distance. Lastly, some sharks and **marine mammals**, dolphins or cetaceans, can be found in this part of the ocean, and even inside the atolls themselves.

Experienced divers who venture into deeper waters with tanks may catch sight of a giant **turtle**, busily grazing on coral or swimming alongside a Napoleon wrasse. This enormous but harmless creature will follow you out of curiosity as long as you remain on its territory. You could easily reach out and touch it, but it's best not to: they are covered in protective mucus, a sort of second skin which provides a natural defence against germs and bacteria.

A delicate balance in need of protection

It is now absolutely forbidden to either touch or feed animals in the Maldives. Doing so would contribute towards destroying a fragile natural balance or modifying the feeding habits of certain species. Batfish, which had developed a taste for bread, have now entirely disappeared from certain lagoons. Although most reef fish are harmless, often indifferent, sometimes inquisitive or even bordering on the sociable, the underwater world is far from being a tamed environment. Many animals have developed formidable natural defences against their neighbours or an unsuspecting visitor. If you are unfamiliar with these waters, and with the spawning, egg-laying or incubation periods of the thousands of different species which inhabit them, it is best to stay on the safe side. The rules are simple: never touch anything in the water, and move away as soon as you spot any sign of aggression.

Forewarned is forearmed

Cone shell	This shellfish has a poisonous dart, which can reach its target from dozens of centimetres away. In some species, it can even pierce diving gloves. Once it breaks the skin, it causes an often fatal muscular and respiratory paralysis.
Sea urchin	Certain species have highly poisonous spines.
Stingray	Difficult to make out against the sandy seafloor, stingrays have a formidable tail spine. But fortunately, they will head off the other way if they spot anyone approaching, so don't hesitate to stamp on the ground or splash the water as you move around.
Sea anemone	Gives a nasty sting. Never touch one.
Stonefish	Very difficult to discern on account of their camouflage, they have dorsal spines which make them very dangerous. They can be found at various depths and all over the seafloor.
Scorpionfish	This term covers all fish which have a dorsal fin covered with erectile spines (including, in particular, the lionfish). Most are red – a clear sign of danger underwater – and their sting can be fatal.
Giant clam	These giant molluscs with their extraordinary fluorescent colours can ensnare an inquisitive finger for hours on end. They can weigh up to several dozen kilograms and you would need a crowbar to move one. You may well hear the story of the inattentive swimmers who put their feet down between the two shells of a clam and drowned, imprisoned on the seafloor.
Morays	Certain species are fairly sociable, but others will attack if you pass too close to their retreat. When diving, always keep your distance from an underwater "wall", their favourite habitat. They don't easily let go of their prey and, because they feed mainly on dead creatures, bites quickly become infected.
Surgeonfish	This fish gets its name from the one or two pairs of scalpels on either side of its tail base. These stand up when the fish are excited (if you feed them, for example). They can brush past you with no risk, and as long as you don't try to touch one, you have nothing to fear.
Jellyfish	Although they can give a nasty sting, they are not really dangerous.
Nudibranch	Some of these extravagantly coloured undulating sea slugs can sting.
Coral	Several types of coral can cause painful burns.
Porcupinefish	Don't mess with this fish, which inflates its body with water into the shape of a ball when feeling threatened. You will often hear true stories of careless divers sliding a finger into its wide-open mouth – only to leave it there for good.
Sea snake	Ten times more poisonous than a cobra, this snake thankfully never attacks humans.
Sharks	Always an impressive sight, but generally harmless. The smaller ones, which can be found in the lagoons, and even very close to the shore, feed on starfish, shellfish, shrimp and tiny fish. You are only likely to encounter the largest and most aggressive ones (white-tip reef shark or tiger shark) when scuba diving in channels or in the ocean. Your divemaster will be able to recognise them and avert an unpleasant encounter.

COMMON FISH

Leopard Moray
(Gymnothorax undulatus)
Longfin Bannerfish
(Heniochus acuminatus)
Teardrop
Butterflyfish
(Chaetodon
unimaculaus)
Clown Triggerfish
(Balistoides
conspicillum)
Parrotfish
(Scarus)
Emperor Angelfish
(Pomacanthus imperator)
H Choimet

Napoleon Wrasse
(Cheilinus undulatus)
Meyer's Butterflyfish
(Chaetodon meyeri)
Lionfish or Turkeyfish
(Pterois volitans)
Moorish Idol
(zanclus cornutus)
Clownfish or Anemonefish
(Amphiprion percula)
H Choimet

LEGEND AND HISTORY

1153	The Maldives convert to Islam following the lead of their king, Dovemi Kalaminja.
1518	The Portuguese open a trading post.
1645	Beginning of Dutch domination.
1796	The British set up a protectorate in the archipelago.
1932	First constitution, limiting the sultan's powers.
1942	Second constitution.
1953	Abolition of the sultanate. Establishment of the first republic, under the presidency of Amin Didi. The sultanate is reinstated during the same year, and Farid Didi becomes the 94th sultan of the Maldives.
1956	Signing of a treaty with the British, who lease Gan Island for 100 years.
1959	Proclamation of the Republic of the United Suvadiva Islands.
1965	The Maldives become independent on 26 July.
1968	Proclamation of the second republic. Amir Ibrahim Nasir is elected president.
1978	Election of Maumoon Abdul Gayoom, following Nasir's resignation.
1998	At the age of 61, Maumoon Abdul Gayoom is elected president for a fifth term.

The official recorded history of what is now known as the Maldives began in 1153 with the conversion to Islam of the king, **Dovemi Kalaminja**, who was thereafter known as Sultan **Mohammed Ibn Abdullah**. It is common knowledge in the Maldives that the islands were once ruled by kings and queens, but their existence falls more within the realm of legend. The history of the archipelago before the 12C is still largely unknown, and several centuries remain shrouded in mystery.

Origins

Some statues of Buddha, a few mounds and *dagoba* ruins indicate a very ancient human presence, but until recently, these vestiges were still being completely ignored, if not destroyed for being pagan relics. Numerous documents attest to this pre-Islamic history: Ptolemy mentions the Maldives in his description of the world in 150 AD; Pappus of Alexandria also mentions them at the end of the 3C, as do the Gujarati travellers in the 4C and some Arabic texts, of which the oldest one, by Sulaiman the Merchant, dates back to 900 AD.

On the spice route

Because of their geographical location, the Maldives are a very ancient place of passage. In order to get from the Andaman Sea or the Bay of Bengal to the Arabian Sea, ships have to sail south of Sri Lanka, avoiding the shallow and reef-filled Palk Strait which separates India from what was formerly Ceylon. The Maldives are thus unavoidable.

On this spice route, the archipelago offered safe mooring, coconut wood, rope fibre and some freshwater wells, so it is hardly surprising that the Indonesians, Egyptians, Arabs, and perhaps even the Phoenicians, landed on Maldivian shores. Through the centuries, various mariners settled there, mixing with a population which was doubtless very limited on account of the scarce natural resources of these tiny islands.

A Maldivian melting pot

Many researchers have devoted their energies to exploring the origins of the Maldivian people, gradually drawing an outline of the various waves by which the archipelago was populated.

Sun worshippers and Hindus – **Thor Heyerdahl**, who was invited to inspect some archeological sites in 1985, discovered some strange sculptures in the south of the archipelago confirming the existence of a very ancient **solar cult**. According to him, 4 000 years ago some peoples, who may have come from north Indonesia and were following the sun around the equator, landed in the Maldives in the north of Gan Atoll. There they built sun temples and carved votive disks and strange statues. Little remains of all of that today, except for some rare vestiges scattered over a few islands (most of which are unfortunately closed to tourists) and a collection which is on display in a small room in the National Museum in Male'.

The Norwegian explorer moreover demonstrated that this was followed, between 2500 and 1500 BC, by an **Aryan wave** originating from northwest India and the Gulf of Cambay, which was responsible for introducing Hinduism and certain traditions, such as ear piercing. The great seafaring merchants from the cities of the **Indus Valley**, Lothal and Baruch, carried on their trade up to Bengal, along the coasts of Malaysia and Indonesia, perhaps even as far as China, and their trade routes ran along the Maldives from north to south. They were the first to bring back **cowrie shells**, which, for centuries, were used as currency. However, all they left in the islands was a few statuettes, some of which can be found in the museum in Male', and they built their Hindu temples on the former sacred sites of the sun worshippers. They left at least one word behind: "*bara baru*", which means "good" in Gujarati, Urdu and Maldivian.

The Tamils – In 1970, **Clarence Maloney** recorded evidence of a Tamil influence and the presence of **Dravidians** from southeast India. Proof of their passage can be seen in the roots of proper nouns and terms relating to the family, sea and navigation, such as the word *dhoni*, which designates the traditional boat of the Maldives. Several dances and customs are also similar to those of Tamil Nadu.

The Sinhalese – The British archeologist, **Henry Bell**, was shipwrecked in the Maldivian atolls at the end of the 19C, as he was travelling to take up his post as civil commissioner in Ceylon. He returned to the islands on several occasions, where he discovered a very strong **Buddhist influence of Sinhalese origin**. He situated this new population wave, coming from Ceylon, between 500 BC and the beginning of the Christian era. Oral tradition and one of the rare known chronicles, the *Loamaafaana*, engraved on copper sheets in the 12C, recount the story of an exiled prince and princess who founded the first Maldivian dynasty. Thor Heyerdahl believed them to be Nagas, Sinhalese aborigines, who had been banished from India by Sinhala Aryans. Indeed, it would appear that a branch of this highly developed people did land in the Maldives at the beginning of the Christian era.

A question of style

The former inhabitants of Giraavaru Island (in North Male' Atoll) consider themselves to be the descendants of the Tamil visitors. They have a few distinctive features: for example, the women have white-embroidered collars on their dresses and wear their hair in a chignon on the left side, whereas the other Maldivian women wear it on the right. The descendants of this ethnic group were forced to abandon their island when the number of men fell below 40, which is the minimum number required to keep a mosque in activity. Today, only a few hundred of them remain, and they almost all live in Male'. As for their little island, it has been converted into a tourist resort.

A book of copper sheets

A legend, engraved on copper sheets in the 12C, links the dynasty's founding myth to the advent of Islam; an account which lightly glosses over ten centuries of history... "At that time, a prince called Koimala Kaloa, undertook a voyage to the Maldive Islands, accompanied by his wife. They reached the island of Rasgetheemu and stayed there for some time, waiting for more favourable winds. When they learnt that the couple were of royal descent, the inhabitants asked them to stay and proclaimed them king and queen of their island. Later, they settled in Male' with the consent of the Giraavaru people and had a son, Kalaminja. The latter, who was a Buddhist, ruled in Male' for 12 years before converting to Islam. He later left for Mecca and his daughter became sultana. She had a son, also called Kalaminja, who married a local girl. All the sultans of Male' are of their stock."

What is certain is that Buddhism replaced Hinduism for over a thousand years, before Islam became the official religion. A few traces from this long-forgotten time still remain: the old form of writing (of many everyday words, particularly in the agricultural sector) and rice cultivation. The Buddhists, in turn, used the old temples of the sun worshippers and Hindus to build *dagobas* and stupas (shrines), of which only a few shapeless mounds remain today.

The bitter struggle for independence

It took six centuries of domination, rebellions, alliances and betrayals for the Maldives to finally free themselves of foreign authority and obtain their own independent republic.

Conversion to Islam

The Arabs knew the Maldives well before the beginning of the Christian era. As an important port of call on their trade routes from the 9C, the atolls, which they called *Dibajat*, served as natural harbours, providing shelter from storms and protected by their rare and difficult channels.

According to legend, a Muslim saint, a certain **Abdu al-Barakaat**, managed, in the name of Allah, to rid the population of an evil spirit *(djinn)* which had been terrorising the inhabitants of Male' and demanding the sacrifice of young virgins. By this feat, he convinced the Maldivians of the benefits of his religion, and they all converted following the lead of their sultan. So much for the legend. It is more likely that he used forceful means to rid the island of Gujarati merchants or Sinhalese pillagers who regularly came to raid Male'.

The Moroccan explorer, **Ibn Battuta**, who spent a year in the Maldives in 1343, left us the most complete record of this period, and his description of the

Account of a 14C traveller

After leaving Ceylon, it took Ibn Battuta ten days to reach the Maldive Islands, which he was later to describe as "one of the wonders of the world". In his account of his journey, he remarked on how all the islanders, rich or poor, walked barefoot; how the streets were swept and shaded by trees; how, at times, one had the impression that one was strolling through a garden. At that time, the Maldivians were using cowrie shells as currency, exchanging them for rice from the Bengalis. Battuta had already seen this form of currency being used during his travels in Mali and Gao, where the exchange rate was 1 150 cowrie shells for 1 gold dinar. The relative freedom of Maldivian women was also something which Battuta remarked upon: he found it rather odd that the islands should be ruled by a woman (Khadija), and that neither she nor the other women covered their heads; they wore their hair swept to one side and nothing but a sort of long loincloth covering them from their waist to their feet.

archipelago almost holds true today. His legacy includes several stories about the ease with which one could marry and divorce there – which is still very much the case – as well as the portrait of a society which barely changed at all up until the mid-20C.
In 1602, a Frenchman, **François Pyrard de Laval**, was shipwrecked on the island of Fulhadhoo while on his way to the trading posts of India, and ended up staying there for 5 years. The account of his voyage, which was subsequently published, matched Ibn Battuta's description.

The Portuguese and Dutch trading posts

The Portuguese arrived in the sultanate at the beginning of the 16C, with the aim of protecting their trade routes between Goa and Ceylon. Coming up against the ruling dynasty of the **Ali Rajahs of Cannanore**, they instigated a coup d'état and placed a protégé on the throne, who, in 1518, granted them authorisation to open a **trading post**.
The Dutch arrived in 1645, on their way to Indonesia. They took advantage of the conflicts between the sultan and the Portuguese – who wanted to convert the Maldivians to Christianity – to supplant them, thereafter managing this protectorate from Ceylon for 150 years. They left barely any trace of their presence, except for the four cannons which can still be seen at the harbour in Male'. History recounts that **Thakurufaanu**, the island chief of Utheemu in the north of the archipelago, joined forces with them to deliver Male' from the hands of the Portuguese, with just a handful of soldiers. He later became sultan and was revered as a national hero.
The Ali Rajahs, now overthrown, seized the pretext of the annexation of Minicoy in the Lakshadweep Islands to form an alliance with the Moplahs of Malabar and, in turn, attack Male'. However, the Maldives, which had signed a treaty with France, called upon Dupleix's troops based in Pondicherry to help repel the invaders.

The British protectorate

In 1796, the British landed in the Maldives to take control of this unavoidable passage between the Indian Ocean and the Bay of Bengal. The Dutch ceded the archipelago to them and they set up a **protectorate** and established a military base on Gan Island, in the south of the archipelago. But soon increasing economic difficulties, the weakness of certain sultans and the arrival of hordes of Indian merchants gave rise to great tension and riots in Male'. In the face of mounting pressure, the British imposed a constitution in 1932 limiting the powers of the sultan, **Shamsuddin III**. The latter tried in vain to regain power but was removed from office and replaced by **Nuruddin II**, who was himself supplanted in 1942, after the adoption of the second constitution.
In 1953, the sultanate was abolished and the Maldives became a **republic**. The new president, **Amin Didi**, immediately adopted a series of very unpopular measures, such as a ban on smoking and the nationalisation of the fisheries, which led to widespread rioting, rapidly causing him to be overthrown.
As a result, the **sultanate** was reinstated on 7 March 1953, with **Farid Didi** becoming the 94th sultan of the Maldives. In 1956, he signed an agreement with the British, leasing Gan Island to them for 100 years in exchange for an annual tribute of £2 000. However, just one year later, the newly elected prime minister, **Amir Ibrahim Nasir**, breached this treaty and called for the return of the island.

E Valentin

Sultan Mohammed Farid Didi

The inhabitants of Gan, for whom the British presence was a source of wealth, rebelled against this decision and, supported by two neighbouring atolls, unilaterally proclaimed the **Republic of the United Suvadiva Islands** in 1959. They elected a president, Abdulla Afif Didi, but he was forced to flee to the Seychelles when Ibrahim Nasir sent the army to quash the insurrection. The British, who were accused of having supported the rebellion, agreed to hand Gan back within 30 years and pay an annual tribute of £100 000. In fact, they were soon to put an end to their protectorate on these rebel islands: on 26 July 1965, the Maldives became **independent**.

The republic

The sultanate was abolished following a referendum, and on 11 November 1968, **Amir Ibrahim Nasir** became the first president of the reinstated republic. This republic did, however, suffer some teething troubles.

In 1972, Nasir took over full personal control of the country. Although he was the first to open the islands up to tourism – the Maldives had around 1 000 visitors that year – he was seemingly the only one to profit from it. In 1974, Sri Lanka, the principal buyer of dried "Maldive Fish", cut back on its imports, causing the market to collapse. Rioting broke out throughout the country and Nasir responded by having shots fired into the crowds. In 1978, faced with increasing popular discontent and fearing for his life, he resigned and went into exile in Singapore.

The Maldives' ambassador to UNO, **Maumoon Abdul Gayoom**, was then elected president and, in 1980, after an attempted coup d'état, the officials of the former regime were ousted. The young president threw himself into developing his country. He encouraged tourism and archeological research, and forged links with many other States. He nationalised the Japanese fisheries of Lhaviyani Atoll, built hospitals and schools, and fought to gain recognition for the Maldives on the world stage. Having defied two successive coup d'état attempts, he was triumphantly re-elected in 1983, and again in 1988, after the military intervention of India, which, at his request, had intervened to thwart a final attempt to overthrow him. He was elected president again in 1993, then in 1998, at the age of 61, for yet another five years and a fifth term of office.

THE MALDIVES TODAY

The hierarchy of political power

Power is exercised at three levels. The **island chief** *(khateeb)* represents the State within the community for which he is responsible. He takes the census, ensures that laws and decrees are applied, and is the guardian of public safety. He is also responsible for the nearest desert islands. He reports to the atoll chief every day, formerly by walkie-talkie, but nowadays by fax or e-mail.

The **atoll chief** *(atholhu verin)*, who is appointed by central government, manages the islands within his district. He is in daily contact with the government agencies which are accountable to central government in Male', and transmits the most noteworthy information to them. So don't expect to pass unseen if you try, in spite of the ban, to land on one of the islands which are closed to foreigners; nothing goes unnoticed here.

The **president** is the head of State. He is chosen every five years by the Citizens' Council *(Majlis)*, which is composed of 48 members. Each of the 20 administrative atolls (including Male') elects two Council members, the remaining eight being appointed by the president. Once the president has been nominated by the Council, his election is ratified by national referendum.

A fragile economy

Although cowrie shells were the country's principal source of wealth for centuries, the Maldivian economy nowadays relies essentially on fishing and tourism.

Dried or smoked tuna was the archipelago's main export – in particular to Sri Lanka – and its essential source of income up until 1971. Now the fish is frozen or canned and sold in the Far East and in Europe. The canning factory in Lhaviyani Atoll produces over 50 tonnes of canned food per day. **Fishing** represents almost 20 % of GNP thanks to the export of mackerel, tuna, bonito and sea bream.

The Maldives were opened up to **tourism** in 1972. Currently, almost one hundred island resorts, and as many small safari boats, welcome **350 000 tourists per year**. By the end of 1998, the hotel infrastructure of the Maldives was able to offer almost 14 000 beds, but the Ministry of Tourism is planning to open new high-capacity island resorts and make a further 10 000 beds available by the year 2010. These developments are, however, being undertaken with great caution, since the preservation of the ecosystem and the traditional structures of Maldivian life are considered a priority. The island resorts are leased for 21-year periods and the government closely monitors their exploitation (quality of services, wastewater treatment, coral and coconut palm protection). The majority of visitors to the islands are Italian (80 000 tourists in 1998), followed by the Germans, British, Japanese and French.

Tourism, which represents nearly 30 % of national income, has become the country's **principal source of activity**. Better still, it generates numerous spin-off jobs in the service sector, cottage industries, boatbuilding, business, construction and crafts sectors. The tourist sector employs around a quarter of the population of the Maldives. The growth of tourism does, however, dictate the massive and costly importation of durable goods, fuel and foodstuffs; the islands' agricultural resources remain limited, despite recent attempts to develop them, including the creation of a poultry island.

Meeting the people

E Valentin

The magical innocence of children

DAILY LIFE

Since the end of the 1960s, tourism and the development of new forms of transport and communication have turned the Maldivians' age-old habits upside down. However, if you have the opportunity to set foot on one of the island villages, you will see that the traditional way of life is still very much in evidence there.

A precarious environment

The population of the Maldives has increased considerably over the last few decades on account of an improved standard of living and a significant drop in the infant mortality rate. Today, the 300 000 inhabitants are spread out between 220 **island villages** and the capital, Male', which alone houses one third of the population.

Set on the largest and most fertile "lands", these villages have, for many generations, housed communities of between 100 and 1 000 people. Their main resources come from fishing and a small number of food crops, but only on those islands where the groundwater is sufficient to enable crop irrigation and provide enough drinking water. These conditions explain why most of the islands, particularly the smaller ones, are uninhabited. So don't be surprised if you see some apparently idyllic islands that are still deserted, while others hold over a thousand inhabitants.

The communities in which the islanders live are extremely close-knit, which can largely be explained by the communal aspect of village life. The precariousness of their environment calls for rigorous organisation and common work rules for fishing, land clearing and farming, as well as for the construction of houses, breakwaters and boats. There is also very little contact between neighbouring islands.

Traditional Maldivian house

Y Keller

The Maldivian habitat

Life in the Maldives is very much centred on the family. On average, each family is made up of between six and eight people, with several generations living together under the same roof on their island *(raa)*.

Outside Male' the habitat has, in almost all respects, remained rather traditional. The houses, which are sometimes no more than simple palm huts, are more often than not made of brilliant white coral stone. Their roofs, traditionally made of woven coconut palm leaves, are sadly now often being replaced by corrugated iron. If you have the opportunity to visit one of them, you will see that the inside is just as stark, very soberly furnished with beds, benches and cupboards made of wood – from the coconut palm, naturally. The kitchen and hearth are always located in an outbuilding, set apart at the end of the enclosure, the sitting room being the main room in the house, where visitors and guests are entertained. Before entering anyone's house, don't forget to take off your shoes and wash your feet using water from the large earthenware jar intended for this purpose. To make the most of the sea breeze, the Maldivians often prefer to relax under a canopy or arbour, where they are often to be seen chatting together, sitting cross-legged on swing-seats.

Home, sweet home...

Whatever the size of the island, the land belongs to the State, which is why even when a Maldivian builds a house, he never really owns it. He is not allowed to sell it under any circumstances and can only pass it down to his heirs. Moreover, in principle you have to have lived on an island for ten years before you can build your own house there. This ancestral rule is certainly often inconvenient but is very rarely flouted in the remote atolls.

The villages stretch over 200 to 500m along white sand paths, kept immaculately clean by the women of the village, who sweep them every day.

Social organisation

Each island village is administered by a *khateeb*, who represents central government, but his official role is counterbalanced by an elected Organisation Committee which manages everyday matters, school, social life and economic development. Two other characters play an essential role: the religious leader and judge *(gazee)* and the schoolteacher.

Although the old caste system disappeared along with the sultanate in 1968, a few traces remain in the language and everyday behaviour. The *Sefalu* aristocracy, which stems from the old ruling families and their courts, still has a certain influence in government, religious matters and business.

Islam: State religion and a way of life

The citizens of the Maldives are all **Sunnite Muslims**, and the influence of Islam extends to civil, religious, criminal and political matters. As the State religion, it is effectively the cornerstone of society, and the 1969 constitution was proclaimed in the name of Allah. The precepts of the Koran are scrupulously obeyed, but there is no sectarianism. You will probably notice that each island has its own mosque, but you should bear in mind that they are not tourist sights but places of worship.

The Maldivians have **five prayer times** every day: at dawn, midday, in the middle of the afternoon, at sundown and at nightfall. The prayers can be recited anywhere, at home, in a *dhoni*, even under a coconut palm, but almost everybody goes to a mosque for the **Friday prayer**. Maldivian Islam has incorporated

An island prison

A few years ago, a German tourist murdered his French girlfriend in a hotel in Male'. He was sentenced to lifelong deportation to a small uninhabited island, where, as in all the best pirate stories, he was left with just a few fishhooks, a dhoni and basic tools. He managed to survive, ended up converting to Islam and, just as in every story with a happy ending, he married a young woman from a neighbouring island, had lots of children and lived happily ever after!

a few local customs, such as the wearing of a charm necklace. And in return, a verse of the Koran is almost always to be found next to the sharks' teeth in amulet boxes.

The Ministry of Justice and Islamic Affairs deals with disputes, and judges the offences and crimes referred to it by the atoll chiefs or *khateebs*. Everyday matters are handled by *gazees*, the religious leaders of the villages or atolls. The most serious offences are punished by exile to a desert island or remote atoll.

The main stages of life

Births are followed by seven days of celebrations, during which time a name must be chosen for the newborn. The infant's father or uncle traces a sura (a chapter of the Koran) in honey, which is then symbolically given to the baby to eat. The infant's head is shaved and the family distributes food and alms to the poor. Circumcision takes place at around 7 years old and constitutes an important landmark in a boy's life, since it marks his passing into the adult world. After the operation, the young boy is laid out on a camp bed beneath a cotton canopy in the centre of the main room of the house. Here he will stay put for seven days, while the father and uncles entertain guests who have come to offer their congratulations.

The islanders tend to get married at a very early age: 15 for girls and 18 for boys. However, the **wedding** is a mere formality and the ties of matrimony are anything but eternal. Indeed, the Maldives is the country with the highest rate of divorce and remarriage in the world. In 1970, the researcher Clarence Maloney recorded 85 separations for 100 marriages. There is no big wedding ceremony and couples are united in the strictest privacy, in the presence of only the *gazee* and two witnesses. Polygamy – which, under Islamic law, allows a man to have up to four wives – is not common. When **death** occurs, the Maldivians don't cremate the body. They wash it and purify it seven times, then bury it on the day after the death. The deceased is buried in a shroud, with only his or her face uncovered, and turned towards Mecca. Women do not attend the burial, prayers or funeral ceremonies, which last seven days. After 40 days, another funeral service takes place, followed by a meal and more alms-giving. Families commemorate the anniversary of the death of their loved ones for many years.

I do I do I do

Although the government, gazee and courts are trying to limit these practices, it is still extremely easy – and commonplace – to divorce in the Maldives: the husband merely has to say "I divorce" three times and inform the religious leader for the marriage to be terminated. In the case of separation, the wife keeps her dowry but must wait three months before remarrying. During this period, her former husband has to take care of her needs. If a couple divorces, the husband and wife must each remarry three times before they can marry each other again. If they break up again, the cycle remains the same and can be repeated ad infinitum. The tradition appears to be of Dravidian origin and helps to explain why some Maldivians have been married to each other more than fifteen times.

Pratt-Pries / DIAF

Studying in the open air

School in the atolls

The population of the Maldives is very young; the number of inhabitants has almost doubled in 30 years and the current rate of increase stands at 3% per annum. Each island village boasts at least one **primary school**, which is just like every other school in the world, except that the schoolyard is covered in sand and the classrooms stand open to the sea breezes. The schoolchildren all wear blue and white uniforms but often go barefoot, at least in the villages. Children from smaller neighbouring islands which have no school either travel to school by boat every morning or if the island is very far away they often board.

For their **secondary education**, which lasts four years, young Maldivians have to go to the atoll capital or to Male', where lessons are given in both *dhivehi* and English. The government has created a School of Hotel and Catering Services and developed **further education** in business and industry, but some Arab and Muslim countries offer grants to students from the Maldives to study at their universities.

The status of women

In the islands, most of the men work as fishermen, merchant sailors or on the staff of island resorts which are often far away. They are frequently away for several months at a time, which explains why the women play such an important role. They run the home, take care of their children's education, work, ply hammer and trowel to build the women's mosques and even build boats, which is actually a predominantly female activity. They vote, take part in all social activities, coordinate numerous women's committees and play a very active part in Male' in administration, tourist organisation, the developing industries and new technologies. The government even has a **Ministry of Women's Affairs**, which is extremely rare in a Muslim country.

As was noted by Ibn Battuta in his 14C chronicles, Maldivian women don't wear a yashmak, just a simple scarf. They can choose whom they marry, keep their maiden name and divorce quite easily, with the consent of their husband. They have almost exactly the same rights as the men, except in matters of inheritance, where their share is less than that of the children or other collateral relatives.

The Westernisation of Male'

Life in the capital differs greatly from that on the island villages. The traditional way of life is rapidly disappearing in Male', which is as much a result of **over-population** as of **urbanisation** and "Western-style" development.

Here, communities are not as close-knit and morals are slackening, women are waiting longer before getting married, and extended families no longer live together under the same roof. Up-to-date means of communication, tourism and the new technologies and industries are changing their vision of the world. Although Islam is still omnipresent, women can move around freely, go to restaurants, window-shop and are more frequently seen without the traditional scarf. You may even spot a few Maldivian businesswomen, looking more like their counterparts in Malaysia and Dubai than their cousins back on the island villages.

Which direction is Maldivian society taking? Many inhabitants of Male' refuse to accept this **Westernisation** and the inevitable standardisation which it entails. Although the government is opening up a few atolls to foreigners, it is never in a great hurry to do so and always proceeds with caution; many islands are thus set to remain forbidden territory for many more years to come. Just like the country itself, Maldivian society, which has remained unchanged for centuries, is very fragile and the Maldivians are doing everything in their power to protect their islands and their way of life.

A village scene

E Valentin

TRADITIONAL FESTIVALS

You are not likely to get the opportunity to attend many festivals, either because they are religious or because they take place in the evening on island villages, which are inaccessible to foreigners after 6pm. However, the resorts organise Maldivian evenings every week, bringing in musicians and dancers from neighbouring islands. Although these events are organised for tourists, they are still relatively authentic.

The main Muslim festivals

Religious festivals are extremely important in the lives of the Maldivians, but will go totally unnoticed on your island resort or on board your safari boat.

Ramadan takes place during the ninth month of the Muslim calendar. This major festival is devoted to prayer and meditation. From sunrise to sundown, everyone must fast and abstain, but everything comes to life in the evening when the Maldivians meet up to feast with their families or friends. If you're staying in a hotel in Male' or Gan, you might be lucky enough to be invited to join in the celebrations: a light meal, *tharaavee*, consisting of "short eats", is served at around 7pm, with a more copious supper, *haaru*, being served around midnight. The end of Ramadan is marked by the **Kuda Eid** festival, with prayers, offerings, meetings, dancing and banquets.

Muslim calendar

As in every country of Muslim persuasion, religious life is governed by the Hegiran calendar, based on the twelve months of the lunar year. Each one begins with the new moon and is made up of 29 or 30 days, which means that the lunar year only contains 355 days and is about ten days ahead of the solar year. Consequently, the dates of the religious festivals always vary from one year to the next.

Bodu Eid is in commemoration of the sacrifice of Abraham (twelfth month). Each family kills a chicken and gathers together to exchange wishes and gifts. This festival falls on the day of the pilgrims' departure for Mecca.

The **Mawlid festival** marks Prophet Muhammad's birthday (third month) and is celebrated by a meal to which every family, however poor, invites a relative living alone or a friend who is just passing through.

Folk dancing and music

The best way to appreciate the diversity of Maldivian dances is to go to one of the festivals organised in Male'. This will also be your only chance to see some of the very beautiful women's dances; only men's dances are performed on the island resorts, and often by the Maldivian employees who work there.

The most famous one, the **Bodu Beru**, is named after the ray-skin drums which provide the accompaniment, and is a very rhythmic dance which can induce a trance. A less common dance is the **Thaara**, performed to the beat of tambourines; two rows of eleven musicians face each other, with the dancers in between. According to tradition, the dancers reach a state of ecstasy by beating their foreheads and lacerating their skulls. The **Langiri**, also known as the "stick dance", is performed by between 12 and 24 teenagers beating their sticks *(langiri dhandi)* to the rhythm of their chant.

The **Raivaru** is an ancient and very moving chant. This solitary improvised recitative is a long poem, delivered *a cappella*, which can sometimes be heard during the afternoon siesta, on a fishing island, or from your boat, in the moonlight. **Modern music** is starting to invade the capital and the island villages.

DO'S AND DON'TS

It is entirely possible to stay in the Maldives without ever meeting any Maldivians other than the employees of your island resort, but that would be a shame. Take advantage of a trip out to an island village or to Male' to get to know this proud people, who are "pious and sincere" according to Ibn Battuta, "subtle and ingenious" according to François Pyrard, sometimes shy, often very reserved, but who still respect their tradition of hospitality, which they unfortunately have little opportunity to extend to foreigners.

Do's

Try to follow the example of the Maldivians: they speak softly, never get angry and take life at a leisurely pace.

They will look at you openly, but never stare or display too much curiosity. You will never be asked about your private life or country, and you will rarely be pestered by sellers, even on the most touristy island villages – which should, of course, be avoided. So for your part, you should also try to be discreet, respectful and extremely polite. Both men and women should wear clothes which cover their legs and shoulders: the Maldivians are extremely modest.

Maldivians usually shake hands upon meeting and leaving, but a mere nod does suffice to say "hello" or "goodbye", even between members of the same family or very close friends.

Female visitors should always behave like a "good Muslim woman", with dignity, modesty and restraint.

Don'ts

– Never visit an island village in swimwear, shorts, sleeveless top or bandeau and don't wear any see-through clothes: you risk being firmly escorted back to your boat.

– Avoid haggling all-out for just a few *rufiyaa*: haggling is an art, and should not be an insult to poverty.

– Don't take too many photographs or remain glued to your video camera: although they are Muslims, the Maldivians do tolerate the photographic representation of the human being, but within reasonable limits. Always be sure to request the permission of the person concerned before filming or photographing anyone, be it man, woman or child, and don't insist if they refuse.

– Male visitors should avoid addressing a woman or girl if there is a man they could speak to instead. At all events, show them the utmost respect.

– Never enter a house without having been invited in; and if you are invited inside, make sure you don't forget to take off your shoes and wash your feet before entering.

– Don't forget that the left hand is considered impure here, so avoid touching people, animals or food (dried fish, fruit, etc) with it.

– Lastly, don't try to impose "your" vision of the world on the people you speak to. The Maldivians jealously guard their way of life, their isolation, customs and religion, and will quite happily keep their distance from foreigners, albeit with great politeness. Our clothes, behaviour, bits and pieces (cameras, watches, etc) and grand "universal" theories tend to provoke irony and suspicion rather than envy and admiration.

Smiling Maldivian faces

LANGUAGE

The official language is Divehi. It is spoken throughout the archipelago, with only a few small nuances in pronunciation between the north and south.
However, the Maldivians who are in contact with the tourists all speak English and you will have no difficulty in making yourself understood in Male', in your resort or aboard your safari boat, during excursions, shopping expeditions or on any administrative business.

Divehi

Related to **Elu**, an ancient form of Sri Lankan **Sinhalese**, Divehi has been enriched over the centuries by words mainly from Asia, left by the sailors, merchants and colonisers who landed on the islands. Being a sea-faring people, the Maldivians themselves brought home some words and expressions from the countries they visited. The result is a learned mixture of Sanscrit, Pashtun, Tamil and Persian influences – traces left by visitors from the north – but the language also contains borrowings from countries of the Indian Ocean, Malaya, Madagascar and Africa. Later, with the arrival of Islam, Divehi adopted many words of Arabic origin.
The oldest form of the language, **Evala Akuru**, bears a great resemblance to the Sinhalese language used in the 3C BC under the reign of the Buddhist emperor Asoka. But a more developed form, **Dives Akuru**, emerged in the 14C and survived until the 17C.
The modern Divehi script, known as **Thaana**, and heavily influenced by Arabic, only became widespread after the departure of the Portuguese. Thaana Divehi is written from right to left, and its alphabet – which resembles both Sinhalese and Arabic – contains 24 letters, with vowels marked in the form of accents above or below.
Divehi is a relatively simple language, and is written by 92.6 % of the Maldivian population. However, it contains **three levels of language**, the legacy of an extremely hierarchical society, which was still very much in evidence only a few years ago.
The first level is **reethi bas** or "nice language", the language of the elite, which is used for official texts and by the media. The **second level** is used for speaking respectfully to a person in a superior position, an elderly person or a foreign guest. The third level corresponds to **common Maldivian**, spoken between people from the same social class or when addressing subordinates.

Other languages

English is the common language and is spoken on all the tourist islands, both by the Maldivian employees and those from Europe or Australia. English, German, Italian, French and Japanese are spoken or understood in all the resorts, at the very least by a few foreign employees.
Some island resorts, which have entered into agreements with European tour operators, have a dominant language. This is how Dhiggiri and Alimathaa in Vaavu Atoll, or Nika in Ari Atoll, for example, came to be known as "Italian" islands, because most of the clients are Italian, and Baros, Kurumba and Kanifinolhu in North Male' Atoll are known as "German" islands. Rihiveli, in South Male' Atoll and the Club Med island are resolutely French-speaking, and the Le Méridien is-

land is also sure to have a strong French influence, since this hotel chain has long been French owned. However, all it takes is for the concessionaire to change or a new agreement to be signed with another tour operator for the dominant language on the island to change too. In fact, all the foreign employees speak at least two, and often three languages, and it is not unusual to find four or five languages being spoken on these islands, which are attracting an increasingly international and varied clientele.

E Valentin

Campaign for literacy

The language of the sea

To describe an environment as unique as the Maldives, it is only natural that the language should develop some original words specifically to describe all the characteristics of the archipelago's physiognomy. Thus there are several words to describe a coral reef, according to its size, shape, position in relation to the island, etc. So you will find it very useful to be familiar with this vocabulary if you intend to explore the islands and ocean depths.

Maldivian diving terms

Kandu	A channel in an atoll's barrier reef, through which the ocean flows and mingles with the waters inside the atoll. Channels are generally excellent places for scuba diving, especially at high tide when large predators are on the lookout for fish, and rays and turtles gorge themselves with plankton. The currents can be very strong here.
Faru	A circular reef located on the outer edge of an atoll. The "walls" and cave formations make this a good place for scuba diving, but it is often not such a good spot for swimming or skin diving.
Faro	A circular or elongated coral reef, located inside the atoll or on its inner edge. Generally of considerable size.
Thila	Smaller than a faro, the thila is very near the surface of the atoll and is a very good site for diving, with or without a tank. Its centre is made up of sand, which gives the water its emerald colour. Over the centuries, sand accumulates there and its level rises, eventually leading to the creation of a new island.
Giri	This word designates a small thila, which is sometimes nothing more than a coral "lump".
Veli	A sandbank, which may eventually – after a few thousand years – turn into an island, if the tides and monsoons don't wash it away.
Finholu	A sandbank which already has a few shrubs.

MALDIVIAN CUISINE

A trip to Male' or a "Maldivian evening" organised by your resort is an ideal opportunity to taste the traditional cuisine, which is highly original and full of subtle flavours.

Maldivian flavours...

Rice and fish are staples in the Maldivian diet and are cooked, flavoured and presented in a multitude of different ways. Most of the dishes are presented in the form of balls or rolls, often fried, sometimes baked in the oven.

"Short eats" *(hedhikaa)*, which you can enjoy in one of the little harbourside restaurants in Male', consist of savoury or spicy side dishes and small delicacies, such as fillets of fish rolled in fine batter *(gulha)* or in the form of a sausage *(keemia)* and fried, or fish tartare mixed with egg and steam cooked *(kulhi bis)*. During your stay, you are bound to come across the famous Maldivian speciality, *Hiki mas*. This is the fish that can be seen all over the islands drying in the sun for days on end before being smoked. *Theluly bombukeyo* is another of the archipelago's specialities, consisting of finely sliced fruit of the breadfruit tree, fried in boiling oil. Certain variations of this recipe suggest replacing the fruit by fish *(theluly kavaabu)*, and adding chillies *(theluly mas)*. For dessert, try *bondi baiy*, a delicious milk and rice pudding, or *roas pan*, fine slices of bread, dipped in egg and sugar, then fried in a frying pan.

The Maldivians drink a lot of steaming weak **tea**, but make sure you try the more exotic *suji*, a beverage made from **coconut milk**, with sugar, crushed nuts, cinnamon and cardamom.

...and cosmopolitan cuisine

The resorts offer **international cuisine**, with some Italian, Japanese, French and English specialities, according to the predominant nationality of the clientele. The quality varies from one extreme to the other with some islands, such as Rihiveli, Sonevafushi and Cocoa, being renowned for the excellence of their cuisine. On average, the food is generally very acceptable, well balanced and made with a good variety of fresh products. Except for the fish, which is caught locally, and the bread and pastries which the resorts bake themselves, all the products are imported from Sri Lanka, southern India, Europe or Singapore.

Breakfast and lunch consist of copious and varied buffets, offering a wide selection of fruit, cakes and cereals. Dinner is served at the tables, but you will always have the option of a candlelit dinner for two on the beach, in front of your bungalow, or even on a nearby desert island.

Hiki mas, the famous Maldivian speciality

Practical information

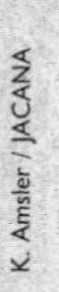

K. Amsler / JACANA

A diver's paradise

BEFORE GOING

• Time difference

The Maldives are 5hr ahead of Greenwich Mean Time, 10hr ahead of Eastern Standard Time, 11hr ahead of Central Standard Time, 5hr behind Sydney, Australia, and 7hr behind Auckland, New Zealand. However, some resorts have introduced their own local time in order to make the most of the sunshine, so you may have to add a further one or one and a half hours to the standard time difference.

• International dialling

Dial international + 960 + the number you wish to call.

• When to go

This country has an **equatorial climate** marked by high temperatures ranging between 26°C and 30°C and by violent winds, followed by showers or tropical storms, which can occur at any time of year. However, the Maldives have two main seasons. During the **summer monsoon** (from May-June to September-October), very humid winds blow from the southwest. During the less humid **winter monsoon** (from October-November to April-May), the winds blow from the northeast. The driest months are between February and April, at least in the central atolls which are open to tourists. So this is theoretically the best time to go.

The sun rises at around 6am and sets at around 6pm all year round, with a half-hour time difference between the north and south of the archipelago.

	J	F	M	A	M	J	J	A	S	O	N	D
rain *(mm)*	90	20	58	104	193	213	146	186	161	175	218	186
sunshine *(hr)*	244	267	293	266	221	200	216	206	223	240	219	217

• Packing list

Clothing

Take light **cotton** clothing, a hat and sunglasses. On your island resort or on board your safari boat you will probably only need swimwear, shorts and a T-shirt, but take along a pair of trousers and a light shirt or dress for the evening. Nudity is forbidden, even on the island resorts. Moreover, you must be decently dressed, with shoulders and thighs covered, when visiting the island villages or Male'.

Diving equipment

Fins, masks and snorkels are available on the islands, but do take your own with you if you are used to them or wear a mask specially adapted to your eyesight. It is also advisable to wear a pair of plastic shoes when swimming to avoid injuring yourself if you should inadvertently step on some coral. *See the "Health and safety" section.*

• A trip for everyone

Travelling with children

If you are taking children with you, be sure to choose an island with a shallow lagoon and remember to take along their own fins, masks and snorkels since the resorts might not have any in their size. It would be a shame for them to miss out on the sights of the coral reefs, especially since children under 12 are not allowed to go scuba diving. All the resorts have at least a few larger bungalows which can accommodate an additional child's bed.

Travelling alone

People travelling alone have nothing to fear in the Maldives – women are highly respected here – but will have to pay a 50 % supplement in the island resorts or on safari boats for a private bungalow or cabin.

Disabled travellers

It is possible to use a wheelchair on the sandy island paths, but make sure that your bungalow is at ground level. There will always be someone to help you into a *dhoni* or onto the plane (stairs are used for boarding). But remember: no dogs, not even guide dogs, are allowed in the Maldives.

• Address book

Tourist information

The only official tourist information centre which exists outside Male' is the Maldives Government Tourist Information Office, Münchener Strasse 48, D-60329 Frankfurt / Main, Germany, ☎ (069) 274 0440, Fax (069) 2740 4422, maldivesinfo.ffm@t-online.de

Embassies and consulates

In Europe – High Commission, 22 Nottingham Place, London W1U 5NJ, ☎ (020) 7224 2135, Fax (020) 7224 2157, maldives.high.commission@virgin.net

In the USA – Permanent Mission of the Republic of Maldives to the United Nations, 820 Second Avenue, Suite 800C, New York NY 10017, ☎ (212) 599 6195, 599 6194, Fax (212) 661 6405, mdvun@undp.org, www.undp.org/missions/maldives

For further information, travellers can also contact the Embassy of Maldives in Sri Lanka, at 25 Melbourne Avenue, Colombo 4, Sri Lanka, ☎ (01) 586762.

• Formalities

ID, visas

You must have a **passport valid for at least 6 months** following the date of your return. Tourist visas are required and are issued free of charge on arrival at Male' airport upon presentation of valid travel documents. Visitors may also be required to show proof of sufficient funds. Visas are valid for 30 days and can be extended for a period of three months, for a fee of approximately US$39.

Customs

When entering the country, remember that it is a Muslim State, so don't bring any pork, alcohol or magazines showing scantily-clad men or women with you. It is also strictly forbidden to take any shells, corals, turtle-shell objects, fish or invertebrates (starfish, sea urchins, etc) out of the country when you leave, even if they are stuffed or mounted.

Vaccinations

No vaccinations in particular are required unless you are travelling from Africa, in which case you must be vaccinated against yellow fever. But do make sure that you are up-to-date with your boosters for the ordinary vaccinations against tetanus, polio, hepatitis A, diphtheria and typhoid.

• Local currency

Cash

The currency is the **rufiyaa** (MVR), which is worth approximately US$0.08 and is divided into 100 *laree*. However, you will pay in **dollars** in your resort or on your boat.

Currency exchange
Don't change too much money, because you will only need a few *rufiyaa* for your purchases in Male' and the island villages you visit. You can change money at the airport, in the capital or at your resort.

Credit cards
The tourist islands accept all the major bank cards.

• Spending money
You are most likely to find the best prices through a travel agency, but if you want to book direct, remember that the cost of living is very high in the Maldives, and that very few resorts (except for Rihiveli and Lily Beach) offer unlimited supplies of drinking water or sports activities free of charge. Make sure you know all the details before you book, because the prices can as much as double from one resort to another.

Full-board **accommodation** in an island resort costs between US$80 and US$200 per person per day, with the return airport transfer costing between US$80 and US$250, depending on the location of your resort.

A **light meal** in a small restaurant in Male', consisting of five savoury and spicy meatballs, three sweet rolls and a soft drink, will set you back around thirty *rufiyaa*.

To give you an idea, here are a few average prices: mineral water, between US$2 and US$5 per bottle; scuba diving, between US$40 and US$50 per dive; windsurfing, US$10 for 1 hour; catamaran sailing, US$25 for 1 hour; water-skiing, US$25 for 15min; fins, mask and snorkel hire, between US$10 and US$15 per day; boat trip, between US$15 and US$40 depending on the distance; trolling, US$10; deep-sea fishing, US$200 for half a day.

• Booking in advance
You can book your trip in advance directly with the island resorts or their agents in Male', and make a deposit by bank card.

• Travel / health insurance
Always make sure you find out whether emergency and repatriation insurance is included in the price of the holidays offered by your travel agent. Also check with your bank, because certain bank cards entitle you to insurance cover abroad. If you are going on a safari, you will have to take out a special insurance policy.

GETTING THERE

• By air
There tends to be a majority of European visitors to the Maldives, with very few Australians and Americans. There are effectively no convenient routes from the USA and Canada, which are literally on the other side of the world, and travellers from these countries must take connecting flights in Europe or Asia. Flights from London – none of them direct – take around 14 hours.

The following airlines operate flights to Male': Austrian Airlines, Condor Flugdienst, Emirates, Indian Airlines, LTU International Airways, Lauda Air, Malaysia Airlines, Martinair Holland, Singapore Airlines, SriLankan Airlines.

Scheduled flights

Prices when purchasing your ticket directly from the airlines are generally very high, so you will be better off going through a travel agent. But remember that there are also seasonal variations in the prices.

From the UK

The following airlines fly to Male' from London:

SriLankan Airlines, ☎ (020) 8538 2000, offers 9 flights per week via Colombo.

Emirates, ☎ (020) 7808 0033, operates 6 flights per week via Dubai.

Lauda Air, ☎ (0845) 601 0934, flies to Male' once a week, on Tuesdays.

From Australia

SriLankan Airlines, ☎ (02) 9667 2750, flies from Sydney to Male' via Colombo 3 times per week.

Emirates, ☎1300 303 777 or (02) 9279 0711, also operates flights via Dubai.

From the USA and Canada

Royal Jordanian and Kuwait Airways have two and three flights respectively per week to Colombo from New York. From there, travellers can take one of the many connecting flights to Male' *(see below)*. Another option is for travellers to fly via Singapore, where there are daily connections to Male' (Singapore Airlines flies to Male' every day, SriLankan Airlines several times per week).

Charter flights

You will find some flights which depart from Milan, Rome, London, Amsterdam, Madrid and Barcelona.

From Colombo (Sri Lanka)

SriLankan Airlines and Emirates between them operate up to 6 flights to Male' per day. The flight takes around 1hr and costs approximately US$84 for a single ticket and US$178 for a return.

From Trivandrum (India)

Indian Airlines operates daily flights between Trivandrum and Male', which means that you can tie in a trip to the Maldives with a journey to southern India. Price: US$75 for a single ticket and US$150 return.

Airport

Hulule is Male's island airport, and the transfer to the capital by boat shuttle takes only 15min and costs around US$5. The resorts or their agents will confirm your return tickets for you. Airport tax is US$10 and facilities at the airport include currency exchange, left-luggage office, bank, post office, shops, duty-free and a bar.

• By boat

Cargo ships sail from Colombo, Singapore and Tuticorin (southern India) to Male' several times per month, but no regular shipping line officially accepts passengers. So it's all down to luck. For further information or if you want to try to persuade a captain to take you on board, contact the harbour master's office at these ports when you arrive.

• Package deals

Rather than trying to organise a trip to the Maldives by yourself, you will find it much easier to ask a travel agent to book your plane tickets, accommodation or safari for you. The traditional travel agencies in Europe offer a wide choice of packages put together by tour operators.

United Kingdom

A two-week holiday (return flight and full-board accommodation, excluding sports activities) will cost you anywhere between US$1 600 and US$3 000 depending on the island and the time of year. Numerous tour operators in the UK offer holiday packages in the Maldives. You can book through your local travel agent and some, including the following, can be contacted directly:

Cosmos – Cosmosair plc, Wren Court, 17 London Road, Bromley, Kent BR1 1DE, ☎ (0800) 015 9528 (Reservations), Fax (0161) 819 7029, www.cosmos-holidays.co.uk

Goldenjoy Holidays – 36 Mill Lane, London NW6 1TQ, ☎ (020) 7794 9767, Fax (020) 7794 9850, reservation@goldenjoy.co.uk, www.goldenjoy.com

Hayes & Jarvis (Travel) Ltd – Hayes House, 152 King Street, London W6 0QU, ☎ (0870) 898 9890 or (020) 8222 7801, Fax (020) 8741 0299, res@hayes-jarvis.com

JMC Holidays Ltd – 29-31 Elmfield Road, Bromley, Kent BR1 1LT, ☎ (0870) 555 0440, www.jmc.com

Kuoni Travel – Kuoni House, Deepdene Ave, Dorking, Surrey RH5 4AZ, ☎ (01306) 747000, Fax (01306) 744497, book@kuoni.co.uk, www.kuoni.co.uk

Thomas Cook Holidays – 12 Coningsby Road, Peterborough, PE3 8XP, ☎ (08705) 666222 or (01733) 418450, Fax (01733) 417784, tch@thomascook.com, www.thomascook.co.uk

Tropical Places – Sussex House, London Road, East Grinstead, West Sussex, RH19 1HJ, ☎ (0800) 083 6662, Fax (01342) 330771, sales@tropical.co.uk, www.tropical.co.uk

Australia

Island Affair Holidays – ☎ 13 10 11 (Australia-wide reservations), siaholidays_au@singaporeair.com.sg, www.singaporeair.com.au

This company is part of the Singapore Airlines group and offers package tours to the Maldives via Singapore either directly or via licensed or AFTA travel agents. A holiday will cost you between approximately US$770 and US$2 225 for a five-night stay, depending on the resort and time of year.

United States and Canada

Very few people travel to the Maldives from North America because of the distance involved. However, **Impex Holidays Maldives** *(see below)* is affiliated with Impex Delaware, Inc, and has a contact number in New York: Fax and Voicemail (212) 658 9044, holidays@mal-dives.com

Travel Wizard, Inc, 5675 Lucas Valley Road, Nicasio, CA 94946, USA, ☎ 800 330 8820, Fax (415) 662 2585, sunshine@tropicalislandvacation.com, www.tropicalislandvacation.com

There are also some companies in the United States which offer diving holidays *(see "Diving holidays" below).*

Specialists in the Maldives

You may like to try the following agencies, based in the Maldives:

AAA Travel & Tours Pvt Ltd – STO Trade Centre 03-02, Male', ☎324933 / 322417, Fax 331726, trvlntrs@aaa.com.mv, www.aaa-resortsmaldives.com

Aqua Sun Maldives Pvt Ltd – Luxwood -1, Boduthakurufaanu Magu, Male', ☎ 316929, Fax 316849, aqua@dhivehinet.net.mv, www.aquasun-maldives.com

Atoll Vacations Pvt Ltd – H Hithigasdoshuge, Hithafinivaamagu, Male', ☎ 315450, 315451, Fax 314783, 321344, atvac@dhivehinet.net.mv, www.atollvacations.com

Capital Travel & Tours Pvt Ltd – M Feylige 2nd Floor, Mirihimagu, Male', ☎ 315089, Fax 320336, capital@dhivehinet.net.mv, www.capitaltravel.com, www.capitaltravel.net, www.faiymini.com (cruise)

Crown Tours (Maldives) Pvt Ltd – H Sea Coast, Boduthakurufaanu Magu, PO Box 2034, Male', ☎ 322432, 312832, info@crowntoursmaldives.com or sales@crowntoursmaldives.com, www.crowntoursmaldives.com

Deens Orchid Agency Pvt Ltd – H Deens Villa, Meheli Goalhi, Male', ☎ 327451, Fax 318992, orchid@dhivehinet.net.mv, www.orchid-maldives.com

Global Voyages Pvt Ltd – 1st, Floor, G Penzeemaage, Alikilegefaanu Magu, Male', ☎ 317537, Fax 315293, info@global-voyages.com, www.global-voyages.com

Impex Holidays Maldives – Ma Kaaminee Hiya, Kaaminee Magu, Male', ☎ 310355, Fax 310697, holidays@mal-dives.com

Inner Maldives Pvt Ltd – H Lady Bird, Kasthoori Magu, Male', ☎ 315499 / 326309, Fax 330884, intermal@dhivehinet.net.mv, www.innermaldives.com

Intourist Maldives Pvt Ltd – Ma Feerumurangage, Dilbahaaru Magu, Male', ☎ 325273, Fax 327203 / 317466, info@intourist-maldives.com, www.intourist-maldives.com

Island Holiday Maldives Pvt Ltd – PO Box 2068, 1st Floor, H - Karanka Villa, Male', ☎ 320856 / 324282, Fax 316272, holidays@dhivehinet.net.mv

Jetwing Maldives – 6th Floor, Aifaan Building, PO Box 20111, Male', ☎ 314037 / 312970, Fax 314038, jetwing@dhivehinet.net.mv, www.jetwing-maldives.com

Lif-Sham Travel & Tours – H Vatheenige, Gulisthaanu Goalhi, ☎ 325386 / 326879, Fax 320381, lift23@dhivehinet.net.mv, www.lifsham-holidays.com

Muni Travel & Trading Pvt Ltd – Ma Carpentervilla, Shaheedali Hingun, Male', ☎331512, Fax 331513, munitrav@dhivehinet.net.mv, www.munitravels.com

Sea N See Pvt Ltd – M Sunny Coast, 2nd Floor, Shaheed Ali Higun, Male', Post Box 20179, ☎ 325634 / 320323 / 320324, Fax 325633, seansee@dhivehinet.net.mv, www.manthiri.com

Skorpion Travel Maldives Pvt Ltd – G Kudhifeyruvaadhee, 1st Floor, Majeedhee Magu, Male', ☎327443 / 320521, Fax 327442, skorpion@dhivehinet.net.mv, www.skorpion-maldives.com

Star Holidays Co Pte Ltd – H Haadhil, Sosun Magu, Male', ☎ 330819, Fax 331572, starco@dhivehinet.net.mv, www.starholidays.com

Sun Travel & Tours Pvt Ltd – H Maley-thila, Meheli Goalhi, Male', ☎ 325975, Fax 320419, suntrvl@dhivehinet.net.mv, www.sunholidays.com, www.vilureef.com

Vista Company Pvt Ltd – Travel & Tourism Service, Bld *no* 4 / 3, 1st Floor, Faamdheyri Magu, Male', ☎ 320952, Fax 318035, sales@vista-maldives.com, www.vista-maldives.com

• Diving holidays

You can book diving holidays through your travel agent or some of the above tour operators, but you may also like to contact the following companies, which are among those specialising in the organisation of live-aboard or resort-based diving safaris:

Euro-Divers – Petersbrunnstrasse 17, A-5020 Salzburg, Austria, ☎ (0662) 84 30 38, Fax (0662) 84 84 38, market@euro-divers.com, www.euro-divers.com

Harlequin Worldwide Travel Limited – Harlequin House, 2 North Road South Ockendon, Essex RM15 6AZ, Great Britain, ☎ (01708) 850346, info@harlequin-holidays.co.uk, www.harlequin-holidays.co.uk
Hayes & Jarvis (Travel) Ltd – *(address as above)*, ☎ (0870) 898 9890 or (020) 8222 7801, Fax (020) 8741 0299, diving@hayes-jarvis.com
Island Dreams, Inc – 8582 Katy Freeway, Suite 118, Houston, TX 77024, USA, ☎ (800) 346 6116 or (713) 973 9300, Fax (713) 973 8585, Ken@islandream.com, www.islandream.com
Regal Holidays – 22 High Street, Sutton, Ely, Cambs CB6 2RB, Great Britain, ☎ (0870) 220 1777, Fax (01353) 777897, info@regal-diving.co.uk, www.regal-diving.co.uk
Seafari Adventures SRL – Via F Frisi 20, 20052 Monza, Italy, ☎ (039) 329338, Fax (039) 328946, seafari_maldives@iol.it, www.seafariadventures.com
Tropical Adventures – PO Box 4337, Seattle, WA 98109, USA, ☎ (206) 441 3483 or (800) 247 3483, Fax (206) 441 5431, dive@divetropical.com, www.divetropical.com

Dive Operators in the Maldives

ProDivers Maldives – Kuredu Island Resort, Lhaviyani Atoll, ☎ 230343, Fax 230344, info@prodivers.com, www.prodivers.com
Sea Explorers Associates Pte Ltd, Waarey Willa, Izzudheen Magu, Male', ☎ 316172, Fax 316783, seaexplo@dhivehinet.net.mv or seafari_maldives@iol.it, www.seafariadventures.com

• Sailing / yacht charters

South Asian Charter – Boduthakurufaanu Magu 35, Male'. Reservations in Belgium ☎ (03) 233 04 18, Fax (03) 232 98 87, Mic@sacharter.com, www.sacharter.com
Some of the above tour operators also organise yacht charters, and the Maldives Tourism Promotion Board has a list of available cruise boats on its Web site *(see Address book below)*.

• Whale and dolphin watching safaris

The Whale and Dolphin Company – PO Box 2074, Maldives Post Ltd, Male', ☎ / Fax 327024, anderson@dhivehinet.net.mv This company runs 7- to 14-day live-aboard whale and dolphin watching safaris around the atolls and is the only one offering this activity in the Maldives.

The basics

THE BASICS

• Address book

Tourist information in Male'

The **Maldives Tourism Promotion Board** in the Bank of Maldives Building on Marine Drive, ☎323228, Fax 323229, mtpb@visitmaldives.com, has maps of the country as well as a list of local travel agencies and resorts, and you can visit its Web site at www.visitmaldives.com Hulule airport also contains a small tourist information office.

Embassies and consulates

There are no foreign embassies in the Maldives and the few local honorary consuls have very limited powers. If necessary, you can contact the embassies of the countries represented in Colombo, Sri Lanka. *See "Embassies and consulates" in the Practical information section for Sri Lanka, p 81.*

Airline companies

The following companies which operate services to the Maldives all have agencies in Male': SriLankan Airlines, Balair, Emirates, Indian Airlines and Singapore Airlines.

• Opening and closing times

Remember that shops and offices close for 10 to 15min during prayer times.

Banks

8am-1.30pm; closed on Fridays and Saturdays.

Post offices

7.30am-6pm; closed on Fridays.

Shops

The shops are open every day from 9.30am to 11pm, except on Fridays, special prayer day, when they open at 2pm.

Restaurants

12pm-2pm / 6pm-9pm (except Fridays). Some restaurants do, however, stay open later.

Offices

The working day begins at 7.30am and ends at 2.30pm. The Maldivians don't work on Fridays or Saturdays.

• Post offices

There is a post office in Male' on Chandanee Magu, and on Gan Island. But all the resorts will post your letters and cards for you. It takes anywhere between five and twenty-one days for airmail to reach its destination from Male', and although the mail service is fairly reliable, it is advisable to send any parcels or enclosures by registered mail.

• Telephone and fax

In Male', card-operated phones can be found everywhere (phone cards are sold in the shops). If you need to use a telex, fax, e-mail, or maritime radio service, contact the Maldivian telecommunications operator, **Dhiraagu**, which also hires out mobile phones. It costs 34 *rufiyaa* per minute to call the UK and 50 *rufiyaa* per minute to call the USA, Canada and Australia during peak hours (8am to 8pm), with the rates dropping to 27 *rufiyaa* per minute for the UK and 40 *rufiyaa* per minute for the USA, Canada and Australia during off-peak hours (8pm to 8am). Add 2 *rufiyaa* to these rates for all mobile calls. Local calls cost between 50 *laree* and 3.5 *rufiyaa* per minute, depending on distance.

On the islands, an increasing number of resorts offer international direct dial (IDD) phones in the rooms. If this is not the case at your resort, you can make phone calls from reception. You should also be aware that most of the resorts do not allow mobile phones to be used outside the rooms. All the resorts have fax machines and often e-mail facilities.

• Public holidays

1 January	New Year's Day.
26 July	Independence Day, celebrating the departure of the British.
3 November	Victory Day, in remembrance of the coup d'état thwarted in 1988.
11 November	Republic Day commemorates the advent of the second Republic in 1968.
10 December	Fishermen's Day.

In addition to these public holidays the Maldivians celebrate **Huravee Day** (anniversary of the victory over the Malabars from India in 1752), **Martyr's Day** (commemoration of the assassination of Sultan Ali by the Portuguese in 1558), **National Day** (first day of the third month of the lunar calendar), as well as the religious festivals, but their dates vary each year according to the Muslim calendar.

GETTING AROUND

The *dhoni* is the most common form of transport in the Maldives. Few of them still use sails, but even with an engine they don't travel any faster than 15kph. Speedboats are rare, because they are expensive and use a lot of fuel. A few large combined cargo and passenger ships sail between Male' and the main islands, but the atolls at which they call are not open to tourists.

Island Aviation Services Limited also operates a small network of domestic lines, but, again, the islands to which services operate are not open to foreigners. The only exception to this rule is the Male'-Gan flight, which takes passengers to the southernmost island, where there is just one hotel, the Ocean Reef Club.

• Getting to your island resort

The resorts will organise transport between Male' airport and your lodgings and will come to meet you at Hulule. These transfers, which will be included in your package deal if you book through a tour operator, cost between US$80 and US$250 return.

By boat

The island resorts of the North Male', South Male' and Vaavu atolls are reached by speedboat. Depending on the distance, it will take you between 30min to just over an hour to travel between the airport and your resort. A culture shock is guaranteed as you step directly from the comfort of your air-conditioned plane into the boat which awaits you at Hulule. You may find the change in climate a little sudden after a night of travelling, but you will immediately fall under the spell of these stunning coconut palm-covered islands set in emerald lagoons. But a word of warning: make sure you're well protected against the sun as soon as you step off the plane.

Domestic flights

The island resorts in Ari Atoll and the atolls which have recently opened up to tourism organise transfers by **helicopter** or **seaplane** with the Hummingbird, Seagull, Air Taxi or Sun Express companies. This means that a resort which would be five or six hours away from the airport by boat, is now only around twenty minutes away. If you are lucky enough to travel to your island by air, take a window seat and don't forget your camera: the view of the atolls from the air is simply unforgettable.

Don't miss the boat!

As a rule, transfers from the airport to the resorts are only made during the daytime. This means that unless you arrive at Hulule airport before 6pm, you will have to spend your first night in a hotel in Male'. Many return flights leave Hulule at night. Your island resort will, therefore, arrange for your transfer in the afternoon so that you arrive in Male' around 6pm. This will leave you with an evening to spend in Male', an excellent opportunity for you to explore the city, its shops and little restaurants. Your hotel rep will look after your luggage for you in the meantime and take you to the airport by boat shortly before the departure of your flight.

• Island hopping

There are no regular links between the island resorts, each one only being linked to the capital. So if you want to stay on two different islands, you will have to return to Male' airport in order to make your way to the next island.

There is always the option of hiring a private boat, but the prices are exorbitant. To give you an idea, a speedboat will cost you between US$300 and US$400 per hour, according to size and speed, and a *dhoni* around US$100 per hour.

The best way to see the islands is, therefore, to take a **safari** on board one of the boats which sail around the atolls open to tourists. You can also hire a **sailing dinghy** in Male', with or without a skipper, but because of the surface-level coral formations which make navigation so dangerous, you will have to follow a set route and will only be able to sail in the two Male' atolls.

• On your island resort

All you will need to get around is your feet – and you won't even need your shoes. Bicycles are available on some of the larger islands.

• Organised tours and excursions

The resorts organise boat trips to the island villages. Alternatively, you can hire a *dhoni*, and the skipper will introduce you to the village chief. Although some of the island villages are very close to the island resorts, it is forbidden to go there alone by catamaran or sail board.

Most of the resorts also offer flights over the atolls by seaplane.

• In Male' and Gan

People get around by foot in Male'. On Gan and the islands of Addu Atoll, which are linked by a 16km-long causeway, you can rent bicycles or take a taxi. A ride from Gan to Rujjehuraa, the most distant island, costs less than US$10.

BED AND BOARD

• Where to stay in the Maldives

You will not be at total liberty to organise your holiday in the Maldives exactly as you wish, and you are very unlikely to be able to escape the tourist circuit. You will have the choice of staying in one of the archipelago's 87 island resorts, one of the ten hotels in Male' or in the hotel on Gan Island. Or you may opt to stay on board a safari boat, but there will be **no possibility for you to stay in one of the island villages**. This option was outlawed as a result of various unhappy experiences. Although foreigners are free to go to any island village within the "tourist zone" (limited to the central atolls), they cannot eat, drink or sleep there, and must leave before sundown. You will need a special permit to set foot on an island which is closed to tourists or to stay on a fishing island. To obtain such a permit, you must first of all have been invited by one of the inhabitants of the island in question, then go through the proper administrative channels. This can take months, sometimes years, and even then your application might end up being refused!

The invaders

At the beginning of the 1980s, some villagers tried to open family guesthouses on their islands to accommodate foreign visitors, but the cultural gap between the islanders' traditional way of life and the practices of the western tourists proved to be enormous. The tourists would take ten showers a day, drink alcohol, walk around half-naked, and expect to be served meat at every meal. On some of the islands, the limited groundwater was used up within a matter of days, as was the village's poultry stock and the very rare supplies of firewood. Several islands consequently became uninhabitable for many years for want of fresh water, and had to be abandoned by their inhabitants.

• Various categories

Most of the 87 island resorts are located in the South Male', North Male' and Ari atolls. The principle is simple: **one island**, **one resort**, and no Maldivians live there other than the employees, who have separate living quarters. These tiny islands range in length from a few hundred metres to 1 or 2km, and are no more than 200 or 300m wide. They are all coral islands, fringed with stunning white sand beaches and covered with lush natural vegetation composed of coconut palms and screw pines.

Since it will be very difficult for you to change islands once you arrive, make sure you choose your resort very carefully.

Resorts

Depending on their size, the island resorts can accommodate from 30 to 200 people, each operating like a **closed world**, where everything is imported. The smallest one (Cocoa) has only 8 bungalows, while the largest one (Sun Island) has 350, but the average works out at 75 rooms. So if you're looking for an idyllic island hideaway, choose one of the less developed islands and a coral-stone (rather than concrete), palm-thatched bungalow giving directly onto the beach. **Water bungalows** built on stilts are becoming ever more popular, which is all very well as long as this is not the resort's way of increasing the number of beds on offer by using the space above the water when there is no longer enough space left on land. But don't forget that you may be better off staying in a bungalow shaded by coconut palms; wood is not very soundproof and the planks soon become burning hot in the sun...

B Gaisne

The level of comfort and luxury offered by the resorts varies greatly from island to island, but always more or less meets **international standards**. With the Ministry of Tourism forcing them to regularly raise their standard of services, many of the resorts now offer mini-bars, hairdryers, personal safes, air conditioning, IDD phones and television in the bungalows. Some establishments provide room service, swimming pools, jacuzzis and saunas.

Accommodation is generally **full-board** (since the islands often have only one restaurant, half-board can leave a large hole in your budget). But it does not always include the price of the numerous sea-related activities which are on offer everywhere: scuba or skin diving, windsurfing, catamaran sailing, water-skiing, boat trips, trolling or deep-sea fishing. The cost of staying in one of these resorts varies greatly depending on the time of year and the island. It costs between US$80 and US$200 per person per day full board.

The hotels in this guidebook have been divided into the following four price ranges: reasonably priced (between US$80 and US$100), mid-range (between US$100 and US$130), expensive (between US$130 and US$160) and very expensive (over US$160). But remember that this information is only intended to give you a rough idea, since some resorts offer different types of accommodation covering the whole price range.

With the exception of **Gan**, which has a tourist hotel, all the other hotels are in **Male'**. Only about ten of them actually live up to this description; the others are, in fact, nothing more than modest guesthouses. The numerous little restaurants in Gan and Male' serve very cheap and tasty food.

Safari boats

Safaris are an excellent way of exploring the archipelago. Around one hundred large *dhoni*, decked and fitted out with between 8 and 12 cabins, cruise the Maldivian waters. Their length ranges between 14 and 22m and their speed between 8 and 16 knots.

You can choose between a **diving safari**, reserved for certified divers and offering the possibility of reaching distant sites otherwise not easily accessible from the island resorts, or a **cruising safari**, which will enable you to explore the islands and do some diving with mask, snorkel and fins. The week-long safaris take in the Male' and Vaavu atolls, while the two-week safaris will take you to the more remote atolls.

If you choose this option, it will cost you on average between US$675 and US$750 per person for a week full board, excluding the dives (between US$40 and US$50 per dive).

SPORTS AND PASTIMES

Most of the leisure activities on offer in the Maldives are sea related. Both the water and air temperature provide ideal conditions for all sea-based activities, as well as a natural invitation to take a dip. Since the lagoons are often shallow and only good for paddling, it is generally easier to swim around the jetty area. But be careful not to stray too far; the currents can be very strong in the channels, even around the house reefs.

• The sea

Catamaran sailing

Some resorts offer this activity, but only **inside the lagoons**. Others have ruled it out because of the danger presented by the barely submerged coral reefs and the proximity of one or more island villages. Despite the fact that it is forbidden to visit these villages in swimwear, there are always a few holidaymakers who shamelessly try to break this rule.

Skin diving

The Maldivian archipelago is a diver's paradise. Even if you are not an experienced diver, just a pair of fins, a mask and snorkel will give you a ticket into a wonderful and spellbinding world. Demanding little sporting skill, skin diving is practised only in the lagoons and requires nothing more than a little attention to currents and not straying too far. Choose an island with a nearby and easily accessible house reef. In general, the round islands, set well inside the atolls, meet these criteria, while the more elongated ones located at the edge of the atolls often have a house reef which is inaccessible from the shore. At resorts where the reef is too far away, at least two *dhoni* outings per day are organised to take divers to the best sites; an instructor accompanies the divers and the sites on the programme are often very interesting. However, the resorts usually ask for a contribution towards the cost of the boat.

Scuba diving

This is, of course, the Maldives' main attraction and the conditions for it are perfect: average visibility is 30m and the water is so warm that you can dive in just a T-shirt. All of the island resorts have a dive base – mostly affiliated with PADI, but sometimes CMAS – with very modern equipment which you can hire per dive or per week. You will find the latest models of jackets, regulators, tanks, dive computers, etc.

Dives are always organised in **buddy teams** with divemasters, and there are **no decompression dives**. Open Water certified divers are allowed to dive up to 20m, the others up to 30m. Spectacular **night dives** are arranged once or twice a week, so that divers can admire the fields of "flowering" corals and see the fish and shellfish which only come out at night.

Most centres offer the possibility of obtaining Open Water Diver and Advanced Diver certificates (this takes around 8 to 10 days), and sometimes even more specialised certificates. If you are a novice, you should sign up for at least an introductory session. By your second dive, you will be all set to explore the fascinating underwater world of the Maldives.

Windsurfing

The shallow inner lagoons make it easy to learn this sport and there is no shortage of boards to hire or borrow. As soon as you leave the shelter of the coconut palms, there will be enough wind to keep you going. However, be careful never to leave the lagoon and don't try to surf to another island: the corals are treacherous and the currents can become very dangerous.

Longline and deep-sea fishing

Longline fishing is a form of trolling which is practised from a *dhoni*. All the resorts offer introductory trips, usually free of charge.

Some of the islands (Rihiveli, Madoogali, etc) are also equipped with expensive modern equipment for deep-sea fishing (around US$200 for half a day). The catches vary greatly depending on the season, winds and currents, but you are most likely to return from your fishing expedition with bonito, sailfish, marlin and dolphin fish.

• Sports activities

Volley-ball

This is the Maldives' national sport. Many islands organise daily tournaments between teams of Maldivian employees and foreign visitors. You will always be welcome to join in a match organised by the Maldivians.

Tennis

The largest islands have tennis courts, which are often floodlit.

Other activities

An increasing number of resorts are offering their guests pedalos, canoes, and sea kayaks. If the lagoon is large enough, you will also be able to try your hand at water-skiing. You can even go jet-skiing at some resorts, although it has been banned in many places because of the noise.

• Relaxation

Should you tire of wallowing in the crystal clear waters of the lagoon and seek other pursuits, you are sure to find a multitude of **games** to keep you occupied in your resort: chess, backgammon, cards, dominoes, table tennis, darts, etc. You will also find informal **libraries** made up of books in many different languages, left behind by guests.

Many resorts play musical recordings, videos and films, or organise **slide shows** on the underwater flora and fauna. They all go to great lengths to keep their guests happy, offering massages, gymnastics (aerobics and stretching), crab races, billiards, etc.

The island resorts all organise **excursions** to fishing islands or to Male', once or twice a week. Some even arrange barbecues on desert islands or bivouacs to give you a "Robinson Crusoe" experience for one night.

The **night-life** is very limited, although some of the island resorts have a discotheque. But they all try to organise theme evenings regularly, such as treasure hunts, Maldivian dancing and "pirate evenings".

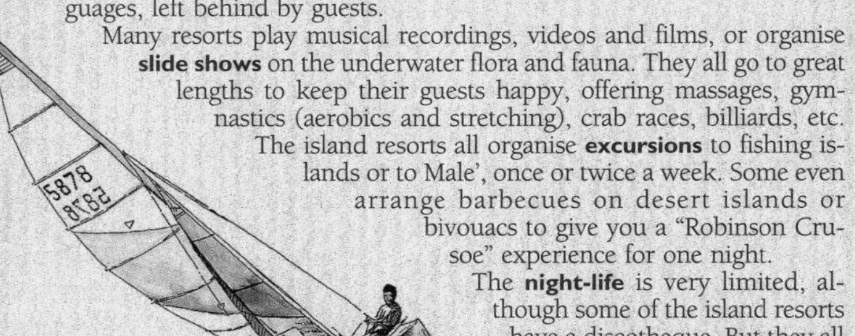

B. Gaisne

Sports and pastimes

SHOPPING

• What's on offer

Lacquerware

The most beautiful lacquered boxes come from Baa Atoll. Cylindrical in shape, they vary in size from the smallest pill box to 30cm high, or even more for the traditional receptacles used for feasts and offerings. These very skilfully crafted objects are decorated with black, red and yellow geometrical patterns, coloured with natural dyes. The more intricate the design, the higher the price.

Gold and silver

Jewellery is crafted using ancestral techniques in the southern atolls of Dhaalu and Faafu. You will find heavy silver bangles, amulets and boxes to put them in, as well as superb and extremely elaborate belts, which are worn wrapped several times around the waist. Very finely cut gold is crafted into delicate neck or wrist chains and some pieces of jewellery even contain branches of polished black coral.

Cloth

Woven by the women of the North and South atolls, the most beautiful cloth *(Thandu Kunaa)* comes from Gaafu and Dhaalu. Bedspreads, prayer mats and ordinary mats are dyed with natural colours, in shades of cream, beige or black. Prices vary according to the fineness of the weave and the intricacy of the geometrical patterns.

Clothes

Don't be fooled, most of the "curios" and material on offer to the tourists (T-shirts, sarongs, pareos, etc) are actually made in Sri Lanka or Indonesia. But why not try dressing Maldivian style, with a sarong *(mundu)* and shirt *(gamis)* for the gentlemen, and a long-sleeved dress *(faaskuri hedhun)*, or *libaas* – with a finely embroidered collar – for the ladies. *Handiki*, which are a sort of cummerbund and are usually black, are also to be found.

Drums

Made out of enormous hollowed-out coconuts or coconut palm trunks with ray skin stretched over the top, these drums are the main musical instrument of the Maldives. They are known as *Bodu Beru*, like the traditional Maldivian dance to which they gave their name.

Local curios

Among the objects which will make an original souvenir from your holiday in the Maldives are the famous **sharks' teeth** – local amulets which you can buy loose or mounted – and **ambergris**, a concretion originating from the intestine of male cetaceans which is used to make precious perfumes. This, along with cowrie shells, was the main source of the Maldives' wealth for centuries. However it is exorbitantly expensive and its export is subject to strict conditions, including a 50% duty. You can find some **cowrie shells** on the beaches, but the most beautiful ones are sold in Male'. And remember that you are only allowed to take a limited number out of the country.

• Regulations on certain articles

The Maldivians fiercely protect their natural heritage. It is strictly forbidden to buy and export turtle-shell objects. Likewise, no corals, shellfish, fish, any animals alive or dead, even if stuffed or mounted, can be picked up, fished, bought or exported from the Maldives. Very heavy fines are inflicted and the sentences (which can involve imprisonment) are strictly applied. So be careful when shopping at the street stalls in Male': the sellers are only allowed to sell you certain species of corals with crafted branches, sharks' teeth and some common cowrie shells.

HEALTH AND SAFETY

• Precautions

There are no endemic tropical diseases in the Maldives.

One of the greatest dangers you will face there is the **sun**, which can be treacherous; never forget that you can still get a nasty burn when the wind is blowing or the sun is veiled by clouds. Very high protection factor sunscreen, a hat and sunglasses are essential, and, to be on the safe side, swim in a T-shirt, at least for the first few days. And don't be fooled by the ambient humidity: **dehydration** is a very real danger. Drink at least 3 litres of water a day – 5 litres for divers, since inhaling dry air accentuates this phenomenon.

Also take great care of your **personal hygiene** in order to avoid fungal infections and maceration. Take frequent showers and dry yourself thoroughly.

Rinse out your ears using a small rubber dropper to get rid of the micro-organisms and coral sand which can cause infection. Take antibiotics (eg neomycin) with you and make sure that your auditory canal is not obstructed by earwax; the heat and humidity can cause swelling.

Watch out for the **corals**, which are at best rough, and usually sharp. Coral injuries won't heal well while you remain in the country. Wounds should be disinfected immediately, but will only heal properly once you return home.

You will not come across any dangerous animals in the islands (snakes, scorpions or spiders), and the only unpleasant insects you will find are mosquitoes and ants. However, the region is not infected by malaria and most of the resorts fumigate certain areas of the islands. The **mosquitoes** are not harmful, but come out as soon as night falls: be sure to have some insect repellent with you and spray yourself and your clothes roughly every 20min between 6pm and 8pm. As for the **ants**, take a couple of "traps" with you. Don't take any pressurised aerosols since you will not be allowed to take them onto the plane.

The marine fauna does have **formidable natural defences**, which it is best not to come into contact with, and some fish do attack if they feel threatened. The rule is simple: never touch anything (corals, shellfish, sea urchins, sea anemones, jellyfish, starfish, etc) and move away from an animal at the first sign of nervousness. *See the section on "Fauna and flora", p 331.*

• Special precautions for diving

The dive centres will ask you for a **medical certificate**. Consult a specialist before you leave or you may have to go for a check-up in Male' or on one of the islands with the necessary facilities (Bandos, Club Med, etc).

– Be careful not to resurface too quickly (never faster than your smallest air bubbles), and watch out for tiredness, alcohol and the various pathologies which favour decompression sickness (obesity, diabetes, fractures, recent surgery, blood circulation disorders, etc).

– Never dive less than 24hr before taking a plane.

– Avoid any "superficial" breathing under exertion, stress or panic and never "strain" if you get caught up in a current or other difficulties, otherwise an embolism is sure to follow within a matter of seconds. Resurface slowly: your boat will be waiting for you.
– Have a dental check-up before you leave. The tiniest cavity can become painful when the volume of air expands upon resurfacing.

• Health

The island resorts all have basic medical supplies but in the event of serious problems, they will arrange for medical evacuation to Male' by seaplane or helicopter, even at night. The main hospitals in the capital are **IGM** (☎ 316647), and the clinics **AMDC** (☎ 325979) and **ADK** (☎ 313553). If you are staying in a remote atoll, the administrative capital will have at least a dispensary. In an emergency, the best-equipped and nearest hospitals are in Dubai or Singapore (daily flights).

• Emergencies

Ambulance, ☎ 102. Police, ☎ 119.

A TO Z

• Alcohol

Since the Republic of Maldives is a totally Muslim country, the consumption of alcohol is officially forbidden. You won't find any in the hotel bars in Male' but alcohol is served on the island resorts and onboard the safari boats (except when in the vicinity of island villages or the capital). The prices are similar to those in hotel bars in Europe.

• Drinking water

Drinking water is available in the form of **imported mineral water**. Bottles cost between US$2 and US$5. Some resorts also offer desalinated and remineralised water.

• Electricity

Generators supply a **220V** and AC 50Hz current, with English or American sockets. Adapters are available for guests from other countries.

• Laundry

All the island resorts offer this service **as an extra**, except for Rihiveli Island, where it is free of charge. However, the level of ambient humidity means that nothing dries easily.

• Newspapers, radio and television

The **Miadhu**, **Haveera** and **Aafathis** newspapers (Divehi-English bilingual) contain only national news. If you want to know what is going on in the rest of the world, you will have to borrow a newspaper from a new arrival.
You can tune into the **BBC World Service** on 17 790, 15 310 and 11 955 kHz in the morning, and on 15 310, 11 750 and 6 195 kHz in the afternoon.
The two local television channels broadcast **a news programme in English**. Some resorts have satellite television with CNN, BBC, TV5 Europe and some regional channels (Dubai, Singapore, India, Sri Lanka).

• Photography

Both on land and sea, use an **ultraviolet filter** and pay attention to the contrast and brightness. You can always hire an **underwater camera** to take photos of the fish and corals. Several resorts hire out such equipment and also provide instruction on how to use it. You will be able to recharge your video camera batteries in your resort or on your safari boat.

• Safety

The Maldives have a very low crime rate, but if you want to put your mind totally at rest, leave your valuables (bank cards, passports, plane tickets) in the resort safe.

• Tipping / gratuities

If you are staying in an island resort, tip the bellboy US$10 and leave as much again for the island's community chest. Also feel free to tip any particularly helpful employee. On a safari, it is customary to give US$20 to the skipper, who will share it out among the crew.

• Units of measurement

Distances in this guide are given in kilometres. As a rule of thumb, one kilometre is five-eighths of a mile: 5 miles is therefore about 8 kilometres, 10 miles is about 16 kilometres and 20 miles is about 32 kilometres.
Consult the table below for other useful metric equivalents:

Degrees Celsius	35°	30°	25°	20°	15°	10°	5°	0°	-5°	-10°
Degrees Fahrenheit	95°	86°	77°	68°	59°	50°	41°	32°	23°	15°

1 centimetre (cm) = 0.4 inch
1 metre (m) = 3.3 feet
1 metre (m) = 1.09 yards
1 litre = 1.06 quart
1 litre = 0.22 gallon
1 kilogram (kg) = 2.2 pounds

LOOK AND LEARN

• General

BELL HCP, ***The Maldive Islands: an account of the physical features, climate, history, inhabitants, productions, and trade*** (1883), ***The Maldive Islands. Report on a visit to Male', January 20 to February 21, 1920*** (1921), ***The Maldive Islands. Monograph on the History, Archaeology and Epigraphy*** (1940), Government Press, Colombo.

GARDINER Stanley, ***The Fauna and Geography of the Maldivian Islands***, Cambridge University Press, 1906.

HEYERDAHL Thor, ***The Maldive Mystery***, George Allen & Unwin, London, 1986.

MALONEY Clarence, ***People of the Maldive Islands***, Orient Longman, New Delhi, 1980.

SALAHUDDEEN Hussain, ***The Story of Mohamed Thakurufaan***, Novelty Press, Male', 1986.

ZUHAIR Mohamed, ***Practical Dhivehi***, Novelty Press, Male', 1991.

• Travel

BATTUTA Ibn, ***Travels in Asia and Africa 1325-54***, Routledge Kegan Paul, London, 1983.
FAROOK Mohamed, ***The Fascinating Maldives***, Novelty Press, Male', 1985.
PYRARD DE LAVAL François, ***The Voyage of François Pyrard de Laval to the East Indies, the Maldives, the Moluccas and Brazil***, translated into English and edited by A Gray, from the third French edition of 1619, Hakluyt Society, London, 1887-90.
SMALLWOOD C, ***A Visit to the Maldive Islands***, Royal Central Asian Society, London, 1961.

• Diving

ALLEN R Gerald and STEENE Roger, ***Indo-Pacific Coral Reef Field Guide***, Tropical Reef Research, Singapore, 1996.
ANDERSON Dr Charles, ***Maldives the Diver's Paradise***, ***Living Reefs of the Maldives*** and ***Divers' Guide to the Sharks of the Maldives***, Novelty Press, Male', 1987, 1991, 1992.
AW Michael, ***Dreams from a Rainbow Sea – Maldives***, Ocean N Environment, 1997.
GODFREY Tim, ***Dive Maldives: A Guide to the Maldives Archipelago***, Atoll Editions, 1998
HARWOOD Sam and BRYNING Rob, ***The Dive Sites of the Maldives***, New Holland Press UK, 1998.
KUITER Rudie H, ***Photo Guide to Fishes of the Maldives***, Atoll Editions, 1998
RANDALL John E, ***Divers' Guide to Fishes of the Maldives***, Immel Publishing Ltd, London, 1992

GLOSSARY

• Pronunciation

A double vowel indicates a slight pause.

a	short *u*, as in *but*	**o**	closed *o*, as in *knot*
aa	long open *a*, as in *calm*	**u**	*u*, as in *put*
e	*e*, as in *red*	**oo**	*oo*, as in *cool*
i	short *i*, as in *pin*	**ai**	*i*, as in *I*
ee	long *e*, as in *tree*	**oa**	*o*, as in *boat*

Common expressions

hello	assalam aleikum	**who?**	kaaku
goodbye	vakivelani	**yes**	aah
how are you?	kihiney	**no**	noon
well	rangaloo	**I**	aharen
please	edhen	**you (s and pl)**	kaley
thank you	shookriya	**he, she**	eyna
how?	kihaa	**they**	emeehun
why?	keeve		

Common words

hot	hoonu	**boy**	firihen kujaa	**sky**	udu
cold	fini	**wife**	anhen meehaa	**rain**	vaarey
go	dhan	**husband**	firi	**sand**	veli

do	kuran	**hat**	thofi	**sun**	hiru
child	kujaa	**trousers**	fatuloonu	**wind**	vai
girl	anhen kujaa	**sarong**	mundu		

Time

before	kurin	**today**	miadhu	**night**	reygandu
after	fahun	**tomorrow**	maadhan	**when**	kon iraku
morning	hendhunu	**soon**	avalah	**late**	las
afternoon	mendhuru fas	**now**	milharu	**early**	avas

Directions and visiting

here	mithaa	**far**	dhuru
where	kon thaaka		

Transport

plane	mathinda	**harbour**	falhu or badharu
boat	dhoni	**car**	caaru

Hotel

room	nidhaa kotari	**bed**	endhu
sleep	nidhan	**toilets**	faakhaanaa or gifili

Restaurant

drink (vb)	boan	**water**	fen	**bread**	paan
eat (vb)	kaan	**fruit**	meyva	**papaya**	falhoa
pineapple	alanasi	**milk**	kiru	**fish**	mas
banana	dhon keyo	**mango**	anbu	**sugar**	hakuru
coffee	kofee	**coconut**	kurumba	**tea**	sai
curry	riha	**egg**	bis	**meat**	eggamu mas

Shopping

money	faisaa	**price**	agu	**too big**	e maa bodu
shop	fihaara	**cheap**	agu heyo	**too small**	e maa kuda
how much?	mi kihaa?	**expensive**	agu bodu		

Emergencies

emergency	emergency	**pharmacy**	beys fihaara	**pain**	thadhoo
dentist	dathuge doktor	**doctor**	doktor		
hospital	hospital	**ill**	balivee		

Numbers

0	sumeh	**13**	theyra	**60**	fas dholas
1	ekeh	**14**	saadha	**70**	hayi diha
2	dheyh	**15**	fanara	**80**	ah diha
3	thineh	**16**	solha	**90**	nuva diha
4	hathareh	**17**	sathaara	**100**	satheyka
5	faheh	**18**	ashaara	**101**	satheyka ekeh
6	haeh	**19**	onavihi	**200**	dhuisaththa
7	hatheh	**20**	vihi	**1000**	eh haas
8	asheh	**21**	ekaavees	**2000**	dhe haas
9	nuvaeh	**22**	baavees	**first**	eh vana
10	dhihaeh	**30**	thirees	**second**	dhe vana
11	egaara	**40**	saalhees		
12	baara	**50**	fansaas		

Exploring the Maldives

E Valentin

Return from a fishing expedition

MALE'

Capital of the Maldives
Approximately 2sqkm (2km east to west and 1km north to south)
Pop 75 000

Not to be missed
The National Museum.
The "dhoni" harbour and fish market.

And remember...
Visit Male' just before catching your return flight if it leaves at night.
Avoid visiting on Fridays, which are holy days, and during the heat of the day.

This small strip of overpopulated "land", lost in the middle of the Indian Ocean and surrounded by a few tiny desert islands, is a real oddity. The only city in the Maldivian archipelago, Male' houses almost one third of the population on a little under 2sqkm – which comes to the incredible figure of almost 100 000 inhabitants, if we include the people who are only passing through. This city, which is the political, administrative and religious centre of the Maldives, has recently started to resemble a **modern capital**. "Sultan's Island" is no more. The peaceful white sand paths edged with little gardens and small traditional coral stone houses have today given way to broad paved avenues and six- or seven-storey buildings. Urbanisation and westernisation are now the key words. Although, unlike our western capitals, the city still has a human dimension and a pleasant atmosphere, the environment and way of life here have nothing in common with those on the other islands in the archipelago.
In order to reclaim extra land from the sea, **polders** have been created on the east coast, which now has an artificial beach. In the Maldives of all places! Villingili (1.5km west of Male') was an island resort until recently, but has now become a residential area, housing around 10 000 inhabitants. An ambitious project is currently underway to build a "second Male'", with polders connecting Hulule airport (1km northeast) to Farukolhufushi, which is currently the Club Med island, but not for much longer. Once completed, this new island should measure almost 6km long and 2km wide, and might be connected to Male' by a bridge.

The city

Allow 2 to 3hr.

An intricate maze of narrow little streets lined with whitewashed houses, the old city occupies the northeast part of the island, while the western and southern parts, built on land recently reclaimed from the sea, follow a grid pattern of thoroughfares at right angles to one another. Marine Drive (Boduthakurufaanu Magu), a long – unfortunately treeless – promenade, which runs along the northern and eastern shoreline, and Majeedhee Magu, which crosses the island from east to west, are the capital's two main roads. This is where all the government and administrative buildings can be found, as well as a large part of the island's business activity (modern shops, headquarters of large companies, etc).
Everywhere you go in Male' you will see the rounded corners of the walls, buildings and streets; this is in keeping with the tradition of the fishing villages and adds an extra touch of charm to the place.

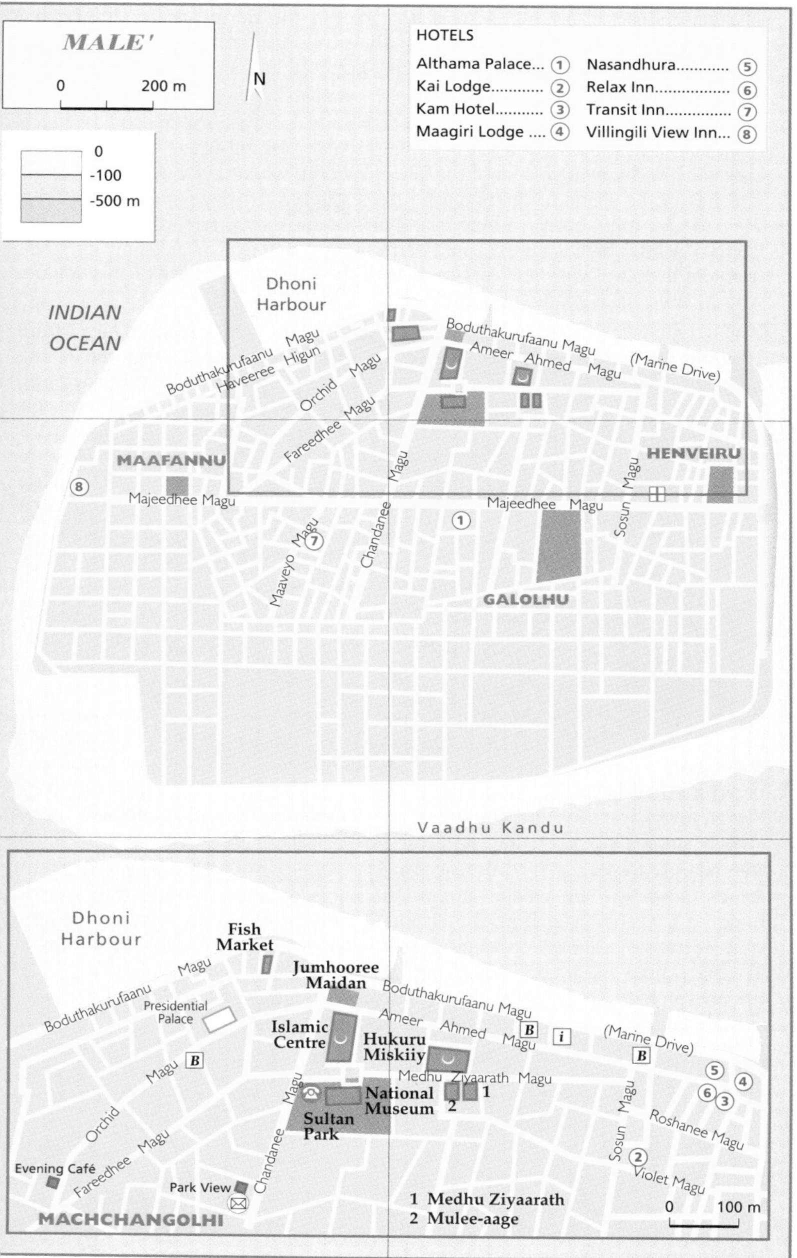
MALE'
0
200 m
N
0
-100
-500 m
HOTELS
Althama Palace... 1
Kai Lodge........... 2
Kam Hotel.......... 3
Maagiri Lodge 4
Nasandhura........... 5
Relax Inn................ 6
Transit Inn.............. 7
Villingili View Inn... 8
INDIAN
OCEAN
Dhoni
Harbour
Boduthakurufaanu Magu
Haveeree Higun
Orchid Magu
Fareedhee Magu
Boduthakurufaanu Magu
Ameer Ahmed Magu
(Marine Drive)
MAAFANNU
HENVEIRU
Majeedhee Magu
Chandanee Magu
Majeedhee Magu
Sosun Magu
Maaveyo Magu
GALOLHU
Vaadhu Kandu
Dhoni
Harbour
Fish
Market
Jumhooree
Maidan
Boduthakurufaanu Magu
Presidential
Palace
Islamic
Centre
Hukuru
Miskiiy
Ameer Ahmed Magu
(Marine Drive)
Medhu Ziyaarath Magu
National
Museum
Sultan
Park
Orchid Magu
Fareedhee Magu
Chandanee Magu
Sosun Magu
Roshanee Magu
Violet Magu
Evening Café
Park View
MACHCHANGOLHI
1 Medhu Ziyaarath
2 Mulee-aage
0
100 m

The various sights are all grouped together in the north around Jumhooree square. This seafront quarter, lulled by the gentle rhythm of the passing ships, is the most pleasant area, with the street stalls and bazaar turning it into a hive of activity in the morning.

Jumhooree Maidan (A3), the real heart of the city, is a vast, shaded square which makes a pleasant place for a stroll. It is a popular meeting-place for local people, especially in the relative cool of the late afternoon, when they relax on the stone benches in the shade of the tamarind trees, discuss the day's events, wait for a *dhoni* to take them home to their island after a day's shopping, or just enjoy the lawns – a little bare, granted, but such a luxury in Male'. You'll find no street hawkers here and very few cars to disturb the quiet tranquillity of this square, which bathes in a gentle, very provincial torpor.

If you follow the quays to the west of the square, you will reach the **Dhoni Harbour** (A3), which is a very lively place in the early afternoon when the fishing boats or cargo ships unload fish and goods to be sold at the nearby **markets**. Sea bream, bluish jacks and gleaming bonito lie alongside bundles of coir (coconut-husk fibre), sheaves of betel leaves, sweet potatoes, chillies, and sacks of saffron and rice. Intense bargaining takes place over the price of bundles of wood, a precious commodity here. Little stalls with a few tables and benches set out under an awning sell weak tea and fried fish, sweet potato and banana rolls.
A stroll around this picturesque quarter will give you a real taste of the Maldivians' daily life.

Singapore Bazaar (A3), this shopping district *par excellence* stretches southwards along Chandanee Magu from Jumhooree square. Full of noise and bustle in the morning when everyone comes to stock up, it empties out almost completely at midday and only comes back to life in the evening, when the heat is less intense. As you wander around, you'll come across **craft shops**, tea rooms and all kinds of stalls selling everyday consumer goods as well as a variety of objects which make good souvenirs to take home (sharks' teeth, cowrie shells, mats, lacquered or unpolished coconut wood boxes, drums). Make sure to choose your purchases carefully, since the products are not always of the best quality and many articles are actually imported from Sri Lanka, India or Indonesia.

The Islamic Centre (A3) *(9am-1pm, closed for prayer between 11.45am and 12.30pm)* stands close by. The golden aluminium dome of this imposing three-storey building is visible even from the airport. Built in 1984 in a resolutely modern style, it houses a **library** containing only religious works in Arabic or Divehi, a Koranic school and a conference centre. If you would like to take a look inside the **prayer hall**, known as the **Grand Friday Mosque**, make sure you are suitably dressed. The beautifully designed interior can hold 5 000 worshippers. It is decorated with carved wood panels and doors, and monumental bronze chandeliers, with swathes of carpets covering the floor. The Maldivians are not keen for this sacred place to become a tourist attraction, but it is freely accessible outside prayer times (the doors are closed to non-worshippers 15min before prayers begin).

Hukuru Miskiiy (Friday Mosque) (B3), which is only a block away on Medhu Ziyaarath Magu, remains Male's most beautiful mosque. Built in 1656 and made of coral stone, it is decorated with **calligraphy** and geometrical patterns carved in the stone or on precious wood (teak, sandalwood, rosewood, etc). The exquisite **traditional lacquer** decorations are superb. Built on the foundations of a pagan temple, this mosque has the rather original feature of not pointing towards Mecca. In theory, you need authorisation from the Ministry of Islamic Affairs (☎ 322266) to visit it, but if you ask nicely at the entrance, and as long as you are suitably dressed, you will be welcome to go inside. The mosque closes a quarter of an hour before the five daily prayers begin. A large number of people, in particular the elderly, attend the Friday prayer here. Next door stands the **Munnaaru**, an entirely white minaret built in 1675, from where the muezzin used to call the faithful to prayer before the construction of the Islamic Centre with its loudspeakers.

On the other side of the street, take a look at the **Medhu Ziyaarath**, a shrine built to honour the memory of Abdu al-Barakaat, who converted the Maldivians to Islam in 1153, and the **Mulee-aage** (B3), which stands just next to it. This palace, built for Sultan Shamsuddin III who was banished in 1936, later became the residence of the first presidents of the republic. Today it houses the offices of the head of State and is used for official receptions; Maumoon Abdul Gayoom usually resides on his private island, Aarah, 4km north of Male'.

After wandering around the city, you may be glad to make a stop in the shade of **Sultan Park** (A3), a little garden hidden away behind a heavy iron gate, opposite the Islamic Centre. Standing on the site of the old sultans' palace which was demolished in 1968, it contains a small pavilion housing the **National Museum** *(9am-1pm / 3pm-6pm, 4pm-6.30pm on Fridays. Entry fee: 25 rufiyaa. No photography allowed)* where many everyday objects are on display, most of them originating from the former **royal court**: there are thrones and palanquins, clothes and embroideries, jewellery, weapons, lacquered boxes, Korans, old photographs, betel boxes, spittoons, hookahs, ewers, parasols, lanterns, crockery, etc. The little room on the ground floor (on the right) contains a display of amazing **pre-Islamic antiques** discovered by Thor Heyerdahl *(see the section on "Legend and History", p 335)*. Few Maldivians come here, and the park is officially only open on Friday afternoons, but since you have to go through it to reach the museum, it effectively has the same opening and closing times.

The Islamic Centre and Dhoni Harbour

E Valentin

Male

Making the most of Male'

GETTING AROUND

You can easily visit Male' on foot. The taxis will hardly get you around any faster and the only advantage they offer is air-conditioning. The main sights are all within one hundred metres of each other. But if you plan on staying here for several days, you can always hire a bicycle from your hotel.

ADDRESS BOOK

Tourist information – ***Maldives Tourism Promotion Board***, 4th Floor, Bank of Maldives Building, Boduthakurufaanu Magu (B3), ☎ 323224 and 323228, mtpb@visitmaldives.com, 9am-1pm.

Bank / currency exchange – ***Bank of Maldives***, head office at *no* 11 Boduthakurufaanu Magu (B3); 5 branches in the city, one at Villingili and one at the airport. ***Bank of Ceylon***, on Orchid Magu (A3). ***State Bank of India***, on Boduthakurufaanu Magu (B3).

Main post office / Telephone – ***Main post office***, Chandanee Magu (A3). ***Dhiraagu***, the Maldivian telecommunications company, stands at the corner of Chandanee Magu and Medhu Ziyaarath Magu, next to the museum (A3). It offers a wide range of services, with a local network linking 140 islands in 20 atolls, and an automatic international network (Quickline). Card-operated phone booths are to be found all over Male'. Dhiraagu provides telex, fax, e-mail, telegram and maritime radio services. It can also host an Internet mailbox for you or rent you a mobile phone during your stay.

Airline companies – They are all located in the city centre or in the vicinity of Jumhooree square. Island Aviation Services Limited, ☎ 322438; ***SriLankan Airlines***, ☎ 323459; ***Balair***, ☎ 323349; ***Emirates***, ☎ 325675; ***Indian Airlines***, ☎ 323003; ***Malaysia***, ☎ 316375; ***Singapore Airlines***, ☎ 320777.

WHERE TO STAY

The Ministry of Tourism lists 26 hotels or inns in Male', but around twenty of them are simple guesthouses with only a few rooms. Many of them close barely a year after opening, or change names when they change hands. You will also have to pay a bed tax of US$6 per night.

Under US$50

Maagiri Tourist Lodge, Boduthakurufaanu Magu, ☎ 322576, Fax 328787 – 7rm. TV CC Mini-bar in the rooms. A very simple hotel, but with a pleasant welcome.

Transit Inn, Maaveyo Magu, ☎320420, Fax 326606 – 10rm. CC Mini-bar in the rooms. You will find a very friendly welcome here.

Between US$50 and US$100

Althama Palace, Majeedhee Magu, ☎313118, Fax 328828 – 20rm. TV CC Hairdryer, mini-bar and safe in the rooms. Located in the business centre, this hotel attracts more businessmen in transit than tourists.

Kai Lodge, Violet Magu, ☎328742, Fax 328738 – 15rm. TV CC Hairdryer and safe in the rooms. With its terrace and little garden, this is a pleasant place to stay.

Nasandhura Palace Hotel, Boduthakurufaanu Magu, ☎323380, Fax 320822 – 31rm. TV CC Mini-bar in the rooms, business centre, gym, billiard table, sauna, jacuzzi. Probably the best hotel in the city, with the additional advantage of a good location.

Kam Hotel, Roanuge, ☎320611, Fax 320614 – 30rm. TV CC Hairdryer, mini-bar and safe in the rooms. A very pleasant and friendly hotel, located in the east of the island. The small swimming pool is welcome indeed. Roof-terrace restaurant.

Relax Inn, Ameer Ahmed Magu, ☎ 314531, Fax 314533 – 12rm. TV CC Karaoke, gym, billiard table, sauna, jacuzzi. Lively and well located.

Villingili View Inn, Majeedhee Magu, ☎ 318696, Fax 325213 – 20rm. CC In the west, towards the harbour. This is not the most interesting quarter, but the hotel is pleasant.

EATING OUT

If you want to taste real Maldivian cuisine, try the little restaurants dotted all around the city, on Marine Drive, around the Singapore Bazaar, the fish market or near the dhoni harbour. Remember that most of them close for 15min during prayer times, but don't worry if you are already at table, they won't ask you to leave!

If you would prefer a restaurant with air-conditioning, here are a few suitable places.

Between US$10 and US$25

Evening Café, Orchid Magu (A3), ☎310661. Indian, Chinese and European cuisine. Seafood. Probably the best fare in Male'.

Ground Six, ☎313431. The restaurant of the Relax Inn, boasting a pleasant setting on the hotel's sixth floor roof terrace. International cuisine and Maldivian specialities.

Nasandhura Palace, ☎ 323380. Restaurant of the hotel of the same name. European cuisine offering some regional, Maldivian, Sri Lankan, Indian and Chinese specialities.

Raaverina, ☎ 318696. Villingili hotel. Slightly out-of-the-way, but in a pleasant setting.

Park View, Chandanee Magu (A3), ☎ 328106. Indian and Italian cuisine. Pleasant setting and quiet atmosphere.

HAVING A DRINK

The friendliest – and cheapest – places to go for a drink are the numerous tea shops scattered around the city. However, if you'd prefer something more chic and with air-conditioning, here are a couple of suggestions:

Cyber café, Faadheyri Magu, ☎ 311122. For Internet addicts.

Seagull Café House, Fareedhee Magu. Renowned for its ice cream.

OTHER THINGS TO DO

Excursions – The former island resort of ***Kuda Bandos***, which is 8km away from Male' and has since been transformed into a national park, has become a very popular weekend destination (Fridays and Saturdays) for the inhabitants of the capital. Here you will find cafés, restaurants and beautiful beaches.

Villingili, a mainly residential area, 2km west of Male' (15min by boat, 5 *rufiyaa*), also has superb beaches lined with coconut palms on its eastern coast.

Bandos, ☎ 440088 – 225rm. Hairdryer and mini-bar in the rooms. Discotheque, sauna, massages. Windsurfing, catamaran sailing, canoeing, water-skiing, dive centre. This is one of the first tourist islands (not to be confused with Kuda Bandos), where many foreign residents go for the weekend. A free boat shuttle makes the outward journey every Thursday evening, returning on Saturday evening. This is the closest island to Male' (8km) with a bar that serves alcohol.

Diving – You will find two excellent dive sites near Male': at ***Kikki Reef***, between Villingili and the refuse island of Thilafushi, and between Male' and the airport, at the wreck site of the ***Victory***, which sank in 1981 (dives between 15 and 35m). Only experienced divers are allowed to dive here, because of the strong currents.

Making the most of Male'

THE MALE' ATOLLS
(KAAFU ATOLL)

Pop 11 000
District of South Male' – Capital: Maafushi
30 islands, of which 3 are inhabited and 16 are island resorts
District of North Male' – Capital: Thulusdhoo
87 islands, of which 8 are inhabited and 26 are island resorts

Not to be missed
The capital, Male', for its museum and atmosphere.

And remember...
Choose your island carefully: these two atolls are among the most touristy, and quality ranges from one extreme to the other.
It's best to stay on one of the more natural islands with fewer bungalows.

The two Male' atolls are located to the north and south of the capital. Open to tourists since the 1970s, they contain the archipelago's most famous islands. North Male' Atoll (60km long and 30km wide) is larger than South Male' Atoll (35km by 15km) and is separated from the latter by a 5km-wide channel, Vaadhu Kandu. The island of Male' stands to the northeast of this channel. Excluding the capital – which in recent years has attracted the majority of the population – these two atolls are, oddly enough, not the most densely populated, despite their central location. They do, however, draw the largest numbers of tourists.

North Male' Atoll

Other than the capital, Male', and its satellite islands – Villingili, Hulule (the airport), Gaamadhoo (the prison), Girifushi (the military base), the president of the republic's residence and the islands where fuel reserves and refuse are kept – North Male' Atoll has only three island villages.

In the southeast of the atoll, **Thulusdhoo**, the district's administrative capital (900 inhabitants), is devoted to industry and houses a bottling plant and a modern shipyard. It is also known for its **drum production**, offering an extensive choice of these instruments which are used to accompany traditional dances, and which you will find much cheaper than in Male'. This industrial island, more westernised than the island villages of the more remote atolls, is rarely visited by tourists. This is a shame because it provides a good insight into part of the modern Maldives which is not selling out to meet the commercial demands of tourism or clinging to a certain vision of the country's past.

Huraa (600 inhabitants) is the island which spawned one of the dynasties of sultans who ruled the Maldives. Trips are often organised here by nearby resorts, and it is still possible to find some good crafts stalls. But **Himmafushi** (600 inhabitants) on the eastern barrier reef is the island which attracts the most tourists, and a few more souvenir shops sprout up on its streets every year. It is certainly not the best example of a traditional Maldivian village.

Although quite far away, the two small atolls of **Kaashidhoo** and **Gaafaru**, are also part of the administrative district of North Male'. Gaafaru is the only island village in the atoll of the same name and has a population of over 800 inhabitants. It receives hardly any visitors, which is also true of Kaashidhoo, a crop-growing island home to over a thousand Maldivians. Although these islands have remained very authentic, the resorts unfortunately don't seem to consider it worth running trips here, seemingly under the delusion that the only purpose of an island-village visit is to buy T-shirts made in Malaysia and trinkets mass produced in Indonesia.

E Valentin

A young Huraa islander

South Male' Atoll

Like its neighbour, the South Male' Atoll contains many island resorts but barely more than three villages. Its administrative capital, **Maafushi**, which occupies a fairly central position on the eastern barrier reef, is the only island to have really kept a traditional way of life. Its activity is mainly centred on **tuna fishing** and it supplies the Male' market. A visit to the island will allow you to see the fishermen at work, busily pulling the nets in on the beach, but the *dhoni* loaded with fish from more distant fishing expeditions tend to take their catch directly to Male'.

Further north, near the capital, **Gulhi** (600 inhabitants) specialises in boat repair and maintenance, and has a dry dock which is used by the large cargo-transporting *dhoni*. The shipyards are generally not open to tourists.

The most well-known island of South Male' Atoll, **Guraidhoo**, was once a reputed natural harbour and used to be an important port of call for all ships heading for the southern atolls. Now set in the heart of the "tourist zone", its activity mainly revolves around tourism. A few fishing families still live here, but most of the men now work in the surrounding resorts, while their wives run the souvenir shops which line the main street in the village. Guraidhoo has a heliport, which is sometimes used by tourists going to stay on neighbouring islands and is also the departure point for trips offering a spectacular bird's-eye view of the atoll.

Dive sites

The dive sites in these two atolls have been listed for many years. Around thirty of them are highly reputed, and rightly so; they are all located on the barrier reef and attract a great number of divers. The best time of year for diving here, like everywhere else in the Maldives, is winter, when the monsoon hits from the

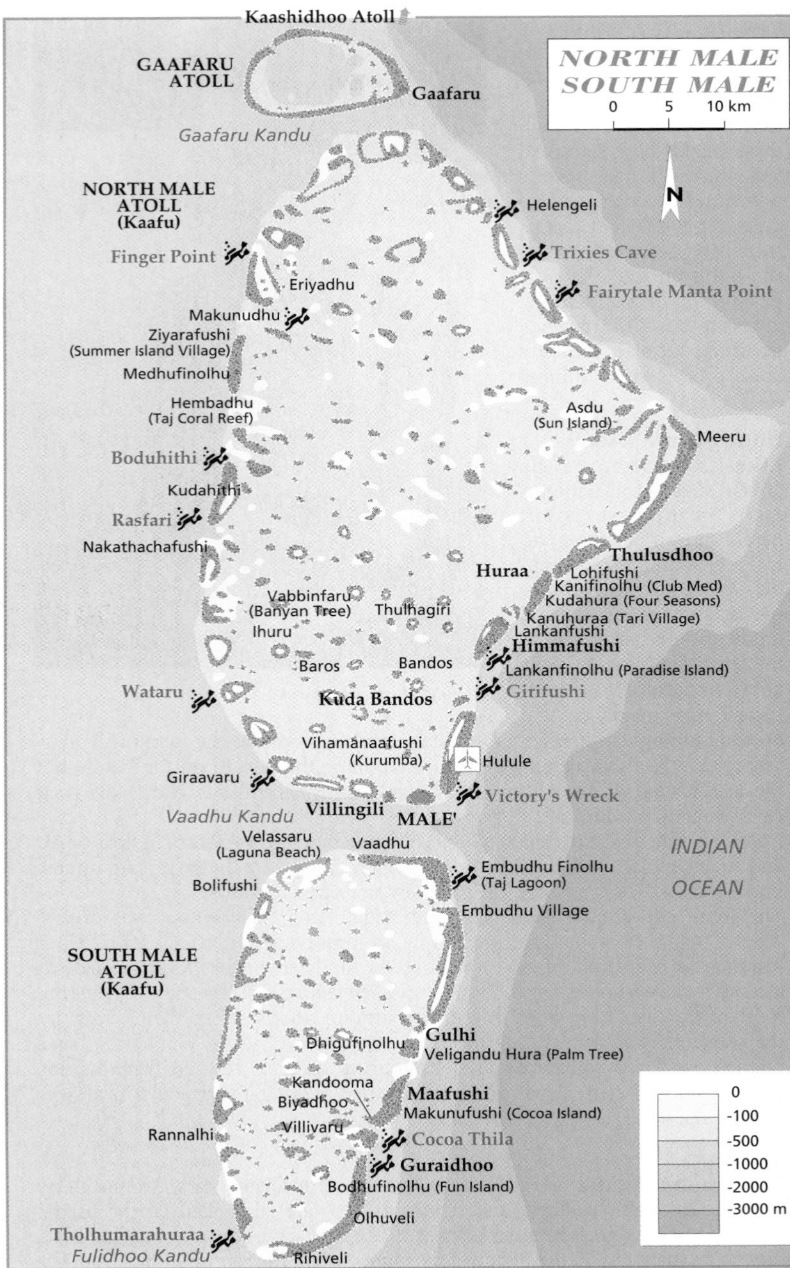
Kaashidhoo Atoll
NORTH MALE
SOUTH MALE
0
5
10 km
N
GAAFARU
ATOLL
Gaafaru
Gaafaru Kandu
NORTH MALE
ATOLL
(Kaafu)
Helengeli
Finger Point
Trixies Cave
Fairytale Manta Point
Eriyadhu
Makunudhu
Ziyarafushi
(Summer Island Village)
Medhufinolhu
Hembadhu
(Taj Coral Reef)
Asdu
(Sun Island)
Meeru
Boduhithi
Kudahithi
Rasfari
Nakathachafushi
Thulusdhoo
Huraa
Lohifushi
Kanifinolhu (Club Med)
Kudahura (Four Seasons)
Vabbinfaru
(Banyan Tree)
Thulhagiri
Kanuhuraa (Tari Village)
Lankanfushi
Ihuru
Himmafushi
Baros
Bandos
Lankanfinolhu (Paradise Island)
Girifushi
Wataru
Kuda Bandos
Vihamanaafushi
(Kurumba)
Hulule
Giraavaru
Victory's Wreck
Vaadhu Kandu
Villingili
MALE'
Velassaru
(Laguna Beach)
Vaadhu
INDIAN
OCEAN
Embudhu Finolhu
(Taj Lagoon)
Bolifushi
Embudhu Village
SOUTH MALE
ATOLL
(Kaafu)
Gulhi
Dhigufinolhu
Veligandu Hura (Palm Tree)
Kandooma
Maafushi
Biyadhoo
Makunufushi (Cocoa Island)
Villivaru
Rannalhi
Cocoa Thila
Guraidhoo
Bodhufinolhu (Fun Island)
Olhuveli
Tholhumarahuraa
Fulidhoo Kandu
Rihiveli
0
-100
-500
-1000
-2000
-3000 m

northeast; this is when a host of turtles, manta rays and even whale sharks are to be seen. But beware of the currents in the channels and *thila*, which can be very strong at this time of year. Wreck dive enthusiasts can explore the remains of the **Lady Christina**, which sank in 1974, and the **Seagull**, which foundered in 1879 north of Gaafaru Atoll. These two ships lie at a depth of 25 metres, but can only be reached in calm weather, because, again, the currents can be extremely strong.

Surf enthusiasts will find around fifteen acceptable sites along the eastern barrier reef of the two atolls, with the best waves in the spring.

Making the most of the Male' Atolls

WHERE TO STAY

• North Male' Atoll

Reasonably priced

Asdu (Sun Island), 32km from Male' (transfer by dhoni: 1hr30min), ☎ and Fax 445051; contact in Male': ☎ 322149, Fax 324300, info@asdu.com – 30rm. CC Windsurfing, canoeing, water-skiing, dive centre. A simple and natural, even rustic island. Maldivian management, but Italian clientele.

Eriyadhu, 42km from Male' (transfer by boat: 1hr), ☎ 444487, Fax 445926; contact in Male': ☎ 324933, Fax 324943, eriyadu@aaa.com.mv – 46rm. TV CC Hairdryer and mini-bar in the rooms. Windsurfing, catamaran sailing, water-skiing, dive centre. A small, peaceful island with a pleasant atmosphere and 46 well-separated beachfront bungalows thatched with palm leaves. Nearby house reef. Swiss, German, British and Scandinavian clientele.

Giravaru, 12km from Male' (transfer by boat: 15min), ☎ 440440, Fax 444818; contact in Male': ☎ 318422, Fax 328505, giravaru@dhivehinet.net.mv – TV CC Hairdryer and mini-bar in the rooms. Massages. Discotheque. Windsurfing, catamaran sailing, water-skiing, jet-skiing, dive centre. This small island has around sixty very simple bungalows with tiled roofs. International clientele.

Kanuhuraa (Tari Village), 13km from Male' (transfer by dhoni: 60min), ☎ 440013, Fax 440012; contact in Male': ☎ 322537, Fax 322798 – 24rm. TV CC Mini-bar in the rooms. Discotheque. Windsurfing, canoeing, water-skiing, surfing, dive centre. The island is due for renovation and will doubtless change considerably.

Ziyarafushi (Summer Island Village), 36km from Male' (transfer by boat: 55min; by dhoni: 2hr30min), ☎ 441949, Fax 441910; contact in Male': ☎ 322212, Fax 318057 – 92rm. TV CC Discotheque. Windsurfing, catamaran sailing, canoeing, water-skiing, dive centre. A small island with palm-thatched bungalows. Shallow lagoon, ideal for windsurfing, but the house reef is only accessible by boat.

Mid-range

Helengeli, 44km from Male' (transfer by boat: 55min), ☎ 444615, Fax 442881; contact in Male': ☎ 328544, Fax 325150, engeli88@dhivehinet.net.mv – 50rm. CC Renowned dive centre. Helengeli is the most northern island in the atoll. Renovated in 1996, this resort has 50 bungalows, which are sadly of modern design and set two by two. Its appeal lies in its magnificent beaches and immense lagoon. No sports activities are offered here, but there are many extremely interesting dive sites on its large house reef (6 channels), which is easily accessible from the beach. A good place for divers or those skilled in the art of doing nothing.

Ihuru, 20km from Male' (transfer by boat: 30min), ☎443502, Fax 445933; contact in Male': ☎ 326720,

Fax 326700, ihuru@dhivehinet.net.mv – 45rm. Hairdryer and mini-bar in the rooms. Windsurfing, catamaran sailing, canoeing, water-skiing, dive centre. With its lush vegetation of coconut palms and its stunning beaches, Ihuru is the most "photogenic" island in the Maldives. Superb house reef, accessible from the beach. Very friendly Maldivian management.

Kanifinolhu (Club Med), 20km from Male' (transfer by boat), ☎ 443152, Fax 444859 – 200rm. Discotheque. Windsurfing, catamaran sailing, canoeing, jet-skiing, gym, omnisports ground, dive centre. House reef accessible only by boat. The Club Med is going to move to this long thin island in autumn 2000. Once the renovation is completed, it should be able to offer 200 bungalows, 38 of them standing above the water.

Lankanfushi (Hudhuveli), 12km from Male' (transfer by boat: 15min), ☎ 443982, Fax 443849; contact in Male': ☎ 325529, Fax 321026 – 44rm. Discotheque. Windsurfing, canoeing, water-skiing, dive centre. This narrow strip of sand is lined with rather simple waterfront bungalows. Its lagoon is ideal for windsurfing, but the house reef is only accessible by boat. British and Italian clientele.

Lohifushi, 26km from Male' (transfer by boat: 35min), ☎ 443451, Fax 441908; contact in Male': ☎ 313446, Fax 318685, lohifush@dhivehinet. net.mv – 127rm. Hairdryer and mini-bar in the rooms. Crèche. Discotheque. Squash. Windsurfing, catamaran sailing, canoeing, water-skiing, dive centre. A large island, 800m long, with a string of over a hundred modern-style bungalows, divided into two categories: "standard" and "suite". Very shallow lagoon, ideal for windsurfing. Difficult access to house reef. International clientele.

Meeru, 40km from Male' (transfer by boat: 45min), ☎ 443157, Fax 445946; contact in Male': ☎ 314149, Fax 314150, meeru@dhivehinet.net.mv – 212rm. Windsurfing, catamaran sailing, dive centre. This immense island with its superb vegetation and amazing beaches is a pleasant place to stay despite the large number of bungalows set in groups of four. Accommodation is in standard rooms, private beach villas, or water bungalows. Large open-air restaurant and three bars, one of which opens onto the beach. Rather young and informal atmosphere. Immense lagoon, but easily accessible house reef.

Medhufinolhu (Reethi Rah), 36km from Male' (transfer by boat: 45min), ☎441905, Fax 441906; contact in Male': ☎ 323758, Fax 328842, rrresort@dhivehinet.net.mv – 60rm. Hairdryer and mini-bar in the rooms. Windsurfing, catamaran sailing, canoeing, water-skiing, dive centre. Sixty bungalows, 10 of which on stilts, with teak terraces. Shallow lagoon, but house reef only accessible by boat (250m away).

Expensive

Bandos, 8km from Male' (transfer by dhoni: 15min), ☎ 440088, Fax 443877; contact in Male': ☎ 325529, Fax 321026, info@bandos.com.mv – 225rm. Hairdryer and mini-bar in the rooms. Massages. Discotheque. Crèche, shops, business centre. Squash. Windsurfing, catamaran sailing, canoeing, water-skiing, parasailing, dive centre (one of the few recompression centres in the Maldives). Bandos is a very popular weekend destination with the expats who live in Male' and airline crews, drawn by the superb beaches and immense lagoon. There are 225 modern bungalows (50 have been added over recent years), including 44 with suites, and no less than 5 restaurants. House reef nearby, with a small shipwreck.

Baros, 14km from Male' (transfer by dhoni: 1hr), ☎ 441920, Fax 443497; contact in Male': ☎ 323080, Fax 322678, sales@unisurf.com – 75rm. Hairdryer and mini-bar in the rooms. Discotheque. Windsurfing, catamaran sailing, canoeing, dive centre. A tiny island with very pleasant palm-thatched bungalows, including 12 water bungalows. Easily accessible house reef, for divers of all levels. British and German clientele.

Hembadhu (Taj Coral Reef), 33km from Male' (transfer by boat: 40min), ☎ 441948, Fax 443884; contact in Male': ☎ 313530, Fax 314059, tajcr@dhivehinet.net.mv – 66rm. Hairdryer and mini-bar in the rooms. Jacuzzi, massages. Windsurfing, catamaran sailing, canoeing, water-skiing, dive centre. This recently renovated resort, which is managed by the Indian Taj hotel chain, has 66 very comfortable and well-designed bungalows, including 14 water bungalows, and offers good value for money. International clientele.

Kudahura (Four Seasons), 13km from Male' (transfer by boat: 20min), ☎ 444888, Fax 441188; contact in Male': ☎ 325529, Fax 318992, info@kudahuraa.com – 106rm. Hairdryer and mini-bar in the rooms. Jacuzzi. Windsurfing, catamaran sailing, canoeing, water-skiing, dive centre. It is rather a shame that during its renovation, the resort's 41 luxury bungalows were sacrificed to make way for 106 modern rooms, with a few suites and water bungalows. However, they are all comfortable and well decorated. Beautiful garden. International clientele.

Lankanfinolhu (Paradise Island), 10km from Male' (transfer by boat: 15min), ☎ 440011, Fax 440022; contact in Male': ☎ 316161, Fax 314565, paradise@dhivehinet.net.mv – 260rm. Hairdryer and mini-bar in the rooms. Jacuzzi, sauna, massages. Discotheque. Windsurfing, catamaran sailing, canoeing, jet-skiing, water-skiing, dive centre. Despite its 260 modern and functional concrete bungalows (including 40 water bungalows), this resort will satisfy visitors looking for standard accommodation who are not bothered by a lack of charm. Three restaurants, two bars and one coffee shop. International clientele.

Makunudhu, 38km from Male' (transfer by boat: 50min), ☎ 446464, Fax 446565; contact in Male': ☎ 324658, Fax 325543, makunudu@dhivehinet.net.mv – 37rm. Hairdryer, mini-bar and safe in the rooms. Windsurfing, catamaran sailing, water-skiing, dive centre. The advantage of this resort is that it has very few bungalows, set two by two but standing well apart from each other. They are fairly spacious and comfortable, and all have a little veranda. Large open-air restaurant and terrace bar. Friendly atmosphere and excellent service. Nearby and easily accessible house reef. International clientele, with an increasing number of honeymooning Japanese couples.

Nakathachafushi, 25km from Male' (transfer by boat: 35min), ☎ 443847, Fax 442665; contact in Male': ☎ 322971, Fax 322678, nakatcha@dhivehinet.net.mv – 51rm. Hairdryer and mini-bar in the rooms. Discotheque. Windsurfing, catamaran sailing, canoeing, water-skiing, dive centre. This small, narrow island has attractive round palm-thatched bungalows which are comfortable and well designed, as well as two restaurants, a grill, and a very pleasant bar. Beautiful beaches and an immense, shallow lagoon. The house reef, which was partly damaged in 1990, has been almost totally reconstructed and is easily accessible.

Thulhagiri, 13km from Male' (transfer by boat: 25min), ☎ 445930, Fax 445939; contact in Male': ☎ 322844, Fax 321026, reserve@thulhaagiri.com.mv – 58rm. Hairdryer in the rooms. Windsurfing, catamaran sailing, canoeing, water-skiing, dive centre. A small round island, once managed by the Club Med, Thulhagiri is a real picture-postcard destination. With its superb beaches and simple but pleasant rooms, it would be just perfect if fewer bungalows had been built during its renovation.

Vihamanaafushi (Kurumba), 3km from Male' (transfer by dhoni: 10min), ☎ 442324, Fax 443885; contact in Male': ☎ 323080, Fax 320274, kurumba@dhivehinet.net.mv – 170rm. Hairdryer and mini-bar in the rooms.

Jacuzzi, sauna, fitness centre. Discotheque. Windsurfing, catamaran sailing, canoeing, water-skiing, dive centre, deep-sea fishing. This island resort was the first to be opened in the Maldives, in 1972, and attracts many weekend visitors from Male'. Its proximity to the airport also makes it more of a transit island. The resort has 170 modern bungalows (standard and suites), three restaurants, bars, a grill and coffee shop, and offers countless activities. Overall good value for money.

Very expensive

Kudahithi, 29km from Male' (transfer by boat: 45min), ☎ 444613, Fax 441992; contact in Male': ☎ 313938, Fax 313939, hcmmale@clubvacanze.com.mv – 7rm. Mini-bar in the rooms. This is the smallest island resort in the Maldives, with only 7 bungalows, all luxurious and each one different from the next. The service is excellent, but the only activities on offer here are canoeing and snorkelling. Magnificent beaches and a very beautiful house reef close by. You can go scuba diving from Boduhithi, a neighbouring island which belongs to the same hotel chain.

Vabbinfaru (Banyan Tree), 16km from Male' (transfer by boat, even at night: 20min), ☎ 443147, Fax 443843; contact in Male': ☎ 323369, Fax 324752, maldives@Banyantree.com – 48rm. Hairdryer and mini-bar in the rooms. Massages. Windsurfing, catamaran sailing, canoeing, water-skiing, dive centre. A small island with luxuriant vegetation, which attracts a very "chic" international clientele. Comfortable and well-designed bungalows, with private gardens, open-air bathrooms and teak terraces. Open-air restaurant and bar. Excellent service, but, unfortunately, a rather impersonal atmosphere. House reef easily accessible for snorkelling.

• South Male' Atoll

Reasonably priced

Embudhu Village, 8km from Male' (transfer by boat: 10min), ☎ 444776, Fax 442673; contact in Male': ☎ 322212, Fax 318057, embvil@dhivehinet.net.mv – 117rm. Hairdryer and mini-bar in the rooms. Windsurfing, catamaran sailing, water-skiing, dive centre. This round island has lush vegetation, beautiful beaches and a wide lagoon. Its air-conditioned bungalows are divided into three categories but are all comfortable and of pleasant design. About fifteen of them stand on stilts. Easily accessible house reef. Mainly young European clientele. It is a shame that there are so many bungalows and that the island is so close to Male'.

Kandooma, 35km from Male' (transfer by boat: 1hr; by dhoni: 2hr), ☎ 444452, Fax 445948; contact in Male': ☎ 323360, Fax 326880, info@kandooma.com – 81rm. Windsurfing, catamaran sailing, canoeing, water-skiing, jet-skiing, dive centre. Kandooma is not the most pleasant island or the most beautiful, but it is one of the cheapest. Its rather simple bungalows are adequate but the beaches are small and the vegetation rather sparse. The house reef is only accessible by boat.

Vaadhu (Vadoo Diving Paradise), 8km from Male' (transfer by seaplane: 45min), ☎ 443976, Fax 443397; contact in Male': ☎ 325844, Fax 325846 – 33rm. Mini-bar in the rooms. Dive centre. A small island with rustic charm – much sought-after by Japanese divers – offering three types of accommodation: a standard two-storey model, "superior" beach bungalows, and 12 water bungalows, which are very pleasant and comfortable. Prices range from reasonable to expensive according to the type of accommodation. Easily accessible house reef.

Mid-range

Biyadhoo, 29km from Male' (transfer by boat: 45min), ☎ 447171, Fax 447272; contact in Male': ☎ 324699, Fax 327014, admin@biyadoo.com.mv – 96rm. Hairdryer and mini-bar in the rooms. Massages. Discotheque. Windsurfing, catamaran sailing, water-skiing, renowned dive centre. A large island with lush vegetation. The

Making the most of the Male' Atolls

rooms, with terraces, are set in 6 two-storey buildings which make the place look more like a classic beach resort than a Robinson Crusoe island. Air-conditioned restaurant serving good international cuisine and some Indian specialities. Excellent service. Easily accessible house reef. Free dhoni shuttle service to the neighbouring island of Villivaru.

Bodhufinolhu (Fun Island), 38km from Male' (transfer by boat: 1hr), ☎444558, Fax 443958; contact in Male': ☎ 316161, Fax 314565, fun@dhivehinet.net.mv – 100rm. CC Mini-bar in the rooms. Discotheque and karaoke. Windsurfing, catamaran sailing, canoeing, water-skiing, jet-skiing, dive centre. A long ribbon of sand stretching over 800m, this island's beautiful beaches give onto a very large lagoon. Pleasant rooms set in modern buildings. Two restaurants and three bars. The house reef is only accessible by boat, but at low tide it is possible to reach two small desert islands on foot.

Bolifushi, 12km from Male' (transfer by boat: 20min), ☎ 443517, Fax 445924; contact in Male': ☎ 317526, Fax 317529 – 40rm. CC Mini-bar in the rooms. Discotheque and karaoke. Windsurfing, catamaran sailing, canoeing, water-skiing, renowned dive centre. A pleasant island with a relaxed atmosphere, ideal for divers, who can enjoy a beautiful and easily accessible house reef. Rather sophisticated rooms and bungalows. European and Japanese clientele.

Dhigufinolhu, 20km from Male' (transfer by boat: 45min), ☎ 443599, Fax 443886; contact in Male': ☎ 314009, Fax 327058, dhigu@dhigufinolhu.com – 97rm. CC Mini-bar in the rooms. Discotheque. Windsurfing, catamaran sailing, canoeing, water-skiing. This narrow island, which is in fact a long sandbank, is surrounded by superb beaches and an immense lagoon, excellent for windsurfing. It is connected by a 1km-long pontoon to the neighbouring island, Veligandu Hura, and to a small island which houses a dive centre and sports complex shared by both islands, as well as all the infrastructures (generators, storehouses, etc). Snorkellers are taken out to the reef by boats.

Expensive

Embudhu Finolhu (Taj Lagoon), 9km from Male' (transfer by boat: 10min), ☎ 444451, Fax 445925; contact in Male': ☎ 317530, Fax 314059, tajlr@dhivehinet.net.mv – 64rm. CC Hairdryer and mini-bar in the rooms. Windsurfing, catamaran sailing, canoeing, water-skiing, dive centre. This island, which is managed by the Indian Taj hotel chain, offers 64 bungalows on stilts, 48 of which are on the beachfront and 16 set in the lagoon; they are all comfortable and well designed, with sun terraces and direct access to the sea. Beautiful beaches and an immense lagoon, but you have to take a boat to go snorkelling. In short, no surprises and good value for money. International clientele.

Olhuveli, 35km from Male' (transfer by boat: 1hr), ☎ 442788, Fax 445942; contact in Male': olhuveli@ dhivehinet.net.mv – 137rm. TV CC Hairdryer and mini-bar in the rooms. Sauna. Discotheque and karaoke. Mini-golf. Windsurfing, catamaran sailing, canoeing, water-skiing, dive centre. This long thin island has 125 two-storey bungalows and 12 water bungalows. The house reef can only be reached by boat. Lacking in charm, but no surprises. Japanese management and clientele.

Rannalhi, 35km from Male' (transfer by boat: 45min), ☎442688, Fax 442035; contact in Male': ☎ 323323, Fax 317993, finance@rannalhi.com.mv – 116rm. TV CC Hairdryer and mini-bar in the rooms. Windsurfing, catamaran sailing, canoeing, water-skiing, dive centre. This island, with its dense vegetation has probably the most beautiful palm trees in the Maldives and recently underwent a complete overhaul. Its bungalows are all set above the water. House reef very close by.

Rihiveli, 40km from Male' (transfer by boat: 50min), ☎ 443731, Fax 440052; contact in Male': ☎ 322421, Fax 320976 – 50rm. Windsurfing, catamaran sailing, canoeing, water-skiing, renowned dive centre, deep-sea fishing. Rihiveli is an unspoiled island whose charm lies in its beauty, service, and the informal atmosphere created by its French managers. It has a well-earned reputation for its relaxed and sporting atmosphere, while being chic and tasteful at the same time. Its individual palm-thatched bungalows have small terraces. Restaurant on stilts serving excellent food. One considerable advantage is that all the sports activities – except for scuba diving and deep-sea fishing – are offered free of charge,. The beaches are superb and surrounded by an immense lagoon. The house reef can only be reached by boat (free) but there are two small islands nearby which can be accessed on foot. French-speaking clientele.

Velassaru (Laguna Beach), 12km from Male' (transfer by boat: 15min), ☎ 445906, Fax 443041; contact in Male': ☎ 322971, Fax 322678, lbr@dhivehinet.net.mv – 129rm. Hairdryer and mini-bar in the rooms. Jacuzzi. Windsurfing, catamaran sailing, canoeing, dive centre. Rather sophisticated, Laguna prides itself on being the closest chic island to Male'. Its bungalows are more or less luxurious, according to their category. They all stand facing the sea, have tiled roofs and are partly separated from each other. Three restaurants (à la carte), a grill, coffee shop and several bars. Good quality service. Easily accessible house reef. International clientele.

Veligandu Hura (Palm Tree), 20km from Male' (transfer by speedboat: 45min), ☎ 443882, Fax 440009; contact in Male': ☎ and Fax 314008, veli@veliganduhuraa.com – 52rm. Hairdryer and mini-bar in the rooms. Windsurfing, catamaran sailing, canoeing, dive centre. This tiny island is linked by a pontoon to Dhigufinolhu and to a third island housing various facilities, which they share. Recently renovated, the number of bungalows here has increased from 16 to 52, which is rather a pity and has taken away much of the island's charm. The house reef is only accessible by boat.

Villivaru, 29km from Male' (transfer by boat: 45min), ☎ 447070, Fax 447272; contact in Male': ☎ 324699, Fax 327014, admin@biyadoo.com.mv – 60rm. Hairdryer and mini-bar in the rooms. Massages. Discotheque. Sixty modern bungalows, 14 of which are on stilts, all comfortable and well designed, with terrace and veranda giving onto the sea, but set very close to each other. Free dhoni shuttle service to the neighbouring island of Biyadhoo, where you can go windsurfing, catamaran sailing, water-skiing and diving. Accessible house reef.

Very expensive

Makunufushi (Cocoa Island), 30km from Male' (transfer by boat: 35min), ☎ 443713, Fax 441919; contact in Male': ☎ and Fax 322326 – 8rm. Windsurfing, catamaran sailing, water-skiing, dive centre. With its long-standing reputation as the "chic" island of the Maldives, Cocoa is very exclusive. Here, the emphasis is placed on nature, sand, sun and sea. Its 8 bungalows with their palm-thatched roofs are simple yet luxurious, comfortable and remarkably well designed, with split-level loggias and sitting rooms. Four hundred metres long and barely 40m wide, this island is one of the most beautiful sandbanks in the archipelago with stunning beaches giving onto a 4km-wide lagoon. Excellent food, and a bar set in the lagoon. House reef accessible only by boat. However, a considerable number of water bungalows are scheduled to be built here, which may well totally disfigure the island.

ARI ATOLL
(ALIFU ATOLL)

Rasdhoo, Thoddoo and Ari districts
60km west of Male' – 74 islands, of which 10 are inhabited and 27 are island resorts
Pop 11 000 – Capital: Mahibadhoo

Not to be missed

Take a trip to Mahibadhoo and Thoddoo Island.
Visit the South Ari Cultural Centre.

And remember...

There are a great number of resorts here, so be sure to choose yours carefully.

A long string of islands stretching over more than 80km from north to south but only 30km from east to west, Ari is the most western atoll in the Maldives. Along with the Male' atolls, it constitutes the heart of the "tourist zone " and contains a large number of island resorts. The small Rasdhoo Atoll stands just off its northeast corner, with the strange island of Thoddoo set all alone in the ocean a further 10km north.

Ari Atoll

The capital, **Mahibadhoo** (1 500 inhabitants), located on the atoll's eastern barrier reef, is an important **fishing centre**. Traditional fishing methods are still practised here, using immense nets stretched out in an arc by five or ten *dhoni*. The return of the fishing boats is an absolutely fascinating sight, with the whole village helping to bring the nets onto the beach and pick up the fish. Lagoon fishing is also practised and involves four or six men standing waist-deep in the water, each one holding the edge of a net, which is laid flat on the sandy bottom, while others beat the water to get the fish to gather above the centre of the net. The fishermen then only have to raise the edges to net their catch.

Coral, the islands' treasure

F. Valentin

The islands of **Fenfushi** and **Maamigili** in the far south are renowned throughout the archipelago for their **coral stone carving**, the former specialising in the production of chiselled tombstones, and the latter in carving blocks of stone for house building. The activities of the other villages consist of fishing or *dhoni* building and weaving sails out of palm leaves. These islands can all be visited easily and you can watch the craftsmen at work, carving or weaving by hand in front of their houses or in the main square.

Also in the south of the atoll stands the now uninhabited island of **Ariadhoo**, whose proximity to the Ari Beach, Holiday Island and Sun Island resorts makes it easily accessible. It was once inhabited by the **Redins**, the Maldivians' more or less legendary ancestors, who may have been sun worshippers and who left some relics on the southernmost islands. Excavations have uncovered a linga almost 40cm long and some carved stones which may have been used to build a temple.

The island housing the **South Ari Cultural Centre** offers an interesting reconstruction of a traditional Maldivian village. This little open-air museum will give you an idea of life in the fishing villages. The centre *(open every day, 10am-6pm, except Fridays. Free entry)* shows three types of dwelling: the home of a local dignitary, with one room set apart for men *(beyru ge)* and one for women *(ethere ge)*, a simple fisherman's house and a more primitive dwelling of the kind that are hardly ever found anywhere other than on the remote islands, where foreigners are not allowed to venture. If you go, remember to donate a few *rufiyaa* for the upkeep and development of the centre. Individual and group visits are organised by the resorts in the southern part of Ari Atoll.

Rasdhoo Atoll

Rasdhoo Atoll, which bears the name of its only village (850 inhabitants), contains only two island resorts. It was an important Buddhist centre before the introduction of Islam. Nowadays it is home to about thirty souvenir shops and is a popular destination for visitors from the resorts in the north of Ari Atoll.

Thoddoo, 10km north of Rasdhoo, is a large isolated island given over to **farming** (watermelons and betel leaves), which reveals a rather unexpected aspect of the Maldives. It owes its celebrity to the discovery in 1958 of the ruins of a Buddhist temple containing – in addition to a statue of Buddha which is now on display in the Male' museum – a Roman coin dating back to 90 BC. However, being two hours north of Ari Atoll by boat, it sadly receives few visitors.

Dive sites

Since most of the islands in Ari Atoll are blessed with nearby house reefs which are accessible from the beach, you will easily be able to go snorkelling, and the marine depths are generally superb. Scuba diving enthusiasts will find spectacular sites near several island resorts. Depending on where you are staying, you will be able to explore the **Mayafushi** *thila*, the wreck of a cargo ship at **Halaveli** (28m below the surface) and another at **Fesdu** (25m below the surface), the **Elliadoo** reef (with a *thila* and a magnificent wall), the **Gangehi** channel (famous for its manta rays in winter) and the **Maalhos** channel (in summer), the **Himandhoo** *thila* (manta rays in winter) and **Bathala** *thila*, and the **Kuramathi** reef. In all, over 30 famous sites await you in Ari Atoll, including the unique **Fish Head***** (Mushimasmigili), which is one of the most beautiful protected marine sites (for scuba divers only).

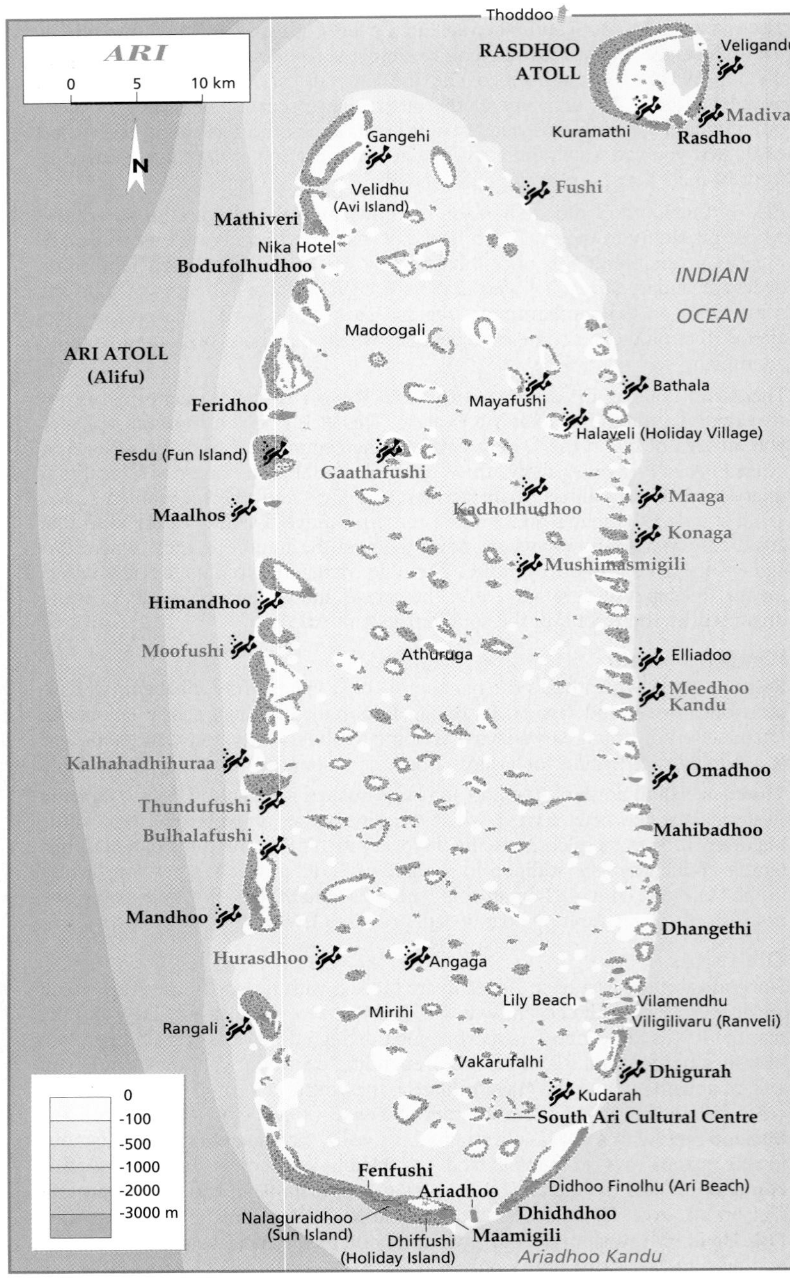

ARI
0
5
10 km
N
Thoddoo
RASDHOO ATOLL
Veligandu
Madivaru
Kuramathi
Rasdhoo
Gangehi
Velidhu (Avi Island)
Fushi
Mathiveri
Nika Hotel
Bodufolhudhoo
INDIAN OCEAN
Madoogali
ARI ATOLL (Alifu)
Bathala
Mayafushi
Feridhoo
Halaveli (Holiday Village)
Fesdu (Fun Island)
Gaathafushi
Maaga
Kadholhudhoo
Maalhos
Konaga
Mushimasmigili
Himandhoo
Moofushi
Athuruga
Elliadoo
Meedhoo Kandu
Kalhahadhihuraa
Omadhoo
Thundufushi
Mahibadhoo
Bulhalafushi
Mandhoo
Dhangethi
Hurasdhoo
Angaga
Lily Beach
Vilamendhu
Mirihi
Viligilivaru (Ranveli)
Rangali
Vakarufalhi
Dhigurah
Kudarah
South Ari Cultural Centre
0
-100
-500
-1000
-2000
-3000 m
Fenfushi
Ariadhoo
Didhoo Finolhu (Ari Beach)
Dhidhdhoo
Nalaguraidhoo (Sun Island)
Maamigili
Dhiffushi (Holiday Island)
Ariadhoo Kandu

Making the most of Ari Atoll

WHERE TO STAY

• Ari Atoll

Reasonably priced

Angaga, 85km from Male' (transfer by seaplane: 25min), ☎ 450510, Fax 450520; contact in Male': ☎ 318136, Fax 323115 – 50rm. CC Windsurfing, catamaran sailing, water-skiing, dive centre. This tiny sand island, barely 200m in diameter, looks just like a picture-postcard. Its individual, palm-thatched bungalows are simple but very pleasant and tastefully decorated; they all have a veranda and their own swing-seat, so typical of Maldivian villages. Guaranteed peace and quiet. Skin diving on a superb house reef, with access from the island. International clientele.

Athuruga, 90km from Male' (transfer by seaplane: 25min), ☎ 450508, Fax 450574; contact in Male': ☎ 310489, Fax 310390, athadmin@dhivehinet.net.mv – 46rm. CC Mini-bar in the rooms. Windsurfing, catamaran sailing, canoeing, water-skiing, dive centre. Good value for money. The rooms don't afford a great deal of privacy but they all have a veranda. Superb dive sites and house reef. Mainly British clientele.

Bathala, 56km from Male' (transfer by seaplane: 25min; by boat: 2hr30min), ☎ 450587, Fax 450558; contact in Male': ☎ 315236, Fax 315237, bir0587@dhivehinet. net.mv – 48rm. CC Mini-bar in the rooms. Dive centre. Three hundred metres long and 150m wide, this island is covered in luxuriant vegetation and fringed by lovely beaches. House reef accessible from the beach. Good dive sites and reasonable prices.

Didhoo Finolhu (Ari Beach), 100km from Male' (transfer by helicopter: 45min), ☎ 450513, Fax 450512; contact in Male': ☎ 321930, Fax 327355, aribeach@dhivehinet.net.mv – 121rm. TV CC Hairdryer and mini-bar in the "superior" rooms. Windsurfing, catamaran sailing, canoeing, water-skiing, dive centre. A long strip of an island with divine beaches surrounded by an immense lagoon. Its bungalows fall under two categories: the standard ones are simple, palm-thatched and set in small buildings with terraces, while the 30 "superior" ones, in the form of an upturned ship's hull, are very pleasant, equipped with beautiful open-air bathrooms and tucked away at the southern end of the island. Since the house reef is far away, you have to take a boat to go snorkelling. Ari Beach has its own heliport.

Elliadoo, 57km from Male' (transfer by seaplane: 20min; by boat: 2hr), ☎ 450586, Fax 450514; contact in Male': ☎ 317717, Fax 314977, mail@travelin-maldives.com – 50rm. TV CC Hairdryer and mini-bar in the rooms. Windsurfing, catamaran sailing, canoeing, water-skiing, jet-skiing, dive centre. Boasting a superb, easily accessible house reef with many interesting dive sites, this tiny island, has around fifty fairly simple, spacious and well-equipped bungalows.

Halaveli (Holiday Village), 62km from Male' (transfer by seaplane: 25min), ☎ 450559, Fax 450564; contact in Male': ☎ 322719, Fax 323463, halaveli@dhivehinet.net.mv – 56rm. CC Hairdryer and mini-bar in the rooms. Discotheque. Windsurfing, catamaran sailing, canoeing, water-skiing, jet-skiing, dive centre. Two types of simple, but pleasant and comfortable bungalows, sporting verandas and set well apart from each other. Lush vegetation and a large lagoon with a superb house reef which can be reached from the beach. Italian clientele.

Lily Beach, 80km from Male' (transfer by seaplane: 20min; by boat: 2hr), ☎ 450013, Fax 450646; contact in Male': ☎ 317464, Fax 317466, info@lilybeach.com – 85rm. CC Mini-bar in the rooms. Discotheque. Boutique. Windsurfing, canoeing, dive centre. Lily is a beautiful little island, 550m long and 100m wide. Its 68 standard bungalows, all bunched together, lack charm, but are comfortable and open onto a lovely beach. The 17 suites set on stilts have direct access to the sea. The resort owes its reputation to a magnificent, easily accessible house reef and its "all inclusive" formula, which includes alcohol (only scuba diving and fishing are not included).

Madoogali, 73km from Male' (transfer by seaplane: 25min), ☎ 450581, Fax 450554; contact in Male': ☎ 317975, Fax 317974, madugali@dhivehinet.net.mv – 50rm. Hairdryer and mini-bar in the rooms. Windsurfing, canoeing, water-skiing, surfing, dive centre, deep-sea fishing. A resort with a relaxed, sporty and friendly atmosphere. Terrace bar and restaurant. Nearby house reef. French and Italian clientele.

Mayafushi, 63km from Male' (transfer by seaplane: 20min), ☎ 450588, Fax 450568; contact in Male': ☎ 320097, Fax 326658, maaya@dhivehinet.net.mv – 60rm. Windsurfing, catamaran sailing, canoeing, water-skiing, surfing, renowned dive centre. Stretching over 400m in length and 150m wide, surrounded by beautiful beaches and an immense lagoon. This island has bungalows set in groups, built in the local style with palm-thatched roofs. House reef very close by.

Vilamendhu, 82km from Male' (transfer by seaplane: 35min), ☎ 450637, Fax 450639; contact in Male': ☎ 324933, Fax 324943, vilamndu@aaa.com.mv – 141rm. Hairdryer and mini-bar in the rooms. Windsurfing, catamaran sailing, canoeing, water-skiing, dive centre. A large island with a relaxed, friendly atmosphere, boasting superb, brilliant-white beaches, and a beautiful big lagoon. The bungalows are of modern design. Nearby house reef. In short, a pleasant island, apart from the recent and hasty addition of 41 extra bungalows.

Mid-range

Fesdu (Fun Island), 75km from Male' (transfer by seaplane: 25min; by boat: 2hr30min), ☎ 450541, Fax 450547; contact in Male': ☎ 323080, Fax 322678, sales@unisurf.com – 55rm. Windsurfing, dive centre. This small, informal and friendly island, boasts attractive vegetation and magnificent beaches. Some water bungalows. Very easily accessible house reef.

Mirihi, 85km from Male', (transfer by seaplane: 30min), ☎ 450500, Fax 450501; contact in Male': ☎ and Fax 325448, mirihi@dhivehinet.net.mv – 35rm. Windsurfing, catamaran sailing, dive centre. This small island offers the advantage of having a limited number of bungalows, 30 of which are set on stilts. Superb house reef nearby.

Nalaguraidhoo (Sun Island), 100km from Male' (transfer by seaplane: 35min), ☎ 450088, Fax 450099; contact in Male': ☎ 316161, Fax 314565, info@sun-island.com.mv – 350rm. Jacuzzi, sauna. Discotheque. Windsurfing, catamaran sailing, canoeing, water-skiing, parasailing, dive centre. This is one of the largest islands in the Maldives, with 350 modern bungalows, divided into three categories. Stunning beaches and a fairly large lagoon, but the house reef is far away.

Expensive

Dhiffushi (Holiday Island), 97km from Male' (transfer by seaplane: 30min; by boat: 2hr), ☎450011, Fax 450022; contact in Male': ☎316161, Fax 314565, holiday@dhivehinet.net.mv – 142rm. Sauna. Discotheque. Boutique. Windsurfing, catamaran sailing, canoeing, jet-skiing, water-skiing, dive centre. Dhiffushi is a typical example of the new, recently converted islands in the Maldives, with a great number of bungalows which have good facilities although they lack charm.

Gangehi, 77km from Male' (transfer by seaplane: 30min), ☎ 450550, Fax 450506; contact in Male': ☎ 323938, Fax 313939, hcmmale@clubvacanze.com.mv – 25rm. Canoeing, dive centre. Peace and quiet guaranteed on this little island with its 25 beautiful bungalows, including 8 luxury bungalows, set on stilts. They are all very comfortable and tastefully decorated.

Vakarufalhi, 90km from Male' (transfer by seaplane: 50min, or by dhoni), ☎ 450004, Fax 450007; contact in Male': ☎ 314149, Fax 314150, vakaru@dhivehinet.net.mv – 50rm. Discotheque. Boutique. Windsurfing, catamaran sailing, canoeing, dive centre. The island, 250m long and 220m wide, boasts stunning beaches and an immense lagoon. Its individual bungalows are pleasant, well designed, and palm-thatched in traditional Maldivian style. À la carte restaurant. Easily accessible house reef.

Velidhu (Avi Island), 85km from Male' (transfer by seaplane: 25min), ☎ 450018, Fax 450630; contact in Male': ☎ 313738, Fax 326264, velidhu@dhivehinet.net.mv – 87rm. CC Windsurfing, catamaran sailing, canoeing, water-skiing, dive centre. This little island has pleasant and comfortable bungalows, including 17 water bungalows. Easily accessible house reef, north of the island. Italian and Swiss clientele.

Viligilivaru (Ranveli Village), 77km from Male' (transfer by seaplane: 30min), ☎ 450570 / 230011, Fax 450523 / 230022; contact in Male': ☎ 316921, Fax 316922 – 77rm. CC. Discotheque. Windsurfing, catamaran sailing, dive centre. Very comfortable two-storey villas. Perhaps slightly too many bungalows to really be described as charming. Restaurant and bar set on stilts in the lagoon. Beautiful dive sites.

Very expensive

Kudarah, 89km from Male' (transfer by seaplane: 30min), ☎ 450610, Fax 450550; contact in Male': ☎ 313938, Fax 313939, hcmmale@clubvacanze.com.mv – 30rm. TV CC Canoeing, dive centre. You will appreciate this island for the peace and privacy it affords, but very few aquatic sports are on offer here. 30 modern-style, spacious and comfortable bungalows, including 5 water bungalows. Magnificent house reef, ideal for snorkelling.

Nika Hotel, 74km from Male' (transfer by seaplane: 25min), ☎ 450516, Fax 450577; contact in Male': ☎ 325091, Fax 325097, nika_htl@dhivehinet.net.mv – 27rm. CC Windsurfing, canoeing, water-skiing, dive centre. Nika Hotel boasts the most beautiful villas in the archipelago: made of coral stone in the shape of nautili, they are thatched with palm leaves and boast vast sitting rooms, open-air bathrooms and private beaches. In the aim of staying close to nature, there is no air-conditioning here, and the gardens are full of luxuriant vegetation. Restaurant and bar decorated "Italian-style". One of the best islands in the Maldives, very exclusive, and set in a superb lagoon. Nearby house reef.

Rangali Hilton, 97km from Male' (transfer by seaplane: 30min), ☎ 450629, Fax 450619; contact in Male': ☎ 324232, Fax 324009, hilton@dhivehinet.net.mv – 130rm. CC Discotheque. Photo lab. Windsurfing, catamaran sailing, canoeing, water-skiing, parasailing, dive centre. This resort consists of two islands with superb beaches, set in the middle of an immense lagoon. There are 100 bungalows on Rangali Finholu, the main island, and 30 more luxurious water bungalows on the small island of Kuda Rangali. An acceptable compromise between a classic resort and a "Robinson Crusoe island". Beautiful house reef.

• Rasdhoo Atoll

Mid-range

Kuramathi, 70km from Male' (transfer by seaplane: 20min), ☎450527, Fax 450556; contact in Male': ☎323080, Fax 322678, resvns@ unisurf.com – 280rm. CC Mini-bar in the rooms. Sauna, massages. Discotheque. Windsurfing, catamaran sailing, canoeing, water-skiing, dive centre, deep-sea fishing. This 2.5km-long island houses one of the largest resorts in the Maldives. It consists of three establishments: Kuramathi Village, with 200 rooms; Kuramathi Cottage, in the centre of the island with 30 rooms set in a small private garden; and Blue Lagoon, the most luxurious part of the resort, offering 50 bungalows with terraces, 20 of them set on stilts. An island shuttle runs between the three villages, which all have their own restaurant and bar. International clientele.

Veligandu, 51km from Male' (transfer by seaplane: 20min), ☎450519, Fax 450648; contact in Male': ☎322432, Fax 324009, veli@dhivehinet.net.mv – 65rm. CC Windsurfing, catamaran sailing, canoeing, dive centre. Peaceful and covered in lush vegetation, Veligandu prides itself on being a nature-lover's retreat, with friendly atmosphere. Pleasant, comfortable bungalows and some water bungalows. Nearby house reef.

Making the most of Ari Atoll

VAAVU AND MEEMU ATOLLS (FELIDHOO AND MULAKU ATOLLS)

District of Vaavu – Approximately 50km south of Male'
26 islands, of which 5 are inhabited and 2 are island resorts – Pop 2 000 – Capital: Felidhoo
District of Meemu – 120km south of Male'
32 islands, of which 9 are inhabited and 2 are island resorts – Pop 4 800 – Capital: Muli

Not to be missed

Diving in the Fotteyo Kandu channel (Vaavu).
A trip to Muli during the tuna fishing season.
The mosque on Veyvah Island (Meemu).

And remember...

The winter monsoon is the best time of year for diving.
Go diving at high tide in the Mulaku channel.

Also known as Felidhoo, **Vaavu** stretches out to the south of the Male' atolls, on the other side of the 11km-wide Fulidhoo channel. On the map, it appears in the form of a large crescent, 30km by 40km, reaching out to mark the easternmost point of the Maldives archipelago. Although it doesn't usually receive many visitors, it is beginning to attract an increasing number of guests staying in the resorts of South Male' Atoll hoping to experience a part of the Maldives less affected by tourism.

Five kilometres south of the Vattaru reef (in Vaavu Atoll), **Meemu** stretches 50km from north to south and 30km at its widest part, forming a triangle with its tip facing south. All of the inhabited islands and the two island resorts are scattered along its eastern fringe. Meemu only opened up to tourism in 1997, and its inhabitants, not yet accustomed to seeing foreigners, still have a very traditional way of life.

Vaavu Atoll

Three islands form the heart of this little atoll: **Felidhoo**, the administrative capital, is a very popular port of call with safari boats though it is only a small fishing village with barely more than 500 inhabitants. It is famous for producing superb **dhoni***, which are apparently the most streamlined, the best-suited for sailing in rough seas and whose prows are the most curved (according to some historians, this is a legacy from the papyrus prows of the Egyptian boats). Don't be surprised to find only women building boats there, since this is an essentially female activity. Further south, the nearby island of **Keyodhoo** is the largest island village in the atoll, with around 600 inhabitants, almost all of them fishermen. Lastly, several hundred metres to the north, stands **Thinadhoo**, a small island with a population of 200. **Fulidhoo**, a small village in the far north, is renowned for the beauty of its surroundings and its peaceful atmosphere, and is a favourite destination of holidaymakers from the South Male' tourist resorts. Vaavu's two island resorts organise day trips and half-day trips to almost all of these islands.

Fifteen kilometres towards the east, **Fotheyobodufushi** is the easternmost island of the Maldives, actually consisting of two small islands joined together by a narrow sandbank. According to one of the many Maldivian legends, it

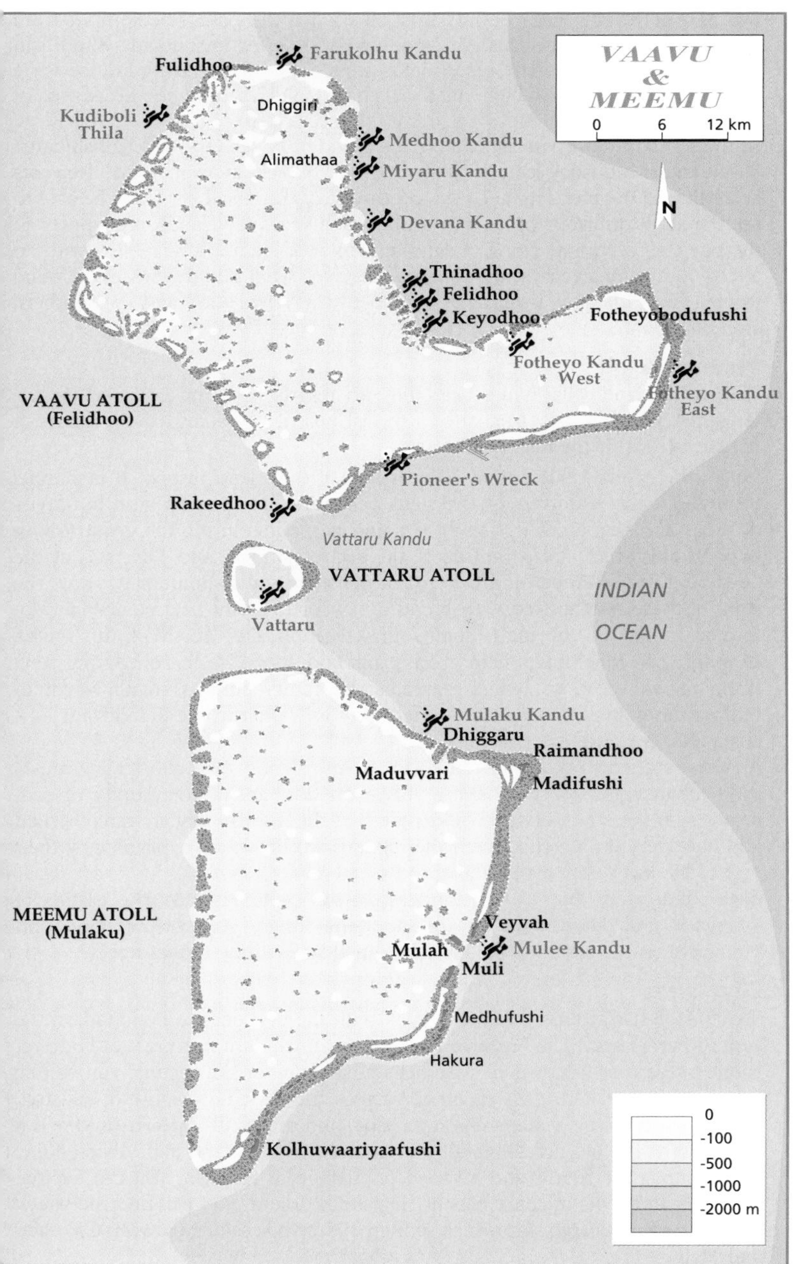
VAAVU
&
MEEMU
0
6
12 km
N
Farukolhu Kandu
Fulidhoo
Dhiggiri
Kudiboli
Thila
Medhoo Kandu
Alimathaa
Miyaru Kandu
Devana Kandu
Thinadhoo
Felidhoo
Keyodhoo
Fotheyobodufushi
Fotheyo Kandu
West
Fotheyo Kandu
East
VAAVU ATOLL
(Felidhoo)
Pioneer's Wreck
Rakeedhoo
Vattaru Kandu
VATTARU ATOLL
INDIAN
OCEAN
Vattaru
Mulaku Kandu
Dhiggaru
Raimandhoo
Maduvvari
Madifushi
MEEMU ATOLL
(Mulaku)
Veyvah
Mulah
Mulee Kandu
Muli
Medhufushi
Hakura
Kolhuwaariyaafushi
0
-100
-500
-1000
-2000 m

was here at the beginning of the Christian era that the exiles or colonisers from Ceylon landed who are thought to be responsible for introducing Buddhism into the archipelago. Their descendants are credited with having founded one of the great dynasties which ruled over the Maldives prior to the advent of Islam.
At the southernmost part of the atoll, the island of **Rakeedhoo** (300 inhabitants) has a rather unusual feature: a surface area which increases and decreases according to the monsoons. To the southwest of the island, you will be able to see the atoll formation process in action: each year, new sandbanks appear in the open sea, creating a ring of sand and coral at surface level *(thila)*, with an already flourishing ecosystem. The small **Vattaru Atoll** is in the process of being formed here, creating a stepping stone between Vaavu Atoll and the southern atoll of Meemu.

Meemu Atoll

The main island villages are near the two resorts and can easily be visited. However, you will have to charter a special boat if you want to visit the more remote islands in the north and south.

Muli*, the capital, is less than 10km north of the island resorts. It is famous throughout the Maldives for the sight of its beaches covered with hundreds of tunas and sharks, caught with nets and harpoons during the **great fishing expeditions** which are organised at the end of January and July, and at the beginning of November and December. Sensitive souls should stay away: the sight of these beaches red with blood is not for the faint-hearted. **Mulah**, the former capital of the atoll, stands directly opposite, north of the **Mulee channel**. The inhabitants here grow **yams** and specialise in sun drying tuna fillets on wicker trays, which explains the rather curious smell. North of Mulha, the island of **Veyvah**** – referred to as Vehoh in the old chronicles – has a 17C **mosque**.
At the southern tip of the atoll, the twin islands of **Kolhuwaariyaafushi** (600 inhabitants) house a fishing village on one, and a community of yam growers on the other. Located 30km south of the resorts, they are rarely visited and have very little contact with the modern world, which explains why their way of life has barely evolved.
Also 30km away, but to the northeast of the central islands, the islands of **Dhiggaru** and **Maduvvari** on the northern fringe, and **Raimandhoo** and **Madifushi** on the eastern side, have remained well off the tourist track.

Dive sites

Vaavu Atoll has around thirty dive sites, with the best ones to be found on the eastern barrier reef. The **Fotheyo Kandu**** channel, 2km northeast of Fotheyo, is one of the most renowned. Whether scuba diving or skin diving, you will be able to spot sharks, turtles, Napoleon wrasses and eagle rays. South of the atoll, be sure to go diving at **Rakeedhoo Kandu***, and the small **Vattaru Atoll**** is a must; both sites are accessible all year round for scuba and skin diving alike. Here, among the sharks and a varied population of reef fish, you can explore the caves and walls of coral. East of Higgakulhi Island, you will find the wreck of the **Pioneer**, a cargo ship which sank in 1958 while sailing between Colombo and Male'.

Meemu Atoll was only very recently opened up to tourism, and most of the sites already listed, which are quite far away from the two island resorts (approximately 30 to 40km), can only be reached by boat. However, you are guaranteed to be the only divers at these virgin sites. The five channels of the northern barrier reef have already been extensively explored, the most famous being the easternmost one, **Mulaku Kandu****. These narrow canyons offer spectacular underwater landscapes, but the currents are also very strong. It is best to dive here when the tide is coming in, which is when you will see hordes of predators on the lookout for prey coming from the ocean. In the middle of the Melaku Kandu channel stands a coral peak covered with magnificent soft corals. Near Maalhaveli, just south of Muli, you can dive at the wreck site of the **Prazere Algeria**, which sank in 1844.

Making the most of the Vaavu and Meemu Atolls

WHERE TO STAY

• Vaavu Atoll

Mid-range

Dhiggiri, 48km from Male' (transfer by speedboat: 1hr30min), ☎ 450593, Fax 450592; contact in Male': Safari Tours, ☎ 323534, Fax 322516 – 45rm. Hairdryer and mini-bar in the rooms. Windsurfing, catamaran sailing, canoeing, aerobics, dive centre. Dhiggiri's beautiful circular cottages, some set on stilts, are made of coral stone or wood and are scattered around the island. They have all been recently renovated and 15 extra bungalows have been added to the original 30. However, the water bungalows stand a little too close to one another, which somewhat mars the appeal of this resort. The island has a house reef directly accessible from the beach, as well as a beautiful big lagoon which is ideal for windsurfing and skin diving. Mainly Swiss and Italian clientele.

Alimathaa, 51km from Male' (transfer by speedboat: 1hr30min), ☎ 450575, Fax 450544; contact in Male': Safari Tours, ☎ 323534, Fax 322516 – 70rm. Mini-bar in the rooms. Windsurfing, catamaran sailing, canoeing, dive centre. This resort too has had all its facilities renovated recently. The bungalows are simple but very pleasant and beautifully designed. They are all grouped together in small blocks on lovely beaches overlooking a superb lagoon. Boats will take you out to go skin diving. Mainly Swiss and Italian clientele.

• Meemu Atoll

Expensive

Hakura, 130km from Male' (transfer by seaplane: 30min), ☎ 460014, Fax 460013; contact in Male': ☎ 313738, Fax 326264, hakura@ dhivehinet. net.mv - 70rm. Discotheque. Windsurfing, catamaran sailing, canoeing, water-skiing, dive centre. Hakura is a tiny little round island, near two small desert islands, which are very popular with resort guests. Located 5km south of Madifushi, on the south-eastern edge of the barrier reef, the island was opened to visitors at the beginning of 1999. Its bungalows are all set on stilts above the water, offering a superb view of the lagoon.

Medhufushi, 125km from Male' (transfer by seaplane: 30min), contact in Male': ☎ 324933, Fax 324943, trvlntrs@aaa.com.mv – 120rm. Hairdryer and mini-bar in the rooms. Discotheque. Windsurfing, catamaran sailing, canoeing, water-skiing, dive centre. A long narrow ribbon of white sand, this island stretches out along the atoll's outer reef 3km south of Muli, just below the fishing island of Naalaafushi and the uninhabited island of Maalhaveli. Medhufushi opened in November 1999 and offers 120 bungalows divided into three categories: standard, suite and water bungalows.

FAAFU AND DHAALU ATOLLS
(NILANDHOO ATOLLS)

District of Faafu – 120km southwest of Male'
18 islands, of which 5 are inhabited and 1 is an island resort – Pop 4 000 – Capital: Magoodhoo
District of Dhaalu – 150km southwest of Male'
30 islands, of which 8 are inhabited and 2 are island resorts – Pop 3 000 – Capital: Kudahuvadhoo

Not to be missed

A trip to the historical island of Nilandhoo in Faafu Atoll.
The two jewellers islands in Dhaalu Atoll.

And remember...

This is an ideal destination for travellers seeking somewhere completely unspoilt.

South of Ari, the small circular **Faafu Atoll** is barely 20km in diameter. It is separated by a 4km channel from the more southern atoll of **Dhaalu**, 35km long and 20km wide, which is also more oval in shape.
Although these atolls are among the smallest and least populated of the archipelago, they are both of great historical importance and are home to archeological sites of inestimable value. You will be among the first to explore these little known islands, which have only recently opened up to tourism and have as yet remained unaffected by any external influence.

Faafu Atoll

Very little is known about the capital, **Magoodhoo**, or Himithi, the only island village on the western side. Its inhabitants were renowned for being highly skilled navigators, but the island was abandoned 10 years ago.
The island of **Nilandhoo*****, situated at the southern tip of the atoll, was made famous by the Norwegian explorer **Thor Heyerdahl**. During his excavations, he uncovered a **tumulus** 45m in circumference, which formed the foundation of an old religious edifice of the Hindus, after having served the Buddhists and sun worshippers. In 1985, he also discovered some stone **lingas** (the phallic representation of Shiva), small votive sculptures, the "parasol towers", and some **shrines**. Moreover, it was he who discovered that the island's remarkable 12C **mosque** was built with much older stones, originally hewn for another building. Next to the mosque, he uncovered some **ritual baths** over 2 000 years old.
Another treasure in Faafu Atoll, **Dharaboodhoo***, south of the capital, is very famous for its **turtle eggs**. The atoll is a favourite breeding ground of the turtles, which are now an endangered species because, although their shells are highly protected, the same cannot be said of their eggs, a very popular delicacy among the Maldivians.

Feeali, in the northeast, houses prosperous **fisheries**, which are renowned throughout the Maldives, while **Biledhoo**, set further inside the atoll, specialises in sun drying tuna fillets. This dried fish, known as *Hiki mas*, was a staple in the Maldivians' diet before the introduction of freezers, and is still one of the main elements of Maldivian cuisine, be it by taste, habit or necessity. But more often than not, Western palates remain immune to its appeal... But don't let these rather pervasive "fragrances" put you off visiting Biledhoo; this is an ideal opportunity to discover part of the Maldivians' traditional way of life.

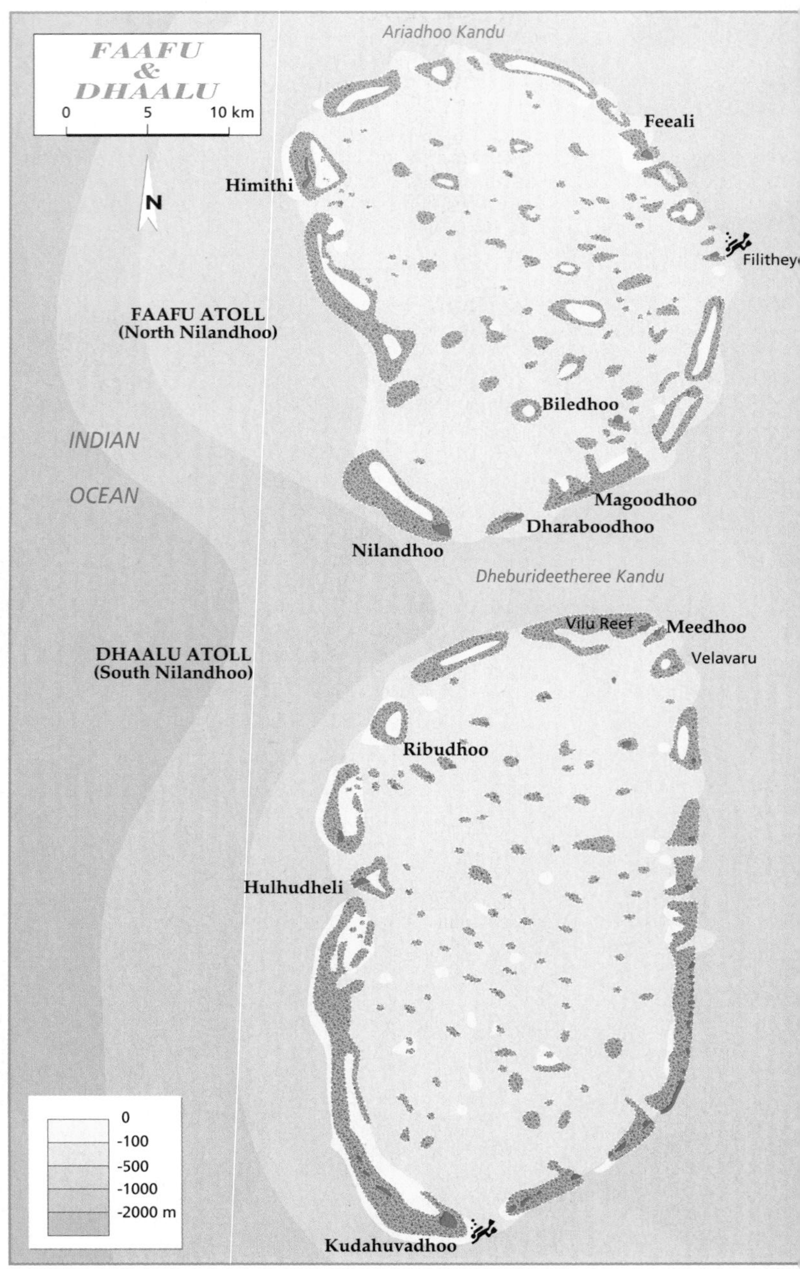
FAAFU
&
DHAALU
0
5
10 km
N
Ariadhoo Kandu
Feeali
Himithi
Filithey
FAAFU ATOLL
(North Nilandhoo)
Biledhoo
INDIAN
OCEAN
Magoodhoo
Dharaboodhoo
Nilandhoo
Dheburideetheree Kandu
Vilu Reef
Meedhoo
Velavaru
DHAALU ATOLL
(South Nilandhoo)
Ribudhoo
Hulhudheli
0
-100
-500
-1000
-2000 m
Kudahuvadhoo

Dhaalu Atoll

Meedhoo, a large fishing island located in the far north, is only a short boat trip away from the two island resorts, and can easily be visited. An attractive alternative is a trip to **Ribudhoo****, which is famous for its **traditional jewellers**. Legend has it that a sultan of Male' once exiled his chief jeweller here for having allegedly stolen some of his gold. The jeweller then taught his art to the islanders, who subsequently became the most skilled jewellers in the Maldives. As you stroll around, you will be able to admire the talent of these craftsmen, who still work in small ancestral forging mills, sometimes even in the street, and produce the most beautiful filigreed jewellery in the archipelago.

Hulhudheli**, on the atoll's western fringe, 30km away from the resorts, is more difficult to reach. Gold jewellery, small chains, necklaces and amulets are also made here and sold at very reasonable prices. But it is mainly worth a visit just to see the craftsmen at work using their time-honoured techniques.

Kudahuvadhoo** is even harder to reach, approximately 45km away from the island resorts (6hr by *dhoni* or 1hr30min by speedboat). Thor Heyerdahl also discovered some **pre-Islamic ruins** here. As on Nilandhoo, near the old mosque he excavated the walls of a ritual bath made of beautifully carved stonework taken from a much older edifice.

Dive sites

The numerous little channels to the northwest of Faafu, and those situated to the northwest of Dhaalu, should be full of pleasant surprises. These sites, just like the *thila* which separate them, have actually never been explored and are sure to contain a wealth of fauna and flora. There are two known shipwrecks at the southern tip of Dhaalu: the **Liffey** (1 400 tonnes), which foundered on the Kudahuvadhoo reef in 1879, and the **Utheem**, which sank in 1960.

Making the most of the Faafu and Dhaalu Atolls

WHERE TO STAY

• Faafu Atoll

Expensive

Filitheyo, 120km from Male' (transfer by seaplane: 30min), contact in Male': ☎ 324933, Fax 324943, trvlntrs@aaa.com.mv – 125rm. Hairdryer and mini-bar in the rooms. Discotheque. Windsurfing, catamaran sailing, canoeing, water-skiing, dive centre. Filitheyo opened at the end of 1999 and has 125 bungalows divided into two categories: beach bungalows and water bungalows.

• Dhaalu Atoll

Expensive

Velavaru, 125km from Male' (transfer by seaplane: 25min), ☎ and Fax 460028; contact in Male': ☎ 324658, Fax 325543 – 92rm. Hairdryer and mini-bar in the rooms. Windsurfing, catamaran sailing, water-skiing, dive centre. Its rooms, which are modern but palm-thatched, are in the shape of turtles ("velaa" means "turtle" in Divehi). Classified in 3 categories – 68 standard, 18 suites, and 6 water bungalows – they are set two by two and are rather lacking in charm. Velavaru is near to several tiny desert islands, for those looking for a Robinson Crusoe experience.

Vilu Reef, 129km from Male' (transfer by seaplane: 25min), ☎ 460011, Fax 460015; contact in Male': ☎ 325977, Fax 320419, suntrvl@dhivehinet.net.mv – 68rm. Hairdryer and mini-bar in the rooms. Discotheque. Windsurfing, catamaran sailing, canoeing, water-skiing, jet-skiing, dive centre. This oval-shaped island, with its prolific vegetation, is slightly smaller than Velavaru and its round, coral stone bungalows are of pleasant, traditional design. Mainly Italian clientele.

SEENU ATOLL (ADDU ATOLL)

District of Seenu – 480km south of Male'
36 islands, of which 7 are inhabited and 1 is an island resort
Pop 17 000 – Capital: Hithadhoo

Not to be missed
A trip to the western isles
to experience the daily life of the Maldivians.
The wreck of the "Loyalty", one of the best-known dive sites.

Addu Atoll is often called Gan Atoll, after its most famous island, the former British **army base** which remained in use until 1970 and was only handed back to the Maldives in 1978. Located south of the equator, this is the southernmost atoll in the archipelago. It is roughly in the shape of an isosceles triangle with 15km-long sides and Gan Island crowning its southern tip.

In 1959, Addu was the headquarters of an independent State, the **Republic of the United Suvadiva Islands**, which included two neighbouring atolls. For obvious economic and political reasons, this State had a merely fleeting existence, but its inhabitants remember this period with nostalgia and have retained a certain independent spirit. They even prefer to be known as the "People of Addu" rather than Maldivians. This is the only atoll where you can

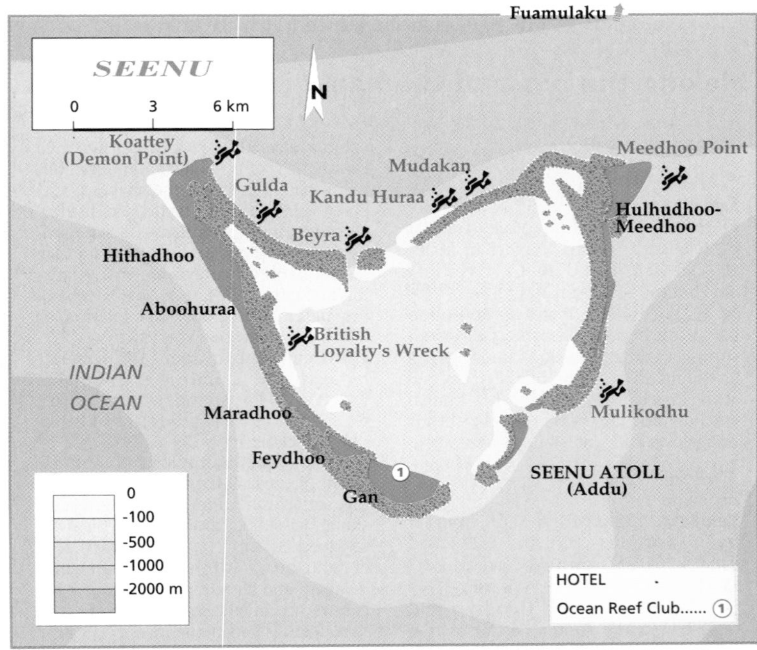

freely visit the villages. Although you will find no accommodation there, they do have some shops and coffee shops.

E Valentin

Muslim cemetery

Gan Island

Boasting an airport capable of handling wide-bodied aircraft, a bank, a hotel and three factories, sewing machine production plants and cloth mills which employ over 1 500 workers, Gan is the **economic capital** of the atoll. Its inhabitants hope that one day the government will turn it into a second Male', now that the Maldivian capital is overpopulated. However, despite the obvious advantages that the island has to offer – its size and relative dynamism – this project appears to be dormant. So, for the time being, Gan is set to remain a sort of large, friendly and lethargic, rather godforsaken village, occupied essentially by the old British army barracks and a golf course, which, over the years, has become an immense piece of derelict land awaiting its improbable metamorphosis.

The island villages

Among other "vestiges" left behind by the British is a 16km-long road linking all of the western islands: **Feydhoo**, **Maradhoo**, the two small islands of Harike and Gaukedi, **Aboohuraa**, and the large island of **Hithadhoo***. The latter is the atoll's administrative capital, and is renowned for the beautiful traditional-style work produced by its **jewellers** and **smiths** using primitive forges, as well as for its many mosques and shrines of venerable Muslims.

Although no special permits are required to visit these islands, they are governed by the same rules as the other islands of the archipelago, and you must return to your hotel in Gan by nightfall. This trip – which is best made by bicycle (there are also a few taxis) – will allow you to discover at leisure the daily life of these authentic, peaceful villages, separated from each other by coconut palm groves and lagoons. Here life goes on at a relaxed pace, following the rhythm of the sun and the seasons. But remember, you won't find any beaches along this rocky coast other than at Koattey, at the northernmost tip of Hithadhoo Island.

In the northeastern part of the atoll, accessible only by boat, the twin islands of **Hulhudhoo-Meedhoo** house the tombs of around fifteen Muslim saints; although this is an important place of pilgrimage for the Maldivians, tourists may find it a little disappointing.

Foammulah Island

30km northeast of Addu, just south of the equator, **Foammulah****, sometimes also known as Fuamulaku, is one of the few islands in the Maldives which are not protected by a coral reef and lagoon. Six kilometres long and 3km wide, this large crop-growing island is very fertile and contains two villages, a dense forest and two freshwater lakes. Archeologists have discovered many pre-Islamic vestiges here, but it is rather difficult to reach. If you want to make a trip here, you will have to obtain a special permit and charter a boat capable of crossing the equatorial channel in all weather from Gan. The trip can be rough, but if you have the time and aren't prone to seasickness, you will discover a totally unexpected aspect of the Maldives on this island, as well as some amazing remains of prehistoric sites.

Dive sites

The British wreaked havoc with the fragile ecosystem of the western part of the atoll by building causeways between the western isles. The best sites are therefore to be found on the northern fringe of the atoll: the **Koattey** plateau, opposite Demon Point beach, the **Gulda** caves, where you can see rays, turtles and sleeper sharks, the small **Beyra** channel and the **Kandu Huraa** channel. Many sharks

Setting off from Foammulah

E Valentin

frequent the waters around the plateau north of Meedhoo Island, and, further south, in the **Mulikodhu** channel, you can see the remains of the anti-submarine net placed there by the British. The wreck of the **Loyalty**** is one of the best-known sites. This 140m-long ship, which was sunk by the Japanese in 1944, lies at a depth of between 17m and 35m and is home to countless reef fish.

Making the most of Seenu Atoll

COMING AND GOING

Island Aviation Services Limited operates regular links with Male', with 2 or 3 flights per day in 40-seater jets. The flight takes around 1hr. The Ocean Reef Club will arrange transfers for its guests.

WHERE TO STAY

Reasonably priced

Ocean Reef Club, 480km south of Male', ☎588721, Fax 320614; contact in Male': ☎321986, Fax 319665 – 78rm. CC Mini-bar in the rooms. Billiard table, discotheque. Windsurfing, catamaran sailing, canoeing, dive centre. This is the only resort in Gan, occupying the former British officers' quarters. The only reminder of its former role lies in the positioning of the cottages, set in military-style lines at right angles to the sea. The British transformed the local vegetation, introducing casuarinas, bougainvillaea, and even grass… The resort offers standard bungalows and suites, all in very close proximity to each other. The rooms are spacious and the old mess still has a very British feel. This is a good spot for windsurfing and skin diving, but there is just one disadvantage: the beach is around 300m away.

EATING OUT

Try some of the little coffee shops in Gan and the other villages.

BAA AND RAA ATOLLS
(MAALHOSMADULU ATOLLS)

District of South Maalhosmadulu (Baa) – 120km north of Male'
64 islands, of which 13 are inhabited and 4 are island resorts –
Pop 12 000 – Capital: Eydhafushi
District of North Maalhosmadulu (Raa) – 150km north of Male'
80 islands, of which 16 are inhabited and 1 is an island resort – Pop 10 000 –
Capital: Ugoofaaru

Not to be missed
Stay in Baa to discover Maldivian handicrafts,
the lacquerware and carved wooden boxes of Thulhaadhoo,
and the woven cloth of Eydhafushi.
Take a trip to Goidhoo.

And remember...
to take the opportunity to visit Raa
while it is still relatively unknown.

The atolls of **Baa** (in the south) and **Raa** (in the north) are separated only by a narrow channel. Although access to Baa has been partly authorised since 1995, on Raa, you will discover a real "virgin" land, where no foreigner has ever resided. The small **Goidhoo Atoll** is set 12km south of Baa and has only one channel on the southern barrier reef and three inhabited islands.

Sun, sand and sea

Pratt-Pries / DIAF

Baa Atoll

The capital, **Eydhafushi**, which is close to the Sonevafushi, Reethi Beach and Le Méridien island resorts, is home to the **last weavers** of *feyli*, the traditional sarongs made of thick white cotton, interwoven with black and brown bands, which are now worn almost only by elderly Maldivians since younger people prefer to wear jeans. The weavers still work using horizontal looms. The island also boasts a beautiful 18C mosque.

About thirty kilometres southwest, near the Coco Palm island resort, **Thulhaadhoo** is renowned for its **wood** and **lacquer** work. The craftsmen here use coconut wood to fashion superb round boxes, simple jewel cases, and the large plates used for offerings during festivals *(maaloodh foshi)*. The colours used – red, black and brown – are all made from natural pigments and the lacquer comes from local resins. As you stroll around, you may see the craftsmen using brushes to spread the lacquer into thin layers which harden in the sun and have to be protected from the insects and humidity by pieces of linen and veils of extremely fine cotton.

South of Baa, little **Goidhoo Atoll** contains only three villages, including **Fulhadhoo**, the most famous one, where the Frenchman Pyrard de Laval's ship, the *Corbin*, ran aground in 1602. He was held prisoner here for five years before making his escape on board a ship which had set sail from Bengal. It is very close to the small island where a German tourist was more recently exiled after being convicted of his girlfriend's murder. Over the centuries, the atoll, with its immense, very well-protected lagoon, became a place where criminals were relegated, and its islands were used as open-air prisons.

Raa Atoll

Further to the north, Raa Atoll was opened to visitors in June 2000, at the same time as the island resort of Meedhupparu. However, only the southern part of the atoll has been included in the "tourist zone", and is thus accessible without a special permit. The majority of the inhabited islands are scattered along the eastern barrier reef, which is the best protected. The capital, **Ugoofaaru** boasts the largest fleet of fishing boats in the archipelago, but the main fishing island is undoubtedly **Kandholhudhoo**, located on the western reef, which is teeming with fish.

The atoll is renowned for the skill of its **boat builders** and the finesse of their *dhoni*. Moreover, most of the safari boats which sail the Maldivian waters were built in Raa or in the small **Alifushi Atoll** (Powell Islands), further north.

It was supposedly on **Rasgetheemu Island** in Raa Atoll that **Koimala** and his royal wife – the legendary founders of the first Maldivian dynasty – landed, and on the island of **Kinolhas** that the explorer Ibn Battuta disembarked for the first time in 1343 *(see "Legend and History" p 336)*.

Dive sites

Many sites remain to be discovered, particularly in Raa Atoll, which has just opened up to tourism. About a dozen excellent sites have been recorded on Baa's eastern barrier reef. It is worth noting that the rather wide channels are less interesting than the *thila* which lie at their centre. Here, you will be able to catch sight of manta rays and even whale sharks, especially at the beginning of the summer monsoon.

Making the most of the Baa and Raa Atolls

WHERE TO STAY

• Baa Atoll

Expensive

Dhunikolhu (Coco Palm), 124km from Male' (transfer by seaplane: 45min), ☎ 230011, Fax 230022; contact in Male': ☎ 324658, Fax 325543, cocopalm@dhivehinet.net.mv – 100rm. TV CC Hairdryer and mini-bar in the rooms. Windsurfing, catamaran sailing, canoeing, water-skiing, dive centre. This resort opened at the beginning of 1999 and boasts magnificent beaches and a vast lagoon, which is ideal for water sports. Its bungalows, 14 of them set on stilts, are divided into three categories but are all comfortable, spacious and well decorated. The resort has a large restaurant open on all four sides, and two bars – at one of them you can even sip cocktails with your feet in the water.

Fonimaghodhoo (Reethi Beach), 104km from Male' (transfer by seaplane: 50min), ☎ 232626, Fax 232727; contact in Male': ☎ 323758, Fax 328842, info@reethibeach.com.mv – 100rm. TV CC Hairdryer and mini-bar in the rooms. Gym, sauna. Discotheque. Windsurfing, catamaran sailing, canoeing, water-skiing, jet-skiing, dive centre. A beautiful big island with dense vegetation, surrounded by a vast lagoon where you can easily go sailing and diving, since the house reef is readily accessible.

Horubadhoo (Royal Island), 105km from Male' (transfer by seaplane: 50min), ☎ 230088, Fax 230099; contact in Male': ☎ 316161, Fax 314565, royal@dhivehinet.net.mv – 150rm. TV CC Hairdryer and mini-bar in the rooms. Gym, jacuzzi, sauna. Discotheque. Windsurfing, catamaran sailing, canoeing, water-skiing, parasailing, dive centre. This enchanting island, which opened at the end of 1999, offers accommodation in bungalows and suites. Bordered by superb beaches, it also has excellent dive sites and a remarkable – and very easily accessible – house reef.

Very expensive

Kunfunadhoo (Sonevafushi), 96km from Male' (transfer by seaplane: 40min), ☎ 230304, Fax 230374; contact in Male': ☎ 326685, Fax 324660, sonresa@soneva.com.mv – 51 villas. TV CC Hairdryer and mini-bar in the rooms. Gym, spa, massages. Windsurfing, catamaran sailing, canoeing, water-skiing, dive centre. This beautiful big island, with its prolific vegetation inhabited by numerous birds, is probably the most exclusive resort in the Maldives. You are guaranteed peace and quiet and very high-class service here. Its superbly decorated villas, each one more luxurious than the last, are divided into three categories, and they all have their own private beach. À la carte restaurant. The lagoon is superb, with a magnificent house reef where you can go skin diving directly from the island or with a guide who will take you there by boat.

• Raa Atoll

Expensive

Meedhupparu (Pearl Island), 130km from Male' (transfer by seaplane: 50min), ☎237700, Fax 235500; contact in Male': ☎323323, Fax 315237, res@meedhupparu.com.mv – 215rm. CC Hairdryer and mini-bar in the rooms. Gym. Discotheque. Windsurfing, catamaran sailing, canoeing, water-skiing, dive centre. This resort opened in June 2000. Its nearby house reef makes it ideal for snorkelling.

LHAVIYANI ATOLL
(FAADHIPPOLHU ATOLL)

District of Lhaviyani – 120km north of Male'
60 islands, of which 6 are inhabited and 4 are island resorts
Pop 8 000 – Capital: Naifaru

Not to be missed
For divers, the Kuredu reef and the Fehigili channel.

And remember...
During the winter monsoon, the islands in the northeast are a better place to stay.

Roughly resembling a trapezium in shape, 35km long and 40km wide, Lhaviyani Atoll is today only a 45min helicopter ride away from the capital. It has a rather

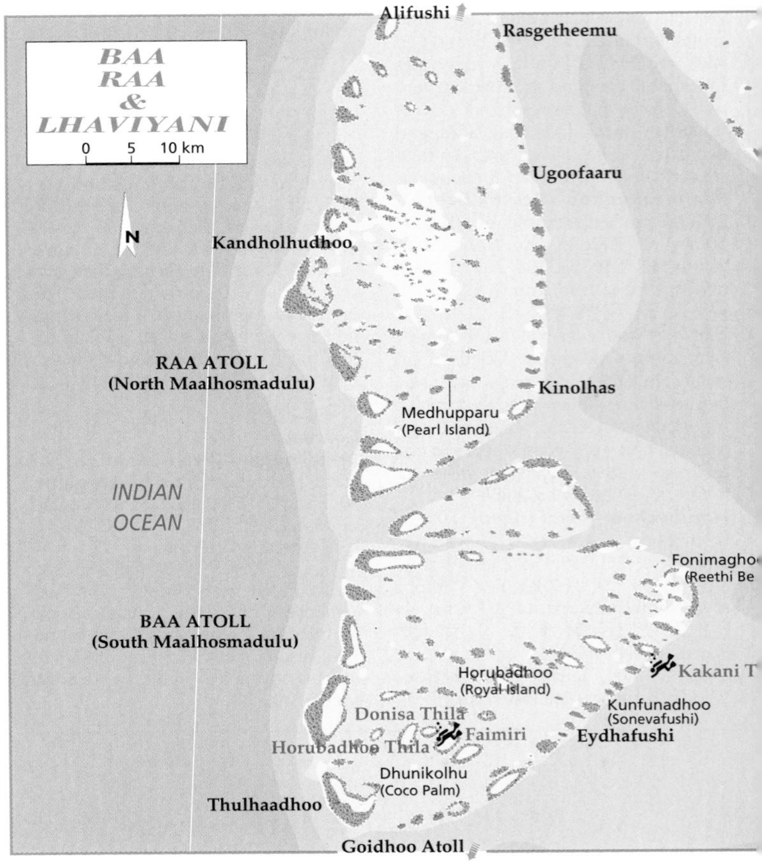

large population of over 8 000 inhabitants spread over six islands, and the main activity here is industrial fishing. As a result of the relative economic development provided by the fish processing factories, these villages offer a very different image of the Maldives from that of the other islands in the archipelago.

The island villages

On the western side, **Felivaru** houses the headquarters of the largest **tuna canning factory**, exporting around 100 000 tonnes of cans each year. The factory was built by the Japanese in 1970, but has since been nationalised by President Gayoom. It makes an essential contribution to the economy of the Maldives and employs some 2 000 people from the two neighbouring islands, Naifaru (to the south) and Hinnavaru (to the north). **Naifaru**, the capital, is a large semi-industrial centre (cloth mills, spinning mills, assembly workshops) and has a very busy harbour which has earned it the nickname of *Kuda Male* (little Male'). Like **Hinnavaru**, however, it suffers from overpopulation and the government is trying to encourage the inhabitants of these islands to move further south to the islands of **Madivaru** and **Maafillafushi**.

In the southern part of the atoll lies **Kurendhoo**, another large island with over a thousand inhabitants who work in the nearby mills and canning factories, while its neighbour to the east, **Olhuvelifushi**, has remained a small, peaceful fishing village, with a population of barely more than 350.

Dive sites

The best sites are to be found on the northern side of the atoll. The most interesting one (with or without tanks) is **Fehigili**★★, just north of Kuredu. It is possible to dive here all year round along the shelves of the outer barrier reef. Reef fish abound here, as do grey reef sharks, barracudas and tunas. The Kuredu reef, which can be reached directly from the beach with or without tanks, also boasts a wealth of marine life. South of **Kanuhuraa**★★ there are five channels where – especially during the winter monsoon – you can admire some of the most beautiful corals in the Maldives. At **Aligau**★, which opens out into the ocean at the southern tip of the atoll, divers can often catch sight of some of the larger sea creatures (sharks, rays, tunas, etc), but the currents can be very strong here. On the southwest side, you can reach **Dhidhdhoo Faru** and **Olhukolhu Faru** with or without tanks; manta rays are frequently to be spotted here. Lastly, there are two shipwrecks to be explored north of Felivaru: the **Skipjack**, at surface level, and the **Gaafaru**, which has remained intact and lies at a depth of 30m. Watch out for the currents.

Making the most of Lhaviyani Atoll

WHERE TO STAY

Mid-range

Kuredu, 117km from Male', at the northern tip of the atoll (transfer by helicopter: 45min; by speedboat: 3hr), ☎ 230337, Fax 230332; contact in Male': ☎ 326545, Fax 326544, info@kuredu.com – 300rm. TV CC Mini-bar in the rooms. Discotheque. Windsurfing, catamaran sailing, canoeing, dive centre. A very large island with a vast lagoon and beautiful beaches which stretch over several kilometres. The resort opened in 1976 and now has 300 bungalows, divided into two categories, "standard" and "superior". In spite of the large number of rooms – Kuredu is one of the largest island resorts in the Maldives – its coral stone, palm-thatched bungalows give it a fairly natural feel. With its four restaurants, two cafés and two bars, this is not really a "Robinson Crusoe island", but it does offer considerable advantages. You can go skin diving directly from the island's north coast, and there are some very interesting sites for scuba diving.

Expensive

Komandoo, 129km from Male', on the atoll's northwest barrier reef (transfer by seaplane: 40min), ☎ and Fax 230377; contact in Male': ☎ 326545, Fax 326544, komandoo@dhivehinet.net.mv – 45rm. CC Mini-bar in the rooms. Discotheque. Windsurfing, catamaran sailing, canoeing, dive centre. This long strip of an island, set a little way inside the atoll, is fringed by stunning beaches and surrounded by a small lagoon which is ideal for skin diving and windsurfing. Its tall coconut palms and small number of wooden, shell-shaped bungalows make this a very pleasant island resort, well sheltered all year round.

Madhiriguradhoo (Palm Beach), 129km from Male', to the northeast of the atoll (transfer by seaplane: 40min), ☎ and Fax 230084; contact in Male': ☎ 314478, Fax 314578, palm-beach@dhivehinet.net.mv – 100rm. TV CC Hairdryer and mini-bar in the rooms. Discotheque. Windsurfing, catamaran sailing, canoeing, water-skiing, jet-skiing, dive centre. Madhiriguradhoo is a long island located on the atoll's outer barrier reef. Its western lagoon is superb and the beaches exquisite. The bungalows are luxurious but of a rather disappointing modern design. The resort opened at the beginning of 1999. Mainly Italian clientele.

Kanuhuraa, 126km from Male', in the north of the atoll (transfer by seaplane: 40min), ☎ 230044, Fax 230033; contact in Male': ☎ 313739, Fax 310549 – 100rm. CC Hairdryer and mini-bar in the rooms. Discotheque, jacuzzi, massages. Windsurfing, catamaran sailing, canoeing, water-skiing, gym, dive centre. Skin diving from boats. This very beautiful island resort, with a superb lagoon and dense vegetation, opened in November 1999. Its bungalows are divided into three categories: standard, suite and water bungalows.

The end...

Notes

Notes

Notes

Notes

NOTES

NDEX

:olombo (Sri): sight or place described in the text
:andaranaike (Solomon): historical figure
'ea: practical information or term explained in the text
ıbbreviation: (Sri): Sri Lanka
(Mald): Maldives

D

E

F

U

V

W

Y

Maps and Plans

Manufacture Française des Pneumatiques Michelin
Société en commandite par actions au capital de 2 000 000 000 de francs
Place des Carmes-Déchaux – 63000 Clermont-Ferrand (France)
R.C.S. Clermont-Fd B 855 200 507

Dépôt légal janvier 2001 – ISBN 2-06-856001-1 – ISSN 0763-1383

Printed in France 01-01/1.1
Compograveur : Nord Compo – Villeneuve d'Ascq
Imprimeur : IME – Baume-les-Dames

Cover photography :
Top : Young Sinhalese girl. A. Even/DIAF
Centre : Fishing with nets at Beruwala, Sri Lanka. Le monde/HOAQUI.
Bottom : Cobra-king guardstone at Polonnaruwa, Sri Lanka. B. Morandi/DIAF.

Your opinion matters!

In order to make sure that this collection satisfies the needs of our readers, please help us by completing the following questionnaire with your comments and suggestions and return to:

Michelin Travel Publications
The Edward Hyde Building
38 Clarendon Road
Watford, UK

or

Michelin Travel Publications
P.O. Box 19008
Greenville, SC 29602-9008
USA

▪ YOUR HOLIDAYS/VACATIONS:

1. In general, when you go on holiday or vacation, do you tend to travel... (Choose one)

- ☐ Independently, on your own
- ☐ Independently, as a couple
- ☐ With 1 or 2 friends
- ☐ With your family
- ☐ With a group of friends
- ☐ On organised trips

2. How many international holidays or vacations of 1 week or more have you taken in the last 3 years? ____________

Last 3 destinations:	Month/Year:
____________	____________
____________	____________
____________	____________

3. What do you look for most when planning a holiday or vacation?

	Not at all	*Sometimes*	*Essential*
Somewhere new and exotic	☐	☐	☐
Real experience/meeting people	☐	☐	☐
Experiencing the wildlife/scenery	☐	☐	☐
Cultural insight	☐	☐	☐
Rest & relaxation	☐	☐	☐
Comfort & well-being	☐	☐	☐
Adventure & the unexpected	☐	☐	☐

4. When travelling, do you take a travel guide with you?

☐ Always ☐ Usually ☐ Sometimes ☐ Never

▪ You and the Michelin NEOS guides

5. About your purchase of a NEOS Guide

How long was your holiday where you used the NEOS guide?
How many days? ____________
For which country or countries? ____________
How long before your departure did you buy it? How many days? ____________

6.What made you choose a NEOS Guide?

Highlight everything that applies.

- ☐ Something new and interesting
- ☐ The layout
- ☐ Easy to read format
- ☐ Cultural details
- ☐ Quality of the text
- ☐ Quality of the mapping
- ☐ Practical Information
- ☐ Michelin quality

7. Which sections did you use most during your holiday or vacation?

Score 1-4	*(1 = least used)*			*(4 = most used)*
"Setting the Scene"	☐ 1	☐ 2	☐ 3	☐ 4
"Meeting the People"	☐ 1	☐ 2	☐ 3	☐ 4
"Practical Information"	☐ 1	☐ 2	☐ 3	☐ 4
"Exploring …"	☐ 1	☐ 2	☐ 3	☐ 4

8. How would you rate the following aspects of your NEOS guide?

Score 1-4	*(1 = Poor)*			*(4 = Excellent)*
Cover design	☐ 1	☐ 2	☐ 3	☐ 4
Chapter Order	☐ 1	☐ 2	☐ 3	☐ 4
Layout (photos, diagrams)	☐ 1	☐ 2	☐ 3	☐ 4
Ease of reading (typeface)	☐ 1	☐ 2	☐ 3	☐ 4
Style of writing	☐ 1	☐ 2	☐ 3	☐ 4
Text boxes and stories	☐ 1	☐ 2	☐ 3	☐ 4
Plans & Maps	☐ 1	☐ 2	☐ 3	☐ 4
Star ratings system	☐ 1	☐ 2	☐ 3	☐ 4
Format	☐ 1	☐ 2	☐ 3	☐ 4
Weight	☐ 1	☐ 2	☐ 3	☐ 4
Durability	☐ 1	☐ 2	☐ 3	☐ 4
Price	☐ 1	☐ 2	☐ 3	☐ 4

9. Did you use other travel guides during your trip? ☐ Yes ☐ No

If yes, which ones? ____________________

10. Please give your NEOS guide a rating out of 20: ____/20 (with 20 as top rating)

Would you use a NEOS guide for your next trip? ☐ Yes ☐ No

If no, why not? ____________________

Which other destinations would you like NEOS to cover? ____________________

11. Any other comments or suggestions: ____________________

____

____

____

____

____

____

Surname/Last Name: ____________________ First Name: ____________________

Address: ____________________

Age: ____________________ Sex: ☐ M ☐ F

Profession: ____________________

Where did you purchase your NEOS Guide: What type of store?
Which country?

Data collected may be used by Michelin Travel Publications for internal purposes only and not for resale.